Roads to Rome

THE NEW HISTORICISM: STUDIES IN CULTURAL POETICS
STEPHEN GREENBLATT, GENERAL EDITOR

1. *Holy Feast and Holy Fast: The Religious Significance of Food to Medieval Women,* by Caroline Walker Bynum
2. *The Gold Standard and the Logic of Naturalism: American Literature at the Turn of the Century,* by Walter Benn Michaels
3. *Nationalism and Minor Literature: James Clarence Mangan and the Emergence of Irish Cultural Nationalism,* by David Lloyd
4. *Shakespearean Negotiations: The Circulation of Social Energy in Renaissance England,* by Stephen Greenblatt
5. *The Mirror of Herodotus: The Representation of the Other in the Writing of History,* by François Hartog, translated by Janet Lloyd
6. *Puzzling Shakespeare: Local Reading and Its Discontents,* by Leah S. Marcus
7. *The Rites of Knighthood: The Literature and Politics of Elizabethan Chivalry,* by Richard C. McCoy
8. *Literary Practice and Social Change in Britain, 1380–1530,* edited by Lee Patterson
9. *Trials of Authorship: Anterior Forms and Poetic Reconstruction from Wyatt to Shakespeare,* by Jonathan Crewe
10. *Rabelais's Carnival: Text, Context, Metatext,* by Samuel Kinser
11. *Behind the Scenes: Yeats, Horniman, and the Struggle for the Abbey Theatre,* by Adrian Frazier
12. *Literature, Politics, and Culture in Postwar Britain,* by Alan Sinfield
13. *Habits of Thought in the English Renaissance: Religion, Politics, and the Dominant Culture,* by Debora Kuller Shuger
14. *Domestic Individualism: Imagining Self in Nineteenth-Century America,* by Gillian Brown
15. *The Widening Gate: Bristol and the Atlantic Economy, 1450–1700,* by David Harris Sacks
16. *An Empire Nowhere: England, America, and Literature from "Utopia" to "The Tempest,"* by Jeffrey Knapp
17. *Mexican Ballads, Chicano Poems: History and Influence in Mexican-American Social Poetics,* by José E. Limón
18. *The Eloquence of Color: Rhetoric and Painting in the French Classical Age,* by Jacqueline Lichtenstein, translated by Emily McVarish
19. *Arts of Power: Three Halls of State in Italy, 1300–1600,* by Randolph Starn and Loren Partridge

St. Vincent de Paul holding a foundling. Henry Bedford, *The Life of St. Vincent de Paul* (New York, 1858).

Roads to Rome

The Antebellum Protestant Encounter with Catholicism

JENNY FRANCHOT

University of California Press

BERKELEY   LOS ANGELES   LONDON

PS
166
.F73
1994

University of California Press
Berkeley and Los Angeles, California

University of California Press, Ltd.
London, England

© 1994 by
The Regents of the University of California

Library of Congress Cataloging-in-Publication Data
Franchot, Jenny, 1953–
    Roads to Rome : the antebellum Protestant encounter with
Catholicism / Jenny Franchot.
        p.   cm. — (The New historicism ; 28)
    Includes bibliographical references and index.
    ISBN 0-520-07818-7 (alk. paper). — ISBN 0-520-08606-6
(pbk. : alk. paper)
    1. American literature—19th century—History and criticism.
2. Anti-Catholicism—United States—History—19th century.
3. Protestantism and literature—History—19th century.
4. Protestantism—United States—History—19th century.
5. United States—Church history—19th century.   6. United
States—Intellectual life—1783–1865.   7. Anti-Catholicism in
literature.   8. Catholic Church in literature.   I. Title.   II. Series.
PS166.F73   1994
810.9′922—dc20   93-25760

Printed in the United States of America

9 8 7 6 5 4 3 2 1

The paper used in this publication meets the minimum requirements
of American National Standard for Information Sciences—
Permanence of Paper for Printed Library Materials, ANSI
Z39.48-1984. ⊗

To My Beloved Mother

Contents

x / *Contents*

Illustrations

Acknowledgments

I owe a debt of gratitude to the many people who have helped to bring this book into being. First I wish to thank the English Department faculty at Stanford University, where I began this project as a dissertation. The encouragement and guidance I received while a graduate student there was critical to this undertaking. I especially want to acknowledge Professor Jay Fliegelman, who not only directed the dissertation but who has continued to share his brilliance and his humor, encouraging me at crucial moments to take heart and complete the book.

I also wish to thank my colleagues in the Department of English at the University of California, Berkeley. In particular, James Breslin, Frederick Crews, Catherine Gallagher, Stephen Greenblatt, and Steven Knapp have all forwarded the progress of this book by their friendship and warm support. I also owe a particular debt to Mitchell Breitwieser for his deeply attentive reading of this work at an earlier stage that opened new perspectives upon the project. In other departments of the Berkeley campus, Margaretta Lovell in Art History, Dell Upton in Architecture, and Larry Levine in History have all been valued colleagues. My especial thanks to Dell Upton for sending me items of nineteenth-century "Romanism" discovered during his own research travels. Farther afield, Norman Grabo of the Department of English, University of Tulsa, has been an irreplaceable friend and mentor who long ago introduced me to the splendors of American literature.

I owe a very particular debt to one scholarly friend who kept this project going when it threatened to languish into private contemplation. Walter Herbert of Southwestern University read the manuscript at an early stage and used it as an opportunity to encourage my intellectual growth and our friendship; in several respects, this book in its final form has emerged from his mentorship and his own profound insights into human motivation that have helped me considerably to understand antebellum Protestantism.

I wish to thank my research assistants who have cheerfully helped me track down many volumes: Anna Chodakiewicz and Carolyn Guile. Two students of mine, Sandra Gustafson and Lori Merish, have also proved to be not only wonderful but patient colleagues as I worked my way through *Roads to Rome*. The quality of their own work has many times been an inspiration and encouragement to me.

During my teaching career at Berkeley, a Doreen B. Townsend Center for the Humanities Fellowship allowed me valuable leave time and the opportunity to converse with scholars from refreshingly different disciplines. A Regents Junior Faculty Research Grant and a Committee on Teaching Minigrant also helped toward completion of the book. I also wish to thank the following institutions for their permission to reproduce documents or pictures in their possession: the Massachusetts Historical Society; the Yale Art Gallery; the Worcester Art Gallery; the Bancroft Library, University of California, Berkeley; the Boalt Law School Library, University of California, Berkeley; the Stowe-Day Foundation; the Archives of the Sisters of Charity, Emmitsburg, Maryland.

The production of this manuscript has been enabled by two wonderful word-processors, Shayna Dubbin and Melinda Colón. Shayna Dubbin especially entered into this project with great generosity of spirit and dedication of her time. At the University of California Press, Doris Kretschmer and Stephanie Fay have been very helpful editors. I wish particularly to thank Stephanie Fay for the patient and scrupulous attention she has devoted to the manuscript.

In addition, I wish to thank Andrew S. Robertson, M.D., for his care and friendship, which have greatly enabled my ability to complete this work.

Nancy Ruttenburg of the Department of Comparative Literature, University of California, Berkeley, has been a close friend to me and this book for several years. Her friendship has given me the strength to survive what have at times seemed insurmountable challenges.

My husband, Thomas C. Dashiell, and our daughter, Lily, have often wondered when this book might be done. But they have always asked with patience and affection and given of themselves whenever and however they could.

Finally, I wish to add that my mother, Janet Kerr Howell, is the guiding spirit behind this project. Truly this book comes from those days she devoted to me as a child, listening to my thoughts and sharing her own. She continues to be my greatest teacher.

Introduction

This book argues that anti-Catholicism operated as an imaginative category of discourse through which antebellum American writers of popular and elite fictional and historical texts indirectly voiced the tensions and limitations of mainstream Protestant culture. The project began from my reading of the New England reformer Orestes Brownson, author of a trenchant analysis of class conflict in antebellum America entitled "The Laboring Classes"—an essay whose focus on class conflict as a source of social and ethical injustice in antebellum America was virtually unique for its time. Within five years of writing that essay, Brownson converted to Roman Catholicism and embarked on a lifetime career as embattled spokesman for the Catholic church in America. How was it that a thinker renowned for his radical politics, fierce rationalism, and impatience with religious orthodoxy could adopt a faith deeply suspected by Protestant America for its absolutism, "Jesuitical" conspiracies, and immigrant challenges to a largely Protestant work force?[1] Was Brownson morally unstable, a man whose ideological shifts from Presbyterianism through Transcendentalism and into Roman Catholicism signaled a familiar, if unenviable, need on the part of wearied post-Enlightenment thinkers for an irreducible certainty? Or did Brownson's conversion signify more than an eccentric (and, to many of his New England contemporaries, perverse) example of the turn toward a mysterious interiority, a phenomenon evasive to culture, obedient rather to psychological imperatives connected to culture only through the private exigencies of biography?

In answering this question, I found that many others emerged. What was the Protestant, and more precisely New England, perception of Roman Catholicism in antebellum America, and how did it determine the understanding of a rapidly expanding American Catholicism? Was that perception reducible to the coherence of an ideology variously inflected by class affiliation, gender, race, and region but not fundamentally altered by them? Exactly what functions did the Protestant image of Roman Catholicism as the "foreign faith" lodged at the heart of American Christendom serve in articulating and organizing a Protestant middle-class identity? Why, finally, was that identity so fragile? As the famous Congregational minister Horace Bushnell warned in his sermon alleging papal conspiracies at work in the American West, "Nothing is necessary to make room for Romanism, but to empty us of all opposing qualities."[2] Why was such a self-emptying seen as potentially so effortless, so imminent? *Roads to Rome* developed as my attempt to answer these questions.

Catholicism (both anti and pro) functioned as a powerful rhetorical and political force during the antebellum decades. The antebellum Protestant encounter with Rome, located along a wide range of cultural enterprises, from intensely private spiritual quests to widespread nativist movements, presents itself as a necessarily interdisciplinary object of study. To uncover the cultural importance of the theological debate fiercely waged between American Protestants and Catholics, this book analyzes a range of generically disparate texts: histories, domestic novels, pulp fiction, poetry, correspondence, and canonical literary narrative. From 1830 to 1860 various events brought Catholicism to the attention of Protestant Americans: the English Catholic Emancipation Bill of 1829, Irish immigration to America during the 1840s, urban labor riots that divided along religious (as well as class) lines, the Mexican-American War of 1846, the rise of the nativist and Know-Nothing movements, and, finally, tourism to Catholic Europe, made possible by the new steamship travel. While markedly distinct social practices, these events nonetheless produced a coherent discourse in which "Romanism" functioned as metaphoric construct and surrogate for Roman Catholicism. That construct embraced not only the Roman Catholic church as a historical institution in nineteenth-century America but also the conflicted political, aesthetic, and gender issues surrounding its troubled reception. In this discourse, the terms *Catholicism* and *Protestantism* functioned as purposeful, rhetorically charged generalizations, abstractions whose impact in large part depended on their ambivalent identification with, and sometimes violent differentiation from, one another.

Unavoidably, the terms of my own analysis in part recapitulate such abstractions, for the very rhetorical features (and creative literary potential) of this antebellum argument are the focus of my investigation.

Wherever possible I specify my own use of broad terms like *Protestant-ism* by reference to the particulars of denomination, class, region, or gender. Moreover, in examining the complex rhetorical edifice of the antebellum encounter with Rome, I frequently borrow what an irritated Bishop England once enumerated as Protestant "nicknames" for Rome, which included "Romish" (or "Romanish"), "Popery" (or "Papish"), the "Whore of Babylon," and, most important for my uses, "Roman-ism." My own dependence on such terms (without quotation marks, for the most part) is in the service of analyzing the specifically Protestant American cultural imperatives behind them. One challenge of my work has been to read these "nicknames" seriously without letting them sub-side into the old and not so interesting waters of theological polemic or into more contemporary psychological terrains of the comic or the pathologically hostile. Because my work aims to describe the intriguing intricacy of this Protestant rhetorical edifice, I have been especially wary of using such terms as *paranoia,* introduced into the historical study of American political and cultural thought by the work of Richard Hof-stadter and David Brion Davis.[3] Although the work of these historians demonstrates the powerful explanatory potential of *paranoia,* my own work focuses on uncovering the often idiosyncratic attractions, fears, and refusals that can hide beneath such social psychological terms.

The assimilation of a rapidly growing immigrant Catholicism into a national culture that had been militantly anti-Catholic from its Puritan beginnings and was, by the mid-nineteenth century, struggling with its own religious sectarianism and secularization generated prolonged and sometimes violent conflict in the decades prior to the Civil War. While appearing in all regions of the Union, this religious conflict received its determining shape from the culture of the Northeast and, consequently, the Protestant sources for this study are drawn almost entirely from this region. Because animus against Romanism was a central determinant in colonial Puritan identity, New England culture in its attendant trans-formations from colony to revolutionary republican society and North American imperial power maintained a persistent identification with popery. Recent scholarship has examined how the still regional culture of New England was bent on claiming itself as the national culture.[4] Such arguments, however, have generally elided the continuing, and by 1830 resurgent, impact of Roman Catholicism on this nationally ascendent regional New England culture. Indeed, one of the larger claims of this study is that Catholicism (as an ideological construct homogenizing key ethnic, class, and regional distinctions among American Catholics as well as among American Protestants) performed an integrative function crucial to New England's pursuit of national primacy. An unintended irony of this reductive process was its eventual disintegrative impact, for the attack on Roman Catholicism, in its enumeration of Rome's suspicious charms, often led to an uncomfortable recognition of the spiritual deficiencies and psychological pressures of Protestant culture. Much of this study is concerned with tracking how a rhetoric of theological attack can twist from enemy back to self and how a religious zone like popery that is made to contain the contaminated, the exotic, and the fearful comes to be entered by the Catholic convert.

American reaction to the large waves of immigrants from Ireland and Catholic Europe during the 1840s ranged from curiosity to a xenophobia that expressed itself in nativist propaganda; in street riots; in church, convent, and Bible burnings; and finally in anti-Catholic political parties dedicated to the "countersubversion" of Rome. In the 1850s the American Know-Nothing party, with its anti-immigration platform, provided a national political forum for such nativism. The party enjoyed meteoric growth until popery was abruptly displaced by slavery as the nation's paramount political and moral issue.[5] Despite continuing and widespread antagonism to their faith, Irish and European Catholics continued to immigrate in such numbers that by 1860, with approximately 3.1 million adherents, their church represented the largest single religious body in America. That figure includes the estimated 700,000 conversions to the church from 1813 to 1893.[6]

The antebellum Protestant attack on Rome drew on an extended international history. Scholars of early modern and later European and English history will undoubtedly recognize pervasive similarities between Old and New World anti-Catholicism. Indeed, many of the more vociferous American opponents or proponents of Catholicism borrowed freely from Reformation and Counter-Reformation polemics. This study largely assumes this Old World background and only briefly addresses Protestantism's emergence from Catholic Europe and the role of Reformation polemics in establishing Anglo-American culture in the New World. Thus although I argue that such an imported discourse was ironically crucial to the assertion of an "original" American culture, I do not claim any uniqueness for that emergent anti-Catholic language. Indeed, an intriguing aspect of American Protestant encounters with Rome is the resilience of anti-Catholic discourse, its ability to cross national, class, and ethnic boundaries and thus unify its rhetorical practitioners, however precariously, behind a "Protestant Way" that was subject to its own disturbing heterogeneity.[7] At the same time, it is crucial to recognize that American anti-Catholicism, while heavily determined by Anglo-European precedent, encountered novel, intriguingly American, factors: the presence of vast and vastly disputed terrains; the competing claims of Native American, Mexican, and African-American cultures; and the establishment of a democracy at once revolutionary and conservative.

If colonial and provincial Americans frequently appealed to Reformation invective against the "Whore of Babylon," this stereotypical polemic was set into powerful new motion during the antebellum decades, resurrected by contemporary challenges to a nascent middle-class identity that for women was domestic and for men, entrepreneurial. Romanism, as envisioned by middle-class Protestants struggling with this division of men and women into "separate spheres," disrupted the formation of this identity by providing novel structures of interiority and public conduct, an alternative psychological landscape that offered to an industrializing, individualist society a populated sacramental tradition, a vastly enlarged sense of temporality, and a reconfigured spatiality of confessional, monastery, and cathedral. Many antebellum literary attitudes toward history, nature, and the individual personality revolved around this Catholic challenge to Protestant being.

For the purposes of this study the three decades prior to the Civil War are additionally crucial, for during this time Catholicism—whether as labor threat to the Protestant worker, alluring aesthetic or spiritual alternative, or menacing political conspiracy—became source material for much literary production. The twinned emergence of immigrant Catholicism and Protestantism's Romanism quickly affected contemporary literature in a way I argue was in many instances formative, shaping both popular and self-consciously genteel writing. American literary engagements with the alien faith surfaced in the romantic historiography of William H. Prescott and Francis Parkman; a voluminous anti-Catholic pulp fiction headed by such bestsellers as Maria Monk's *Awful Disclosures of the Hotel Dieu Nunnery* (1836); a steady stream of travel literature fed by the "cathedral pilgrimages" of genteel authors like Charles Eliot Norton, James Russell Lowell, and James Jackson Jarves; and finally the ambivalent fictional treatments that appear in both male- and female-authored fiction of the American Renaissance.

Such works indicate the degree to which Catholicism in its imaginary and actual forms penetrated nineteenth-century American writing. As a religious, political, and literary force it involved (and sometimes spliced together) low and high culture, generating a distinctive rhetoric ranging from the "paranoid" denunciations of Edward Beecher's *Papal Conspiracy Exposed* to the elegiac poetry of Longfellow's *Evangeline*. The resurgence of Puritan antipathy toward Rome in antebellum America is less remarkable than its appearance alongside a new wave of sympathetic, and at times voyeuristic, fascination. Indeed, the ambivalent Protestant struggle with Romanism informed and interrelated such opposing fictional modes as the crypto-pornographic anti-Catholic tales of abduction and seduction, the sentimental sketches of Italy that filled contemporary magazines, the self-consciously Protestant histories of Prescott and Parkman, the doctrinally ambivalent fiction of Hawthorne, Melville, and Stowe. In short, the discourses of anti- and pro-Catholicism informed and at points ironically sustained each another. Just as the notorious destruction of the Ursuline convent in Charlestown, Massachusetts, by a mob in 1834 occurred during the time when Gothic edifices were being constructed in American cities, so extreme prejudice and imitative desire uneasily coexisted in many individual minds. While nostalgia for a lost medievalism had its provenance among an educated, increasingly agnostic (but still Protestant) elite and bigoted terror of Catholic iniquity was one marker of an embattled Protestant working class, antebellum writings often reveal the structural links between these sensibilities. The animosity of the working class toward the Irish Catholic immigrant inheres in genteel reveries of a return to Rome just as refined nostalgia inflects the popular literature exposing the atrocities of the "Whore of Babylon." When examined from this perspective, antebellum literature reveals how an intricately metaphorized Catholicism operated in effect as a strategically confused language of spiritual desire and ethnic repudiation for middle-class Anglo-Americans. Prevented by its enforced marginal status from being assimilated too rapidly, antebellum Catholicism served many masters, justifying or criticizing Victorianism, emblematic simultaneously of premodern gaiety and the repressions of the Industrial Age. Prescott paints his Aztecs as priest-ridden Catholics obsessed with sacrifice while straining to depict Cortés as a New World Protestant hero; Hawthorne persistently analogizes Hester Prynne's abandoned Elizabethan world of aesthetic richness to Catholicism, Longfellow the modern world's lost pastoralism to Catholic Acadia, Harriet Beecher Stowe the safe purity of female childhood to little Catholic Eva.

The gradual assimilation of Catholicism into antebellum culture inevitably exacerbated a number of cultural tensions. At issue were political questions of allegiance, hierarchy, tradition, and reform; aesthetic quarrels over iconography, ceremony, and theater; moral and spiritual dilemmas about the nature and extent of sin, the efficacy and proper form of confession, the availability of salvation. Controversy over how to resolve these issues in an American democracy influenced the narrative structures, characterizations, and thematic resolutions of the antebellum literature that forms the focus of this study.

To map the complexity of the controversy and its multiple effects on literary production, I have chosen the somewhat perilous route of abstracting several key Protestant preoccupations with Romanism, although such concerns inhabit different, sometimes competing, logical categories. Thus in analyzing confession in Hawthorne's fiction or monasticism in Melville's tales of captivity, I understand confession as at once a "foreign" ecclesiastical practice and a transcultural psychological impulse to unburden the self, and monasticism as both the life of Roman Catholic monks and nuns and a variously elaborated antebellum suspicion about celibacy and retreat from the public space. The vitality of Protestantism's rhetorical construction of Romanism resides precisely in this imprecision of reference, a terminological slippage that enabled not only the incendiary suggestiveness of popular fictions but also the subversive insinuations of Hawthorne and Melville. I hope to demonstrate the cultural and literary power of such taxonomic confusions and, secondarily, to illustrate the explanatory utility of seriously engaging such theological issues. These semantic transactions in the American Protestant image of Rome do not, however, argue for interchangeability. Preoccupations with ceremony, celibacy, monasticism, or priesthood function more intriguingly than as exchangeable instances of, for example, the conspiratorial mind. They lead rather into the rhetorical and philosophical character of particular individuals and texts.

The Protestant American encounter with the estranged world of Catholicism provoked a characteristically conflicted response of repulsion and longing, a fear of corruption and a hunger for communion. When a literary artist confronted Catholicism, deeply associated in the post-Reformation mind with the dubious attractions of art, the encounter proved peculiarly self-reflexive. Catholic art, especially the statuary, architecture, and picture galleries of Renaissance Rome, loomed large for antebellum painters, sculptors, and writers. Hawthorne, Melville, Poe, and Stowe all used such art as a symbolic commentary on their own creative and philosophical struggles and those of their fictional characters. In particular, I argue that the tourist response to Italian Catholicism—in its demonized formulation as Whore of Babylon and in its sentimentally divinized image as the "bosom of the mighty mother"—partially legitimized Catholicism's status at home as national menace and potential contaminant by appealing to its rapidly developing international status as aesthetic commodity. Ritually ostracized and cordoned off from the Protestant public at home, Romanism's dangerous domestic powers of contagion ironically sustained the touristic reproduction and commodification of its repudiated sacred.

Divided into four parts, my book situates this complex literary engagement with Catholicism within and against larger cultural discourses of historical inquiry, gender formation, and spiritual conversion. Part 1, "History: The New and Old Worlds," examines the competing projects of Francis Parkman, William Prescott, and lesser-known figures (including dissenting Catholic historians) to fashion an ideologically coherent American historical narrative about the cultural consequences of the great post-Reformation schism. My analysis places issues of ethnic and gender conflict in dialogue with religious difference and argues that converging conflicts over the disturbing mixtures represented by the "feminine," by invalidism, and by popery profoundly influenced American romantic historiography. Specifically, I attempt to map the connections between white Protestant historiography in antebellum America and ethnographic and racial divisions between these New England authors and their various imagined Catholic others: the French Jesuit, the North American Indian, the Spaniard, and the Mexican. Especially in my treatment of Parkman's second volume of his seven-volume account of Catholic France's defeat by an "Anglo-Saxon" America, I argue for the centrality of the historian's suffering body. Like Prescott, Parkman endured a lifetime of invalidism for which his histories served as therapeutic control, if not cure, his fascination with Catholicism inspired by his perception of the foreign faith's more spectacular representation, and hence management, of bodily pain.

Parkman's and Prescott's histories narrated and ambivalently legitimated the creation of a Protestant America in the vast regions north and south of New England; behind the historians' assertion of national boundary lies a tortuous dialectic between the failed body of the elite male author and the imperfect (but powerful) body of the heretical Catholic other. It was not only the French Jesuit (or the idolatrous Aztec kingship of Montezuma in Prescott's 1843 best-seller, *The History of the Conquest of Mexico*) that attracted Protestant scrutiny. The rhetoric generated by the 1846 war with Mexico suggests a coincidence of fears—of the body of the Mexican (product of racial mingling) and, more generally, of miscegenation—that incited the Protestant repudiation of popery's blasphemous minglings of flesh and spirit.

Part 2, "American Protestantism and Its Captivities," explores the best-selling pulp fiction of Maria Monk and Rebecca Reed to argue for the centrality of gender issues in popular anti-Catholicism. These best-sellers deployed a European (and English) literature of anticlericalism and Gothic horror to expose the iniquities of life behind American (and Canadian) convent walls. This convent fiction also developed, however, from an indigenous tradition of Indian captivity narratives that in their original Puritan instance frequently posited priests and savages as strangely twinned evils of the American wilderness.[8] The "savagery" and "priestcraft" of the American wilderness, in turn, drew their malignant energies from anterior conceptions of seductive and devouring womanhood. Not only is this blending of European and indigenous literary genres a fascinating instance of the much-discussed antebellum struggle to create an original New World literary culture, but the anxiety about American cultural purity also suggests deeper struggles over racial and religious homogeneity and how, if at all, to enclose slavery within a democratic nation.

The best-selling convent exposés participated in a larger cultural debate as well—over the proper nature of the bourgeois family. In popular advice manuals advocating the new middle-class domesticity, monastic life (among many other practices) functions as a threatening and frankly heretical alternative. As the frontispiece of St. Vincent de Paul cradling an infant suggests, the rejection of standard reproductive roles could enable startling deviations: the nun could claim a suspicious autonomy from marriage and motherhood, and the monk could appropriate the role of mother. Both the celibate male body and the sentimental female body were central to the Protestant attack on convents. Widespread political agitation over convents focused on the seduction of Protestant virgins by a licentious priesthood, disguised behind the pretense of celibacy. To many Protestant authors and readers of convent tales, such deviant sexual states logically generated disease, most typically surfacing in the figure of the consumptive nun. In its varied formations as intemperate immigrant Irish worker; as pallid, consumptive nun; as lustful, duplicitous priest, the Catholic body marked the boundaries of a normative Protestant self intent on a purity that would signal the attainment of perfection. The imaging of these various bodies culminated in ruminations on the human proclivity for "mixture" and "excess"—twinned forms of the impure that generated the tainted expressivities of Rome.

Part 2 ends with a discussion of how these "popular" issues of seduction, suspicion, and abasement operate in such elite fiction as Melville's *Benito Cereno* and Poe's "The Pit and the Pendulum." The sectional crisis of the 1850s illustrates, in turn, how these texts transformed elements from popular anti-Catholic literature into profound meditations on enslavement. Melville's famed ambiguity and Poe's equally notorious theatricalism are skilled manipulations of the popular Catholic captivity tale.

Part 3, "Conversion and Its Fictions," deals with the language of pro-Catholicism—a more diverse and motivationally complex discourse than that of anti-Catholicism. Both Part 3 and Part 4 deal dialectically with the "convert prose" of neglected figures like Mother Elizabeth Ann Seton, Sophia Ripley, Isaac Hecker, and Orestes Brownson and such religiously nostalgic but studiously "unconverted" works as Longfellow's *Evangeline*, Hawthorne's *Scarlet Letter,* and Harriet Beecher Stowe's *Agnes of Sorrento.* The interraction of faith (or its absence) with gender conflict and narrative structure is the focus of my discussion. What are the formal or broader ideological implications of the manifest imitativeness (or even "doubling") of these writings? To answer this question, I turn in Part 4, "Four Converts," to the writings of the Catholic converts mentioned above, figures who have remained peripheral to contemporary literary critical studies, in part because they passionately assert the priority of object over subject, the existence of truth over and above any linguistic representation. The didactic (or rhapsodic) rhetoric of conversion bears within it anti-Catholicism's fervid preoccupation with the body as well as romantic historiography's concern with the founding of an original American self.

Although this is a book emphatically about Protestantism, it presents what I hope is a convincing argument for the religious "other" in its midst. The role of Protestantism in the development (or nondevelopment) of various genres, from the colonial captivity narrative to the sentimental novel of seduction to the "metaphysical" fiction of Melville, has been frequently and often brilliantly explored. The writings of Sacvan Bercovitch and Ann Douglas, developing from those of Perry Miller, have persuasively argued for the impact of New England Puritanism and nineteenth-century evangelical discourse on our national literary culture. An unintended result of such scholarship is an ever more Protestant America, a critical view that nonetheless has still to account for the overt Catholic concerns of so much antebellum writing.[9]

I hope my study will supply, however partially, the competing voice at the heart of (and on the excluded edges of) antebellum Protestantism. Ideally, this study would give equal attention to the antebellum Catholic psyche and how it contributed to or evaded the Protestant construction of Romanism. In puzzling through how to present the unduly neglected voices of antebellum Catholics, I decided, for reasons of scope and conceptual coherence, to devote most of my attention not to those who grew up in the Catholic church but to those who converted to it. The voice of Protestant converts to Rome who publicized (often strenuously) their new Catholic viewpoint offers an intriguing summation of my subject by its very struggle to exchange Romanism for Catholicism. Because of their hybrid status, antebellum converts spoke a language of competing alliances that offers a fascinating study of the embattled transformation of religious identity.

Finally, it is worth noting that the voice opposing this antebellum language of religious outrage or conversion was that of religious indifference. Although *Roads to Rome* largely skirts discussion of secularization and the specific impact of the Higher Criticism, the Protestant invective against and fascination with Rome were clearly symptomatic of the modern West's withdrawal from a cohesive spirituality. Indeed, I read the attack on Catholic absolutism as part of liberal Protestantism's struggle to divest itself of absolutist Calvinist orthodoxy while attempting to control its own debilitation by rallying forces against a malevolent Rome. From the liberal Unitarian perspective of the day, the real enemy facing Boston was not Rome but a ghostly skepticism that would soon destroy even Rome's power:

> a dreary spectre, weaponless, passionless, mute,—bidding her no defiance, declining close engagement, overcome by no disaster, elated by no success, but lurking by her side, waiting and watching, destroying her by a steadfast, ghastly look, blasting all objects on which it rests, desolating, petrifying like the gorgon of old.[10]

1

HISTORY:
THE NEW AND OLD WORLDS

ONE

Protestant Meditations On History And "Popery"

Spokesmen for Anglo-America in the New World, nineteenth-century American historians constructed a national history that traced America's development from colonial settlements of religious refugees and adventurers to an industrializing society whose progress was the joint result of Protestant and republican reformist energies. In the words of one Philadelphia journal, antebellum Americans would succeed in their pursuit of exemplary nation building if they could simply "bear in mind that they are the patriarchs of modern emancipation."[1] Such progress, however, depended on a sustained rearguard action against a European past conceived of as contaminated by monarchism, aristocracy, and Roman Catholicism. If the revolutionary struggle had successfully deposed royal power, the struggle against Roman Catholicism continued. An enemy conventionally figured over the course of four centuries as popery, Romanism, or, more graphically, the Whore of Babylon, the Catholic church infiltrated the American Protestant historical imagination as a principal impediment to progress and at times as a principal attraction. If, as Cotton Mather proclaimed in his *Magnalia Christi Americana*, the workings of Providence demanded the defeat of the remaining *"Baits of Popery"* yet left in the church, those vestiges of Romanism proved curiously resistant, even against the postmillennial optimism of later revivalists like Jonathan Edwards, for whom America, after enduring an anticipated "very dark time," was to conquer the Antichrist and enjoy the coming of the millennium.[2] In part because he thought the "power and influence of the Pope is much diminished,"

3

Edwards fought infidelity more than popery; but in claiming the dynamism of evangelical Protestantism as America's identifying possession, Edwards implicitly lodged Catholicism in the darkness of contemporary spiritual indifference.[3]

Events in the decades following Jonathan Edwards's death in 1758 threatened such confidence in an American providential design. Especially in the aftermath of the American Revolution, Protestantism contended with disestablishment and the consequent rise of voluntarism, sectarianism, and secularization.[4] Initially fought during the Reformation, the Protestant battle against Rome, in its variant denominational aspects, was reenacted and precariously legitimated by the spread of English Protestant culture in the New World. Catholicism continued to be silenced by a providential history that in the sixteenth century had performed two momentous and interrelated feats: the Reformation and the Puritan settlement of America. Antebellum America understood its privileged status as emerging from the doctrinal revolutions of the Reformation and from the ethnic superiority of those early "Teutonic" rebels against "Latin" tyranny. "The genius of Northern, Scandinavian life thenceforth asserted its supremacy," explained one essayist of America's emancipatory origins, "and reformations, discoveries of new worlds in the physical and mental sphere, free institutions, and popular governments were necessary, unavoidable facts."[5]

The British Puritan imagination, analogizing from its understanding of the New Testament's typological fulfillment of the Old, conceived of the New World as both separating from and seeking to purify Europe. The Puritan reforming spirit, stemming directly from God and later strengthened by the alleged racial superiority of the Teutonic genius, continued to enact the divine will in nineteenth-century America's "manifest destiny" to extend its territorial boundaries.[6] The major antebellum historians of America's southern and northern frontiers, William H. Prescott and Francis Parkman, stressed the "Anglo-Saxon" cultures' destined conquest of the land, its native American inhabitants, and European Catholic power. Intent on claiming the Puritan Christian teleology for the New World, early American Protestants like Mather and Edwards as well as later historians like Prescott and Parkman insisted that the Reformation had rescued the progressive workings of the spirit from the stasis or even regression of papal captivity.[7]

This resuscitated evangelical force, heroically transported to the New World in the Puritan migration, reemerged in the nineteenth century as the Protestant Way, a cultural route invoked to unify an increasingly fragmented Protestantism and to fight the threats posed by Irish and German Catholic immigration. Since the Reformation had freed believers from a church deemed tyrannical in part because of its philosophical resistance to the notion of change, "history" and America's Protestant sects were firmly identified, an alliance that occasionally extended to all of time itself: time was endowed with the same invincible commitment to reform. Thus the European Reformation, argued one New Englander, was a natural outgrowth of a universal phenomenon: "The reforming process, of which Luther's resistance was one of the stages, began before he existed, it survived when his wars were over, and will keep on long after our generation is in the dust." That Catholics should still exist after having been directed offstage nearly four centuries earlier greatly disturbed both conservative and liberal American Protestants, who alike concluded that their very position in the vanguard of history called for constant vigilance against the immigrant Catholic to maintain, even perfect, the virile autonomy of the "native" Protestant American self. As Emerson argued in his 1849 essay "Power," the "necessity of balancing and keeping at bay the snarling majorities of German, Irish, and of native millions, will bestow promptness, address, and reason, at last, on our buffalo-hunter, and authority and majesty of manners." But if the emancipatory narrative unfolded initially in Puritan historiography pervaded antebellum periodical literature, sermons, and speeches, its consensus about the Protestant victory over a Catholic past was rendered internally fragile by the disputing Arminian and Orthodox persuasions—an internal schism that required a concerted resistance to the menacing Catholic immigrant and to the ahistorical, largely invisible, and profoundly magnetic power of popery.[8]

Antebellum New England efforts forged a national identity that was not only oppositional but even "negative" in its essence, for it was profoundly shaped by a continued rejection of and rivalry with Roman Catholicism. Seeking to confirm a still provisional, self-consciously Protestant nationhood by contrasting it with what was familiarly called the "foreign faith," the romantic historians drew on colonial and eighteenth-century attitudes toward the repudiated church for their new progressive historiography. If the papacy had receded in political influence with Anglo-America's triumphs against both New Spain and New France, as an ideological figure known as popery or "Romanism" it received an alarmed scrutiny during the antebellum decades from ministers, novelists, statesmen, and historians, who often invoked the unlikely threat of papal overthrow to divert attention from intractable national problems that finally had little to do with religion. Divisive sectionalism, urbanization, immigration, industrialization, race slavery, and finally the stresses in the formation of the middle-class family all challenged the notion of a national identity made coherent by its allegiance to Protestantism. To assert a national selfhood that was essentially religious enabled American Protestants of varying and often antagonistic denominations (and social classes) to minimize, if not resolve, racial, sexual, and economic divisions in the American nation.[9]

If nineteenth-century American Catholics defensively divided the world between the one, holy, and apostolic church and the unchurched cosmos, American Protestants had their own troubling divisions to deal with. In several respects, conservative Catholic invective against the evils of Protestantism touched on painful truths of the national culture. The practiced controversialist Archbishop Martin Jay Spalding of Baltimore described the Reformation in extravagantly reactionary terms that pointed, however, to interpretive quandaries liberal Protestants were indeed struggling with, although of course they would have disagreed with Spalding's Catholic diagnosis:

> It was not a merely local or transient rebellion against Church authority which was at hand, but a mighty revolution, which was to shake Christendom to its very centre; and to endure, with its long and pestilent train of evils, with its Babel-like sound and confusion of tongues, with its first incipient and then developed infidelity, probably to the end of the world![10]

American historians like Prescott and Parkman, the novelists of the American Renaissance, and writers of popular and domestic fiction were indeed troubled by a confusion of tongues, perplexed in part by a bisection of cultural time into an iconic Catholic "past," sealed off from the present and available for aesthetic and psychological rumination, and an emphatically text-oriented Protestant "history," extending from the Reformation into the antebellum present. The ideology of American Reformed Christianity constructed this vanquished, static, regressive Catholic "past": it appeared most commonly as a conglomeration of ruins and foreign cultures, Italian Renaissance and Baroque art (made available through new processes of reproduction), and a foreign "Latinate" or "Celtic" selfhood, seen by American tourists abroad and, with the onset of Irish immigration in the 1840s, confronted at home as well. Against this ideological construction of an imagistic, "idolatrous," and politically regressive Catholic past (itself a regressive construction that became very much "present" in antebellum America), Old and New

World Protestant "history" upheld the power of the "Word" against that of the "Image" and, by extension, the power of biblically allusive historical and fictional narratives against the suspiciously flesh-bound powers of Rome.[11] Both Protestant religious polemics and American travel accounts opposed ahistorical Catholic "ruins" to Protestant "history" and the perilously attractive ahistorical corruptions of the Catholic body to the progressive and cleansing powers of the Protestant voice. Between Catholic matter and Protestant spirit snaked the dividing line of the Reformation, which had initiated a new religious narrative against the allegedly calculated falsehood of the pope's story and which reiterated crucial oppositions between autonomy, purity, and self-regulation, on the one hand, and the dangers of submission and "excess"—whether liturgical, aesthetic, or political—on the other.

The conflict between Protestant enlightenment and popish duplicity was early fashioned into epochal drama by John Foxe in his famous (and to Catholics, notorious) history, *Actes and Monuments* (1563). When, as Foxe recounts, "coloured hypocrisy, false doctrine, and painted holiness, began to be espied more and more by the reading of God's word," the revolutionary dynamic revealing the Word's power over the image was set in motion.[12] Such an asserted triumph of textuality over European humanity's imagistic, duplicitous past could only be sustained by endowing the Word (in the confines of what early Dissenting preachers denoted the plain style) with the charismatic power, if not the palpable contours, of the abandoned image.

Modeling his history on the French Calvinist Jean Crespin's *Book of Martyrs,* Foxe in his martyrology displays a series of significations that interlock the sacred, the political, the aesthetic, and the technological. Thus he proclaims the invention of printing as a divine intervention in earthly affairs that makes possible the production of authentic history; the Word, made newly available to humanity by the printing press and soon thereafter by Foxe's heroic historiography, rivals and finally transforms the flesh of Foxe's martyrs into pointedly articulate and distributable text. In the transformative medium of fire that consumes a series of Marian martyrs Foxe's words themselves assume the rhetorical authentication of the passional suffering they record. Conversely each victim, in the agony of incineration, achieves the evangelical potency and historical permanence of Gospel text. Thus Foxe punctuates his historical account with execution tableaux in which text and flesh dramatically coalesce; martyrs read aloud from the Bible as they burn, words and flesh consumed in a synchrony that argues in turn for their mutual incorruptibility. Heretical and heroic like each martyr, the

Word in turn enforces the identity between martyr and reader of martyrdom:

> There was a company of books cast into the fire; and by chance
> a communion-book fell between his hands, who receiving it joy-
> fully opened it, and read so long as the force of the flame and
> smoke caused him that he could see no more. Then he fell
> again to prayer, holding his hands up to heaven, and the book
> between his arms next to his heart, thanking God for sending
> him it. (392)

Such tableaux, then, fuse the Book and the Body, reading and corporeal suffering, into a spectacular and revelatory historical action
whose permanence derives not from the tangibility of the Catholic icon
but from the gruesomeness of the icon's extinction. One particular
polemical benefit of Foxe's martyrology, then, is its incorporation of the
body's iconic and commemorative power into the new Protestantism.
Foxe's history establishes distinctions between text and flesh specifically
to deny them; the Word, as made present through Foxe's words, engi-
neers the paradox by which the martyrs become new relics for their
iconoclast audiences, translated from venerated body to venerated text.
The Gospel sufficiently anesthetizes the flesh so that Foxe's Marian
martyrs comment theatrically on their grisly transfiguration by clapping
their burning hands to signal the absence of pain. That same Word
interprets such theater for the populace. In a transformation extremely
important for later Protestant historiography, the Word becomes the
words of the historian, authenticated by their revelation of "popish" evil
and consequent conversionary impact on the reader. Exposé and conversion are rhetorically and theologically linked, for conversion to Protestantism critically depends on the exposure of Catholic duplicity and
wickedness. Thus in Foxe's accounts each burning is preceded by a ritual
dialogue (of forgiveness, temptation to recant, etc.) between the martyrs
and their Catholic persecutors, followed by the victims' invocations to
the audience before the lighting of the fires. These spontaneous sermons
by the bound victims provide cameo lessons in history, explaining how
the imminent holocaust will contribute to the great battle against
Antichrist predicted in the Book of Revelation.

Because Foxe's record of these sacred sacrifices assumes a power
kindred to that of the Gospel, advertising to the world the horrors of
Bloody Mary just as the Gospels published the persecuted glory of Jesus
Christ, the Foxean imitation insists that exposure of Catholic iniquity
serves as humanity's new access to revelation. Like Christ, Foxe must not

only expose and exorcise but also convert; in his professedly impartial documentary record of the burnings, the Protestant historian-martyrologist draws his readers into the conversionary state of the spectator by enforcing a parallel between witnessing the martyrs' deaths and reading of that witness: "And the fire flaming about them they yielded their souls, bodies and lives into the hands of the omnipotent Lord, to whose protection I commend thee, gentle reader" (418). While Foxe's history was influential enough to be chained to lecterns in English churches, its charismatic blend of hagiography and invective sounded increasingly anachronistic to nineteenth-century readers. The martyrologist Cotton Mather, a self-styled American Foxe, offering "unto the Churches of the Reformation, abroad in the World, some small Memorials, that may be serviceable unto the Designs of Reformation," was particularly distrusted by liberal antebellum Protestants, not only for his role in the Salem witchcraft executions but also for more generally symbolizing the persecutorial energies latent in American Calvinism.[13]

For nineteenth-century Americans, religious liberation had lost its gritty detail of slow-burning wood and agonized flesh and had assumed the vague contours of humanistic freedom. Although a Catholic priest could still cause a national uproar by burning Protestant Bibles, the Word in its temporal expression as history was losing its numinous force.[14] History had forsaken none of its progressive dynamic, but its goal had become increasingly abstract, even hypocritical, disguising beneath its optimistic terminology of emancipation and improvement the unsavory realities of imperialist expansion and race slavery. If nineteenth-century American schoolbooks pictured Western history as a "Hegelian process for the realization of the idea of freedom," neither the process nor the freedom was especially apparent.[15] Depleted of its previous urgency and salvific aura, and challenged by denominational disputes in Protestantism itself, Reformed Christianity—particularly liberal New England Congregationalism and Unitarianism—could no longer easily dismiss the countertext of Catholic iconography and ceremony. Although declared discontinuous with the present, that iconic past, palpable in image and statue, cathedral and catacomb, lithograph and engraving, now intruded on the purified and printbound present.[16] Thus as the Reformation receded, so too did the insurrectionary and purifying powers of the Word. New England Puritans had created and sustained their subversively conservative identity through a still rare written word that recounted the human conquest of an inarticulate past bent on silencing the Gospel. But by the mid-nineteenth century, Scripture was everywhere competing with the encroachments of a developing mass-printing market.[17]

Although anachronistic, Foxe's drama of the cleansed "text" of Reformed Christianity overcoming the diseased embodiments of Roman Catholicism by the incendiary enumeration and publication of its fleshly corruptions still informed American sensibilities in the 1840s. A contemporary essayist, for example, distinguished Luther from Loyola precisely in terms of Lutheranism's textual supremacism: "But while Luther swore allegiance to the Holy Scriptures, the Jesuit gave himself to dreams and rhapsodies and to a chivalrous devotion to our Blessed Lady."[18] Many accounts of Protestantism's historical development stressed the crucial cultural contributions of printing and of reading, particularly lay reading of the Bible, to the individual exercise of "private judgment."[19] In describing his English ancestry, early America's most famous citizen, Benjamin Franklin, proudly noted how his Dissenter forebears ingeniously thwarted Anglican regulations against Bible reading.

> They had got an English Bible, and to conceal and secure it, it was fastened open with Tapes under and within the Frame of a Joint Stool. When my Great Great Grandfather read in it to his Family, he turn'd up the Joint Stool upon his Knees, turning over the Leaves then under the Tapes. One of the Children stood at the Door to give Notice if he saw the Apparitor coming. . . . In that Case the Stool was turn'd down again upon its feet, when the Bible remain'd conceal'd under it as before.[20]

Early republican novelists like Susanna Rowson (*Charlotte Temple,* 1794) and Hannah Foster (*The Coquette,* 1797) appropriated Protestantism's legacy of individual judgment to justify the writing and reading of female didactic fiction about the sexual temptation and destruction of women in the New World. At the same time, however, these novelists, uncomfortably aware that Protestantism could lead the independent soul astray, warned against the potentially anarchic effects of solitary reading, especially when the prerogatives of "private judgment" were extended to a young girl's reading of seductive letters: Mademoiselle LaRue's invidious injunction to her student Charlotte Temple to "open the [seducer's] letter, read it, and judge for yourself," abruptly perverts Charlotte's readerly devotion to Scripture; henceforth, she reads only the language of seduction and descends into sexual error, pregnancy, and death.[21] When the Vatican in the nineteenth century tried to curb Catholic reading of the King James Bible and when American Catholics demanded that the Protestant Bible be excluded from public schools if Catholic Bibles were to be prohibited, American Protestants had further evidence of the tyrannical opposition of popery to the democratizing effects of private (unguided) reading of Scripture. Indeed, when a Roman Catholic priest publicly burned Protestant Bibles in 1842, an event known as the Champlain Bible Burning, it recalled Foxean images of Protestant martyrs reading in the flames and was even proclaimed a revival of the Spanish auto-da-fé in the United States.[22]

Combined with Scripture into a single progressive sacred text, *history* as a conventional term of antebellum Protestant periodical prose enjoyed the redemptive power of a language close to "nature" and hence divorced from the contaminations of culture. Americans who understood their country as "Nature's nation" relegated Catholicism to the realm of culture—an ideological region of artifice, complexity, and immorality.[23] New World Christians, empowered by the lands apparently made theirs by divine fiat, strove to free themselves from the restraining grip of European culture as well as the insidious effects of urbanization and the inevitable artifices of a developing cultural life.

If fire was Foxe's primary image of release and self-purification from institutional corruption, water was central to the American Protestant symbolic imagination. For the early immigrant generations of religious exiles, the Atlantic ocean crossing powerfully suggested a renewed baptism into the life of the spirit and the land of promise.[24] But water imagery also continued to convey antebellum America's cleansing from Catholic pollution. The German church historian August Neander (1789–1850) imagined history, in the approving words of one American critic, as a liquid flowing from the Old to the New World:

> He [Neander] thus was pre-eminently qualified to trace the flow of Christian doctrine and influence from its sacred fountains down through its discolouring channels of transmission, through ages of darkness and eras of renewed light, through corruptions, heresies, and partial reformations, to these latter days, in which its still divided current rolls on to become one again in that happier future foreshadowed in the Saviour's prayer at the Last Supper.[25]

By the antebellum decades, such transatlantic crossings had lost their typological force, in part because Catholic immigrants were now making that voyage. Purification was no longer accomplished by crossing the Atlantic, but, more metaphorically, by journeying from Europe to the American frontier. History flowed from the Old into the New World and then, quickly enough, from the eastern seaboard to the "Adamic" western frontier, in harmony with the imperialist notion of empire's westward course, first popularized by Bishop Berkeley. Like English Protestants, historiography was itself freed of discolorations in this westward course. Since the "pure light of the Gospel, in penetrating the thick mist which enveloped the heathen world, became itself discolored at once,"[26] it took the discovery of the New World to restore that light to purity, to liberate the divine schedule of events from the discolored, clogged impediments of the Old World. This formative symbolic opposition between European contamination and American purity played itself out not only in the triumph of the Protestant word over the Catholic image but also in the triumph of heuristic clarity over "Jesuitical" obfuscation. American Protestants were accordingly obliged to pursue their clarified vision with moral strenuousness. "Under the patronage of our free institutions," explained the anti-Catholic agitator W. C. Brownlee, "the religion of Christ enjoys an opportunity of working itself clear from the sediment of misrepresentation which has been cast into its pure fountain."[27]

The Protestant historical vision, then, claimed a virtually redemptive function precisely by defining history as Protestant, as a dynamic that cleansed the spiritual of its material dross by separating out the entangled strands of sanctity and corruption. For liberal New Englanders, in particular, Christian worship had grown steadily less Catholic by continuing to separate itself from the earthy, the inarticulate, and the literal. Unitarian Christians (who were greatly interested in Roman Catholicism during the 1830s and 1840s) placed themselves in this vanguard movement toward a fully literate, increasingly bodiless, "spiritual" religion; indeed, liberal Unitarians demonstrated their allegiance to the Word rather than worldly ecclesiastical power and theological incarnationalism by an increasingly symbolic reading of Scripture, a willingness to interpret the Word as a congeries of images, metaphors, and symbols.[28] Religion's progress from the material to the spiritual, the ceremonial to the verbal was finally successful, then, because of the way providential history worked. As one Unitarian contended, sacrifice, as religious ritual, had already progressed from corrupt material offerings to pure spiritual ones because the "mode of historical development is that of a separation of things mixed, allowing individual representations to both of the contending principles." It was not just that, for example, communion tables were no longer to look like altars in Virginia's churches after disestablishment but also that American history was thereafter dedicated to the segregation of altars from tables, a continued disentangling of "things mixed."[29]

Liberal Protestant voices performed this anti-incarnational function of extracting spirit from flesh, text from image to gain a righteously empowered purity. But in separating the elements of sacrifice one from another, these voices also spoke a new language of radical simplification. By the mid-nineteenth century, the false could more readily be distinguished from the true thanks to history's personified capacity for organizing life into a drama of Catholic regressive "matter" conspiring against Protestant progressive "spirit" but ultimately vanquished by it. What individuals encountered when they personally inquired into the past was another matter. But for influential contemporary periodicals like the *North American Review,* the *Christian Examiner,* and *Harper's Magazine,* history's main role was as organizer and judge of a past whose ideological message was purposefully simplistic. It was in this judgmental, clarifying sense that Protestant history laid claim to a God-like function. While liberal Protestant clergy and novelists struggled to overthrow the aggressive exclusionism of orthodox Calvinism, which dismissed most souls to eternal perdition, they still clung to Calvinism's predilection for separation and purification in their meditations on national identity; if Protestant souls increasingly enjoyed the benefits of a liberalized theology that democratized the availability of the spirit, Protestant citizens were building a national identity ever more exclusionary.[30] And if "foreigners" were no longer overtly "damned," they were frankly, and at times violently, excluded from the privileges of republican union.

The Roman church, naturally catalogued as ahistorical by the liberal antebellum religious press, its own histories invalidated as fiction or reactionary polemic, nonetheless guarded itself zealously from innovation, in part to protect itself from Protestant attack but also to maintain its divinely commissioned mandate to preserve its truths from the vagaries of historical change. Protestant critics, flatly refusing this redemptive view of changelessness, insisted that Catholic ahistoricity had little to do with the Eternal and much to do with the disguised tyranny of reactionaries. Many Americans were uncertain, however, whether Catholics opposed the purifications of history intentionally and conspiratorially, were victims of the divine plan, or, worse yet, were psychological and political dupes of "priestcraft." Was it even possible to distinguish among Catholics, or was papal authority so monolithic that it crushed any distinctions of gender, class, national origin, and temperament? From one perspective, the Roman church menacingly "set itself in systematic opposition to the Christian ideas of freedom and development announced by Jesus and his Apostles,"[31] thus requiring Protestants of whatever denomination to militantly oppose any Catholic presence on American shores and to ferret out alleged papal conspiracies against American republican ways. From another perspective, because Catholicism was seen as a human fabrication excluded from the divine-natural world of providential history, it was impotently mired in its own duplicities and suffered the consequent frailties of the human. It was not a global power but an uncanny survival of a European, even feminine, consciousness. From this patronizing (but potentially more sympathetic) perspective, the Roman church was to be pitied, even studied, and perhaps celebrated, but finally dismissed. Associated with the fabulous, with the world of fiction instead of fact, with stasis instead of progress, Catholicism represented the false narrative of Western culture to which one could respond with outraged, even paranoid, indignation or with tentative explorations of the motivations behind this Romish falsity.

Having been excluded from the nation's forward movement and the history that had articulated and continued to promote it, Roman Catholicism ironically attained a crucial place in defining New World Protestantism and maintaining that self-definition through the antebellum decades. It played the fiction to Protestantism's truth, the failure to its progress, the weaker femininity to its superior masculinity. Observers called the Roman church a yarn spinner, turning out ever taller tales to meet the "pressing and practical" demand for miracles in Rome. A typically condescending description of the process of beatification assures readers that "no story or miracle can be invented, so preposterous that it may not be overmatched by what is received, sanctioned and magnified in the Sacred City to-day."[32] The spectacle of such a globally institutionalized power intricately allied with fantasy nonetheless intrigued suspicious empiricists. Understood as fictional rather than authentic, the Roman church could then exert the proverbial seductions of fiction. Emerson, writing in 1847, faulted Protestantism for its sectarianism while praising the collectivist aesthetic of Catholicism as most natural and hence amenable to the transcendentalist imagination:

> The Catholic religion respects masses of men and ages. . . . The Protestant, on the contrary, with its hateful "private judgment," brings parishes, families, and at last individual doctrinaires and schismatics . . . into play and notice, which to the gentle, musing poet is to the last degree disagreeable. . . . The Catholic Church is. . . . in harmony with Nature, which loves the race and ruins the individual.[33]

Indeed its delusions were understood as hoodwinking its most intelligent defenders; even the famous Catholic convert and controversialist Orestes Brownson was disoriented by its illusions. So Brownson's efforts to explain (and defend) Catholicism—efforts that by 1870 had amounted to some twenty volumes of essays and fiction—were compared to Captain Perry's efforts to reach the North Pole by unwittingly hiking north on an iceberg moving south. Against the "current" of the age, Brownson was laboring vainly to "reach the north pole of a frozen and arctic religion."[34]

If Orestes Brownson, ex-Transcendentalist and very much ex-Protestant, uncomfortably personalized the threat of Catholicism's attractions, New England observers often disguised their discomfort by incorporating the Roman church into the very drama of Protestant reform. Thus one essayist declared that "somewhere the antagonist should stand forth to give battle, and occupy the strength of heart, head, and arm of the youthful era of a better social organization; and the Catholic Church is that embodiment and that antagonist."[35] Those who prided themselves on being above the bigotry of anti-Catholic nativists (who campaigned for punitive restrictions on Catholic immigration and voting rights) consigned Catholics instead to a parental role in the family romance of Protestant self-development. In this drama, popery played a ritual parental figure—a menacing but eventually impotent opponent, one whose defeat had already been decided and whose threat was finally an intriguing one.

By contrast, religious alarmists like Samuel F. B. Morse, painter, inventor of the telegraph, and anti-Catholic agitator, saw the Roman church actively contending against the nation's republican principles. Ironically, Morse's paranoid nationalism endowed the immigrant church with a genuine, if menacing, vitality. Shocked by public indifference to alleged papal conspiracies, Morse reminded his readers that the blood shed by Catholicism was "still wet upon the dungeon floors of Italy" while the "spirit of '76" lay sleeping.[36] But for those relatively uninfected with nativist emotion, Catholicism was simply not strong enough to pose a serious threat. Its role in history was effectively finished. "In the providence of God it had a purpose to fulfill, and it has fulfilled it," declared one journal with quiet confidence.[37] It was a sentiment echoed by many other genteel voices of the day as they took turns at politely interring Catholicism. Somewhat less graciously, the Reverend Nicholas Murray (a Catholic turned polemical Presbyterian minister) exulted that "popery" was "like unto a bladder once blown to its full extension, but now dry, beyond the power of holy oil or water to soften, and rent beyond the power of priests to patch up, and utterly incapable of a new inflation."[38]

TWO

"The Moral Map of the World"

American Tourists and Underground Rome

From the 1830s on, American Protestants were challenged not just by internal dissension and Catholic immigration, but by the surprising aesthetic attractions of Catholic Europe, made possible by steamship travel. "Americans," declared the *North American Review,* "have a special call to travel. It is the peculiar privilege of their birth in the New World, that the Old World is left them to visit."[1] Travel itself was both a cultural activity necessary to the continued formulation of national identity and a spiritual enterprise. But increasing contact with Catholic Europe on the part of monied New Englanders complicated the construction of a coherent historical account of national development and of the character of "Antichrist." These ideological constructs of clerical and nativist rhetoric had abruptly to include a constellation of stunning visual elements: European cathedrals, museums, and public architecture frequently overwhelmed admiring American tourists with their astonishing display of human genius and the expansive potential of the senses. Those who at home expressed confidence in the genteel or apocalyptic defeat of Antichrist were often those who, once abroad, found themselves embarked on a disturbing exploration of the repudiated Catholic world, an experience frequently described as an uncanny, potentially guilty return to the cast-off, specifically maternal, parent culture.

Americans who returned thus as travelers to Europe were often aware of reversing New England's legendary separation from Old World corruptions. With mounting and increasingly reverential exposure to the Catholic artworks and architecture of Italy, in particular, the American Protestant victory over popery no longer seemed as complete as previously claimed. If Puritan America was to accomplish the destruction of Antichrist, by the mid-nineteenth century many Protestant Americans found themselves visiting the home of Antichrist, studying it with fascination, and purchasing reproductions of Italian or Spanish art and souvenirs to decorate their parlors back home. The "Grand Staircase of Burgos Cathedral" (Fig. 1), engraved for American readers of the *Illustrated Magazine of Art,* offers for scrutiny one such intriguingly elaborate religious space, in which the "dim light impart[s] an air of mystery to the intricate workmanship of the decorations."[2]

In contrast to the destinarian promises of Protestant or, more narrowly, "Teutonic" victory (arguments that would become increasingly racialist and often frankly racist by the 1850s), personal encounters with Catholic culture, specifically with architecture and liturgical rites, created a nexus of troubled sensations that argued against Protestant doctrinal supremacy while confirming Americans of northern European descent in their ethnic superiority. The complexities of a Catholic "past," both suddenly available and carefully arranged by the new tourism, competed against the triumphant abstraction of "history" in contemporary magazine writing. Travel narratives of the period contradictorily advertised the triumph of Protestant history over the visible evidence of contemporary Italy's pagan ruins and allegedly Vatican-induced poverty while acknowledging the overwhelming force of the visual encounter with classical and papal Rome. If Rome, as Leslie Fiedler long ago observed, provided the site for Americans to encounter themselves, to discuss troublesome questions of self and national identity in a safely foreign and leisured environment, the visual experience of Catholic Rome insinuated itself into these ideological ruminations and often disturbed their conclusions. While the staircase of Burgos cathedral astonished by its scale, Catholicism also offered mysteries of a powerfully compressed, populated, and hidden interiority. Inside a "huge black den hung with broken stalactites," the young tourist Francis Parkman was led by a priest toward the shrine of Santa Rosalia. What the future historian finally discerned in the darkened light impressed him deeply.

> The priest kneeled before a grating beneath the altar, and motioned me to look in between the bars. Two or three lamps were burning there, but for some time, I could discern nothing else. At length, I could distinguish a beautiful female figure, sculptured in marble, and clothed in a robe of gold, lying with a crucifix in her hand and a scull [*sic*] beside her. The white transparency of the marble showed beautifully in the light of the lamps.[3]

Parkman's gradual discovery of the "beautiful" female form hidden within an interior that strangely combines golden riches and bones in the

Fig. 1. "Grand Staircase of Burgos Cathedral." *Illustrated Magazine of Art*, 1853.

lambent features of marble disrupts customary viewing relations, inviting him into a privatized and novel aesthetic in which artificiality testifies to authenticity, morbidity to feminine beauty. Whether encoded in famous travel novels like Nathaniel Hawthorne's *Marble Faun* (1860), George Hillard's best-selling *My Six Months in Italy* (1850), or the brief sketches that appeared frequently in the major magazines, travel to Rome challenged Americans to absorb the defamiliarizing power of such images. While many, like Parkman, recorded astonishment at the Italian religious aesthetic, some found their faith disabled or reconfirmed by these often spectacular images.

⟨≈⟩

While repudiating the Roman church's self-proclaimed vision of a single global Christian church, Protestant tourists abroad could not help reading their European Catholic past ambivalently, witnessing Italian culture through the revisionist lens of Protestant history. That perspective divided historical time into the apostolic, the papal, and the reformed eras and further organized the nineteenth century into a lingering Catholic past existing behind or beneath a vital Protestant present that yet remained ambiguously attached to it. As American tourist rhetoric continually implied, such Protestant attachment was preoccupied with issues of psychological and cultural loss, the loss of a mighty, avowedly maternal, Rome whose comforts of the spirit included those of semantic certitude—one born, however, of the image rather than the text.

Antebellum Americans who possessed a spiritual past in Scripture but felt the lack of a sufficient national heritage selectively, if awkwardly, appropriated a cultural ancestry from their tourist experiences in Catholic Europe.[4] This tourist "discovery" was kept in guarded relation to the present back home, available for middle-class tourists and readers but strenuously dissociated from contemporary theological and political domestic issues. In several respects tourist literature resolved the dilemma of a nation hungering for a past yet fearful of the burdens such a past might entail. The American republic could neither originate from a European past, frequently figured as a tainted maternal origin, nor derive from the New World, whose native cultures also threatened to contaminate a fledgling democratic selfhood.[5] Struggling to create an undefiled, self-originating identity, antebellum Protestants maintained at home a tense proximity to both sites of suspect origin. The advocates of democracy—in sermon, history, travel sketch, or novel—poised the country, like Hawthorne's Donatello, midway between "savagery" and "civilization," somehow meant to grow without growing older, to develop without risk of decay.

But as Hawthorne suggested in *The Marble Faun*, many affluent American tourists experienced an ardent, even dependent, attraction to this decayed Catholic Europe—a Europe whose offerings to the American ambiguously shifted between the spiritual and the aesthetic and in so doing called into question the reality of any strict division between the two regions and, more disturbingly, between the two religions. While American travels to Europe in the nineteenth century were shaped by the eighteenth-century tradition of the Grand Tour, American travelers themselves showed an additional and marked religious preoccupation that lent a sectarian edge to conventional pursuits of the picturesque and the sublime. In numerous travel sketches, the tourist experience of moving through and looking on Catholic Europe emerges as a valuable aesthetic acquisition that can offset the losses resulting variously from the disruptive forces of disestablishment, immigration, and urbanization back home. "I would be free even to declare, that, in the light which played between those lips and lids," an American clergyman wrote of the Dresden Madonna, "was Christianity itself,—Christianity in miniature for the smallness of the space I might incline to express it, but that I should query in what larger presentment I had ever beheld Christianity so great."[6] It was a delicate task, however, to remain distant from Romanism and close to Rome's splendors—a balance necessary to the spiritual and aesthetic enterprise of national identity formation. Beneath the triumph proclaimed by Protestant ideology lay an uneasiness that threatened not the defeat but the embrace of the enemy—an embrace that led not so much to religious conversion as to an aesthetic and emotional appropriation of the enemy's powers. If Harriet Beecher Stowe's Puritan heroine, Mary, of *The Minister's Wooing* (1859) is too modestly circumstanced to tour abroad, the ocean waves themselves bring her a da Vinci "Madonna" to hang on her bedroom wall, "a picture which to Mary had a mysterious interest, from the fact of its having been cast on shore after a furious storm, and found like a waif lying in the seaweed."[7] Mary's discovery on the Newport beach is meant to be extraordinary, the logic of realism discreetly ruffled by the contravening interests of evangelical sentiment to demonstrate the heroine's transcendent status. Mary's serendipitous art acquisition keeps her safe from the contamination of travel, the dross of contemporary Italy through which American tourists looked to the ideal region behind. Although one's first impressions of Italy would undoubtedly be mundane and ugly, let the traveler "bide his time," counseled the most popular travel writer of the

1850s. "The Rome of the mind is not built in a day . . . the unsightly and commonplace appendages will disappear, and only the beautiful and the tragic will remain."[8]

Italian travels inevitably reminded American Protestants of their Reformation roots, the poverty of the Italian populace and the opulence of the Vatican returning them imaginatively to the heroic age of Lutheran and Calvinist reform. If class divisions back home were becoming uncomfortably apparent with industrialization and immigration, that domestic menace receded before Italy's extremes of deprivation and wealth. "They draw life," wrote Parkman of priests he observed in Messina, "and sustenance from these dregs of humanity—just as tall pig-weed flourishes on a dunghill."[9] Italian travel presented New England tourists, in particular, with a heroic Catholic past that not only diminished the disturbing impressions of the Catholic present but also embellished the dreary realities of the Protestant present. If Americans generally expressed confidence in their national future, they had no such simple emotions toward their present or past. Like English and European neomedievalists who invented a past of benevolent authoritarianism and organic communitarian values to compensate for the gross disruptions of the Industrial Revolution, some Americans found in Europe the pleasures of a recovered Catholic medievalism, especially as imaginatively projected by Walter Scott, Thomas Carlyle, and William Cobbett. But a culturally pervasive romancing of the Middle Ages did not characterize American culture until after the Civil War, at which point medievalism served as one rallying cry against the manifold psychic deprivations of modernization.[10] For the vast majority of antebellum tourists to Italy theology and aesthetics were crucial, not, as in neomedievalism, psychology and aesthetics.

Tourism to famed sites of European Catholic art relinked what ideology and geographical distance had severed; having returned from Italy and the Holy Land, Melville, in the formulaic tones of the lyceum, expressed what was quickly becoming a conventionalized sense of reconnection to the Old World: "On entering Rome itself, the visitor is greeted by thousands of statues, who, as representatives of the mighty past, hold out their hands to the present, and make the connecting link of centuries."[11] The Protestant Word and the words of accusation and self-defense it generated were surprisingly vulnerable to this "connection" experienced by American tourists in Rome. Archbishop Spalding in his *History of the Protestant Reformation* (1860) somewhat uncharitably decided that his Protestant historian colleagues were necessarily baffled by history because they had abjured Christ's promise to protect his Church, a promise that was the "thread of Ariadne, which would have conducted them with security from the tortuous windings of the labyrinth of history, in which they appear to have been lost."[12] Protestant historians largely denied such confusion, but Protestant tourists frankly expressed their amazement and religious disequilibrium in the labyrinthine Italian streets and catacombs. Reconnection with a repudiated past and the disorientation of foreign travel coalesced to produce a sense of uncanniness for American visitors to Rome. The first recorded use of the term *sight-seeing,* in 1847, indicated the spread of a new, touristic, form of seeing but one that was still not carefully distinguished from sacramental vision, the looking on the raised Host. Antebellum sightseers in Rome struggled constantly to convert sacred sights (and sites) into touristic ones while yet pondering with genuine theological intensity not only what they saw but also whether (and how) they believed in what they saw.[13]

While journals back home declared their confidence in the Protestant principle of "private judgment," American tourists and artists abroad wandered psychologically between the conflicting worlds of two faiths. The *North American Review* assured its readers that "it is wonderful to see how one of those principles of the gospel, when received in the living letter, illuminates every region of the soul, and casts light so broad and far on the way of life, that no one can wander, if the heart is only true." But it was no easy task to maintain a true heart once outside a society rife with evangelical certainty about the "living letter." The reassuring "spirit of preciseness" that even Unitarians claimed for the Bible, in contrast to the antiscriptural mysteries of the Catholic church, began to blur before Rome's imprecise but powerful collections of images.[14] As a context that undermined Protestant Scripture, the Eternal City burdened visitors with its novel, elusive, or simply excessive meanings. So condensed were Rome's significations that they reminded Hawthorne of the epistolary cross-writing popular in the pre–Civil War era in which letter writers—to save paper, to preserve privacy, to create a disguised intimacy of two—superimposed vertical onto horizontal script. Displayed before Hawthorne's weary and intimidated gaze, Rome appeared like the "broadest page of history, crowded so full with memorable events that one obliterates another; as if Time had crossed and re-crossed his own records till they grew illegible."[15]

Confusion before this Roman world was aggravated by two rival Protestant versions of the past: those encountered in written histories and religious polemics and those personally encountered in travel. This division of American time into a moribund Catholic past (encountered in travel) and a dynamic history (connoting beneficent change and denying the sad workings of time and human evil) was reinforced by the habitual splitting of the Western world into Old and New.[16] According to Nicholas Murray, all one had to do was look at the "moral map of the world" to see the division.[17] What many anti-Catholic Americans saw was a globe divided between New World industry and Old World indolence, the "one portion of the earth's surface reminding us of the powerful, ever-advancing Gulf-Stream,—the other of the weedy, motionless Sargasso Sea."[18] Such a moralized geography dictated that history—as the study of change—was a Protestant possession; the stagnant terrain of the past belonged to Catholics. The New Testament, Protestant history, and America's Manifest Destiny moved jointly forward; Catholicism, divorced from time and Scripture, stood still.[19]

Supposedly left to eternal stagnation, Roman Catholicism emerged as vitally, even shockingly, alive to antebellum tourists. Cast as ritual antagonist rather than historical force, the Roman church had long enjoyed a certain borrowed power from the sheer force of Protestant invective. And having declared that Romanism was dead, Protestant tourists in particular found themselves not so much rid of popery as faced with palpable images of an elaborate morbidity, an excess largely constituted by their own religious preoccupation with self-regulation and the cultivation of the perfectionist powers of voice and text over the recalcitrance of the body. Disease, death, and decomposition were frequently identified with a faith continually pathologized as dead. "The taste of Roman Catholics for the morbidly horrible in death's doings is strangely general," declared *Harper's New Monthly Magazine* in 1854.[20] As increasing numbers of Americans descended on Italy, this same opinion became strangely general among them. The Catholic past and present, graphically displayed in bone reliquaries and sarcophagi, loomed as an uncanny challenge to Protestantism's anticorporeal aspirations and increasing efforts to sentimentalize death as an antiseptic transition into resurrection.

In one of her typically exasperated dialogues with the Presbyterian Oswald, the Catholic heroine of Mme de Staël's best-selling novel *Corinne; or, Italy* (1804) insists that Rome is "not simply an assemblage of dwellings, it is the history of the world."[21] While tourists throughout the nineteenth century responded to this melancholy universality of Roman ruin, American visitors were notably occupied with the physically morbid aspects of the Eternal City. At home Walt Whitman saluted the past as a "corpse . . . slowly borne from the eating and sleeping rooms of the house," a corpse that seemed to end up in Rome where Americans visited it with troubled curiosity.[22] Travelers repeatedly singled out from the plethora of visual novelties the presence of the Italian dead, buried in catacombs, lying on biers, their bones seemingly displayed everywhere for veneration or, worse yet, decoration. At its most literal and grotesque, this "past" exposed itself with an indecent, even erotic, energy before American viewers. The dreamy nostalgia perfected by Washington Irving as he wandered discreetly through Westminster Abbey's "wilderness of tombs" was frankly inadequate in Rome, where graveyard romanticism often gave way to hysteria at this bone-filled world.[23]

Catholic churches appeared stuffed with death, "full of bones and skulls, and coffins," repositories of biological decay that seemingly ignored any hygienic or moral etiquette.[24] Or rather, that etiquette was a foreign and vulgar one that violated American Protestant notions of propriety and aesthetic organization. Young Parkman, himself in revolt against conservative Unitarian proprieties, uncomfortably noted in his Italian journal that the dead virgins of the Capuchin convent catacombs "all wear crowns of silver paper, from beneath which they grin and gape in a most alluring fashion."[25] Traveling to recover the health he had professedly lost through excessive physical exercise, Parkman confronted the crowned female skeletons with a sexual unease apparent in many tourist accounts. That these females were virgins only exacerbated the anxiety; their vows of celibacy, their rejection of sexual experience, irritated Parkman's developing preoccupation with virility even as their display of asceticism intrigued him. Parkman was hardly eccentric in his dismissive but carefully detailed reports of "alluring" Catholic skeletons. Having proclaimed their freedom from Old World bonds, tourists often felt compelled to reenter a specialized experience of deathly enclosure once overseas—a surrender not only of the eye but of the body as it roamed through a variety of novel, and at times conspicuously morbid, architectural interiors. Accounts of being captivated by the Italian experience include familiar emotions proper to the sublime and the picturesque; but conventional enchantment could easily resolve into disgust or even panic before relics or skeletons. Such temporary experiences of aesthetic discomfort were in turn conventionalized as a false "literary" captivity that frankly imitated the titillating details of the Gothic. And like Gothic narratives, American tourist accounts wavered between simulated and authentic terror.

In particular, the descent into Rome's catacombs elicited fears of incarceration, even live entombment. Descending from the New World to Rome's literal underworld, American explorers of Roman catacombs experienced a psychological captivity that strikingly contrasted with the vastness and perceived emptiness of their still largely rural landscapes back home.[26] If the symbolic terrain of American Protestantism figured itself as clean, empty, and magically capable of change without decay, that of Catholicism was clogged with the filth of bodies. Emptied of Catholic artifacts, New England and Virginia churches presented studiously cleansed interiors to subordinate the distractable eye to the aural experience of the Word. Such interior emptiness, architecturally speaking, facilitated the Protestant's unmediated relation to the Holy Spirit; but the ideological affection for emptiness also influenced the perception of the American landscape as empty of inhabitants and hence available for settlement. John O'Sullivan's seminal 1845 essay in the *Democratic Review* explained that America's "Manifest Destiny" was to construct a national interior from an "empty" wilderness. When American Whigs and Democrats stood in the catacombs and dusted the powder of bones from their hands, they hesitantly acknowledged an altogether different destiny that tied them to earth and bones, holding them captive to neither Jehovah nor American Indians but to biology. In the Roman catacombs such tourists experienced a confused merging of the literal and the metaphoric, of corpses and the past. That combination produced a pleasing metaphysical shiver, a carefully measured dose of romantic melancholy that, once conveyed in nationally printed travel essays back home, offered a safe alternative to the fiction of elite writers like Hawthorne and Melville, whose visions of America's past and future recorded the more subversive anxiety that led Melville to declare of the Galapagos Islands that it "is but fit that like those old monastic institutions of Europe, whose inmates go not out of their own walls to be inurned, but are entombed there where they die; the Encantadas too should bury their own dead, even as the great general monastery of earth does hers."[27]

Roman monastic practices of burying the dead beneath the living horrified yet pleased American visitors. If back home they prided themselves on orderly cemeteries discreetly positioned in churchyards or, increasingly, in separate areas on town perimeters, they consciously sought out the horror of European burial pits; visiting the famous Naples cemetery, the "traveller invariably gave the guard a small tip to lift one of the stone slabs so that he could look within, and he invariably reported the most horrible sight of decaying forms that he had ever seen."[28] Such burial pits luridly challenged the theological optimism of liberal American Protestantism, which increasingly figured heaven as an extension of the middle-class home and promised to close the distance between God and person originally insisted on by Calvin, who argued that in heaven "our glory will not be as perfect as to allow our vision to comprehend the Lord completely . . . there will be a wide distance between Him and ourselves." Properly organized cemeteries in the antebellum decades now ideally functioned as "nurseries of piety for an everlasting home"; one sat or walked through a collection of the dead, each safely, separately, encased and textualized beneath commemorative stones. The developing suburban American cemetery extended the design principles of sentimental, genteel domesticity that stressed purification, ventilation, and the studied arrangement of household furnishings to inspire pious character development.[29] Increasingly distanced from the dead at home by these habits of sentimental commemoration (memorably satirized by Mark Twain in his portrait of Emmeline Grangerford in *Adventures of Huckleberry Finn*), the American tourist's proximity to corpses in Rome enabled the recovery of an illicit but finally safe authenticity. The dead, after all, were not their own and were not from their class, religion, or ethnic group. Italian burial pits presented grisly subterranean interiors that starkly contrasted to cemetery parks; the pits substituted the pleasures of visceral astonishment for those of contemplation, the threat of engulfment for the "upward" pull of sorrow. Liberal, genteel Protestants who meditated in graveyards back home found that in Italy funerary text was boldly displaced by shocking image, the meditative tempo of reading by the instantaneousness of bodily spectacle.[30]

Rome's distinctive geography, then, confirmed Protestant convictions of Catholic morbidity, whose crowdedness pressed upon the tourist with an eerie but consoling pressure. The American George Greene, who begged permission to accompany a Jesuit archaeologist on his inspection of the catacombs, afterward wrote that he "never walked the streets of Rome again without feeling that with every footfall I was awakening an echo in the caverns of death."[31] Rome's deathly underground competed against its romantic ruins for tourist attention; the ruins above ground provided access to the favored experience of European romanticism, involving a textually scripted imitation of an anterior European self, either fictional (Corinne) or historical (the historian Gibbon sitting in the Coliseum). Such identification with English or European characters' experience of the Italian sublime was undermined by the vernacular Roman sights of catacomb and burial pit that pulled the tourist down from the sublime to the "lower" sensual Gothic world, where terror was born of titillation and disgust. Rome's juxtaposition of sublime art (and ruins) to contagious "malarial" soil legitimated the vulgar desire to detect the rottenness at the heart of the sublime or, in the inflammatory misogynist rhetoric of anti-Catholicism, to expose the Whore of Babylon at the heart of Mother Church.

This change in "genre" registered by tourists' descent from the sublime into Rome's contagious soil also figured as a partial loss of control, specifically the control enjoyed by the traveler gazing discreetly on the foreign. The fascination with walking atop the pagan and Catholic dead derived in part from being able to establish both contact with them and dominion over them. Indeed tourist accounts of descending into the catacombs nervously monitor the level of aesthetic and psychological intimacy by trivializing or frankly mocking the terrors of the site. A catacomb anecdote related by Greene points to this careful positioning of the American Protestant tourist before the Catholic dead. An interpolated vignette recounts how an eighteenth-century artist lost his way in the catacombs, having let go of his guiding thread. Minutes of panicked searching for the lost thread produced only a sickening realization of loss and impending death in the clammy, dark labyrinth. But just as he began to faint in panic, his hand fell on the thread and, grabbing hold, the artist made his way back to daylight, experiencing a hysterical glee. This artist of a century back offers a fantasy of resurrection for the antebellum narrator and his readers, the tourist who shares this tale providing the Gothic pleasure of both incarceration and euphoric exit. As these doubled eighteenth- and nineteenth-century narratives of escape suggest, fleeing the catacombs and the surrounding morbidities of papal Italy was fraught with difficulties that pointed less to Roman wickedness than to the imperatives of their Protestant manufacture.

Like the anecdote of the lost thread, other magazine accounts of escape from Italian interiors sound a similarly contrived, hastily evasive note: if the psychic challenges of international encounter imbued with ethnic and religious prejudice were confronted by tourists in Rome's underground, they were scarcely resolved. Rediscovery of the lost thread abruptly, if unconvincingly, enables an otherwise unseemly flight. In a long essay entitled "A Reminiscence of Rome," an American tourist recounts his descent, with a companion, into monastic burial vaults. Initially the two men seek to disguise the discomfort born of intense religious ambivalence by cataloguing the anatomical features of their macabre surroundings. Minimizing the mystery of the monastery vault interior by satire, the narrator crumples the supernatural significance of the skeletal displays beneath the biological, reducing Catholicism to the gruesome absurdity of the dismembered human body—a strategy that assuages doctrinal hostility by heightening a generalized religious anxiety. "The acanthus-shaped sacrum and os coccygis formed a rich cornice for the walls and arches, while ribs, fingers, toes and disconnected vertebrae served for the mouldings of the curiously wrought panel-work of the ceilings."[32] The foreign religion and the intimacy of the body's promise to decompose are jointly repulsive. Like Ishmael's ponderings on the enormousness of the whale skeleton in Melville's *Moby-Dick*, the bony interior of this narrative prompts uneasy, finally frenzied reflections on the relation of the bony bodily "inside" to the invisible cultural "outside"—a relation imagined as a Catholic interior detected and pathologized by Protestant observers. Amid the skeletal decor, the visitors regress, not to originary, childlike selves, but rather toward a desiccated masculinity as they try to sketch and eventually dance with one of the skeletons, their monastic skeletal partner pointing to their own future decomposition and the exposure of their bony interiors. Released from the individual bodily boundaries they enjoyed in life, the various skeleton parts of deceased monks display a queasy democracy where hierarchy is replaced by what the two tourists report to be a promiscuous mingling of the "bodies," which submit to such jumblings to meet the vulgar demands of a grisly Catholic aesthetic. When the tourist pair seek to master this interior decor by asking permission to sketch it, they unwittingly forfeit their fragile superiority, for the attempt to draw the lurid enclosure precipitates nervous collapse. Left alone in his "voluntary entombment" while his companion goes to retrieve his sketching equipment, the solitary amateur artist, "locked in with silence and death," becomes hysterical. While he sings and dances with the skeletons, his horrified companion listens outside, certain the hellish fiends are carrying off his friend. But once back inside the walls, he finds to his bewilderment that his hysterical friend has been, in his word, the "aggressor" (745).

That these masculine visitors should not only disturb but frankly assault the dead imitates the syncopated tempo of aggression and haphazard self-control that typifies female Gothic narrative. As Harriet Beecher Stowe revises Gothic conventions of female vulnerability in *Uncle Tom's Cabin*, positioning the fugitive slave Cassy as a living ghost who haunts Legree, so "A Reminiscence of Rome" recounts a hostile American haunting of the tyrannous Italian dead. In so doing, this particular essay offers a rare glimpse into the violence of the American tourist-interloper, whose dance with the skeletons desecrates the foreign interior. The tourist's frenzy emanates not just from hostility to death but, more particularly, from the materiality and plurality of these monastic bodies whose various parts he forcibly removes from their sacred design to the secular (but hardly less troubling) intimacies of the dance. The American tourist's "minuet" with the Italian skeleton is a memorable instance of a foreign bodily contact that forbids genuine communication. Appearing in the genteel pages of *Harper's New Monthly*

Magazine, "A Reminiscence of Rome" even finally evades the very audience courted by its Gothic excitement; frankly refusing further dialogue with his readers, the narrator concludes that the events gave him "an insight into the mysteries of psychology; but upon this subject I do not wish to be confidential with everyone" (745). Thus does the narrative encase its own hostility to the materiality of the Catholic body—both its fragility *and* the obtrusiveness of its lingering presence. In a replication of this cultural distancing, the narrator thwarts his readers, refusing confessional disclosure to preserve the enclosure, the psychological privacies, of his Protestant subjectivity.

The narrative's retreat into secrecy is a coy maneuver that reduces the possibility of any ecumenical or interethnic communication to the insignificance of flirtation. Neither the Roman dead nor the author's "mysteries" overcome these tourists (or implicitly their readers); indeed, enough of their sketches survive to illustrate the essay quite elaborately and, in so doing, guide its reception (Fig. 2). Surrounded by engravings of skeletons, the magazine text replicates the vault experience of bony encirclement, its prose closed in upon by the grinning monks. Such typographic claustrophobia further invites the reader into the American touristic experience while simultaneously reducing it to the manageable level of the decorative. In this latter sense, the article's illustrations perform an evasion similar to that of the narrative voice that refuses further disclosures under the presumed necessity for privacy. The article's graphic presentation thus registers the successful assertion of American identity against the foreign, for, having regained control of themselves in the burial vault to the extent that they can sketch what has made them hysterical, the tourists further advertise their management of the Catholic menace by the commercial display of their encounter.

Both celebratory accounts of the catacombs and the accounts of other American tourists who attempted to claim rather than repudiate this Catholicized terrain of the dead contrast to such derisive portraits of unseemly Catholic intimacy. Instead of relegating the foreign religion to a prehistory of bone-ridden archives, some visitors tried to insert parts of Catholicism into Protestant time—tried, in other words, to convert elements of Italy's troubling, morbid "past" into America's mainstream "history." A principal site for this reappropriation was the catacombs. Turning from the artificial ruins fashionable in the late eighteenth century, nineteenth-century American visitors exploited Rome's ruins for

THE THREE BROTHERS.

Fig. 2. "The hideous mummies leered at me from beneath their moth-eaten cowls; their eyeless sockets seemed to gleam with fiendish intelligence, and their idiotic grinning put on a devilish motive and character." "The Three Brothers," from "A Reminiscence of Rome," *Harper's New Monthly Magazine*, 1857.

ammunition in their contemporary religious disputes.[33] According to this revisionism, the skeletal remains and decorated sarcophagi of the catacombs were not instances of a vulgar Catholic morbidity but rather a "rebuke to the Papal Rome above"—the indisputable evidence of a primitive Christianity ennobled by persecution and free from contaminating relations to the state.[34] The very earthiness of such newly opened archaeological sites reassured the more skeptically inclined, who, having denied the papacy's supernatural sanctions, were casting about for alternative authorities and empirical guidelines to support their "private judgment." Americans easily extended the Reformation rhetoric of "restorationism" (the attribution of Protestantism to the early days of the Church) to include the silent catacombs recently discovered beneath Rome. Viewed from this perspective, the dead harbored in the catacombs were seen as free from the objectionable exhibitionism of monastery burial vaults; they became virtual Protestants for some American tourists and thus their spiritual parents, ancestors who exerted a magnetic authority over a modern progeny who were confessedly suffering the discomforts of theological uncertainty and a consequent fascination with violent (and violated) religious conviction. Such an "American" Roman past supported domestic Protestant polemics against American Catholic claims of the church's unbroken allegiance to the apostolic era. The catacombs that provided this much-needed Protestant antiquity with a vision of an extensive and pure history that could compete with the vast but contaminated past of Rome did so, importantly, without threatening to mingle with the American present; as "ruins" they were not only overseas but also underground. Doubly distant, they enjoyed tremendous appeal.

Such appreciation for early Christian martyrs, then, effectively converted a portion of the Catholic "past" into mainstream American Protestant "history," enabling American tourists to subversively imagine their national origin in the Roman catacombs. Rome's past became America's future in the dual sense that catacomb martyrs pointed to the English Puritan exodus to America while themselves epitomizing an ideal Protestantism for antebellum American emulation. In preserving America's ancestors, the catacombs pointed to a redeemed future for an ailing Protestantism; containing the "exhibition and the promise of a purer Christianity," they served as both origin and destination for the providential vision of New World onlookers.[35] From the liberal New England perspective, the catacombs, as underground church, belied the contemporary pagan Christianity above. Indeed, the persecuted catacomb dead collapsed classical and papal Rome aboveground into a single text of dangerous, if dazzling, corruption. Discussing Charles Maitland's *Church in the Catacombs* (London, 1846) and the anonymous *Rome, Pagan and Papal by an English Resident* (London, 1846), one Unitarian underscored the religious obligation of American tourists to detect this underground truth. While "old Pagan Rome seems to have risen from her ashes and still to live in the prevailing rites and usages of the 'eternal city,'" a Protestant past lies encapsuled beneath, waiting to be deciphered by tourists of sufficient spiritual insight.[36] To look on the skeletons of these early Christians offered a vicarious experience of grace; N. P. Willis, writing of the "humble traces of the personal followers of Christ" in the catacombs of St. Sebastian, suggested the excitement of this return to apostolic times. "We saw the skeleton as it had fallen from the flesh in decay, untouched, perhaps, since the time of Christ."[37]

New World tourists in Rome positioned this recovered Old World ancestry in the horizontal (if intermittent) sequence of earthly history, rather than in a vertical, thoroughly mediated, Catholic continuum from earth to heaven. The catacombs were proof positive, serving as archives from which tourist-explorers, as New World Protestants, reconfirmed their temporal history of persecution, martyrdom, flight, and perseverance. The historical continuity produced by these tourist experiences of Protestant ancestral bonding was distinct from the traditional Roman Catholic vision of a cosmos in which the sainted dead lived on in anxious heavenly supervision of the earth's struggling souls. For American Catholics, the dead lived eternally, not historically. Affirming the link between the earthly and heavenly cities (and implicitly disputing the Protestant focus on Rome's supposed morbidity), the American Catholic journal the *Metropolitan* declared: "Nowhere in this world, we believe, is there a more living, real, exultant life than in old Rome; and who are more living than those whom we call the dead?"[38] Challenging the American tourist's preoccupation with Catholic Rome's political and erotic deathliness, with an antiquated institutional papacy atop and mingled monastic bodies beneath, American Catholics appealed to New Testament promises of life-in-death to defend Rome, whose ruins and skeletons were precisely the evidence for eternal vitality.

Like C. Auguste Dupin of Edgar Allan Poe's detective narratives, Protestant tourists searched the catacombs for clues to their religious identity by constructing narratives of ecclesiastical crime from a disorderly collection of mute details. The accounts they fashioned conscientiously opposed the distrusted conventions and imagery of Italian Catholic art. Trying to imagine the early saints afresh, one such amateur historian-detective revealingly wrote that it is "from the catacombs that we must seek all that is left to enable us to construct the image that we desire."[39] As the Vatican had allegedly conspired to suppress the Bible, so these detective-tourists unburied it, citing their discoveries as further contributions to American biblicism. Although they assured readers of their "faithful and honest exploration" (33), what they discovered rather naturally confirmed their reading of church history. Denizens of the catacombs turned out to be model believers whose faith had little need of institutional support.

> In those first days there was little thought of relics to be carried away,—little thought of material suggestions to the dull imagination, and pricks to the failing memory. The eternal truths of their religion were too real to them; their faith was too sincere; their belief in the actual union of heaven and earth, and of the presence of God with them in the world, too absolute to allow them to feel the need of that lower order of incitements which are the resort of superstition, ignorance and conventionalism in religion. (519)

The early Christians emerge in this idealized portrait as ancestors to their modern day Protestant celebrants; together they disdain Rome's "superstition, ignorance and conventionalism." But they also emerge as rivals to their visiting modern Protestant progeny, for it was not only Catholics who needed the material dimension but also Protestants, who were carrying away relics and for whom the "eternal truths" were decreasingly persuasive.

Shaped by such a nostalgic and self-deprecating revision, the dark, twisting catacombs ironically emerged as symbol for devotional clarity and straightforwardness. Their labyrinthine interiors opposed the obfuscations of the papacy, the quandaries of liberal Protestantism hoping to illuminate what church tyranny had disguised and what modern subjectivity could not find. Representing an era when the "mystery of the mass and the puzzles of transubstantiation had not yet been introduced among the believers" (521), the early martyrs sanctioned a bumptious "scientific" hubris on the part of these Americans; archaeological efforts to bring corpses to light and to reconstruct the history they mutely evoked imitated God in his acts of revelation. Thus the "Cuvier-like" archaeologist De Rossi was credited for discovering the remains of St. Cecilia by an "inductive process of archaeological reasoning" (683) just as the "Lord discovereth deep things out of darkness, and bringeth out to light the shadow of death" (685). In a final irony, such an appropriation of divine power for the developing science of archaeology signaled the secularization of the catacombs, a process that rapidly converted them from sacred mausoleum to museum and tourist attraction. As underground Rome was recovered and organized, its mortality, initially so overwhelming to American visitors, was gradually transformed by the light of science into purified historical evidence against papal fictions. What remained above ground represented for many of these tourists the true city of the dead, a degenerate conglomeration of pagans and popes whose tombs possessed little of the redemptive, revelatory power of the catacomb dwellers.

Thus, in Protestantizing Christian antiquity, American tourists obtained partial control over a Catholic past whose dead (along with the funerary art and architecture devoted to their memory) initially overwhelmed them. Disputing the Catholic dogma of Apostolic Succession, one antebellum nativist insisted that the Holy Spirit had escaped the corruptions of a priest-ridden civilization in full accord with the Book of Revelation. "They say it is the *first* form of Christianity. That is a mistake. It is the *second*. The first appeared for a while, then 'fled into the wilderness, where she had a place prepared of God,' and re-appeared at the Reformation."[40] For many antebellum tourists, the catacombs had become that wilderness refuge.

THREE

The American Terrain of W. H. Prescott and Francis Parkman

For mid-century Americans, this moribund Catholic world of catacombs and ruins did not reside in Italy alone. For those who wrote and many of those who read the popular romantic histories of William Hickling Prescott, author of the best-selling *History of the Conquest of Mexico* (1843), and Francis Parkman, author of the seven-volume *France and England in North America* (1865–92), tourist images of Catholic Europe influenced their historical "tour" of America's past. Visiting the Catholic Old World served in effect as the experiential counterpart to reading the consciously literary histories of America's national formation unfolded by Prescott and Parkman. Like many other New England authors of their day, both historians had visited Italy as young men and later incorporated their vision of Catholicism into their mature histories. What they encountered early abroad and wrote later at home constituted a sequential narrative that legitimated (if regretfully) Anglo-America's victory over ecclesiastical corruption and political authoritarianism.

Although both historians emerged from Unitarian Boston, their stories of America's historical development returned obsessively to the question of Catholicism. As the two principal historians of America's struggle against Catholic imperial powers, they argued for the overriding historical agency of a virtually hypostatized Protestant selfhood made narratively coherent by its opposition to a contradictory and irrational Romanism. In their historiography the European Catholic world, as aestheticized ideological construct intricately composed of antebellum tourist images and post-Reformation Protestant polemics, shapes the New World terrains of their histories. Indeed European Catholicism, according to their historical narratives, had deviously situated itself at the very origin of the English and Spanish New Worlds. In an 1853 oration on the discovery of America Edward Everett, the famously eloquent clergyman, Harvard College president, and Massachusetts senator, claimed that Columbus's fateful landing had in fact enslaved the New World to the Spanish: "When on the following morning the keel of his vessel grated upon the much longed for strand, it completed with more than electric speed, that terrible circuit which connected the islands and the continent to the footstool of the Spanish throne."[1] But the deeper meditations of the New England historical mind uncovered a pre-Columbian Catholicism already entrenched in the Western hemisphere. It was carried in the minds and cultures of North American and Mesoamerican Indians, whose faintly understood cultures seemed to resemble Romanism in sufficiently astonishing ways that at points they simply merged as twinned images of popery. Modern Americans who read Prescott and Parkman could thus "tour" an elaborate and morbid aesthetic of Catholicized savagery just as they physically explored the gloom of cathedral and catacomb overseas. Revealing the continued difficulty of New England Protestantism's separation from Rome, these histories positioned Catholicism at the root not only of America's repudiated European origins but of its New World past. In their exodus to the New World, "Anglo-Saxons" encountered the very enemies of sensualism, ritualism, and mystery from which they had fled.

Prescott's and Parkman's post-Puritan romantic accounts of the necessary demise of Amerindian ritualism betray a volatile touristic combination of fascination with the foreign and disdain for it. Native American representatives of indolence, superstition, and decadent materialism must eventually surrender to Anglo-Saxon energy, ideality, and modern efficiency. But the Indian (whether Aztec or Huron) entices the melancholic New England historical gaze that searches for a redemptive primitive; once engaged, that gaze on the vanishing aboriginal American reveals the shadow image of a New England "native" self, vanishing beneath its own repressions. This latter self demands its own form of therapeutic control, one accomplished through the historiographical construction and eventual elimination of an aboriginal Catholicism. It is the disappearance of this secondary "native" Protestant self that energizes the elegiac attention of these histories. Their providential plots master Aztec, Iroquois, Spanish, and French Catholic cultures but resist surrendering the imagery and implications of New World Catholic heroism, ritualism, and tragic asceticism, a subordinate but persistent text whose essence contains an autobiographical narrative of the "native" masculine self in combat with its New England "Brahmin" cultivation.

If these antebellum histories of national formation resolve the problem of Anglo-America's eradication of allegedly unassimilable native cultures by continued appeal to an unassimilable Catholicism, that Catholicism in turn discloses a drama of Protestant selfhood resisting its own proprieties.

Like their various heroes in pursuit of New World territory and souls, both narrative historians made great efforts to capture a past prior to Anglo-America, to track it down and encircle it with language vivid enough to resurrect the triumph and the cost of this mastery. Although contemporary reviews frequently praised Prescott and Parkman for their impartial realism, the past they presented curried to the political and psychological needs of their educated readership while disavowing the ideological (and compositional) labor of their works. Especially anxious to distance himself from the excesses of the religious minded (of whatever creed), the agnostic Parkman repeatedly advertised the documentary empiricism of his history's second volume, *The Jesuits in North America* (1867). "I have studied and compared these authorities," he declared of his missionary and other sources, "as well as a great mass of collateral evidence, with more than usual care, striving to secure the greatest possible accuracy of statement, and to reproduce an image of the past with photographic clearness and truth."[2] Such assertive realism arguably rendered his romantic historiography more vulnerable than it might otherwise have been to contemporary novelistic conventions, for speaking as documentary investigators, Parkman and Prescott also distributed a carefully elaborated religious allegory through their scenic narratives. What later readers detect as a religious and ethnic Brahmin myth of Amerindian tyranny and sloth possessed the charismatic transparency of truth to these historians and their readers—a truthfulness born of their self-distancing from the religious bigotry of their Puritan ancestors and the anti-Catholic nativism of their conservative Protestant contemporaries.[3] Prescott and Parkman simply refuse to engage in any overt doctrinal debate with Rome. In its place they offer the superior authenticity of romantic narrative, whose truth claims depend on its proffer of a "psychological" Catholicism, a constellation of (still disabling) personality traits that explain the collapse of native cultures. Symptomology and diagnosis replace religious polemic.

As conservative Whigs and religious liberals, Prescott and Parkman pride themselves on the psychological realism of their characterological histories and frequently contrast their cautious empiricism to the allegedly irrational and exaggerated Catholic chronicles on which their narratives uncomfortably depend. The subject matter and the majority of historical sources for both historians dwell in a prehistoric morbid atmosphere of superstition and religious enthusiasm. An unscientific, antiprogressive, stagnant world, it calls for the greatest investigative skill combined with the conquering dynamism of picturesque romantic historiography. Armed with ironic wit, both historians forge their route through a tangle of untrustworthy sources, searching for the scenic distillation of reality their romantic methodologies are designed to disclose. In so doing, they present their readers with painterly images of an exotic, violent past crucially severed from contemporary America. Just as the Old World divided irrevocably into pre- and post-Reformation time, so they split their New World into superstitious and enlightened eras. History, conceived of as those events leading to the establishment of Anglo-American culture in North America, effectively begins only with the arrival of (English) Protestantism. What exists before that event is a "past" as morbidly compelling as that found in any Roman catacomb.

Prescott and New Spain

In 1843 William Hickling Prescott published *The History of the Conquest of Mexico,* which became a best-seller for that year and has since remained a classic achievement of nineteenth-century romantic historiography.[4] *Mexico* begins with a lengthy essay on Aztec civilization, then narrates Cortés's expedition and later career, and concludes with an appendix consisting of an essay, "Origin of the Mexican Civilization— Analogies with the Old World," and three translations of "original documents": the Spanish historian Bernardino de Sahagún's account, "Advice of an Aztec Mother to Her Daughter"; an Aztec "Poem on the Mutability of Life"; and Ixtlilxochitl's "Of the Extraordinary Severity with Which the King Nezahualpilli Punished the Mexican Queen for Her Adultery and Treason." This overall structure—the lavish introductory resurrection of a native culture, the account of its conquest, and the concluding fragmented meditations on Aztec culture's seeming resemblance but actual profound difference from European civilization— recapitulates the very dynamics of conquest as they proceed from initial invasion to ambivalent commemoration.

Published three years before the United States' 1846 war with Mexico (a war that concluded with Mexico's sale of California, New Mexico, Nevada, and parts of Colorado, Arizona, and Utah to the federal government in exchange for fifteen million dollars and with the establishment of the boundary between the two nations at the Rio Grande),

Prescott's *Mexico* provided a narrative rehearsal for that event. Adolph De Circourt, one of Prescott's fervent European admirers, wrote in June 1847: "You seem to have, while describing so eloquently the *past* Conquest of Mexico, foretold the *future* one."[5]

If to write history was to reenact it, so too the reading of *Mexico*'s romantic duplication of the first conquest prepared the way for the second. Prescott himself characteristically conceived of his compositional procedures as a military calculation, struggle, and triumph that competed against, even while emulating, those of his "genius" Cortés; similarly, readers of *Mexico* absorbed its ideological and even literal directives for the 1846 war. General Winfield Scott virtually followed Cortés's route in 1519 from Vera Cruz to Mexico City, and it is likely that not only Scott but also a fair number of American soldiers were reading Prescott as they advanced on Mexico City. On a trip in 1846 to Washington, where he socialized with Webster, Polk, and Calhoun, the already famous Prescott wrote home that his *Mexico* had become a campaign manual of sorts. "Mr. Mason, former Secretary of the Navy told me that the sailors on board the Delaware had sent in a petition that the 'Conquest of Mexico' should be entered among the books of the ship, and that it was now ordered to form part of the library of every man-of-war in the navy. He said he considered this as the greatest compliment I had received."[6] As it turned out, the second conquest was easier than the first. In April 1848 Prescott commended the Yankee general Caleb Cushing for his expedient military conquest, which triumphantly duplicated the sixteenth-century invasion while forming a corrective sequel to his own 1843 history.

> You have closed a campaign as brilliant as that of the great *conquistador* himself, though the Spaniards have hardly maintained the reputation of their hardy ancestors. The second conquest would seem, *a priori* to be a matter of as much difficulty as the first, considering the higher civilization & military science of the races who now occupy the country. But it has not proved so—and my readers, I am afraid, will think I have been bragging too much of the valor of the old Spaniard.[7]

Prescott's *Mexico,* together with its companion volume, *The Conquest of Peru* (1847), represents antebellum America's principal account of the rise and decline of the Spanish empire in the New World; both volumes provide a crucial rationale for North American imperialism and the superiority of "Anglo-Saxon," in particular New England, culture over the racially mixed cultures of the south. Prescott's account of the

Spanish discovery, invasion, and conquest of the Aztecs (and then the Incas) participates in the 1840s Anglo-American campaign to convert a specifically Catholic foreignness into the "native" through the extension of a strenuous, if self-doubting, Protestant imperialism.

Mexico subtly modulates into a critique of the vitiated Hispanic civilization that results from the conquest, thus providing an ancestor narrative justifying Mexican subordination to an expansionist Protestant United States. Prescott's Cortés, the "young adventurer, whose magic lance was to dissolve the spell which had so long hung over these mysterious regions" (*Mexico,* 130), functions as a charismatic agent in this cultural mystification, enabling white North Americans to identify with "Spain, romantic Spain" (537) while divorcing themselves from contemporary Mexico, indicted by one contemporary newspaper for its "idol worship, heathen superstition, and degraded mongrel races."[8]

The assimilation of a foreign territory and culture into a "native" Anglo-Saxon America was a pressing issue on the domestic as well as the international front. While Prescott was composing his history, "native-born" Americans in his hometown of Boston were struggling against Irish Catholic immigrants; Prescott's *Mexico* records Anglo-America's confrontation not only with Mexicans in the Southwest, then, but with Catholic foreigners on the northeastern "frontier" as well. As an affluent Bostonian of the 1840s, Prescott faced not only the specter of racial mixture in the Southwest, a contamination of the industrious, liberty-loving Anglo-Saxon "gene" with that of the Mexican (who was already a disturbing compound of Indian, African, and Spanish ancestries) but also the threat of ethnic mixture in his hometown. Of the Irish immigrant, Prescott mused: "What can he know of these [the "sympathies," "feelings," and "ways of thinking which form the idiosyncrasy of the nation"], who has never been warmed by the same sun, lingered among the same scenes, listened to the same tales in childhood, been pledged to the same interests in manhood by which these fancies are nourished; the loves, the hates, the hopes, the fears that go to form national character?"[9] If the body politic precariously depended, as Prescott's rhetorical question suggests, on a uniformity of domestic experience (listening to the "same tales in childhood"), Prescott enabled this provincial American self to surmount the challenge of ethnic and religious difference by producing for its consumption a native-born Bostonian history about America that records the subordination of difference into national uniformity. The demise of Prescott's "gloomy" Aztec afforded a therapeutic consolation for native-born Americans faced in the East with large numbers of Irish Catholic immigrants and in the West with Catholic

Mexico, which (according to the logic of Manifest Destiny), occupied lands destined to be enclosed in the providentially disposed borders of the continental United States.

Finally, if Prescott's *Mexico* points to these frontier struggles with both Mexico and Irish Catholic immigrants, such violent boundary disputes presaged escalating sectional differences within—specifically, between southern and northern whites. Prescott's imaginative reconstruction of an antidemocratic and indolent southern kingdom, doomed to submit to the morally purified violence of Cortés, transplants to the American hemisphere European distinctions between the Teutonic and Mediterranean, the northern and the southern; those distinctions then figure not only *in* the rhetoric of North America's invasion of Mexican territory but *as* the rhetoric for civil war hardly more than a decade later. Indeed, Prescott's conservative Whig vocabulary plays off one version of the South against the other: Polk's campaign against Mexico represents a suspiciously land-hungry American South in debatable action against a southern enemy. Northern suspicions of southern slaveholders' ambitions combined with distaste at the notion of any racial mixture to create a composite image of the South as a region of unregulated appetite and violated purity. Acknowledging that "we are going on triumphing to the Halls of Montezuma," Prescott wrote to his sister during the war that "the Spanish blood will not mix well with the Yankee, and the Southern scale of our republic is already getting a good deal too heavy."[10] Although a social conservative, Prescott was not unsympathetic to contemporary radical Whig opposition to the Mexican War that saw in the conflict the inner workings of slavery, metaphorized by one radical abolitionist as a maternal pathology: "The egg was laid surreptitiously in the nest of the American Eagle, who now loves its ghastly and hideous disclosure better than all her legitimate brood, whose food that young cormorant devours apace, defiling what is not destroyed."[11]

Notwithstanding his conservative Whig suspicions of a conspiratorial slave power, Prescott saturated his narrative with the sacrificial, even providential, violence that characterized Democratic annexation rhetoric. Anticipating the decline of the Aztecs after the establishment of New Spain's first colony at Vera Cruz, he predicts in his history's opening pages that Spanish culture will have a purgative effect on that of Mesoamerica, destroying it with the "light of a consuming fire" (191). Confiding to his memorandum book that the story of Cortés and Montezuma was remarkable chiefly for its "resistless march of *destiny*,"[12] Prescott finally submerged his New England mercantile distaste for an agrarian southern imperialism beneath a destinarian discourse of romantic historiography; in so doing, he effectively translated questions of national guilt (and sectional dispute) into his signature literary effects of irony and nostalgia. *Mexico,* which sold an estimated ninety-one thousand copies by 1860, was so popular in part precisely because of this ambivalent authorial agreement with imperial expansion; Prescott's narrative stance both entertained proponents of the war and spoke to the war's large opposition, which consisted of an unstable coalition of abolitionists, conservative Whigs, and a significant number of southerners reluctant to assimilate the racially suspect populations of Mexico.[13] Prescott's cautious opposition to expansionism and slavery and his support for the racial and religious superiority of North American (and especially New England) whites supply the history's generative tension and its distinctive melancholic voice as it negotiates its burdened route between contradictory allegiances. The history resituates the nation's divided conscience over slavery and annexation in the literary tropes of chivalric exploit and religious doom, nostalgically resurrecting the losses attendant on the ascendency of a capitalist, avowedly Protestant culture over inferior native civilizations. "Brave Moctezuma [*sic*]," who appears in the history's appendix as hero of the Indian "Poem on the Mutability of Life," serves as prime elegiac instance of the universal instability of empire and thus offers "native" sanction for the antebellum destruction of Mexican culture. Figure of mourning and of the violence that produces it, Montezuma provides as well an indigenous aristocratic genealogy for a New England Brahmin class anxiously detecting its own decline in status.

␥

As a sixteenth-century enactment of vehement antebellum debates over the legitimate boundaries of the nation, Cortés is himself a violent, wily creator of boundary, who, as instrument for the extension of Spain's boundaries, enjoys the vaunted boundlessness of the immigrant European male. As the history tracks Cortés from the ocean toward the center of the Aztec empire, the reader "experiences" the expansion of Spanish Catholic territory. But the text just as rapidly converts this Spanish conquest into an Anglo-American religious one as Cortés sheds his Catholicism for Protestant self-reliance, demonstrating that he is "as usual, true to himself" (429). Cortés's diminishing Catholicism and increasing Protestantism refer the history in turn to its contemporary imperialist context, the impending conversion of Mexican Catholic territory into North American Protestant possession. Cortés's coherent identity, in which his interior symmetrically issues into a representative exterior (a coherence reflected by the conquest's easy resolution into narrative sequence), is opposed by Montezuma's disintegrating and opaque selfhood: degenerating under the burden of his "priest-ridden" and materialist culture, Montezuma forsakes any autonomous identity, vacillating between fierce monarch and cowed "savage" until lapsing into "effeminate" despair. This decomposition of Montezuma's personality into conventional configurations of the effeminized native is both a key instance of the European's providential achievement and a reason for it.

In its rhetorically charged portraits of an indolent Cortés transformed into an energetic Protestant hero who delivers just retribution on the Aztecs' sacerdotal culture for its idolatry and ritualism, the history reveals the extent to which anti-Catholicism structured New England historical constructions of American origin. Termed by Prescott the "Dominicans of the New World" (50), Aztec priests, for example, are at once Catholic and barbarian, living in monastic seclusion and practicing flagellation, baptism, confession, and absolution. If to one reviewer such resemblances demonstrated how "thin is the partition that sometimes divides the heathen from the Christian world,"[14] to Prescott the gulf between Aztec and Roman Catholic monkishness and Protestant Christianity is unbridgeable.

Such a powerful coincidence between sixteenth- and nineteenth-century America is achieved through a Unitarian indictment of Catholicism, whose allegedly illicit comminglings of spirit and matter, transcendence and institutional power, link Aztec, Spaniard, and Mexican. Situated at the root of both America's problematic European origin and its "savage" New World past, Catholicism, as historical and transcendental category of difference, is the enabling device by which native Mesoamerican culture is rendered dismissible in familiar terms for New England readers. Prescott, disengaging Catholicism from its institutional and geographical framework and transplanting its uprooted traits to Aztec culture, extends Walter Scott's technique of extrapolating attributes from European (principally Italian and Spanish) Catholicism to create a Catholic "character," one defined principally by its incongruous extremes. Such a character then dramatizes cultural otherness whose destruction needs justification or whose meaning remains problematic. Once Aztecs become sufficiently Catholicized (Catholicization being a process finally of southern Europeanization), their annihilation becomes prerecorded, as it were, in the Reformation's triumph over the papacy. As Italy, lingering on for aesthetic perusal, provided American tourists with a symbolic terrain from which to produce for sale ruminations on their own white American identity, so Mexico, as Prescott offered it up, was a New World Italy—a "wilderness of sweets [in which] lurks the fatal *malaria,*" a "land of enchantment" (10)—a land, in short, of past grandeur and present mongrelization, of seductive exterior and corrupt interior. Even the region's volcano speaks to the fearful tourist eye: its "long, dark wreaths of vapor, rolling up from the hoary head of Popocatepetl, told that the destroying element was, indeed, at work in the bosom of the beautiful Valley" (335).

Such an anti-Catholic discourse ironically places Europe at the very center of the Americas; scrutinizing the Aztecs, Prescott, like nineteenth-century Americans in Italy, repeatedly focuses on the problem of Catholicism's adulterous mixtures. The ancient Mexicans, like their Italian Catholic colleagues four centuries later, betray an intractable confusion of matter and spirit. The resemblance of such Aztec religious mixtures of "pure philanthropy . . . and of merciless extermination" (44) to Catholicism's own mixtures is surprisingly close, claims Prescott. Aztec inconsistencies "will not appear incredible to those who are familiar with the history of the Roman Catholic Church, in the early ages of the Inquisition" (44–45).

The degenerative character of the Aztec is due finally, then, to the indigenous Catholicism that constitutes the interior of that character. Positing a superstitious interior to be investigated by an enlightened Protestant outsider, the Catholic-Protestant opposition shaped not only Prescott's vision of both America's western and southern frontiers but also more general views of perception and interpretation. Nourished by "nature," the enlightened mind is spontaneously able to perceive intended meanings. The superstitious mind, by contrast, is imprisoned within a Poesque interior, baffled by its own distorted perceptions and unable to exert sufficient interpretive control. The Poesque interior is one of excess mediation where superstition verges on lunacy—a transgression that, in the words of one popular medical critic of the "superstitious" mind, marks a discursive shift from religious deviance to psychological pathology:

> The straggling sunbeam from without streams through the stained window, and as it enters assumes the colors of the painted glass;—whilst the half-extinguished fire within, now smouldering in its ashes, and now shooting forth a quivering flame, casts fantastic shadows through the chambers of the soul. Within the spirit sits, lost in its own abstractions. The voice of nature from without is hardly audible.[15]

The superstitious mind in this and other accounts assumes the qualities of a Catholic cathedral; falsely mediating between self and reality, it imprisons the human creature in his or her own delusions. Rather than functioning correctly as a transparent medium between self and "nature," the superstitious mind is a cluttered, muffled piece of Old World architecture whose windows discolor perceptions precisely as the Catholic church, both theologically and architecturally, impedes the Gospel's pure light. In effect, the superstitious mind is that church in miniature, for it intercedes duplicitously between consciousness and world as the papacy does between believer and God. The spectacle of this primitivized mind, unable to extricate itself from its own gloomy fantasies and finally collapsing into its own interiority, like Brockden Brown's Wieland or like Prescott's Montezuma, who was "deeply tinctured . . . with that spirit of bigotry" (437), provided a fascinating psychological investigation for "enlightened" Americans.

As the story *of* the antebellum moment, Prescott's history of the collapse of dual Spanish and Aztec origins into a single European (finally English) origin—of native America supplanted by North America—is a story of uncanny religious resemblances converted into racial difference, of an insider's ecclesiastical narrative translated into an outsider's racial one. As the racial other, Montezuma, whose "hard fate," Prescott admits, is to be "wholly indebted for his portraiture to the pencil of his enemies" (280), is nostalgically expelled from the cultural body of America, and a new genealogy is established from the white Cortés. Ideological contradictions at work in this transaction fuel rather than impede the narrative, for they provide the crucial narrative trope of "sacrifice" of the Catholic other that functions as Prescott's central, ostensibly apolitical, rationale for this new genealogy. Focusing his scenic narrative talents on Aztec rituals of human sacrifice and cannibalism, Prescott argues from them to the necessary "sacrifice" of Mesoamerican culture.

> How can a nation, where human sacrifices prevail, and especially when combined with cannibalism, further the march of civilization? . . . The heart was hardened, the manners were made ferocious, the feeble light of civilization, transmitted from a milder race, was growing fainter and fainter, as thousands and thousands of miserable victims, throughout the empire, were yearly fattened in its cages, sacrificed on its altars, dressed and served at its banquets! The whole land was converted into a vast human shambles! The empire of the Aztecs did not fall before its time. (612–13)

Seen as a primitive, sanguinary ritual in need of clarifying extermination, Aztec religion nonetheless provides the primary site for the history's confusion, for the perceived uncanny resemblance of Aztec religious practices to European Christianity, and Spanish Catholicism in particular, forms the interpretive crisis at its core. Prescott's subtle anti-Catholicism functions as the principal medium through which this crisis is enacted, for the resemblance between Aztec and Roman Catholic practices of confession, baptism, priestly hierarchy, and punitive ritual provides the history's compelling ideological argument *and* confusion, identifying the New and Old Worlds while enforcing a new distinction between the papal-Indian amalgam and Protestant North America. "The existence of similar religious ideas in remote regions, inhabited by different races, is an interesting subject of study; furnishing, as it does, one of the most important links in the great chain of communication which binds together the distant families of nations" (38 n.5).

In recording this providential triumph, *Mexico* and its Aztecs, who were "another, yet the same," open a consolatory, therapeutic space for readers to ponder the irrevocability of difference—a reading space that paradoxically emerges from (and just barely contains) a subversive text of religious resemblance and hence potential identification. Reviewing George Bancroft's historiography of the Old and New Worlds, Prescott observed:

> The analogy is much more striking of certain usages and institutions, particularly of a religious character, and, above all, the mythological traditions which those who have had occasion to look into the Aztec antiquities cannot fail to be struck with. This resemblance is oftentimes in matters so purely arbitrary, that it can hardly be regarded as founded in the constitution of man; so very exact that it can scarcely be considered as accidental.[16]

But if religion, specifically in its bloodthirsty outbreaks, revealed to Prescott the universality of human nature, it also demonstrated the perplexing phenomenon of incongruity. "The forms in which it [religion] is expressed are infinitely various," Prescott continued in his essay on Bancroft, "but they flow from the same source, are directed to the same end, and all claim from the historian the benefit of toleration."[17]

Remarking that his concluding essay, "Origin of Mexican Civilization" (which finds that the evidence argues against the New World's derivation from the Old, notwithstanding the numerous resemblances), was first written as part of his introduction, Prescott suggests a certain circularity to his historiographical enterprise. The appendix, adjudicating issues of origin, derivation, resemblance, and difference, was "originally designed to close the Introductory Book" (Mexico, 688) and was written as part of the introduction. It is in this appended essay that Prescott isolates the vexed issue of religious resemblance and difference. Religion functions as the crucial evidence in support of the initial obligation of his romantic narrative history to convert cultural and historical difference into resemblance, to transform distant Aztecs into psychological verisimilitudes of human nature (universalized beings on whom the reader's involvement with the text depends). But unlike New Spain's "monkish chroniclers," who superstitiously perceived resemblances between Indian and Catholic rituals, Prescott promises to offer his readers "only real points of resemblance, as they are supported by evidence, and stripped, as far as possible, of the illusions with which they have been invested by the pious credulity of one party, and the visionary system-building of another" (692).

Yet if Prescott gently mocks his Catholic sources for perceiving theological affiliations between Spaniard and Aztec, he readily analogizes the inconsistencies of Catholicism to those of Montezuma. In the process, that is, of asserting his differences against the imagined religious resemblances chronicled by Catholic missionaries, he acknowledges cultural analogies that emerge from "nature, common to all" (699). The various subversive potentialities of resemblance (Is the New World the same as the Old? Are the Aztecs one of the Lost Tribes of Israel? Is the Aztec like the North American Indian? Is the Catholic Cortés like the Emersonian hero? Are the Mexicans like New Englanders?) are regulated by acknowledging the innocuous resemblance of all to "human nature." As the concluding essay demonstrates, the key analytic terms in Prescott's narrative of the conversion of foreign Americas into the familiar "New World" of North American Protestants are finally those of religious resemblance and difference, the difficult object of the history being to extract the racial difference from a constructed religious resemblance, to break any continuity between native and European to justify the latter's imperialist mission. Thus what is original to this peculiar, indeed "original," Aztec character of Montezuma is precisely the contradiction of Prescott's vision of unique human natures residing within the universal. The incongruous Aztec character achieves its morphological expression by its volatile intermediate position in the world's civilizations. "The Aztec had plainly reached that middle station, as far above the rude races of the New World as it was below the cultivated communities of the Old" (330). At the same time, the "Egyptians were at the top of the scale, the Aztecs at the bottom" (56). But like the developing middle classes of capitalist America, the Aztecs' middle station harbors the uneasy prospect of decline. Prescott's Aztecs are on their way down, not up.

Preoccupied by the threat of both miscegenation and ethnic assimilation, Prescott's history broods over what it declares to be the mixtures of Aztec culture, implicitly arguing that Aztec heterogeneity is the polluted origin of the contaminated difference of the nineteenth-century Mexican, theorized by one editorial as a "sickening mixture, consisting of such a conglomeration of Negroes and Rancheros, Mestizoes and Indians, with but a few Castilians."[18] Such mixtures confirmed not only the racial but also the religious purity of the Anglo-American reader.

Saturated with the historian's self-conscious investigative voice, supplemented by lengthy footnotes, and surrounded by an extensive, extratextual correspondence with Spanish and English historians, however, Prescott's history reveals him to be no simple polemicist against popery but rather a skilled mythologizer of archival materials whose self-consciously antique "chivalric" narrative speaks to the nativist political moment. As an aristocratic historian speaking for and to America's "democracy," Prescott advertises the accuracy and coherence of his account by contrasting his cautious empiricism to the superstition of his Catholic sources. He is Cortés on the narrative plain, constructing a new account of white America from prior Aztec and Hispanic texts that are flawed by primitive faith. Throughout, the Unitarian historian sounds a wry, nostalgic, skeptical note before a spirit-ridden pagan world of Aztec and Spanish Catholic beliefs. "It is impossible to get a firm footing in the quicksands of tradition. The further we are removed from the Conquest, the more difficult it becomes to decide what belongs to the primitive Aztec, and what to the Christian convert" (694 n.18). His is an agile act of interpretation, like the Unitarian reading of Scripture; Prescott both believes and discredits his sources, invalidating them as history while paradoxically relying on them as eyewitness accounts of a lost era. Famous for introducing critical bibliographical footnotes to the writing of history, Prescott creates from this religious drama a two-tier text whose typographical organization—romantic narrative on top, scholarly footnotes beneath—plays out the dominion of liberal Protestant historiography over Catholic chronicles that themselves blend disturbingly with their indigenous Aztec double. This troubled confrontation between Catholic source and Protestant revision is reduced to a mock combat that finds symbolic typographical expression: the encounter invariably occurs in footnotes accompanying but never usurping the mainstream narrative. Such encounters are frequently reenacted within individual notes. Pondering the pagan-papal flaws of one Tezcucan source, Prescott writes in a footnote:

> All these advantages are too often counterbalanced by a singular incapacity for discriminating—I will not say, between historic truth and falsehood (for what is truth?)—but between the probable, or rather the possible, and the impossible. One of the generation of primitive converts to the Romish faith, he lived in a state of twilight civilization, when, if miracles were not easily wrought, it was at least easy to believe them. (561 n.10)

Prescott's papal and Reformed Christianities, one associated with bias, the other with truth, enact a historiographical conflict beneath his avowed impartiality. American historians attain their greatest control over Catholicism by practicing a courtly tolerance, even ambivalence, toward a faith notorious for the intolerance of its Inquisition. The voice of Prescott's inherited Unitarianism is objective, self-consciously masculine, and committed to disclosure; that of Catholicism, as implied by his portraits of Aztec and Spanish Catholic character, subjective, effeminate, and bent on deception. Drawing on while simultaneously questioning his missionary Catholic chroniclers, Prescott, maintaining a studiously modest dominion over his sources (one of whom, he notes approvingly, was "purified in a great measure from the mists of superstition" [35 n.41]), subtly replays the great defeat of the papacy represented by the establishment and growth of Protestant America. At the very base of the history, then, an intricately politicized relation to prior Catholic texts is at work, an ideologically loaded interchange that determines the structure and intention of the history, enabling it to be not only a disclosure but an exposure of past and present Catholic contaminations. Embedded at the core of the history, this gentrified confrontation between falsehood and truth, Catholic eyewitness and Protestant judge provides a view of cultural dissent otherwise obscured by the seductions of scenic narrative.

◄∾►

Mexico provided an enormously influential legitimation of European ascendance in the Americas not only because of its ambivalent endorsement of the Mexican War but also because of its careful commercialism. Emerging from Boston's Brahmin culture, Prescott's "amateur" history frankly aspired to a popular status at odds with its author's Anglophile pretensions. Writing to Fanny Calderón de la Barca (the wife of the Spanish ambassador to Mexico and the author of a Mexican travel narrative closely consulted by Prescott for his history), Prescott happily described his history as a popular, even Gothic, tale: "The 'Conquest of Mexico' goes off bravely. More than three thousand copies have been disposed of in little more than two months. I am quite popular among children, and for aught I know the *tiers état*. It is a child's story as much as any of Monk Lewis's tales of wonder."[19] If this commercialism broached class lines, it didn't breech them. For a man who claimed never to have "worked for the dirty lucre,"[20] the pursuit of a mass readership offered a reasonably decontaminated access to public power—a literary mastery free of the vulgarity of politics that Prescott at times associated with feminine corruption. The gendered tension between the purified province of historiography and the suspiciously female, potentially class-less precinct of politics emerges in his criticism of his fellow historian (and lifelong friend) George Bancroft's unseemly involvement with the Democratic party: "How a man can woo the fair Muse of history and the ugly strumpet of faction with the same breath, does indeed astonish me."[21] For Prescott, the reading public, unlike the political public, was not an obstreperous or seductive woman but a site where class, gender, and generational differences might be molded into consensus through the powers of romantic narrative.[22] But if he was writing for fame rather than for "dirty lucre," for consensus rather than the "strumpet of faction," the issue of profit was not inoperative but rather was resituated onto the literary. Prescott's conservative Whig indictment of the vulgar femininity of Bancroft's Democratic partisanship had no vulgar mas-culine correlative. If the public was associated with a disreputable fem-ininity, America's masculine crudities displayed the promise of progres-sive development into a malehood free of class mingling. Prescott declared that even Polk's misadministration would not harm America's virility, which proceeds "like a great lusty brat that will work his way into the full size of a man, from the strength of his constitution, whatever quacks and old women may do to break it."[23]

Prescott's flight from the political into the historiographical produced a powerful ideological prose that consistently advertised its emptiness, transparency, and lucidity. If Prescott's prose style was compared by one enthusiastic reviewer to the "manners of a well-bred gentleman, which have nothing so peculiar as to awaken attention,"[24] the history was meant not only to entertain without provoking "attention" but also to maintain class structure. The history's apparent lack of partisanship led its most vehement critic, Theodore Parker, to attack it for "lack[ing] philosophy to a degree exceeding belief" and hence for having been composed with and for an "average sense" of mankind.[25] That quality of emptiness was far more typically read, however, as indicating the work's truthfulness. *Mexico* was elsewhere admired for being preserved in the "embalming" effects of pure "truth" rather than being encased in the "varnish" of bias that would speed any work's "dissolution."[26] Such language mimics the colonizing procedures of Prescott's historiography that sentimentally embalm Aztec culture while recounting its destruction. Indeed, Prescott's own sense of the complex distancings and artifice of romantic historiography suggests how crucial was this achievement of transparency. His was to be not only a theatrical text but a simulacrum of theater. As one reviewer explained, "One of the 'primal duties' of a historian is . . . to produce an effect resembling as nearly as possible the illusion created by seeing the events he narrates represented by well-trained actors, with appropriate costume, scenery, and decorations. Here, too, Mr. Prescott has been signally successful."[27]

These literary theatrics, then, not only shroud the political but, more fundamentally, stand in for it; explaining why he chose not to write a history of the Mexican War, which began three years after his history's publication, Prescott confessed that he "had rather not meddle with heroes who have not been underground two centuries at least."[28] But as a reviewer of *Mexico* suggested, Prescott's historiography was, in its very evasion of contemporary politics, redolent of a political and religious dominion over foreign material. "The most superficial reader perceives, that he has made himself a perfect master of the subject, and that he writes down upon it from a superior position."[29]

Among the many accolades for his work, Prescott received no higher compliment than that from his close friend Charles Sumner, famed opponent of the extension of slavery in Texas and equally famed victim of a vicious caning on the Senate floor in retaliation for his inflammatory speech, "The Crime against Kansas." "Since I first devoured the Waverley novels, I have read nothing by which I have been so entirely entraîné," Sumner wrote to Prescott.[30] Sumner's selection of the French term *entraîné* to convey his absorption indicates a careful appropriation of the French language to register social standing—both the one the two men shared and that of Prescott's text. Such aristocratic status was confirmed through the self-silencing of one's ethnic and religious prejudices before the hypnotic force of romantic historiography. This effort to be free of "national or party feeling," as Prescott phrased it in the preface to his earlier history of Ferdinand and Isabella, emerges as well from the strategy of liberal Unitarianism in the face of denominational dissension: an assertion of tolerant, relativistic selfhood via the unifying power of the symbolic imagination.[31] Situated in the destabilized interpretive field of liberal Protestantism, Prescott's romantic history borrows from fiction to gain the allegedly bipartisan authenticities of the literary and whatever convictions of sentiment might be gleaned from a skillfully aestheticized past.[32]

Prescott's text was not to be a sensationalist exposé of Spanish perfidy, for vehement anti-Catholic bias belonged neither to genteel Unitarian society nor to its histories. In the case of Cortés and Montezuma, whose story appeared in schoolbooks throughout the nineteenth century, Prescott's own schoolbook history distinguished itself from sectarian treatments that reveled in details of Spanish cruelty and, in so doing, won Archbishop Hughes's gratitude for a fair treatment of Catholics. Contemporary reviews sometimes chided Prescott for not judging the Spanish more harshly, but he consciously avoided descending into the middle- and lower-class discourse of anti-Catholicism in favor of a genial relativism that sophisticated rather than dismissed his discomfort with Rome.[33] Prescott displaces Catholicism onto the Aztec, replacing the "Black Legend" of Spanish conquistadorial cruelty with tales of chivalric heroism, and thus merges an aristocratic Spanish Catholicism into American Protestantism. *Mexico* presents the conquest as a single text blending nature and literature that brings Cortés within the precincts of an antifeudal providentialism. "Nature," Prescott mused in his diary, "does not often work out epics like the Mexican conquest."[34]

The assertion of cultural and racial superiority by a sentimental identification with subordinated Indian cultures operates finally at the foundation of the history's composition where Prescott grafts one European genre onto another, as preliminary to the later engrafting of Europe onto the Americas. Prescott compared his narrative at its earliest stages of composition to Italian epic poetry; it is "as romantic and as chivalrous as any which Boiardo or Ariosto ever fabled," he noted in his memorandum book.[35] Having turned toward the study of Spanish history after reluctantly abandoning the field of Italian literature to his close friend George Ticknor, a Harvard professor of romance languages, Prescott inscribed "Italy" onto "Spain." But he transcribed not only chivalrous Italy but also contemporary Roman Catholic Italy, its Romanism alluring, commingled, and ultimately doomed—a construct not simply disguised by the historian's liberalism but a constituent feature of it. Writing to Lucas Alamán in 1846, Prescott listed the various sectarian readings to which he had been subjected:

> It is true you think I savour something of the old Puritan acid
> in my anti-Catholic strictures. A Roman Catholic Dublin review

speaks of it as doubtful from my writings whether I am a Catholic or Protestant. A Baltimore Catholic journal condemns me as a deist. The Madrid translator of *Ferdinand and Isabella* (Rector of the University of Madrid) condemns me for my hostility to the Inquisition. So I think between them all I may pass for a very liberal Christian.[36]

As another reviewer suggested, the ambiguities in Prescott's estimation of the Aztec empire set a crucial boundary for readers in a secularizing age. Approving of Prescott's acknowledged uncertainty about the origins of pre-Columbian Mexican civilization, one reviewer converted his ambivalence into a salutary metaphysical mystery: "It is one of those mysterious questions, which, from the insuperable difficulties they present, administer a tacit rebuke to the pride of human intellect, by the bounds which they set to its progress, presenting depths which it cannot fathom and heights which it cannot scale."[37]

If Prescott's struggles with the literary origins of his text yield to the history's preoccupation with the impure genealogy of the Aztecs, that impurity in turn recoils upon the conflicted nature of their religious culture. Prescott's representation of the racial, religious, and national otherness of the Aztec, which substantiates contemporary efforts to subordinate and even demonize the Mexican people, unfolds from the history's key trope of incongruity: "In contemplating the religious system of the Aztecs," Prescott writes in the introduction, "one is struck with its apparent incongruity, as if some portion of it had emanated from a comparatively refined people, open to gentle influences, while the rest breathes a spirit of unmitigated ferocity" (37). Such a hybrid national type supported the era's sustained invective against miscegenation, and in particular the hybridized character of Mexico, vilified by Polk's secretary of the treasury as a country of "mixed races, speaking more than twenty different languages, composed of every poisonous compound of blood and color." The vitiated character of both Aztec and contemporary Mexican further served as sacrificial double for the "miscegenated" selves produced under American slavery. Speaking in 1853 against any further acquisition of Mexican territory, Senator John Clayton voiced a typical fear of being overrun by mulattoes: "Yes! Aztecs, Creoles, Half-breeds, Quadroons, Samboes, and I know not what else—'ring-streaked and speckled'—all will come in, and instead of our governing them, they, by their votes, will govern *us*."[38]

Such incendiary rhetoric over the annexation of Mexican lands reveals a preoccupation with "character" similar to that in Prescott's history. The insistent focus of Prescott's historiography upon the powerful individual engineer of historical events thus represents a literary confirmation of the contemporary racial preoccupation with character. As fictional construct and political device, "character" works in the service of a cultural defense against foreign contaminants, a pure substance that forestalls the dangers of mingled social existence. In his attack on the moral and religious disintegration of frontier settlements, the easterner Horace Bushnell argued for the insidious connection between aboriginal cultures and Roman Catholicism and their combined threat to Protestant character. "Let us empty ourselves of our character, let us fall into superstition, through the ignorance, wildness and social confusion incident to a migratory habit and a rapid succession of new settlements, and Romanism will find us just where character leaves us." Bushnell's specter of a Catholicized American West incorporates the southern frontier as well; Mexico and South America "have been descending steadily towards barbarism, in the loss of the old Castilian dignity."[39] Since character, literarily speaking, must be reasonably consistent to attain representational verisimilitude, contradictions must be carefully regulated: A character who advertises irresolvable contradiction meets fictional eradication. The contaminations of feudalism and Catholicism become the property of the doomed, effeminized Aztec—a character at once profoundly literary and inimitable because of its peculiar inconsistencies, which arise not only from the extreme climate and the Aztecs' positioning in the "middle station" between aborigines and Spaniards but also from Catholicism itself.

The contradiction between feudalism and modernism at the base of Cortés's character shifts, therefore, as the history proceeds, onto Montezuma. "The Aztec character was perfectly original and unique. It was made up of incongruities apparently irreconcilable . . . the extremes of barbarism and refinement" (91). It is these very imperfections of Aztec character that make it amenable to picturesque representation, fueling the literary production that is dedicated to their enfeeblement.[40] Precisely because of the impurity born of such contradictions, the incongruous Aztec culture lays claim to the history's therapy. Prescott's history, as we have seen, monitors a crucial shift in the elaboration of cultural difference from religion to race; if its first trajectory serves the mandates of racial purity, dedicated to the aligning of whites (Catholic or Protestant) against native cultures, the second, conflicting, trajectory serves the dictates of class anxiety, the stratification of New England culture into various Protestant masters and Irish Catholic subordinates. Initially eager to differentiate between his Catholic Indians and his Catholic conquerors, Prescott eventually collapses this crucial distinction. His overriding concern with the delusions of Catholic piety and ritual finally consumes the very oppositions initially constructed by it. Both Aztec and Spaniard exhibit a disjunction between (and mingling of) spirit and letter—difficulties Unitarianism had allegedly solved. Catholic and Indian cultures, as unfolding paradigms of the feminine, indulge in beautiful forms that disguise corrupt contents. Protestant fears of an aestheticized Roman conspiracy—of being duped and captured by a malignant ecclesiastical beauty—underscore Prescott's fascinated depiction of Aztec culture, whose prayers are "often clothed in dignified and beautiful language, showing, that sublime speculative tenets are quite compatible with the most degrading practices of superstition" (53 n.36).

Posited against this deviant, heterogeneous Aztec character is Prescott's own, one universally hailed for its geniality, its capacity to transmute difference into consensus. One panegyric review presents the historian as ideal simulacrum for expansionism itself. "His knowledge, patiently acquired and long reflected upon, has become assimilated and blended with the substance of his mind, and is not the crude and half-digested result of a hurried process of cramming."[41] Celebrated alike for the transparency of his prose and his personality, Prescott, who declared that his history was "nothing but a plain tale," presented a racial and narrative homogeneity set in (genial) opposition to a heterogeneous America.[42]

Indeed, Prescott's ambivalence toward the violent "character" of Cortés permits the diffusion of ambivalence to political events. Prescott pondered becoming a biographer in 1825 because of the "deeper interest which always attaches to minute differences of character, and a continuous, closely connected narrative."[43] In biography, character and hence cultural differences can be converted into the unities of romantic narrative. The finely calibrated character analyses of Prescott's history not only prefigure and commercialize images of the ideal racial and religious character central to annexation debates but also speak to Prescott's preoccupation with the regimentation of his own character. According to his first biographer and close friend George Ticknor:

> He made a record of everything that was amiss, and examined and considered and studied that record constantly and conscientiously. It was written on separate slips of paper,—done always with his own hand,—seen only by his own eye. These slips he preserved in a large envelope, and kept them in the most reserved and private manner. From time to time . . . he took them out and looked them over, one by one. If any habitual fault were, as he thought, eradicated, he destroyed the record of it; if a new one had appeared, he entered it on its separate slip, and placed it with the rest for future warning and reproof.[44]

That the agnostic Prescott should so closely follow Franklinian textual practices of character reformation testifies to his powerful attraction to asceticism, an attraction embedded in and disguised by his persevering efforts to create a leisured rhetoric.

Just as his history, in its conclusion, backs onto its introduction and thus suggests a continued preoccupation with origin, so his conception of the Spanish and Aztec confrontation reverts to Europe's classical origins. Of an early battle between the Spaniards and Tascalans, Prescott surmises: "It was, in short, the combat of the ancient Greeks and Persians over again" (238). As Prescott's identification with Cortés's militarism makes clear, such a Europeanization of New World history struggles to subordinate conquistadorial violence to a superior Protestant moralism. Cortés's violent and labored campaign into the Mexican interior is reproduced by the historian's Protestant moralism, itself a campaign directed not only at the world but also at himself, specifically his indolent self. "My pen is my good lance," wrote Prescott in his journal, "with which I may fight the battles of humanity—for the diffusion of truth, and virtue, and civilization. And shall I let it rust from slothfulness?"[45] Of his lengthy introductory essay on the Aztecs, Prescott recorded in his diary that he had "given the reader, or, at least, myself—a sweat in the Introduction. The rest must be play for both of us."[46] As the terms of both entries suggest, Prescott understood the narration of the conquest as a recreation that disguised the labor involved in both the construction and the consumption of the historian's panoramic display of Indian culture and landscape. This opposition between work and play figured at the heart of expansionist rhetoric prior to and during the Mexican War since it was precisely Mexican indolence and inability to improve the land that often justified invasion by the industrious Anglo-Saxon.

The socialite son of a successful Boston lawyer and politician, Prescott lived with his wife and children and parents in the parental home for twenty-four years, establishing his own home only after his father died. While diary entries and correspondence indicate satisfaction with this protracted filial status, they also monitor a continuing struggle against the psychological burdens of leisure, the "effeminate native of Hispaniola" within. Struggling to oppose the temptations of socializing with his Franklinian regime of self-imposed labor, Prescott vowed: "To the end of my life, I trust I shall be more avaricious of time and never put up with a smaller average *than 7 hours* intellectual occupation *per diem.*"[47] The irony was that this self-regimentation was dedicated to the creation of leisure reading, to providing a "narrative for intelligent loungers."[48] Blinded in one eye during a food fight while an undergraduate at Harvard, Prescott also suffered partial blindness in his remaining eye and composed most of his histories on a noctograph (an instrument to guide the handwriting of the blind), having absorbed his data from dictation and composed his text in his head. Figure 4 shows him sitting erect at this instrument, composing his portrait of Montezuma for "loungers," the body of the historian in disciplined contrast to the ornate and melancholic figure of Montezuma that appeared as frontispiece for *Mexico* (Fig. 3). As the recipient of some eight thousand pages of unpublished source materials for his *Mexico,* the invalid historian understood his historiography as in part the display of his heroic will over the indolence and disability born of encountering the "Rome" within:

> Many, very many, all too many ways lead to Rome. Idleness leads there; for Rome saves the trouble of independent thought. Dissoluteness leads there, for it impairs moral vigor. Conservatism, foolish conservatism, leads there, in the hope that the conservatism of the oldest abuse will be a shield for all abuses. Sensualism leads there, for it delights in parade and magnificent forms. Materialism leads there, for the superstitious can adore an image and think to become purified by bodily torments, hair shirts, and fastings, turning all religion into acts of the physical organs.[49]

Opening with a voluptuous travelscape, Prescott's introductory depiction of Aztec culture, most fully epitomized in Montezuma's character, is the labor-intensive artifact he built to protect himself against these internal Roman encounters—a creation the ensuing recreational narrative violently dismantles. The history's narrative structure, then, enacts Prescott's potency over the foreign religious object as the partially blind

Fig. 3. "Montezuma, II. Emperor of Mexico." From William Hickling Prescott, *The History of the Conquest of Mexico* (1843). Courtesy, The Bancroft Library, University of California, Berkeley.

Fig. 4. W. H. Prescott at his "noctograph," a writing instrument designed for use by the visually impaired. Courtesy, The Bancroft Library, University of California, Berkeley.

historian writes the text of his own character regulation onto that of Montezuma's dissolution.

Travel excursions, the writing of history, the extension of imperial power, and the construction of a national self from the disciplining of the invalid body function as reciprocal activities in Prescott's *Mexico*. Reviewing Mme de Calderón de la Barca's *Life in Mexico* (which he consulted for his taxonomy of Aztec character and landscape), Prescott fashions key connections between the sacred, the chivalric, and the touristic.

> The taste for pilgrimage, however, it must be owned, does not stop with the countries where it can be carried on with such increased facility. It has begotten a nobler spirit of adventure, something akin to what existed in the fifteenth century, when the world was new, or newly discovering, and a navigator who did not take in sail, like the cautious seamen of Knickerbocker, might run down some strange continent in the dark; for, in these times of dandy tourists and travel-mongers, the boldest achievements, that have hitherto defied the most adventurous spirits, have been performed: the Himmaleh Mountains have been scaled . . . and the mysterious monuments of the semi-civilized races of Central America have been thrown open to the public gaze.[50]

In this key passage for understanding the Anglo-American representation of the Americas as theater presenting an aestheticized southern drama for northern beholders (a bifurcation that typified Mexican War propaganda in its focus on the erotic Mexican woman), Prescott's language locates the origins of tourism in a religious spirit that subsequently issues into the ahistorical but solidly gendered field of adventurism. Chivalric exploits rescue those "dandy tourists and travel-mongers" from the twin threat of unstable gender and class constructs, from effeminacy and vulgarity. For Prescott, who himself never traveled west of Niagara, "travel" jointly defines fifteenth-century European voyages of discovery and conquest and the nineteenth-century opening of foreign cultures "to the public gaze."

What Prescott articulates here is not only a conventional pictorializing of the foreign (and its disguise of imperial appetite) but the domestication of the alien by a touristic vision that converts an external foreignness into a psychological possession internal to the Anglo-American subject. The democratic implications of Prescott's rhetoric of mysteries now opened to the public gaze are in turn recontained by the sentimental privacies of the history's printed pages. If travel registers the freedom of the mobile New World eye penetrating the contradictory ("mysterious") body of the foreign—a freedom largely unavailable to the nearly blind historian—Prescott further insists that such democratic motions will issue, not into communication with the tourist's constructed other, but rather into a meditation with one's self while in its presence. This dynamic is not unlike the experience of reading his romantic history. For Prescott, history enacts on the narrative plane the disciplining of both the personal body and the democratic fantasia of travel. His history is travel corrected of the latter's potential transgression of ethnic and religious difference. Travel's disruption of boundary threatens national identity and, in so doing, the aesthetic particularity, the discernible foreignness of the other. "Nations are so mixed up by this process, that they are in danger of losing their idiosyncracy; and the Egyptian and the Turk, though they still cling to their religion, are becoming European in their notions and habits more and more every day."[51] In short, Prescott valued the cultural separateness made available through imagining but carefully avoiding travel, for such separateness supplied the material for the production of romantic historiography.

In a New World empty of architectural enclosures to investigate, the mind of the "superstitious" savage served as the Catholicized interior for anti-Catholic readers to tour without risk of contamination. Empowered by the interpretive guidelines of reformed Christianity, American tourist-readers of Prescott's *Mexico* could peer into the mind of Montezuma, whose effeminate "Catholic" distresses reduced the threatening complexities of New World racial difference to the familiarities of Old World religious difference.

Because the representation of the Aztec forms the charismatic center of his historical narrative and makes manifest the virtuosity of his ambivalent, melancholic prose, Prescott's Aztec culture carries within its self-destructive contours the possessiveness and excited mastery of the invalid historian's power. Elegy, which disguises the necessary work of imperialism, also serves as expression for the author's labored and masterful self-effacement. Indeed, the very structure of the history suggests that while it consistently argues for the inevitable sacrifice progress entails, its interior drama is preoccupied with vulnerability and the protection of an inner aboriginal self. As Prescott's journal entries on the experience of composing his history imply, the text's therapeutic workings enable readers to reconstruct their own lost alterity as text, itself explored, conquered, yet always possessed on the bookshelf in its pre-invasion defenselessness. Aztec society, sumptuously evoked, then, affords the opportunity both to locate supposedly internal Catholic pathologies that will lead to its collapse and to experience that foreign body's wholeness in religiously familiar terms. This Mexican "past" as romantic-historical construct becomes, finally, the touristic other with whom the middle-class reader (adult and child) can mingle without danger of religious or racial corruption. Further, the reader is given access to the interior not only of Montezuma, "prey to the most dismal apprehensions" (289), but also of Cortés, whose initially coherent European identity is eventually disclosed as also harboring the opposing "extremes of barbarism and refinement" (91) and whose character is finally, like the Catholic faith, "marked with the most opposite traits, embracing qualities apparently the most incompatible" (681). If the hero sweeps away the Aztecs, he is "civilized" only by contrast to his "barbarian" victims; having performed the work of Protestant culture by killing the Indian, Cortés resumes an incongruous character that will invite the same fate. Like Montezuma, he is removed from providential time and locked in the stasis of his equilibrated oppositions. Internal heterogeneity comes to mark the Spaniard as well as the Aztec as unnatural, deviant, and appropriate for sacrifice. Cultural heterogeneity or, put more locally, the conversion of 1840s Boston from Protestant preserve to immigrant plurality is deposited (and provisionally contained) in the interior of both their Catholic characters. At the end of Prescott's history, Mexico is powerfully excluded from the destined precincts of North America to remain foreign until its Protestant domestication three years later, in 1846. The self that Prescott's history constructs, the self that his judicious but intimate Unitarian voice claims as its own definitive and sacrificial "character," is constituted precisely at this narrative boundary between American Protestantism as heroic suppression of bodily deficiency and Aztec Catholicism as melancholic collapse into the flesh.

Francis Parkman and New France

I was led into a convent by the same motives that two years later led me to become domesticated in the lodges of the Sioux Indians at the Rocky Mountains, with the difference that I much preferred the company of the savages to that of the monks.
          Francis Parkman, "A Convent at Rome," 1890

In 1855 Thomas D'Arcy McGee published the first Catholic history of America, attempting on a popular level what John Gilmary Shea's massive *History of the Catholic Church in the United States* attempted on the scholarly: the revision of American history to acknowledge the role of Catholics in the founding, settlement, and growth of the nation. Addressing his immigrant readers, McGee's *Catholic History of North America* sought to raise Irish self-esteem through the familiar, if troublesome, tactic of illustrating the minority's membership in and affection for mainstream culture.[52] As he struggled against nativist prejudice by Americanizing Catholics, he also worked to Catholicize America, a country that from McGee's perspective had been discovered by the great Catholic explorer Columbus under the especial patronage of the Virgin Mary. Irish immigrant laborers, as the instruments of the nation's industrial development, were the true pioneers, not Emerson's "buffalo-hunter." Resisting the Anglo-Saxon prejudice of contemporary histories and novels, McGee pushed aside the Natty Bumppos and Davy Crocketts of frontier mythology: "I claim that the first highways which crossed the Blue Ridge and the Alleghenies were the work of the Irish Hercules—the true pine-bender and path-preparer of the new world" (131).

To McGee, the central fact of American culture was not Anglo-America's defeat of Catholic power but the church's triumphant expansion, a growth that had paralleled (and was largely responsible for) the progress of the Republic. Beneath this patriotic picture of Catholicism's productive liaison with democracy is an insecure assertion of its secret victory over Protestantism. With Hawthornesque sensitivity to the interplay between the two Bostons, McGee offers his ironic account of American development: "The Puritan was to become rich; and the Catholic in his poverty was to come after him, to win wages from him by industry, and to erect in the land of the Puritan, with the money of the Puritan himself, the cross the Puritan had so long rejected" (105).

McGee's narrative of the church's disguised entry into Puritan culture and sly mastery of it alternates with his other, more public, version of history: that America was initially and powerfully Catholic. According to this latter interpretation, Catholicism originally possessed what it later would have to recapture in the nineteenth century. But in either of McGee's perspectives, the Roman church controlled access to the New World and its development, in large part because of the Jesuits, whom McGee depicts as sentry figures in American history, demanding deference from antebellum inquirers into the American past: "I might almost assert that every Catholic order is represented in the history of this continent. Why be at war with history? The Jesuits are there, in the outer gate of all our chronicles. Speak them civilly as you pass on" (66).

In the context of contemporary anxieties about Jesuit conspiracies and a pervasively "Jesuitical" reasoning that could bewilder and even enchant the susceptible Protestant, McGee's claim was intentionally provocative. The revival of the Jesuit order in 1814 unleashed suspicions that had hardly been laid to rest, and the Jesuit resumed his powerful status in the American Protestant imagination—an invisible, impenetrable figure of celibate masculine power. The *American Protestant Vindicator,* a major nativist publication, inflamed such fears by claiming as an "ascertained fact that Jesuits are prowling about all parts of the United States in every possible disguise, expressly to ascertain the advantageous situations and modes to disseminate Popery."[53] While Jesuits loomed large to the nativist, they seemed pitiable to the refined Unitarian: "Poor owls," wrote one Jesuit-watcher in the *Christian Examiner;* "surprised by the broad sun in their nocturnal rambles, the Jesuits are groping about from court to court for a shelter, proffering the cooperation of their foiled policy and exploded hypocrisy, acting the part of satellites of those monarchs of the earth, of whom they were formerly the terror."[54] Such condescension disguised a vestigial unease. Inappropriate, even grotesque, the Jesuit "owls" continued to haunt nineteenth-century Americans, especially the theological liberals of New England.

Parkman's *Jesuits in North America* (1867) is deeply informed by this conflicted cultural context of renewed paranoia and studied condescension toward Jesuits. Throughout this work, the second of his seven-volume history, the historian both disputes that the Jesuits were in any way central to the nation's development and demonstrates that they were indeed of great importance to antebellum American attitudes about the national past. As Parkman explained in the midst of his historical narrative, "The Jesuit was, and is, everywhere."[55] Parkman's extended and complex inquiry into this ubiquitous figure narrows into a profound study of the Jesuit missionary "mind," which he reveals as pervaded not by conspiratorial intentions but by a religious enthusiasm so ardent as to elevate the missionaries into a heroic, if not saintly, asceticism. Like Prescott in his *History of the Conquest of Mexico,* Parkman celebrates the violent encounter between Old and New World cultures through his agnostic, often lavishly scenic, display of Catholic features. Catholicism symbolically inhabits the allegedly indolent and superstitious Canadian Indian cultures, an aboriginal "wilderness" that must be vanquished before Protestant America can properly begin. But while Prescott genially delivered his Catholic-Aztec world to sentimental extinction, Parkman's profound attraction for that exterminated world more seriously complicated his historical enterprise. No matter how he worked to infuse "local color" and the correct degree of impartiality into his romantic historical narrative, Parkman produced a heavily literary history. Although famous for his traveling of the forests that figure in his histories, he maintained a simultaneously deferential and dismissive relationship to previous written accounts, creatively arranging them to conform to his narrative point of view. Following the example of Prescott (who was the first to append lengthy critical notes to his text), Parkman produced a history similarly characterized by a curious flirtation between New England historian and Catholic sources—a relationship that lends a distinctive tone of bemused skepticism and suppressed admiration to Prescott's genial and Parkman's baroque histories.[56]

Professedly empirical, Parkman organized his historical data according to the novelistic techniques of Sir Walter Scott and James Fenimore Cooper, whose visual tableaux, heroic characterizations, and suspenseful plots were deemed more faithful to wilderness history than those contained in the Canadian government's 1858 republication of *The Jesuit Relations* (referred to hereafter as the *Relations*)—the principal source material for Parkman's *Jesuits*. The eyewitness accounts of the *Relations* recorded events from a supernatural perspective that always seemed unrealistic, if not duplicitous, to the Unitarian-bred historian. Although he declared the Jesuit *Relations* "trustworthy," Parkman associated them with the theater and his own historical consciousness with the technical superiorities of the new photography: "Nearly every prominent actor in the scenes to be described has left his own record. . . . I have studied and compared these authorities, as well as a great mass of collateral evidence, with more than usual care, striving to secure the greatest possible accuracy of statement, and to reproduce an image of the past with photographic clearness and truth" (*Jesuits*, vii). Jesuit accounts provided data, not structure; material, not meaning. Thus Parkman's professional estimation of the *Relations* rested upon an appreciation of their scenic value rather than their substantive content and purpose. "In respect to the value of their contents, they are exceedingly unequal. Modest records of marvellous adventures and sacrifices, and vivid pictures of forest life, alternate with prolix and monotonous details of the conversion of individual savages, and the praiseworthy deportment of some exemplary neophyte" (*Jesuits*, vi). It is important to set against this view, however, the praise Parkman garnered for the range and depth of his research; the work led the Abbé Casgrain in 1872 to see in *Jesuits* "a reparation and a work of justice which our enemies have too long refused us" and to claim that the "facts" uncovered by Parkman's assiduous scholarship outweigh any "erroneous interpretations."[57]

Combining Scott's narrative techniques with his own ethnic and aesthetic prejudices against Irish and Italian Catholicism, Parkman abstracted various attributes from popery to create a Catholic "character" who functions as the principal agent of historical change and historical explanation in his volume on the Jesuits. Such a character not only dramatizes the colonial moment and justifies the destruction of one culture by another but also, as the Protestant's principal symbol of "mystery," importantly provides the terms through which Parkman conceives historically problematic issues. For example, once the Huron culture becomes sufficiently Catholicized (a process, finally, of mystification), their annihilation becomes permissible, if not desirable. Through this religious dynamic, Parkman not only organizes his colonial historiography but also voices the ambiguities of his Protestant consciousness, which practices a strenuous reserve toward both the heroic asceticism of the Jesuit martyrs and the mysterious assaults of his own estranged body, crippled by lifelong and ultimately mysterious illnesses.

In his history of the seventeenth-century Indian civil wars and failed Jesuit missions, Parkman's post-Unitarian and frequently dark agnosticism converts supernature into innermost human nature, a secularizing process that finally ties the foreign church to the Boston psyche. Translating the foreign sacred into the psychological, Parkman depicts the holy and the satanic as emerging jointly from a pathologically energized bodily interior. Thus Parkman's rhetorically charged inquiry into the Jesuit "mind" extends the conspiratorial mode conventional to Protestant views of the Jesuit into an even more radical claim for his ubiquity. He is not only "everywhere" out in society but "everywhere" inside the Parkmanian historical imagination.

The complexity of Parkman's portrait of the Jesuit derived partially from the guilty nostalgia toward American nature that characterized mid-nineteenth-century thinking. As the supremely civilized being who threw himself into the worst of wildernesses, the Jesuit missionary was inevitably implicated in widespread antebellum debates over the relative merits of nature and civilization; conflictedly engaged with the romanticism of the Jesuit in the wild and the romanticism of the advance of Anglo-Saxon civilization, Parkman's writing celebrates the violence of the latter while indulging in a deeply imagined identification with the Promethean excesses of Jesuit asceticism. In their willed pursuit and endurance of torture and death at the hands of the Iroquois, these seventeenth-century missionaries hardly resemble the indolent Catholic sensualism of Prescott's Montezuma. Rather, they emerge as virtual icons of masculine self-control, confronting through their missionary activity horrendous temptations to self-surrender—temptations they heroically refuse. If for New England romantics, in particular, Protestantism claimed for itself a spiritualized nature that struggled against corrupt and materialist Catholic civilizations, this drama depended upon a deeper and more troubling correspondence between Catholicism and biological matter. The uncultivated nature of the New World that existed prior to the advent of a spiritualizing Protestantism belonged, according to this symbolic logic, to Catholicism; and it was this New World nature—flesh-bound, violent, superstitious—that called for annihilation. Catholicism, then, represented the extremes of barbaric nature and overrefined civilization, while Protestantism existed in between, quarantined from the twinned corruptions of the wild and the artificial.

The *Christian Examiner,* reviewing the Catholic apologist Reverend J. Balmes's *Protestantism and Catholicity Compared in Their Effects on the Civilization of Europe* (1851), revealed the violence implicit in this liberal Protestant dichotomy between nature and civilization. Pondering the complexity and alleged barbarity of Catholic Europe, the article condones the often brutal and reductive procedures of Protestant civilization. "Man has been placed by his Creator upon this earth, as upon a great theatre of action. Vast stores and wonders it contains, adapted to his convenience and comfort. But these do not lie upon the surface. They require to be sought and searched for,—the earth requires to be scrutinized and 'subdued,' before they can be reached."[58]

In such a view of colonization as a struggle against the secrecies of the earth, there is no mention of native inhabitants but rather the suggestion that the New World, like a text, invites a scrutiny that will eventually yield the gift of meaning. To rest content with what the earth offers upon its "surface" is to risk divine displeasure, for such a refusal to extract the earth's true essence would constitute a refusal to be a spectator at the Creator's theatrical performance. Like many of their New England contemporaries, Prescott and Parkman located Catholicism upon the deceptive surface that must be carefully studied and finally "subdued" by the Protestant historian. Moreover, in the symbolic terrain of Parkman's celebrated forest histories the "surface" of indolent Indians, fanatic priests, and interminable wilderness must be brilliantly reconstituted—for this historiographical effort marks the scrutiny necessary to the acquisition of the secrets beneath that surface.

Thus Parkman's New World does not become truly new until Britain gains control; before that providential event America remains an aged world that breeds danger and chaos. Elaborating on Buffon's Eurocentric vision of a sodden, imperfect New World, Parkman introduces his Jesuits with a portrait of a decrepit, diseased land, its politics and nature anarchic. "America, when it became known to Europeans, was, as it had long been, a scene of wide-spread revolution," declares the historian in the opening sentence of his volume. His landscape's revolutions are natural in an aboriginal, not Protestant, sense; cyclical and chaotic, they bear little resemblance to the orderly, divinely sanctioned (and divinely contained) American Revolution. Within this anarchic zone, the organizing imprint of history is little evident, and without it the romantic historian has difficulty embarking upon his interpretive enterprise. No plot can be fashioned from the welter of repetitive biological processes that constitute the Amerindian cosmos; nor can any moral vision be summoned up. As Parkman explains: "These Canadian tribes were undergoing that process of extermination, absorption, or expatriation which, as there is reason to believe, had for many generations formed the gloomy and meaningless history of the greater part of this continent" (341).

What distinguishes this volume of Parkman's history not only from Prescott's work but from later volumes in Parkman's own series is that in recounting the white man's arrival, he does not inevitably shift into the progressive thematics of romantic history. The appearance of the Jesuits, among the most able representatives of European civilization, introduces into this "meaningless" history, not meaning, but rather a new element of chaos. Entering an ongoing struggle between Huron and Iroquois, the Jesuits eventually become, like the Indians, victims of New World processes of extermination. An already unstable mixture of the savage and the civilized, Parkman's missionary French Catholicism finally fractures and collapses in the wilderness world, which itself already possesses so many popish qualities. As a latter day and discreetly ironical martyrology, the *Jesuits* depicts an abortive New World where savagery and superstition fight their final battle—a battle in which the white missionary meets his doom as surely as the native. The Jesuits and the Canadian Indians, representing the extremes of civilization and nature, confront each other like Poesque doubles, mocking and soon outwitting each other, their resemblances increasing as their mutual destruction approaches.[59]

As devious materialists, Jesuits and Indians skulk along the underbelly of Parkman's historiography, embodying a rejected, compellingly conflicted cosmos of contaminated matter and heroic asceticism. That cosmos first made its literary appearance in Parkman's travel journal of

1843. Suffering the first of a series of physical and psychological disorders that he would later organize under the rubric "the enemy," Parkman set off for Europe, recording in his journal the discordant responses that Italy, in particular, provoked in him. The European travel was intended as therapy for the nervous prostration he acknowledged was induced by his own obsessive physical exercise (and unacknowledged psychological regimentation) while at college; the trip initially afforded him reassuring confirmation of his own self-management techniques. Sailing to Malta (on a British troopship), Parkman, the son of a prominent Unitarian minister, approvingly noted Europe's radical cultural difference from Unitarian Boston:

> A becoming horror of dissenters, especially Unitarians, prevails everywhere. No one cants here of the temperance reform, or of systems of diet—eat, drink, and be merry is the motto everywhere, and a stronger and hardier race of men than those round me now never laughed at the doctors. Above all there is no canting of peace. A wholesome system of coercion is manifest in all directions.[60]

The attractions of such coercion were manifold, for they promised a utopian dynamic of simultaneous restraint and release of bodily appetite, the silencing of its complaints and vulnerabilities to enable a virile expression at once conformist and physically autonomous. Parkman's early tourist experiences with European Catholicism are crucial for understanding his historical exploration of Jesuit missionaries composed more than twenty years later, for it was as a tourist that he first encountered actual Jesuits, whose eloquence surprised him. Their powers threatened to encircle his reserved and frustratingly invalid New England self.

> It is as startling to a "son of Harvard" to see the astounding learning of these Jesuit fathers, and the appalling readiness and rapidity with [which] they pour forth their interminable streams of argument, as it would be to a Yankee parson to witness his whole congregation, with church, pulpit, and all, shut up within one of the great columns which support the dome of St. Peter's —a thing which might assuredly be done.[61]

In his later history of the Jesuits, the specter of Protestant encasement within a column of St. Peter's is thoroughly banished by the historian's own masterful and lavish rhetorical performance, which unfolds an ironically doubled battle between Indian and Jesuit in which the only victor is the wry, heroically invalid historian who recounts their sacrificial confrontation. Not only do the Huron and Iroquois fight civil wars that fatally weaken them and thus deprive the Jesuits of any chance for missionary success, but the Jesuits themselves also indulge in a lust for self-extinction. Combined with what Parkman sees as the almost ludicrous otherworldliness of Jesuit piety, Indian and Jesuit unwittingly forfeit the victory to the British, who make their appearance in later volumes.

The forces of Anglo-Saxon liberty remain outside the purview of the *Jesuits*, the second volume in Parkman's series. What absorbs this narrative instead is the deathly and ironic struggle between missionary and savage, a fight between slaves before the master arrives. If what interested the invalid Parkman was "struggle in general as the condition of life,"[62] that struggle appears in its most compellingly futile form in the encounter between Indian and missionary. Without the Indian, there would be no Jesuit, no martyrdom, no ascetic, but emotionally ardent greatness. In 1852 Parkman wrote his cousin-in-law, Mary Dwight Parkman, of his personal struggles with an intermittently recalcitrant body, one that voiced itself by coercing him into stasis, a painfully lesser version of the glorified afflictions later suffered by his Jesuit martyrs in his 1867 history. To his cousin, he recounts his suffering in characteristically action-filled prose:

> At present I am fast bound—hand and foot—and there is little possibility of my ever regaining even a moderate share of liberty. Yet, if by God's mercy, a single finger is unloosed, its feeble strength will not lie idle. In *achievement* I expect to fail, but I shall never recoil from endeavour, and I shall go through life, hoping little from this world, yet despairing of nothing.[63]

Not surprisingly, Parkman was enamored of both the fierce endurance displayed by Indian and Jesuit and its futility—a theatrical display of masculine transcendence of bodily pain that was purged of the contemptible Gothic inauthenticities so apparent in his early tourist sight of a "granite column, to which he [a Franciscan monk] said that the monks were bound when condemned to the penance of flagellation—it would have made a very fair scene for Monk Lewis."[64] While a spokesman for Protestantism's superiority, then, Parkman reveals himself in this volume as the supreme analyst not of Gothic captivity but of tragic bondage. Anticipating the breakdown of romantic optimistic history in the work of Henry Adams and the "scientific" historians, Parkman's ironic, pain-filled vision haunts his faith in the progressive powers of Anglo-Saxon culture to rid the New World of its "gloomy" and chaotic materialism.

By definition the Protestant world, where order and freedom prevail in a "meaningful" pattern perceptible to the historical imagination, could not be tragic. Nor was it intriguing enough to engage Parkman's polarized consciousness. In his Harvard College oration, he dismissed the American Revolution as a fit subject because it had "no display of chivalry or of headlong passion, but [showed] a deliberate effort in favor of an abstract principle." By contrast, the Lake George terrain was an ideal site for a narrative history because "blood has been poured out like water over that soil!"[65] That collegiate view remained relatively unchanged in the mature historian, for whom the creation of the New (English) World, while associated with the desirable anticorporeal spirituality of Protestantism, was powerful only literarily in its struggle with a prior materiality, one both "savage" and "Catholic." Without this struggle, the spirituality of the Anglo-Saxon rapidly converted into what Parkman saw as the despicable effeminacies of liberal Protestant culture, which he fled by writing his histories of the forces that created them. This theological conflict worked to make Protestantism psychologically inaccessible to many Protestants, who professed an increasing inability to feel its substance as their own. Only by setting this "bloodless" Protestantism against the feminine, embodied, violently ascetic materiality of Catholicism, could Protestant piety claim a renewed virility. One contemporary essayist thus compared the difference between Luther and Loyola: "When we consider, that Luther's struggles with himself arose from the action of conscience and intellect, were waged by means of his intellect, and terminated in a doctrine,—while Loyola's came from conscience and a past life of wrong-doing, went on by the instrumentality of imagination and feeling, and resulted in a new life, we see no ground for any comparison between the two."[66]

The implied feminization of Catholicism in this character sketch of Loyola underlies Parkman's ambivalent attitude toward Jesuit piety as both excessively female in its religious enthusiasm and paradoxically male in its endurance of bodily deprivation and torture. The blood-drenched soil of New France superficially advertises the virtues of masculine force, but at base it is a feminine terrain, self-sacrificing and indulgently visionary. Thus feminized, the historiographical terrain quickly assumes threatening qualities of unreason and sensuality as the confusions of religious difference turn to the polarizations of gender for relief. Parkman's pursuit of this Catholic world and its thematized sexual excesses (an inquiry that, narratively speaking, enjoys its own running border dispute with hagiography), is the secret drama that transpires beneath the created surface of his historiography.

A Huron in the crowd, who had been a convert of the
mission, but was now an Iroquois by adoption, called out,
with the malice of a renegade, to pour hot water on their
heads, since they had poured so much cold water on those
of others. The kettle was accordingly slung, and the water
boiled and poured slowly on the heads of the two
missionaries. "We baptize you," they cried, "that you may
be happy in heaven; for nobody can be saved without a
good baptism."
Francis Parkman, The Jesuits in North America

The boiling baptism of two Jesuit missionaries, Jean de Brébeuf and
Jérôme Lalamant, is only one of several tortures described in the culminating chapters of Parkman's history. But it is perhaps the most
symbolic, for its diabolic version of a central Christian rite underscores
the complex theatrical kinship between savage and priest that generates
and organizes the imaginative intensity of this history. It is a kinship of
reciprocal violence, of failed purpose, and finally of mutual extinction.
Unlike Prescott's accounts of the subterfuge between Cortés and Montezuma, Parkman's passage leads us to feel that, oddly enough, Jesuit and
Indian fundamentally understand one another; like the antebellum Catholic apologist Orestes A. Brownson's claim that Protestants have "stolen
the livery" of Catholicism, the Indians reject Christianity by skillfully
maiming its rituals. Paradoxically, ceremony comes to dominate Parkman's allegedly chaotic wilderness world, and in their rituals of intim-
idation and imitation the two doomed cultures mime their murderous
sympathy for one another.

Thus while Parkman structures the events of his history around tribal
warfare and the fight to impose salvation, he organizes his historical
meanings around the ironic resemblance between adversaries and the
pathos of their combat. Beneath the initial, sharply sketched, opposition
between pagan and Catholic cultures lies this troubled kinship that
voices within itself Parkman's militarized affiliation with his own "fast
bound" but skeptical body. Catholicism is the "only form of Christianity
likely to take root in their crude and barbarous nature" (418) because
it represents the European double to Indian religion. The resemblance
soon erupts into a rivalry between the two cultures as each struggles to
dominate the other by adopting foreign practices to their own indigenous
and conflicting purposes. Baptism, the bestowal of the opportunity for
eternal life, becomes the chosen ritual that each culture enacts in the
effort to eradicate the other. What the Jesuits perform symbolically, the
Indians practice literally; the Indians "baptize" Jesuits by torturing them

into submission to their religion, the priests having plied them with Catholic trinkets, rosary beads, and crucifixes, haranguing them all the while as black-robed medicine men. These distinctions only partially describe the intentional rhetorical and ideological confusions of this baptismal scene, where Indians "baptize" Jesuits by deviously meta-phorizing their creed and where Jesuits refute this corruption by their studied refusal to verbally counter the heretical claim. Christian dogma adopts Indian ceremonial form quickly but finally less effectively than Indian culture mimics Christian ritual. Conversion plays a poor, if dra-matic, second to torture.

In Parkman's historical reconstruction of this and other scenes vividly reported in *Jesuits,* he underscores the ironic affinities between Indian and priest to heighten the psychological intrigue of their cultural combat. While the missionary and the savage intuitively (or as the baptism scene demonstrates, theologically) understand one another, the two remain confessedly impenetrable to the author. Parkman writes that the Nation of the White Fish "proved tractable beyond all others, threw away their 'medicines,' or fetiches [*sic*], burned their magic drums, renounced their medicine-songs, and accepted instead rosaries, crucifixes, and versions of Catholic hymns" (416). American readers had already been intro-duced to such ironic appraisals of missionary settlements over eighty years before, when Jedidiah Morse made much the same observation on Jesuit colonies in Paraguay in his *Geography Made Easy* (1784): "Most of the country is still inhabited by native Americans who are gross idolaters, worshipping the sun, moon, stars, thunder and lightning; but the Jesuits boast that they have now made a great number of them Roman Catholics, an exchange not much for the better."[67]

To heighten the ideological power of these culminating resemblances between Indian and missionary, Parkman devotes the introductory sec-tion of his history to detailing the differences between them. Following Prescott's example in *Mexico,* he opens his history with a lengthy ex-position on Huron society that provides his readers a leisurely, imagistic survey of the doomed cultural victim. A puerile and degenerate group, enfeebled by gambling, sorcery, and torture, Parkman's Hurons are a stagnant culture living in "perpetual fear" (81) of their spirit-ridden environment.[68] Their numerous deficiencies justify their extinction; us-ing the same ominously innocent verb as Prescott, Parkman claims the Indians have "melted" away, not because civilization destroyed them but because their own "ferocity and intractable indolence made it impossible that they should exist in its presence" (418). If the white man is not responsible for the destruction of the Indians, neither are the Iroquois especially accountable for their rabid destruction of Huron and Jesuit, for these "human tigers" (346) are more animal than human, creatures whose "organization and . . . intelligence were merely the instruments of a blind frenzy" (538).

Parkman opposes his fatalistic portrait of the Indians almost point for point in his following chapter on the Jesuits. While uncontrolled violence, sensualism, formless democracy, and superstition dissipate Huron and Iroquois, the Jesuits function as an army of disciplined idealists, empowered by their hierarchical, finally totalitarian, organization to accomplish heroic feats. Parkman's Jesuits emerge, somewhat paradoxically, as representatives of the modern state out to cultivate and systematize the savage remnants of the globe.

But this dramatically imaged antithesis between chaotic paganism and rationalized piety soon shifts into a confused identity between the two cultures. Although the Jesuit mentality is motivated and disciplined by a professedly spiritual organization, it turns out to be as polluted by the material realm as that of the savage. Indeed, Catholic piety is so immersed in the corporeal dimension that its practitioners, like the Iroquois tigers, cannot be justly condemned. The various contaminants of their superstitious faith, for example, corner the Montreal settlers like animals, as the minds of these New World settlers struggle, like those of Prescott's Aztecs, against the confinements of Catholicism. "Surrounded as they were with illusions, false lights, and false shadows; breathing an atmosphere of miracle; compassed about with angels and devils; urged with stimulants most powerful, though unreal; their minds drugged, as it were, to preternatural excitement,—it is very difficult to judge of them" (300–301). Parkman's judgmental-nonjudgmental portrait of this imprisoned Catholic mind implicitly depends upon a system of counter-values that remains significantly unarticulated in his history—a Protestant worldview that projects its mastery by the quietness of its survey. Nature not supernature, mind not imagination, God not angels are what the authorial consciousness tacitly opposes to the lurid enthusiasms of his various historical actors.

While Indians grow mysterious when exiled to the mute and irrational animal world, Jesuits grow strange in their association with the borders of human nature; so bizarre is their piety that it finally provokes an imaginative and comic association with crime. In one telling metaphor, Parkman compares the missionaries' speed at baptizing savages to the "nimble-fingered adroitness" (207) of pickpockets.

Positioned midway between diatribe and hagiography, Parkman's "realistic" history, then, prides itself on discerning the indiscernibility of

Catholicism. On the surface it presents the keen-eyed, Protestant persona, investigating and appraising the Jesuits, whose virtues "shine amidst the rubbish of error, like diamonds and gold in the gravel of the torrent" (553). But even those virtues are depicted as problematic. Echoing Hawthorne's and Brownson's sense that negation formed the basis of Protestantism, Parkman favorably opposes the ardent missionary Brébeuf to a nihilistic Protestantism; Brébeuf's Counter-Reformation piety, however, borders on an abnormal fertility: "Not the grim enthusiasm of negation tearing up the weeds of rooted falsehood, or with bold hand felling to the earth the baneful growth of overshadowing abuses: his was the ancient faith uncurtailed, redeemed from the decay of centuries, kindled with a new life, and stimulated to a preternatural growth and fruitfulness" (143).

Because Parkman was a practiced horticulturalist himself, his imagery for this reinvigorated piety is suspect; while this Catholic fecundity is superior to a Protestant revolutionary enthusiasm that, like the American pioneer, rips the wilderness apart, it dangerously approaches the terrain of organic decay. The Catholic enthusiast feeds off his church. Thus Parkman describes the "fanatical Chaumonot, whose character savored of his peasant birth,—for the grossest fungus of superstition that ever grew under the shadow of Rome was not too much for his omnivorous credulity, and miracles and mysteries were his daily food" (471–72). This parasitism, gluttony, and rank organic growth result from the church's mixture of spirit and matter, an adulterous activity that produces such omnivorous contaminated progeny as Chaumonot. The original "sordid wedlock" (172) of Holy Mother Church to secular governments abnormally involved the spiritual life with the body and the exhilarations of power. Such adulterated piety manifests itself in the excesses of asceticism or worldliness—alternatives whose very extremity of rejection or embrace betray their engagement with the body. The pollution is so powerful that it spreads outside its institutional boundaries into the psyches of individual priests who suffer the same "mixture" that defines the structure of the church. With Chillingworth-like accuracy, Parkman detects the unconscious corruption in the priestly heart as it compels obedience from its flock:

> His conscience, then, acts in perfect accord with the love of
> power innate in the human heart. These allied forces mingle
> with a perplexing subtlety; pride, disguised even from itself,
> walks in the likeness of love and duty; and a thousand times on
> the pages of history we find Hell beguiling the virtues of
> Heaven to do its work. . . . The unchecked sway of priests has

always been the most mischievous of tyrannies; and even were they all well-meaning and sincere, it would be so still. (251–52)

Catholic missionary power stems, then, from its deceptive combinations of pride and love, dominance and desire. But priests, who practice this seductive duplicity, are finally deceived by themselves. Fooled in the innermost recesses of their own psyches, they can entrap others with magnificent cunning, their power limitless because unconscious.

Often vociferously opposed to monastic asceticism (its rejection of society, matrimony, and worldly work for the suspect virtues of seclusion, celibacy, and contemplation), antebellum Americans like Parkman anxiously struggled with bodily appetites and ailments without the guidance or cultural sanction of traditional forms of asceticism. Newly secularized efforts to link psychological ailments to physiological imbalances, to pinpoint the physical rather than the metaphysical as determinant cause for the still intractable emotional regions of the self, particularly focused on the melodrama of the female constitution. As one psychology journal put it, "When the young female suffers from irregular action of the ovaria on the system, the natural astuteness and quickness of perception degenerates into mere artfulness or monomaniacal cunning."[69] Such portraits of women became increasingly prevalent in the "therapeutic" culture of postbellum America; in the antebellum decades, such physiological formulations inevitably called up theological discourses, specifically the doctrinal debate over the proper mixture of spirit and matter. Woman, with her modest exterior and potentially cunning interior, was capable of Jesuitical intrigue, her volatile uterine constitution commingling ovaries and rage into "artful" behavior. If the female constitution was, to a troublesome extent, inherently Jesuitical, the male was endowed with the superior capacity to transcend such fleshly modes. Efforts to control the body's influence extended into the ultimately physical event of martyrdom; even at that moment the ideal Protestant victim was to maintain his independence of the physical, as manifested in visions and heavenly visitors. As to how Protestants were meant to endure agony without the "bodily" consolations afforded Catholic martyrs, W. Newnham explained in his *Essay on Superstition* (1830):

The Christian has nothing to fear from this view of the subject; the promised strength from on high, strength equal to his day, *is* vouchsafed, but it is afforded by the ordinary assistance of the Holy Spirit: it is conveyed through the medium of second causes, and *not* by the intervention of a supernatural creation;

by leading the mind into all truth, and not by the perversion of its imagination; by the sure word of God, and not by the presence of an angel. The latter fancied appearance is a brainular illusion, from which the disciple of Christ should pray to be delivered.[70]

There is no such deliverance for Parkman's Jesuits and Indians; they remain interred in their separate but nearly identical mental confinements until the end, twin victims of "brainular illusion" who pursue but never gain the other. Their sufferings, therefore, remain somehow suspect—implicated in the falsity of matter, whether because of their dependence on ritual, on crucifixes in the flames, or on hallucination in the forests. Heroic, they are never finally granted sanctity. As the judicious historian who nonetheless chafed under his own studied agnosticism and Unitarian proprieties, Parkman hovered about the edges of this priest-savage relationship, fascinated by religious enthusiasm, as he admitted in his 1890 article entitled "A Convent at Rome," which recalls his stay in a Passionist monastery when a young tourist in Italy.[71] What so compelled Parkman was less the God-man relationship and the divinity that inspires such enthusiasm, than the mind-body relationship such enthusiasm can create. In short, he invests Jesuit spirituality with such imaginative intensity because he perceives that it splits the self in two and thus divorces it from the anxieties of the flesh. Jesuit endurance and stamina assume not a numinous but a dissociative grandeur to the invalid historian, the intimate pains of existence finding their most violent expression and denial in the ritual torture-deaths of the Jesuits.

Parkman's youthful experiments in asceticism, in part a revolt against a Unitarian minister father who, according to one Parkman scholar, "made a fetish out of clerical proprieties and formalities," were self-confessed failures, for his efforts to perfect himself brought on crippling headaches, arthritis, impaired vision, and chronic insomnia.[72] Abandoning his strenuous exercise program to redirect his physical and psychic drives, Parkman spent the rest of his life admiring external and internal restraint, celebrating in his volume on the Jesuits the joint pursuit and transcendence of physical affliction. But finally his various illnesses constrained him far more effectively than any purposeful discipline; by forbidding the more active life he coveted, however, they also enabled the achievement of his art. In a rare confiding letter to his close friend George Ellis, Parkman described in 1864 the "mania" of his young manhood that his ensuing invalidism unconsciously, if painfully, remedied: "The condition was that of a rider whose horse runs headlong, the bit between his teeth, or of a locomotive, built of indifferent material, under a head of steam too great for its strength, hissing at a score of crevices, yet rushing on with accelerating speed to the inevitable smash."[73] Parkman's only novel, *Vassall Morton* (1856), exhibits (with mawkish sentimentality) the romantic desire that remains unmentioned in the letter to George Ellis. Morton's emotions threaten to overcome him as the machinations of his romantic rival unjustly confine him to an Austrian prison; there the hero practices a virile repression of his "girl-hearted" temptation to despair and finally wins his girl.[74]

Thus in their relentlessly intimate relationship to their bodies—in the grotesque bodily recesses of the Indians and the baroque extremism of the martyrs—Parkman found the missionaries and the Indians jointly compelling. In their frankly exhibited closeness to the body, the domain the invalid Parkman took great pains, literally, to subdue, lay their peculiar triumphs over the flesh, their capacity for silence in the face of pain. The Jesuits, paradoxically, match their corrupting proximity to a materialist theology with a disdain for bodily comfort that unleashes an ascetic fortitude that often, in turn, provokes additional Indian violence. If, as Brownson claimed, "of the motives which governed the missionaries, of their faith and charity, as well as of their whole interior spiritual life" Parkman understood "less than did the 'untutored Indian,'"[75] it was this very lack of understanding that enabled him to render Jesuit martyrdom with such dramatic intensity. As an outsider to both Iroquois and Euro-Catholic viewpoints, he scrutinized their mysterious interiority unrelentingly in an effort to focus, recurrently displaying in his footnotes the accuracy of his scenic accounts while implicitly confessing the strange nonsense of his story. Having virtually secularized the Jesuits with his dark Unitarian perspective, the historian is then left with the phenomenon of their inexplicable power, an unrivaled spectacle of masculine, not divine, energy, a reincarnation of his own practice in his college days, when he made long, even heroic, treks into the forest, preparing to accomplish his already formed "plan" to write the history of the French defeat in Canada. He recollected his younger self in the third person:

> As fond of hardships as he was vain of enduring them, cherishing a sovereign scorn for every physical weakness or defect, deceived, moreover, by a rapid development of frame and sinews which flattered him with the belief that discipline sufficiently unsparing would harden him into an athlete, he slighted the precautions of a more reasonable woodcraft . . . stopped neither for heat nor rain, and slept on the earth without a blanket.[76]

In the *Jesuits,* the Indians display a similar awesome asceticism, impassive in the face of torture and the grinding deprivations of the wilderness. But theirs is an animal rather than a masculine power. Parkman is content to let them go.

While Parkman's fervid admiration of Jesuit stoicism betrays the idiosyncratic depths of his personal illness, it also accords with contemporary Protestant visions of Ignatius Loyola and the organization produced from his militaristic piety. Amid their widespread accusations of priestly depravity and debauchery, antebellum periodicals consistently praised Jesuit missionary strength. Although Ignatius, as we have seen, was implicated in the feminine precincts of an emotionally ardent visionary nature while Luther claimed the masculine world of the text, the Jesuit founder also displayed the organizational genius that flowered from ascetic self-discipline, thus yoking obedient community and autonomous individuality in a way that inspired Protestant admiration. Anticipating the "cult of the strenuous" that would attract privileged Americans in the postbellum decades as an antidote to hypercivilization and neurasthenia, one writer approvingly noted of Loyola: "We may call him fanatical, mad, hypocritical, perhaps; but call him what we will, he was training his nature to endurance and labor such as few men have ever encountered."[77]

The Ignatian spiritual exercises called for long periods of concentrated mental attention upon internally formed images of Christ—attention guided by the use of the body (especially the hands) as mnemonic aids. The contrast between Ignatian spiritual directives and Parkman's lifelong focus on his illness forms an intriguing opposition, for what Parkman, who produced some twenty-six volumes of prose, found so difficult to do was to concentrate. His difficulties were threefold as he described them: "an extreme weakness of sight, disabling him even from writing his name except with eyes closed; a condition of the brain prohibiting fixed attention except at occasional and brief intervals; and an exhaustion and total derangement of the nervous system, producing of necessity a mood of mind most unfavorable to effort. To be made with impunity, the attempt must be made with the most watchful caution."[78] Because Parkman so closely identified with Jesuit powers of concentration—powers he claimed not to possess yet manifested on a heroic scale in his writings—the Jesuit missionaries of his history are subjected to the same mystification with which he viewed his illness. Beneath their cultural ambiguity as wielders of powers both archaic and visionary, modern and systematic, Parkman's Jesuits wield the creative power of the invalid historian, whose "vehemence" for his historical vocation broke the bounds of bodily propriety, with the crucial difference that while the missionaries aggressively released their enthusiasm onto Indian cultures, Parkman made sure to keep his "from being a nuisance to those around."[79] In Parkman's history, Loyola is described as a man of tremendous inward emotionality who manages the critical feat of externalizing his powers before they disable him. "In the forge of his great intellect, heated, but not disturbed by the intense fires of his zeal, was wrought the prodigious enginery whose power has been felt to the uttermost confines of the world" (95). As Promethean figure, Loyola attracted other romantic spokesmen for subversive pastoral retreat, like Emerson and Thoreau. But for Parkman, the Jesuit venture into the wilderness, while indeed Promethean in its flouting of fate, exhibited a masculine power tragically aware of interior ailment. In his balancing of "worldly wisdom" with the "highest flights of his enthusiasm" (466 n.2), the individual Jesuit missionary is accessible to the rationalist historian. But Parkman is finally interested in this Jesuit balance not for the political power it can produce (which figures centrally in conspiratorial attitudes toward Jesuits) but for its ascetic genius, specifically its capacity to master zeal without risking its slightest diminishment.

Reluctant to admit that papist "superstition" could produce such masculine heroism, more conventional admirers of Loyola instead preferred to see two contradictory sides of the saint's personality. As holiness became an increasingly feminine and therefore suspect quality, the male saint, looked at spiritually rather than politically, tended toward freakishness. Protestant gentility dictated that men practice a subdued piety, avoiding the seeming abasement and self-exposure of holiness. Emersonian and, even more, Melvillean heroism was achieved through harboring and controlling, rather than surrendering, the self; in the terms of this masculine logic, true sacrifice consisted of abnegation, not communion; of restraint, not expressive release.[80] The Jesuits (and the Huron and Iroquois on a secondary, "animalistic," level) achieve the supreme Parkmanian feat of expressively refusing to disclose themselves. Celebrating Jesuit and Indian as emblems of virtually numinous restraint, Parkman displaces their ardent rituals and religious rhapsodies to the psychic sidelines where his own illness dwells, a "bodily terrain" with which the historian cannot directly communicate. It is this marginalization that irritated Orestes Brownson, but it is precisely this authorial denial of the Jesuits' Christian love, of their dialogue with God, that renders them baroque figures, strangely lit and excessive. In constructing this luridly pictorial narrative, Parkman inverts anti-Catholic ideology: if the Catholic minds of his ritualistic missionaries and savages are polluted by the corporeal, their bodies are redemptively implicated in the spiritual. Cleansed of all dross, the tortured body becomes the true, if unconfessed, zone of the sacred in this history.

Ironically, the tortured body is the safe one, for it is freed of the tormenting routines of the historian's irritable constitution that finally escape the considerable powers of Parkman's language, his headaches, "endurable in comparison with other forms of attack which cannot be intelligibly described from the want of analogous sensations by which to convey the requisite impressions."[81] Like Parkman's linguistically evasive illnesses, the Jesuit missionaries, to the extent that they can be represented, emerge in terms of contradiction and paradox that yet fail to describe their most identifying feature, their love of Christ. This assertion of authorial incomprehension becomes Parkman's signature analytic mode, an ironical claim "not to see" that historiographically reproduces his own physical inability to endure light, which forced him, like Prescott, to use a noctograph.

Obsessively pictorializing a Catholicism that he professedly cannot see, Parkman can only "sketch" the infinitude of Jesuit features:

> Of this vast mechanism for guiding and governing the minds of men, this mighty enginery for subduing the earth to the dominion of an idea, this harmony of contradictions, this moral Proteus, the faintest sketch must now suffice. A disquisition on the Society of Jesus would be without end. No religious Order has ever united in itself so much to be admired and so much to be detested. (99–100)

Parkman's rhetorical impotence in the face of Jesuit complexity disguises an effective ideological attack on Rome, for had he claimed to understand Catholicism, the skeptical historian would have partially reduced its alien status and to some extent legitimated it. Like more militantly Protestant writing, his history depends on maintaining, indeed nourishing, Catholicism as an alien structure in its midst. Thus while Parkman's history accedes to the generic constraints of romantic historiography, in which heroic character motivates events and providentially patterned scenic narrative dominates analysis, his work carefully avoids judging one side against the other. Although Parkman claimed to be a realist, working, not "to eulogize" the missionaries, "but to portray them as they were" (100), he was, more profoundly, a brilliant allegorist of Protestant selfhood in quest of its American origins.

In his bodily identification with the missionary priests, Parkman achieves his final unsettling insight, that Catholicism, like the Jesuit, is everywhere. It has broken out of the confines of history and lives in the present, its spectacular visibilities potently allied with the invisible suffering interiors of both priest and historian. Less a subject to be investigated than a bodily truth to be endured, Parkman's Catholicism is human nature, its powers those of humanity: "Clearly, she is of earth, not of heaven; and her transcendently dramatic life is a type of the good and ill, the baseness and nobleness, the foulness and purity, the love and hate, the pride, passion, truth, falsehood, fierceness, and tenderness, that battle in the restless heart of man" (173).

With this declared psychological affinity, Parkman's romantic historiography overcomes the ideological schism that forms the larger subject of his historical inquiry into New World imperial conflict. If Parkman's narrative of Jesuit folly, duplicity, and grandeur achieves the brilliance of a therapeutic empathy, the bonds formed are those of the body, not the spirit. Priest and Protestant historian alike are invalids of the "restless heart."

Coda to Part 1

Catholicism, conceived of not as a historical institution but as a series of proliferating traits, assumed increasing powers of personification for antebellum Americans. Its morbid interiors, which alarmed and beckoned American tourists and historians, were similarly personalized by contemporary periodical prose, and in a further, implausible, development of this abstracting process, some writers catalogued the human mind itself as either Protestant or Catholic in its proclivities and capabilities. In a New World relatively empty of built religious enclosures, the minds of the Jesuit missionary and the superstitious Aztec became Catholic interiors that Protestant readers might explore without risk of entrapment.

Whether those interiors were finally evaluated as pathetic or heroic, they remained psychologically exotic and intimately Romanish. Because Prescott's Unitarian perspective and Parkman's darker agnosticism converted supernature into innermost human nature, the foreign church was particularly tied in their works to the compelling needs of their leisured but strenuous lives. Both historians depict the holy and the satanic as emerging jointly from a pathologically energized interior that reflects their own embattled encounters with illness and the related temptations of indolence.

The spectacle of the superstitious Roman mind collapsing, like Brockden Brown's Wieland, into an eroticized and violent interiority, incapable of extricating itself from its own gloomy fantasies, fascinated "enlightened" Americans, whether they were touring Italy, described by one critic as "the best show the nineteenth-century had to offer,"[1] or reading about Aztec captives or Jesuit missionaries. Empowered by the interpretive clarities of Reformed Christianity, American tourists and readers peered into the Catholic mind and its elaborate architectural or historiographical structures. But as we have seen, antebellum tourists and historians were both troubled and excited by this inquiry into the aboriginal "Catholic" interior. Wasn't that interior a Christian one after all? Were Prescott's readers meant to indulge in a traditional hostility to Cortés or an equally traditional hostility to New World "savages"?

One solution was to shroud both sides of the issue in the mystifications of a conspicuously deferential liberalism. Thus one reviewer, critical of Prescott's cautious judgment of Catholic Spain, turned the vexations of cultural imperialism and individual culpability back to the God from whom Prescott (and Parkman) had so ambivalently wrested their narratives: "We shall but tell the impartial story. God, the searcher of all hearts, can alone unravel the mazes of conscientiousness and depravity, and award the just meed of approval and condemnation."[2] Such a return to a sovereign God, who alone can survey the "mazes" of the human heart, was for many antebellum Protestants an unsatisfying solution to the perplexities facing their "native" faith. Better to focus on a foreign Catholicism whose labyrinthine interiors, at once fearful and familiar, beckoned Protestant investigation and promised to disclose not deity but the truths of domestic identity.

2

AMERICAN PROTESTANTISM AND ITS CAPTIVITIES

FOUR

Rome and Her Indians

America's long and absorbed engagement with the threat and thematics of captivity—with real or imagined bondage to Indians, witches, slave-holders—shadowed the country's official vision of itself as the land of liberty. While political rhetoric enumerated the blessings of freedom, imaginative discourse was preoccupied with the often exoticized threat of confinement. By the mid-nineteenth century, middle-class audiences had become veritable connoisseurs of captivity, eager and practiced readers of its agonies, its mysteries, and its lessons. Hungry for the vicarious experience of confinement as an imaginative control of their turbulent democracy, antebellum Americans avidly read several versions of the captivity genre: anthologies of seventeenth- and eighteenth-century Indian captivity tales, a steady stream of slave and convent-escape narratives, and numerous popular novels including such best-sellers as George Lippard's *Monks of Monk Hall* (1844) and Harriet Beecher Stowe's *Uncle Tom's Cabin* (1852), that righteously exposed the horrors of economic and racial captivity.

Two hundred years of literary treatment had produced an elaborate rhetorical edifice of confinement and escape initially founded upon a scriptural model, structured according to religious, racial, and sexual fears and mysteriously illuminated by the pleasures of torment and deliverance. In many respects, this American captivity tradition represented a domestication of the European and English Gothic. But conditions specific to America—the imperial conquest of indigenous peoples and the establishment of chattel slavery—uniquely shaped the genre of the American Gothic. The essentially psychological focus of such Old World novels as *The Mysteries of Udolpho* by Ann Radcliffe and *The Monk* by M. G. Lewis was invested with imperial and racial conflicts specific to nineteenth-century America. Thus the "savage" and the "dark" were at once actual peoples stigmatized as impediments to Anglo-American settlement and forms of psychological being suppressed by the advent of modernization. American Gothic narratives functioned more directly in antebellum politics, capable not only of legitimating ongoing social oppressions but also, in particular instances, of inciting violence against them.[1]

Roman Catholicism figured crucially in this American captivity tradition as a principal and historically resilient captor of the New World Protestant settler. Changing its guise in response to the psychosocial anxieties of successive generations of Protestants, the specter of Romanism played captor to each in turn, looming as menacing figure in the New England forests, the Southwest, and the Mississippi Valley region. The tradition of Protestant bondage to Roman evils originated with Luther's claim in 1520 that "the church has been taken prisoner" by a greedy and theologically misguided papacy.[2] Lutherans and Calvinists thereafter characterized their reformation as not only a purification but also an escape from an outraged and sometimes pursuing Rome.

As the genre of Indian captivity narratives shows, the experience of "Roman" captivity was a highly self-conscious one in colonial America, a trauma of ethnic confrontation that attracted intense religious and aesthetic responses, which in turn produced highly popular narratives advertising the conflicted formation of national identity. Detailing the drama of white captivity in an Indian New World, many such narratives phrase the trauma of cultural and racial estrangement as a spiritual tribulation essential to the formation of an American selfhood. Such development involved an often protracted separation from forms of European worldliness that were at the same time claimed as critical to the success of white Christian civilization in the New World. Roman Catholicism played a crucial historical and symbolic role in this simultaneous extraction of the pure from the corruptions of Europe and assertion of European purity against the seductions of Indian America; profoundly familiar yet rendered foreign by the Reformation, Romanism was a force that threatened to disrupt the forming of the American self.

In writing the earliest New World Indian captivity narratives, Spanish and French Catholic authors had themselves suggested an essential, if violent, kinship between their Catholicism and that of their captors. Puritan and later Protestant captivity narratives agreed that such a kinship did indeed exist between the Catholic European and the American Indian, only that kinship was a demonic, not a potentially sacramental, one. Endowed with a treacherous autonomy in Puritan narratives, Catholicism enjoyed a shifting power of personification, a wilderness enemy who conspired with the Indian to master the Protestant settler and, with the later Jacksonian "removal" of Indians, intrigued by itself for dominion over the Protestant body and soul.

≈

In the century prior to English colonization, when Spanish explorers and priests knew America, a time that nineteenth-century Protestant historians and filiopietistic celebrants of America's pilgrim beginnings dissociated from the nation's official origin, the first recorded captivity occurred. In compensation for returning "naked" from the New World, a Spanish adventurer humbly offered his king a narrative of his experience. *The Journey of Alvar Núñez Cabeza de Vaca and His Companions from Florida to the Pacific, 1528–1536,* published in 1555, recounts the Spaniards' eight-year captivity among North American Indians.[3] Its stunning depiction of both the ambiguous interchange of authority between Spanish captive and Indian captor and the subtle, resilient sacerdotal power of Catholicism prefigures later Anglo-American ruminations upon a vagrant Spanish Catholicism circulating invisibly through antebellum America—a power whose apparent charisma attracted vehement nativist criticism for its "foreign" forms of authority and submission.

Núñez's narrative implicitly articulated a formative irony that characterized many Indian and, later, religious captivity tales—namely, that captivity, for all its coercion, deprivation, and suffering, covertly registered the benefits of imprisonment. The subversive note of voluntarism, if not complicity, so noticeable in antebellum fictions about Rome accompanied the captivity genre from its American beginnings. In a reportorial style noticeably alien to the later, melodramatic language of New England's Scripture-bound Puritans, Núñez described for his king an imprisonment fraught with skewed intentions and accidental exchanges of power; his documentary style only enhances the account of his evident awe before the marvels of ethnic estrangement and provisional assimilation. When his Florida exploration dwindled to baffled wandering, he finally and desperately gave himself over to the Indians, captivity his only way to survive. Half captives, half tagalongs, Núñez and his small group followed the famished tribes as they roamed in search of roots—the only El Dorado in this New World landscape being rumored fields of prickly pears two days' march away.

In a remarkable interaction between the numinous influence of Núñez's white skin, his political acumen, and the famine and religious expectations of his tribal captors, the captive explorer soon claimed a charismatic authority born of his marginal ethnic status. Over the course of eight years, he walked from Florida to Mexico, accompanied by thousands of Indians who looked to their white god for healing, blessing, and guidance. That his divine status produced a new, more problematic, captivity was not lost on him; he confided to his king that "frequently we were accompanied by three or four thousand persons, and as we had to breathe upon and sanctify the food and drink for each, and give them permission to do the many things they would come to ask, it may be seen how great to us were the trouble and annoyance" (95).

If the assumption of the priestly role felt burdensome to the layman Núñez, his familiarity with its rituals proved immensely valuable. Curing and blessing as he proceeded, he negotiated his way from tribe to tribe, the worshiping horde increasing as the caravan moved west. Throughout this captivity-turned-journey he claimed that Spaniards and Indians communicated perfectly by gesture, the two cultures spontaneously sympathizing by means of the hybrid religious rituals created in their meeting—an achievement later Protestant captives neither desired nor could attain. By the time Núñez reached the Spanish settlements around the Gulf of California, his captivity had become a virtual anticaptivity; in a final reversal, he stepped forward as the protector of his Indian prisoners, warning them against the traitorous schemes of the Christians before embarking for Spain. As anticaptivity, the narrative signals the colonial moment only to deny it, offering a suspended pastoral before the work of colonization begins in earnest.

The captivity narrative of the famed Jesuit missionary Father Isaac Jogues, written a century after that of Alvar Núñez, is a second crucial antecedent to colonial English narratives, for as a document of missionary zeal rather than exploration, it displays the workings of a professional Catholicism in competitive conflict with Iroquois shamanism. Núñez became, as it were, a priest with little reference to his private piety, whereas Jogues the priest was stripped of all ritual until in his martyrdom he attained a radically autonomous piety perfectly independent of priestly accoutrements. Acutely sensitive to the potential spiritual benefit of captivity (specifically, martyrdom), Father Jogues wrote one of America's most powerful early narratives of Christian imprisonment in the "heathen" New World: *The Captivity of Father Isaac Jogues, of the*

Society of Jesus, among the Mohawks (1655). His narration of captivity, torture, eventual escape from, and final sacrificial return to the Iroquois records a martyrology at work in the New World that ardently transcends the polemics of Reformation and Counter-Reformation. If Jogues's physical heroism and eventual martyrdom figure importantly in Parkman's discreetly polemical *Jesuits in North America* as a compelling instance of an exemplary, even charismatic, masculinity, Jogues's account is uninterested either in such translations of religious force or in the apostolic management of the Canadian tribes. Rather his narration unfolds a contest between spiritual powers in which Catholicism triumphantly transcends all aspects of the material world—a sacral force that within fifty years would be inversely portrayed by New England Puritan captives as the primary power of deceit, corruption, and bondage in the New World.[4]

In 1642, the Iroquois captured Father Jogues and his lay assistant, René Goupil, near Albany, New York. As Núñez had done more than a century before, Jogues, a man later characterized by Parkman as "indomitable and irrepressible," transformed his captivity into an anti-captivity through a language of ardent subjection in which power and liberty accrue in direct proportion to bodily helplessness.[5] Jogues's white skin draws upon him all the ritual violence the Iroquois can bestow—a violence that lingered below the surface of the adulation Núñez engineered, one kept at bay by his passive mimicry of priestly functions and careful avoidance of any missionizing. In one of the most torture-ridden of American captivity narratives, Jogues wrote to his superior in 1643 of his agonies and, more important, of his repeated refusal to flee them, his missionary zeal aggressively transforming Iroquois rage into proof of sacred love. Enduring a year of captivity before being ransomed by the Dutch at Albany, Jogues, less ambivalently than later Puritan captives like Mary Rowlandson, embraced the European divinity he perceived at work in the New World. His Ignatian spirituality was entirely separate from its New World "theater," for he was intent upon martyrdom more than colonization; thus Jogues, as missionary, is always in motion even while bound to the stake, moving through the New World as fallen temporality rather than settling within it as colonist of the New Zion. Nonetheless Jogues, like the Puritan Rowlandson, anxiously pondered the possibility that Indian captivity spelled divine wrath or, worse, abandonment.[6] When a savage mysteriously desists from cutting off his nose, a mutilation that by Iroquois custom would have necessitated his death, Jogues writes to his superior that that one restraint showed that "God watched over us, and was trying us rather than casting us off" (11).

Supported by the passionately inclusive discourse of martyrdom that swiftly positions any potentially deviant carnal detail in a proliferating series of indications of divine presence, Jogues compares his torture to the pains of childbirth, quoting the apostle John in explaining to his superior that "we were like to 'a woman in travail' [John 16:21]," the agony of torture preceding the joys of eternity as surely as labor precedes those of maternity. Vitalized by this procreative vision, the celibate Jogues denies that the Indians are agents of their own violence, insisting that their attack on him is actually his own ethnically and spiritually inviolate self-birthing. Powerfully engaging monastic traditions of asceticism and self-mortification, Jogues conceives of his torture as a masculine ascesis necessary to a feminine new birth, the sexually transgressive metaphor testifying to his creative powers of endurance and authorship. In asserting their connection, however, the metaphor promptly discloses the excruciated distance between tortured priest and laboring mother—a disclosure that recalls the distance between religious experience "then" and "now," a gap always apparent in the carnal deadness of language used to convey the living spirit.

Within a wilderness occult, Jogues improvises his own indigenous piety, carving the name of Jesus on the forest trees, seizing every opportunity to convert and to baptize, aggressively countering Mohawk violence with his sacred, the meaninglessness of pain with the inexorable significance of martyrdom. The teleology of martyrdom reveals that even his own seemingly anomalous behavior is part of a pilgrimage home that converts New World tortures into reenactments of the Jerusalem crucifixion. Thus Jogues, explaining to his superior why he did not flee his Iroquois torturers when the opportunity arose, voices a classic formulation of New World captivity as a voluntary exile necessary to regain one's spiritual home: "Although I could, in all probability, escape either through the Europeans or the savage nations around us, did I wish to fly, yet on this cross, to which our Lord has nailed me beside himself, am I resolved by his grace to live and die" (38).[7]

Alternating between accounts of his torture and of his contemplative retreats from the "Babylon" of Indian villages into the forest, Jogues's narrative contrasts the apparently aimless wanderings of the Iroquois to the transcendent orderings of his Ignatian piety. Unless captured and reorganized by conversion and baptism, the Indians, from Jogues's perspective, are wandering, in soul as well as body, the violence they inflict on the missionary a sign not of cultural agency but of a randomness that signifies the confusion of the damned. But in the contrast lodges a spiritually revelatory identification, an exegesis made visible only through the Indians' ostensibly random violence. For Jogues records a certain gruesome intimacy between torturer and victim (precisely the intimacy that Parkman so powerfully misappropriated), one that dimly but perceptibly reflects the transcendent bond between martyr and God: at one point, abruptly spared death, Jogues comments that the event has taught him that "I should not fear the face of a man when the Almighty was the protector of my life, without whose permission not a hair could fall from my head" (25). Not only does the excess of pain, in its un-controllability, resemble the sublime powers of divinity, but its unspeak-ableness also urges the victim to rephrase it as divine speech. These two captivities, then, incite and sustain one another, the torture necessitating the descent of grace, the grace welcoming the further intrusions of torture: "But God justly ordained that the more I pleaded, the more tightly they drew my chains" (18).

This reciprocal dynamic effectively transforms the captivity from a demonic imitation of heavenly intimacies to their numinous enactment. Tied to a stake, Jogues experiences his bodily fixity as mobilized spir-itual combat in which the terrors of cultural estrangement are contained within the theologically (and ethnically) familiar precinct of the satanic. The primitive, the savage, the demonic never attain to the status of the unknown, a rank Jogues carefully reserves for his God. Thus in Jogues's continuance of his crucifixional experience, sin and holiness, abandon-ment and grace reciprocally construct one another, creating a narra-tive (and theological) interdependence that skirts the heretical percep-tion that God and Satan are one. That he is no longer on the cross at the time of writing his narrative emerges in his rhetorical efforts to con-tinue upon it. While his narrative insists upon his continued nailed closeness to the cross, the writing of the narrative depends upon his escape from it.

In their production of grace, Jogues's afflictions yield as well aston-ishing narrative power. Markedly contrasting to the silences of Melville's *Bartleby, the Scrivener,* to the unspoken recesses where agnostic sensi-bilities retreat when in pain, Jogues's torture generates an eloquent and disciplined articulateness precisely because his pain unleashes a speci-ficity of meaning.[8] The more he is tortured, the more invincible the author becomes, asserting an ever stronger verbal reprise of his agony. When his thumb is hacked off, he raises it up in thanks to the Lord that his writing hand has been preserved from mutilation. Paradoxically, Jogues uses the torture that is designed to enforce recognition of his captive status to empty that captivity of any political reality. No longer torture but crucifixion, Jogues's experience mirrors, but finally cannot be, the desired captivity to Christ, a captivity that can be perfected only in death. Reduced to a simulacrum of an inaccessible communion, the torture, by destroying the body it works upon creates the conditions of its own temporal thwarting as well. De-realized into sacred metaphor, bodily experience functions as a necessarily partial conduit to the numinous; Indian unreality becomes a sign of Christ's living but still invisible presence. Yet Jogues's narrative reconstruction of this dynamic must retemporalize this crucifixional epiphany in order to publicize to Europeans the creative logic of New World captivity.

Forced in his wilderness exile to practice a Protestantized piety, Jogues explains to his superior how "passages which my memory had retained taught me how I should think of God in goodness, even though not upheld by sensible devotion" (30). Later Puritan captives showed little such flexibility, however, when confronted with the "sensible" accoutrements of Catholic piety. As pawns in the extended North American conflict between France and England, many New England colonists were kidnapped by Indians allied to Catholic France. Schooled in Reformation polemics, these seventeenth- and eighteenth-century New England prisoners to Catholicized tribes interpreted rosary beads and crucifix, whether handled by missionary priest or "savage," as the insignia of a devilish Rome vengefully pursuing them in the New World.

The ambiguous relationship to captivity unfolded in the narratives of Núñez and Jogues also characterized the accounts of Puritan captives, for whom attack and kidnap heralded the presence of the divine. Impelled by Christian zeal, many cultivated, if they had not actively pursued, their captivities as instances of "merciful affliction" and hence divine attention. Seventeenth- and eighteenth-century New Englanders were especially adept at articulating the processes by which the trauma of abduction and often violent acculturation into Amerindian societies revitalized their European piety. The narration of kidnap into the wilderness could generate a radical spiritual excitement, for it made palpable the elusive paradox of New Testament Christianity: that life itself is a bondage and that liberty can be found only in entire dependence upon an unpredictable God. More precisely, the experience of captivity that apparently testified to God's potentially traumatic changeableness was revised to read as a primary index of his loving concern. Evangelical Christian subjectivity had long understood the unconverted state as one of radical captivity to the powers of Original Sin; in the words of one seventeenth-century English Quaker, "Man is a captive, his understanding captive, his will captive, all his affections and nature in captivity."[9] For American Puritans, an actual captivity to "savages" theatrically enacted this truth, confirming their Calvinist theology and controlling it by depositing it, at least temporarily, in the precincts of the foreign; Indian captivity, by externalizing their internal phenomenology of subjugation, afforded psychological, if not bodily, release from its pressures. In the abjection of forced surrender to heathens more depraved than themselves, Puritan captives partially escaped their own depravity; the burden of Indian violence additionally urged them to depend entirely on Christ, the real, yet merciful, captor.

This psychological and rhetorical understanding of Indian captivity as a New World stage for an Old World Christian pilgrimage was critical as well to the development of the Anglo-American national self, which sprang free of Europe by strenuously applying European Christianity to the American environment. The problem became how to preserve this new liberty once ransomed from captivity. If the providential reading of abduction and ransom depended on the victim's survival, his or her return to some psychological and literal place from which to formulate that reading also signaled a new distance between self and God's chastening afflictions—a distance in which the control over the past required to narrate it might issue in spiritual torpor, the loss of an ecstatic living in the Word.

Colonial Puritan acculturation to New Zion propelled New England saints against the twinned trials of "savagery" and "popery."[10] Unlike Jesuit missionary perceptions of Protestant heretics as themselves in need of conversion and as ideologically adjacent to rather than commingled with the Indian, Puritan captives located French Catholicism, when they encountered it, at the heart of heathen America, inextricably fused with the savage. Thus positioned inside the often violent enterprise to establish Anglo-America, the Romanism emanating from France and its Indians demanded a concerted military and spiritual response to ward off the danger of spiritual backsliding or foreign imperial conquest.

But like the Indian and the wilderness itself, popery covertly served to incite piety, an integral (if more problematic) part of Puritan efforts to achieve a stark and ever-watchful gratitude toward God. When acting in concert, all three agents of the "demonic" verged upon the "gracious," for they produced in Puritan captives that vigilant dependence on God that was perhaps their most coveted subjective state. Like later antebellum nativists, Puritans exploited popery as catalyst and justification for their own spiritual and political vitality.

Because of its ideological utility in the mythology of Puritan captivity, popery developed a powerful literary presence: allied with the threatening but ultimately impotent forces of primitivism, Catholicism itself became a virtual character, one "who" dwelled within the charged but politically marginal domain of melodrama. Such a theatrical and instrumental personification would influence later antebellum attitudes toward Catholicism as a foreign, even "uncanny," agent, one both powerful and impotent, threatening yet farcical. Unlike Indian cultures, popery was ineradicable kin to the Puritan reformed consciousness, and hence helped translate the North American wilderness into a familiar psychological terrain of merciful, if not penitential, afflictions boldly designed for the spiritual betterment of Reformed Christians. Puritan astonishment at encountering the anomaly of Catholic Indians was rapidly grafted onto already conventionalized emotions of fascination and contempt toward the Mother Church, who, as cast-off parent, haunted her errant children. Guilty ambivalence over having broken the unity of the Christian family translated into suspicious avoidance of an angry Roman parent, unleashed in the wilderness and intent on recovering her flock—her vigilance matching that of the New England saints. Not surprisingly, then, the Roman church constructed by this theological family romance emanated a puzzling villainy in which forcible estrangements disguised profound recognitions. Catholicism's strangeness differed crucially from that of the Indian: it was "uncanny" rather than wholly new, tempting the Anglo-American Puritan with reacculturation to Europe rather than abandonment into wilderness ways. When Puritan captives confronted the convergence of these temptations in the figure of the Catholic Indian, they were forced to the disturbed acknowledgment that "home" had come with them into the wilderness.[11]

With the onset of King Philip's War (1675–78), the violence of the Iroquois combined with the calculated efforts of missionary priests to form an enduring Protestant suspicion of popery's rival sacramental power as at once punitive and unpredictably seductive. The most influential Puritan account of subjection to this "Catholic" wilderness was John Williams's 1707 best-seller, *The Redeemed Captive Returning to Zion.*[12] Williams's narrative focuses recurrently on the strange anachronisms of his experience. Captured with most of his family and parishioners in 1704, Pastor Williams survived a forced winter march from Deerfield, Massachusetts, to Montreal. En route, he endured what seemed to him the bizarre tyranny of his Catholicized Indian master, who, like a New World inquisitor, forced his Congregational prisoner to cross himself and to attend the "great confusion instead of gospel order" (185) of an Indian mass.

Captivity was at once a forced march into an anarchic wilderness and a weird regression into coercive Old World spiritual ritual. The combination of violence and mysterious ornamental behavior strangely recalled the ceremonialism and persecutions of Catholic monarchies. But Williams's narrative of "myself and so many of my children and friends in a popish captivity" finally focuses less on Indian and Roman violence than on missionary seduction. The true threat to this Deerfield minister emanated from the priests who split up Puritan families, luring or coercing the children into the worst captivity of all: conversion to Catholicism. Included in his captivity narrative is a lengthy epistle to his son Samuel on the follies of transubstantiation and purgatory that presumably persuaded the boy away from the foreign doctrine.

Williams's epistle to Samuel tellingly reveals how captivity already provided a compelling explanatory construct for Christian subjectivity, especially for Anglo-American Puritans, who anxiously insisted that their purified New England culture represented and further enabled the workings of a rigorously disembodied spirit. As Pastor Williams explained to his son, their Indian captivity logically derived from a generative captivity lodged at the heart of Catholic theology: the doctrine of transubstantiation, which profanely embodied and hence incarcerated God. "[It is] a blasphemy to pretend to a power of making God at their pleasure," Williams writes, "and then eat Him and give Him to others to be eaten or shut Him up in their altars, that they can utter the same words and make a God or not make a God according to their intention" (216). Thus Williams pictures the Eucharist as capture and cannibalism: a closeting of the Deity that, in permitting consumption, provokes a terrifying specter of God's instability and vulnerability: If God can be eaten, he can disappear. From this original act of confinement issue a proliferating series of enclosures by which Catholics, already expert cannibals of God, seek to trap (and, by implication, devour) their fellow humans. Purgatory is, Williams reminds Samuel, one such device, "a fatal snare to many souls who sin with hopes of easy getting priestly absolutions at death and buying off torments with their money" (217). The analogy between Catholicism's theology of captivity and the wilderness experience of the Williams family was conclusive: Catholicism and Indian captivity were not only synchronic representations of Original Sin, manifesting the universal phenomenon of bondage in a fallen world, but in diachronic relation as well, for Indian captivity emerged from Roman Catholicism, its tyrannies and rituals those of popery. Such arguments convinced Samuel, for he returned to New England and the professed liberty of Congregationalism.

Ironically, Pastor Williams became famous not so much for this victory over popery as for his defeat. Struggling to retrieve two of his children from the dread fate of conversion, he recovered Samuel, but not Eunice; to the scandal of her Mather uncles and the grief of her father, Eunice chose to remain in captivity. Rebaptized a Catholic, she took the name Marguerite and, at age sixteen, married a Caughnawaga brave named François Xavier Arosen. From this traumatic childhood of abduction and coerced assimilation, Eunice later emerged as a steadfast Indian wife, mother, and Catholic, one of the earliest in a long and interesting line of American converts to Rome. Although her brother Stephen eventually persuaded her to visit Deerfield, she refused to move back, for fear, she said, of losing her soul.[13]

Thus, as John Williams had learned too well, the freezing Canadian wilderness contained a seductive magic by which Indians cannibalized their slain enemies to ingest their strength and priests transubstantiated God to ingest his conversionary powers. Against such heretical incorporations of matter, Puritan captives shielded themselves as ascetically as they could. Another young captive, John Gyles, who suffered the (to him) dire fate of being purchased from the Indians by a Frenchman, responded in revealing fashion to a Jesuit priest's efforts to ransom him. "He gave me a biscuit," Gyles reports, "which I put into my pocket, and not daring to eat it, buried it under a log, fearing he had put something into it to make me love him."[14] Gyles's fear of Catholic wizardry points to residual superstitions in Puritanism that erupted in the Salem witchcraft crisis. But his unease points as well to emergent anxieties in American Protestantism. If his hurried burial of the Jesuit menace shows his youth and historical era, his fear of contact with seductive Catholic matter would be shared by many later Americans. Indeed, many nineteenth-century narratives of Protestant captivity to Catholicism would focus precisely on such dynamics of involuntary love.

FIVE

Nativism and Its Enslavements

As the Indian was forcibly removed from America, Catholicism occupied an enlarged cultural arena for the identity-confirming drama of piety and violence, of ritual resistance to the torments and seductions of the profane initially fashioned in Indian captivity and conversion narratives. Having made its American literary debut in Jesuit and Puritan narratives of captivity, Catholicism thereafter figured crucially in the construction of antebellum Protestant subjectivity.

The powerful link between piety and sadism seen in a narrative like Jogues's resurfaced in the nineteenth century in the immensely popular tales of captivity to a punitive Catholicism. In imagining Americans trapped in convents, confessionals, and the dungeons of the Inquisition, militant Protestant nativists battled against Roman intrigue and persecution. Anti-Catholic narratives, while developing the conventional but still compelling association of the violent, the exotic, and the hidden that had structured the Indian captivity genre, moved the site for these psychic challenges from the forest to the parochial school, the nunnery, and the confessional. In the words of one "escaped" nun: "Where do you place the abode of cruelty and of curiosity? Where, but in the mysterious seclusion of the convent?"[1]

Many antebellum Protestants imagined that a resurgent, disturbingly immigrant Catholicism aimed for their land, their children, their very souls. Embattled by this Protestant nativism that peaked in the 1830s and then again in the 1850s, Catholic leaders sometimes took the reckless offensive. In 1850, Archbishop Hughes, for example, brashly declared: "Everybody should know that we have for our mission to convert the world—including the inhabitants of the United States—the people of the cities, and the people of the country, the officers of the navy and the

99

marines, commanders of the army, the legislatures, the Senate, the Cabinet, the President, and all!"[2]

Such statements threw conservative Protestants into angry panic. Lyman Beecher, whose evangelical rhetoric drew much power from artfully terrifying depictions of an imperial power that dared compete with the Anglo-Saxon, imaged the papacy as the archcaptor, holding "in darkness and bondage nearly half the civilized world" and threatening to swallow America whole. As Beecher went on to explain in his *Plea for the West* (1835), papal machinations were already at work to overtake the American West since Catholic policies had always sought to "compensate for losses at home by new efforts to extend their influence abroad."[3] Only if New England funneled funds westward to establish Protestant schools could Americans hope to compete ideologically against popery, whose successful and rising number of parochial schools and dangerously populous settlement of the Mississippi River Valley promised a Roman Catholic frontier.

Fears of educational takeover paralleled visions of political usurpation, for the mind of the child and that of the voter were figured as similarly impressible. The confessional—as a mysterious architectural interior closed off from public surveillance, a place where secret dialogue transpired beyond the alleged democratizing influences of print—attracted enormous political and sexual anxiety. In the confessional, according to the nativist Protestant imagination, women were seduced and men suborned by priests who as confessors could discover the workings of home, marketplace, and polling booth and manipulate all invisibly. To nativist sections of the Whig and, later, Republican parties, the Irish immigrant was particularly susceptible to both the priest and the Democratic party machine, leagued to overthrow republican America.

Fears of political conspiracy were greatly enhanced by Anglo-American prejudice against the Irish that flared up when the Great Famine (1845–52) sent 1.25 million impoverished Irish to America in the space of a decade. Could America's still nascent democracy, one that in the 1830s actively battled the tyrannies of "King Jackson" on the one hand and the "Money Power" on the other, withstand the massive foreign influence of these spiritually "docile" Irish? Or would American politics regress to the despotism and cabalistic intrigues that typified Old World political culture?[4] Nativists typically described the pope's impending political dominion in terms that indirectly implied their own powerlessness in an electoral system increasingly afflicted by fraud and graft. If the will of the people was divided by sectional quarrels and economic conflict, the Vatican's will was reassuringly united by its malevolent intention. Thus the author of *Pope or President? Startling Disclosures of Romanism as Revealed by Its Own Writers* (1859), for example, sought to convince American voters that the "hand of popery, secretly moving, misdirecting or holding in check the rights of the people," was about to grip America by the throat.[5] This "hand of popery" operated as demonic counterpart not only to Adam Smith's invisible hand of the market but to evangelical Protestantism's hand of the Lord, a hand whose providential management of New Zion was increasingly impeded by denominational schism and the spiritual paucity of American civil religion.[6] The Vatican hand invisibly guiding schoolchild and confessional visitant meant that any Roman Catholic with public power would be psychologically incapable of observing the constitutional separation of church and state. One popular anti-Catholic novel incited readers with "the extraordinary spectacle of the entire Postal Department—which controls the transmission of the public and private intelligence of the country—confided to the hands of a Roman Catholic, with upwards of fifty thousand offices in his gift."[7]

Political phobias in particular were shaped by the centuries-long tradition of suspicion toward the Jesuits, confessors to generations of European royalty and hence the supposed masterminds behind domestic and international politics. As missionaries in New France, as an educated elite, and as highly placed confessors, Jesuits, as one nativist explained, "have cords drawn all around the world."[8] Even more than Napoleon, Loyola (as we have seen for the theologically liberal Parkman) epitomized an absolute power based on the fusion of political, intellectual, and spiritual energies. According to one antebellum Protestant biographer, a single idea inspired Loyola: "that of an absolute domination over the spirits of men, and of a centralization of all powers on earth, in the bosom of one master of souls."[9] With the revival of the Jesuit order in 1814, the passage of the Catholic Emancipation Act in 1829, and the sharp rise in immigration from Catholic Europe between 1845 and 1855, a renewal of papal despotism, engineered by the Jesuits, seemed near, and "Jesuitical" intrigue became the target of Protestant missionary reprimand.

Writing for the Home Missionary Society, the liberal Congregational minister Horace Bushnell spoke in tones of Gothic alarmism, condemning Pope Gregory XVI for his politics, in which, "with few exceptions, every centre of power is the seat of some cabal; and creatures, male and female, glide about the precincts, who are able, by the base and criminal secrets in their keeping, or perhaps, by terms of partnership well understood, to open or shut at will, the gates of favour."[10] Behind this

Gothic image of spectral figures gliding through conspiracy-ridden interiors stood American party politics (and for Bushnell in particular, Hartford church politics), whose invisible workings and all too visible corruptions propelled many citizens to abandon traditional party affiliations and subscribe to the anticonspiratorial platform of the American, or Know-Nothing, party.[11]

It was finally difficult, however, for Americans to act decisively against the papal threat of electoral captivity. For all its ominousness, the precise nature of the popery overwhelming America remained vague: "Few have any exact knowledge of the doctrines of that Church which, through her servants, whispers seductively into the ear of a monarch, or mingles in a popular election, in order to compass her end of universal mental despotism."[12] One writer even confessed his bewilderment in the face of his own conspiratorial suspicions; if the Jesuits achieved global dominion, "the question still comes up, what did they intend to do with the world and in it?"[13] This elusiveness at the heart of Catholic agency was crucial to its continued vitality as a conspiratorial menace, always beckoning nativist fears toward social spaces where the figure of Romanism invisibly mingled. If to those unconvinced by the charges of Protestant alarmists such elusiveness simply signaled the absence of malign papal intentions, lack of evidence only worked to heighten nativists' certainty of intrigue. They turned for evidence of their unsubstantiated fantasies of global domination to the local mysteries of language deceitfully shared between unsupervised individuals. Captivity was to occur not through military invasion or overt political gesture but through the seemingly casual minglings of an increasingly heterogeneous and urbanized social space.

While alarmed Protestants had trouble arriving at very precise notions about their Catholic enemy, they also had correspondingly few ideas about how to ward off impending captivity; notwithstanding their meteoric rise to political power in 1854, Know-Nothing legislators failed to issue any new laws. Know-Nothing demands for a twenty-one-year naturalization period, restriction of officeholding to native-born citizens, and legislation requiring periodic inspection of convents succumbed to the greater appeal of the new Republican party platform calling for "free labor"—an appeal in which the South and slavery were cast as the nation's principal menace. Nativists' efforts to stigmatize the Catholic immigrant were thwarted both by economic realities and by the manifestly vague conception of the foreign threat, which enabled its appropriation by abolitionists in their campaign against the southern "Lords of the Lash." But if abolitionists borrowed the terms of anti-Catholic invective to bolster their righteous attack on the tyranny and sensual excess of plantation life, their rhetoric hardly accorded black slaves the purity of the Protestant martyr. Rather, that status was reserved for the New Englander, intent on asserting his or her section's vision of America against the Romanish iniquities of the South.[14]

New England hostility to immigrant Catholicism in the three decades prior to the Civil War facilitated the mounting regional attack on slavery by popularizing a usefully improbable and clearly regional rhetoric of purity and contamination, a discourse legitimized by appeal to a religious supremacism that left racial loyalties intact. One could attack the South for the Romanism of its slaveholding practices rather than the white supremacism of such customs. Thus Harriet Beecher Stowe's evangelical critique of the Catholic household of the St. Clare family in *Uncle Tom's Cabin* indicts slavery for its spiritual tyranny over the soul more than for its racial tyranny over the body. That little Catholic Eva attends Methodist meetings with her spiritual colleague Uncle Tom discreetly registers her escape from Romanism's toils—toils that entwine her neurasthenic punitive mother and her indolent father.

It is difficult, finally, to position anti-Catholic discourse in the sectional crisis of the 1850s; if Stowe and more radical abolitionists "Romanized" southern slaveholders, the Louisville Bloody Monday riots of 1855 found Know-Nothing agitators on the side of the South, preventing immigrant (often radical and antislavery) German Catholics from voting, thus "converting the election into a perfect farce."[15] The increasing tensions that followed the passage of the Kansas-Nebraska Act splintered nativism into competing sectional alliances; for example, New England nativists allied themselves with antislavery forces against Irish Catholic immigrants while siding with southern planters who attacked German Catholic immigrants in Kentucky. Such contradictory uses of anti-Catholicism illustrate its strategic flexibility to antebellum politics and render problematic any one formulation of its position in the slavery crisis. Indeed, alarmist southerners themselves borrowed the terms of anti-Catholic discourse to depict the threat of a slave conspiracy that was seemingly confirmed by Bishop England's opening of a school for slaves in Charleston, finally closed by protests.[16] The elusiveness of anti-Catholicism in antebellum politics enabled sectionally divided Americans to express their regional animosities while imagining their united opposition to the pope. If popular and elite fictions of Protestant captivity to Rome functioned in the 1830s and 1840s to contain the threat of the Catholic immigrant, by the 1850s they permitted North and South alike to imaginatively resist white America's impending fratricidal violence. To fight the machinations of Rome was to displace the specter of civil war; more generally, to imagine Rome as protean conspiratorial agent, confusingly allied with both pro- and antislavery forces, was to imagine an America still joined by common religious concerns.

Alarmed anticipations of an impending national captivity to popery form a revealingly distorted commentary on troubling issues of immigration, urbanization, and democracy. If the nativist efforts of the American party to purge the nation of heterogeneous "Catholic" elements represent one aspect of a recurrent American xenophobia, the literary-historical importance of antebellum nativist discourse resides in its use of an increasingly anachronistic vocabulary of theological conflict to describe and obfuscate the crises of America's transition from a "union" to a "nation."[17] Nativist "religious" purity powerfully supplemented appeals to ethnic supremacism and racial purity, projecting contaminations of the Republic, like the capitalist regimentation of the Lowell textile mills or the miscegenation of the races, onto the foreign and tyrannous papal father. The widening controversy over the validity or permissible extent of slavery clarified this focus on Catholicism, the "foreign" religion a powerful surrogate for the "foreign race" enclosed in white America. The image of captivity to Rome, then, not only expressed the slave's captivity for the Protestant abolitionist and the slave conspirator's for the planter class but also revised the estrangements of a modernizing economy and social space into the righteous simplicities of filial revolt against Rome.

Thus in its obsessive fantasies of an impending Protestant surrender to papal mastery, much anti-Catholic writing resituated the divisive and pluralistic public sphere—whose tensions infiltrated the strenuously asserted privacies of the "domestic sphere"—in the manageable confines of an enclosed and melodramatized privacy of religious sentiment. Perplexed by the strain of conveying the "indelicacies" of slavery "delicately," even the fugitive slave Harriet Jacobs appealed to the ritual theatrics of anti-Catholicism in her pseudonymous *Incidents in the Life of a Slave Girl* (1861). Referring to her master's hidden fathering of eleven slaves, Jacobs's persona, Linda Brent, reminds readers that "the secrets of slavery are concealed like those of the Inquisition."[18] Jacobs's invocation of the Inquisition signals her owner Timothy Flint's licentious exploitation of women slaves and her own righteous exposé: she will reveal the illicit excesses of his private and at times frustratingly invisible dominion. Her Inquisitional metaphor also dramatizes the intensity of her victimization and the justice of her revolt in terms profoundly familiar to her white northern readership. Such metaphorizing of herself as Protestant victim to the subtle and largely hidden tortures of the Inquisition perilously borders on the salacious associations of anti-Catholic rhetoric widely popularized by the dime novelist Ned Buntline, who wrote, for example, of the titillating tortures of the Inquisition: "For, oh! upon that rack lay stretched the fair and half-naked form of Genita, its symmetry convulsing in matchless tortures, the bosom palpitating awfully with the pangs of that earthly hall and the exquisitely modelled limbs enduring all the pains of dislocation."[19]

Intent finally on disclosing the intricacies of Linda Brent's psychological as well as bodily enslavement, Jacobs's narrative renders the sexual theatrics of Inquisition literature ironically: rather than eroticized torture in basement cells, she images for her northern evangelical readership a far more subversive interiority, as she tells of hiding herself first beneath kitchen floorboards and then for seven years in her grandmother's garret, from where she looks down on the master who still pursues his fugitive slave. In artfully removing herself from captivity within the sexually contaminated domesticity of Flint's household and his threatening interrogations, Linda Brent simultaneously sidesteps the nativist melodrama of anti-Catholic discourse—not only its prurient focus on female violation but also its consoling promise that ideological complexities are nothing more than Romish mysteries to be indignantly deciphered. Linda Brent's garret interior—in its solitude, its aerial superiority to masculine persecution, its surveillance of the white world—resolutely forbids the reader's "religious" arousal.

In contrast to Jacobs's suspended, calculating, and painfully protracted escape from slavery, nativist literature of the convent, the confessional, and the Inquisition recurrently imagined the pleasures of a serendipitous, instantaneous flight. The intensity of fantasied emancipation was fueled by a sentimental logic of vicarious identification with the imagined prisoners of antebellum culture. George Lippard's best-selling *Monks of Monk Hall* (1844) lavishly multiplied the forces of imprisonment and their (usually) female captives; Lippard's Philadelphians, though sometimes villainous, are at bottom helpless captives of capitalism, libertinism, and religious (Protestant, Catholic, and visionary) opportunism—forces not so much woven into a coherent plot by Lippard as melodramatically dismembered into the various spaces of the long-ago Catholic interior of Monk Hall.[20]

Many contemporary observers, reluctant to acknowledge the relationship of righteous anti-Catholicism to racial and ethnic conflict, claimed that the religious paranoia and violence were incited by the flood of anti-Catholic sermons, pamphlets, and novels that saturated the antebellum literary marketplace. Some of this literature, such as the reformist priest Scipio de Ricci's *Female Convents, Secrets of Nunneries Disclosed* (1829), was directly imported from England, where agitation over the promulgation of the Catholic Emancipation Act (1829) produced a spate of anti-Catholic works. Other works made their way to America from more distant times, such as Anthony Gavin's *Great Red Dragon; or, The Master-Key to Popery* (London, 1725). Gavin's work was reissued three times in America (Philadelphia, 1816; Boston, 1854; Philadelphia, 1855), its popularity indicating the contemporary efficacy of such an anachronistic text. From 1800 to 1860, a partial count of anti-Catholic publications shows some 25 newspapers, 13 magazines, 210 books, 40 fictional pieces, 41 histories, and scores of giftbooks, almanacs, and pamphlets dedicated to the anti-Catholic cause.[21]

As a strategic displacement for actual and ongoing captivities in antebellum America, anti-Catholic narratives exhibited a characteristically farcical tone. A sense of theatricality and insincerity pervades not only the frankly commercial dime-novel literature but more elite literary productions as well. Many Americans detected the imposture, sham, and simple profiteering that accompanied the often violent ideological tensions of this period. By 1835 anti-Catholicism had become a moneymaking venture that many entered into with entrepreneurial gusto. "The abuse of the Catholics," noted one magazine, "is a regular trade, and the compilation of anti-Catholic books . . . has become a part of the regular industry of the country, as much as the making of nutmegs, or the construction of clocks."[22] The observation points to a paradoxical dynamic in American anti-Catholicism—namely, the indigenous production and consumption of an ostensibly foreign, Catholic commodity. Indeed this Old World religion, as conceived by nativist propaganda, became one of the basic ingredients in the developing American identity. Catholic perceptions corroborated the pervasive anti-Catholic slant of contemporary writing. Declared the leading Catholic journal: "There is not a single work of fiction, emanating from Protestants, which does not directly or indirectly assail the faith or morals of the Catholic Church."[23]

The inauthentic strain at the base of the hysteria troubled some observers because it revealed a disturbing resemblance to hated popery. If the domestic manufacture of popery was aimed at bolstering the Protestant Way, it quickly assumed an ironic function as well. Much anti-Catholic writing unwittingly revealed that Protestant Americans could be as scheming and exploitative as the papists they despised. The vocabulary of Protestant disdain was fast turning in on itself as self-critical Americans applied it to their society. Thus one review of an anti-Catholic text defined Jesuitism as

> referring to all those of every religious denomination who are more zealous for their church than for Christianity, more particular about ends than means, who resist the teachings of their instincts as solicitations from the devil, who estimate their virtue by what they suffer rather than by what they enjoy; who take pride in concealing an appetite which they intend to mortify; and who, in time, form a habit of deception which spreads over the whole surface of their character, perhaps without their ever suspecting its existence.[24]

Thus while Jesuits, as the menacing other, continued in symbolic counterpart to the developing entrepreneurial masculine identity, they were also beginning to appear as an indigenous feature of that identity. Nativist discourse was escaping from its confines and attaching itself to the interior of Protestant subjectivity. To the minister Calvin Colton, anti-Catholic writers were themselves "Jesuitical," for they used religious zeal to disguise their own greed and pornographic inclinations. The phenomenon so disturbed him that he wrote a book, significantly entitled *Protestant Jesuitism* (1836), which detailed how Protestantism and Catholicism ironically converged in a salacious nativist literature: "The taste for these publications and the excitement produced by them, are the natural product of that false alarm which the Jesuitism of our own country has attempted to raise against the Jesuitism of Rome. Here is rogue chasing rogue—Jesuit in pursuit of Jesuit—but the older rogue is the wiser, because he has been longer in practice: he will not be overtaken, for the sufficient reason that his pursuer is on the wrong scent."[25]

As Colton's statement suggests, the antebellum struggle to fend off the Catholic enemy manifested a curious doubling effect that disrupted the traditional captivity model in which Protestants righteously fled from Catholic persecution. Protestants, increasingly corrupt in the same ways as their enemy, were now pursuing Rome. It was not only that Americans, by indulging in their taste for the pornographic, the inquisitional, and the violent, were practicing the very vices they ascribed to their enemy but that their conspiratorial fears also came to function as a surrogate religion, which inevitably resembled its Catholic nemesis because its shape and meaning developed through enumerating the myriad evil tenets of popery. The high ritualism and secrecy of the nativist Order of the Star-Spangled Banner is one prominent example of this surrogate effect. As a doubled representation of Protestant selfhood, the image of

Romanism attracted obsessive scrutiny precisely because it covertly promised access to the self modeled upon it. This strangely solipsistic pursuit produced a voluminous literature denying its self-bound origins. As David Reese declared in his *Humbugs of New-York: Being a Remonstrance against Popular Delusion; Whether in Science, Philosophy, or Religion* (1838): "Indeed the class of Anti-Popery literature, including volumes, pamphlets, tracts, and newspapers, have become so numerous, that it is impossible to read them all, unless indeed all other reading be postponed to the all-absorbing inquiry into the abominations of Romanism."[26]

Such an "all-absorbing" fascination with Catholic iniquity indirectly confirmed the purity and unity of Protestantism.[27] Because the Roman church had been traditionally associated with the complexity and corruption of culture, it served as an ideal antagonist in the fervent, if not entirely sincere, struggle against materialism. The threat of captivity to Catholicism's dread interiors, to its alluring and perilous worldliness, gave shape and limit to American democracy; the menace also functioned, however subliminally, as a desirable alternative to the pressures disguised beneath the optimistic rhetoric of democracy. Here as elsewhere, the Jesuits figured importantly as symbols of an alternatively constructed masculine power. Isaac Taylor's eccentric but revealing biography *Loyola and Jesuitism in Its Rudiments* (1857) diagnosed Protestantism's antagonistic fascination with Catholicism as symptomatic of the loss of human agency in the antebellum age, an insight unusual for the period. For all his hatred of the Jesuits, Taylor, like Francis Parkman, betrayed a self-critical curiosity about them. But unlike the famous historian, Taylor carried his analysis one step further in claiming that the fascination was not in fact with the Jesuits but with the early modern culture that produced them. At its zenith, the Jesuit order represented an era when individual agency clearly counted. By contrast, in the modern era individual power had been eroded by a vast, impersonal, and uncontrollable system:

> The cessation—or the apparent cessation—of human agency, as related to the movements and progress of the moral system, seems to invite attention to the times when its power was at the height; and when the individual peculiarities and the personal history of illustrious men gave a well-defined direction to the mind of nations, and left a strongly marked image upon their forms of belief, and upon their permanent institutions.[28]

Like many others, Taylor sought refuge from his newly "systematic" age in studying (and creating) a historical past that validated individualism and nourished convictions strong enough to resemble the "marked image." Paradoxically, the Jesuits, representing an absolute obedience to absolute authority, enjoyed freedom from cultural enervation. They epitomized at once the captive mind and the power of individual will.

The nostalgia for a zealous but disciplined agency evinced by Taylor and others figured at the center of evangelical opposition to Catholicism and explains some of the conflicted and self-reflexive nature of Protestant fears of captivity to Rome. To many contemporary observers, their democratic age, in suppressing the rule of charismatic authority, enfeebled convictions of all sorts, religious ones included. Antebellum criticism of Rome, especially in the recurrent portraits of the malign but attentive Jesuit, aim at the recovery of agency and, for ministers in particular, the recovery of audience as well. Many of the most vocal anti-Catholic agitators, such as George Bourne and the Reverends Brownlee and Beecher, were ministers on the defensive, struggling to maintain prestige in a heterogeneous religious marketplace. From their alarmist perspective (which registered in heightened tones a queasy unrest at their decline in status) America could more easily brave a Catholic plot than the rapid proliferation of Protestant sects that apparently mocked any notion of theological design to the Christian universe. Lyman Beecher, who owed much of his fame to his crusade against Catholicism, suggested as much in outlining the Austrian-papal plot to gain dominion of the American West: "If such complicated indications of design may exist without design, as well may the broader mechanism of the world be regarded as the offspring of chance."[29] For many antebellum Protestants, the supposed Catholic conspiracy to capture them proved not only that their faith was still vital but that their ministers were too.

Captivity structured nativist perceptions not only of papal machinations but also of Catholic dogma itself. Bondage characterized popery in all its aspects, thus presenting a satisfyingly coherent text for observers to decipher. To Nicholas Murray, the development of Catholic dogma and practice since the early Middle Ages revealed, as they did for Pastor Williams in his Canadian captivity, Catholicism's innate relationship to captivity. "These tenets," Murray explained, "artfully linked together into a great chain, forged for the purpose of binding the soul at the feet of the priest, were quietly received in those days of darkness; and the darkness was cherished by the locking up of the Scriptures from the people, and by the inculcation of an implicit faith."[30] Murray's identification of Catholic piety with confinement, with the locking in of Scripture and of the soul, characterized liberal as well as nativist attitudes.

Illustrating this distribution of nativist discourse across theological "class lines," liberal New England Protestants even borrowed images of Catholic captivity to depict their own fear of entrapment by any orthodoxy, the specter of confinement figuring prominently in Unitarian and agnostic thinking about the spiritual life in general. Orthodoxy, whether Catholic or Calvinist, threatened to imprison the soul. From the perspective of one Unitarian writer, acceptable spirituality was closely associated with images of space and escape. In his article entitled "Sacrifice" he describes the spiritual life as poised between the alternatives of interiority and exteriority, confinement and release.[31] Significantly, no explicit reference is made to Protestantism's quarrel with Rome, for by avoiding any hint of polemics he effectively dismisses the possible validity of their separate claims. Nonetheless, a clear ideological division remains. Liberal Protestantism implicitly figures as the way of release, Calvinism and Catholicism as the way of confinement. Presenting an amiable version of the labyrinthine interiors of Gothic fiction, the author depicts the self as a maze through which the divine spirit seeks to pass, God's chief desire being to flow through us and on into the world. The divine spirit "waits with sublime imperturbable serenity at every closed avenue, and enters at every open one" (320); our religious duty is to remain open to this spirit by emptying ourselves through a constant self-expenditure, or "sacrifice." Having let the divine enter us, we must let it exit into the world. We must not "make our bosom a terminus, rather than conduit, for the river of life" (332). Ideally, the individual should behave like a fountain, then, circulating the divine spirit through society; any attempt to confine the Deity, to horde it or hold it captive, will deform the person, for to constrain or repress this divine spirit generates the vices of "bigotry, self-mutilation, and every species of conscientious suicide" (316)—vices commonly ascribed to a monastic and penitential Rome.

Captivity to Romanism, be it on the national or individual level, was complicated by the threat of complicity. Many accused the Catholic church of luring people into its grasp, of charming their senses with the magnificence of its art or befuddling their reason with Jesuit casuistry. The widespread conviction of Catholicism's spellbinding properties suggests the discomfort yet usefulness of the felt attraction; the passivity of enchantment was psychologically safer than the activity of desire. Nativists were expert politicians of this theology of mesmerism; in effect, they created and controlled this enchanting menace in their self-appointed efforts to alert the American public to its presence. To Samuel F. B. Morse, artist, inventor, and Protestant propagandist, Catholics lurked hypnotically and evilly like serpents in the "cradle of the embryo giant [America]." Moving quickly from pagan fantasies of America's Herculean infancy to Genesis imagery of sexual temptation, Morse hopes that the infant America, having grasped these serpents, will "neither be tempted from his hold by admiration of their painted and gilded covering, nor by fear of the fatal embrace of their treacherous folds."[32]

Morse's use of Edenic imagery to describe Catholicism's serpentine sexual and moral temptations was typical of his time; earlier Americans had also understood the foreign religion as an extension through time of the devil's seduction of Eve. John Adams, for example, wrote to his wife, Abigail, of Catholicism's deceptive allure: "Here is everything which can lay hold of the eye, ear, and imagination. Everything which can charm, and bewitch the simple and ignorant. I wonder how Luther ever broke the spell."[33] By Morse's time, many Americans were convinced that Luther had not successfully broken the spell. Catholics hardly needed to conspire against America, for the nation's citizens were already spellbound, dangerously ready to sample Rome's delusions further. Morse's role in this prelapsarian drama was to alert Americans "who, with a facility most marvellous, fall into every snare and pleasant baited trap that Popery spreads for them."[34] Anti-Catholic activity like Morse's could reenact the Fall in order to repair it, resurrecting Satan in order to triumph over him.

The continued reimagining of the horrors of captivity to Catholicism's labyrinthine, despotic interiors, past and present, provided an acceptable access to racial and economic worlds of subordination and dispossession disturbingly enclosed in, and forced beneath, middle-class existence. Unlike Lippard's eccentrically lurid fiction, anti-Catholic fiction more typically confined its treatment of such dispossession to the racially and economically "pure" precincts of the domestic where powerlessness could be safely figured as maidenhood trapped in the architectural complexities of the convent rather than the mazes of politics or economics. Narratives of imprisoned Protestant virgins offered a tantalizing confluence of theological and sexual preoccupations—a discursive convergence that was itself as provocative as the contents of convent life that it disclosed.

SIX

Sentimental Capture
The Cruel Convent and Family Love

As nineteenth-century Americans shifted their focus from the transcendent to the social, they reconceived captivity in psychological rather than religious terms. Captivity to "savages" accordingly yielded less information about the divine, for in a middle-class (and increasingly anti-Calvinist) America that newly insisted on the benevolence, even domesticity, of the Deity and the agency of the believer, such exotic and tortured bondage only faintly recalled the desired Christian relationship with God. Torment—whether physical or spiritual—became increasingly detached from holy authorship, and bodily suffering like that exemplified in Parkman's historiography provided more information about the psyche in society than about Jehovah's mysterious ways. As antebellum Indian captivity tales, slave narratives, and convent escape stories illustrated, captives no longer typically responded to their plight by abandoning themselves to God, for their captivities signified new but potentially surmountable horrors of imprisonment to humanity and its corruptions. One no longer sought through captivity to obtain a cleansed and grateful awareness of God's power, of the reality and glory of one's existential dependence, but simply, if no less desperately, to escape. Captivity became a drama, not of being kidnapped into the American wilderness, boundless and frightening, but of being entrapped by built spaces—cathedral, confessional, and convent—with Romanism providing an antidomestic cultural architecture for Protestant habitation.

In this new preoccupation with issues of flight rather than submission, of sentimental release rather than orthodoxy, piety was often subtly transfigured into the afflictions of burdensome emotion.[1] Faith operated less successfully as counterpart and rigorous antidote to torment; sep-

112

arated by the forces of middle-class domesticity and market capitalism, the sacred and the violent parted ways in middle-class fiction, meeting again in the marginal, subversive terrain of the convent exposé or the elite artistry of Melville and Emily Dickinson. Middle-class fictions like *Uncle Tom's Cabin*, even when arguing for the transcendent and evangelical potential of captivity, connected such spiritual power with the lavish cultivation and expression of sentiment. In nineteenth-century Indian captivity narratives, although vestiges of faith remain in formulaic acknowledgments of Providence for escape or rescue, the kinesis and mystery of piety have shifted their domain to the heart. As the dogma of redemptive suffering that structured earlier captivity narratives gradually eroded, and as Christian apologists staved off post-Enlightenment attacks by arguing that religion was finally a question not of disputable dogma but of autonomous emotion, feelings assumed many of the attributes of the sacred.[2] One no longer suffered at the hands of God so much as by the demands of one's privatized subjectivity; antebellum middle-class fictions and sermons, in dethroning an unjustly severe Calvinist God, installed new and conspicuously feminine powers of sentiment whose grip was sometimes experienced as equally harrowing and unmanageable. The "heart" came to represent an internal domain as sacred (if not as forbidding) as that wherein had dwelled the "soul," and like Jehovah, the heart now became both captor and redeemer. America's greatest Protestant revivalist of the 1820s and 1830s, Charles Grandison Finney, described this new evangelical phenomenology in his 1836 sermon "Sinners Bound to Change Their Own Hearts":

> The term *heart*, as applied to mind, is figurative, and recognizes an analogy between the heart of the body, and the heart of the soul. The fleshly organ of the body called the *heart*, is the seat and fountain of animal life, and by its constant action, diffuses life through the animal system. *The spiritual heart, is the fountain of spiritual life, is that deep seated but voluntary preference of the mind, which lies back of all its other voluntary affections and emotions, and from which they take their character.* In this sense I understand the term heart. . . . It is evidently something over which we have control; something voluntary; something for which we are to blame, and which we are bound to alter.[3]

Participating in this larger cultural trend toward sentimentality and domesticity, many nineteenth-century captivity narratives focused on the trials of this white "heart," at once ambiguously fleshly and spiritual, as it underwent a drama of emotional burden and release. Objective experiences of Indian captivity, for example, were interpreted less as an encompassing metaphysical bondage to the Lord than as a subjective confinement to emotion. The crucifixional ironies that had structured earlier Christian tales of captivity subsided before a simpler but no less powerful melodramatic strain, while a fierce drive toward authorial expressiveness and readerly intimacy replaced the ambiguities and symbolic inventiveness perfected by spiritually zealous captives like Isaac Jogues or John Williams. Accounts of captivity and release aimed to produce an emotional catharsis, a freeing of the socially constrained, implicitly urban, eastern self as it vicariously tasted the excessive tribulations of southern slave or western Indian captive. In this sentimental identification with such captives, exposé came to replace revelation as the horrors of captivity, rather than its providential lessons, gained narrative priority.

The *Narrative of Henry "Box" Brown* (1849) brilliantly illustrates antebellum America's newly sentimental perspective on captivity. As Brown's name suggests, the fugitive slave reached freedom after a twenty-seven-hour journey through the U.S. mail, nailed up in a three-by-two-foot box. The narrative focuses less on the captive's spiritual development within his box than on the reader's emotional release in imagining another's incarceration and escape. In the preface to this mythic story of a literal living letter, forced to travel to freedom upside down in the fetal position, Brown's editor urges his readers to let their feelings "burst forth from their enclosure."[4] The editorial passage connects Brown's live internment to a vaguer unbounded captivity at work in the reading audience—that within the "enclosure" of selfhood. Like the black fugitive bursting open his box in Philadelphia, readers of Brown's tale are encouraged to use his story to break free from the inhibitions of middle-class existence by a vicarious indulgence in another's plight. As Stowe argued in *Uncle Tom's Cabin*, it was precisely the refusal "to feel" that maintained the system of slavery; in her conservative abolitionist logic, to develop sympathy for the captive was the necessary precedent to urging southerners to release their slaves.

As Henry "Box" Brown's story indicates, sentimentalism permitted many nineteenth-century captivity narratives to locate transcendence in the release of emotion. Just as captivity was redescribed in terms of an emotionality broader (and less subversive) than the earlier sense of "enthusiasm," so the interior world of the captive self was increasingly depicted in an affectional vocabulary of imprisonment and escape. The attack on emotional repression and the invitation to sentimental release allied protagonist and reader in a newly intimate reading space where the burdens of the social became those of an exaggerated expressivity that could be at least partially dispelled through the act of reading.[5] The increasing pursuit of grace by both conservative and liberal evangelical Christians through the cultivation and release of feeling meant that such Christians continually wrestled to keep emotional excess from vitiating pious sentiment. Thus the Christian heroine of Susan Warner's 1850 best-seller *The Wide, Wide World,* to purify and unleash her refined powers of sentiment, must painfully repress the grief and rage that are deemed excessive. If Ellen Montgomery's spiritual pilgrimage becomes, as a result, a painful conflation of asceticism with repression and of charity with an upper-middle-class consumerism that disdains British aristocrats and America's urban underclass alike, antebellum Indian captivity narratives detailed an even more precipitous decline into insincerity.[6]

Ironically, this inauthenticity appeared precisely when the captivity genre no longer advocated theological tenets but aimed to elicit the inner truth of feelings. Problematically theatrical, nineteenth-century accounts of captivity to slaveholders, Catholics, or Indians displayed an intense, explicit concern with audience, the apparent displacement of God as primary interlocutor initiating an aggressive search for the suitably responsive human reader. The challenge of establishing connection (and making sales) to a mass reading public that was increasingly female and ethnically diverse urged authors even more toward the sentimental voice. While members of a declining eastern elite, like Hawthorne, quietly (if no less commercially) cast about in a sea of faces for that "ideal reader," middle-brow writers of popular captivity narratives hounded readers to win their involvement, reiterating the horrors of bondage as if to ward off the twin phenomena of religious indifference and reader insensibility.[7] In this transformation of the genre, a palpable anxiety about readers' indifference (their turning away from the text before them) supplants previous fears of divine wrath or abandonment.

R. B. Stratton's *Captivity of the Oatman Girls* (1859), for example, recounts the Indian captivity and torture of two frontier sisters in order to stimulate readers with Indian atrocity rather than awe them with the workings of divinity.[8] Like other sentimentally indignant nineteenth-century narrators, Stratton interrupts and repeats one sister's descriptions of torture, heedless of narrative awkwardness in his obsessive pursuit of the reader. If nativist paranoia toward Jesuits and the pope reflected an intense need for audience, that same dynamic figured in Stratton's melodramatization of Indian torture. Other authors of nineteenth-century captivities practiced a similarly stylized and self-conscious courting of excess, approaching captivity's dark regions of sadism, mourning, and possible redemption through a formulaic incitement of emotion, a patterned excess as orderly in its way as the prior use of Scripture to generate and structure the recollections of kidnap and escape.

The Narrative of the Capture and Subsequent Sufferings of Mrs. Rachel Plummer, Written by Herself (1839) suggests, finally, that the real bondage to be endured is not to God or Indian but to the heart and its affectional ties.[9] Plummer's story of abduction and enslavement by the Apaches—a two-year saga that begins with the witness of her child's murder—is perhaps the finest example of the sentimentalization of the captivity genre and its new concern with the developing "tortures" of family love. Plummer's implied readers are not Christians dulled by life in the settlements but rather parents who exist not in a state either of sin or of grace (each condition representing a reasonably intact, if not invincible, selfhood) but instead in a theologically emptied zone of vulnerability to irremediable loss: the death of children. The focus of the narrative is not pain on its way to heaven but pain that remains in a critical stasis, unable to go anywhere. The narrator's burden is the secular, finite, but eventually incommunicable one of extreme maternal anguish; the comparatively unwounded parental sensibilities of her readers function as the only shared text available for interpreting this captivity. Not the soul but the heart must suffer and endure this newly domesticated frontier anguish; Plummer concludes her description of the torture-death of her infant with this warning: "Parents, you little know what you can bear. Surely, surely, my poor heart must break" (342). Plummer's pathetic address is hardly less ominous (and certainly less manageable because more isolated) than conservative evangelical portraits of the Lord's impending afflictions. There is finally little escape from the condition of suspended catastrophe created by her poignant warning; hence enormous pressure is brought to bear upon the therapeutic action of sentimental narrative to avoid what Plummer implies is the age's new experience of damnation: the broken parental heart.

Plummer's treatment of Indian captivity in terms of family love and insurmountable woe finds partial symbolic resolution in a remarkable episode where she descends into a cave—an adventure that follows the death of her infant and occupies the bulk of her narrative. In a burst of seemingly arbitrary psychic need and heroic rebelliousness, the prisoner inexplicably beats up her Apache mistress, not to gain freedom but to explore a cave. Leaving her mistress behind, Plummer, like tourists in the Italian catacombs, pursues her journey "in the bowels of the earth" (350), imagining the candlelit chambers as grand church interiors.[10] Writing with the trenchant imagery and orchestrated movement of an original mythographer, Plummer then shifts her account from cathedral to psyche. Following an underground stream for over a mile, she finally falls into a deep sleep by an underground waterfall, and "in the confused roar of the waters," she reports, "I fancied I could hear the dying screams of my infant" (350). Her literalized submergence in maternal grief, far beneath the ego and an earth's surface afflicted by race wars over possession of the land, yields a therapeutic dream vision; a "stranger" (who functions as Christ but who remains significantly anonymous) appears before the sleeping woman and bathes her wounds. After two days Plummer emerges from the cave, still a prisoner (and still prisoner to her maternal grief) but newly heroic to her Indian captors. Ransomed, she concludes her narrative with no sense of theological or psychological resolution but with a poignant plea for the return of her other child, abducted and separated from her.

Thus where Indian captivity tales had formerly functioned as a symbolic discourse that confirmed one's significance to a punitive but merciful deity, they now addressed America's increasingly sacralized entity: the family. As Plummer's narrative memorably demonstrates, captivity had become increasingly involved with the burden of affectional ties—how to endure their loss or, more disturbingly, how to escape their confines.

In this newly sentimentalized association between the bonds of captivity and family, Roman Catholicism emerged not only as devious captor of the individual Protestant soul but also as sentimental competitor to the Protestant family. With the near eradication of Indian cultures, the discourse of anti-Catholicism was released into the domestic sphere of middle-class culture, where it voiced anxieties about that domesticity, its gender dissymmetries, its isolation from the public sphere, its polarized adulation of sentimental womanhood and entrepreneurial manhood. Anti-Catholic attacks on the alternative family structures represented by the convent, the celibate priesthood, and devotion to both the Virgin and the intercessory community of the sainted dead exposed Catholic familial structures as intriguing and dangerously collectivist—elaborate institutional structures that suppressed the autonomous individual, that confusingly both elevated and oppressed women, and that finally evaded distinctions between public and private central to liberal democracy and middle-class heterosexuality. A dangerous irony of Protestantism's antagonistic and sentimental response to this Romanism was that in inciting readers to identify with victims of its affective powers, Protestantism sometimes urged them to an unsentimental violence against it.

Perplexed about the just extent of their pluralistic, individualist ways and attracted to, yet suspicious of, the notion of contemplative retreat, convent captivity narratives like George Bourne's *Lorette, The History of Louise, Daughter of a Canadian Nun: Exhibiting the Interior of Female Convents* (1833) and the later best-sellers Rebecca Reed's *Six Months in a Convent* (1835) and Maria Monk's *Awful Disclosures of the Hotel Dieu Nunnery* (1836) domesticated the metaphysical concerns of their American literary prototype, the Indian captivity narrative. As frenzied re-presentations of issues initially formulated in Indian captivity narratives, they recounted forced flights from home into an exotic, marginal culture and the cultivation of captivity's afflictions. Like the colonial model, where kidnapping frequently disguised a subversive longing to escape the settlements and the dulled pieties of civilization, convent narratives depicted escapes not so much from convents as from the tyranny (or the absence) of a parental roof. To enter the Catholic prison was to achieve a vitalizing sense of contested selfhood, but one that was conspicuously independent of God.

Nonetheless, these feminine (but often male-authored) revelations of affliction and eventual escape confirmed the "providential" lessons of those colonial predecessors who discovered the satanic within the popish denizens of the wilderness; so these nineteenth-century "maidens" claimed to have met savagery behind the religious guise of priest and nun. But the manifest concern with spiritual enlightenment in seventeenth- and eighteenth-century Indian captivity narratives that powerfully linked captivity to biblical revelation, imprisonment to spiritual freedom, was now submerged by murkier connections between captivity and exposé, imprisonment and disillusion. By the mid-nineteenth century, the captivity genre, whether exposing frontier savagery or urban convents, dedicated itself to revealing the corrupt and cunning ways of man in his relations to the defenseless, rather than the mysterious ways of Jehovah. Indicative of a profound shift in America's understanding of the relationship between suffering and knowledge (and of the relation between the sexes), the discovery of the sinner inside the confessor, of the void inside the prison, figured at the center of both popular and American Renaissance fictions.

If often explicit in the fiction of major nineteenth-century authors, the breakdown of metaphysical certainty remained largely implicit in popular anti-Catholic fiction, which absorbed the loss of religious faith and the attendant problems of identity and vocation into the drama of Protestant male interest in female incarceration, a middle-class fiction at once self-righteous and erotic. Any analysis of Rome's intentionally deceptive surfaces was bound to fail, reduced to the status of perennial suspicion. Worse yet, so powerful and subtle was Romanism's duplicity that to read it was to risk believing it. "This semblance of the true faith," wrote one observer, "which her 'articles of religion' exhibit, while united to other articles which are utterly at variance with the former, is the secret of her power and influence, since it serves to clothe error in the habiliments of truth."[11] Like Catholic theology and ceremonies themselves, the Catholic clergy disguised their true nature behind an alluring holiness. The distinctive robes of the priesthood summoned up images of post-Edenic secrecy and malice; one alarmist description from *Priestcraft Exposed,* a semimonthly journal published in 1834, portrayed priests as "covering their hypocrisy with the cloak of *religion,* and with more than the serpent's guile, worming themselves into the confidence and affections of their unsuspecting victims."[12] Indeed, the celibate priest circulating through civilian spaces of the marketplace and the home enjoyed a perplexing masculine mobility that made him both captive and exiled. "The situation of the priest *alone,* yet not alone," mused one author, "free and not free, in the midst of a world in discord with him, reminds us of that of a man condemned to the cellular treatment, who should carry his cell about with him. Nothing would be more likely to make him mad."[13]

The suspicions aroused by this variously deceptive Catholic surface register the social anxieties provoked by the new mobility, heterogeneity, and competitiveness of the antebellum decades. How was one to determine another's origins, motivations, and objectives? Melville's portrait of a confidence man at work in the turbulent steamboat world of the *Fidèle* delights in exposing the middle-class American as virtually predestined to imposture, made vulnerable by his obtuse faith in the supposedly purified commercial transactions of the New World. Similarly, the Jesuit, prowling everywhere, is not only the figure of the foreign conspirator working to convert America's "heart" but also the mobile American male himself, suspicious of neighbors whom he no longer knows and calculating in his social interraction. Persistent evangelical conviction of the depravity of the soul enhanced this dread of the Catholic imposter and his "prisons of confiding girls"; even the discerning self-control developed in the protective privacy of the family could fall victim. John Claudius Pitrat's *Paul and Julia; or, The Political Mysteries, Hypocrisy, and Cruelty of the Leaders of the Church of Rome* (1855) was one among scores of novels opposing familial ties and romantic affection to the seductions of the church; when the young monk finally discovers the corruption of his father confessor, he returns home to find his beloved dead and himself dies on her grave.[14]

Concern over the potential duplicity of strangers increased suspicions that priests intrigued for control of the Protestant family. Proffering the inviting interiors of convent and confessional, priests lured young women from their sheltered domesticity to even more privatized spaces, where their spiritual and sexual purity could be violated—a violation that resulted either in the pitiable death of the Protestant victim or her conversion to Catholic licentiousness, responses conventional to novels of seduction, religious or not. As M. G. Lewis's famous novel *The Monk* (1796) explained, the priests' abuse of women emanated from their vows of celibacy, for these vows repressed their sexual energies to the point of madness. Formerly Madrid's holiest monk, Lewis's sexually wild protagonist, Ambrosio, typifies the perils of a masculine sanctity itself conceived of as an instance of excessively willful control. Understood as an illicit suppression of the natural self (and specifically its reproductive obligations), continence is the original violent action that needs but a slight catalyst to erupt into its opposite. Protestant or Deist masculine outsiders figure in Lewis's (and other Gothic) narratives as curious bystanders, whose inability to interrupt this sexual traffic from the daylight world to the dark monastic interior both aggrandizes monastic power and, as important, suppresses the power of the father in civil society. Thus the evasion of secular patriarchy dramatized in the monastic landscape of male rampage and female violation images a catastrophic and childish heterosexuality whose safe containment in castle or monastery permits its narrative publication.

For Jacksonian Americans fashioning the new middle-class domesticity, the monastery, like the communitarian ideals of such reform movements as Brook Farm, rivaled the domestic project. The capture of virgins and their rape inside convent walls, their psychological subjection to tyrannical abbess and lecherous father confessor, and the titillating exposure of these indignities for middle-class readers refashioned the seclusion of women inside the domestic sphere of civil society as liberty, their subordination to patriarchial authority as voluntary, their sexual repression as "purity."[15] The attack on convents in Jacksonian and antebellum America intricately voiced Protestant perplexities over the ongoing construction of the "cult of domesticity." Whether because of its ardent female mystics, its veneration of Mary, its convents, or its traditional negative image as the Whore of Babylon, Roman Catholicism advertised a constellation of alternative femininities conspicuously excluded by antebellum theoreticians of the family who constructed, instead, a region of sentiment that, though run by women, was overseen by husbandly authority. Catholic sentimentality was inferior to the rationality of this Protestant sentiment—more bodily, ardent, and regressive. An article in *The Christian Parlor Book,* "John Knox and Mary,

Queen of Scots," sets an unreasoning Catholic womanhood against the masculine logic of Protestantism as the narrator imagines a weepy Queen Mary coolly surveyed by the emotionally contained church reformer. In case the political dimensions of this sexual and religious hierarchy remain unclear, the author reminds readers "that the interests of freedom and Protestant Christianity are on one side reaching through ages and extending to nations, and on the other, [is] one frail heart stained with crime, and one fair face bathed in tears."[16]

Such regret over the vanquishing of one frail woman in the name of Protestant imperialism enabled parallel processes of masculine mystification of the bodily interiors of Catholicism and women, mirrored structures of exterior allure and recessed corruption. Cathedrals architecturally represented this masculine Protestant configuration, for their architectural splendors held the dark confessional and its sexual secrets. The historian Jules Michelet's *Le Prêtre, La Femme, La Famille* (1845), a book quickly translated and distributed in America, provides a remarkable tour of this eroticized architecture whose salacious moments reside in the historian's anticlerical imaginings of intimacy:

> Delightful hour of tumultuous, but tender sensations! (Why does the heart palpitate so strongly here?) How dark the church becomes! Yet it is not late. The great rose-window over the portal glitters with the setting sun. But it is quite another thing in the choir; dark shadows envelope it, and beyond is obscurity. One thing astounds and almost frightens us, however far we may be, which is the mysterious old painted glass, at the farthest end of the church, on which the design is no longer distinguishable, twinkling in the shade, like an illegible magic scroll of unknown characters. The chapel is not less dark on that account; you can no longer discern the ornaments and delicate moulding entwined in the vaulted roof; the shadow deepening blends and confounds the outlines. But, as if this chapel were not yet dark enough, it contains, in a retired corner, a narrow recess of dark oak, where that man, all emotion, and that trembling woman, so close to each other, are whispering together about the love of God.[17]

Michelet's architectonics of a verbal intimacy that simulates, even transcends, the pleasures of sex is a memorable example of anticlerical eroticism that reveals how well known Catholicism, the supposed "unknown," is. There is nothing unpredictable about Michelet's tour through an interior made dim by the "illegible magic" of stained glass; as he proceeds, not down the nave to the altar but, purposeful in his deviance, over to a "retired corner," Michelet guides the reader to the inner scandal of Catholicism: intimate conversation between the sexes about God. The disgrace is not only that such conversation occurs, and that it does so privately, but also that it avoids sexual intercourse as the grounds for its exchange: the insistence of anti-Catholic discourse on the "seduction" of confessional and convent always includes, in addition to a theatrics of sexual violation (or intimacy), this peril of unsupervised conversation between the sexes. Anti-Catholic writings move the implicitly Protestant tourist-reader from the church and confessional to the convent, often figured as covertly attached by hidden corridors to the church—a geography of subversive intimacy in which Catholic masculinity commandeers Protestant femininity in a recurrent drama of illicit sexuality and religious conversion. As one "escaped" American nun confessed of her vertiginous experience with this priestly power: "As the fluttering and terrified, but irresistibly attracted bird, flies in gradually lessening circles, around the venomous snake, as it lies coiled in its serpentine folds, so did I fly from, yet return to, the witchery of Romanism."[18]

Notions about the female heart further structure the anticlericalism of Michelet's *Le Prêtre, La Femme, La Famille.* The heart resides in the family, itself a precarious sanctuary from the stress of the capitalist world; Catholicism threatens to invade both. "The question is about our family," Michelet declares in his opening sentence, "that sacred asylum in which we all desire to seek the repose of the heart, when our endeavors have proved fruitless, and our illusions are no more" (xli).[19] If Orestes Brownson was accurate in labeling Michelet's volume "a compound of ignorance, infidel malice, prurient fancy, and maudlin sentiment,"[20] that volume nonetheless throws revealing light on Protestant fears of captivity by suggesting that their real animus was the affective separation demanded by the new bourgeois economic order, not any incarceration threatened by the Catholic church. Michelet's anticlerical tirade disguises a convoluted critique of the bourgeois world, whose pressures leave one open to priestly intrigue and seduction. This world isolates a woman from her husband (the preoccupied businessman) and separates her from her child (sent away for early schooling); she soon falls victim to ennui and then, inevitably, becomes the prey of the priest, who is the wife's counterpart in the modernizing order, a creature with no discernible work to perform yet free from economic pressure.

In the suffering and envy of his own perverse celibacy, the priest intrigues to rob the husband of control over his wife by gaining complete spiritual dominion over her. Failing this (as he will since, according to Michelet, a part of the soul always eludes capture), he consoles himself with the seduction of her body. Michelet's text culminates in a melodramatic analysis of the attraction between women and Catholicism, a bond derived from the passional domain of female biology that renders the need for seduction obsolete. Michelet's own heartfelt narrative establishes an interlocking exchange of influences between the church's cult of the Sacred Heart, the sentimental-erotic bond between a woman and her confessor, and the female body itself.

> The heart!—that word has always been powerful; the heart, being the organ of the affections, expresses them in its own manner, swollen and heaving with sighs. The life of the heart, strong and confused, comprehends and mingles every kind of love. Such a sentence is wonderfully adapted to language which is meant to have a double meaning.
>
> And who will understand it best?—Women:—with them the life of the heart is everything. This organ, being the passage of the blood, and strongly influenced by the revolutions of the blood, is not less predominant in woman than her very sex. (138)

Like Donald Grant Mitchell's Ik Marvel of *Reveries of a Bachelor; or, A Book of the Heart* (1850) or Hawthorne's Coverdale of *The Blithedale Romance* (1852), Michelet tracks the minute details of this "life of the heart," of sexual surrender—a simultaneous unveiling of Catholicism and of women in their bourgeois households. In his conspiratorial erotics, the woman's bloody "sacred" heart lies subversively inside the sentimental heart. Although American Catholics subscribed to much contemporary sentimentalism, writing many novels of marriage and conversion expressly linked to the sentimental heart, hostile Protestants nevertheless persisted in excluding them: Catholics belonged in Gothic dungeons, not domestic parlors, their hearts bloody, not pure. As isolate voyeur of woman's confused interior (which can yet decipher language of "double meaning"), Michelet fashions his own authorial intimacy with his readers. American women could speak in these sexualized intimacies as well, artfully blending the perspectives of victim and voyeur as they unfolded their captivity in the confessional for Protestant readers. In a passage even more redolent of Aztec sacrifice than of the French bourgeois bloody heart, one American former nun describes "confession" as a sacrificial machine that grips its victim in a desired fixity while animating Catholicism into a galvanized "figure":

> Superficial observers ascribe the influence she [the church] exerts to the charm of her ostentatious ceremonies and her imposing ritual; to the theatrical display and sensual appeal of her worship. These are indeed the agencies that at first *attract*, but it is the revealments of the confessional that *retain*. These are the bands of flowers thrown around the youthful victim to draw her to the altar; but the ordinance of confession is the sharp hook of steel that grapples her till the sacrifice be accomplished. The robes, the crucifix, the pictures, the incense, the mass, the invocation of saints, the thousand and one enchanting and gorgeous rites, make up, indeed, an attractive image, apparently possessed of vitality and vigor; but confession, as it were, completes the galvanic circle that keeps the form erect and active. Detach this, and the figure falls, a pale, corrupting corpse, to the ground.[21]

If confession could grapple someone with a hook, it was because the spirit was increasingly identified with the body, in part because of liberal Protestant efforts to dispel the Calvinist heritage of depravity (which exaggerated the distance between spirit and flesh), in part because of the middle-class cult of domesticity that endowed the persons and objects of the home with an affectional aura that bordered on the sacred. These efforts to familiarize and feminize the Deity were prevented from becoming eroticized by the expulsion of such bodily excesses onto Catholic spirituality. If, as the nativist Nicholas Murray explained to the Roman Catholic chief justice Roger Taney in one of his famous letters, "like sin and death, confession and seduction follow each other in Rome,"[22] it was because Catholic spirituality was becoming powerfully eroticized by the "feminization" of Victorian Protestantism.

The insistent identification of spirit and body is prominent in much of this sentimental writing, whether in more didactic examples, like Susanna Rowson's best-selling *Charlotte Temple* (1791), or in a riotous version like George Lippard's *Monks of Monk Hall* (1844). In countless novels of sentiment, be they feminized or masculinized, genteel or titillating, heightened emotion assumes the dominance of a corporealized, finally eroticized, character in its own right. Like the body they have replaced, the feelings of sentimental characters exist in a state of excited vulnerability, are roused and soothed, violated and sometimes redeemed. Conversely, the female body is etherealized until, like Hilda of Hawthorne's *Marble Faun* (1860), it offers itself as sentimental surrogate for the Crucifixion and ascension of Christ. There are few better icons of this capacity of the nineteenth-century sentimental body to deny itself by appeal to its affective religious power than Hiram Powers's *Greek Slave* (1843); as Powers explained of his famous sculpture of the nude, bound girl, "It is not her person but her spirit that stands exposed."[23] Powers's Swedenborgian faith in the consubstantiality of the divine and the natural enabled him to confidently deny any suggestion of prurience; in addition, his visionary piety accorded well with the sentimentalism of more theologically mainstream middle-class Protestants intent on affiliating the female body to the soul by means of sentiment. If an intended conclusion to this domestic affective logic was the sexualization of Catholic piety, an unintended one was the antebellum Protestant "heart's" usurpation of its own soul as that heart became the site not only for romantic but also for spiritual union, for metaphysical aspiration as well as erotic desire. Because confession, according to anti-Catholic fictions, involved disclosing the repressed contents of the heart of bewitched Protestant maidens, Protestants saw it as tantamount to illicit sexual intercourse. "How terrible, my dear sister," explained a convent escapee to women still outside the celibate enclosure of the convent, "is the power of these men, who pry into the most secret recesses of our hearts."[24]

Thus the encounter between celibate priest and young woman in the hidden interior of the confessional was attacked as an unavoidable occasion for seduction and sexual captivity because unsupervised talking, as suggested in Michelet's depiction, was itself seen as a surrogate sexual act. As "Rosamond" declared in her widely read captivity narrative of priestly rape and concubinage in Cuba: "Filthy communication is inseparable from the Confessional."[25] The inquiries of the confessor signaled the sacrilegious invasion of language into the unspeakable region of sex. Masculine and feminine hearts were alike vulnerable to these sexual depredations of verbal intimacy: "There is a Holy of Holies in every man's heart which no stranger has a right to penetrate," declared an Episcopalian minister. "They are things secret and sacred—which the heart reserves to itself and to God."[26] Joseph Berg's *Great Apostacy, Identical with Papal Rome; or, An Exposition of the Mystery of Iniquity, and the Marks and Doom of Antichrist* (1842) focused even more directly on the connection between speech and sexuality. "God is a God of decency and order," Berg intoned, "and he never would authorize a sinful man to catechise his fellow creature on subjects concerning which nature and conscience declare that it is a shame even to speak."[27] Nativist criticism of the salacious capacity of discourse to beguile and inflame an otherwise modest woman virtually identified confessional booth and female body and played an important part in the developing cross-denominational socialization of woman into the "pure." To one writer, the confessional was the "key-hole" into the bedroom, the female penitent figuring as a capacious house within the home, both maternally vast and consolatory. The excluded husband "is allowed to rest his head on the cold marble of the outdoor steps; but the confessor triumphantly walks into the mysterious starry rooms, examines at leisure their numberless and unspeakable wonders; and, alone, he is allowed to rest his head on the soft pillows of the unbounded confidence, respect, and love of the wife."[28]

This Protestant drama of confessional intrusion into the sacred enclosures of the heart provided the sentimental structure for antebellum convent captivity narratives. Even the most ephemeral nativist fiction betrayed a self-conscious control of these issues, playing off one interior against the other, the convent against the home, the Catholic bloody heart against the Protestant purified one. In Charles Frothingham's *Haunted Convent* (1854), for example, a politician consents to send his daughter, Agnes, to a Montreal convent in exchange for the Catholic vote. For his part, the priest demonstrates the conventional willingness to capture each and every Protestant maiden, the prize apparently well worth the rigging of a state election. Bidding farewell to her lover, Justin Peoples (a hardy young democrat who will later rescue her), Agnes describes her impending convent incarceration with revealing coyness. "The Bleeding Heart! What a funny name. It is emblematic of yours after my departure, I suppose."[29]

Vehement objections to these "prisons of confiding girls" (all nineteenth-century American nuns adhered to the rule of enclosure) derived from twinned anxieties of middle-class masculinity: an envious hostility toward the unbridled sexuality allegedly enjoyed by the priest, who, free from the burden of economic competition and family responsibility, circulated like a vagrant pleasure principle through the minds of Protestant clergy, workers, and professionals and a competitive attack on a rival form of masculine authority, which, in its theological and often ethnic difference, formed part of a dangerous public space that encroached on the privacy of the family. Convent interiors, then, registered the tensions of Protestant familial interiors while thwarting domesticity's hegemonic claims. As a subversive re-formation of the self's relation to family and the family's position in society, convents also challenged middle-class Protestant boundaries between public and private. Too intimate, too collective, too formalized, convent communities departed from republican ideals of neighborly individualism. Or, as one Unitarian essayist explained, they were simply antibiblical, for the New Testament was "saturated" with the "social feeling."[30] Seclusion, celibacy, and collective living all violated this carefully poised sociality. To join a convent was to escape into an indolent space, unregulated by the demands of reproduction or labor, "to fly from the scene of trial," declared a former nun, "and to abandon the relations of our providential position, and to waste, in a condition of passivity and mental vacuity, the precious moments of probation."[31] Such images of female wastage were paralleled by the masculine surplus of monasticism, because of whose evils, according to an antebellum essayist, "the deserts of the mountains, the bowels of the earth resounded with the groans of a thousand victims, who thought they were pleasing God by abjuring his gifts."[32]

This rhetoric of wastage and live entombment, the cloistral existence nothing less than a "burying [of] the heart in a living sepulchre,"[33] far outweighed romanticized images of monastic life. During the antebellum period, the medieval revival (a movement that was Protestant in origin and aimed at Protestants), was still largely confined to England, where such figures as William Cobbett and Thomas Carlyle fashioned from medievalism a sentimental, aristocratic counter to the dislocations of industrialism. If Carlyle's portrait of Abbot Samson argued for the utopian potential of medievalism, it had little such impact in antebellum America, which had yet to experience the profound class dislocations of industrialization and which had little affection for the frank elitism of the British medieval revival. The Episcopalian Reverend Field's subdued approval of the monastery typified that of the few Americans who saw anything to favor in the cloister. "Another winning feature of the Catholic Church," muses Field, "is *the repose* which its numerous institutions offer to the weary—the broken heart."[34] If repose was a scarce commodity in the entrepreneurial Northeast—where it was associated with the potentially subversive artistic productivity of such creative "loungers" as Walt Whitman—it also bordered on the problematic specter of exhaustion and defeat. The convent's supposed invitation to leisure was typically represented in contradictory images of sexual license and mindless obedience, of a self both rampaging and passive that in both guises rejected republican and Protestant ideologies of self-government and industriousness.[35] Cloistered nuns dramatically contrasted to other American middle-class women, who, as European travelers frequently observed, enjoyed a notable physical freedom and masculine deference, prerogatives dependent on their exclusion from remunerative labor. "This deference [to women] does great honor to the intelligence of the Americans," wrote one European tourist, "who have realized in the midst of the pêle-mêle of democratic life, that woman ought to be placed above the general level; and yet nothing in this affects the idea of equality, since she remains a stranger to the struggles of active life."[36] Inverting this structure, the cloister physically curtailed women while hiding them from the observation of Protestant men.

The Roman (and the Anglican) church had legendarily schemed against the Protestant family as the locus of an autonomous, potentially heretical, piety. Roman Catholics, having betrayed their own domestic allegiances by pledging filial obedience to their father in Rome and to their priest in the confessional while urging their daughters to lives of cloistered chastity rather than marriage and motherhood, then sought to disrupt the naturalized structures of Protestant family life and replace them with the mazelike structures of priestly hierarchy, confessional, and conventual living. Antebellum domesticity's sacralization of the family understood itself as carrying forward the traditions of early reform. John Foxe's *Actes and Monuments* (1563) glorified the sanctity of lay piety, upholding the family as central to the creation of the "priesthood of all believers," by depicting the martyrs in the context of their families.[37]

The *Actes and Monuments of Martyrs,* while celebrating the religious heroism of the Marian martyrs, presented powerful portraits of the martyr family that influenced generations of dissenters and lay behind the domestic preoccupations of antebellum nativist fiction. Foxe's Protestant martyrology situated religious heroism within a newly articulated domestic piety, one practiced at the heart, not the altar, and organized along new lines of unmediated obedience to Christ, the natural family, and the national government. Throughout, Foxe struggles against the disturbing implication that Henry VIII's own antidomesticity has triggered the horrible persecutions; as Protestant ideologue, Foxe could only choose to assert a precarious distinction between the false family and the genuine. Henry's first wife and the pope belong to the first category. Foxe strained to formulate Henry's first divorce: "Thus the king being divorced from his brother's wife, married this gracious lady, making a happy change for us, being divorced from the princess and also from the Pope, both at one time" (113).

To curtail the troublesome implications of Henry VIII's divorces, Foxe mythologized Catholicism into a virtual demon of antidomesticity, accusing the pope's evil family of subverting the civil precincts of lay piety. This religious melodrama is central to eighteenth- and nineteenth-century novels of seduction that decried the intriguing seducer as well as to novels of sentiment that celebrated Protestant domesticity. Thus Foxe portrays a murderous Catholic husband carrying his heretic wife to the

Fig. 5. Martyred Women, from the 1583 edition of John Foxe's *Actes and Monuments* (1563). Courtesy, The Bancroft Library, University of California, Berkeley.

"bloody bishop" (400) and certain death while a Catholic mother spurns her heretic son in a callous identification with the state: "Faggots I have to burn thee: more thou gettest not at my hands" (373). The Protestant victim family achieves its apotheosis in Foxe's description of the martyrdom of the pregnant Perrotine, whose child bursts from her burning womb only to be thrown back into the flames (Fig. 5). To Foxe, the episode epitomized the "Herodian cruelty of this graceless generation of Catholic tormentors" (380). Catholic iniquity could reach no further than the sacred interior of the womb.

In contrast to Rome's sadistic attacks on the family, Foxe repeatedly linked Protestant domesticity to the divine—the natural and heavenly fathers leagued against the false political and spiritual fatherhood of the Catholic priesthood. The family unit must be celebrated as autonomous (from Rome) but dependent (on Christ), a precarious status that informs the story of the nineteen-year-old martyr William Hunter, whose death provides a "singular spectacle, not only of marvelous fortitude in the party so young, but also in his parents, to behold nature in them striving with religion" (244). William's parents voluntarily participate in the transfiguration of domestic into saintly anguish, the mother's gracious suppression of her maternal emotion implicating parents in the deaths of their children; together, the stake of martyrdom and the affectional bonds of the earthly family bind the martyr against the temptations of Rome's false family. Just prior to his execution, young William revealingly dreams that he "met his father as he went to the stake, and that there was a priest at the stake who went about to have him recant, to whom he cried 'Away, false prophet!'" (248). True to his dream, William meets the opposing figures of father and priest en route to the stake and performs his rehearsed repudiation of the corporate for the nuclear family, confirming his allegiance to his natural and heavenly fathers by offering himself as a burnt sacrifice from the one to the other.

The new conceptions of the proper exercise of parental authority that influenced the American colonial rejection of English royal authority strengthened this opposition between the affectional intimacies of Protestant domesticity and the coercive familial structures of monarchy and papacy. American revolutionary rhetoric, in attacking the parental injustices of George III, struggled to reassert the legitimacy of a properly benevolent patriarchal authority in the new nation, a reassertion that benefited from the continued stigmatizing of monarchism and popery.[38] One American immigrant nun wrote to her French superior of American hostility to nuns: "Nothing is more odious in America than the office of superior, for from it flow dependence and submission, virtues which the Americans do not recognize. To bear the name of superior in the United States of America is to acquire the inalienable right to the public hatred, contempt, and so forth."[39] She might also have added that the specter of female authority particularly disturbed many antebellum Protestants, influenced by such phobic portraits of powerful females as Jules Michelet's of the mother superior, "who, more absolute than the most absolute tyrant, uses the rage of her badly-cured passions to torment her unfortunate, defenceless sisters."[40] Nativist fiction assured Americans that the benign constraints of patriarchy would prevent the outbreak of such womanly Old World absolutism.

Against these images of an aristocratic (and in the convent, administrative) womanly power, the antebellum family claimed an informal metaphysical structure, free, like liberal Protestantism's anti-Calvinism, of undue dogmatism or coercion, organized instead by expanding practices of affectional tutelage. Maternal authority, credited by Catharine Beecher and Harriet Beecher Stowe with redemptive spiritual and (indirectly) political power, operated through promptings, not commands, its authority indicated precisely by its invisibility. Protestant maternal power was discreet, not in being hidden from the eye of the community, like the power of the mother superior, but in being hidden from the mother herself.[41]

Affectional family religion established itself not only in the advice literature and novels of the domestic movement but also in the related discourse of antipopery. At the base of Edward Beecher's *Papal Conspiracy Exposed, and Protestantism Defended in the Light of Reason, History, and Scripture* (1855) lies an evangelical, sentimental theology of marriage and domesticity in which Protestant familial love appears in its historical posture of provocative vulnerability to the antidomestic evils of Catholicism, calamities generated by the original sin of celibacy. The family, Beecher explains, is "a little model of the universal system under God and the church; and the love on which it is based is an emblem of the highest love of the universe—even that which exists between God and the redeemed."[42] Bitterly lampooned in Melville's *Pierre* (1852), this domestic metaphysic nonetheless displayed enormous commercial power, generating a best-selling women's fiction that shaped the antebellum literary marketplace—a fiction of domestic interiors whose psychic and bodily asceticisms balanced the lavish expansion and mobilization of female sentiment with women's physical circumscription.

The description of Protestant domesticity in the 1850 best-seller Susan Warner's *Wide, Wide World* voices this unremitting but affectionate coercion of emotion into sentiment, a transaction whose psychic violence, perhaps because of its adherence to the mandates of Protestant invisibility, remained largely unapparent to its readers. Contemporary reviewers praised novels like Warner's for the "quiet" they afforded, such stories of the hearth providing a surrogate contemplative retreat for a culture strenuously opposed to monasticism.[43]

Many writers besides Edward Beecher seemed oblivious to Christ's warning about excessive family attachment in their celebration of domesticity. Mitchell's best-selling *Reveries of a Bachelor,* for example, offered readers sequential fantasies of wife worship that do not guide family members to the "highest love" so much as inspire their spiritual hunger in order to satiate it with domestic "reveries." Mitchell's lonely bachelor Ik Marvel peers (like the voyeur priest of nativist fiction) from his hearth into "all the phases of married life" (viii), imagining home and the "presence" of a wife with a prayerful ardor that coyly transgresses into idolatry: "The *Lares* of your worship are there; the altar of your confidence is there; the end of your worldly faith is there; and adorning it all, and sending your blood in passionate flow, is the ecstasy of the conviction that *there* at least you are beloved."[44] Mitchell's masculine surrender to the sacred middle-class woman and his picture of the male recovery of an unconditional love, offer escape from the challenges of the marketplace that are just as frankly embraced by the commercial appeal of such reclusive sentiment. That the text's worshipful fantasies are conjured by a bachelor, a dreamer who typically concludes his individual reveries by mourning the often violent destruction of his imagined women, children, and domestic interiors—a venting of iconoclastic wrath on these household gods that disguises male rage as sentimental grief—reveals the fury locked within the idolatrous imaginings of Protestant domesticity.[45] When Mitchell's readers objected to the obvious fictionality (but not the violence) of Ik Marvel's reveries, the author appealed to the higher justification of sentiment. "What matters it, pray, if literally there was no wife, and no dead child, and no coffin in the house? Is not feeling, feeling, and heart, heart?" (43). Mitchell's juxtaposition of coffin, house, and heart points not only to the claustrophobic violence of domesticity but also to its generative enclosures of sentiment. Stories of convent captivity are deeply engaged with the emancipation of such a closed selfhood, a release paradoxically imaged as the seduction, violation, and ruin of the Protestant heart.

Against these rival forms of piety created by the Protestant defense of sacred domesticity, antebellum Catholics ventured to defend the monastic system as completing, rather than conspiring against, the family. Explained one writer for a Catholic journal, the *Metropolitan,* the cloister did not usurp the heart so much as perfect it, at least in places other than antebellum America: "In Catholic times, the tendency of the family was towards perfection: from a natural it passed to a spiritual condition, and from the fireside it extended to the cloister."[46] Protestants persisted, however, in contesting precisely this terrain between fireside and convent.

James Jackson Jarves, a prominent art collector of the 1850s, was typical in responding to the sight of Italian nuns by asserting the superior (uncostumed) sanctity of Protestant motherhood: "Nor do our sisters of charity wear other garb than that in which they so faithfully perform their duties as Christian mothers," he declared in his aptly entitled travel book, *Italian Sights and Papal Principles Seen through American Spectacles* (1856).[47] That such defenses of the family borrowed from Catholic terminology only underscores the perplexing nature of a rivalry in which the Protestant annexation of the rival discourse served to register distance from it. Thus a reviewer of the British medievalist Kenelm Digby's *Mores Catholici* (1844) speaks in the language of canonization to chastise the church's apparent indifference to matrimony and motherhood: "A faithful mother is most truly sainted by revering children, and next to her claim to canonization comes that of . . . a wise teacher, or an humble village priest. Rome has forgotten her truest saints."[48] Such discursive borrowings enhanced the competition between two ideologies of the family while folding into it Protestant anxieties about exclusion from the "flock." Thus the ceremony of taking the veil compared unfavorably to the saintly practices of the unmarried Protestant woman, according to an 1858 article in *Harper's*, "The Ladies of the Sacred Heart."[49] Like the bachelor dreamer of Mitchell's *Reveries,* the author of this article enjoys his position on the threshold of imagined feminine interiors; voyeuristically poised between cathedral and home, he elaborates the differences between these forms of female enclosure. From the dark chapel where he witnesses the taking of the veil, he moves with relief to the sunlit world of connubial bliss enjoyed by his friends.

As a bachelor, he is notably preoccupied, not with his own, but with female celibacy, for once inside the sunny home, he focuses on the husband's older unmarried sister, whom he dubs the "Protestant lay Sister of Mercy" (206). While the nun proper has just "sacrificed" herself to a false familial vision, her Protestant counterpart enjoys the fruits of both earthly and heavenly households, "the one a life of gloom and sterility, in fancied subservience to a stern Diety to be propitiated by penances and mortifications; the other, a cheerful, loving, filial service, rendered to a benign Father" (206). This critique of convent life establishes parallel oppositions between slavery and service on the one hand, sterility and fertility on the other, the image of Catholic enslavement heightened by corresponding notions of a sexual dysfunction that avoids not only procreation but its possibility. In a tellingly biological application of the parable of the vineyard, he pities the young woman, who in assuming the veil has strayed from the "appointed vineyard" and gone "into a desert where there is neither spring nor summer, seed-time nor harvest" (205). Such vagrancy from the womanly potential of her vineyard collapses the biblical parable's injunction to labor for the Lord into the injunction to do so for the family, a labor opposed by the spiritual and reproductive errancy of the nun.

While consistently stigmatized, the figure of the nun still whispered the attraction of emancipation. Another *Harper's* essay, "Margaret—the Lay Sister" inverts the terms of the debate to offer a penetrating (if finally undermined) critique of marriage.[50] Twice refusing the narrator's marriage proposal, the heroine Margaret offers the following indictment of domesticity: "The thousand harsh words, reproving looks, recriminations and petty irritations, that form the staple of much domestic society, would either kill or craze me" (810). Ironically, this self-described Protestant "nun" depicts herself to her baffled but admiring suitor in the heroic terms of Emersonian self-reliance. Disdainfully saluting her transcendentalist, quasi-Catholic, feminine insurrection, the rejected suitor concludes that "the nun yet lives outside the cloister to

> "Show us how divine a thing
> A woman may be made"
> —even a single woman!
> (813)

The figure of Margaret dodging the tyrannies of "woman's sphere" under the rhetorical guise of the self-reliant nun offers covert, if ambivalent, validation of female separation from domesticity; the attraction of such imagery for Protestant men and women was that it suggested a flight from privacy that studiously avoided disturbing the boundary between household and marketplace. American Catholics were naturally less reluctant to criticize the confinement of Protestant womanhood in her separate domestic sphere. In 1835, Bishop John England favorably compared the voluntary cloistered life to the settled coercion of marriage. Before an audience of more than seven hundred curious onlookers, the bishop addressed a young woman about to join the Ursuline order. To those who saw the monastic life simply as incarceration, England rhetorically inquired: "Have they no compassion for those who, forced by a variety of authorities or powers, are compelled, in contracting marriage, to sacrifice their own long-cherished and reasonable preferences to the caprice or to the calculations of another?"[51]

SEVEN

Two "Escaped Nuns"
Rebecca Reed and Maria Monk

Rebecca Reed's *Six Months in a Convent* (1835) and Maria Monk's notorious best-seller *Awful Disclosures of the Hotel Dieu Nunnery* (1836) provide the two most significant examples of nineteenth-century American anticonvent literature. Both texts offer fascinating examples of a popular historiography that contrasts intriguingly to the elite historiography of William Prescott and Francis Parkman. As we have seen, both Brahmin historians made plausible their working assumption of America's Protestant origins by insisting on the analogy and finally identity of Indian "idolatry" and Catholic "papadolatry," inscribing the corruptions of Old World (principally Italian) Catholicism on little understood Amerindian cultures. Thus Prescott viewed the Aztecs and Parkman the Hurons and Jesuit missionaries through a lens of racial and religious difference that, at least within the discursive terrain of their histories, functioned to construct and reveal the American "past." That "savages" were not (except in French and Spanish territories) really Catholics and Catholic conquistadores or missionaries not really "savages" only permitted a more successful functioning of the ideological resemblance between them.

A similar dynamic, simultaneously privileging European origin and repudiating its Old World impurities, characterized antebellum Protestant clerical discourse about America. That process of purification depended, as we have seen, on importing and depositing the "sediment of misrepresentation" onto New World terrain and tribal cultures. Only thus could Protestant America define itself as a "pure fountain" and maintain its alleged ethnic superiority to Europe. A key means for doing so, as Prescott's and Parkman's histories show, was through the rhetorical appropriation of "Catholicism"—for as the primary index of

European corruption, the "foreign faith" could be transplanted to native cultures, thus permitting white American Protestants to declare themselves the authentic "natives" by divorcing themselves one more time from popery. In the process, these white American Protestants could legitimate their subordination of Indian cultures *and* renew their racial connection to English and Continental culture, now conceived of as "white" rather than as "Catholic."

Such elite historiographical and clerical struggles with the issues of racial and theological difference, encoded in the strategic antinomy of "past" and "present," can illuminate our understanding of popular historiography's account of Protestantism's American struggles. Specifically, the preoccupation with purity enables us to decipher history that was written as "event," enacted by working- and middle-class people who were by no means historians but who were very much concerned with the historiographic issue of how to correct America's potentially or actually impure development from its vaunted pure origin.

The event I focus on and interpret as a popular historical text dedicated to reasserting an origin that promises the achievement, rather than the loss, of an artisanal Protestant republicanism is the notorious mob attack and burning of the Ursuline convent outside Boston in 1834. Arguably the most important political event in Massachusetts prior to the agitation surrounding the passage of the 1850 Fugitive Slave Law, the Ursuline convent riot signaled the renewal of anti-Catholicism and provided a model for escalating popular demonstrations against hated popery and what were called its priests' prisons. One rioter claimed of the convent, according to a witness at the ensuing trial, "that the institution was a bad one; that the nuns were kept there for a bad purpose; for a certain purpose. He said bishops and priests pretended to live without wives, but that the nuns were kept to supply the deficiency in this particular. He said this in vulgar language."[1] The riot (and the trials that followed) received indignant national attention because of the violence of the working-class mob, composed largely of Scots-Presbyterian bricklayers. For a culture occupied with the supposed perils of Roman Catholicism, the convent burning, occurring at the time of an increasingly profitable Protestant evangelism spurred by a New England religious revival in the winter of 1833, enacted Protestant hostility toward the "foreign faith," exposing working-class Protestant prejudice and its persecutorial energies.[2] The riot and trials enabled Protestants of various social classes to vent their anger against Romanism and also to distance themselves from the "mob." The violence led many observers to fear that Jacksonian democracy could not contain working-class uprisings, much less enjoin necessary discipline on the American male. "It will be in-scribed in our history," declared the attorney general at the trial of one of the ringleaders, "that here, at least the age of chivalry is gone. The mob put down everything and every body."[3]

When a Protestant Bostonian later sought an audience with Pope Gregory XVI, the pope asked him, much to his humiliation, "Was it you who burned my convent?"[4] The question—undeniably parental in its reproachful tone—disturbed not only that New England tourist but many other educated observers as well. What motivated the mob vio-lence, and who was responsible? To the English diarist Frederick Mar-ryat, the convent burning presented Americans another opportunity for self-mystification, not self-examination—a mystification born from nar-rativizing the event as an allegorical, even Edenic, confrontation between secrecy and curiosity:

> The Americans are excessively curious, especially the mob: they cannot bear anything like a secret—that's *unconstitutional*. It may be remembered, that the Catholic convent near Boston, which had existed for many years, was attacked by the mob and pulled down. I was enquiring into the cause of this outrage in a country where all forms of religion are tolerated; and an American gentlemen told me, that although other reasons had been adduced for it, he fully believed, in his own mind, that the majority of the mob were influenced more by *curiosity* than any other feeling. The Convent was *sealed* to them, and they were determined to know what was in it. "Why, sir," continued he, "I will lay a wager that if the authorities were to nail together a dozen planks, and fix them up on the Common, with a caution to the public that they were not to go near or touch them, in twenty-four hours a mob would be raised to pull them down and ascertain what the planks contained." I mention this con-versation, to show in what a dexterous manner this American gentleman attempted to palliate one of the grossest outrages ever committed by his countrymen.[5]

～

On July 28, 1834, Elizabeth Harrison (Sister Mary John), suffering from "delirium," left the Ursuline convent in Charlestown and sought shelter with a neighboring farm family. Shortly thereafter she returned to the convent, escorted by her superior—an episode that (aided by the Boston papers) sparked rumors of the incarceration of helpless females in the convent, females who included not only nuns but boarding school students. At the time, the Ursuline convent was providing an aristocratic French education for some forty-seven girls—two-thirds of whom were, ironically enough, the daughters of Boston's Protestant, largely Unitarian, elite, irritated by the conservative Congregationalism of the public schools. Only one-eighth of the students at the Ursuline Academy were Catholic. To the working-class mob of Scots-Presbyterians, Catholics and Unitarians had formed an upper-class combination against Congregationalism.[6] This seemingly paradoxical alliance of Unitarians and Roman Catholics signaled that new rifts in Protestant orthodoxy itself were beginning to displace the traditional antagonism between Protestantism and Catholicism. As many educated Americans already knew, the simplified religious antipathy to Catholicism demonstrated by the mob was fast becoming an anachronism as well as a dangerous diversionary tactic, a false simplication of divisions within Protestant orthodoxy and within the national economy.

Shortly after Elizabeth Harrison's ambiguous flight, one concerned neighbor was given a full tour of the convent and boarding quarters, but his report, scheduled for publication in the Charlestown newspaper, came too late to prevent the riot, which occurred two weeks later. On the Sunday night before the riot, Lyman Beecher delivered three anti-Catholic sermons to huge congregations in three different Boston churches. On the following night, August 11, 1834, a mob of some sixty men, watched by an estimated two thousand spectators, burned the convent to the ground and returned the next night to rip up and burn all the plantings. Early in the attack the twelve nuns, three women servants, and forty-seven students fled the main building and hid in the garden. From their hiding place, they watched the rioters light bonfires in the dormitories, hurl cherished pianofortes out the windows, don the girls' clothing, and then proceed to the convent cemetery to pry open the coffin of a recently deceased nun. Protestant rioters pursued Protestant girls into a peculiar captivity: recalled one schoolgirl fifty years later, "We were shut up in that garden as closely as if we were in a prison, with no place even a temporary refuge from the rioters but the tomb, and the poor girls held the tomb in as much horror as they did the rioters."[7] According to this same student memoir, the rioting did not conclude for over seven hours. A later committee report speculated that the two thousand spectators did not interfere because "from the omission of magisterial influence, doubt and mistrust existed, whether the work were not so sanctioned by popular opinion, or the connivance of those in authority, that resistance would be hopeless."[8]

The exhausted students made their way into Boston the following morning, after a night of walking and hiding in various farmhouses. Sandwiched between Sister Mary John's delirious weekend flight and Reed's soon-to-be-published memoirs of her own imprisonment and escape from the Ursuline convent, this hurried walk of nuns and children emerges as the only genuine escape in a complicated cultural movement of staged invasions and exits. Like antebellum convent fiction itself, historical accounts of the event betray a curious sense of commingled calculation and frenzy. At the trial of the riot leaders, the attorney general sought to convey an image of the crowd violence as precipitate and savage, comparing it to colonial Indian attacks on white settlers, the women and children suddenly "awakened by frightful yells, like those which startled our ancestors, when the warhoop of the *native* savage burst upon their midnight slumbers."[9] But nearly all accounts suggest that, contrary to the notion of an Indian attack, most inhabitants of the convent knew of the riot in advance; one memoirist of the event even concluded that "there was a strange fatuity in all the proceedings."[10] Louisa Whitney, one of the Protestant scholars, remembers that the day of the riot was a long one of anticipation that turned Monday into "an unexpected holiday."[11] Indeed, the slowed tempo of the experience—the daylong anticipation, the night hours of waiting, the hiding in the garden and then in two consecutive homes, and finally the children's long wandering walk into Charlestown—remained perhaps its most distinctive feature to Whitney, one that led her to suggest its strangely fictive status: "All this has taken nearly as long to tell as it did to happen."[12] Indian captivity served Louisa Whitney, however, to convey not so much the surprise attack of savages as the girls' peculiar experience of rescue. When the exhausted children were finally loaded onto stagecoaches for Boston in the early morning, they met the returning crowd of rioters, who turned around and became their escort, offering an ambiguous protection that to Whitney seemed like Indian captivity made real: "We slowly rode the gantlet between a double file of amiable ruffians."[13]

The intense awkwardness of this processional, in which upper-class Boston adolescent girls consented to forced rescue by working-class men, can be sensed more fully in the realization that the girls were evidently already practiced, even disdainful, readers of Gothic accounts of convent captivity. A fascinating glimpse of their reading habits emerges in an account of the selectmen's tour of the convent on the day of the riot—an inspection that was marked by a "large number of pupils coming to the windows, and addressing us in a very rude and improper manner, inquiring, 'have you found her? Did you find her in the tomb? Was she buried alive?' "[14] Embedded in such antagonism, however, was a covert sympathy between these "rude" schoolgirls and the ominous emancipatory crowd that soon arrived. Schoolgirl fantasies about the spaces forbidden the boarders in the convent formed a secret anti-Catholic catalyst for the riots that arose from within, not from outside, the convent. "I do believe these ridiculous fancies, held by Protestant children to account for a novel discipline which they could not comprehend," wrote Louisa Whitney later in life, "obtained circulation among certain classes outside the Convent, and assisted in bringing on the catastrophe which destroyed the school."[15] Such an account intriguingly suggests that the schoolgirls themselves had a hand in the writing of this riot.

The riot and the ensuing trials of eight men (all of whom were eventually exonerated) for the capital offenses of arson, burglary, and murder were presided over by Melville's father-in-law, Chief Justice Lemuel Shaw. They attracted national publicity as a sensational exposé not only of convents but also, as mentioned earlier, of the dangers of "mobocracy." The dual nature of the sensation significantly links the nun and the American worker as joint figures of unrest. The rioters were not so much mobocratic, they declared in their defense, as chivalric, for they were bent on the rescue of imprisoned maidens and refrained from setting fire to the convent, according to trial testimony, "till they were satisfied there was no woman in the house." Trial testimony by one bystander confirmed that he "heard them say that no females should be hurt, but the cross must come down."[16]

A frankly misogynist dislike of the mother superior accompanied such chivalry, however; she was described in trial documents as the "unconscious cause of all this loss, trouble, sensation, and disgrace."[17] Virtually all the trial documents imply that violently contested proprietary rights over the female were at the base of the rioters' chivalric nativism. This contestation was further complicated by the implicit class antagonisms between the working-class male rioters and the upper-class females they "rescued." Thus one of the riot leaders, James Logan, vocalized the volatile proximity between the "feminine" (figured alternately as a foreign haughtiness and a native-born helplessness) and the inequities of private property. Of the rioters' pursuit of the mother superior, Logan testified: "They searched, and gave up endeavoring to find her, and then began breaking up the furniture."[18] Described in other testimony as a "figurehead made of brass," the superior attracted an invective conventionally reserved for the pope (as Antichrist) and one that categorized her as property, and fraudulent property at that.

But for all the hostile focus on the mother superior, human beings finally emerge in the riot writings as curiously passive agents—secondary to the more compelling activity of property, specifically the illicit investigation, theft, and destruction of Catholic church possessions by the Protestant worker. An 1870 anonymous compilation of newspaper accounts and trial materials surrounding the convent episode suggests the charismatic aura that clung to this plunder:

> On the Wednesday after the conflagration, Henry Creasy of Newburyport, a man about thirty-five years of age, committed suicide at the Bite Tavern by cutting his throat. Many rumors were circulated about the deceased,—that he had the communion chalice of the Convent in his possession, etc.; but it was only discovered that he had stated, just before he killed himself, that he had some of the sacramental wafer in his possession; and afterwards two pieces of the consecrated bread, which came from the chalice, were found in his pocket.[19]

As the crowd oscillated between the rescue and destruction of the Catholic female (ambiguously figured as captive nun and indoctrinated boarder), the propertied figure of the Protestant daughter remained untouched by the mob—islanded as the representation of inaccessible wealth. One of those Protestant daughters herself spoke these architectonics of provocative property, reminiscing that the convent's "handsome building . . . invited the curiosity that it repelled."[20]

In the advertisement of its curriculum, the convent frankly identified its educational services as designed to inculcate an aristocratic and highly self-controlled femininity in its students. The school's disciplinary agenda (the curriculum required students to maintain silence for nine hours daily) subjected boarders to a regimen excluded from but similar to that of the convent nuns.

From our historical distance it is possible to read in the anticonvent literature's depiction of the Ursulines' collectivized, regimented curriculum and ownership of luxury goods a veiled attack on the perplexing transformation of the workplace in New England's economy from traditional to incipiently rationalized—a change that manifested itself early on in the routinized factory labor of the new mill towns of eastern Massachusetts. The market's encroachment on the domain of the "native" New England agrarian economy and the added threat of immigrant labor to overturn the ideology and prerogatives of artisanal republican-ism lie encoded in this conspicuously gendered convent discourse. The Scots-Presbyterian bricklayers who formed the core of the mob and who understood themselves as chivalric agents vented their anger over their own decline in status and decreasing wages on a convent community of leisured women, hidden from public view, supported by foreign capi-tal—and, to the extent that the Ursulines garnered the allegiance of Protestant women, a community that disrupted masculine control of the family. Paradoxically, then, the convent emblematized not just reac-tionary Old World power but also fearsome economic inequities of American industrialization. In this translation of the economic into the religious, convents were frequently called factories of the spirit that subjected their inhabitants to unnaturally long hours of repetitive tasks for the antiscriptural sake of instilling obedience to a superior, conven-tionally accused for her own repudiation of the maternal. As an anti-reproductive, authoritarian system, the convent held up linked images of mechanization and aristocratic wealth, both of which excluded a "na-tive" artisanal class.

For a nation growing uncomfortably aware that its own revolution had confirmed rather than reformed unequal property and gender relations, the link between Boston's propertied class and the "Whore of Babylon" articulated a conspiratorial duplicity at the heart of American republi-canism. Built, inconveniently enough, within sight of Bunker Hill, the Ursuline convent desecrated the terrain of revolutionary struggle. The wave of anticonvent propaganda that followed the convent burning often resorted to the twin appeal of seduction and revolution, violated woman and nation, as if to perfect a still incomplete American Revolution. Pamphlets and ephemeral tales reiterated that it was imprisoned femi-ninity on *revolutionary* soil that justified the mob violence. Thus Charles Frothingham's *Convent's Doom: A Tale of Charlestown in 1834*—a brief work that sold forty thousand copies in its first week of publication—claimed that the need to rescue stolen daughters, sisters, or fiancées was the legitimate reason behind the burning. Patriarchal and patriotic duties called for the convent's destruction since, as one virtuous arsonist ex-plained, the Founding Fathers "thought not that within site of Bunker Hill, where the blood of heroes flowed, a Convent would be established, and their granddaughters become its inmates."[21] The convent exposé genre, as developed with Ursuline riot materials, applies the conventional features of Catholic imprisonment, indoctrination, and persecution in-herited from the English and European Gothic traditions to address the failures of the American Revolution; feminine violation and Catholic secrecy obliquely critique the limitations of democratic republicanism and even the suspicious new powers of the court. One handbill circulated at the trial's opening even extended the promise of revolutionary heroism for those who resisted the nunlike deceptions of a sacerdotal Superior Court: "Liberty or death! Suppressed evidence, Sons of Freedom! Can we live in a free country, and bear the yoke of priesthood, veiled in the habit of a profligate Court?"[22] The prosecution countered that the riot offered the sad spectacle of generational decline from the heroic Founding Fathers and that the glory of Bunker Hill was offensively disfigured by the "black embattlements" on Mount Benedict.[23]

Imagining every conceivable iniquity behind the impassive exterior of convent walls, American Protestant authors formulated a conspiratorial rhetoric that identified Catholicism's deviant metaphysic not only with the reduced promise of democracy but also with the burdens imposed by the new privacy of the middle-class family. The cloistered celibate women of the Ursuline convent attracted hostile scrutiny from passersby; what sort of family life was practiced behind convent walls? Even more disturbing, what sort of power was given to women in the relative absence of men? Responding to the suspicion that Catholics practiced what Protestants termed Mariolatry and, in so doing, gave earthly women aside from Mary too much power, the mother superior was called on at the trial to explain the political and familial hierarchies that ordered the Ursuline community. Chief Justice Shaw, who had dismissed the anti-Catholic prejudices of the jury as irrelevant, ruled that such inquiries had bearing on the trial proceedings. Yet when Rebecca Reed later took the stand, he intervened in her cross-examination to rule that "neither party could go into the internal character of the institution," a decision that reportedly "greatly disappointed many present, who wished to have all the inside arrangements of the Convent revealed to them."[24] While Reed was protected by Shaw's intervention, the mother superior was forced to reveal the internal familial relations that supported her authority. The superior's attempt to normalize her position against Reed's specific charges of having been coerced into worshiping the mother superior speaks to the collision of two family structures, Protestant patriarchy and Catholic ecclesiastical hierarchy. On the second day of her testimony, the superior thus attempted to explicate the convent's communal structure and to stabilize her position within it.

> The community sometimes call me *mother;* sometimes *President,* but usually "ma mère." The words *divine mother* are never applied to me. Confessions are never made to me, but to the Rt. Rev. Bishop, or in his absence to some other clergyman.

> I confess to the bishop. The confessions are made once a week. We apply the word *divine* only to the divinity. I do not represent the Virgin Mary, but am considered in the light of the mother of a family.[25]

Convent life inverted and subverted acceptable patterns of female mobility: women were physically constrained but, from the perspective of the Protestant patriarchy, ideologically unavailable. The rule of enclosure symbolized an imprisonment that ambiguously contained female escape. Cloistered women, then, were captives in need of rescue but also, as the interrogation of the mother superior makes clear, cultural deviants in need of control.

In addition to the superior's masculine, aristocratic hauteur, further instances of female pathology circulated in the riot documents. According to the Charlestown citizens' committee, when the attack began the convent harbored "one . . . in the last stages of pulmonary consumption, another suffering under convulsion fits, and the unhappy female, who had been the immediate cause of the excitement, [and] was by the agitations of the night in raving delirium."[26] Virtually all the documents imaginatively oppose the "delirium" of Elizabeth Harrison and the masculine control of the mother superior. "Of the Lady Superior, to whose stern and unyielding course during the excitement and difficulties which preceded the riot, the disaster has been often attributed, there have been strange and contradictory rumors, both before and since the time of the trials. She was a woman of masculine appearance and character, high-tempered, resolute, defiant, with stubborn, imperious will."[27] Indeed the riot and ensuing trials continually reverted to the issue of female impropriety, for during the riot the superior allegedly provoked the mob by an ill-timed assertiveness that contravened customary female deference. The defense counsel for four of the rioters, in his opening remarks, argued that notions of conspiracy were groundless; rather the superior had brought on the attack herself. His key proof "was the language of the Lady Superior to the rioters; in relation to which the counsel said that had she addressed them in different terms, it was his firm belief that the Convent would be now standing on Mount Benedict."[28]

Unfortunately, Attorney General Austin's main example of violated female American virtue—this same mother superior—continued her un-American bearing in court, appearing heavily veiled when called to testify and admitting under cross-examination that two days prior to the riot she had responded to a neighbor's warning of impending trouble by threatening that "the Right Reverend Bishop's influence over ten thousand brave Irishmen might lead to the destruction of his [the neighbor's] property, and that of others also."[29] At the later trial of three rioters, a witness to the riot testified that the superior even more pointedly refused the protection of Protestant chivalry for one of her companions:

> This witness, it will be remembered, stated that when he went up with the mob at the earlier part of the evening, they were addressed by a lady from a window, whose observations almost induced them to disperse; that he and others then offered the lady their protection, upon which the Superior appeared at another window and told them she did not require to be protected.[30]

In the vocabulary of this chivalric anti-Catholicism, convent walls held not only kidnapped maidens but women whose tyrannous faith mysteriously enabled a troublesome autonomy.

❧

I was troubled in various ways by Romans.
　　　　Rebecca Reed,
　　　　Supplement to "Six
　　　　Months in a Convent"

Rebecca Reed's *Six Months in a Convent* (1835) was complexly implicated not only in the riot and its aftermath but in the larger American project to assert a native Protestant cultural origin. The text, written by Rebecca Theresa Reed, a self-described "escapee" from the Ursuline convent who had lived there for six months as a "charity scholar" three years prior to the riot, sold ten thousand copies in Boston in its first week of publication.[31] Reed's editor argued that it was absurd "to trace the origin of a formidable conspiracy to a mere girl!" (Introduction, 17). Nonetheless, Reed's narrative of captivity and abuse in the Ursuline convent was a significant incitement to the mob violence, the trial verdicts, and the Ursuline community's eventual failure to receive any reparation from the Massachusetts legislature for the total loss of their property. Reed later claimed that her book was not an incendiary exposé but rather a spiritual autobiography and, even more, a confession of theological errancy written to argue for her readmission to the Episcopal church.

Although not published until 1835, Reed's story circulated locally prior to the riot, for at school one student remembered having "assisted at various disputes held among the girls about that notorious book, 'Six Months in a Convent,' and the character of its author."[32] Following the riot, Reed's text served as the event's chief product and legitimation, both parent to the event and its most dazzling offspring. A key witness at the ensuing trials of the rioters, Reed testified with "modest deportment" to the truth of her narrative, one that details her naive desire to retire from the world, subsequent realization of her imprisonment as a "novice," and final escape to a neighboring house through the convent gate, which, she rather charmingly confesses, she found "unfastened" (174). Her narrative and her testimony provoked in their turn an indignant rejoinder from the mother superior titled *An Answer to Six Months in a Convent Exposing Its Falsehoods and Manifold Absurdities* ... (1835)—a document that incited Reed and her editor to collaborate in writing the document called *Supplement to "Six Months in a Convent" Confirming the Narrative of Rebecca Reed* ... *by the Testimony of More Than One Hundred Witnesses*" (1835). The mother superior declared ludicrous Reed's captivity to "Roman bondage," priestly mind reading, and austere regimentation and especially her escape, since Reed might have just as easily "used the front door."[33]

This swirl of documents and their characteristic alternation between terror and violence on the one hand and ridiculous farce on the other testify to a volatile confusion—between fiction and historical event, between exposé and legal testimony—characteristic of anti-Catholic discourse in this period. Emerging from and in turn inciting the "mob," Reed's "insider" fiction of female captivity, disillusion, and escape is marked as well by developing processes of mass literary production. Designed for quick consumption, her narrative speaks an abbreviated, hasty language of scandalous exposure. And as a collaborative project between an "escaped nun" and her "editor," the convent exposé marks the anomalous, incendiary, and highly profitable appropriation of the amateur and sentimental female voice by the male nativist. As such, Reed's *Six Months* stands as an intriguing example of popular female authorship, a text ambiguously dictated, edited, and eagerly publicized by market-conscious anti-Catholic clergy who enjoyed exclusive profits to the best-seller.

Simultaneously slipshod and compelling, Reed's narrative denies any interest in formal composition, offering instead a fractured structure whose very defects oddly mimic the authentic voice of victimized childhood. Thus she recounts her early ascetic preparations for joining the Ursulines: "I knew of no greater sacrifice I could at that time make, than to give up all the treasures my dear mother left me. I also gave my globe and goldfish" (65–66). Reed's story develops a further plausibility of sorts through breezy disavowals of any need for detail. "For some days," she informs us, "I was not well, and my mind, as may naturally be supposed, sympathized with my body, and many things occurred that were to me unpleasant, which I shall pass unnoticed" (166). Like America's first best-seller, Susanna Rowson's *Charlotte Temple* (1791), Reed's convent exposé ignores the etiquette of the belles lettres tradition to create a newly intimate voice of exploitation that produced legions of true believers. If generations of *Charlotte Temple* readers visited the Trinity Church graveyard where Charlotte supposedly lay interred, leaving tearful mementos on her unmarked grave, readers of Rebecca Reed responded by insisting that convents in their vicinity be inspected, their captives liberated, their buildings burned. And like Rowson before her, Reed shows a skillful ability to convert the language of female victimization into aggressive indictment. Thus in a public letter defending herself against having caused the riot, Reed suavely directs the rioters' own vernacular against her accusers: "That it should be publicly said of me, by one who holds a seat upon the judge's bench, that I have been the cause of the 'popular feeling' . . . is an invasion of defenceless female innocence, if possible, more barbarous than that invasion of private rights, which has called forth so much public discussion" (Introduction, 30). Reed's rhetorical stance shows the precariousness of her position, for she violates the sentimental literary conventions of female victimization (chief among which, if we are to believe *Charlotte Temple,* is that one should die rather than speak), by writing an exposé that, while claiming her own continuing need for "retirement" from the world, promptly invades and manipulates the public arena of the courtroom.

If the Unitarian upper class disdained the bigotry of Calvinist Lyman Beecher's antipopery sermons and coveted the European refinement offered their daughters by the French-educated Ursulines, their daughters still read fiction such as Reed's. One Ursuline boarder, for example, remembers reading a similar narrative, Mrs. Sherwood's *Nun,* shortly before the riot occurred. Orthodox Congregationalist (or Presbyterian) working-class readers read anticonvent literature like Reed's with a scriptural conviction one imagines lacking in the Unitarian schoolgirl reader. Orphan girl and "charity scholar" (neither nun nor affluent boarder), female author, and, as she later described herself, "Catholic Episcopalian," Reed locates herself in no interpretive camp. Rather, she functions as connecting link, permitting an explosive confrontation between the propertied and the dispossessed. If the riot circulated through Reed's text, the contradictions of New England culture circulate through her voice, the seduced and violated voice of the "orphan girl."[34] The motif of the abandoned child emerges fully in the mother superior's response to Reed's literary production. "I had discovered her to be a foolish, romantic girl, and felt no interest in her" (*An Answer to Six Months*, 30). Reed's complaint against the superior was precisely that she refused to play the nurturing maternal role central to sentimental Protestantism. In Reed's indignant words: "I had then permission to go to the choir, where I immediately fainted, at which the Superior was angry, and said in a whisper she had told me *I ought not to have any feelings*" (98–99). Sensitive to the manipulation but not the motives behind it, the superior pictures Reed as a swindling trickster who "could always find ready listeners, by whom the supposed secrets of a cloister or a nunnery must have been greedily listened to" (*An Answer*, 2). Convent life, in the superior's estimation, did not incarcerate this Protestant girl, as nativists believed, but rather gave Reed "an opportunity of indulging her idle habits, her wanderings from house to house, her talents for mimicry, her desire of display without the labor of preparation, and her enthusiasm in the cause of a new religion,—all at our expense" (*An Answer*, 2).

The story Reed records of the Catholic seduction of the Protestant girl finally serves to seduce American readers into submerging their class and gender antagonisms for the sake of acquiring a "native" American identity. In evident contrast to the multivolume histories produced by Prescott and Parkman, the welter of material surrounding the Ursuline convent riot is marked by divided and divisive political agendas and philosophical affiliations—conflicts that problematize the status of the writings precisely because the protracted and often vehement debates over what or who caused the riot, over who should be punished and how, and finally over the "meaning" of the event prevented any single text from claiming a coherent generic identity. Thus fictional accounts like Frothingham's *Convent's Doom* and Reed's autobiography and spiritual confession both represent themselves as factually responsible history, whereas much of the trial testimony, as oral history, is frankly saturated with references to various anti-Catholic fictions like Reed's *Six Months*, Mrs. Sherwood's *Nun*, and Beecher's *Plea for the West*—all variously pointed to as evidence explaining, if not justifying, the behavior of the rioters.

This confusion over evidential boundaries extended from the various quarrels, before and after the riot, about the Ursuline convent's "trespass" on the holy ground of America's revolutionary struggle to the stories of alleged trespass on convent grounds by neighboring (Presbyterian) laborers. Coincident to the riot, Charlestown selectmen were also prosecutors in a trespass lawsuit against Bishop Fenwick; having purchased land on Bunker Hill for a Catholic cemetery, the bishop was then forbidden to bury two Catholic children there. He did so anyway and was sued by the city of Charlestown for violating city health regulations.[35] The bishop's "pollution" of a Protestant terrain made sacred by the civil religion of the Revolution was soon countered with a Protestant invasion of the convent's sacred precincts. In the days before the riot, three women trespassed on convent grounds to get to the turnpike road; ordered by the superior to turn the women back, her Irish servant Peter Rossiter directed them off convent grounds. For this, Rossiter was severely whipped by John Buzzell, a ringleader of the riot.

One of the most revealing characteristics of the convent captivity fiction of the 1830s is its determined imaginative trespass into Romanism's illicit and alluring interiors. Directly after the riot, a citizens' committee established to investigate its causes declared the Ursulines reputable only because their public function as teachers excused the otherwise debatable features of monastic life; as teachers, the nuns "devote themselves to those services and the cause of humanity which render them at all times subjects of public observation; and expose their personal deportment, as well as the character of their institution, to the strictest scrutiny."[36] The "trespassings" point us back to the confusion over the nature of convent family life and the contested boundary between private behavior and "public observation." As in the mother superior's struggles to define and not define herself as "mother," the riot material everywhere betrays a preoccupation with boundary; the consequent fluidity of textual genre attaches to Reed herself, the convent victim who still advocates retirement from the world after her escape back into it, and to Reed's editor, who expresses discomfort at the convent's institutional ambiguity. "The Convent," he declares in his introduction to Reed's narrative, "was either a religious establishment, for the worship of Roman Catholics, or it was a seminary of learning for the education of Protestant young ladies. If it were the former, it was no place for Protestant children. If it were the latter, then it is entitled to no sanctity" (Introduction, 43).

Such fluid boundaries characterize elite antebellum historiography as well. One thinks not only of Prescott's Cortés as an imperial creator of boundary, forging the outline of New Spain as he progresses into Mexico's interior (an activity accompanied by Prescott's shifting meditations on the proper boundaries between civilized, "barbarian," and "savage" groups), but also of elite history's generic preoccupation with the assertion of boundary. The tableaux that dramatize Prescott's account of Cortés's invasion and Parkman's "forest history," the elaboration of the "characters" of the principal historical actors, the pictorial displays of landscape, and even the ambivalent appeal to providential design, destinarianism, and Anglo-Saxon superiority—all constitute fictive narratives designed not only to vivify romantic historiography but also to supply essential explanatory systems that can give data the ontological status of "facts." Romantic narrative history adroitly mixed novelistic and archival materials to serve an evolutionary progression toward a racially and spiritually monistic world. Reviewing Prescott's Catholicized account of Aztec sacrifice, for example, one sympathetic Unitarian approvingly noted that sacrifice had progressed from the corruption of material offerings to the superior purity of spiritual ones because the "mode of historical development is that of a separation of things mixed, allowing individual representations to both of the contending principles."[37] To find historical texts where that separatist dynamic is contested, we must turn away from elite histories, for the processes creating their narrative coherence, if not their complexity and elegance, are the same ones creating their persuasive, potentially punitive ideological coherence. There is an unmediated connection, in other words, between Prescott's melodramatic felicities of style and characterization and his overarching "point": that Mesoamerican culture, vitiated by its cult of human sacrifice and tyranny, very properly gave way to the moral and racial superiority of Cortés.

The Ursuline convent riot, occurring some nine years before the publication of Prescott's *Conquest of Mexico,* provides us with just such a vernacular historiography that voices rather than controls ethnic, gender, and economic difference and that betrays not just antagonism but an equally volatile confusion. The discursive freedom that manifests itself in the characteristic volatility of Reed's speaking "I"—whose outrage backs onto a poignant sense of abandonment—promptly infects the stability of the event reported on by that "I." Thus Reed, describing the burial of a nun, appends this footnote to her description of the funeral: "My feelings were much hurt to witness the manner in which the lid of the coffin was *forced* down to its place. The corpse had swollen much, and become too large for the coffin" (138). Such generically inappropriate detail infantilizes Reed's historical voice but, in so doing, ironically authenticates the voice of the "escapee"; it marks the narrative as ineluctably "female," amateur, and outside classic historiography, where the management of point of view makes visible the point of access to foreign cultures and registers the epistemological control of genteel New England over the dispersed, subordinate groups that have neither points of view nor a viewing point onto the superordinate culture.

Reed's intriguing, sensational, and sense-bound exposé of iniquities behind convent walls seemingly advertises a blatant point of view—that of Protestant working-class animus against Irish Catholic immigrant labor and Protestant clerical animus against its major ecclesiastical rival—an ideological stance whose simplification and vehemence contrast to the almost luxuriant ambivalence of writers like Prescott and Parkman, whose rhetorical "mixture" of nostalgia and Protestant supremacism accompanies the strenuous work of separation and cleansing of "things mixed" in their histories. But their continual questioning of source materials and their self-conscious musings on the historian's tenuous perspectival position—precisely the constituent features of their point of view—enable their historiography to achieve representational dimensionality and a relative philosophical coherence. Reed's convent history works precisely otherwise: its refusal to entertain ambiguity, its all-out attack on the villainy of popery, and its "pure" reading of the riot as necessary American return to a cleansed Protestant origin signal a paradoxical inability to maintain difference. Even the operative identification between the "savage" and the "Catholic"—inherited by Prescott and Parkman from seventeenth-century New England captivity narratives and put to such effective rhetorical use in their representations of the "frontier" as a terrain disabled by its primitivism and tainted affiliation with Catholic Europe—is disrupted in the Ursuline riot discourse.

As we have seen, Massachusetts Attorney General Austin, in his closing argument for the prosecution, labeled the white "American" laborers, not the Catholics whom they attacked, as the "savages" attacking defenseless women and children in the middle of the night. But this wholesale attack on the "foreign," while arguably serving the same rhetorical and ideological enterprise as elite historiography's Anglo-Saxonism, accomplishes something else entirely: a calling into question of the very practice of reading, a breaking through the distances that organize textual interpretation into an intimate rhetorical terrain of lawless proximity, of trespass and even touching. These problematics of touching surface in Reed's indictment of convent life when she claims that "never to *touch anything* without permission" was one of the community's chief rules, a taboo meant to symbolize the excesses of Catholic totalitarianism and exclusivity. Her divulgence of this prohibition makes her exposé itself a bold and excessive touching, one that breaks out of not only Protestant boundaries but also the generic boundaries that enforce literary proprieties. If the mother superior constantly bans the gratification of curiosity, Reed's book will solicit and satisfy it.

Reed's *Six Months in a Convent* dwells in a stasis of unresolvable conflict that characterizes itself not as ambiguity (as it does for elite male writers like Prescott and Parkman) but as rhetorical disjointedness. A collision between religious and class antagonisms makes it impossible to decide which was worst: the foreign religion, the anarchist threat of the native-born working class, or the emancipated woman. This confusion suggests a disordered symbolic landscape beneath (or alongside) American master narratives of revolutionary origin and purified separation from the contaminants of the Old World and the racially "inferior" cultures of the American hemisphere. This terrain, along with Catholic iniquity, is what this vernacular history written by an "orphan girl" exposes. A lengthy "supplement" to Reed's novella, published to defend Reed's allegations and to respond to the mother superior's own devastating "answer" to Reed's story, suggests what we might call the reproductive confusion between "foreign" and "native" at work in Reed's narrative. The supplement's author writes of the convent:

> It was wholly *foreign;* having been founded, in 1820, by two *foreigners,* who imported four Ursuline *foreigners* into this country for that purpose, and in 1826 and 1827 [established] the Nunnery of *foreign money,* collected by a Mr. John Thayer in Rome and Ireland, (an American, we blush to add,) who rejoiced in the American Revolution only as the means of accomplishing a "much more happy revolution," in the supremacy of the Pope in America![38]

In contrast to the separation of "things mixed" that characterizes the canonical romantic historians, Reed's novella, the mother superior's "answer," and Reed's editor's "supplement"—whether individually anti- or pro-Catholic, anti- or pro–working class—demonstrate a frenetic involvement in the foreign, even an attachment to it, that presents itself alternately in the guise of vehement denunciation and desiring curiosity. Thus Rebecca Reed characterizes the mother superior as someone fantastically interested in her. "Presently the Superior joined me, wishing to know how I liked the garden, the flowers, etc. Observing a pocket album in my hand, she asked what I had hoarded up there. . . . She took it, and examining it, desired to know if I wished to keep some money I had in it. . . . She also requested me to sing" (71–72). Even this brief excerpt of Reed's prose shows how little her ephemeral style appeals to the organizing and suppressive powers of genre.

Reed's convent story and the mother superior's "answer" advertise only one generic affiliation—that of the exposé, whose indiscriminate conclusions, yoking the demonic, the sentimental, and the trivial in episodic historical account, are meant to authenticate the discriminating power of what Reed's editor calls the "Protestant eye." Reed and her mother superior, as two amateur historians of an event in which both serve variously as author, perpetrator, and victim, construct unmethod-ized, unpredictable accounts that are undisciplined by any circumventing generic requisites. Exposé quite simply problematizes explanation just as narrative history enables it. What are we to make, for example, of Reed's diagnosis of her quasi-tubercular condition, which, like her portrait of the consumptive nuns coerced into an exhausting regime of austerities, is meant to endow her with the charismatic status of victim to Catholic iniquity?

> My lungs were also very sore in consequence of repeating the offices; so much so, that when present at recreation, when I had permission to speak, it gave me pain rather than pleasure. I have, since leaving the Convent, consulted several physicians, who have expressed it as their opinion, that the cause of my bleeding at the lungs, which frequently occurs, was originally the repeating the office and other services, in *one long, drawling tone,* which any one can know by trying to be very difficult. (108n.)

This improbable diagnosis, which targets Catholic liturgical practices as probable pathogen for lung conditions still beyond the therapeutic control of American medical practice, betrays its own instability in the narrative's conclusion. There, such diagnoses evaporate in the face of Reed's startling return to Protestantism's strenuously advertised depen-dence upon "private judgment"—a dependence that, as Orestes Brown-son famously charged, backed precariously onto indeterminacy and a self-imprisoning subjectivism.[39] Reed closes her exposé of Ursuline au-thoritarianism and corruption with a Protestant challenge to the reader's autonomous interpretation that finally subverts the claims of her own history. "And I leave it with the reader to judge of my motives for becoming a member of the Ursuline Community, and for renouncing it" (186). This sudden, almost cavalier retreat from her claim to provide a true history is presumably meant to advertise her invulnerability to such inspection. But as the conclusion to her lengthy indictment, this very Protestant invitation unsettles the historical project.

Reed's history of life in the convent, then, as it lurches from one inappropriate juxtaposition to the next, alerts us to the coercive smooth-ness of classic romantic historiography. Ironically instituting itself through a nativist discourse adamantly claiming to read the Catholic other, to decipher its deceptive ways, and, in so doing, to regulate the relation between a purified past and present, Reed's history disrupts that agenda, unwittingly supplanting the protective and stratified structures of class, religious, and ethnic antagonisms with a rhetoric of undifferentiated anxiety—indiscriminate in diagnosis, negligent of boundary, resistant to closure.

After several unsuccessful attempts to gain reparation from the state of Massachusetts for an estimated property loss of one hundred thousand dollars, the impoverished Ursuline community was finally forced to leave for Canada in 1838.

In January 1836 the most widely read convent captivity narrative, Maria Monk's *Awful Disclosures of the Hotel Dieu Nunnery,* was published, selling three hundred thousand copies before the Civil War—to be outsold only by Stowe's great exposé of slavery, *Uncle Tom's Cabin.* An intriguing instance of collaborative writing, Monk's story was originally fabricated with the help of a little-known former priest named Hoyt and taken from Monk's dictation by a group of nativist and abolitionist men, adept at creating and projecting the sentimental voice of the captive Protestant heroine. Among these men was Jonathan Edwards's probable great-grandson Theodore Dwight, who tried, unpersuasively, to claim that Monk's work was a historical romance: "The story, short as it is, for simplicity and pathos is not unworthy the genius and talents of a Scott."[40] But as recognized then and since, Monk's story was hardly directed to a genteel audience, for her salacious revelations of life in a Montreal convent, while intended to bolster the claims of middle-class domesticity (and benefit from the success of Rebecca Reed's convent narrative), were meant to be read somewhere ambiguously outside but near the sacred precinct of the home.[41] If the composition of Monk's actual readership remains difficult to trace, her story of female victimization, partially written by and for men, is a "masculine" tale that registers middle-class "feminine" concerns with domesticity. At once quasi-pornographic and sentimental, the *Awful Disclosures* defends its own violations of readerly etiquette as necessary to warn parents, "even if delicacy must be in some degree wounded by revealing the fact."[42] Thus, like Harriet Jacobs, who later struggled with the delicate exposure of her indelicate sexual enslavement, Monk reaches for her "virtuous reader" by detailing the depth and breadth of her most unvirtuous captivity, enough so that the lower-class licentiousness of her narrative comes to function as an index of her middle-class propriety. Unable to gain the dignity of a court appearance like Rebecca Reed, forced therefore to "make my accusations through the press" (5), Monk works all the harder to write a middle-class best-seller of womanly trials and fortitude.

Unlike Rebecca Reed, Maria Monk had never been a charity scholar or even a novice but was in fact the nun's alter-image, a prostitute, who in 1834 had been taken into the Magdalen Asylum and was dismissed when she became pregnant (raped, she claimed, by a priest; Fig. 6). From there she made her way to New York and literary notoriety. Picking up where Reed left off, Maria Monk lavished on her readers fantastic descriptions of convent lechery and murder, a fantasia of captivity and escape from popish perils that encloses the largely unspoken drama of her "fallen womanhood" and its appropriation by a righteous male nativism to attack the "Whore of Babylon." As Maria "Monk" she is also a curious double of the licentious priests whom she exposes as the cause of her own prostituted status—the sexual chaos and shame of her prostitution explained and contained by its resituation in the convent. Its vague clipped style reminiscent of Reed's, Monk's *Awful Disclosures* portrays the frailty of Protestant girlhood, a vulnerability ultimately traceable, as for Charlotte Temple and Rebecca Reed, to the perils of "private judgment," which fails to decipher the calculations of the seducer. The abbreviated quality of Monk's narrative indicates more particularly the shared familiarity of her readers with this anticonvent discursive terrain of a Protestant feminine judgment bewildered by the labyrinthine structures of priestly power and desire.

Accusing her mother superior of an aggressive (hence depraved) female sexuality, Maria Monk claims that the superior played the role of brothel director, assigning sexual duties to her nuns and regulating the procedures for the murder of their infants. Of the priests, Maria confessed, somewhat disarmingly, to her readers that "often they were in our beds before us" (128). Monk depicts the Hotel Dieu Nunnery as the New World counterpart to Rome's "corrupt" topography, on which Protestant tourists ruminated; the priests soon inform her that "the chambers of pollution are above, and that the dungeons of torture and death are below; and that they dread the exposure of the theatre on which their horrific tragedies are performed" (344). This architectural hierarchy of vice provided by the priestly guide renders iniquity reassuringly organized and tangible—a demimonde version of Fourier's phalansteries of pleasureful living but also, perhaps more significant, a materialized architectonics of suffering that enables the representation of an otherwise unspeakable dimension of the profane: that inhabited by "fallen" women.

At the core of Monk's Gothic narrative of sex and infanticide is a troubled revelation of the perils of family estrangement. Like Rebecca Reed and the young heroine of Susan Warner's *Wide, Wide World* (1850),

Eng.ᵈ by W. L. Ormsby

Bring me before a court

Maria Monk

Fig. 6. Maria Monk holding her infant and demanding of her reading public: "Bring me before a court." From *Awful Disclosures of the Hotel Dieu Nunnery* (New York, 1836).

Monk is a virtual (if not actual) orphan, distanced from her mother and beset by her arbitrary maternal power, confessing at one point:

> I shall not attempt to justify or explain my own feelings with respect to my mother, whom I still regard at least in some degree as I ought. I will merely say, that I thought she indulged in partialities and antipathies in her family during my childhood; and that I attribute my entrance into the nunnery, and the misfortunes I have suffered, to my early estrangement from home, and my separation from family. (269)

Monk's criticism of her mother's violation of the maternal ideals of Protestant domesticity underlies her attack on the convent's antifamilial project. Her fragmented narrative voice (one further primitivized by the compositional processes of dictation and editorial interpolation) speaks in the tones of the outraged child, forced into an adulthood of prostitution that "cloisters" her from middle-class existence. As a translation of orphanhood into the parallel thematics of sexual violation, Monk's *Disclosures* travels adjacent corridors of abandonment and rape, her prostituted voice moving confusedly between isolation and violation, a condition that follows her even in escape when she confesses, "Sometimes I think I can hear the shrieks of helpless females in the hands of atrocious men" (325).

Monk's histrionic divulgence of sexual caresses and punishments illuminates a civilian world of emotional absence and physical exploitation, supplying a fawning priest in place of the lost father, a dominating mother superior in place of the indifferent mother who fails to provide any religious instruction, thus leaving her daughter entirely without traditional Protestant theological equipment. "I had no standard of duty to refer to," explains Maria Monk of her malleability, "and no judgment of my own which I knew how to use, or thought of using" (50). Leaving her convent schooling, Maria returns home but "soon became dissatisfied, having many and severe trials to endure at home, which my feelings will not allow me to describe" (22). These unspeakable tribulations of home propel her to a novitiate, a training from which she soon "escapes" for another brief and troubled expedition through civil society that includes a marriage (and separation) and her theft of her mother's military pension, funds she uses to regain admittance to the convent. Among her many gestures of bewildered complicity once she is back in the convent is her gathering of the mother superior's hair combings, which she wears as an amulet around her neck. This gesture of abject daughterly dependence, however, is roughly thwarted when the superior "told me I was not worthy to possess things so sacred" (30).

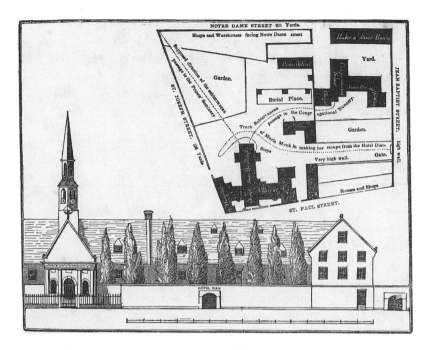

Fig. 7a. Exterior view of the Hotel Dieu Nunnery, the site of Maria Monk's "captivity." The inset (*above, upper right*) shows the "track of Maria Monk in making her escape," a route that intersects twice with the alleged subterranean passages between seminary and convent that enabled licentious contact. From *Awful Disclosures* (New York, 1836).

After taking the veil, a ceremony that called for her to lie down fully draped in ceremonial garb in a coffin ("My thoughts were not the most pleasing during the time I lay in that situation" [46]), Maria Monk is fully informed of the convent's true life. The first night she suffers "brutal" (53) treatment from three priests; she is also forced to kneel on dried peas and, perhaps most damaging of all, to surrender her most interior thoughts in the confessional: "While at confession, I was urged to hide nothing from the priest, and have been told by them, that they already knew what was in my heart, but would not tell, because it was necessary for me to confess it" (78).

If Maria has trouble revealing her interior thoughts to the priest or, worse yet, gaining access to the emotional interior of her mother superior, she nonetheless develops a bold and precise knowledge of the convent's secret recesses, traveling the subterranean corridors, expert in her later narrative reconstruction of its architectural intricacies for her readers (Fig. 7). During one of her explorations of the convent cellar, she

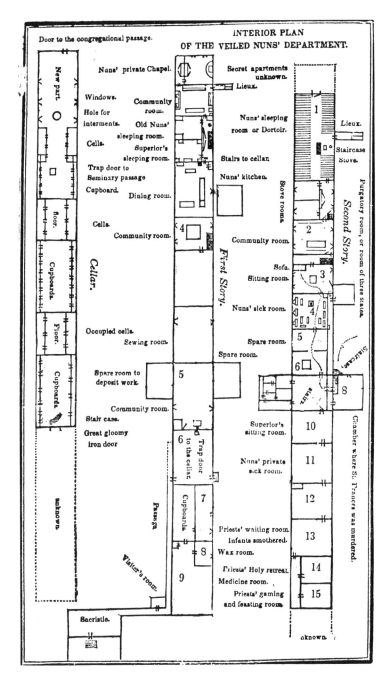

Fig. 7b. Interior of the nunnery. The segments marked "unknown" serve to authenticate Maria Monk's otherwise precise architectural recall.

finds herself on the edge of an enormous pit, "in a spacious place, so dark, that I could not at once distinguish its form" (81). Here in this pit Maria discovers the lime that has been thrown to disintegrate the bodies of murdered infants, and at its edge she ponders the familial atrocities of Rome. Outraged American readers of her narrative sought to make their way to this pit and demanded the right to investigate the Hotel Dieu convent to discover where indeed those sites of sexual intercourse and infanticide were located.

Incredibly, thousands of Americans believed Monk's narrative. Soon, however, her exposure of the infamy of convent life degenerated into an exposure of her own imposture, her mother somewhat improbably claiming that her daughter had been damaged by a slate pencil driven through her head when a child; Monk's mother further claimed that a Protestant minister had approached her to see if she would agree to the fabrication that her daughter had been seduced by a Catholic priest when in fact Maria had been impregnated by the minister himself, a story that was offered as profitable solution to an unwanted pregnancy. To her credit, Monk's mother turned down the bribe, declaring in later interviews that she had spent her maternal energies trying to curb the vagrancy and unpredictable stories of her daughter. When a New York lawyer named William L. Stone found himself in Montreal, he determined to inspect the Hotel Dieu Nunnery for himself, later producing a document entitled *Maria Monk and the Nunnery of the Hotel Dieu, Being an Account of a Visit to the Convents of Montreal and Refutation of the "Awful Disclosures"* (1836). Admitting that he inclined toward believing Monk's account before his tour of the convent, lawyer Stone (with the Montreal bishop's permission) inched his way through it in search of evidence of Catholic iniquity. Like his fellow Americans exploring the Roman catacombs, Stone evidently relished his role as detective assigned to pierce the veil of Catholic deception. What he discovered, however, helped him to see why Montreal's citizens, in his words, "seemed to look upon the intelligent denizens of the United States, as laboring under a widely extended monomania!"[43] For Stone discovered nothing beyond a group of nuns who were living in apparently tranquil accord. In fact, the nuns—to Stone's still slightly baffled perspective—appeared to beat Protestant families at their own game, leading him to admit, "I have never witnessed in any community or family more unaffected cheerfulness and good humor, nor more satisfactory evidence of entire confidence, esteem and harmony among each other" (26).

Failing to find any mysteries of iniquity in the Hotel Dieu, Stone investigated the mysteries of Maria Monk. As he soon recognized, the secrets dwelled less in Catholicism than in the strange impostures and seductions of a newly anonymous and commercialized public space. Monk's evident helplessness before her clerical exploiters and her seeming belief in her religious victimization signaled the troublesome powers of publicity available in the nascent mass-print culture. Therein lay true perplexity. Discovering what he could of Maria Monk's true history, Stone was quick to detect the pathos of the young unwed mother, not yet the "prostitute" of later legend. Unlike her collaborators, she made hardly anything from her best-seller, and Stone could see why: "Indeed she is a fitful credulous creature—a child of freak and impulse—who has probably been as much of a dupe herself, as the public have been dupes of her" (48). Catholicism had become curiously implicated in the swirling deceptions of capitalist culture, the exposure of Roman iniquities a way to profit from the public. Stone's Protestant mission now swerved from the exposure of Romanism to the "emancipation of my own countrymen from the bondage of prejudice, superinduced by the most flagrant imposture" (56). The great theme of captivity to Roman Catholicism was threatening to give way to a more troubling bondage—to the impostures of one's fellow (clerical) Americans and the impulsions of one's own need to believe.

Not suprisingly, Stone's mission of liberation failed to take effect on Monk's patrons, the Reverends Brownlee, Bourne, and Slocum and Mr. Theodore Dwight. After discussing his findings with them, Stone could only marvel at their curious submissiveness to the girlish pretender. Their continued support of Maria Monk indicated to him an unnatural regression to an infantile dependence on the mother. "How melancholy, methought, while wending my steps homeward, to see grave theologians, and intelligent laymen thus pinning themselves to the aprons of such women!" (46).

On August 15, 1837, Maria Monk fled from New York to Philadelphia; once there, she refused to be escorted back by her alleged guardian, the Reverend Slocum. Instead, she had him arrested and said "that she had fled the Hotel Dieu and Catholic Jesuits only to fall into the clutches of Protestant Jesuits, who 'all made well by my books.'"[44] What Maria (whom a Philadelphia doctor declared incapable of caring for herself) did for the next twelve years is unknown. But as the *Philadelphia Times* noted on July 28, 1849: "Since the publication of her book of 'discourses,' she has plunged into every excess of female iniquity."[45] Reportedly, she died in 1849 like a female Bartleby—silenced and impoverished on Welfare Island.

EIGHT

The Inquisitional Enclosures of Poe and Melville

The closely imagined relationship between popery and captivity initially established in the Indian captivity narrative developed, in nineteenth-century convent exposés, a crucial thematics of artifice. As we have seen in the narratives of Rebecca Reed and Maria Monk, convent terrors strategically deployed sham fears of Rome to voice the pressures of an emergent middle-class Protestant domesticity. As productions of a deviant female and popular voice, convent narratives imagined perverse domesticities in which an errant female voice, ambiguously positioned between working-class melodrama and middle-class sentiment, gained entry to Protestant parlors by cleansing itself of the impure attraction to Rome. The artifice at the heart of convent narratives—of persecuting figures dispatched from Rome—firmly situated the Protestant language of Romanism in the precariously privatized domain of family romance as well as the public terrain of political contestation. Rome was not only imaged polemically as the ethnic interloper in nativist conspiracy tracts but also figured sentimentally as a haunting memory, itself characterized by uncanny metaphor and fragmented, even implausible, narration, marks of fictional contrivance that point to submerged authenticities.

Antebellum Protestants experienced and contributed to this "dream logic" of Rome in varied ways.[1] But critical to our understanding of Romanism as a shaping force in the antebellum literary marketplace are the collective aspirations of this cultural logic that infiltrated from popular into elite fictions. In the "ascent" into higher canonical regions, this dream of Rome—nightmarish, comical, and baffling—found powerful vocalizations in writers of the American Renaissance, themselves imaginatively preoccupied with the terrors and representational challenges of alienation. In particular, Edgar Allan Poe's "Pit and the Pendulum," and

Herman Melville's *Benito Cereno* translate the "womanly" dream logic of convent captivity into a "manly" logic of inquisitional or shipboard imprisonment.[2] Both texts displace overtly female preoccupations with the familial perversion of convents with images of the masculine psyche closed within Catholic powers or ambiguously excluded by them. Voices of maidenhood and prostitution are supplanted by the voice of an ambiguously celibate masculinity whose largely unspoken patriarchal dominion in the familial enclosure of middle-class domesticity enables its exploration of extrafamilial spaces. Such expeditions finally deposit these celibate explorers in Romanized interiors that speak, not a dispossessed female language of hyperbolic conflict and sexualized violence, but an elite language of densely symbolic ambiguity. Thus Poe and Melville draw upon the language of Protestant captivity, Poe to dramatize the enigmatic pains of consciousness and Melville to construct the "knot" of slavery and racism embedded in the New England conscience.

Like convent captivity narratives, "The Pit and the Pendulum" and *Benito Cereno* picture the sufferings of an exaggeratedly privatized subjectivity, one rendered critically alone by virtue of its fascinated dread of Catholic power. If Puritan Indian captivity narratives figured the afflictions of papal bondage as genuine instances of the clash of imperial powers (both temporal and supernatural), these antebellum captivity narratives enjoy no such clarified relation between private and public. In these eminently self-conscious fictions, Roman Catholicism is no longer a rival imperial power but, to the contrary, a conspicuous anachronism, peripheral to the narratives' contemporary urgencies. Positioned off center, the Romanism of these captivity tales, particularly in its elusive religious malignity and the uncertainty of either capture or escape, distracts protagonists and readers alike from the true meanings of their victimization. Amasa Delano's "dreamy inquietude" aboard the *San Dominick* and Poe's narration of sickly fear inside the dungeon of the Spanish Inquisition are registered in the accents of a Protestant paranoia subjected to an ironic metanarrative gaze. If entrapment by Catholic powers exploits the nativist passions of Poe's and Melville's readers, Poe's narrator and Melville's Amasa Delano quickly transcend such crude simplicities of audience manipulation. Both tales consistently undermine the anti-Catholicism they invoke—not only to mock the nativist susceptibilities of the reading public but, in so doing, to question the very pretensions of narrative.

The unsettling combination of suffering and parody, of imprisonment as a sly, if not a playful, event, owes its peculiar tenor to the artificiality, even theatricality, of nativist captivity literature, with its characteristic blend of opportunism and genuine dread, of safe distance and dire involvement. The virtuosity of both narratives stems from their sustained and ambiguous mingling of sham and terror, their translation of nativism's exploitative melodramas into the aggressions of art. If the fraudulence of much nativist fiction reflected not only commercial opportunism but underlying doubts about the Catholic menace, Poe and Melville forged new authenticities, born of narrative elusiveness, from the inauthenticities of nativism.

In their religious manifestation, captivity narratives exerted a fascination born of the drama of suspended forgiveness. While the surface action of a narrative like Isaac Jogues's unfolded structures of merciful affliction, of the Lord forgiving and drawing his creature to him again, the interior drama threatened the reverse. Any number of seventeenth- and eighteenth-century narratives implicitly portrayed the suffering creature's forgiveness of God, the transition from anger to love, from insufferable fury to the prized condition of gratitude. As the popularity of the genre testifies, it was an absorbing dynamic, this adamant revision of resentment into bliss. With their developing capacity to reduce suffering, nineteenth-century Americans located in domesticity the pleasure of converting resentment and found it ever more difficult to perform an authentic submission. Increasingly, where suffering was concerned, the only bliss available was its cessation or, more realistically, its sentimental regulation.

Notwithstanding their release, such captives as Isaac Jogues or Mary Rowlandson sought to prolong their captivity, to dwell permanently inside the region of affliction. In the concluding lines to her captivity narrative, for example, Rowlandson jealously guards her battered consciousness from the soothing effects of the settlements and confesses to a new condition of sustained vigilance: "When others are sleeping, mine eyes are weeping!" Ironically, her greatest hope and necessity is to extend her captivity indefinitely, to maximize the moment of redemption by avoiding the closure of her experience. Thus she concludes in the atemporal, transcendental posture of the contemplative, bidding her readers, as Moses did the fleeing Israelites, to "stand still and see the salvation of the Lord."[3] In stark contrast to Rowlandson's newfound vigilance, Poe's narrator inches his way through an obsessively wakeful discourse in pursuit of the swoon, angling not for immortality but for oblivion. All he achieves is the horror of exposure, enduring the ceaseless recognition not of God but of his own consciousness: the eyes of punishment have replaced the gaze of faith: "Demon eyes, of a wild and ghastly vivacity, glared upon me in a thousand directions, where none had been visible before, and gleamed with the lurid lustre of a fire that I could not force my imagination to regard as unreal" (695).

I pondered upon all this frivolity until my teeth were
on edge.
                    "The Pit and the Pendulum"

Having tripped and landed with his chin on the edge of the pit, the agonized hero of "The Pit and the Pendulum" congratulates himself for the second in a series of accidental deliverances. His lips suspended over the clammy vacancy of the pit, he enjoys to the full, like Maria Monk before him, the pleasures of the threshold; as another observer of popery's evil interiors, the narrator scrutinizes its gloomy recesses, eager simultaneously to pursue and escape its secrets. Grateful that live burial, the "most hideous of fates" (685), does not await him, he ventures into the perils of undifferentiated space, his curiosity enticed by the "blackness and vacancy" (685) through which he gropes. As prisoner of the Inquisition, Poe's narrator is lodged at the foundation of the edifice of Romanism—a visually duplicitous location where mechanical ingenuity endows his presumptively Napoleonic Age inquisitors with the technological powers of an industrializing America. The technical precision with which these inquisitors dominate the interior of the prison, invisibly engineering the movement of walls, floors, and swinging pendulum, registers envious antebellum suspicions of Rome's efficient technologies of the spirit. One contemporary observer of Catholicism commented on "the resources of that marvellous ecclesiastical system"—that is "so ingeniously contrived, so adroitly defended, so cunningly accommodated to human pride and weakness both."[4] Demoniac Catholic techniques to control both spirit and body marginalize Protestantism to an ever dwindling space of evasion. Progressively displaying its insidious creativity, the narrator's dungeon seemingly manipulates its own interior, from pit to pendulum to mechanized inferno, treating its victim to a series of spectacular disclosures whose unspeakability is cited in an ever more loquacious prose.

Unlike Maria Monk, who must be hit before she falls to the floor, Poe's narrator performs his own prostration, swooning before his own religious terrors. Enthralled by the pleasures of infantilization before the monkish power, this self-identified "recusant" (690) gazes up at the gleaming pendulum "as a child at some rare bauble" (691). Like other Protestant explorers of convents, catacombs, and confessionals, the narrator struggles for mastery by acting the detective, out to deduce not only the extent of Catholic iniquity but the intentions behind it. If Rebecca Reed and Maria Monk partially negotiate the challenges of this detective imperative by at least escaping, though in a state of continued bafflement, Poe's narrator frankly, luxuriously fails. His rationalist investigation cannot compete against the technical ingenuity of his captors, and in the face of their spectacular and disciplined violence he trails off into "vain, unconnected conjecture" (695). His attempts to decipher his plight are entirely secondary to the ardent predatory power of the wrathful church, which in pendulum form descends to the bound and childlike narrator, who can look *up,* but not *at* his persecutors.

The tale's pleasuring in the Inquisition recalls that of the New York showman who in 1842 exhibited a building of the Inquisition replete with common instruments of torture.[5] By the time of Poe's tale, the Inquisition and its ingenious tortures had become a form of popular entertainment. If the confessional offered the attractions of illicit intercourse, the Inquisition offered its own erotic intimacies. Bound in his oily bandage, Poe's narrator submits to the embrace of dungeon rats: "They pressed—they swarmed upon me in ever accumulating heaps. They writhed upon my throat; their cold lips sought my own" (694). The feminized posture of his plight disguises an aggressive, distinctly masculine desire to enter the persecutorial intimacies of Romanism. Juan Antonio Llorente's *History of the Inquisition of Spain* (London, 1826) describes how, on the opening of the Madrid Inquisition in 1820, a prisoner was discovered who was to die the following day by the pendulum method.[6] Whereas Llorente reports with objective restraint on the Inquisition as a thing of the past (albeit recent past), Poe invests his source material with the radical intimacy of his anonymous and confessional "I." This voice of suffering resurrects and appropriates the Inquisition as immediate antebellum context and symbol of its own indeterminate anguish.

The private taxonomy of captivity that forms the gruesome and comic focus of Poe's narrative neatly organizes the range of Protestant confinements in the ideological enclosure of Romanism; the spatial removes into Indian country of Puritan and Jesuit narrative become vertiginous descent into unconsciousness. Of the many horrors that surround us, which is the worst? Poe, given to insistent scrutiny of the possible incarcerations available in this life, asks, in this tale above all, which captivity is the worst? Live entombment or the loathesome abyss?[7] The pit or the pendulum, the indifference of the void or the exquisite intimacy of the blade? Enamored of classification, the narrator must repeatedly submit to the Inquisition's sublime dismissal of his categories. The hero's hierarchy of punishments is subject to constant revision, as one torment leads into another, issuing finally into a competition of sufferings that renders distinction futile. "To the victims of its tyranny," explains this student of the Inquisition, "there was the choice of death with its direst physical agonies, or death with its most hideous moral horrors" (687). As his clinically precise discourse proceeds in its effort to survey the features of inquisitional captivity, the confinement becomes more boundless and uniform, the narrator's proliferating physiological detail finally pushing his captivity narrative to the edge of the ludicrous, where it is left to hover.

Thus the perceptual bondage suffered by Poe's bewildered "I" is both tortured and funny, a combination that forces the reader to dwell in a space as narrow as the narrator's—an uncomfortably shifting surrender to the tale's mimetic power where trust continually incites suspicion. Captivity as authorial joke is also authorial menace. Objective tortures are endowed with a technological excess that incites reader engagement only to mock it, just as the original authenticities of the Protestant captivity tradition are rendered artificial to convey the emergent authenticities of a surrealist art in which the text's frank confession of its artifice testifies to its author's engagement with the finally unspecifiable urgencies of his idiosyncratic consciousness. Or in the authorial tones of Poe's captive to the Inquisition: "I saw the lips of the black-robed judges. They appeared to me white—whiter than the sheet upon which I trace these words—and thin even to grotesqueness" (681).

A virtuoso of studied authenticity, of a deflected sincerity like that of his artfully descending pendulum, Poe mimics the ambivalent blending of farce and dread that characterized conspiracy-minded nativists, for whom the foreign religion was sufficiently present yet unknown to make their accusations plausible. As the ultimate stylist of Protestant captivity, Poe uncovers the self-preoccupation at the heart of a tradition of practiced tremblings before the specter of the Inquisition.

As the primary vehicle of his religious burlesque, Poe's relentlessly physiological language supplants the "recusant" soul with a Protestant body as primary target of Catholic captivity, intrigue, and torture. While the narrator invokes the classical captivity narrative tradition by citing Scripture, confessing, like Hezekiah, to being "sick unto death" (Isaiah 38:1), his objective is hardly the education of the soul's ascetic powers by incarceration within the torments of the fallen world. His enclosed self immediately abandons the consolatory achronicity of biblical citation for a narrative of obsessive temporal precision, his rationalist language focusing on the flesh, a gaze that converts the pleasures of exegesis into those of "nausea" and "thrill." Intercessional wisdom fades into impotent spectral images as the "angel forms" of candle flames shift into "meaningless spectres" (682). This dissolution of scriptural context discloses a region of bodily obsession in which even the political menaces of Romanism, its proverbial systematized ingenuities, revert to a meaningless mechanization; thus the "inquisitorial voices seemed merged in one dreamy indeterminate hum" that simply suggests circularity, not revolt, the mere "idea of *revolution*—perhaps from its association in fancy with the burr of a mill-wheel" (681). In this sensationalized, and hence depoliticized, incarceration, religious captivity metaphorizes the impingements of consciousness, whose pressures urge one not toward God but toward the "sweet rest" (682) of the grave. Catholic persecutors become identified with the masochist energies of the modern subject—an "I" whose nationality, religion, and individual history are suppressed beneath a newly sensational language of disorientation and dispossession.

This deposit of the Inquisition at the heart of the narrator's dehistoricized subjectivity participates in the logic of convent captivity narrative, where maiden subjectivity can experience its purity only through identifying the mother superior as fallen mother. So Poe's narrative pictures the abjectly filial autobiographical subject as one pursuing contact with, and knowledge of, his inquisitional fathers. That he awakens already confined in a space that proceeds to dwindle makes of his every evasion an inevitable drawing closer. Poe's narrative, then, affords us a choreography of antebellum Protestant movement upon the shifting stage of Romanism. A benevolent version of this mobility appears in Hawthorne's admiring efforts to describe an Italian church: "Perhaps the best way to form some dim conception of it, is to imagine a little casket, all inlaid, in its inside, with precious stones, so that there shall not a hair's breadth be left un-precious-stoned; and then imagine this little bit of a casket increased to the magnitude of a great church, without losing anything of the intense glory that was compressed into its original small compass."[8] While Hawthorne can imaginatively shrink and then magnify the cathedral interior that so dazzled him, Poe's narrator is the hapless victim of such aesthetic play as his colorful dungeon looms large or shrinks at another's will.

Hope whispers falsely to the bound narrator, writhing before the pendulum's descent; so too his narrative, in its garrulous unspeakabilities, degrades the incarcerated logic at the heart of Jesuit or Puritan capture—a logic in which the bound body, imitating Christ's sacrificial immobility, gains access to a fluid, mobile subjectivity, one that not only can move into but also can move meanings. Here the body's fixity registers an exegetical fixity: the "heart's unnatural stillness" registers the "sudden motionlessness throughout all things" (683). Nor can the hero measure the site of his captivity, its beginnings and ends rendered identical by the "perfectly uniform" (685) wall. The hero's inability to decipher the meaning or measurements of a captivity transpiring within the "shadows of memory" (683) gains its cultural authenticity by reference to the "thousand vague rumors of the horrors of Toledo" (685)—imagined by antebellum Protestants as countless, incapable of final measurement.

Taunting the very religious fears he elicits, the narrator describes with studied artifice his fumbling along the slimy wall: "I followed it up; stepping with all the careful distrust with which certain antique narratives had inspired me" (685). Coyly alluding to the contemporary context of "no-popery" literature, Poe's captive urges his readers to understand his experience as authenticating their unease; glimpsing the pit, he assures us that the "death just avoided was of that very character which I had regarded as fabulous and frivolous in the tales respecting the Inquisition" (687). His horrors of consciousness are consistently subject to the satirical effect of this intertextuality. "Of the dungeons there had been strange things narrated—fables I had always deemed them—but yet strange, and too ghastly to repeat, save in a whisper" (685). With a teasing regularity that mimics the methodical enumeration of his sensations and gestures the narrator hints at the conventionality of his predicament, finally suggesting that his (and the reader's) real captivity is to no-popery literature. Thus his first trembling retreat from the pit's edge occurs within a sly reference to his past career as a reader of anti-Catholic fiction: "Neither could I forget what I had read of these pits—that the *sudden* extinction of life formed no part of their most horrible plan" (687).

Abruptly enabled by a "sulphurous lustre" (688) to see the true nature of his enclosure, the narrator confirms that the psychic void is reassuringly peopled with Catholic images, the walls everywhere "daubed in all the hideous and repulsive devices to which the charnel superstition of the monks has given rise" (689). These culturally self-reflexive motions of consciousness are doubly recontained by this invocation of monkish aesthetics, the skeletal forms displayed, as they were for American tourists in underground Rome, for his gruesome enjoyment. While the masochism of black vacancy yields to the sadism of monks who finally depict themselves as separate from the narrator so that the monologue of live entombment can at least become the dialogue of "inquisition," Poe's eccentric narrator is himself recontained as a character in no-popery literature. Like any reader of familiar texts, he appreciates his tormen-tor's deviation from the pit to the pendulum as an admirable instance of authorial ingenuity, aimed at preserving readerly interest: "The plunge into this pit I had avoided by the merest of accidents, and I knew that surprise, or entrapment into torment, formed an important portion of all the grotesquerie of these dungeon deaths. Having failed to fall, it was no part of the demon plan to hurl me into the abyss" (690). The captive's anticipatory knowledge of course is inverted by his narrative to cast him as a figure whose private reasonings are fully anticipated by his invisible persecutors. They have carefully kept his bound body from the descend-ing path of the pendulum, their deep monkish intimacy with his most spontaneous unvoiced speculations rendering his every revelation al-ready known, as happened to Rebecca Reed and Maria Monk before him. As past reader, current captive, and future author of anti-Catholic fictions, the narrator finds that his most frantic work is to disguise his entire knowledge of his inquisitors as their entire knowledge of him.

As one who knows all there is to know, he finally turns his rhetoric of teasing disclosure toward his readers, enticing and thwarting their engagement, refusing, unlike Maria Monk, to divulge what he sees in the pit's "inmost recesses" (696). Inquisitorial dalliance with his agonies models his own flirtation with the reader, enough so that the ingenuities of Catholic torture come to articulate how a burlesque of authorship simultaneously conveys the perils of its reading. Enticing the victim to cooperate in his own extinction, the inquisitors delight in surprise and protraction to enforce his acknowledgment of their punning, intertextual imaginations. As heretic pushed toward a mechanized auto-da-fé, in doubled bondage within a dungeon that itself flattens into a red hot lozenge, the narrator confesses to his captors' ingenious identification of deliverance and perdition. Springing away from the pendulum, he merely leaps toward their next narrative episode on the edge of the pit. "Free!— and in the grasp of the Inquisition!" (695) he cries as the walls begin to move. His best efforts to decipher and elude the "doom prepared . . . by monkish ingenuity in torture" (690) have failed, for the pendulum has sliced him free precisely that the walls might shove him into the pit.

In drawing the parallel between his narrator's frantic efforts to de-cipher the intentions of his inquisitional captors, his equally perplexed attempts to construct a sequential narrative from his memory fragments, and finally the reader's struggle to believe and disbelieve the manifest artifice of the narrative, "The Pit and the Pendulum" translates the legendary unspeakable filth within the recesses of Romanism—its im-postures and secrecies—into the recalcitrant processes of a psychological realism struggling to represent a "memory which busies itself among forbidden things" (683). If captivity to Rome's agents in the New World formerly implicated Catholicism in the pleasures of regained spiritual vigilance and a revivified gratitude, it now belonged to the circuitous expeditions of the swoon into the unconscious and ambiguously beyond it. Captivity to Catholic mysteries has yielded to imprisonment in the menacing and maddeningly trivial confines of the writing psyche. The "seared and writhing body" (697) of Poe's narrator, a body whose "soul took a wild interest in trifles" (688), is the self-bound sequel to the heroic incandescence of Foxe's burning martyrs.

The Spaniard behind—his creature before: to rush from
darkness to light was the involuntary choice.
                                                                Benito Cereno

In 1841, the nativist Joseph Berg uttered a revealing diatribe against the confessional:

> We hear a great deal said about slavery in our day; and I abhor oppression in every shape; but I count the poor slave, who hoes his master's corn under the lash of a heartless overseer, a freeman, when compared with the man who breathes the atmosphere of liberty, and yet voluntarily fetters his soul, and surrenders himself, bound hand and foot, to the sovereign will and pleasure of a popish priest.[9]

Berg was not alone is his astonishing opinion that the slave was better off than the Roman Catholic. His statement reveals a depressing capacity to rationalize chattel slavery as one (and not the worst) among a series of enslavements, a reasoning that suggests how images of bondage to papal captivity could minimalize objections to race slavery. The priest is more fearsome than the slaveholder because Berg, racially and regionally, cannot identify with African Americans beyond the abolitionist stereotype of "the poor slave." The priest, unlike the planter, also enjoys the voluntary surrender of his victims. Berg's focus on this voluntarism at the heart of Catholic bondage reveals the uneasy masculinity of the Protestant temperament, which had long struggled with the theological imperative to enact a willing surrender to Christ.[10] If the seduction of females by priests registered the pressure of Protestant domesticity on the errant desires of women, the alleged psychological seduction of the male by priests violated cultural expectations of masculine autonomy—expectations that arose in order to legitimate the proliferating demands of the developing capitalist economy. Male victims of masculine power risked effeminization. As the fugitive slave Frederick Douglass well knew, the oratorical display of his own victimization at the hands of his former white masters encroached dangerously on the virility he also proudly claimed.[11]

Put simply, male victims always had to contend with the implication of complicity, a specter indeed more threatening than that faced by the slave, who, if "poor," at least did not volunteer for his or her fate. Perversely applying traditional Christian distinctions between spirit and flesh to condemn Romanism's spiritual tyranny or the bodily tyranny of slavery, northern nativists voiced their dread of such potentially all-male confessional intimacies. Like the fearsome image of miscegenation that haunted both pro- and antislavery white Americans, the threat of spiritual miscegenation as figured in anti-Catholic writing argued that mingling inevitably led to mixture—and in such mixtures all claims to purity were dangerously forsaken.

Melville's *Benito Cereno* (1855) probes these sexual, racial, and religious comminglings at work in the Protestant masculine imagination and brilliantly extends the logic of embattled purity to the challenges of narrative itself. Does purity afford one its vaunted insight into the workings of the contaminated enemy, casting light on its darkness? Or is purity a self-blinding force, repressing America's all too evident disturbances beneath a surface rhetoric of bemusement that genially minimizes what little remains to be seen? In the perceptions of Amasa Delano as he boards the *San Dominick*, Melville images slavery in the New World as the secret text layered within the Protestant text of Rome. Delano's repeated deflection of a murderous racial reality into a fading world of ecclesiastical conflict was a familiar feature of nativist and abolitionist thought. *Benito Cereno* forcefully identifies the papal threat with the slaves and to that extent folds a southern voice of conspiratorial anxiety into Delano's northern ruminations that eventually lead him to conclude that Spaniard and African are piratically leagued against him. Delano was hardly unique in his misreading. Like Poe's "Pit and the Pendulum," Melville's Protestant captivity tale dramatizes the captive's plight as a protracted series of interpretive quandaries. But if Poe internalizes Catholicism to register the panic at the heart of his marginalized southern subjectivity, Melville insists on endowing it with the representational density and plausibility of conspiratorial narrative.

In 1853 the great diarist George Templeton Strong observed of a no-popery riot in New York: "If Roman Catholicism as transplanted here shall retain all its aggressive and exclusive features, in other words, its identity, I don't see but that a great religious war is a probable event in the history of the next hundred years; notwithstanding all our national indifference to religious forms."[12] Strong was right about the war but wrong about the issue; his false prediction only too clearly recalls Amasa Delano's notorious naïveté aboard the *San Dominick*—a naïveté ideologically and aesthetically enabled by the suggestive convergence of black habit and black skin. Delano, the polite racist from Nantucket, is, we might argue, a representative northeasterner in his identification of slave ships and monasteries and a representative southerner in his perplexed musings on the black masks everywhere around him.[13]

When *Benito Cereno* was published in *Putnam's* in 1855, readers were well familiar with the ambiguous and ominous associations between Catholicism and slavery that Melville developed in his story, and with the narrative stance of confused and confusing perceptions of spiritual and bodily oppressions. In no-popery literature, the Catholic church itself moved treacherously across the boundary between profane and sacred—a division that powerfully informed domesticity's doctrine of "separate spheres," of prohibitions against interracial marriage, and of mounting northern hostilities to the South. Delano's voluntary captivity in what he initially views as a structure "like a white-washed monastery" (48), his alternately smug and frightened musings before its Old World secrets once aboard the *San Dominick* (nautical metonym of the Dominican-led Inquisition), reembody the hystericized interior of Poe's "Pit and the Pendulum" with the contemporary specifics of religious, racial, and regional conflict. If Poe's Seville dungeon is located at the geographic heart of the Spanish Inquisition, Melville's *Benito Cereno* sets that interior afloat; on the margins of European imperial power the self-described "little Jack of the Beach," Amasa Delano, meets up with the monasticized mysteries of the *San Dominick* "at the ends of the earth" (77). The *San Dominick*'s travels down the South American coast and its eventual forced passage back to Lima under the escort of the New England *Bachelor's Delight* free that Catholic interior from both its Old World touristic context and its domestic American context of Indian or convent captivity.

Only, like any traveler, Delano carries those domestic captivity narratives within him; he steps between the hatchet polishers "like one running the gauntlet" (59), compares a sailor peering at him to "an Indian [peering] from behind a hemlock" (74), a collapse of African and native American finally voiced by the narrator outside Delano's consciousness, when Africans are described fighting "Indian-like" as they "hurtled their hatchets" (101). Delano speaks as well a language of

American travel abroad, transplanting the tourist rhetoric of European Catholicism onto the floating monastery. Like American tourists in Italy, baffled by their simultaneous exclusion from convents and confessionals and inclusion in the dazzling interiors of cathedrals and picture galleries, Delano is intrigued by the ship's visual self-presentation but mystified by the inhabitants. Indeed, just as the interest of antebellum tourist writings about Catholic Europe resides largely in the alternating collusion and confrontation between anti-Catholic ideology and the heterogeneous sights of Italy (in particular), so Melville fashions his narrative's intrigue from similar slippages among the conflicting forces of conventionalized anticipation, troubled perception, and disturbing memory. If those slippages occasionally enjoy the familiarity of the organic, his "old trepidations" recurring "like the ague" (78), they more frequently contradict one another forcefully enough to seem estranged, even uncanny. The circuitous inquiries and odd atmosphere of Delano's New World captivity, then, exhibit the suspended, rapt Protestant pace of exploration through convent, cathedral, and catacomb. As tourists pondered America in Rome (and convents back home), so Delano moves ideologically (and hence perceptually) through Europe to understand the Catholicism floating strangely before him. Whether readers shared in or disdained the nativist campaign against pope and immigrant, they would certainly recognize the narrative's peculiar tone of genial condescension flecked with abject dread, for it characterized discussions of the interlocking menaces of the 1850s: Romanism and slavery.

But if Delano, off the coast of Chile, must encounter the baffling metamorphoses of inquisitional power aboard the *San Dominick,* Melville carefully denies him the assurances of the Protestant captivity tradition. Its accoutrements are there and not there, vital yet absent, like the metaphors that enclose them. The ship appears "like" a monastery; its appearance "almost" leads Delano to imagine a "ship-load of monks" (48). That Delano first sees the Spanish slaver as crowded cloister registers the cultural error of nativism, in which racial blindness is enabled by religious illumination, a purifying light that mistakenly transforms slaves into monks. The ship, qua ship, enjoys a peculiarly intensified interiority by virtue of the sea's surrounding blankness; it is a particular kind of Catholic interior, for the malevolent fatherly power of Jesuit, of pope, and of the Dominican inquisitor in particular has been usurped— not conquered by Protestants but subversively appropriated by Africans. Many antebellum Protestants would agree with Delano's groping effort to situate Spaniards in the familiarites of Protestant English history by claiming that "the very word Spaniard has a curious, conspirator, Guy-

Fawkish twang to it" (79). The blurred grammatical focus and casual tone of Delano's musings genially recognize the familiarity of the anti-Catholic code and the gentility of his partial refusal to believe in time-worn conspiracy. If to be a Spaniard still resonates with a "Guy-Fawkish twang," Delano subdues his conspiratorial gullibility, for he and his *Putnam's* readership know just what a "Guy-Fawkish twang" is—a threat rendered sufficiently absurd by Protestant imperial power that it now sounds like a "twang."

While directing their suspicions toward immigrant Irish and (to a lesser extent) German Catholics, Protestant Americans accorded an aristocratic superiority to Spanish Catholicism. As home to the Jesuits and the Dominican Inquisition, Spanish Catholicism represented an ultimate (and in both senses of the word, a refined) fanaticism, one far superior in class terms to the impoverished and spiritually "docile," if politically threatening, Catholicism of the Irish. Indeed, the Catholic Cereno's symptoms are aristocratic ones, according to Delano's diagnosis: "Shut up in these oaken walls, chained to one dull round of command, whose unconditionality cloyed him, like some hypochondriac abbot he moved slowly about" (52). The Nantucket captain's sympathy with Cereno's burdens of command also suggests the shared commercial and class interests of northern "merchant princes" and southern "cotton kings"—alignments that only reluctantly succumbed to sectional animosity in the late 1850s. Indeed the "fraternal unreserve" (114) enjoyed between the two on the voyage back to Lima, while silent Babo lies imprisoned beneath, transiently recovers the solidarity of such alliances before the Negro's "shadow" (116) again interrupts the southerner's ability to communicate with his northern friend.

Melville's Catholic imagery invokes the Roman church's role in spurring the development of African slavery—a role that began, ironically, with the efforts of Las Casas to protect New World Indians from enslavement by suggesting the greater suitability of Africans.[14] Slavery in its later manifestation in Melville's narrative (set in 1799) is resolutely an affair of New Spain, not New England. Delano's suspicions of the apparently neurasthentic and morbidly reserved Cereno are traced to the pathology of Cereno's national type, his behavior "not unlike that which might be supposed to have been his imperial countryman's, Charles V., just previous to the anchoritish retirement of that monarch from the throne" (53). Delano's sentimental and sociable racism, which allows him to imaginatively berate Cereno as a bitter master and hence to locate him in English Protestant legends of Spanish cruelty in the New World, also allows him to chastise Cereno for his excessive familiarity with Africans.

Reminding himself that "Spaniards in the main are as good folks as any in Duxbury, Massachusetts" (79), Delano minimizes national difference to ponder the internal mysteries of spirituality and temperament.

Thwarted by Don Benito's enigmatic reserve, Delano, in a series of unspoken ruminations, attempts to penetrate Don Benito's psychological interior. Indeed, until the long-delayed illumination of the racial meaning of the events surrounding him, Delano recurs to a religious, and at times medical, interpretation of the lassitude, disorder, and morbidity of life aboard the *San Dominick*. His Protestant exegesis of the "hypochondriac abbot" Don Benito, tended by Babo, his "friar" (57) on this "shipboard of monks," however, remains on the level of metaphor as Delano compares this baffling New World community to Old World Catholic morbidities. Anomalous and, as it turns out, finally unspeakable relations between Africans, English, and Spaniards in the New World gain a partial expressibility through their uncanny resemblance to the religious schism at the heart of Christianity. The cleansed and orderly procedures of Anglo-American subjectivity thus appraise with dismay the mingled items of Don Benito's cuddy, whose indiscriminate Catholic clutter contains both an actual and a metaphoric Catholicism. Delano notices a "thumbed missal" and a "meager crucifix" and then proceeds to metaphorize other items in the cuddy into his own ideological edifice of Romanism: thus the rigging lies "like a heap of poor friar's girdles"; the malacca cane settees are "uncomfortable to look at as inquisitors' racks" (82); and the barber chair "seemed some grotesque, middle-age engine of torment" and the sink "like a font" (83). This rush of remembered artifacts dismembers Catholicism into an assemblage of books, clothing, and furniture that chaotically invokes the Franciscan order, the Inquisition, the sacrament of baptism, the Catholic liturgy. Delano's construction of this popish interior develops its grotesquerie from this jumbled collection of reminiscences and Roman artifacts. "This seems a sort of dormitory, sitting-room, sail-loft, chapel, armory, and private closet all together" (83), he remarks, troubled by the mixture of functions. As this paraphernalia prophesies the collapse of an antiquated Spanish imperial power before a modern Anglo-American one (whose interiors are well organized in their domestic rather than ecclesiastical piety), so the genre of Catholic captivity slips into Delano's subconscious, inhabiting the subordinated regions of fleeting intuition, suspended revelation, and haunting resemblance. Part of the tale's ideological subtlety is its simultaneous use of Delano's anti-Catholicism to voice his provincial views of New World politics and race and the rise and subsidence of the narrative's truth.[15]

In documenting the passage of a Protestant mind from naive confidence to vague suspicion, then to revelation and hard-hearted revenge, and finally to denial and forgetfulness, *Benito Cereno* forces apart and temporally orders the entangled skeins of ideology. Delano must forgo the religious for the racial narrative, must realize that the ship is no floating monastery of Old World tyrannies and impurities but a slave ship in which the Spaniard is not the powerful agent of Catholic imperial power but a feeble white man swooning before the ingenious tyrannies of the African.

In imagining the enslaved African as New World monk, Delano implicitly compares the masculine autonomy enjoyed on his ship, the *Bachelor's Delight,* to the suspicious collectivism of the slave ship's Catholic celibates. If New England bachelors advertise (without participating in) an unthreatening familial version of middle-class marriage, Catholic monks menace by their very numbers and anonymity. "Peering over the bulwarks were what really seemed, in the hazy distance, throngs of dark cowls; while, fitfully revealed through the open port-holes, other dark moving figures were dimly descried, as of Black Friars pacing the cloisters" (48). As an intermittently revelatory Catholic enclosure that entices Protestant exploration in order to punish it, the *San Dominick* enjoys the cover of Delano's religious blindness. Unable to see into monasticism, he is doubly distant from the truths of race slavery it disguises. Indeed, because his religious narrative imagines a superstitious, sickly Catholicism, Delano can exaggerate the difference between himself and Cereno; contemplating the Spaniard's seeming fear of the deceased, Delano muses, "How unlike are we made!" (61). The New England captain recurrently imagines Cereno's captivity in a morbid Catholicism that radically excludes the very idea of race slavery. Thus Cereno is strangely attended by Babo, who is "something like a begging friar of St. Francis" (57); Babo indeed is more a metaphor than a character, for his self is only partially revealed in the later trial depositions as the former "captain" of the slaves. That Delano understands Cereno as a religious rather than a political captive preserves both the racial hierarchy and Babo's unknowability. To recognize that Babo is a subversive African rather than a "deprecatory" (57) friar is to forgo the supremacies of Protestantism for the crisis of race war.

Ironically enough, the safety of this Protestant Gothic vision that enables Delano to imagine an impenetrable "subterranean vault" (96) rather than, as Cereno later describes it, a fully intentional inhabited community whose "every inch of ground [was] mined into honey-combs under you" (115) also provides him the hint. In his famous misreading of the shaving scene, Delano's focus on its inquisitional aspect truthfully communicates Babo's murderous power. The barber's seat does indeed work like "some grotesque, middle-age engine of torment"; musings on Babo's unwitting mimicry of the Inquisition do generate "the vagary, that in the black he saw a headsman, and in the white, a man at the block" (85). Babo's shaving of Don Benito, in its ceremonial, even ritual, precision, resonates with the legendary (and historical) calculations of a religiously motivated violence. At the same time, it possesses the vitality of historical anachronism; as countless Gothic narratives testify, psychic meaning accrues in proportion to a setting's historical displacement. Thus the Catholic imagery through which Delano haltingly approaches his enlightenment operates both sardonically and prophetically, simultaneously illuminating the limitations of his Massachusetts sensibility and pointing toward the presence of a novel malevolent power in the New World that jointly inhabits the story's exterior deceptions and its interior truth.

Like the blacks' staged reenactment of their former enslavement, Delano's interpretive recurrence to the enclosures of monastery and Inquisition (a recurrence in which the two are equated) appeals as well to anterior narratives of oppression. Each retrospection enables the other; Delano's monastic ruminations, in their focus on Cereno as the authoritarian "abbot" and Babo as faithful victim to the Spaniard's gloomy rule, make possible Babo's deception. Similarly, the slaves' staged reenactment of their former status—a collective theater that is always on the verge of disruption—fuels Delano's religious interpretation. The moments of near disruption—when Delano witnesses violence from black boy to white, when the knot is thrown to him, when he bids the "slaves" stand back—urge him to speculate on Cereno's improper use of authority as an instance of religious excess, one that resembles Charles V's "anchoritish retirement" from power. In constructing a New England subjectivity that persistently pathologizes the religious other in order to organize an otherwise baffling scenario, Melville satirizes its interpretive pretensions. Indeed, while Delano, precisely because he has categorized Cereno as the Catholic other, consigns himself to "again and again turning over in his mind the mysterious demeanor of Don Benito Cereno" (67), unable to decipher the catacomb environment, his own interior is seemingly transparent to the mutineers, who strike their hatchets "as in ominous comment on the white stranger's thoughts" (67).

Thus if Melville exploits antebellum preoccupations with the conventional monastic secrecies of Catholicism to introduce the radically unconventional duplicities of the African American, he endows the black man with monkish powers of collective organization and devious spiritual insight. Delano's uncertainties about his Catholic double—is he an invalid, an incompetent youth, an imposter?—finally urge him to embrace his own bewilderment as he concludes that "to the Spaniard's black-letter text, it was best, for awhile, to leave open margin" (65). The moment is an important one, for it signals the supersession of his conspiratorial religious vision, in which the sentimental vagaries of his anti-Catholicism falsely schematized black and white as abbot and monk to obscure the murderous racial schism between them.

If neither Cereno nor Babo has access to Delano's Romanism, the narrative's concluding extracts from Cereno's deposition and the remarks upon that deposition invite the reader to marvel at Romanism's serendipitous contribution to Babo's conspiracy. Providing access to the interlocking processes of religious and racial conspiracy, Delano's language of mysterious interiors disguised by black cowls, black skins, and "black vapors" (69) is finally the language Melville uses to describe the elusive interior meanings of his fiction. If the deposition serves "as the key to fit into the lock of the complications which precede it, then, as a vault whose door has been flung back, the San Dominick's hull lies open to-day" (114). The force of this passage is not only to connect 1799 to the "today" of 1855 but also to register the ingenuity of authorial constructions over that of religious or racial conspiracy. The story finally wrenches Delano from his charitable musings on the twinned excesses of Catholics and slaveholders and violently repositions him within a vengeful vision of racial pollution. Delano's insidious transition is registered when "he smote Babo's hand down, but his own heart smote him harder. With infinite pity he withdrew his hold from Don Benito" (99). Delano's Gothic dread of Cereno is thus replaced by racial hatred, as the shadow of the Negro now covers that of the pope.

Cereno's leap toward Delano and the white man's conquest of the black rebel that ensues force the punitive logic of this polluted interiority onto the African. The blacks' bodies are open to white transgression while the sailors of the *Bachelor's Delight* are sealed off from penetration. The blacks' "red tongues lolled, wolf-like, from their black mouths. But the pale sailors' teeth were set" (102). Such racial thematics abruptly scissor Delano's musings and replace the recesses of papal iniquity with those of black bodies whose dark interiors are not uncanny so much as radically different—a difference that provokes the violent suppressions of the imperialist instead of the gingerly probings of the tourist.

Both the deposition extracts and the postdeposition narrative reintroduce the Catholicism that has been so abruptly jettisoned by the revelation of racial conspiracy. As a mark of the new sympathy between Spaniard and New Englander, Cereno, "courteous even to the point of religion" (115), acknowledges Delano's fraternal religious status; both men agree that they are protected by the "Prince of Heaven" (115); and Cereno even forgives Delano's misjudgment of the "recesses" (115) of his character. But this (racially homogeneous) ecumenical spirit, by which narrative sequence and white supremacy are restored, lapses again into the uncanny fragmented world of monasticism and narrative uncertainty. Prostrated and largely silenced by the "shadow" of "the negro" (116), Cereno retires once more, this time not to his cuddy but to a monastery, "where both physician and priest were his nurses, and a member of the order volunteered to be his one special guardian and consoler, by night and by day" (103). Thus the silenced, soon-to-be decapitated Babo is replaced by the monk Infelez; the illicit proximity practiced by the subversive African Babo, whose plotted narrative had forced whites to become his characters and no longer his author, reorganizes back into the European proximity of monk and spiritual patient. In larger narrative terms, Melville finally extracts the reader from the metaphoric to the deictic, from Delano's interior musings on the *San Dominick*'s resemblance to a monastery to an omniscient narrative that points, first, to the truths of slave conspiracy and, second, to those of monasticism. Cereno leaves Delano's "shipload of monks" for an omnisciently narrated pilgrimage to the monastery on Mount Agonia.

From these last exits of Babo and Benito Cereno, Delano is excluded. With his last words, which include his injunction to "forget it" (116), his world of New England Romanism vanishes from the text, replaced by the hidden monastic intimacies of Infelez and Cereno. That the text ejects Delano after he has urged us to forget what has happened does not signal the forgetting of the Protestant captivity tradition. On the contrary, the narrator supplants Delano and appropriates his mystified Romanizing gaze, enticed and thwarted by a foreign Catholic interiority. If the ship's hull has disclosed that antebellum America's secrets are those of race, not religion, those aboard retreat back into the mute Catholic interior. Babo's and Cereno's passage into voicelessness recontextualizes race within religion as the conspirator's decapitated head gazes toward (and into) St. Bartholomew's Church and toward (and onto) the monastery on Mount Agonia. In positioning these concluding narrative moments as all emanating from Babo's gaze, one directed on the Catholic "vaults" (117), Melville forcibly identifies his antebellum reader with Babo. We look at Babo's head, which, "fixed on a pole in the Plaza, met, unabashed, the gaze of the whites" (116), only to be suddenly looking with that head toward the church and monastery that enclose the vanishing Catholic slaveholders, Aranda and Cereno.

Babo's gaze recuperates and extends that of antebellum Protestantism, for it promises that one can gain access to the Catholic interior; not only does Babo stare into the vault that holds Aranda's bones, but his gaze, in following Cereno's funeral procession toward the monastery, is also there, narratively speaking, to greet him, for Babo's authorial inscription beneath Aranda's skeleton, "seguid vuestro jefe," is repeated in the narrator's final description of Cereno's end: "Benito Cereno, borne on the bier, did, indeed, follow his leader" (117). If Babo is victim finally to the allied Catholic and Protestant slaveholding powers of New Spain and New England, his displayed head, a "hive of subtlety" (116), suggests that he reclaims the cellular organization and ingenuities of the monastery for his own. Emerging as the conclusive monastic interior—collectively empowered and ingenious—that brain lodges itself in New Spain's literal Catholic edifices and in New England's metaphoric ones. As a final icon of religious difference, the monkish Babo subversively imitates New Spain to mock New England, master of both their guilty interiors.

NINE

Competing Interiors
The Church and Its
Protestant Voyeurs

Catholic captivity literature unfolded in the context of Protestant orthodoxy's internal quarrels and its efforts to construct a new consensus by sacralizing the family. Like the narratives of Henry "Box" Brown and Rachel Plummer, convent escape tales were preoccupied with the strange new gods of modernization and modern capital and inconclusively involved with issues of psychic and familial confinement. Ironically, the ostensibly religious polemics of anti-Catholicism provided a major channel for this new focus on a profane privatized world of sentiment and its psychological confinements while increasingly secular conceptions of captivity in turn played a formative role in the generically diverse antebellum portraits of Catholicism as seducer of the heart and senses more than the soul.

The continued deployment of specifically Protestant tensions about captivity to Rome depended on endowing it, as we have seen with the fictions of Poe and Melville, with a punitive interior, one disguised by any number of duplicitous architectural or behavioral exteriors. Whether nativist or genteel critics of Rome, antebellum Protestants characteristically envisioned the foreign religion as a monolithic Gothic edifice containing intricately organized and perilous interiors, privacies deeper than those increasingly claimed for middle-class family life, and differently constructed. These Roman privacies resisted the eyes of the citizen and the open spaces of democratic life, inviting speculation about unjust incarceration and illegal conversations, bodily or otherwise. Protestants created in Romanism an imaginary container whose alluring multifaceted surface disguised a violent, even devouring, interior, images drawn from the sexually fearful and punitive rhetoric of the Book of Revelation. Rome, as the Scarlet Woman and the Whore of Babylon, had "polluted" female recesses and an alluring female surface. Protestant womanhood, undergoing its own strenuous purification through the "cult of true womanhood," was thought especially vulnerable to Rome's unbridled female sensualism.

If American Protestant women were engineering a problematic escape from centuries of misogynist speculation about their tempting, corrupting interiors by denying themselves an interior, by struggling to become transparent vehicles of a domesticated Holy Spirit, these displaced thematics of erotic depth, both either misogynist or sensual in representation, menaced the newly delicate identity of the Protestant woman. In Hawthorne's *Marble Faun,* Kenyon shudders to think, when the delicate Hilda has disappeared, that she might have suddenly fallen through Rome's precarious surface into some "abyss" or "cavern" or "chasm"—terms that pervade the terrain of the novel and of Romanism as Kenyon imagines it. Figured as a corrupt feminine topography that could engulf the near transparent Protestant woman, Rome transported the Edwardsian image of hell back to Europe, from whence it had fled. Many antebellum tourists shared Kenyon's lingering Calvinist suspicions of the Roman surface and, whether at home or abroad, understood themselves as inheritors of the Enlightenment, out to disclose and enumerate the workings of superstition. The revolutions of 1848 seemed to promise the culmination of this Protestant exposé; as one self-styled historian of the Inquisition exulted at the opening of its chambers during the short-lived Roman Republic, "The inmost recesses of its interior have been explored, and all its abominations are now set before an astonished world."[1] Invading this Catholic enclosure entailed, as we have seen, a range of literal and vicarious explorations—including cathedral visits, convent attacks, and the writing and reading of anti-Catholic narratives. Dispersing the gloom in the light of Protestant reason would subject Catholicism's regressive privacies to the democratic collective and, by so doing, make apparent the energy and purity of Protestants' antisensual subjectivity.

But the logic of this Protestant exploration dictated a continuing exposure of Catholicism as dangerous interior; the coherence of Protestant subjectivity, then, could be guaranteed only by positing interiors within interiors, an infinite regress designed to satisfy the theological tourist-investigator. Catholicism as global abstraction was itself theorized as imprisoning container so that no matter how many of its specific chambers were exposed, more remained because of its capacity to generate them. As one writer declared, Dante's inscription above the entrance to hell actually described the prison of religion from within which the poet wrote: "It was needed that the appropriate motto should be engraved in unmistakable characters upon its portals: 'Ye who enter here, leave all hope behind.' "[2]

Liberal and conservative antebellum Protestants prided themselves on having no such treacherous distinction between inner and outer, spirit and letter; their faith had no gilded covering, no outside and inside, but was instead an integrated, and hence largely invisible, spiritual process, one coincident with the "invisible" church of their Reformed piety. Protestants, in insisting on their piety as one relatively unmediated by human intervention and hence pure—a single substance ideally unmarred by divisions between flesh and spirit—implicitly struggled against the palpable divisions of the ostensibly sovereign self in democratic society. When that sovereign self experienced the numerous circumscriptions of property, gender, and ethnicity as curtailments on its autonomy, it transcended them by imagining a recurrent escape from Romanism, whose spaces, infinitely bounded by rules, costumes, and religious practices, were, furthermore, capable of exhibiting fascinating transformations from "inlaid casket" to "sublime cathedral." Protestant thinkers dwelled, like the hero of "The Pit and the Pendulum," on a slippery spiritual topography, one that descended into this protean Catholic materiality. The further one traveled from Reformed piety toward Roman Catholicism, the more embodied and potentially confining the landscape grew. Of course, those made uncomfortable by such material forms were not insensible to their benefits, even if the need for them suggested a certain spiritual weakness.

Nathaniel Hawthorne, for example, wrote to his wife about their daughter Una's worrisome leanings toward Anglicanism: "Would it be well—(perhaps it would, I really don't know)—for religion to be intimately connected in her mind, with forms and ceremonials, and sanctified places of worship? Shall the whole sky be the dome of her cathedral?—or must she compress the Deity into a narrow space, for the purpose of getting at him more readily?"[3] Hawthorne's image of Anglicanism as a compression and incarceration of God recalls the claustrophobic discomforts of Pastor Williams with the closeting and consumption made possible by transubstantiation. Only Hawthorne's unease with such enclosures is additionally inflected by a note of worrisome womanly aggression. Una, after all, is credited as agent, one who performs this compression to get "at him more readily." Hawthorne was not unusual in imagining High Church Anglicanism (and Catholicism) as an aggression against the Deity, an unleashing of humanity's imaginative and technical powers to create rival temples, built spaces of splendid artifact and ceremony that registered the confines of psyche rather than its communions, its aesthetic ingenuity rather than its purity.

~

Melville's satire of American Episcopalianism in "The Two Temples" unfolds as allegorized exploration of twinned ceremonial enclosures: that of New York's Grace Church and that of a London theater.[4] Dedicated to Sheridan Knowles, a well-known actor turned Baptist preacher whose antipopery sermons attracted wide attention in the 1850s, Melville's diptych was initially rejected by *Putnam's* magazine for its potential religious offensiveness. Knowles's career, which involved the theater, antipopery, and evangelical Protestantism, registered the principal concerns of Melville's story. Knowles's nativist sermons attacking the evil of Catholic theatricality inform Melville's ambiguous thematics of captivity in the ecclesiastical impostures of High Church Episcopalianism. But like so many Melvillean protagonists, the narrator only points to the folly, bitingly aware of the absence of charity in the modern world without himself being capable of any.[5]

Melville's narrator, speaking confidentially with his magazine readership, presents himself as Protestant captive to Catholic materiality, except that the material enclosure is, importantly, not a Catholic one but one of the "new-fashioned Gothic Temples" (304) of the Protestant bourgeoisie. Similarly, he is not so much a captive Reformed Christian as a spokesman for the urban under- and working classes. The proud materiality of this seemingly Catholic edifice, "marble-buttressed [and] stained-glassed" (303), excludes the penniless pilgrim with his prayer book; in retaliation, the self-described "caitiff" (304) exposes the suspect neo-Catholicism of the propertied classes, whose money punishes with an impious authority like that of the pope. After the corpulent beadle has turned him away, the pilgrim impishly explains to his readers: "I suppose I'm excommunicated; excluded, anyway" (303). As the Gothic edifice displays the newly comprehensive powers of capital to destroy both the republican equality and austerities of American Protestantism, captivity is no longer a question of the forced exploration of a taboo interior but of exclusion among the dispossessed, who suffer the constriction of "invisible" market forces rather than of the Inquisition. The "Puseyitish" (308) interior marginalizes the narrator from worshiper to awed spectator. His captivity in a structure of "richly dyed glass . . . flaming fire-works and pyrotechnics" (304) yields, not providential wisdom, but a new imperialism of aerial perspective, an ability to look down on members of the congregation and to see the structure of market relations and priestly theatrics that sustain them. Perched above the oblivious worshipers, the narrator claims his invisible "pew" is closer to Heaven, his righteous perspective converting the humanity below into "heads, gleaming in the many-colored window-stains . . . like beds of spangled pebbles flashing in a Cuban sun" (306). If the topography of Melville's captivity narrative sardonically inverts that of "The Pit and the Pendulum," placing the prisoner's gaze high above rather than desperately below and looking up at his inquisitional judges, the subjectivities of the two narratives nonetheless share a compressed, defensive space, anxiously monitoring and seeking to thwart the ecclesial authorities pressing upon them.

When the narrator's ascent brings him to a "gorgeous dungeon" (304) of stained glass, his first impulse is to pierce through these Romish mediations to an objective daylight view of the outdoors by "scratch[ing] a minute opening in a great purple star forming the center of the chief compartment of the middle window" (304). But when he does, his unmediated view fails to win him the promised Protestant objective of intimate communion with Christ—communion authenticated by the independent processes of private judgment. Instead, his peephole reveals the church beadle far below, driving off impoverished boys—a sordid inversion of Christ's rage at the money changers.

If Melville's theological critique of mediation frames his critique of the workingman's exclusion from the egalitarian promises of republicanism, concern with the divisive workings of capitalism nonetheless remains entangled with the delusions of the worker's gaze. Having ascended to his highest perch, the narrator is no longer subject to the visual confinement of stained glass, one that identifies his oppression as ecclesiastical; freed from that captivity, he must now contend with the oppression of mortality itself, for a wire screen obscures his view, "casting crape" (306) on the scene below, thwarting his visual mastery and revealing him to readers as but another marred point along the profane perspective. This authorial shading of the utopian narrative eye registers Melville's characteristic suspicion of reformism and also underscores the seclusion of the Protestant voyeur, whose spectatorial attachment to illicit material forms, be they the "dim-streaming light from the autumnal glasses" (307–8), the "enrapturing, overpowering organ" (307), or the "noble-looking" (306) priest, forbids participation in them. Indeed "Temple First" dramatizes the connection between economic dispossession and spiritual incarceration, implying that exclusion from bourgeois consumption leaves one not only "outside" but confined "inside" one's deprivation: thus the narrator, fleeing the church, finds the beadle has unknowingly locked him in, an indifference to his existence that renders the workings of authority simply paradoxical: "He would not let me in at all at first, and now, with the greatest inconsistency, he will not let me out" (307).

Melville's translation of antebellum Protestant concern with the confinements and intrusive mediations of Romanism into his studies of urban alienation refuses, however, the nativist subtext of that concern: the hero of "Temple First," having been arrested and fined for his anti-Catholic trespass, flees to London, where his adventures in "Temple Second" pointedly expose America's inferiority. The doubled structure of the diptych enforces the resemblance of Victorian America to England—the narrator again "outside," destitute and isolate amid the crowds of "Babylonian London" (310) that surge aggressively against him in a kind of Malthusian apocalypse. As Babylon, "Leviathan" (310), and Tartarus, the city forms a vast and infernal container, whose object is not to compress and torture but to segregate and silence the self, a fate coyly resisted by the chatty, intently allusive, and punning narrator, who looks to "rest me in some inn-like chapel, upon some stranger's outside bench" (310–11). Looking again for ecclesial refuge from the crowded anonymity of urban spaces, the narrator stumbles on a street that ends "at its junction with a crosswise avenue" (311), a topography he imagines as crucifixional. This passional cityscape promises to convert his urban wandering into the pilgrimage that has been continually invoked and foreclosed by the narrative's sheer plethora of scriptural allusions. The crossed streets promise a therapeutic quieting of his chatty questing, a psychological and spiritual relief that he compares to "emerging upon the green enclosure surrounding some Cathedral church, where sanctity makes all things still" (311). The rural simile, however, signals not the attainment of the sacred but an encounter with its simulation—not as Episcopalianism but as theater.

The London experience henceforth functions as the double of the New York experience, imitating its autonomous structures only to thwart them. Entering the alluring theater through the proverbial low side door, the narrator begins another heavenly ascent to imperial spectatorship, with humanity far below; but this time, as he quickly admits, "I had company" (313). Ensconced in empyreal intimacy with a working-class audience, the narrator rejoices in his position at the "very main-mast-head of all the interior edifice" (314), a position from which he can enjoy a "sovereign outlook, and imperial downlook" (314) and yet not be alone. Ironically the theater's frank simulation—as opposed to the duplicitous artifice of Grace Church—allows the "enraptured thousands" (315) to feel the sacred sensation of fraternal inclusion. The moment signals the emergent importance of mass entertainment in Victorian culture, particularly its utility in quelling working-class dissent by charismatically miming the oppressive state. The narrator's companions rise to give the actor Macready a spontaneous, "unmistakably sincere" (315) ovation for his performance in Bulwer-Lytton's *Richelieu; or, The Conspiracy* (1839)—an embrace of aesthetic mimesis that exposes the New York priest as hollow actor while praising the charismatic impact of the professional Macready.[6] Indeed, the imperial perspective of "Temple Second" on "Temple First," with the charity of working-class theater-goers exposing the churlishness of New York Episcopalians, depends on a pointed religious defense of Macready's theatrical incitement and skilled management of audience euphoria—his construction of a perfectly controlled space in which "nothing objectionable was admitted" (314). If the narrator's concluding praise for the charity found in the London theater disturbingly links such virtue to the self-forgetfulness of entertainment, the theater world still enjoys a sacred power. The American church of "Temple First" is disabled by the theatrical analogy while "Temple Second" is finally bolstered by the religious analogy, for the London theater demonstrates an enviable capacity to absorb what it resembles into the matter of its own self-representation.

Conceived of as something one "entered," Catholicism's palpable presence attracted those who felt the oncoming drafts of religious infidelity, or who, like the wanderer through Melville's two temples, longed for community. But that same physicality also indicated corruption and potential suffocation. The church's ornamental exterior was necessarily deceptive, a false visualization of what Protestants claimed must always remain invisible to avoid the taint of idolatry. Melville's conversion of the theater and church, actor and priest in "The Two Temples" extends the language of dissent beyond its traditional target—the vestiges of popery in Anglicanism—and inverts its conventional moral geography. Melville's New York now claims the ornament and corruption of Old World culture while the theater, a traditional target of reform animus, contains the sacred. While ironically locating the sacred in the theatrical, Melville continually invokes traditional suspicions that the Roman church staged magnificent theatricals to bedazzle and manipulate its flock. Its ceremonial revelation of the Godhead in the elevation of the Host was at once mesmerizing and blasphemous, for it restaged an

Incarnation that to Protestants had occurred once, and only once. Indeed, the priest's sacramental enactments, in making visible the invisible workings of spirit, violated the privacy of God's gaze, profaning his theatrical space with that of the human gaze. In the words of one concerned Unitarian:

> The Church of Rome is dramatic in all its features. It seems to be its office, and its very essence *to act* Christianity, and to hold out in exterior exhibition that, which, in its true light, no eye but God's can see. No wonder the Church of Rome is fond of sacraments, when the definition of one so admirably suits herself;—she is "an outward and visible sign of an inward and spiritual church."[7]

If a dangerous exhibitionism hovered over Catholic ritual, converting its priests into performers and its theology into entertainment, Protestant critics of such spectacle defensively theorized their own intrusive gaze as different from the dazzled eye of the Catholic believer. While the Catholic "spectator" looked gullibly on the priest's theater, Protestants directed their "pure" gaze of detection and ethnographic curiosity on this figure. One journalist observed of Americans who included mass-watching among their activities as tourists abroad that "during the interesting part of the performance, they stand on tip-toe on the kneeling-board to obtain a good view; when the music pleases them they listen in silent admiration; when the interest of either Mass or music lags, conversation, not always confined to an under tone, beguiles the time."[8] Even sympathetic Protestants persisted in identifying Catholic ritual as secular theater. Loyola's antebellum biographer Isaac Taylor muses on his subject's ostensibly theatrical behavior as the cause of his own uncertain religious views: "The things said and done are in themselves, perhaps, good and approvable; but they are so done and said as if a harlequin were doing and saying them. At every turn of the bedizened performer we are inwardly perplexed, not knowing whether we should admire or scorn what is passing before us."[9]

Fascination and disdain, enchained attention and alienation coexisted in the Protestant observer who watched Catholicism constrained to perform theatrical spectacles before its critics. Thus did Protestant spectatorship bind together the displays of captivity and theatricality, enforcing a privileged exposure (and degradation) on those "perverted" to Rome. Even the age's most respected convert, Cardinal Newman, described himself as a captured wild beast on display.[10] One could spy prayerfully, as it were, like the tourist Hawthorne, who recorded in his

Italian notebook that "yesterday I saw a young man standing before a shrine, writhing and wringing his hands in an agony of grief and contrition. If he had been a protestant, I think he would have shut all that up within his heart, and let it burn there till it seared him."[11] In watching someone else in an "agony" and then recording what he sees for further narrative elaboration, Hawthorne memorably enacts the religious voyeurism at the heart of Protestant spectating.

Against charges of imposture and demonic counterfeiting of the divine, Roman Catholics defended the redemptive possibilities of spectacle, seeing in the unembarrassed exhibition of the crucified body the prime signifier of triumphant spirit. From its original instance—Christ displayed on the cross before the mocking crowds—on through the annals of the Jesuit missionaries (Father Jogues dragged as "spectacle" from one Indian village to another), the spectacular features of Christianity, particularly the image of the male body in extremity, became identified with foreign Catholic representational practices. For American Protestants constrained by the sexual sublimation of Victorian gender relations, a bare cross carried scandalous associations, and a crucifix stirred even greater unease. Thus did Elizabeth Seton's sister try to prevent her from attending mass at St. Peter's church (where José Maria Vallejo's *Crucifixion* hung over the main altar), by whispering, "They say, my sister, there is a great picture of Our Savior ALL NAKED—!"[12] When Charles Eliot Norton confronted ubiquitous images of crucified Saviors on his Italian travels, he found their principal effect was "to substitute the coarsest fancies for the most solemn and pathetic truths, and to minister to a diseased craving for unnatural and detestable excitements."[13] Norton's language of an illicit substitution that provokes a diseased and deviant desire resonates with antebellum medical and clerical attacks against masturbation, whose pleasures not only enervated the ideal entrepreneurial self but also distracted it from the duties of reproduction. The beauty of the male body, exposed on the crucifix, posed a peculiar challenge to male members of New England's Protestant elite (a group whom Emerson had described in his 1830 address "The American Scholar" as "lined with eyes"). American masculine unease before the Italian Catholic aesthetic found no greater expression than in a journal entry by Francis Parkman:

> I saw an exhibition of wax figures, among which was one of a dead Christ, covered by a sheet which the showman lifted away with great respect. The spectators, who consisted of five or six young men, immediately took their hats off. Yet, in spite of their respect for the subject on which the artist had exercised

his skill, they did not refrain from making comments on the execution of the figure.[14]

The responses of both Parkman and Norton must be considered in relation to the age's competing Protestant icon of sacred femininity: Hiram Powers's *Greek Slave,* a statue that, as we have seen, afforded a purified spectacle of the female body. While Powers's sculpture was repeatedly hailed for its spiritual power, its triumphant dematerialization of a naked girl in chains, images of the Crucifixion were customarily accused of dragging spirit into flesh. The sculptor Horatio Greenough wrote in 1846 that no "American has, until now, risked the placing before his countrymen a representation of Our Saviour. The strong prejudice, or rather conviction of the Protestant mind has, perhaps, deterred many."[15] Catholic nakedness, its exposure of the male body a taboo representation of erotic arousal and moral degradation, thus differed from Protestant nakedness, in which the exposed female body functioned as fetishized image of the middle-class masculine and feminine discipline of lust.

Such issues of spectatorship, theatricality, and subversive nakedness informed cultural attitudes toward Catholicism-as-theater. In contrast to Peter Cartwright's famed Methodist revivalism techniques that organized conversion into a tripartite architecture of audience, "anxious pen," and space of conversion, three areas of reciprocal vigilance that could shift unpredictably into disorder, Roman Catholic practices unfolded a series of controlled spectacles, radically different from the revival, with its improvisational atmosphere, but no less astonishing in performative skills. The church's "visibility," its sanctified spaces and elaborate "meanings," presented themselves as rarefied aesthetic for many sympathetic Protestant viewers. "As the procession was gliding into the Sacristy, in their pure white albs, like spirits," wrote Sophia Ripley of priests during Easter service, "they fell on their knees like snowflakes, in front of the pavilion. We ignorant children supposed it was only a slight act of reverence and a silent prayer, when they burst forth in the Stabat Mater."[16]

An antebellum painting by the American Episcopalian and West Point painting instructor Robert Weir beautifully portrays this spectatorial fascination with Catholic ritual. Entitled *Taking the Veil,* Weir's canvas depicts a young woman in bridal array kneeling before the officiating priest (Fig. 8). Himself reluctant to paint the figure of Christ although deeply interested in the neo-Gothic movement, Weir explained of an earlier work that "I painted the *Two Marys at the Tomb,* but left the

Fig. 8.   Robert W. Weir, *Taking the Veil*, 1863. Courtesy, Yale University Art Gallery.

figure of Christ to be imagined. I have often so left it. One feels a delicacy in even attempting the delineation."[17] Troubled by the Catholicism he saw in visiting Italy, Weir was studiously modest in his solemnly theatrical composition of taking the veil. He developed the painting from an 1826 sketch of a consecration he had witnessed in Rome. To the viewer's left stand a crowd of entranced spectators, who fill the hazy background of the cathedral interior and approach the illumined precincts of the main sanctuary. While the eyes of the multitude are fixed on the ceremonial transaction, the viewer's gaze alternates between the bridal figure and the crowd, witnessing its own spectatorhood on the faces of the witnesses. Weir, as American artist-onlooker, relocates himself from a main to a side gallery. The unreciprocated gaze between painter and crowd is transacted across the downcast eyes of the girl, who kneels in opulent self-effacement, head bowed, appropriately unconscious of her theatrical celebrity. On the verge of being veiled and eclipsed from public scrutiny, she affords one last backstage view of womanhood before retreating from the Protestant eye, her heavily clothed body a discreet substitute for the naked Christ whom Weir hesitated to paint.

3

CONVERSION AND ITS FICTIONS

TEN

The "Attraction of Repulsion"

Writing his spiritual autobiography in 1857, America's most outspoken convert, Orestes Brownson, claimed that "the secret history of my own country for several years prior to 1844, would reveal a Catholic reaction in the more serious portion of the Protestant sects, that would surprise those who look only on the surface of things."[1] That "Catholic reaction" comprised not only early conversions like that of Elizabeth Ann Seton in the first decade of the century and the later ones of several Transcendentalists but also a complex movement of sympathy toward the church on the part of such major antebellum writers as Harriet Beecher Stowe, Henry Wadsworth Longfellow, Nathaniel Hawthorne, and James Russell Lowell. Variously engaged with the idea of "secret history" themselves, these writers were drawn to Catholicism as a site not for truth so much as expressivity—an aesthetic and psychological region that enabled their literary production. While converts spoke in polemical or mystical language of the Truth they now possessed, these novelists and poets practiced an ambivalent strategy of partial appropriation and conversion of this Catholic "Truth" into literary effect. Antebellum Protestant authors, in their investigations of Catholicism as charismatic aesthetic, constructed a language of figurative conversion whose plot often held at its center the mystery of religious conviction. The fictional representations of Catholic history, theology, ritual, and "character" in Longfellow's *Evangeline* (1847), Hawthorne's *Scarlet Letter* (1850), Stowe's *Agnes of Sorrento* (1862), and Lowell's *Fireside Travels* (1864) are not simply manifestations of a reactionary nostalgia but explorations of contemporary forbidden regions, explorations intricately structured by competing Catholic and Protestant versions of the sacred and the profane.

Such theologically preoccupied novels as Charles Brockden Brown's *Wieland,* Hawthorne's *Marble Faun,* and Oliver Wendell Holmes's *Elsie Venner* critiqued religious conversion by unfolding the ironic and often brutal dynamic by which transformations into ideal selfhood reveal themselves as degeneration into an unintended animality. Novelistic portraits of conversion as a psychopathic delusion or, in the case of Holmes's *Elsie Venner,* as a physiological impossibility found an apposite text in Catholicism, itself viewed as a "hybrid" religion commingling the ideal and the animal, the saint and the tyrant. "Convert prose," situated in and often against these fictional investigations, actively engaged issues endemic to them, offering resolutions to the vexed relation between flesh and spirit, individual and community, freedom and authority. If read not simply as manifestations of a transcendent (hence unanalyzable) force or as symptoms of various psychic infirmities that finally issue in an uninteresting lapse into spiritual nostalgia, convert prose reveals its powerful cultural voice. The convert writings of Elizabeth Seton, Sophia Ripley, Isaac Hecker, and Orestes Brownson illustrate that theological preoccupations with problems of sin and regeneration, conviction and vocation were deeply informed by cultural and aesthetic questions of autonomous selfhood and its fashioning into an authentic identity. In contrast to an increasingly sectarian "invisible" Protestantism, the "visible" and unified spirituality of Roman Catholicism was, both for converts and for sympathetic Protestant literary artists, concretely available for personal and aesthetic inquiry. One could travel to it, get inside it, describe and emplot it, its very materiality and intricacy of symbolic meaning rendering it a compelling subject for fiction as well as spiritual autobiography.

Like those who converted, many antebellum Protestants felt themselves oppressed by cultural stereotypes that characterized their Catholic sympathies as mere lapses into inauthenticity. Sophia Ripley, for example, wrote to her cousin Ruth Charlotte Dana about the inhibitions felt by a mutual unconverted acquaintance: "Horace says he did not express to Julia and yourself half the sympathy he felt, because there is so much sentimentalism nowadays about Catholicism that he thought you would not know that it was a deeper feeling with him."[2] Ripley's stratification of religious emotion into "sympathy," "sentimentalism," and "deeper feeling" suggests the subtle prohibitions at work on the borders between the two faiths, constraints peculiarly apparent to the Catholic converts who, in engineering their disaffiliation from Protestant culture, frequently experienced themselves as beset characters in a larger drama. As Ripley's own correspondence testifies, the self-conscious interaction between the language of conversion and various fictional models of "deeper feeling" reveals entangled discourses of political and literary authenticity in which the felt imperatives of spiritual and psychological development voiced themselves through the often confessed inauthenticities of fictional narrative, with its contrivances of character, metaphor, and plot. This often anxious relationship between the authenticities of faith and those of fiction involved for Catholic converts a particularly vivid sense of the entwined relation between the Incarnation, the visible church of Rome, and the incarnationalism of language's mimetic powers. For those Protestant authors who gazed into Catholicism while remaining carefully outside it, the foreign faith at times constituted the intimate matter of their art, a substance they strove to reconstruct as part of their aesthetic property and as integral to the power of their voice. As one Catholic somewhat disingenuously observed of this Protestant phenomenon: "Our everyday life is the romance of their dreams."[3]

The preoccupation of nineteenth-century American literature and art with Catholic subject matter suggests a culturally specific conversation between a situational and affective (or rational) Protestantism and a "transformational" Catholicism that functioned as an alternately vilified and sanctified "other."[4] Within that "other" occurred spectacular and haunting transformations, as the spirit infused the flesh, converting bread into the Godhead, men and women into saints, artifacts into relics—an infiltration of the material world that Protestantism claimed to have repudiated. Celebrating such sublime interactions between flesh and spirit in his biography of St. Vincent de Paul, Jedediah Huntington dramatized the Catholic manipulation of the flesh as a culturally transcendent force: "Gory and pale, wasted with fasting, but with erect fronts and invincible eyes, do they stand, at last, on the threshold where all must stand sooner or later, and then it is seen who are the truly great. These men—yes, and these women, for it is grace and not sex that inspires courage for this war—these men and women, you know, are the saints."[5]

Such fascination with the spectral wastings of the flesh manifested itself in the superficially opposed but finally linked cultural practices of church burnings and mass watching. At home or abroad, Protestant spectators accused contemporary Irish and Italian Catholicism of all the deficiencies (and then some) of lived reality while simultaneously discovering within its corrupt spectacles the dangerous plenitude of a fleshly sublime. In watching Catholicism and, even more, in writing about it, one claimed its bodily transformations for those of one's art. But to practice it was to lose not only social but creative power. About the possibility of actually subscribing to the Catholic faith, of believing in the literal as well as aesthetic authenticity of St. Peter's, Hawthorne observed: "It would be but compelling myself to take the actual for the ideal; an exchange which is always to our loss, in things physical and moral."[6]

Occurring alongside a widespread hatred of popery, the pro-Catholic movement baffled antebellum observers of both persuasions. Reluctant to claim the Protestant engagement with things Catholic as divinely engineered, one Catholic writer vaguely concluded that "we are only conscious that some mysterious and irresistible agency is gradually augmenting the proportion of the Catholic element in American society and weakening the Protestant."[7] Nativist Protestants relied on equally mystified descriptions of cultural change, typically imaging such irresistible power as masking an elaborately calculated papal or Jesuit intentionality, the American fascination with Catholicism the result of insinuation conspiring with enchantment. Samuel F. B. Morse, subordinating images of Catholic violence and persecution to even more dubious claims of designing seductiveness, declared that the hated papists had "but one aim in this country, which absorbs all others, and that is to make themselves popular."[8] At the heart of Morse's xenophobic imagery of oppressive authority lay the puzzling specter of religious curiosity and spiritual desire. Morse's own career expressed that conflicted dynamic. As a gifted young painter he traveled through Italy, simultaneously developing the prejudices that would soon thereafter issue in virulent nativist writings and painting such tranquil canvases as *Chapel of the Virgin at Subiaco* (Fig. 9). Completed in January 1831, Morse's painting of a young woman kneeling before a roadside shrine depicts a sheltering Catholicism in which shepherds and female worshiper are framed without being constricted by the shrine. The balanced openness and community of this pious pastoral confirm its safety, although such comfort frankly depends upon the consolations of anonymity. The worshiping female is an unknown, half-seen figure whose function is essentially architectural as her bent shape corresponds to that of the shrine. As a painterly form, the worshiper is conspicuous while the Virgin is hidden and the body of the retreating shepherd even further distanced from our view.[9]

In contrast to such carefully spatialized compositions, nativist tracts by Morse and others advertised a melodramatic thematics of abduction, claustrophobic interiority, and precipitate surrender that led one Episcopalian minister to observe that "people talk as though the Catholics

Fig. 9. Samuel F. B. Morse, *Chapel of the Virgin at Subiaco*, 1831. Courtesy, Worcester Art Museum, Worcester, Massachusetts.

were masters of some jugglery by which men could be bewitched out of their religious faith without knowing it."[10] Nativist fears of papal seduction found unwitting confirmation in the language of converts, who themselves felt subject to a mysterious enticement. Isaac Hecker wrote to Brownson in 1844: "The life that leads me to the Church is deeper than all thought and expression and if I attempt to give a reason or to explain why I am led to the Church afterwards I always feel that it never reaches the reason and I feel its inadequacy."[11] In an age when the term *romance* figured frequently to describe narrative prose, the Protestant identification of Rome with the seductive mysteries of the imagination endowed the church with the controversial powers of fiction. To the nativist Reverend Sparry, this meant that all literature was logically in the church's province:

> It is a fact which has attracted but little notice, which nevertheless is worthy of serious consideration, that much of the popular literature of the day is tinctured with a spirit of mysticism and romance, which embosoms and embalms, which gives beauty and power to the Romish system. . . .

> We love to contemplate objects and scenes invested with pomp and glory and mystery, and the Romish system provides largely for the gratification of this feeling. Hence it may be called the *religion of romance*. Poets and novelists have drawn largely from this source of inspiration, and paid it back with interest. . . . Scarcely does there a poetic fragment or a novel appear, but you find this infusion of Romish superstition and idolatry. Thus the poison of their system is infused in our literature; the mind is imperceptibly corrupted and ensnared, and the way gradually prepared for the spread and triumph of the Romish religion.[12]

If papist romance contaminated the nativist sense of realism, it formed an intriguing ornament to some of New England's liberal Protestant elite. Writing to Margaret Fuller from Baltimore in 1843, Emerson condescendingly delighted in what the Reverend Sparry so feared, the "romance" of the mass:

> It is a dear old church, the Roman I mean, and today I detest the Unitarians and Martin Luther and all the parliament of Barebones. We understand so well the joyful adhesion of the Winckelmanns and Tiecks and Schlegels [German converts]; just as we seize with joy the fine romance and toss the learned Heeren [historian of the ancient world] out of the window; unhappily with the same sigh as belongs to the romance: "Ah! that one word of it were true!"[13]

Catholicism and romance are disposable commodities available for buoyant gestures of consumption or repudiation, material items external and inferior to idealist essence. For Emerson, Hecker's conversion, in particular, violated manly etiquette, less because of its cultural deviance than because Hecker disturbed the aesthetic illusion of Catholic romance by persisting in talking about it. "We are used to this whim of a man's choosing to put on and wear a painted petticoat," Emerson recorded in his journal of Hecker, "as we are to whims of artists who wear a medieval cap or beard, and attach importance to it; but, of course, they must say nothing about it to us . . . but if once they speak of it, they are not the men we took them for and we do not talk with them twice."[14]

Portrayed by nativist rhetoric as importing a threatening ethnic heterogeneity, the "immigrant church," like its converts, was endowed with virtually magical powers of communal cohesion. If Protestants discredited the papacy's apostolic theology as a presumptuous commingling of the human and divine, they remained deeply attracted by its organizational and doctrinal unity—an ambivalence that typically manifested itself by simultaneous attacks on the church and praise for various individuals in it. Catholic saints, in particular, attracted repeated Protestant praise for their charismatic individualism. As Ignatius Loyola inspired Francis Parkman's admiration for his virile asceticism, so other saints were similarly celebrated for their masterful bodily control and institutional power. Even Theodore Parker conceded to the alien faith a cohesive and not wholly undesirable energy, concluding his conflicted portrait of St. Bernard by acknowledging that "by the might of his spirit alone, this emaciated monk kept the wide world in awe."[15] Like St. Bernard, whose charismatic will enforced a connection between spirit and society, St. Ambrose embodied the church's doctrinal unities of spirit and letter, faith and works. "Thus he stands among those heroes of history," wrote an essayist for the *North American Review,* "those nobles of God's own court, who have renewed their strength by divine grace, and wrought out eternal life from the imperishable tissue woven by faith and good works. Honor to Ambrose for this union, we say, sturdy Protestants as we are."[16]

Longfellow, however, soon demonstrated that the romance of the church was inextricably bound into the Protestant imagination, incapable of being tossed about and finally out. As the Reverend Sparry sensed, one could toss aside neither the romance nor the faith; rather they combined to form a burden of peculiar weight for some New England authors and their readers.

As in the days of her youth, Evangeline rose in his vision.
H. W. *Longfellow,* Evangeline, *II,v,1367*

America's most popular nineteenth-century example of Catholicism as Protestant romance, *Evangeline,* took Longfellow fifteen months to write and reached its sixth edition within three months of publication in 1847.[17] Although Hawthorne reportedly rejected the legend because it had "no strong lights and heavy shadows,"[18] the story of Acadian exile and Evangeline's lifelong pursuit of her bridegroom, Gabriel, emerged in Longfellow's treatment as shadowed indeed. While the Catholic maiden's failed search for her beloved intermittently appears as a purifying affliction, her story is one of overpowering loss, of the protracted thwarting of desire and its punitively brief consolation. Anticipating the postbellum wanderings of Melville's Clarel through a dessicated Holy Land, those of Evangeline across the American continent embody directionless pursuit and spiritual suffering.

Expelled from the sacred domesticity of her Catholic home, an Acadian settlement that enjoys an equilibrated distance from the contamination of both the Old World and the New ("Alike were they free from / Fear, that reigns with the tyrant, and envy, the vice of republics"),[19] Evangeline wanders through the wilds of America, an early and desperate tourist. Although her Acadian home is in the New World, its domestic interior, prior to the British invasion, claims the protective quiet of a European cathedral.

> As in a church, when the chant of the choir at intervals ceases,
> Footfalls are heard in the aisles, or words of the priest at the altar,
> So, in each pause of the song, with measured motion the clock clicked.
>
> (I,ii,215–17)

What remains of this pre-industrial religious serenity after the British have expelled the Acadians is the clicking clock; as an extended and hushed rendition of a story about waiting, Longfellow's two-part poem transforms this cathedral quiet into the silence of an American void. Unrolling its ten cantos of somber, uncertainly suspenseful hexameters, the poem displays the primeval geography of Evangeline's search and memorializes the stasis of her unremitting devotion. "Slowly, slowly, slowly the days succeeded each other" (II,iv,1207) intones the poet, his murmuring, meandering tone invoking the mournful hemlocks and wandering rivers of his poetic landscape. Copying the day's work on large sheets at night without using his eyes, then again in ink the next morning, Longfellow labored to create this impression of meander, later remarking that "*Evangeline* is so easy for you to read because it was so hard for me to write."[20] Like many others, Oliver Wendell Holmes delighted in the narcotic spiritual effect of Longfellow's hexameters: "The hexameter has been often criticized, but I do not believe any other measure could have told that lovely story with such effect, as we feel when carried along the tranquil current of these brimming, slow-moving, soul-satisfying lines."[21]

Although *Evangeline* anticipates the spiritual sterility of Melville's *Clarel,* its author was still ideologically committed to the redemptive worth of suffering; unlike the dialogic intensities of Melville's pilgrims, whose querulous conversations presage the final stages of metaphysical hysteria, the characters in *Evangeline* remain courteously silent, encased in the dirge-like narrative voice. Heard throughout the poem is the clicking of time, for the mute suffering of Longfellow's exiled Catholic Acadians is still young with the shock of lost union. Constructing and memorializing this exiled faith, the Protestant narrative voice imagines the Catholic Evangeline as heroic sufferer, one whose foreign piety permits a profound sentimental identification between the male author and his female subject. Orestes Brownson may well have been thinking of *Evangeline* in diagnosing the morbidity of sentimental fiction and attributing it to Protestantism: "There is a deep melancholy that settles upon the world as it withdraws from Catholicity. All Protestant nations are sad."[22] Brownson's diagnosis of his era's sadness, while characteristically exaggerated, nonetheless suggests an important connection between the felt sense of deficiency expressed by many antebellum Protestants and the consolation of their sentimental fictions of Catholicism.

As Longfellow's narrative poem implies, the relevant context for such melancholic wandering was the antebellum tourist nostalgically revisiting Catholic Europe. If eighteenth-century America is the poem's ostensible text, nineteenth-century Europe is its other, suppressed, location. Weaving Christian Americans' sense of exile (from Eden, from the Virgilian pastoral, from Egypt, and from Europe) into his Acadian drama, Longfellow articulated his own lifelong attachment to European culture and his New England sense of exile from an unrecoverable Catholic community. Longfellow had visited Europe extensively and had made a career of translating its literatures and teaching its languages; his identity as American tourist abroad enhances his identification with the traveler Evangeline, an identity between Unitarian poet and French Catholic heroine symbolically confirmed by a sculpture that greets visitors to the Longfellow house in Cambridge: the bust of the poet with the figure of Evangeline behind him. Even Evangeline's parental home, floating in the timeless present of a natural solitude emptied of culture ("This is the forest primeval"), is implicated in the genteel alienation of the New England tourist who travels in remote European regions, witnessing their Catholic features while recording his exclusion from them. Thus Longfellow describes the property surrounding Evangeline's Acadian homestead as an analogue to a Catholic European tourist site:

> Under the sycamore-tree were hives overhung by a penthouse,
> Such as the traveller sees in regions remote by the roadside,
> Built o'er a box for the poor, or the blessed image of Mary.
> (I,i,87–89)

Anonymously reviewing his friend's poem in the *Salem Advertiser*, Hawthorne adroitly converted its relentless sadness into a more acceptable, if finally unpersuasive, spiritual redemptiveness. Of Evangeline's discovery of Gabriel after a thirty-eight-year search and his immediate death in her arms, Hawthorne wrote:

> It is a theme, indeed, not to be trusted in the hands of an ordinary writer who would bring out only its gloom and wretchedness; it required the true poet's deeper insight to present it to us . . . its pathos all illuminated with beauty. . . . We remember no such triumph as the author has here achieved, transfiguring Evangeline, now old and gray, before our eyes, and making us willingly acquiesce in all the sorrow that has befallen her, for the sake of the joy which is prophesied and realized within her.[23]

Perhaps already embarked on the creation of his own Madonna-like heroine Hester Prynne, whose long-suspended reunion with Dimmesdale similarly occurs with his death in her arms, Hawthorne rightly sensed that the burden of Longfellow's plot was the achievement of willing female acquiescence to an almost crucifixional suffering. As the implied "ordinary writer" who would bring out an undesirable gloom, Hawthorne excused himself from the burden of Longfellow's repressive Unitarianism, creating, instead of the heroic Evangeline, the ambiguously righteous Hester.

As Catholic maiden expelled by the inhumane English troops from the sacramental order of her Acadian village, a town where chimney smoke rose "like clouds of incense ascending" (I,i,50), Evangeline figures as a compelling poetic heroine for readers of the domestic novel, themselves absorbed in the attainment and maintenance of a private sphere secure from the depredations of economic or imperial power. Longfellow's evocation of a lost domesticity drew the convert Sophia Ripley's praise: "You will forgive it to the fanaticism of a newly received child of the church, if I say," wrote Ripley, "that the tribute of devotion you have offered to this our Holy Mother by the expression of your Catholic sympathies seems to me to have been repaid to you by a deeper inspiration than your Muse had ever before received."[24] Although Ripley claimed that the inspiration of the poem was Catholic, its preoccupation is less with Evangeline's deepening religious commitment than with her romantic loss, and it argues, accordingly, that her travels constitute not so much a pilgrimage as a psychological endurance contest, for "before her extended, / Dreary and vast and silent, the desert of life" (II,i,683–84). Although she eventually attains spiritual peace, the evangelical maiden's existential martyrdom as she wanders "Bleeding, barefooted, over the shards and thorns of existence" (II,i,732) occupies all but the poem's final stanzas, a disproportion that suggests the compelling attraction of thwarted female gratification for Longfellow.

On first hearing the story, he reportedly declared that "it is the best illustration of faithfulness and the constancy of woman that I have ever heard of or read."[25] Enamored of this image of wifely fidelity, Longfellow was also imaginatively preoccupied with evading its reach and frustrating its aspirations. Thus, having endured considerable time apart, Evangeline and Gabriel suffer one of the great missed reunions of sentimental literature. After panoramic journeyings that have finally led Evangeline down the Mississippi, the lovers are suddenly revealed by the poet to be only feet apart; the weary heroine, accompanied by her priest, sleeps on an island in the "lakes of the Atchafalaya," while the grieving Gabriel and his companions

> glided along, close under the lee of the island,
> But by the opposite bank, and behind a screen of palmettos,
> So that they saw not the boat. . . .
>
> (II,ii,836–38)

If the proximity of the exiled lovers is a sublime coincidence, their failure to meet is an equally stunning coincidence that crystallizes the poet's psychological fascination with failed union (missed encounters recur with ritual regularity through the story) and an accompanying aesthetic attachment to the exquisiteness of such pain.

This famous failed meeting of Catholic lovers transpires in the tropical intricacies of bayou country, where the mosses "Waved like banners that hang on the walls of ancient cathedrals" (II,ii,771). Derived from the travel sketches of a "fugitive monk," Karl Anton Postl's *Life in the New World; or, Sketches of American Society* (1844), Longfellow's Louisiana landscape invokes both the enclosures of the medieval past and the sentimental interiority of Evangeline's tribulations, sufferings that seclude her in a radical privacy of affectional attachment, even as she relentlessly travels through America's public spaces. If the vestigial medievalism weaves its Gothic details through a New World wilderness to invoke a mythic time of united Christendom, it finally accedes to a distinctively American ennui.[26] The Gothic dimness and allure of the Louisiana lowlands emphasize that Evangeline's is a psychological journey to an American underworld, whose primordial "roar of the grim alligator" (II,ii,805) finally absorbs the cathedral interiors of the Old World, closeting her in emptiness. Unaware of Gabriel's proximity, Evangeline and her priest paddle hopelessly through the bayou's "shadowy aisles" (II,ii,788) toward and beyond the failed reunion, proceeding through a luminous watery landscape whose reflections double the lovers' images without permitting their encounter.

This stasis of thwarted desire keeps safely at bay even the possibility of French Catholic reproduction and homebuilding while endowing Evangeline with the sentimental credentials of wifehood. Involuntarily celibate, Evangeline testifies to the transcendent claims of domesticity by virtue of her persistent exclusion from them. Generically poised between prose and lyric, the poem too struggles against its own alternatives. Thanking Hawthorne for his kind review of the poem, Longfellow fashioned a graceful witticism from his poem's prosiness, its very lack of differentiation: "This success I owe entirely to you, for being willing to forego the pleasure of writing a prose tale, which many people would have taken for poetry, that I might write a poem which many people take for prose."[27] At an early stage of the poem's composition, Longfellow had planned to entitle both his heroine and the poem "Gabrielle," but because Gabrielle sounded reportedly too masculine in the American pronunciation of the name, Longfellow settled on the relatively rare name of Evangeline, the female derivative of Evangel.[28] Longfellow's transfer of his heroine's original name to her bridegroom suggests an underlying lack of difference between them—a mirrored characterization that contributes to the poem's almost punitive stasis as Evangeline moves around within herself rather than pursues an individuated other. Out West, Evangeline sits in the tent of a Jesuit missionary only to hear that Gabriel has been there the week before and told the same tale of lost love, another near encounter that enables this Unitarian romance of Catholic suffering to further delay its end.

As one of the primary agents of these thematics of suspended consummation, nature reflects but never converges. From her island slumber, Evangeline awakes and climbs back in her boat for a sunset journey across waters reminiscent of Cooper's Lake Glimmerglass.

> Hanging between two skies, a cloud with edges of silver,
> Floated the boat, with its dripping oars, on the motionless water.
>
> (II,ii,868–69)

This luminous tableau displays the poem's identification of the sacred and the romantic. Catholicism, in the figure of Evangeline's priestly companion, has officially sanctioned her romantic quest, bidding the girl to "accomplish thy work of affection!" (II,i,724). Evangeline can then participate in numerous such illuminated exchanges between sky, water, and spirit; no mediating others mar her union with the inspirational transparencies of sentiment.

Touched by the magic spell, the sacred fountains of feeling
Glowed with the light of love, as the skies and waters around her.
(II,ii,871–72)

Such lexical reunions of the aesthetic, the sacred, and the sentimental
entice the lovers (and readers) to keep working for union while at the
same time suggesting an underlying crisis of sameness that renders the
project futile. Her ardor gradually transformed into a sacrificial labor,
Evangeline's joint pursuit of God and Gabriel finally subordinates the
thematics of exile to the baffling circularity of the Protestant romance
that recounts it. The lovers' failed pursuit of one another eventually
emphasizes the elusive proximity and distance of the Deity. "Art thou so
near unto me, and yet thy voice does not reach me?" (II,iii,1047),
soliloquizes Evangeline from the bayou, her own unconsummated marriage invested with the vanishing communion between God and his New
England Unitarian worshipers. Catholic imagery, representing what has
been simultaneously lost and repudiated, powerfully informs this liberal
Protestant poetics of foreclosed union. Even the Louisiana flowers come
to know the painful wastage of this subjectivity that voices itself in
isolation, denied communication by the retreating Catholic other.

Nearer and round about her, the manifold flowers of the garden
Poured out their souls in odors, that were their prayers and
    confessions
Unto the night, as it went its way, like a silent Carthusian.
(II,iii,1031–33)

Such moments of fragrant expressivity are silenced then as the flowers
confess to a night intent on its own contemplative seclusion. If the
American landscapes carry the burden of Protestantism's disaffiliation
from Euro-Catholic unities—the maize of the Jesuit missions forming
"Cloisters for mendicant crows" (II,iv,1211)—the forlornness of Longfellow's American epic reveals the imperial dimensions of that New
England melancholy.

Like the retreating Carthusian night, the poem practices its own
denials, twice proffering repetitions of itself in the squaw's tales of the
Mowis and of the lovesick Lilianau and in the women at the poem's
conclusion who repeat among themselves the legend of Evangeline.
These inset retellings quietly assert the supremacy of the narrative's
touristic movement over any particular resolution. As the narrative voice
unrolls its landscapes, exchanging one for the other with the detachment
of the sightseer, it offers duplications rather than consummations of itself
that aspire to the sublime proportions of the painter John Banvard's

"Moving Diorama of the Mississippi," which Longfellow saw while working on the poem. Longfellow's journal entry for December 19, 1846, captures the dreamy dissociation provoked by his sight of the twelve-hundred-foot-long moving canvas: "One seems to be sailing down the great stream; and sees the boats and sand-banks crested with cotton-wood, and the bayous by moonlight. Three miles of canvas; and a great deal of merit."[29] Imitating Banvard's moving panorama, which emphasized the attractions of passivity before an episodic scenery that simulates the viewer's movement into it, Longfellow's hexameters unfold the American landscape through the immobility of a suffering Catholic womanhood.

Of the poem's several inset narratives, the most significant occurs early on when on the eve of exile, the village notary, Father Leblanc, reassures his worried neighbors that justice will prevail by recounting the story of an orphan girl wrongly executed for the theft of some pearls. At the moment of her death, thunder strikes a bronze statue of Justice, whose scales fall to the ground, disclosing the pearls (woven by a magpie into his nest) lodged within them. Gabriel's father, Basil the Blacksmith, remains unconvinced by the story, and rightly so, for the next day the British brutally expel the entire village. Although Evangeline later recalls the girl's story to console herself in the midst of her own afflicted orphanhood, the tale's grisly sentimentality broods over the poem's conclusion, which, like the fortuitous discovery of the pearls, dislodges even as it speaks the language of redemption.

Having finally given up her search, Evangeline returns to Philadelphia—her choice of city motivated by an intuitive affinity with Quaker piety but also, undoubtedly, by Longfellow's having seen only that landscape of all those in the poem. In contrast to the nation's recently declared Manifest Destiny to expand westward, Evangeline's is a reverse migration: down the Mississippi, out West to the Jesuit missions, through northern Michigan, and back East to urban poverty. There she experiences a religious conversion that enables her to humbly forsake her romantic quest, a transformation that accords her a perspectival control over her former wandering, panoramic viewpoint: "So fell the mists from her mind, and she saw the world far below her" (II,v,1273). Notwithstanding her conversion, Evangeline hardly experiences the joyful resolution of exile expressed in mythic terms by the convert Bishop Ives, who wrote of his converted self: "I felt, as one may be supposed to feel who in his unconscious childhood had been borne off asleep from his native shore on some wreck to a desert Island, and then, in his manhood, after long subjection to want and hardship, becomes convinced of the disaster and returns to the father that begot him, and the mother who cherished his infancy."[30] In pointed contrast to Ives's return in adulthood to the parental home, Evangeline, as fictive Catholic progeny of the Protestant imagination, remains subordinate to the pathos of exile and orphanhood.

Swiftly completing her transition from marital pilgrim to religious servant, Evangeline reenters society as a Sister of Mercy who tirelessly nurses the urban poor, dying by the scores in Philadelphia's 1797 yellow fever epidemic. Quite by chance, the aged nun one day discovers her Gabriel among the dying. Embraced for one brief moment after a thirty-eight-year separation, Gabriel slumps back on his pallet and dies. Holding him to her again, Evangeline then bows her head and performs her most stunning devotional surrender, murmuring to God, "Father, I thank thee!" (II,v,1380). If this concluding embrace satisfyingly joins domesticity and celibacy in the image of the nun who loves, it more disturbingly voices the continuing imperatives of the antebellum Protestant romantic imagination to dissolve the mixtures of human intimacy into the purity of the solitary self. When approaching his own death, Hawthorne reportedly asked his son to read the reunion scene aloud, and afterwards responded, "I like that."[31]

To conservative Protestants, Catholicism's involvement with "romance" only partially explained its appeal. The Old World religion was paradoxically enmeshed as well with the suspect innovations of bourgeois culture. Observed one nativist clergyman: "Modern Liberalism, Infidelity, Ultra High Church Doctrines, the principles of expediency, all these things conspire to aid the march of Popery."[32] The felt insufficiencies of Protestant reform became increasingly confused with the pressures of modernity and led many to attribute superior, if ultimately illegitimate, powers to the marginalized Roman church. As William Ellery Channing (1780–1842), the foremost Unitarian minister of the day, explained in an open "Letter on Catholicism" to the editor of the *Louisville Western Messenger*, Protestantism was in decline, its ministers precocious instances of bourgeois alienation. According to Channing, whom Emerson called the "star of the American Church," "The great danger to a minister at this time is the want of life, the danger of being dead while he lives."[33]

How had republican freedoms produced such a sense of impenetrable exteriority, of walking deadness? Could one sufficiently ease the burden of inauthenticity and loss of intimacy by indulging in the sentimental experience of popular narratives like *Evangeline?* If the pleasures of even Evangeline's reunion with God and her beloved were insufficient, could one somehow, as Channing's "Letter" vaguely suggested, extract Catholicism's vitality while remaining outside it? Channing's admission of ministerial inadequacy situates traditional Christian struggles with spiritual indifference or hypocrisy within American Protestantism's struggles to thwart Catholicism's threatened sway over the West. From the Bostonian's Unitarian perspective, the "chains" (446) of tradition enclose liberal New England, not, as in the image's traditional referent, Catholic Europe. An enviable power invigorates both the American West and the Catholic church while the debilitating constraints of culture now enfeeble New England. Channing's critique of Romanism further confesses a personal failure to break either the "chains" of Boston tradition or the "habits, rules and criticisms" (446) of his rational faith. All that he can finally offer the younger clerical colleague to whom he addresses his "Letter" is an uncertain promise that virtue, devoid of exclusionary forms and rigid dogma, will prevail.

Channing saw clearly that republicanism and Protestantism had given powerful impetus to a competitive capitalism that shunted its ministers to the periphery of society. Like Hawthorne in the Custom House, sporting the "hang-dog look of a republican official, who, as the servant of the people, feels himself less than the least, and below the lowest, of his masters," Channing chafed against the humiliating dependencies of democratic culture.[34] Thus his conflicted support for liberal religion— his recognition that his parishioners' freedom in many ways spelled the minister's loss of authority and liberty—is the operative concern of his "Letter." In it, Channing's Unitarian rivalry with an immigrant Catholicism barely suppresses a largely unresolved vocational quandary. As Channing defensively explained, the expanding technologies of the print media only exacerbated the minister's loss of cultural status and his impotence as puppet orator. From within this competitive market, the Catholic priest emerges as Channing's empowered double—one who wraps chains around others, not himself. Although "nothing too bad can be said" (441) of the confessional, it is precisely its powers that engage Channing's admiration. As he suggests to his correspondent, the Unitarian clergy must somehow imitate the confessor's access to individual minds rather than continue to speak in generalities from the pulpit. Thus does Channing's critique of Catholicism seek to appropriate what conservative Protestants sought to banish from the shores of America: the confessional and its notorious powers of seduction. Channing's 1841 sermon "The Church" reiterated his defensive support of Unitarianism by again critiquing Catholic claims of sacramental power.

> When we come down to facts, we see it [the church] to be not a mysterious, immutable unity, but a collection of fluctuating, divided, warring individuals, who bring into it, too often, hearts and hands anything but pure. Painful as it is, we must see things as they are,—and so doing, we cannot but be struck with the infinite absurdity of ascribing to such a church mysterious powers, of supposing that it can confer holiness on its members, or that the circumstance of being joined to it is of the least moment in comparison with purity of heart and life.[35]

Beneath Channing's rejection of institutionalized supernaturalism operates a formative hierarchy of privatized spirit over collectivized letter. Channing's Unitarian distrust of Catholic claims even shares more orthodox Protestant fears of captivity within Catholic enclosures as he urges his congregation to "shudder at the thought of shutting up God in any denomination" (33). But Channing's was no simple attack on Catholicism, for while he defended the spiritual efficacies of the minister's "character" against the claims of apostolic ordination, he was far from convinced of the superiority of Protestant community. He had spent many years in Boston admiring the untiring charity and pastoral warmth of Bishop Cheverus, whose efforts he had celebrated in his 1829 essay "Remarks on the Character and Writings of Fénelon."[36] Like his conflicted appraisal in his "Letter on Catholicism," Channing's sermon "The Church" amiably denies the powers of any priestly counterpart while conceding the attractions of Catholicism's global unity. Delivering his sermon from a Congregational pulpit in Philadelphia, Channing artfully stages his subversive admiration by presenting himself as sitting in an unnamed Catholic church, studiously partial in his attention: "The voice of the officiating priest I did not hear; but these sainted dead spoke to my heart, and I was sometimes led to feel, as if an hour on Sunday spent in this communion were as useful to me, as if it had been spent in a protestant church" (29). His cautious approach to Catholicism through dialogue with the "sainted dead," rather than the living, records as well a normative sociability that evades the suspicious privacies of Catholic interiors.

Channing's worried efforts to recover clerical and personal authority figured as a primary factor in several conversions to the church among Episcopalian clergy. Recognition of the problematic connection between authority and authenticity or, in the terms of convert prose, between apostolic succession and the pastoral efficacy of the Catholic priest motivated several such conversions. For the Vermont minister Daniel Barber, his denomination's "fanciful scheme of ministerial powers given immediately, and invisibly to one another" finally could not compete against the Catholic doctrine of apostolic succession.[37] Barber's uncertainty over his professional authority had spurred his earlier switch from Congregationalism to Episcopalianism. That he then converted to Catholicism thirty years later suggests the tenacity and depth of his struggles for vocational legitimacy.

Bishop Ives was similarly preoccupied with Episcopalian ministers' lack of lawful authority. Ives's sense of the spuriousness of his clerical powers, his felt inability to give "infallible" assistance when needed, produced a dread incapacity to offer any help at all to his parishioners. When an Episcopalian priest, he "felt in my conscience wholly unable to tell with certainty, and in many vital particulars, what that [Christ's] will is."[38] Worse even than his own uncertainties and Episcopalianism's neglect of the poor, Ives declared, "was the absence, in my view, of any instituted method among Protestants for the *remission of post-baptismal sin.*" After years of reflection, Ives concluded that his authority as Episcopalian bishop ultimately derived "from the Church of Henry through Elizabeth"—an adulterous and certainly carnal heritage that compared dismally with Ives's converted view that Christ "united Himself to her [the church] in indissoluble and eternal bonds in the womb of the ever-blessed Virgin."[39] The combined impact of these issues finally motivated Ives to forsake his career and livelihood as Episcopal bishop of North Carolina and become a Catholic layman who ministered to the urban poor.

Although some appreciated the motives behind the conversions of such figures as Barber, Ives, and Joshua Huntington, the Catholic church continued to provoke deep suspicion. Even those Protestants who acknowledged how "faithfully and how tenderly the Church sought to gird life with a zone of sanctity" were still acutely sensitive to the boundaries and restraints necessary to that zone.[40] Voluntary entry into that sanctified region still indicated forms of weakness or delusion popularized by convent captivity literature, although converts like Isaac Hecker rejoiced that such captivity enabled true liberty when he wrote to Orestes Brownson that he was "freed from myself and in the hands of a God-commissioned man."[41] Antebellum Catholicism, endowed with an autochthonous power from its imposed cultural marginality, exerted a powerful attraction, especially for the liberal Protestant.[42] Sharing Channing's palpable sense of inadequacy before the spiritual equipment of the Catholic priest, other Unitarian sons felt vulnerable, even shamefully so, before the aggressively creative force of the subordinated church. James Russell Lowell explained to readers of his *Fireside Travels* (1864) that "in approaching St. Peter's, one must take his Protestant shoes off his feet. . . . Otherwise the great Basilica, with those outstretching colonnades of Bramante, will seem to be a bloated spider lying in wait for him, the poor Reformed fly."[43]

A genial redaction of ritual dramas of disrobing and initiation, Lowell's ceremonial directives to his domestic audience invited their rapt attendance at his impending passage into the hungry interior of St. Peter's. Like much tourist rhetoric, Lowell's metaphor of the bloated spider referred not only to things abroad but also to certain predatory developments at home, specifically the rapid growth of the "immigrant church" into a political power bloc, making it by 1850 the largest single religious group in America. Horace Bushnell, embattled spokesman of liberal Congregationalism, suggested the depths of the liberal Protestant fear of the immigrant when depicting Catholicism's perceived threat to the common school system: "Growing more hopeful of their ability, by the heavy vote they can wield, to turn the scale of an election one way or the other between opposing parties, and counting on the sway they can thus exert over the popular leaders and candidates, they have lately attempted a revolution of the school system of Michigan."[44] An informal cultural logic convinced Protestant observers that any who entered these predatory and insurrectionary precincts necessarily came from other marginal cultural locations, so that Protestant conversions to the church were understood as an exchange of positions from one periphery to another. Summing up the church's likely targets, one writer underscored the connection between these metaphoric configurations of predation and insurrection and the vexed issue of vocation for those excluded from the entrepreneurial marketplace: "It appeals to the tender devotion of woman, the sensitive, fastidious nature of the artist, and the discontented, restless spirit of the baffled philanthropist longing for some haven of peace."[45]

If it made sense for artists and social reformers to convert, their decision was still denoted in contemporary discourse as a "perversion" rather than a conversion. Josephine Bunkley, for example, the notorious "escaped" nun from Mother Seton's community at Emmitsburg, Maryland, referred to Newman as the "distinguished pervert from Oxford," while Harriet Beecher Stowe wrote of listening to a sermon in England by the "celebrated pervert Archdeacon Manning."[46] Although the term would not assume an almost exclusively sexual connotation until the

1890s, its mid-century meaning signified a deviation from a normative theological condition only slightly less troubling.

As a cultural landscape, Catholicism was considerably complicated by this new, ostensibly more favorable (if "perverse"), romantic association with the feminine, the artistic, and the politically progressive. Those "traits" formed an awkward alliance with conservative Protestant suspicions of Jesuitical intrigue, inquisitional torture, and rank superstition. As an imaginative category, how could Catholicism contain these extremes of feminine and masculine excess, the "sensitive, fastidious nature" of the artist and the brutality of the Inquisition? Unable to forgo such blatant contradictions, liberal Protestant observers resorted to a vocabulary of yoked alternatives that became the particular preserve of those sympathetically inclined to Catholicism. In contrast to the insistent opposition between purity and corruption characteristic of nativist rhetoric, this developing language of Protestant sympathy practiced a studied ambivalence. Addressing the Home Missionary Society in 1847, Bushnell, one of America's most innovative strategists of Protestant conversion, relied on such ambivalent language to appraise recent conversions to Rome. Implicitly referring to the Oxford movement's impact both in England and America, Bushnell sought to downplay Rome's competing conversion model by explaining how a "cultivated man" could enter the "gate of superstition":

> These are only caprices, accidents, idiosyncracies, which support no general conclusion, save that between opposite superlatives, the sublimities and follies of mankind, there is often a natural brotherhood. Thus, over-cultivation may sometimes join hands at the church door with barbarism, both entering as fellow proselytes together.[47]

Bushnell's single "general conclusion" is a significant one, for it suggests how Rome (and its various detachable insignia) functioned as a primary rhetorical site for the production and expression of ambivalence. Just as the displacements and projections of the American tourist in Rome produced a characteristic discursive structure of alternating extremes (the Episcopalian Reverend Field's response of "admiration and disgust" was typical),[48] so these tourist dynamics informed Protestant clerical discussions of Catholic conversion at home. Bushnell offered his hypothetical model of yoked opposites to explain an otherwise inexplicable phenomenon: the conversion of educated individuals to Catholicism. Rendered plausible by appeal to a hypothesized familial kinship (the notion of a "natural brotherhood"), Bushnell's explanation in fact provided another mystification, itself designed to "join hands" with his determinate conception of the church as the proverbial "gate of superstition."

The widespread perception of deviation from the straight line of Protestantism suggests that an ideologized topography covertly structured attitudes about those who followed the various "roads" to Rome—a topography crucially inflected by a language of tourism that often conflated going to Rome and becoming a Catholic. Having compared prosperous Protestant cities to the impoverished and malarial suburbs of Rome, the art collector James Jackson Jarves applied this tourist topography to that of conversion, explaining that "the path to her [Rome] lies over the plain of death."[49] Through the "perversions" of this contaminated topography cut the vertical path of purified piety, a path followed by the properly circumspect tourist abroad as well as the cautious observer of Romanism at home.

As linked terms, then, conversion and perversion spoke powerfully of the temptations and contaminations of the ethnically and sectionally divided antebellum political landscape—dangers to which American Catholics felt susceptible as well, only in reverse. Not roads to Rome, but roads to America and assimilation led to perversion for Hugh Quigley, who wrote of Irish priests in his Irish-American novel, *The Prophet of the Ruined Abbey; or, A Glance of the Future of Ireland* (1855): "If such be their high vocation, they ought not to blend with, but rather remain separate from, the people which they are ordained to regenerate and reform! But, if they become absorbed in the amalgam of races which form the population of these United States, and as a consequence adopt their prejudices and vices, their usefulness as missionaries is at an end, and instead of converting others, they become themselves perverted."[50] Newly sensitized to the cultural deficiencies and coercions of antebellum America, Catholic converts frequently adopted this defensive immigrant perspective, at times provoked into a sexual disgust at the license (and implicitly, the allure) of Protestant pluralism. The convert John Bryant, for example, wrote in his well-received treatise *The Immaculate Conception of the Most Blessed Virgin Mary, Mother of God* (1855):

> Three hundred years have now expired since the impetuous, turbulent, and petulant geniuses of the sixteenth-century first began to play harlot against the Church of Christ. The impure sects which then arose were confessedly conceived and born in lust. . . . America has had the misfortune to receive some of all these Sodomitic Sects, but has added to them by swift and sure

degrees, until it holds the unenviable distinction of having given open and public license to *seraglioism*.[51]

   Contemporary sympathetic attempts to uncover the precise relationship between Mother Church and her erotically deviant convert offspring only mystified it further. Like Longfellow and Evangeline, the two religions seemed strangely intertwined—the world of religious prejudice oddly adjacent to that of conversion, their antagonisms and affections in reciprocal and often sentimental interaction. As the figure of the cherubic boy dressed up in monk's clothing suggests (Fig. 10), antebellum Protestants at times displaced this mimetic dynamic into the safer domain of child's play; there, the child could be jovially reproached for an otherwise troublesome inauthenticity, envious curiosity, and even appetite for a religious transvestism. Struggling to articulate this relation, David Reese, a New York doctor intent on exposing the "ultraisms" of his age (a list that included animal magnetism, phrenology, homeopathy, "ultra-temperance," and "ultra-Protestantism"), finally characterized Catholic-Protestant relations as an "attraction of repulsion." In Reese's mechanistic conception, the centrifugal forces of "repulsion" were mysteriously yet scientifically linked with the centripetal motions of "attraction." Like Jonathan Edwards's earlier attempt to rephrase the Calvinist language of the covenant in a novel rhetoric of "attraction," Reese's imagery replaces prevailing nativist notions of coercion and conspiracy with an interior movement of the psyche, if not the soul.[52]
   Such Catholic apologists as New York Archbishop John Hughes resorted to a similar gravitational model when discussing the phenomenon of conversion. Like individual believers, Protestantism and Catholicism were mutually engaged by an interactive dynamic of dispersal and centralization that Hughes predicted would eventually exhaust Protestantism: "The declension of Protestantism is in two opposite directions, as the positive or negative principle prevails—the negatives all rushing off, every one in his own way, and the positives all gathering towards a Catholic centre, under the influence of a prudence that dare not reject divine authority."[53] Delivered to a New York audience in 1850, Hughes's address implicitly equates religious with political secession, his rhetoric resonant with the nation's mounting sectional rivalries; if the effort to reposition an increasingly divided America around a Catholic "centre" failed in practice, Hughes's language of "gathering" and "influence" participates in the political dilemmas of the 1850s over what constituted the grounds for a legitimate national union.

Fig. 10.

How truth is better than a lie;
Straightforwardness than mystery;
How heads amount to more than *chapeaux*,
Or e'en (see Willis) ladies' "abbos";
How cheats are cheated, biters bit,
And all rogues get the worst of it;
This little shaver in disguise
Shows now to everybody's eyes.

For taking cowl, and cord, and cape,
  And holy gown, from an old trunk, he
Trying a reverend man to *ape*,
  Only appears A LITTLE MONK-Y.

"The Disguise"
Boston Miscellany of Literature (1842)

In describing the systemic quality of his age's great religious quarrel with popery, Reese's "diagnosis" provides cultural grounding for the spiritual ambivalence so central to popular and elite fictions of the antebellum decades. If the novels of Melville and Hawthorne often explained to their readers that spiritual hatred and love were metaphysically and narratively linked, made manifest in the transcendent bonds between Claggart, Vere, and Billy Budd or between Chillingworth, Dimmesdale, and Hester Prynne, cultural spokesmen like Reese and Hughes explained those bonds as emerging from the peculiar reciprocities of contemporary religious controversy.

ELEVEN

The Protestant Minister and His Priestly Influence

The rhetorical configuration of a mystified, "perverse" Catholicism and a touristic Protestant discourse of sympathetic inquiry struggling to maintain its linear progress in its passage through Catholic perversity informs Hawthorne's short story "The Minister's Black Veil." First published in *The Token* in 1836, Hawthorne's tale of a Connecticut minister's enigmatic decision to live life shrouded in a black veil exploits the growing fascination with the secrets of Catholicism and, more particularly, as shown by the Ursuline riot, with the potentially incendiary provocations of the veiled. Like Rebecca Reed's glowing and phobic description of the Ceremony of the Black Veil in *Six Months in a Convent,* Hawthorne's story, published one year later, proposes a sinful gratification, a sensationalism at the heart of such self-abnegation. Does Parson Hooper's veil represent humility, or does it, as Reed and other nativists charged of veiled nuns, disguise shameful deeds and a devious countenance? Perplexed and suspicious, Hawthorne's narrator and spectator of this ministerial exhibition can only wonder whether the veiled and praying face signifies unmentionable crime. "Did he seek to hide it from the dread Being whom he was addressing?"[1] As a detachable piece of the metaphorical fabric of anti-Catholicism, the veil carries powers of concealment and illicit knowing lodged by nativist rhetoric in the confessional interiors of the immigrant religion. Synecdoche for this immigrant power, the veil is subversively positioned as the ethnically and theologically foreign element in Hawthorne's historical romance of indigenous New England Calvinism while the congregation's gaze upon the veil draws its particular power from the antebellum Protestant touristic gaze on the spectacular obscurities of Rome.

Just as Reed and other anti-Catholic writers attributed magical powers to those immured behind veils and monastery walls, so Hawthorne
suggests that Parson Hooper's "mysterious emblem" (39) endows him
with moral acumen and a suspicious spiritual power. Although when
summoned by the dying, he stoops to "whisper consolation" (49) rather
than administer Last Rites, the implied parallel between Parson Hooper
and Catholic priest is clear; like the keys of the priesthood, Hooper's veil
provides him a supernaturally efficacious supplement that clothes and
empowers his otherwise naked Protestant ministerial authority—so
much so that in later years, he becomes known as "Father Hooper"
(49)—a name that studiously ignores the minister's transvestism. With
his veil, after all, he more nearly resembles a nun than a priest.

After veiling himself, Hooper delivers a masterful Edwardsian sermon, unfolding a series of eschatological threats with "melancholy
voice" (40).[2] While Hooper embodies the potentially egocentric indulgence of Great Awakening revivalism and, more particularly, the dangers
of an evangelical dependence on Scripture (the veil throwing "its ob-
scurity between him and the holy page" [39]), these dangers of Protestant
revivalism are rendered seductive by their association with cloistral
ritual—a seductiveness born not only of things Catholic but also of the
sexual transgression implicit in Hooper's simulation of the veiled nun.
Unfolded with reference to a dual historical horizon—that of eighteenth-
century New England Calvinism and the story's contemporary Jacksonian context of charged debate over the burgeoning attractions of
nunneries—Hawthorne's tale subtly appropriates anti-Catholicism to
critique the separationist excesses of Protestant revivalism and nativism.
Thus the minister's transgression against his congregation invokes alleged Catholic violations of communal norms; like the spectral figure of
the Jesuit of popular nativist discourse, Hooper's veil transforms him
into a dematerialized and predatory figure, walking with "an almost
noiseless step" (39) through his village.

The tale's constituent oppositions between enclosure (within the black
veil and its terrors, or within the "veil, that shuts in time from eternity"
[51], or, most generally, within the veil of Original Sin that lies over all
our faces) and disclosure, between concealment and revelation, organize
Hawthorne's dissatisfactions with the pallor of Protestantism, exposed,
like the story's "pale-faced congregation" (39), to an alternative, enigmatic, and visually absorbing spirituality. Although the twin celestial
lights of conversion and eternity imagistically balance the blackness of
Hooper's veil, the superior strength of such Protestant illuminations is
provisional at best, for the diffuse perspective of the narrative gaze

suggests a persistent depth of attachment to the veil's sexually and theologically enigmatic aesthetic. Mapping the contours of the minister's evasive self-presentation, the narrative voice usually adopts the bewildered perspective of the parishioners, who "but darkly understood him" (42). At key moments, however, the narrative voice can and does assume Parson Hooper's phobic perspective from behind the veil, surmising at one point that the "congregation was almost as fearful a sight to the minister, as his black veil to them" (39). Enclosed within the vulnerable, if radically asserted, privacy of this pulpit perspective, the reader looks first upon the pallid audience, then into the readerly self, subjected like the fictional parishioners to the all-seeing eye of God: "The subject had reference," explains the narrator of the veiled Hooper's sermon, "to secret sin, and those sad mysteries which we hide from our nearest and dearest, and would fain conceal from our own consciousness, even forgetting that the Omniscient can detect them" (40).

The joined gazes of parishioner and reader are obsessively drawn toward but perpetually excluded from the veiled rhetorical power of minister and author—a seduction that borders on the illicit intimacies of necrophilia. Thus, when Hooper bids farewell to a corpse, Hawthorne identifies the reader's perspective with that of the corpse: "As he stooped, the veil hung straight down from his forehead, so that, if her eye-lids had not been closed for ever, the dead maiden might have seen his face" (42). Tantalizingly offering the imagined disclosure of Hooper's face (of the nun's face behind the veil), the moment recapitulates the story's other significant instance of taboo intimacy, Hooper's cemetery visits, during which he is seen by the "stare of the dead people" (48). Lodged uneasily between the inaccessible perspectives of the veiled Hooper and the dead, the reader lapses, like Hooper's parishioners, into the subordinated status of object for that gaze.

As if heeding William Ellery Channing's troubled admission that Unitarian generalities from the pulpit were no match for the confessional's "access" to individual minds, Hawthorne's spiritually awakened minister has abandoned the torpor of a deinstitutionalized Protestantism, enabled by the veil's separation to obtain a radical intimacy with his listeners. Among the many aggressive disclosures that the enclosing crape paradoxically makes available are views into each parishioner's interior. "Each . . . felt as if the preacher had crept upon them, behind his awful veil, and discovered their hoarded iniquity of deed or thought" (40). The story's adjacent discourses of Calvinist revivalism, confessional intimacies, and the authorial powers of the historical romancer led Hawthorne to speculate in a later journal entry about its further potential: "A Father Confessor—his reflections on character, and the contrast of the inward man with the outward, as he looks round on his congregation—all whose secret sins are known to him."[3] Intrigued by the morally perilous power of such a confessional vision, Hawthorne's Parson Hooper remained, however, his most fully articulated image of a sacrilegious and charismatic Catholic figure, deploying an unsettling combination of anonymity and intimacy on the exposed and vulnerable Protestant reader.

As suggested by Hawthorne's use of the black veil to expose the limitations of Calvinist piety, the American romantic preoccupation with symbolic indeterminacy gravitated toward an increasingly influential immigrant Catholicism. The rhetorical structure of this ambivalence, apparent in Bushnell's imagery of conjoined cultivation and barbarism or in Hawthorne's "ambiguity of sin or sorrow" ("Minister's Black Veil," 48), contributed to wider cultural debates over what constituted true conversion amid the multiform "perversions" of a voluntarist, pluralist society. As elsewhere in Hawthorne's fiction, the sincerity of individual piety depends finally on the quality of social relation, for the narrator evaluates the spectacular power of the veiled minister according to communal issues of religious separatism and the Catholic cloister. While Hooper's conversion may indeed have been a genuine acknowledgment of "secret sin" (46), its exclusionism distorts his various obligations to his congregation and to his betrothed. Emblem of the blinding (and shaming) truth of Hooper's vision and agent of further conversions within his congregation, the veil stands aligned with the iconographic and efficacious spiritual power exchanged between priest and individual sinner; emblem of Hooper's imprisoning exclusionism, the veil conversely advertises the antisocial perversions of Edwardsian separatism. The only community that survives its alienating effects is a fragile one between the minister and those parishioners who are poised between the agony of conviction and the pleasures of assurance. "His converts always regarded him with a dread peculiar to themselves, affirming, though but figuratively, that, before he brought them to celestial light, they had been with him behind the black veil" (49).

But the story's reiterated obscurities dim such spiritual illumination. Having endured the effects of the veil in their church, the congregation's deputies sit uneasily before it in the minister's parlor, their anxiety registering the transgressive presence not only of the sacred within profane space but also of unbridled clerical authority within domestic space. During this exquisitely uncomfortable encounter, Hooper enjoys even greater than priestly confessional powers, for through his crape he can see both the faces and the hearts of his parishioners, his domination quite complete: "Thus they sat a considerable time, speechless, confused, and shrinking uneasily from Mister Hooper's eye, which they felt to be fixed upon them with an invisible glance" (45). The symbolic indeterminacy of the veil only serves to strengthen Hooper's grasp over his neighbors while the proliferating enclosures of death that conclude the story confirm the eerie persistence of his invisible dominion. As the narrator ponders the minister's veiled and shrouded corpse inside its coffin underground, the multiple captivities barely constrain a lingering sense of the priestly Protestant eye looking upward.

Unlike Parson Hooper, with his obsessively private involvement with the "stare of the dead people" (48), Channing, in his 1841 sermon "The Church," projected an image of himself communing with the dead (but not with the priest) to voice a Christian sociality, not a Gothic deviance into the obsessional psychic recesses of Catholicism. The theologically progressive Channing wanted such community less for its reformist capacities than for the security it offered, while the increasingly orthodox Orestes Brownson chose Catholicism as the only path to genuine social reform. Writing to Hecker in the year before his own conversion, Brownson explained that

> no work of reform can be carried on with any prospects of suc-
> cess, till we have recovered the unity and catholicity of the
> Church as an outward visible institution. . . . no theory, how-
> ever true it may be, if born as pure theory, can ever embody
> itself in a practical institution. It must be born in union with its
> institution, as the child, if living, is born the union of soul and
> body. It is as impossible for men to embody spirit, as it is for
> them to animate a body in which the spirit is not.[4]

For Channing, Catholicism's union of spirit and letter signified shelter, not social reform. His political and psychic conservatism tacitly expressed itself in the appendix attached to his sermon "The Church," an 1841 essay from the *Edinburgh Review* entitled "The Port-Royalists" that implicitly confirms Channing's cautious ministerial investigation of Rome's possible sanctity. Attempting to remedy the ill effects of sectarianism, the article analogizes the diversity of churches to those of species united under one class; all are "members in common of the one great and comprehensive church, in which diversities of forms are harmonized by an all-pervading unity of spirit," a Linnaean credo that aims, however, not to defend Reformed churches, but to assure their members access to the Catholic community.[5] The essay concludes by assuring Protestants that they too belong to Catholic Christendom and its empowered sacred. "For ourselves, at least, we should deeply regret to conclude that we are aliens from that great Christian Commonwealth of which the Nuns and Recluses of the valley of Port-Royal were members, and members assuredly of no common excellence" (57). The competition between the desire for such community and the fear of enclosure within its constraints issues finally in the awkward assurance of vicarious membership. Like the heroines of convent-captivity literature, Channing, staunch opponent of ecclesiastical dogma and authority, concludes his discourse by covertly voicing his attraction for the precincts of the cloister.

Thus to Channing, Catholic theology perverted genuine spirituality while its conventual communities embodied an ideal, organic connectedness. Broader cultural anxieties about association, defined by one Channing scholar as the "epidemic protest that men *could* challenge their given station, that they could link themselves in voluntary union,"[6] shaped this conflicted perspective. Paradoxically, Roman Catholicism was implicated in this new and threatening development of liberal democratic culture, for its populous, voluntary solidarity was a prototype for various associationist movements of reform. Directing his polemical tract *Protestant Jesuitism* (1836) against all moral and religious reform associations, Calvin Colton accused them all of being "Jesuitical in their organization." By Jesuitical, Colton meant "that state of mind . . . which creates a religious empire of its own, independent of God and man,"[7] a sacrilegious independence originating from an anterior and pathological obedience derived from the Jesuits' excessive devotion to their founder.

Frightened like Colton of the new political power of the immigrant electorate, Protestant commentators on Catholic conversion saw it as a social and psychological gesture whose deviance emanated from a jointly excessive dependence and independence, a violation of professedly precarious cultural boundaries between the sovereign individual and the communal authorities of family and state. The characteristic aggressiveness of antebellum Protestant conversions to Rome surfaces in Isaac Hecker's expressed desire to break through cultural boundaries and to overwhelm the freedoms of his local culture with the constraints of a foreign divinity. Hecker wrote to Brownson in July 1845:

> I would be consumed by God. . . . I do not find here the room
> to loose [*sic*] my life. I feel the need of being met. . . . I want
> someone to kill me stone dead, or make me cry out enough,

enough. . . . The Church is all. . . . I want her to crush me, so
that she may be all in me, which she now is not. There is no
use of compromise. There can be no looking back. I want a
discipline that sinks deeper than what I have yet experienced. I
have too much liberty. This liberty abridges my freedom.[8]

Such abandoned rhetoric implicates conversion in the perils of a
consuming, uncompromising materiality. Hecker's language of mortification, crushing, and consuming knowingly pressed against the proprieties of his own German-American immigrant culture and its quest for
bourgeois autonomy. If for Hecker the "idea of an invisible Church is
a sheer piece of subterfuge to escape her claims to allegiance," many
sympathetically inclined Protestants wanted the pleasure of such allegiance but not its discipline, preferring, like Emerson, a Swedenborgian
vision of a universe laced through with correspondences yet free of ritual
and hierarchy.[9] The proper place for unity, as Emerson's essays reiterated, was not within, but behind form. By implication, the mendicant
hungers of Hecker's dialogue with God vulgarized the Emersonian soul,
which inhabited the elevated precincts of soliloquy, unsullied by the
foreign importation of dialogue. Tacitly referring to the alternative ar-
dors of Catholic spirituality, Emerson exclaimed against its faults and
labyrinthine architecture in "Self-Reliance":

In what prayers do men allow themselves! That which they call
a holy office is not so much as brave and manly. Prayer looks
abroad and asks for some foreign addition to come through
some foreign virtue, and loses itself in endless mazes of natural
and supernatural, and mediatorial and miraculous. Prayer that
craves a particular commodity, anything less than all good, is
vicious. Prayer is the contemplation of the facts of life from the
highest point of view. It is the soliloquy of a beholding and ju-
bilant soul. It is the spirit of God pronouncing his works good.
But prayer as a means to effect a private end is meanness and
theft. It supposes dualism and not unity in nature and consciousness. As soon as the man is at one with God, he will not
beg.[10]

Against this repellent humiliation of petitionary prayer, Transcendentalism was to practice an ideologically purified action of assertion
that would protect the self from mendicancy. But the weakness of such
fortified solitude lay in its inability to establish community. As one
Unitarian explained, "Protestantism, from its very nature, can never
consolidate its strength around a central point of dogma. It must be held

together by a spirit."[11] Such hopeful solidarity was bolstered by the nation's political organization, the structure of the federal government providing a plausible reassurance that Protestant sectarianism would not destroy Protestantism: "We sometimes wonder if Providence should permit such a multitude of sects," confessed another essayist, "and yet on further reflection we must perceive that they constitute that balance of power among the different communities, which, in the church as in the state, is a check upon each, and the security of all."[12]

Catholic apologist or nativist, sympathetic observer or convert shared a conviction that "influence," whether exerted conspiratorally, sentimentally, or educationally, was critical to the formation of democratic community. In the increasingly divisive 1850s, rhetorical appeals to or warnings against the workings of "influence" were frequently invoked to ascertain noncoercive grounds for sustaining not only political but also religious solidarity. One article, entitled "Sphere of Human Influence," explained: "As by the law of gravity the material universe, and by that of love the spiritual world, so by the law of association of ideas is the world of thought bound into one whole, whereof you cannot move one thought but that thereby you move the whole."[13] Gravity, love, and association were parallel phenomena powered by the same bio-spiritual forces of influence.

Theorists of domesticity and romantic liberal Protestant spokesmen for organic unity as well as Emerson's Swedenborgian theory of correspondence all argued for networks of (largely benign) reciprocal forces— forces that established communal connections without the contaminating intrusion of any coercive authority. Such "influences," however, claimed a dark side, for their noncoercive ways could insinuate themselves, exerting a hidden authority potentially more profound than one more frankly wielded. Even Stowe's unequivocal celebration in *Uncle Tom's Cabin* of the Quaker Rachel Halliday's maternal influence over her household and family suggests the velvet controls behind her motherly paradise, where kettle and daughter move in ritual obedience to the mother, the steaming kettle "a sort of censer of hospitality and good cheer. The peaches, moreover, in obedience to a few gentle whispers from Rachel, were soon deposited, by the same hand, in a stew-pan over the fire."[14]

Related contemporary theories of the body also depended on notions of influence to describe physical health as an interactive unity of ingoing and outgoing forces, all highly susceptible to an equilibrium of various "influences." If vulnerability to malign forces was an unfortunate internal feature of the human constitution, the power to exert benevolent force was ascribed particularly to the mother by advocates of the new sentimental domesticity. Lydia Maria Child's best-seller *The Mother's Book* (1831) argued that parenting involved a delicate management not only of environmental but also of specifically maternal forces surrounding the child, since not just the world but the domestic interior harbored threats of contagion and radical moral disequilibrium. Children, in Child's manual, are biologically vulnerable to deficient psychological nurture; according to the compensatory logic of sentimentalism that ascribed enormous powers to womanly feeling, a mother's parenting could dominate the competing forces of nature (if not patriarchy). "Children have died in convulsions, in consequence of nursing a mother, while under the influence of violent passion or emotion; and who can tell how much of *moral* evil may be traced to the states of mind indulged by a mother, while tending the precious little being, who receives everything from her?"[15] While such language was potentially accusatory in the extreme, it was therapeutic in intention, Child's informal theory of maternal nurture serving to diagnose otherwise mysterious illnesses that too often robbed parents of their offspring. Possessing in reality very little control over childhood disease, antebellum women focused on strategies of emotional mastery over the physiological; mothers, not germs, could save or kill their children. As Longfellow's and Stowe's Evangelines proved, feelings were one area of life susceptible to discipline, a discipline that ultimately (if still partially) negated the traumas of loss, illness, and death.

The most important liberal Protestant theoretician of marshaling influence and domestic nurture toward religious conversion, Horace Bushnell, argued in his 1846 sermon "Unconscious Influence" that the Protestant influences of domesticity were themselves shaped by covert competition with various forms of Catholic influence. Published the year before *Christian Nurture,* his famous work that advocated the soul's natural growth in grace, Bushnell's sermon before a Protestant missionary audience submerges his nativist concern with popery beneath a liberal religious rhetoric of depoliticized organicism.[16] In the sermon's imagery of the workings of conversion, Bushnell's anti-Catholicism lies embedded in his liberal Congregationalism: the sermon depicts a two-tiered world in which conscious intentions sit atop a far more powerful region of "unconscious influence," a terrain composed of the impressions one's vocal tones, facial expression, and gestures ineluctably exert on others.

As if anticipating the perils of his developing theory of language's symbolic resources, Bushnell constructs a compensatory region of interpretive certitude in this sermon; if verbal constructs are essentially metaphoric, a person's unconscious expressions are referentially precise. Individual "gestures" always reveal truth and in so doing penetrate oppressive barriers to social interaction and genuine community. "You inhabit a house which is well nigh transparent; and what you are within you are ever showing yourself to be without, by signs that have no ambiguous expression" (178).[17] Unlike the duplicities of behavior, unfortunately increased by the reasserted symbolic resources of language, Bushnell's involuntary influences transparently reflect the truths of an otherwise hidden intentionality. Contradicting a more narrow Protestant ideology of the sovereign self, one fortified against priestly or other authoritarian intrusions, Bushnell's romantic phenomenology insists on the self's fundamentally social identity, one fashioned by an unmediated, perpetual, and revealing communication between individuals. Unlike the feared social intimacies of the confessional, Bushnell's dialogic contact claims for its own an invisible architecture in which "the door of involuntary communication . . . is always open" (173).[18]

So pervasive and decisive are Bushnell's involuntary influences that they transform social existence into a web of mutually captivating associations. Explicating his scriptural text ("Then went in also that other disciple" [John 20:8]), Bushnell explains that like John following Peter into Christ's sepulcher, "just so, unawares to himself, is every man, the whole race through, laying hold of his fellow-man, to lead him where otherwise he would not go" (145). Like the prolific unity of the Catholic apologist John Milner's "Apostolical Tree" (see Fig. 12), Bushnell's unconscious influences invisibly lace together otherwise dispersed and isolated selves. While people remain in one sense individuals, they are "in a certain other view, parts of a common body, as truly as the parts of a stone" (173). But in contrast to Roman images of the faithful as stones in Holy Church or branches on the Apostolical Tree, Bushnell's slightly odd depiction of "the parts of a stone" invokes a geological rather than an ecclesiastical formation. The revelation of Christ's divinity and the apostolic continuation of his teachings are not the source of unity. Rather, an organic society derives from an unconscious psychic communicativeness between individuals that enables their receptivity to Protestant ministerial power. It is a union developed from below rather than from on high: "Far down in the secret foundations of life and society, there lie concealed great laws and channels of influence, which make the race common to each other in all the main departments or divisions of the social mass—laws which often escape our notice altogether, but which are to society as gravity to the general system of God's works" (174). Suppressed within this subterranean landscape lies Bushnell's polemical intention: to reassure his clerical audience that American society, notwithstanding its absence of visible constraints, is capable of receiving ministerial guidance toward its (Protestant) salvation, of being manipulated, even, toward that end.

Like the young women of numerous domestic novels who practice a studiously "unconscious" influence over others, Bushnell is imaginatively compelled by innocent power, his theology of unconscious influence at once sentimental and anti-Catholic. The link is further suggested by the similarity between Bushnell's internal organic system and Edward Beecher's later anti-Catholic vision of invisible government. Against the skillful and malignant influences emanating from Rome, Beecher asserts the benign workings of a divine influence that obviate any such blasphemous intermediary as the papacy: "It is the true glory of God, by a direct and omnipresent yet invisible influence on all men, to reduce the world to such order that all human governments will become so simple that men will scarcely feel their existence."[19] Similarly, Bushnell's purified mechanisms of attraction and self-revelation consistently invoke a Catholic countertext of corrupt influence and authoritarian community.

That this alternative world is a Catholic one becomes apparent in Bushnell's description of malign influences; the dangers of priest, confessional, and religious iconography hover behind Bushnell's warning against the potentially malevolent workings of influence—forces so strong that one must avoid visual (or aural) contact with them. Shrinking from the confessor's habitual exposure to others' sins, Bushnell seeks to appropriate the power and intimacy of that knowledge through his private psycho-theology of gestural influence. As we unconsciously influence, so too do we expose ourselves. The source of our sway over others ("that which flows out from us unawares to ourselves") also exposes our innermost selves. This dynamic of spontaneous disclosure reveals the duplicity of voluntary action and, implicitly, the feebleness of the conscious will. Furthermore, Bushnell's language of infection and dangerous diffusion uncovers a fundamental connection between his implicit and ambivalent struggle with popery and notions of pathology. Bushnellian influence not only travels in submerged channels through society but also spreads according to a "law of social contagion" (169), a preoccupation with disease, concealment, and polluted waters that also informs antebellum historical thinking about the nation's emergence from Europe. Of society's manifold unconscious influences, Bushnell writes: "They go streaming from us in all directions, though in channels that we do not see, poisoning or healing around the roots of society, and among the hidden wells of character" (170). If Christ is the ideological goal of Bushnell's sermon, even that center is potentially occupied by pestilence and confinement. The workings of Protestant influence ironically create psychic enclosures as imprisoning as any Old World interiors, for since the self always exerts its influence, "it is impossible to live in this world, and escape responsibility" (178).

This interpenetration between exterior and interior, arguably the central preoccupation of the Catholic-Protestant debate, reasserts itself at the core of Bushnell's sermon and forms a significant thread in his argument for the interpenetrating regions of human and divine in *Nature and the Supernatural* (1858). But "Unconscious Influence" significantly transposes cultural arguments over the relationship between subject and object into the language of disease, Bushnell's ministerial preoccupation with contamination increasing until it castigates the self who lives in the sermon's community of contagion and shameful self-revelation: "If you had the seeds of a pestilence in your body, you would not have a more active contagion, than you have in your tempers, tastes, and principles" (178). Such latent pathology is so potent that one can catch it by looking on another's sinful countenance or communicate it by merely glancing at someone else. Thus recalling Emerson's fascination with the sublimated violence of seeing ("Eyes are bold as lions . . . they wait for no introduction . . . but intrude, and come again, and go through and through you in a moment of time"), Bushnell's sermon articulates ancient phobias about the mythological evil eye, recast to diagnose the perils of antebellum social experience.[20]

From the midst of this epidemic, Bushnell issues appropriately somber directives. Like Lydia Child in her advice to nursing mothers, Bushnell, theologian of family nurture, warns everyone to "first make it sure that you are not every hour infusing moral death insensibly into your children, wives, husbands, friends, and acquaintances. By a mere look or glance, not unlikely, you are conveying the influence that shall turn the scale of some one's immortality" (178). And like Channing, who lamented Unitarian impotence in his "Letter on Catholicism," a powerlessness acknowledged by the numerous clerical converts to Catholicism, Bushnell in his sermon returns finally to ponder the fragility of Protestant ministerial authority. If Protestantism fails, it is not the minister's fault but the congregation's.

In the final analysis, it is not papal conspiracy but popular indifference that threatens Bushnell. Reproaching his audience of peers, he summons an apocalyptic vision of freezing waste to condemn the seeming or potential indifference of his clerical audience. Bushnell's preoccupation with the opposing forces of mediation and transparency, with the intervening impediments of conscious intentions and the spontaneous disclosures of unconscious behavior, converges with his secondary (but no less serious) concern over his professional authority. Counterpart to the light of the Gospel, Bushnell's concluding indictment of resistant ministerial hearts that are "banks of ice" (179) enacts a negative mediation, one that refracts rather than communicates the light. His prior depictions of humanity's extraordinary susceptibility to interpersonal influences suddenly invert into a spectacular image of his colleagues' invulnerability to his message. The ice of the clerical heart arrests the potentially redemptive workings of influence, whose powers, previously endowed with such intensity, suddenly lose all impact. Thus this Protestant meditation on the dilemmas of Christian community remains mired in the competing organizations of popery, the Protestant minister's loss of status, and a bodily thematics of influence and contagion that mediate feverishly between.

Ironically, those who failed to understand the delicate power balance of Protestant sects were sometimes accused of precipitating conversions to Catholicism by liberal New Englanders who blamed nativists and anti-Catholic mobs (mobs composed largely of working-class men who were in fact excluded from "the balance of power") for swaying public sympathy toward the church. Chiding Samuel F. B. Morse for the bigotry of his tracts on papal conspiracy, the *Christian Examiner* criticized this unintended effect of such conservative Protestantism: "Notwithstanding all that has been said about a 'foreign conspiracy against the liberties of the United States,' it will yet be found, we suspect, that the reaction, occasioned by the spirit manifested in this country against the Catholics, will do more to establish Catholicism here, a thousand times over, than his Excellency Prince Metternich, or the St. Leopold Foundation."[21] As this censure indicates, growing theological and class differences between liberal and conservative Protestants rendered conspiracy rhetoric especially suspect to some of New England's liberal elite. Appearing shortly after the Ursuline convent riot, this 1836 review article of a convent exposé entitled *Female Convents* (1834) is a cool appraisal of nativist rhetoric that defends Catholicism to discredit conservative (and lower-class) Protestantism. But as the ministerial fictions of Hawthorne and Bushnell demonstrate, to borrow Catholic influences to depict (and enhance) the purity of Protestantism was to risk its intrigue and contamination.

TWELVE

The Bodily Gaze of Protestantism

In the cautious turn toward the redemptive powers of the material dimension, issues of the body, of church architecture, of art, and of food converged to form a distinctive Protestant gaze on Rome, a gaze that acknowledged its spiritual desire, celebrated Catholicism as spectacle, and fantasied the consumption of this foreign substance rather than conversion to it. This Protestant gaze was forged from the terms of anti-Catholic discourse in its preoccupation with Romanism's bodily excesses, ranging from decomposition to nakedness, mortification, and frankly displayed crucifixion. Puzzled by the turn toward Old World orthodoxy among liberal Protestants, one writer could not decide whether an excessive or deficient sensibility caused conversion. Having traced the problem to an uncontrolled sensibility, he concluded: "Her converts have been from among those who were impenetrable to the inspirations of the new age,—the dead, and not the living."[1] Significantly, this reactionary impulse was formulated in terms of a bodily excess emanating from an undisciplined femaleness or morbidity. Not only Catholic conversion but also Catholic art summoned up just such images of bodily deviance to the Protestant observer.

The rhetorical appropriation of Catholic language complicated these ambiguities of Protestant spectating. As if to diminish his own guilty self-consciousness, one viewer of a Catholic painting even used the vocabulary of benediction to convey his spiritual alienation and aesthetic discomfort. Looking at Jan van Eyck's painting of the Pascal Lamb, he wrote: "One gazes with a gentle, half smile at the long jet of blood bending in parabolic curve, and falling, with the accuracy of a well-aimed bombshell, into the vessel below, and as he gazes, he blesses the simple-hearted and childlike artist of other days, who, having no irreverent mirth in his own bosom, suspected none in others."[2] With its commingled language of faith and infidelity, sanctity and deception, the passage points to a growing implication of fraud in the language of liberal Protestant faith; this author in particular was able to express his suspicion effectively only through a faintly ironic use of the language of benediction. Antebellum Protestants who resisted conversion were often entangled in the dubious morality of such curiosity. It was not only that spectating carried the proverbial taint of the stage but also that the spectacle was undeniably Christian. Increasingly, it was observers rather than participants who were implicated in imposture and who sensed themselves dwelling in the recesses of a strange religious voyeurism, of being moved by another's faith but not adopting it for their own.

From this intimacy between tourist-spectator, Catholic worshiper, and American reader emerged a pseudo-confidentiality similar to that practiced by Melville's protagonist in *The Confidence-Man: His Masquerade.* But while Melville's text dodges any concession to conviction, contemporary Protestant literature about Rome often perplexedly confided in its readers; the evasions and conflicted identifications characteristic of sympathetic Protestant writing were not ironic strategies so much as bewildered movement within the constraints of the spectator model, itself dependent on a disturbing alliance between freedom and self-distrust, a psychological and epistemological model that, as one Unitarian writer made clear, entirely opposed Catholic notions of infallibility: "We hold that all true liberality is founded in a proper distrust of our own judgment; in a practical sense of our fallibility on all subjects."[3] Liberal New Englanders simultaneously upheld such a system and lamented the enervating burden of such self-distrust, both disparaging the bodily excesses of Catholic piety and hoping somehow to exceed that piety's heroic conviction.

These thematics led to an absorbed gaze on the alternately redemptive and repulsive spectacle of the Catholic "body," visible in a plethora of graphic and sculptural representations in Europe and available for reproduction and transport home to embellish the interiors of the Protestant household. One of the most popular of such "sacred" artifacts was a Raphael engraving. Universally admired by Americans for his spirituality and, in particular, his domestic, nurturing Madonnas, Raphael functioned as a compelling imaginative aid to the beleaguered Protestant spectator, an excerpt, as it were, from the Catholic "whole" that could be imported for domestic consumption. *The Transfiguration,* the favorite Raphael painting of American tourists in Italy, displays Christ rising above Mount Tabor between Moses and Elijah in the presence of Peter,

James, and John; below the Savior, a possessed boy is being led to the apostles to be cured. This painting, repeatedly engraved, was a deeply satisfying representation of the transformation of suffering flesh into spirit or, more precisely, of the moment of triumphant doubleness when man and God are simultaneously visible. With arms extended and robes swirling around motionless legs, Christ replicates the posture of the crucifixion, simultaneously memorializing and negating the humiliation of the flesh.

Meditating on Raphael's canvas, John Singleton Copley thought that the moment represented "one of the most Sublime Subjects" and must have utterly possessed the apostles with "Holy Wonder" although they had already been "spectators of the Power of Christ exercised in [a] Miracle of a Stupendous Nature."[4] Capturing that moment of transient joining and incipient separation of flesh and spirit, Raphael's Christ presents a view of redemptive imitation with none of the attendant horrors customary to Gothic fictions of the double. If Christ was escaping the burdens of matter, He did so with palpable (and consoling) physicality. When the Hawthornes returned home from Europe in 1860 and settled at the Wayside, Emerson made them a house present of *The Transfiguration*. Protestant tourists who returned home to hang their Raphael engraving on the wall could observe or evade at will its absorbing view of spirit and flesh converging, its manipulation by new processes of mass reproduction minimizing an otherwise objectionable Catholic iconographic power. Subject to competing crosscurrents of evangelicalism, Protestant Americans found such suspended transformations into the spirit especially compelling; painterly images like Raphael's Christ, even led Henry Ward Beecher to describe his viewing of European art as an "instant conversion."[5]

Shaped by the antebellum Protestant rhetoric of Catholicism as spectacle, claims of aesthetic restoration or conspicuous imitation of the Catholic "body" informed the discourse of Catholic conversion as well. For many Americans, conversion occurred within an aestheticized context of beholding visual discords and harmonies. To be "restored" to the Faith metaphorically invoked a complex cultural reaffiliation phrased as aesthetic restoration. Emma Forbes Cary (Louis Agassiz's sister-in-law) explained how her upbringing in the high ideality of the Channing School led with ironic inevitability to her Catholic conversion: "As if I had found a precious bit of mosaic and sought for the work of art from which it had been severed," wrote Forbes of Channing's sermons, "I hid these maxims in my heart and pondered on them."[6] That Forbes traveled toward this unity along the byroads of secrecy, subversively hoarding

Channing's Unitarian wisdom for eventual restoration to its rightful context, points to lingering Protestant guilt over both the rupture of Christendom and the repudiation of Protestant ministerial authority. If Forbes's pursuit of spiritual and aesthetic unity was, as for many other converts, mediated through cultural betrayal, she justified it by restoring to the parent church what rightfully belonged to it.

As a new Catholic, Sophia Ripley delighted in this same experience of the thrill of theft and the satisfaction of restoration, claiming a new understanding of her "blessed books": "How every sweet spiritual flower of thought, that attracts us even in our Protestant reading, faded and wilted as it may be by transplantation there, blooms out fresh and fragrant in its own rich, Catholic soil. Oh what born thieves are *we* Protestants!"[7] While converts self-consciously restored their intellectual experiences (and themselves) to those whom they now saw as their original Catholic owners, others continued to extract pieces from the Catholic whole for the ambiguous adornment of their Protestant (or secular) culture.

As Weir's *Taking the Veil* (see Fig. 8) suggests, what absorbed those gazing on Catholicism was not the life of the cloister but the "spectacular" decision to enter it. Weir's painting captures liminality at its most dramatic: the young woman is neither a secular nor a religious. She wears a bridal dress, not a habit, and can thus be imagined to carry suspended within her the profane and the sacred, her freedom and the constraints of holiness. It was the crossing into the space of the Catholic sacred, then, rather than the experience of interior life that functioned as true spectacle. Emerson spoke directly to this fascination with boundaries and transitions when he observed in his 1848 essay "Power" that "everything good in nature and the world is in that moment of transition, when the swarthy juices still flow plentifully from nature, but their astringency or acridity is got out by ethics and humanity."[8] In short, the necessities and perils of transformation and spiritual display, not the complexities of the spiritual life after conversion, intrigued antebellum Protestant observers.

For Emerson, the liminal zone between nature and culture generated a power that saturated the world and inspired his problematic celebration. The church's dramatic display of the distribution and deployment of its sacramental authority, particularly in its conversion of young women into nuns and wafers into Hosts, and in its absolving of sin in confession, was, in this Emersonian context, a profoundly interesting display of "power." But even the transition from the pictorial to the theatrical, from looking at paintings to observing Catholics worshiping, frequently disturbed the equilibrium between furtive sympathy and disdain, the interior purity and safety of spectating and the legitimacy of the worship being witnessed. Only other Protestants could fully understand the peculiar emotions of dissociation and veneration released, for example, in the activity of watching mass. As Weir's painting suggests in the two groups of observers stationed around the female novice, antebellum Americans both watched Catholicism and watched one another doing so. Their self-reflexive spectatorship in effect created a nervous aesthetic space, one animated by competing ideologies of the proper relation between spirit and flesh. Were the various Catholic materializations of spirit inevitably contaminants? Or were they necessary, even desirable, vehicles for developing, as phrenologists called it, the "organ of veneration"?

As the "body" of Christ, the Roman church aroused contemporary anxieties about the susceptibility of the Protestant spirit to the Roman body. Catholic theologians like Johann Möhler reiterated incarnationalism as the key dogma of the visible church, the only antidote to the ailments of those outside Rome, whose diseased symptoms of religious indifference or faddish interest in the occult imitated, to him, the oscillations of tuberculosis. "Our age is doomed to witness the desolate spectacle of a most joyless languor, and impotence of the spiritual life, by the side of the most exaggerated and sickly excitement of the same."[9] Whereas Catholic apologists defended their church as Christ's mystical body, suspicious Protestants saw in such mystic corporeality a sublimated, potentially predatory eroticism. Protestant comment on Catholic converts often mapped such conversions onto a topography of the unreliable and indulgent flesh.

The potential contagion between mothers and children apparent in Lydia Maria Child's argument for maternal influence, as in Bushnell's imagery of subterranean social influences, lent credibility to such diagnoses of Catholicism's fearful bodily influences. Even Prescott's proliferating instances of a deviant physicalization of the spirit linked the maternal attractions of Rome to the constitutional predispositions of the Protestant body. "In the tone of certainty, which the Catholic uses," warned another, "there is a charm and authority, which addresses itself with great power to the credulity and latent superstition of the human heart."[10] It was thus not so much a psychological as a physiological susceptibility that explained the surrender of the Protestant "constitution" to Rome: "Another is relying and affectionate. A doubt in religion tortures him. He wants some certain rule of faith. He needs some visible authority on which to lean. If in addition to this he is imaginative, and endued with senses quick to perceive the beautiful in sounds and forms, he is by constitution predisposed to be a Catholic."[11]

American tourists in Rome imported their domestic rhetoric of bodily influence to explain the emotional impact of this witnessed Catholicism. Watching a Roman congregation kneel at the elevation of the Host, the Unitarian minister Orville Dewey rationalized his own illicit desires as an automatic response to Catholic "influence," further distancing the response from himself by describing it as hearsay at two removes: "When every knee bows, and an immense body of troops fall prostrate on the pavement, as if awe had struck them like death, I can easily believe what a gentleman told me, that he had known a man remarkably devoid of all religious emotion to burst into tears at the sight."[12] Intrigued by this spectacle of masculine release, Dewey suggests an element of sexual transgression in Catholicism's dominating theatrical displays: its power to enthrall and control could finally issue in the "feminization" of the self by breaking down its emotional reserves. As technocrats of the sacred, skilled at its production, distribution, and consumption, Catholics, in the Protestant view, gained a technical expertise over the emotions as well; the perception was widespread that the church's professionally adroit transactions between the institutional and the individual or, in bodily terms, between the psychological and the physiological, endowed its members with a power at once magical and professional.

The pseudonymous female author of the popular novel *Stanhope Burleigh: The Jesuits in Our Homes* (1855) acknowledged that such talismanic forces at the heart of Jesuit "influence" were superior to those of maternal domesticity: "One young, genial, clear-headed boy of genius, may, by a breath of influence, that would not disturb a leaflet, have his heart gained for Loyola forever."[13] The nativist William Nevins complained as well against the "magic" of Catholic conversion that craftily detoured the time-consuming nurturing of faith for a spontaneous conviction wrought by an artifact passed from one body to another. "We do not understand converting people as the Catholics do. They can *regenerate* and *pardon,* and do all the rest in a trice. We have to bring before the *mind* of the sinner the great-saving truth of Christ *crucified;* but they have only to put the little *crucifix* in his *hand*."[14] While a caricature, Nevins's account nonetheless resembles what many educated Protestants felt and what even converts, in their excited adoption of the church's apostolic theology, parental authority structure, and persuasive iconography seemed to confirm. If anti-Catholic rhetoric consistently invoked the malignant charisma of the pope, converts attributed a benign magic to the church. Explaining to Charlotte Dana why she did not write to her cousin Eunice, Sophia Ripley wrote: "I do not write to her, because I could not do so without expressing to her how much more peace one little prayer to our Blessed Mother—one pressure of the cross to her heart—one benediction from a Rev. Father would give her than all the instruction she has had from her youth up."[15]

The magic emanated from Catholicism's allegedly impure mixtures of human and divine—adulterations that for converts became powerful instances of a novel purity. It was less the specific content of Catholic doctrine than the mingling of sacred and profane that explained popery's power to many antebellum Americans. "Why will they in their devotions," queried Nevins, "associate creatures with the Creator?"[16] This dangerous "association" in Catholic worship, the mingling of what should remain disparate, threatened not only the emotional boundaries of the Protestant observer but his or her class boundaries as well. The Catholic mass, enthused Sophia Ripley, attracted "all classes of persons,"[17] a foreign simulation of the egalitarian democracy proclaimed by American republicanism. Unlike the strenuous pursuit of social or spiritual purity in various Protestant denominations (pursuits parodied by Melville's "Two Temples"), the church's minglings, Brownson freely admitted, had the potential for corruption. "The Catholic Church makes no selection of the elect, but, like civil society, takes the whole people into her communion bodily. She is the net that gathers all kinds of fishes, the field in which tares grow together with the wheat until the harvest. . . . The causes which produce decay and death can work on the individual and on the nation even when they are within her fold."[18]

A vocabulary of substance and negation, food and hunger further structured antebellum ruminations on these Catholic minglings as Protestants pondered which was worse, contamination or starvation. Addressing the contemporary cultural concern with adulteration (and of course his own novelistic concern with the issue of adultery), Hawthorne confided to his Italian journal that such fears could well produce a more troublesome deficiency. "In however adulterated a guise, the Catholics do get a draught of devotion to slake the thirst of their souls, and methinks it must needs do them good, even if not quite so pure as if it came from better cisterns, or from the original fountain-head."[19] A polluted theology, in short, was better than none. Emerson spoke similarly in his journal about the rumored inclination of a Boston Unitarian girl to join the Catholic church: "If the offices of the Church attract her, if its beautiful forms and humane spirit draw her, if St. Augustine and St. Bernard, Jesu and Madonna, Cathedral, Music and Masses, then go, for thy dear heart's sake, but do not go out of this icehouse of Unitarianism all external, into an icehouse again of externals. At all events I charged her to pay no regard to dissenters but to suck that orange thoroughly."[20] Emerson's patronizing approval alternates between traditional Protestant suspicions of externality and an emergent romantic, post-Protestant language that speculates on the revelatory powers of matter, of aestheticized matter that can be as satisfyingly consumed as an orange.

Dante, as a historical and imaginative figure, was crucial to this wary Protestant consumption of Roman substances, a figure subject to repeated "translation" by such major formulators of New England culture as Longfellow, Charles Eliot Norton, and James Russell Lowell. According to one early nineteenth-century reader of the *Commedia,* Dante's force was magnetic and ultimately indefinable; of importance, however, to the inscrutable attraction Dante represented was that he was imagined as incapable of being fully consumed by the reader: "He possesses a power, partly resulting from the varied excellencies which we have attempted to point out, and partly from a certain something, which we confess ourselves unable to describe, of producing in his readers the most undivided and unwearied attention."[21] Decades later, Longfellow, Lowell, Norton, and others devoted themselves to isolating and describing that "certain something." "With Dante, taking him as a guide and companion in our privater moods," wrote one essayist for the *Atlantic Monthly,* "we may, even in the natural body, pass through the world of spirit."[22]

As anti-Catholic discourse projected Protestant fears onto the figure of Loyola, so pro-Catholic rhetoric invested Dante with the power to satisfy twinned longings for doctrinal certitude and a perfected material aesthetic. Emerson's compliment that "Dante's praise is that he dared to write his autobiography in colossal cipher, or into universality" suggests the dimensions of this fantasied masculine other.[23] Even Longfellow, who was not given to such trumpetings, praised Dante for his masculine control. Assessing how Dante's use of the vernacular contributed to Italy's developing nationhood, Longfellow explained that Dante's strength was needed to "fix the uncertain foundations of their national language and literature broad, deep and massive."[24] While Loyola epitomized Catholicism's unbridled domination of human nature in its collective and most private aspects, Dante embodied his beneficent opposite, inspiring rather than subjugating the troubled soul, keeping particular company with the New England Brahmin elite. Lowell explained in his lengthy essay on the poet: "He is not merely a great poet, but an influence, part of the soul's resources in time of trouble."[25]

Unlike the Madonna, whose iconographic power was qualified by Protestant fears of both female power and the potentially idolatrous imagination, Dante invited an unrestrained veneration from these men, his poetry exerting an aesthetic power that invoked (without usurping) Christ's incarnation, embodying an ideal union of flesh and spirit, poetry and doctrine—a pure "hybrid" for readers perplexed by such failed combinations as Hawthorne's Donatello. As the charismatic alter ego for the New England male writer, Dante was completion to their fragmentariness, a superiority that yet resolved itself down to their level. James Russell Lowell explained: "Though Dante's conception of the highest end of man was that he should climb through every phase of human experience to that transcendental and super sensual region where the true, the good, and the beautiful blend in the white light of God, yet the prism of his imagination forever resolved the ray into color again, and he loved to show it also where, entangled and obstructed in matter, it became beautiful once more to the eye of sense" (42). The prism image is key here: like many of his contemporaries, Lowell articulated anxieties about purity and contamination through references to whiteness and color. As indicated in the dubious mediation of stained glass (which Melville capitalized on in "The Two Temples"), color and Catholicism jointly embodied the contamination of matter; Protestantism, whether through purgation or its successful blend of abstractions (Lowell's "the true, the good, and the beautiful"), enjoyed the privileged domain of "white light." The strategic importance of Dante is that he enabled a successful negotiation between the blended heights of white godliness and the lower human regions of disparate color. Indeed, the brunt of Lowell's admiration for Dante rests on the latter poet's depiction of this lower region. His imagery of entanglement and obstruction, so resonant with the terrors of the captivity tradition, suggests a new kind of beauty—bounded and fragmented, but enchanting because so. Or as Lowell summarizes: "Dante was a mystic with a very practical turn of mind" (43).

Nonetheless, the liberal rejection of Calvinist austerities at times implicated this corporeal Catholic sensibility in issues of tainted heredity and generational contamination—a region of the body incapable of claiming Dantesque beauties. New arguments for the physiological determinism of heredity rather than the spiritual influence of an inherited Original Sin led Oliver Wendell Holmes to ponder Catholicism's position in his anti-Calvinist novel *Elsie Venner* (1861).[26] Written to dispute Calvinist predestination, Holmes's story of the snake-girl Elsie, like Hawthorne's of the faun-boy Donatello, explores the moral problem (and errant erotic spectacle) of a sinless sinner. Because of her congenital physical and moral disorder (her serpentine nature communicated to her in utero when her mother suffered a snake bite) Elsie, according to Holmes's anti-Calvinist polemic, cannot be held responsible for her behavior; she is several levels removed, then, from the guilt of the "fallen woman" that plagued Maria Monk. Her moral innocence is voiced with reference to related anxieties about bodily infiltration; Elsie, as morally impervious as she is physically permeable, inverts the boundaries maintained by the sentimental heroine, whose heart is as open to every influence as her virginal body is closed. Like Hawthorne's *Marble Faun*, Holmes's "romance" of hybridity unfolds against a background of Roman Catholicism, the hybrid religion. Both mixed phenomena, the imperiously sexual snake-girl and Romanism focus a Protestant patriarchal gaze on the adulterous and adulterated female, a gaze that finally asserts purity over heterogeneity in the death of Elsie Venner. Unlike the hybrid Elsie, whose partial animality exempts her (as Donatello is also exempted) from the "need" for religion (an autonomy as attractive to the agnostic Holmes as to Hawthorne), the more human characters of *Elsie Venner* fall under Catholicism's animalistic sway. Resorting to a convention of Protestant tourist literature—the enumeration of Catholicism's repellent fleshly morbidities—Holmes constructs a powerfully biologized Catholicism in what he called his "medicated" novel. An ostensible conspiracy against the hero's (and author's) muscular Protestant masculinity links the foreign piety to the seductive corruptions of the female body.

When the weak Unitarian minister of the novel, the Reverend Fairweather, approaches conversion to Catholicism, he dreams an elaborate nightmare in which hordes of the dead overrun a gorgeous cathedral. "Then, as his dream became more fantastic, the huge cathedral itself seemed to change into the wreck of some mighty antediluvian vertebrate; its flying-buttresses arched round like ribs, its piers shaped themselves into limbs, and the sound of the organ-blast changed to the wind whistling through its thousand-jointed skeleton" (409).[27] Shifting the dream imagery from human skeleton to prehistoric creature, Holmes delivers an especially severe indictment of the Catholic church. Older than the Old World, Catholicism now belongs to the newly emergent inhumanity of geologic time. So antiquated that it can only be labeled prehistoric, the great Catholic fossil (unlike the aspiring spirituality of Holmes's "Chambered Nautilus") never participates in history's progressive dynamic. Over the skeletal hulk, the pathetic minister, a good example of Brownson's uprooted and spiritually desperate Protestant, voices the suppressed anger of his "feminized" powerless status by dreaming of becoming a Catholic bishop.

Holmes's novel attacks Calvinist predestination by appealing, not to the freedom of the will, but to heredity, an influence that mimics the Edenic narrative to subvert it. The irony is that in opposing Original Sin, Holmes appeals to an even more encompassing authority: the irreversible laws of one's private "constitution." The juxtaposition of this medical destinarianism with a secondary plot recording Fairweather's conversion to Rome establishes Elsie and the Roman church as doubled icons of hybridization that together exert an unavoidable power. The two plots argue the poverty of both Calvinism and Arminianism as Fairweather is drawn toward Rome and Elsie to her serpentine destiny.

Holmes intended, as he wrote to Harriet Beecher Stowe, to critique a judgmental Calvinism and the sanguinary individualism of evangelical piety, "under cover of this [plot] to *stir* that mighty question of automatic agency in its relation to self-determination."[28] But that "mighty question" of free will covered other concerns about the contamination of sexual release, the threatened effeminacy of spiritual hunger, and the perils of a maternal power accorded new privileges by the cult of domesticity. While Protestantism offers an array of fresh dishes, according to the narrator, Catholicism, the "Old Mother," offers to feed you leftovers, "broken victuals" (407), with a gold spoon. Elsie, who has lost her mother and has suffered the penetration of the snake, is one such "broken victual," symbolically slain by the rigorously pure dictates of this medical novel. Fairweather is the other broken victual, for he too is a hybrid who must be exported from the domain of the novel through conversion.

Fairweather's particular heterogeneity emerges not from crossed species but from a more contemptible deficiency of virility. To the extent that his deviance (his conversion to Catholicism) is due not to brute physiological mixings but to an even more ambiguous adulteration of genes, temperament, and church affiliation, Fairweather is culpable where Elsie is not. Described as a cold and spineless man, Fairweather manifests supposedly Unitarian flaws, which are diagnosed as the cause of his "engrossing passion" (251): to be in the majority, and to enjoy the solace of collectivity. Physiological, theological, and political accusations converge as the aristocratic Holmes indicts Fairweather for fleeing the dull isolation of Unitarianism for a voyeuristic peep at a Catholic service. Fairweather, manifesting Holmes's own anxieties about the loss of identity and the concentrated energy made available by such collective worship, longs to "enjoy that luxury of devotional contact which makes a worshipping throng as different from the same numbers praying apart as a bed of coals is from a trail of scattered cinders" (64). The desire for a tactile spirituality renders the convert Fairweather a man of suspect lower regions. If he shows the weaknesses of democracy in his hunger to conform to the (immigrant) "majority," such conformism is finally an unmanly insecurity. With covert allusion to the strenuous polemics of the converted Orestes Brownson, Holmes stigmatizes Catholic conversion as an unnatural repudiation of one's "inherited" Protestantism:

> But to see one laying a platform over heretical quicksands, thirty or forty or fifty years deep, and then beginning to build upon it, is a sorry sight. A new convert from the reformed to the ancient faith may be very strong in the arms, but he will always have weak legs and shaky knees. He may use his hands well, and hit hard with his fists, but he will never stand on his legs in the way the man does who inherits his belief. (418)

Holmes was so interested in Fairweather's crippled stature in part because he felt himself a religious victim as well. An admirer of Stowe's successful flight from Calvinism into Episcopalianism, Holmes hoped to repair his own damaged nature through proximity to spiritually recovered individuals like her. He wrote to her in 1867 of his Calvinist childhood in revealing terms: "So I think the stain of my boyhood may wear off in some degree by intercourse with sweet and straight and wholesome natures, whose nurses never let them fall, as they are wont to say of the poor hunchbacks."[29] Holmes's poignant self-image of his spiritual deformity as the product of a violent adult carelessness suggestively undermines his fictional condemnation of the convert Fairweather. The hereditary faith rather than the adopted one carried the disabling blow. The weak-legged Fairweather can be read, then, as the broken-backed Holmes's alternative self, and the account of Fairweather's surrender to Romanism as Holmes's expression of contempt for his own childhood surrender to Calvinism. That he surrendered helplessly (the infant fallen from the nurse's arms to permanent injury) only increases his rage.

Thus Holmes's insecure physiological vision forbids the self-reparation of religious conversion, such therapeutic transformations rendered illusory by the overwhelming constraints of heredity and environment. The only available recourse is that of somehow shedding religious belief, specifically one's early Calvinist training. But as Holmes's confiding letters to his fellow ex-Calvinist Harriet Beecher Stowe suggest, escape from childhood religious instruction was virtually impossible. The doctrine of the Fall of Man, wrote Holmes in his "autobiographical notes," was "not only wrought into the intellectual constitution of a New

England child, coloring his existence as madder stains the bones of animals whose food contains it, but it entered into his whole conception of the universe."[30] Such language acknowledges the growing appreciation for the power of environmental (and specifically familial) influences on childhood development—but this potentially progressive view is tinged with apprehension and Holmes's penetrating fatalism.

If Hester Prynne's scarlet letter was ambiguously internal and external to her sexually adulterous constitution, a stain both flung aside and reclaimed in the forest, Holmes's Calvinism more thoroughly clings to the interior of his being. In a later letter to Stowe, Holmes revealingly situates his own confidences about Calvinism's scars in the language of confession: "I do not say you have been through all this,—I do not want you to say you have,—you are my confessor, but I am not yours." Holmes's surrender to his epistolary confessional, as well as another admission to Stowe that "Romanism is to me infinitely more human than Calvinism,"[31] further underscores his connection to Fairweather. Notwithstanding its greater "humanity," however, Catholicism was never a live option for Holmes. Instead, he shifted the burden of the soul's psychological inheritance to the diseased but potentially curable secular body, whose chief glory was to resolve the problem of moral guilt by putting it physically beyond reach, in a body that, unlike Elsie's, cannot be opened:

> God lets me move my limbs—these he would trust me with. But he shut my heart and my breathing organs and all the wondrous mechanism by which I live, in a casket beyond my rash meddling, of which He keeps the key. So I know that he has entrusted me with many precious interests which I can use well or ill; but I will not believe that he has ever trusted the immortal destiny of my soul out of His own hands.[32]

Developing liberal Protestant convictions about the interactive unity of the physical, moral, and aesthetic worlds situated the phenomenon of Catholic conversion in perilous cultural regions of influence and contagion. In the new environmentalism of anti-Calvinist discourse that advocated the maternal nurture of the Christian child, "climate" emerged as a formative trope, posing Protestant (especially Unitarian and orthodox Calvinist) "coldness" against Catholic "warmth." One of the most significant novelistic examples of this moralized geography was *Agnes of Sorrento,* a historical romance written by Holmes's anti-Calvinist confessor, Harriet Beecher Stowe.[33] First appearing in the *Atlantic* from May 1861 to April 1863, Stowe's novel of fifteenth-century Italy is an extended rumination on the relative merits of the Catholic and Protestant faiths, an exploration structured around the workings of "influence" in the construction of ideal community. Stowe organizes her story of the young Catholic Agnes, virtuously battling various papal and masculine iniquities, around the contrasting climates of northern and Mediterranean Europe. To borrow Reese's phrase, "the attraction of repulsion" between these two climatic zones structures the novel's uncertain celebration of Catholicism. Coincident with the eruption of the Civil War, Stowe's novel pits a disembodied northern European piety against the "mediistic" substantiality of southern European Catholicism.

> The Northern mind of Europe is entirely unfitted to read and appreciate the psychological religious phenomenon of Southern races. The temperament which in our modern days has been called the mediistic, and which with us is only exceptional, is more or less a race-peculiarity of Southern climates, and gives that objectiveness to the conception of spiritual things from which grew up a whole ritual and a whole world of religious Art. (97)

Stowe transports her domestic romantic racialism from white and black American southerners to the "race-peculiarity" of Catholic Italy. As the doctor explains to the good Calvinist minister of *Elsie Venner:* "Everybody knows that Catholicism or Protestantism is a good deal a matter of race" (317). Stowe's novel similarly situates religion in terms of race, arguing (if more sympathetically than Holmes) that the Protestant quest for an "objective" faith, one external to private judgment and happily "mediistic," nonetheless improperly mingles itself with attraction to an inferior "race." The novel's reluctant yet self-righteous dismissal of Catholic Italy's objective "conception of spiritual things" offers an expatriot justification for American northern assertions of superiority over the American South (with its "picturesque and voluptuous ideality") and its enslaved population of African Americans (earlier described by Stowe as "exotic[s] of the most gorgeous and superb countries of the world").[34]

When published in book form in 1862, *Agnes of Sorrento* appeared with a letter from the author explaining its origins in a story-telling contest in Salerno between Stowe and her traveling companions. Intent on divorcing her work from any historical or political context, Stowe insists that her almost four-hundred-page romance of Renaissance Italy is "a mere dreamland" (ix). Recalling the supernatural assistance she had allegedly received ten years earlier in the writing of *Uncle Tom's Cabin*, Stowe presented her new novel as an effortless (if more secular) production of the touristic imagination, secured by images of happy matrimony. "It merely reproduces to the reader the visionary region that appeared to the writer.... All dates shall give way to the fortunes of our story, and our lovers shall have the benefit of fairyland; and who so wants history will not find it here, except to our making, and as it suits our purpose" (ix). Stowe's appeal to an ahistorical sentimentality enables her evangelical adjustment of Old World Catholic history to her "purpose," the fictional reconstruction of a lost Catholic past for an American Civil War readership. In a poem she wrote during this same Italian tour, entitled "The Gardens of the Vatican," an imperial righteousness mingles with a pronounced nostalgia; convinced that Rome is her deserted home, one abandoned by Jesus (and implicitly by herself), the poet begs Christ to return and banish the "money-changers." Following this intervention and purification, the poet imagines their joint reappropriation of the Vatican grounds.

> Gardens of dreamy rest, I long to lay
> Beneath your shade the last long sigh, and say,
> Here is my home, my Lord, thy home and mine.[35]

Agnes of Sorrento voices a similar interest in recovering a Catholic home by cautiously appropriating selected features of its "southern" sensibility, the novel's reconstruction of fifteenth-century piety and papal intrigue forming the seductive challenge to Stowe's antebellum Protestant "conception of spiritual things." That conception portrays Catholicism as a force of gendered excess, its (feminine) ardent piety and (masculine) unprincipled power yoked in a union that disrupts the gendered, separated spheres of American middle-class domesticity. Stowe's submissive Catholic maiden, Agnes, enjoys an intuitive and ritualistic faith that thwarts papal iniquity and monkish ingenuity, although the author's faith in the saintly powers of girlhood (developed most memorably in the character of little Catholic Eva) reappears slightly adjusted by Agnes's national difference. Agnes's sacred femininity, more than that of Eva (whose Catholicism is modified by her attendance at Methodist meetings and her Scripture-based friendship with Uncle Tom), is distanced from the author's Protestant gaze, which in scrutinizing this southern, Catholic, and Italian femininity oscillates between identification and cautious critique. Ambivalently defending the church's celebration of the feminine, *Agnes of Sorrento* participates in the larger antebellum Catholic feminization of a sectarian and avowedly deficient

Protestantism while simultaneously evangelizing the Old World from which America had emerged.[36]

Stowe's imperial yet needy evangelicalism endows her adolescent Catholic heroine with a pure piety sufficiently free of the largely masculine corruptions of papal tyranny and monastic lust to make her the spiritual ancestress of America. Continually mediating between her unreservedly Catholic heroine and her American Protestant readers, the narrator lyrically evokes Agnes's devotionalism only to assert its genealogical connection to American Protestantism. Against conservative Protestant and nativist insistence that an unbridgeable gap divided the static Catholic "past" from America's dynamic Protestant "history," Stowe argues for an unbroken transmission through a devotional femininity that purifies this Christian truth of its masculine (popish and monarchical) contaminants.

> The Christian faith we now hold, who boast our enlightened
> Protestantism, has been transmitted to us through the hearts
> and hands of such,—who, while princes wrangled with Pope,
> and Pope with princes, knew nothing of it all, but in lowly
> ways of prayer and patient labor were one with us of modern
> times in the great central belief of the Christian heart, "Worthy
> is the Lamb that was slain." (134)

Thus articulated, the inner project of this historical romance, which culminates in the martyrdom of Stowe's "Protestant" hero Savanarola and the marriage of her heroine, is to argue for the essential, immutable, and intimate unity of the Christian "heart." As in other depictions of female subversion of established theological power in Stowe's fiction, Agnes's Catholicism can dispel the menace of Catholic defilement and its potential threat to America because it is fundamentally the same as Stowe's Episcopalianism, the two faiths identified by an evangelical femininity that preserves and transmits an essential Christianity independent of national church and "race peculiarity." Such a feminized spiritual union of Italian "passion" and New England "purity" depends on Agnes's (and Stowe's) studied obliviousness to papal history.

Like the Mercersburg theologians, the novel argues that there had been no great schism in Christendom that prevented an unbroken transmission of the true faith because the Christian's spiritual inheritance remained conspicuously independent of apostolic authority. And like Bushnell's social theology of "unconscious influence," Stowe's religious unity is forged by invisible, unconscious links. The hymn of Agnes's beneficent uncle, the monk Father Antonio, exemplifies the workings of this Italian Catholic–American Episcopalian faith, which is capable of entertaining mixture without defilement, conflict without rupture.

> The words were those of the old Latin hymn of Saint Bernard, which, in its English dress, has thrilled many a Methodist class meeting and many a Puritan conference, telling, in the welcome they meet in each Christian soul, that there is a unity in Christ's Church which is not outward,—a secret, invisible bond, by which, under warring names and badges of opposition, His true followers have yet been one in Him, even though they discerned it not. (134)

The narrative itself extends these Christian bonds of unconscious union with anachronisms whose expressed casualness underscores Stowe's argument for a feminized Christian unity. Approving the hymns written by the novel's offstage hero, Savanarola, Stowe presents them as pietist Protestant productions: "The soft and passionate tenderness of the Italian words must exhale in an English translation, but enough may remain to show that the hymns with which Savanarola at this time sowed the mind of Italy often mingled the Moravian quaintness and energy with the Wesleyan purity and tenderness" (223). But while such cordial ahistoricity Protestantizes (and "Anglo-Saxonizes") Renaissance Italy, Stowe's discursive practices, by imitating the liturgical practices celebrated by the plot, Catholicize her narrative. Thus, characteristically interventionist in her narrative voice, she appropriates the intercessory powers of the Catholic community of saints by frequently "interceding" for her characters before the reader. Stowe's affection for the communal companionship of the Catholic doctrine of intercession was especially relevant for her wartime readers, whose griefs and religious (and political) doubts would soon be assuaged by such reassurances of heavenly reunion as those offered in Elizabeth Stuart Phelps Ward's *Gates Ajar* (1868). In her pamphlet "The Ministration of Departed Spirits," Stowe argued that God takes people so that their "ministry can act upon us more powerfully from the unseen world."[37] Such a solution to the agony of loss meant that Stowe experienced the intercession of the "personal" as well as the sainted dead in almost palpable proximity, an animation of the spiritual landscape that she describes in her poem "The Other World," where the afterworld "palpitates the veil between / With breathings almost heard."[38]

Stowe's continued quest for communion with dead loved ones was shared by converts to Catholicism, for whom anti-Catholic rhetoric of "Romanism's" garish morbidity yielded to a reassuring sense of the

Catholic community of the dead. Recalling the motives behind his own conversion, Isaac Hecker acknowledged that he too shared the need that had driven so many into the alternative ranks of spiritualism: "One thing I wanted was the satisfaction of that feeling and sentiment which has made so many persons Spiritualists. I found that in the Church there was no impassable barrier dividing the living from the departed. That was an intense delight to me."[39]

Compelled by a similar ambition to overcome the separation between her hard-won Episcopalian sensibility and her more conservative Protestant readership, Stowe as narrator even intercedes for the doctrine of intercession: "Whatever may be thought of the actual truth of this belief, it certainly was far more consoling than that intense individualism of modern philosophy, which places every soul alone in its life-battle, scarce even giving it a God to lean upon" (124). The presence of the saints watchfully attending the spiritual progress of those on earth exerts a consolatory force; the ideologically suspect aspects of such intercession are themselves contained by the benevolent intrusions of the narrator, who keeps maternal company with her readers and guides them to a clearer understanding of this communal Christian life. Living in a secluded grove of orange trees, the devout Agnes enjoys a community that antebellum Protestants could find, perhaps, only in historical romances.

> To the mind of the really spiritual Christian of those ages the air of this lower world was not as it is to us, in spite of our nominal faith in the Bible, a blank, empty space from which all spiritual sympathy and life have fled, but like the atmosphere with which Raphael has surrounded the Sistine Madonna, it was full of sympathizing faces, a great "cloud of witnesses." The holy dead were not gone from the earth; the Church visible and invisible were in close, loving and constant sympathy,—still loving, praying and watching together, though with a veil between. (71)

Catholic community emerges not only in the intercession of the saints, whose concern for struggling souls below eases the Protestant (and particularly Calvinist) burdens of isolation, but also in the bond of the confessional that enables Father Francesco, Agnes's confessor, to discover her sympathetic soul. In Stowe's description of the priest's joy, the intimacy of the confessional portends not indoctrination and seduction but a release from the punitive legacy of individualism.

> Such is the wonderful power of human sympathy, that the discovery even of the existence of a soul capable of understanding

our inner life often operates as a perfect charm; every thought, and feeling, and aspiration carries with it a new value, from the interwoven consciousness that attends it of the worth it would bear to that other mind; so that, while that person lives, our existence is doubled in value, even though oceans divide us. (36)

This inner union between Francesco and Agnes models the ties of sympathetic affinity constructed by the historical romancer who tours the Renaissance Catholic past to retrieve its consolatory essence for Protestant readers doubly bereaved by theology and civil war; as romancer, Stowe establishes a therapeutic union with those suffering the various ailments of individualism, although her curative maternal gestures depend on a strategic exclusion of largely masculine forces of deviance. Stowe's politics of the unconscious, in which the purity of Christendom's unity relies on the exertion of innocent, not calculating, influences, dictates that both heroine and narrator remain adroitly unaware of their own powers.

Paradoxically, then, the potent communalism of Catholic piety can only emerge from Agnes's radical separation from herself. Every motion of her spiritual being registered by vigilant saints and priests, Agnes knows nothing of herself, the proverbial liberation from selfhood enjoyed by saints rephrased by Stowe's theories of sacred girlhood as sexual and intellectual innocence. Agnes's psychic wholeness emerges not from conflict with culture but from the pure autonomy of gender, a virtually transcendent essence of self-forgetfulness. Stowe's description of the consequent inversion of authority between the fantastically obedient girl and her increasingly demanding confessor asserts the power of this unconscious femininity, whose unawareness permits evasion of both masculine authority and female consciousness.

> Nay, it sometimes seemed to him as if the suggestions which he gave her dry and leafless she brought again to him in miraculous clusters of flowers, like the barren rod of Joseph, which broke into blossoms when he was betrothed to the spotless Mary; and yet, withal, she was so humbly unconscious, so absolutely ignorant of the beauty of all she said and thought, that she impressed him less as a mortal woman than as one of those divine miracles in feminine form of which he had heard in the legends of the saints. (35)

The passage aligns the accomplishments of Agnes's "humbly unconscious" sanctity with those of female authorship. Like Stowe in her introductory portrait of herself as passive medium, Agnes enjoys a spontaneous creativity that transforms Francesco's sterile directives into spiritual fruit without any conscious (hence presumptuous) intervention on her part. The model for such a receptive fertility is, of course, the Virgin Mary, from whose immaculate being masculine divinity flowered, an achievement "unconsciously" imitated by Agnes and her author. Both Mary, avatar of sinless matter and merciful intercession, and Agnes, virginal repetition (rather than progeny) of this womanly creative sanctity, receive celebratory material embodiment by the female Protestant historical romancer, who exerts her own intercessory maternal dominion over the matter of history. Or as Stowe explains of her story's birth in her introductory letter: "Whether it ever find much favor in the eyes of the world or not, sure it is, the story was a child of love in its infancy, and its flowery Italian cradle rocked it with an indulgent welcome" (viii).

Stowe's novel imperially dismisses more orthodox Protestant suspicions of the Catholic veneration of the Virgin as Mariolatry, for Stowe and others saw in Mary the same transfigurative powers as those claimed for American Christian domesticity. James Jackson Jarves, including a description by the English art historian Anna Jameson of Raphael's *Sistine Madonna* in his own *Art-Hints: Architecture, Sculpture, and Painting* (1855), approved of this sacred female power: "There she stands, the transfigured woman, at once completely human and completely divine, an abstraction of power, purity and love, poised in the empurpled air, and requiring no other support; looking out . . . quite through the universe, to the end and consummation."[40] The Protestant cult of domesticity, then, enabled a partial recovery of a repudiated incarnational and intercessory "aesthetic" by such celebrations of the Madonna. Arguing against the age's fascination with spiritualism, the converted Brownson explained in "The Worship of Mary" (1853) that the Virgin and the saints, not the Protestant mother, provided the only legitimate intercession, one that would never fail the supplicant. "We see not our guardian angel, yet he as a pure intelligence sees and hears us, and can instantly report all to the company of heaven, or to the saint that we invoke, so that the saint can never be ignorant of the petitions we proffer."[41]

But if Agnes's creative chastity draws on the celibate yet fertile Virgin, it inspires as well the deviant eroticism American Protestants feared so vehemently in Catholicism. Struggling against her growing love for the cavalier Agostino Sarelli, Agnes confesses her most minute transgressions of maidenly affection to Father Francesco, who, influenced by such submissive candor, quickly deteriorates into a lust-ridden and guilty priest; Dimmesdale-like, he inflicts unnatural austerities on himself to vanquish his desire. The confessional, which had provided the site for a praiseworthy intimate communion between spiritual colleagues, now facilitates the growth of Francesco's sexual iniquity, for the more Agnes confesses, the more she reveals her spotless nature and hence her desirability. Tormented by jealousy of the girl's innocent love for Sarelli, her confessor decides to enforce a painful scrupulosity on Agnes as well. The mortifications he imposes all address the eroticism painfully apparent to himself, the narrator, and the Protestant readership but censored from Agnes, the erotic drama's original "author." Thus he directs her to wear a hair shirt against her delicate skin only to watch its sexually aggressive torment nullified by her sublime unawareness of its real purpose. While the girl's escape from Francesco's spiritual sadism into the safe piety of marriage with the anticlerical Sarelli concludes Stowe's Protestant romance, Agnes's unwitting participation in the novel's sexual underground remains unresolved. As the main vehicle for the plot's Gothic descent from sanctity to lust and sadomasochism, Agnes's exaggerated creative purity virtually solicits the shift of Francesco's pastoral attentions into demoniacal sexual obsession, a solicitation necessary to demonstrate the evasive powers of sacred femininity over and against male invasion.

Whereas Agnes and her suitor Sarelli enjoy Stowe's appreciation for a decorative and ardent ritualism, Francesco receives the brunt of her antipathy to Calvinism, the repudiated religion of her youth. Francesco degenerates into the hell-preoccupied sensuality of popery, a domain that ironically resembles the Calvinist hell of such distrusted "New Light" forebears as Jonathan Edwards. Dante, as elsewhere, mediates in this novel between a sublime and dreadful Catholicism: the poet's relationship to Beatrice conveys the redemptive potential of Francesco's exposure to Agnes's transcendent femininity, while Stowe invokes his *Inferno* to frame the monk's masochistic decline. Unable to quell his passion for Agnes, Francesco finally descends into the sulphurous crater of Vesuvius, his penitential journey recapitulating what New Englanders felt to be Dante's deviant preoccupation with hell. Five years after the publication of *Agnes of Sorrento*, Holmes wrote to Stowe of Dante's *Inferno*: "How often I have said, talking with Lowell, almost the same things you say about the hideousness, the savagery, of that medieval nightmare!"[42]

Having "fairly landed on the dark floor of the gloomy enclosure" (232), Francesco writhes and fulminates like the worst of Dante's lost souls. His plight in the volcano recalls the many desperate inmates of

Catholic-captivity fiction, perversely enamored of the mortifications that oppress them and the confinement into which they have fled. Unlike nativist writers, however, Stowe, in indicting Catholic mortification, pointedly recalls the self-punitive excesses of Calvinism. "It was not the outcry for purity and peace," explains the narrator of Francesco's desperate prayers from within the crater, "not a tender longing for forgiveness, not a filial remorse for sin, but the nervous anguish of him who shrieks in the immediate apprehension of an unendurable torture" (234). In her portrait of a sulphurous and tortured Catholicism, Stowe vents the psychological duress of her own rebellion against her father's Calvinism, an effort whose aggressive energies were more typically submerged by the benevolent sentiments of her liberal Protestantism. The underground affinity between the anti-Catholic stance of her Calvinist upbringing and this Dantesque Catholicism betrays itself in the narrator's lavish interest in Francesco's hell-imbued piety; his scorched soliloquies from the pit of the volcano contain the novel's finest writing.

Representing that specter of excess that haunts the precincts of Stowe's "fairyland" story, Francesco's desire precipitates frequent narrative ruminations on what constitutes false and correct self-control. Forced by his vow of celibacy to repress what Stowe and others understood as man's natural connubial instinct, Francesco suffers a sexual anguish that leads to the (implicitly) masculine heretical stance that life is an "unendurable torture." Excluded by his celibacy from the nurturing female expressivity of true piety (a piety this historical romance provisionally identifies with the artistic exuberance of Renaissance Italy), he undergoes a protracted crisis of generativity, unable to emigrate either to a northern Protestant topography of coldness or into Stowe's Catholic southern landscape of maternal expressivity. Instead he must writhe inside the volcano of male desire, a revenge rendered all the more complete by Stowe's confinement of the volcano in the maternal Italian landscape, innocent yet mighty: "It would seem as if humanity, rocked in this flowery cradle, and soothed by so many daily caresses, and appliances of nursing Nature," writes Stowe of Italy, "grew up with all that is kindliest on the outward—not repressed and beat in, as under the inclement atmosphere and stormy skies of the North" (8).

By exposing the latent class violence of anti-Catholic propaganda, the Ursuline convent attack (see Chapter 7) forced New England's periodical press to revise its estimation of Catholic community and, in particular, monastic life; the incendiary results of the nativist rhetoric of conspiracy and captivity (as many as twenty churches were burned between 1834 and 1860) greatly contributed to liberal Protestant support for the Catholic community, if only because of the "sanctity" of private property.[43] In discussions ensuing on the convent burning, the personalism of conspiratorial theories was complicated by Protestant middle-class suspicions of the working classes, whether Catholic or Protestant. Sensitive to the inflammatory potential of antimonastic rhetoric, several writers attempted more impartial readings of Catholicism, like the reviewer who set about to dismiss *Female Convents* by providing his readers with a "correct" history of monasticism. His defense of the Desert Fathers indicates a self-conscious shift from wholesale denunciation to an admission of the perplexities of religious faith, independent of doctrine: "Whoever denounces them [the Desert Fathers] as mere imposters," warns the author, "does but portray his own ignorance of the subject and of human nature."[44] Having arrived at his unconventional opinion that Catholic asceticism involved complexities of "subject" and "human nature," however, the reviewer reaches an impasse typical of contemporary liberal Protestant assessments of the relation between the powerfully individualized saints and the institutional powers of the church.

In his biographical essay "Joan of Arc," the steadfast Transcendentalist James Freeman Clarke provides one such conflicted account of Joan as a "Protestant heroine" who refuses to forsake her voices and submit to the authority of the church. Clarke's revisionist portrait of Joan of Arc effectively deploys the post-Ursuline strategy, in which authorial impartiality subtly works to discredit both Protestant nativism and Catholic piety. Clarke concludes that the crucial issue of whether the saint's visions were real or delusory "must remain a problem; perhaps always."[45] Such complacent bewilderment at the phenomenon of a religious genius only partially normalized by his revisionary claim for her essential Protestantism leaves Clarke's readers wondering whether sainthood is mental pathology or a foreign instance of the Transcendentalist "Oversoul." Clarke's uncertainty about his religious heroine's stability contrasts sharply to the widely held view that Catholic men, like Hawthorne's veiled Parson Hooper or Stowe's Father Francesco, possessed a profound, if calculating, grasp of human nature; Loyola, as we have seen, was credited with masculine discernment, a "gift to feel his way unerringly through the intricacies of human nature, and to dive into every bosom; and whoever possesses this intuition, comes, by consent of all, into the place of leader in his circle; for the discerning of spirits is the foundation of power."[46] In contrast, Joan of Arc, like Stowe's Agnes, is at best the passive vessel of prophetic powers, at worst a victim of clinical disorders.

Significantly, the first issue of the *Dial* offered a narrative rendition of this New England impasse before a fantasied and variously gendered Catholic power, an impasse born of the Transcendentalist resistance to nativism. Contributing a sketch, "Ernest the Seeker," to the new Transcendentalist periodical, Ellery Channing, the wayward and eventually pathetic nephew of William Ellery Channing, structures his brief tale on the voyeuristic model favored by Hawthorne.[47] The story consists principally of reflections by Ernest, the tale's protagonist, as he reads from his friend Constant's journal. While Ernest sits in his Boston home, perusing his friend's innermost thoughts, Constant is in Rome studying for the priesthood. Ellery Channing's self-distancing authorial strategy, characteristic of pro-Catholic discourse, enfolds author, narrator (Ernest), subject (Constant), and reader into a self-conscious drama of displaced authorship and covert gratification. Looking over Ernest's shoulder, we too spy on Constant's first response to Rome, as recorded in his journal: "It was no dream! I, a child from a far land, was really taken home to the bosom of the mighty mother, who has fed the world with her holiness, and learning, and art" (50). Eagerly reading on, Ernest is suddenly interrupted by his own Bostonian version of mighty Rome—his own disapproving mother. The situation recasts the New England family romance as one conspicuously devoid of any patriarchal figure: the idle and spiritually confused son leans devotedly on the "bosom" of Rome while intruded on by his actual (masculinized) mother, who promptly dismisses her imaginary Roman rival.

Like Lowell's image of the Reformed fly approaching Rome, the bloated spider, Ellery Channing's sketch of maternal Rome is anxiously formed to thwart a competing domestic text of filial impotence before a dominant maternalism. Having lost his own mother when a boy, Channing displaces the dilemmas of orphaned existence onto an imagined Rome, investing his story's Ernest with the shame-faced hostility he felt as a failed son before his socially prominent father and uncle.[48] Parental control over Ernest survives his encounter with a charismatic Catholic bishop, who, in response to Ernest's questions about the Inquisition's persecution of Galileo, exerts a proverbial Catholic mastery over the questing Protestant psyche. "The bishop looked at him steadfastly, for a moment, as if with his luminous gray eye he would throw a light into the most secret chambers of Ernest's consciousness" (240). Such a hypnotic gaze implicitly acknowledges Transcendentalist uncertainties about Catholicism in a filial drama of backward-looking flight from the parent. On the one hand, that "parental" truth is sufficiently persuasive to generate the bishop's penetrative power; on the other, it remains so inaccessible that it yields no articulation whatever. The bishop looks but never says a word, and Ernest strolls off, still entertaining doubts, still unchurched, still a son at home. The proximity of such fiction to the contemporary reality of Catholic conversion emerged not long after when at Brook Farm in 1843 George Curtis nicknamed Isaac Hecker "Ernest the Seeker."[49]

Thus if Emerson chose the fields of Concord over the psychic landscapes of the Vatican, other New Englanders were less successful in doing so. In 1847 Ellery Channing went on to publish *Conversations in Rome: Between an Artist, a Catholic, and a Critic,* a text that illustrates the internalization of tourist Rome into the dilemmas of a home psyche tormented by a lack of professional and spiritual direction.[50] In Channing's book, the model of political pluralism, so frequently cited by the liberal press to justify Protestantism's sectarian disputes, threatens to become that of psychic disarray. Channing explains in his introduction that his book's conversational format aims "to introduce several sides without opposition"; but the author's pluralistic model is hardly an optimistic one, for his "several sides" do not converse so much as alternately speak their discordant claims. Arguing over Rome's beauties and corruptions, the three mouthpieces in effect produce an unsettling portrait of the divided Protestant tourist-spectator, locked in unproductive debate with himself.

Significantly, Channing reserves the "I" of the *Conversations* for the Catholic, whose views are further confirmed by the Artist's opinion that "the old religion was not superficial or perplexing, but productive and profound. They enjoyed it, which is better than can be said of religion with us" (53). By contrast, the Critic emerges as a vulgar and ineffectual voice, evidently burdened with authorial guilt and hostility toward his own skeptical impulses. Both he and the Artist are helpless before the lyricism of the Catholic, who effortlessly deploys a language of domestic trial and transcendence bound to flatter most American readers. Describing a nun's hymn, for example, the Catholic isolates the moment as one of ultimate sentiment: echoing Ernest the Seeker's search for the "bosom of the mighty mother," the Catholic recalls that the nun's voice "stole within the heart, like the Mother's voice, when she calls upon her Child, in her dying hour, to keep good the promise of his youth" (131).

The peculiarity of Channing's volume is that its voices are both internal to the authorial mind and sufficiently externalized to precipitate ritual gestures of trespass and propitiation before this maternal Rome.

Because the Eternal City is both inside and out, both imaginary and confusedly real, Channing's adulation alternates between self-depreciation and self-protection. In the volume's introduction, having yet to split himself into three voices, Channing confesses to a painful sense of sterility, of abject derivativeness in the presence of objective Rome, in a language of trespass that recalls the anxieties of the Ursuline riot: "Let me ask pardon for trespassing in these rich domains. I enter these cultivated grounds, to devote something to the beautiful Monuments around, if it is merely the dry leaf of an uncultivated plant, possessing a color and not a fragrance of its own" (xiv). But these same artistically superior and taboo-laden Roman grounds are also the constituent elements of the narrator's imagination; Channing's opening poem "To the Reader" clarifies this romantic identification between Rome and his Transcendentalist psyche:

> Let the Soul journey in the land of dream,
> And never may the day, with flattering beam,
> Look in and light that land; let us see Rome,
> As she stands firm within the Fancy's home.
>
> (x)

Channing's internalization of Rome as Transcendentalist romance detours the class entanglements of nativism or conversion for the aristocratic privacies of the romantic imagination. Once removed from class issues, Rome's powers can infiltrate and invigorate the enfeebled Unitarian son, the fantasied appropriation of the Old World easing the frustration of imitating an inaccessible ideal: the poem assures its readers that they need "seek no more; / The sands of Europe gleam on Salem's shore" (xi). This Transcendentalist dialogue with Rome operates finally as a de-conversion narrative; the self does not move toward the sacred but wrests it from its European context and internalizes it as the property of the romantic imagination, thus transforming the pluralist model of "conversation" into the politics of an imperial, if lonely, imagination. And as Rome is mixed into the sands of Salem, its sacred powers are scattered into competing regions of the New England mind.

THIRTEEN

The Hawthornian Confessional

Perhaps the finest antebellum romance of Catholicism is Hawthorne's *Scarlet Letter* (1850), which, as conversion narrative and detective story, explores the protracted processes of sin's tortured confinement, devious display, and eventual disclosure.[1] Acutely sensitive to the deficiencies of Calvinist and liberal Protestantism, Hawthorne constructed a Puritan Boston suffused by the meditations on Catholicism of a nineteenth-century spectator who, like Dimmesdale, is implicated in various strategies of evasion and partial appropriation of the "old, corrupted faith of Rome" (144). Incapable of "disentangling" Hester's "mesh of good and evil" (64), the Boston clergy label her "a scarlet woman, and a worthy type of her of Babylon!" (110). Thus labeled in anti-Catholic terms familiar to the novel's antebellum audience, Hester is a Babylonish confusion, inciting a therapeutic Puritanic discourse against the sins of a concupiscent woman who refuses to divulge herself except through her sewing, an activity that partially vocalizes an otherwise iconic silence. Hawthorne's evasive authorial voice, intermittently present in the narrative, both criticizes her sexuality and imitates the duplicitously expressive workings of Hester's needle.

Readers have interpreted Hawthorne's assignment of certain obviously Catholic features to his characters as evidence that the novel opposes a banished Anglo-Catholic past of iconographic richness to a Puritan past (and, by implication, a nineteenth-century Protestant present) of cold intellection and self-inhibition. Certainly, Roger Prynne's emergence from the "study and the cloister" (58) and his adoption of the pseudonym Chillingworth (the name of a seventeenth-century Protestant apologist), Dimmesdale's various identifications with monkish excess and his seclusion of himself within his "dim interior" (130), Hester's embodiment of Mother Church in her dual aspect as the Whore of Babylon—notorious for adulterous union with the sins of the flesh—and as the "image of Divine Maternity" (56), and finally the scarlet letter's persistent reminder of a recently repudiated Anglo-Catholic ceremonialism all invoke the religious tension between Old and New World cultures. But Hawthorne's narrative voice unpredictably distributes these competing terms, enough to dispel any simple nostalgia for a Catholic world repressed by an incipiently bourgeois and pallid Protestantism.[2]

As the pre-text to a story of adulterous union and illicit investigation, the Custom-House sketch mingles itself with the upcoming narrative by establishing freighted symbolic alliances between the "continually prying" (39) narrator and the sacrilegious meddlings of his characters, who like him obsessively investigate one another and, even more dubiously, themselves. Transforming her child into an animate scarlet letter, Hester imitates the narrator's suspicious idolatry of the image; the banished woman "carefully wrought out the similitude; lavishing many hours of morbid ingenuity, to create an analogy between the object of her affection, and the emblem of her guilt and torture" (102). That the morbid Hester serves as the narrator's (as well as the community's) double and chosen scapegoat ties her to the simultaneously invasive and self-absorbed activities of narrative.[3] Further disturbing analogies emerge between the Custom-House sketch and its offspring novel: between the stain of the author's sanguinary ancestry and that of Hester's and Dimmesdale's adultery; between the author's creative "numbness" (35) and Hester's "burden" (79); between the author's struggles with excessive dependence and creative vitiation and the wasting minister, dying "for very weakness" (196) and finally destroyed by his "dread of public exposure" (153); between the author's political "guillotining" at the Custom-House that enables him to write the novel and the symbolic executions suffered by Hester, Pearl, and the minister in their various fugitive appearances on the scaffold. Such covert alliances between the juxtaposed texts, between the historical romancer and his variously criminal characters in their joint perpetration, investigation, and invidious elaboration of sin, suggest that the novel's evident Catholic themes might also emerge from its formal origins in the Custom-House sketch. Indeed, the numerous thematic concerns shared by the two texts, specifically those of circumspect violation, wasting, dreaded exposure, and confession, argue that the Catholic imagery of the novel derives from the exigencies of its composition.

Completing her "term of confinement" (78), Hester begins her dubious wanderings within the prolonged social captivity wrought by wearing the letter that closes "her in a sphere by herself" (54). Her invisible confinement enables an eventual, if partial, liberation. In contrast to Chillingworth, who emerges from his Indian captivity with a vision bent on damnation, Hester and her adulterated family partially extricate themselves from the novel's "cunningly contrived" (85) sentence. Like Pastor Williams's 1707 captivity narrative, Hawthorne's account of sexual lapse and protracted resistance to confession argues the connection between Indian and papal captivity. In introducing Mr. Dimmesdale's nocturnal encounters with his "bloody scourge" (144), however, the novel subverts the logic of Pastor Williams's Congregational polemic (which exiled the alien theology of Catholicism to a wilderness of priest-infested savagery) by depositing the deviant Catholic piety at the heart of the Puritan commonwealth. Hidden like the scourge in Dimmesdale's "secret closet" or flagrantly imaged on Hester's breast, Catholic practices of excessive materiality supply the truculent matter that entices and legitimates the Protestant gaze.

The letter—as Hester's "mark of shame" (63)—persistently identified with religious spectacle, with the shameful and redemptive branding of the stigmata, and the "marks" of the visible church, is implicated, moreover, in the romantic (and nativist) Protestant conception of Romanism, an ideological terrain of semantic conflict, visual sublimity and torture, crucifixional passion and fraud. As an imaginative construct of the Protestant mind, that Catholic domain inhabits a marginal space in the narrative, hedged in by conspicuous ironic disclaimers; Hester's association with the Madonna, for example, depends on a series of conditionals that retract, in the very process of asserting, her Catholic aura: "Had there been a Papist among the crowd of Puritans, he might have seen in this beautiful woman . . . an object to remind him of the image of Divine Maternity, which so many illustrious painters have vied with one another to represent; something which should remind him, indeed, but only by contrast, of that sacred image of sinless motherhood, whose infant was to redeem the world" (56). Tentatively present only through the hypothetical (and entirely unlikely) "Papist among the crowd," the Madonna imagery is subjected to further distancing and dismantling when the narrator extends his imaginative identification with his imaginary Catholic observer. Hester's resemblance to the Virgin is "only by contrast" (56); hers is a deceptive resemblance, the narrator insists, obliged (like many antebellum Protestants who detected in the features of the Virgin, to their dismay, those of the painter's mistress) to expose the duplicities of the image.[4] "Here, there was the taint of deepest sin in the most sacred quality of human life, working such effect, that the world was only the darker for this woman's beauty, and the more lost for the infant that she had borne" (56). Such rhetorical cancellations and disavowals do not diminish the vitality of the Catholic image, however. For that "Papist in the crowd" is no one so much as the novel's narrator and readers, alike fascinated by such romantic excavations and examinations of the Catholic icon.

While underscoring the limitations of Catholic piety, these narrative dynamics also critique Calvinist piety. The absence of the confessional aligns Puritanism with a tortured hypocrisy that transforms the self into a spectral shadow, the minister's vitiation standing as symbolic counterpart for the enervated antebellum Protestant subject, freed from monastic enclosures but plagued by the isolating effects of a culturally imposed reserve. Hester is continually set within the frame of Catholic discourse and found wanting. Both representing and diverging from the Catholic model, she clothes the poor ("it is probable that there was an idea of penance in this mode of occupation" [83]) but forbears to pray for her enemies, a narrative view that reasserts itself in Hester's gradual transformation into a "Sister of Mercy" (161), whose whispering neighbors are disarmed by the crucifixional power of the letter. "It was none the less a fact, however, that, in the eyes of the very men who spoke thus, the scarlet letter had the effect of the cross on a nun's bosom" (163). But unlike Evangeline's full translation into a Sister of Mercy that signals her achievement of otherworldly fidelity and endurance, Hester only fugitively inhabits the nun's role; her letter possesses a "kind of sacredness," its "effect" that of theatrical exhibitionism rather than that of interior piety. Walking with her "cross on a nun's bosom" (163) into the forest, Hester tosses it aside, claiming the emancipated prerogatives of the "escaped nun" of convent-captivity fictions, in flight from the authoritarian cloister. In its transformation from Babylonish stigma to nun's "cross," the scarlet "rag" incorporates the alien religion's dual imaginative aspect of fraud and heroic sanctity. The narrative voice invokes Protestant suspicions that behind the letter's pious exterior lurks the corrupt interior of Hester's proud mind and unsubdued sexuality. Between his relenting community and his nunlike heroine, the narrator inserts the lingering possibility that Hester, like Parson Hooper, might be a fraudulent nun or, worse yet, a mother superior. "Interpreting Hester Prynne's deportment . . . , society was inclined to show its former victim a more benign countenance than she cared to be favored with, or, perchance, than she deserved" (162).

If Hester incompletely resembles a Sister of Mercy, Dimmesdale more fully achieves the Catholic prototype of excessive bodily preoccupation.

"It was his custom, too, as it has been that of many other pious Puritans, to fast,—not, however, like them, in order to purify the body and render it the fitter medium of celestial illumination,—but rigorously, and until his knees trembled beneath him, as an act of penance" (144). The narrator, articulating vis-à-vis the heroics of Catholic piety a Protestant distaste that judges its torments pointless or, worse, a covert encouragement to egotism, views Dimmesdale as sufferingly attached to his spiritual narcissism, his "Catholic" morbidity a displaced representation of the pressure of his Calvinist "constant introspection" (145) and a distraction from it.

These residual gaps in Hester's and Arthur's imitation of Catholic spirituality register the deficiencies of their Calvinist psyches. In this sense, Catholicism is presented as the site for authenticity that makes apparent their fallen status. But the narrative voice intermittently presents such an implicitly Roman ideal in the terms of anti-Catholic discourse, which labeled Catholicism the primary locus of the inauthentic. Is it Hester's duplicity or the hidden hypocrisies of the nunnery that account for her character? Is it Dimmesdale's narcissism or that inherent to penitential practices that accounts for his?

The letter's simultaneous involvement in the discourses of pro- and anti-Catholicism, with martyrdom and hypocrisy, redemption and duplicity, is replicated on a formal level by *The Scarlet Letter* as historical romance. Discovering this "rag of scarlet cloth,—for time, and wear, and a sacrilegious moth, had reduced it to little other than a rag" (31), the narrator resurrects its worn iconic meaning, restoring it to life through his self-professed powers of romance. As described in "The Custom-House," such romance achieves its signature combination of defamiliarization and verisimilitude by scrupulously dividing and admixing various colors of moon-, fire-, and daylight—activities that, in their evident preoccupation with purifying the pollutants of realism and of maintaining a precarious authorial proximity to the materials of the story, invoke ideological struggles between the white light of Protestantism and the stained-glass corruptions of a mediated Catholicism. This moonlight conception and many-hued presentation are refracted throughout the novel by the religious violence of a decade of English Puritan revolution and regicide that spawned in the New World a revolutionary culture as perilously "dis-colored" by sin as the novel's probing, insinuating narrator. The larger psychological and theological question raised by the novel is the extent to which the polluted can save the pure or even issue into the pure, a question that leads Hawthorne to identify the corruptions and materiality of Catholicism with those of the imagination. The "lonely eye witness" to the meteor, for example, views it through the "colored, magnifying, and distorting medium of his imagination" (155). The contamination of such mediation is firmly reconnected to the perils of Catholicism, which also invites a corrupting mediation of egotism between subject and object. Thus the narrative diagnoses Dimmesdale's private revelation when he looks at the meteor as "the symptom of a highly disordered mental state, when a man, rendered morbidly self-contemplative by long, intense, and secret pain, had extended his egotism over the whole expanse of nature, until the firmament itself should appear no more than a fitting page for his soul's history and fate" (155).

For the historical romancer, the distortions of the estranging "medium" (35) of moonlight do not corrupt but rather purify the substances of his domestic world and promise to remove the bodily impediment of his creative torpor. Like Protestantism, moonlight renders the spirit visible while conspicuously avoiding the indolence and sensuous captivities of matter: "All these details, so completely seen, are so spiritualized by the unusual light, that they seem to lose their actual substance, and become things of intellect" (35), the narrator says of his parlor furniture (and, by implication, of the emergent elements of Hester Prynne's story). Hawthorne's verisimilitude in the liminal terrain of romance fiction, "where the Actual and Imaginary may meet" (36), depends on the addition of "coal-fire," whose reddish warmth "converts" the "snow-images" (36) into characters. The merging and separation of scarlet Hester and pale Dimmesdale, then, reenact a mingling whose "consecration" remains subject to recurrent narrative doubt. Hawthorne's narrative alchemy is a notoriously private one that struggles to distill his plot from the torpid, self-punitive, and confessing self—enough so that, rendered secure from autobiographical contaminants, it can risk reengagement with the coloration of matter. Gazing into his carefully adulterated twice-distanced light in the midnight mirror, the narrator anticipates that his "imaginary scenes" will tomorrow "flow out on the brightening page in many-hued description" (35). But even as it culminates in the intensified light of the meteor, this light fails in its conflicted project of revelation and purification, for all four characters stand "in the noon of that . . . splendor, as if it were the light that is to reveal all secrets" (154). Thus, if the historical romance's ritual distancing from the pollutions of the Actual aligns it with the pure light of the probing Protestant imagination, the material product remains deeply implicated with the tinctured obscurities of Catholicism.

Hawthorne's "many-hued" test of variable and disturbing significance centers finally on Pearl, a child whose "depth of hue" (90) and killing gaze reenact the novel's emergence from its own adulterous commingling of chaste historical romance and immodest autobiographical confession. As a creature "imbued with a spell of infinite variety," (90) Pearl as "treasure" represents the scarlet letter as book and child as well as object of the narrative's shameful diggings. With her broken lineage, Pearl recalls the abandoned Anglo-Catholic culture of "dear old England" (206); her clerical interrogator, the Reverend Wilson, claims to have "seen just such figures, when the sun has been shining through a richly painted window, and tracing out the golden and crimson images across the floor" (109–10). Pearl's wild materiality wrenches such nostalgia into the present perplexities and hostilities of antebellum Protestant views of Catholicism. If Pearl is animate stained glass to the Reverend Wilson, she refuses her vestigial status as something "left behind us, with other relics of Papistry, in merry old England" (110). Nonetheless, she is eventually made to submit to the antebellum purifications of sentimental domesticity. In digging for the "treasure" of Pearl's lineage, this detective novel relocates her, not in the past, but in the hysteric penalties of its own middle-class domesticity. Another victim of its exaggerated maternal powers and sexual repressions, Pearl has nursed "all the turmoil, the anguish, and despair, which pervaded the mother's system" (70), a contamination of female rage that articulates itself through the Catholic corruptions of the "stained-glass" Hester: "The mother's impassioned state had been the medium through which were transmitted to the unborn infant the rays of its moral life; and, however white and clear originally, they had taken the deep stains of crimson and gold, the fiery lustre, the black shadow, and the untempered light, of the intervening substance" (91). If the narrator implicitly succeeds at controlling such admixtures of expressive emotion in his evasive, reserved ("moonlit") romance, Hester fails to constrain the contagion of her sin, the crimson stain of Catholicism and adultery seeping from her body into Pearl's. The anxiety and hostility the child provokes in mother, father, and narrator are contextualized in the unlawful dimensions of the Catholic image and its potentially hell-bound commingling of spirit and flesh: "how could they doubt that their earthly lives and future destinies were conjoined, when they beheld at once the material union, and the spiritual idea, in whom they met, and were to dwell immortally together?" (207).

In its sustained preoccupation with such concerns as mediation, confession, self-mortification, and the attractions of the image, *The Scarlet Letter* testifies powerfully to the disturbing depths of the mid-century liberal Protestant engagement with "popery." Centrally important issues of spectacle and spectatorship emerge in Hawthorne's narrative of shaming scrutiny, one dedicated to the production of repeated bodily exposures—a novel whose four characters, alike endowed with preternatural spiritual intuition and powers of detection, thwart public scrutiny only to borrow its punitive energy to afflict one another. If an alien Romanism manifests its compelling influence in the plot's preoccupation with the limits of ministerial self-control, the necessities of confession, and the seductive, even numinous perils of the image, that same deviant spirituality sounds in a narrative voice engaged in the partial confession and suspended disclosure of its story—activities justified by the narratorial appeal to the uncertain significance of the scarlet image.

To untie the "inextricable knot, the agony of heaven-defying guilt and vain repentance" (148) of Dimmesdale's heart, the narrator slowly confesses his plot, the hesitant tempo depending on the minister's competing capacity for reserve, which, like Hester's "erring woman's heart" (64), evades the narrator's efforts to appraise his guilt concisely. If the novel's conversion plot of affliction, repentance, and redemption subscribes to the ideological imperatives of Hawthorne's Protestant domesticity (and, specifically, his allegiance to female purity), its detective plot belongs rather to the more compelling anti-domestic domain of Catholic sensuality and secrecy. The narrator's protracted efforts to discover, disguise, and finally disclose the perpetrator of the crime suggest that the figure of a father confessor whom Hawthorne eight years before had imagined as possible protagonist ("his reflections on character, and the contrast of the inward man with the outward, as he looks round on his congregation—all whose secret sins are known to him") has indeed appeared, not as a character, but as a narrator. With its privileged confessional knowledge of the characters' sexual crimes and penitential practices, the narrative voice provokes readerly curiosity in order to thwart it. Imagining that his ideal reader, "a friend, a kind and apprehensive, though not the closest friend, is listening to our talk" (4), the Custom-House narrator offers his fiction as overheard confession, maintaining a precarious balance of intimacy and anonymity that will permit communication while preserving privacy, so that "we may prate of the circumstances that lie around us, and even of ourself, but still keep the inmost Me behind its veil. To this extent and within these limits, an author, methinks, may be autobiographical, without violating either the reader's rights or his own" (4). Hawthorne's image of himself as a veiled yet autobiographical speaker invokes Catholicism's alleged violations of the Protestant American's political, sexual, and spiritual "rights" to assure his readers that his will be a properly managed confessional.

This Hawthornian confessional paradoxically registers its propriety by its reserve, its resistance to the Roman confessional's excessively intimate communications. As the suddenly alerted Dimmesdale says to the prying Chillingworth: "There can be, if I forebode aright, no power, short of the Divine mercy, to disclose, whether by uttered words, or by type or emblem, the secrets that may be buried with a human heart" (131). Author of Dimmesdale's "strange reserve" (125), the repository of its undivulged contents, the narrator indicts Chillingworth's sexually predatory scrutiny only to maintain his own impenetrability. Having claimed, however, the virginal integrity of his Protestantized confessor status, the narrator then indulges in the aggressive inquisitiveness of a father confessor (as characterized in antebellum Protestant discourse). The narrator presses forward through Dimmesdale's fantasied pseudo-confessions from the pulpit ("The minister well knew—subtle, but remorseful hypocrite that he was!—the light in which his vague confession would be viewed" [144]), to the inarticulate confession of his Election Day Sermon ("The complaint of a human heart, sorrow-laden, perchance guilty, telling its secret, whether of guilt or sorrow, to the great heart of mankind" [243]), and finally to the minister's public acknowledgment on the scaffold before the gaping crowd. Thus while faulting Chillingworth for his sadistic probing, the narrator pursues with equal cunning Dimmesdale's dread of exposure. And while Hester's refusal to disclose Dimmesdale's identity to either Chillingworth or the authorities is justified according to a sentimental (and nativist) Protestant thematics of violation ("it were wronging the very nature of woman to force her to lay open her heart's secrets in such broad daylight, and in presence of so great a multitude" [65]), her refusal to confess Chillingworth's identity to the suffering minister exposes him to seven torturous years of unconscious "confession" to Chillingworth. Those years form an extended interlude whose horror exceeds the traditionally gendered anti-Catholic images of female rape in the confessional, spilling over into the disgust of a homoeroticized display: "And the shame!—the indelicacy!—the horrible ugliness of this exposure of a sick and guilty heart to the very eye that would gloat over it!" (194). By punishing Chillingworth for his blasphemous probings, for daring to "thrust himself between the sufferer and his God" (137), the narrator can then legitimate his own probings, secure that his intimate location in the interior of his characters will be read not as sexual violation but as the pure attention of the Protestant gaze. "No eye could see him, save that ever-wakeful one which had seen him in his closet, wielding the bloody scourge" (148).

While a literary character as father confessor might have fatefully risked the sovereignty of the masculine subject, the narrator as confessor, prying into and pondering the stories of his characters, represents Hawthorne's masterful recovery of poise. Breaking down the Reverend Dimmesdale's "vast power of self-restraint" (66), the narrative then curtails the anxiety of this masculine release by withholding Dimmesdale's secret from the reader, allowing only a choice "among . . . theories" (259). Similarly, the letter, emerging in part from the suppressed iconographic dimension of Catholicism, is a "most curious relic" (33) that inspires the Custom-House narrator's conventional antebellum perplexity before the abandoned church of Rome; throughout the narrative it provokes multiple and finally inconclusive "private judgments" as to its import. As the chosen instrument of the Puritan hierarchy, the letter serves as insignia for the new culture's anti-Catholic values while provocatively commemorating the loss of that despised popish world.

Coda to Part 3

The language of antebellum Protestant observation of "Romanism," unlike Emerson's vision of unmediated selfhood as "transparent eyeball," depended on a continued surveillance of Rome's alternative sacred as a splendid and repellent exhibition of the body. The transactions between the anti-Catholic attack on the spiritual despotism of Romanism and the pro-Catholic language of fascinated desire for Rome occurred through a mediating thematics of spectacle and "influence" that issued finally from the contradictions of embodiment. Imaged as containing (and even indecently exhibiting) the body, Rome functioned as aesthetic substance for Protestant consumption, an imperial logic that achieved classic expression in Lowell's brief chapter from his *Fireside Travels* (1864), "A Few Bits of Mosaic."[1] Like Emma Forbes Cary's metaphor of the mosaic that describes her restorative conversion to Catholicism, Lowell's "mosaic" figures the Protestant tourist-self as a deciphering intelligence at work amid the fragments of his own alienated spirituality. Standing on the threshold of St. Peter's, the author is bent on tracking down "what that secret is which makes a thing pleasing to another" (288), a pilgrimage of spiritual detection and regeneration problematically involved in profane issues of taste and consumption. Lowell's quest involves neither negation nor acceptance but a complex revision of Catholic dogma into a Protestant "consumable," a dramatized incorporation of Catholicism as commodity that occurs in an imaginary southern European terrain that combines the easeful pleasures of a Boston drawing room and a Mediterranean landscape. "Suppose that a man in pouring down a glass of claret could drink the South of France" (289), the narrator muses for his American magazine audience. Southern France is a seductive vista that provides all the light and space so powerfully absent from the interior of St. Peter's, the predatory place from which the tourist-narrator (as a "poor Reformed fly") has begun his Mediterranean reverie. But the narrator can reach his fantasized French landscape only through the dark interiority of the "real" cathedral into whose confines he is propelled: "As he lifts the heavy leathern flapper over the door, and is discharged into the interior by its impetuous recoil, let him disburden his mind altogether of stone and mortar" (288–89).

Once inside St. Peter's, the erotically frightened Protestant tourist abruptly shifts to southern France in his imagination, a flight that enables him to practice an imperialist consumption that implicitly competes against the papal dynasty, which he declares "the most powerful the world ever saw" (289). What Lowell drinks is not claret but France entire, its agriculture, its culture, its people, a hungry violence that energizes his description of the connoisseur who "could so disintegrate the wine by the force of imagination as to taste in it all the clustered beauty . . . of the grape, all the dance . . . and sunburnt jollity of the vintage" (289). Consumption of this commodity enables him to break it into its constituent elements and thus overcome his own alienation: He drinks not only to taste sunny beauty but also to recapture the joy of unalienated labor, the proverbial harvest merriment that lies concealed in the wine.

But this rural plenitude is only a prelude to the tourist's recurrent concern with Italian Catholicism, to which he returns through an imaginary act of ingestion: "Or suppose that in eating bread, he could transubstantiate it with the tender blade of spring" (289). This is hardly an orthodox transubstantiation but one itself "transubstantiated" by Lowell into a poetic approximation; the narrator's French bread leads not to Christ's body but to a Thomsonian parade of seasons that traces the wheat's growth to the autumn harvest, a transubstantiation whose regress from bread to "tender blade" reverses the orthodox progress from bread to spirit. Present beneath the palimpsest of romantic discourse and rendered immobile by it, Christ is a dispossessed figure whose sacerdotal powers are now claimed by the priestly poet, who reveals the spirit behind the letter to be the grapes behind the claret.

Lowell's role as vatic poet supplants his former, painfully inferior, status as the "poor Reformed fly," his powers of poetic transubstantiation equivalent to "what the Roman Church does for religion" (290). In this amiable identification, Protestantism functions as the hypostatized invalid, weakened by an unnamed physician who offers only "a drop or two of the tincture of worship" (290), a mere tint that cannot sustain the soul. Like these untherapeutic medicinal drops, Protestantism represents an extracted "essential religious sentiment"—a finished deadening product, an "extinguished Q.E.D." (290). Following the logic of this physiological contrast, Catholicism conversely yields access to an unfinished plenitude of the past, one that unfolds panoramically before viewers and permits them to feel "one by one all those original elements of which worship is composed" (290). Lowell's celebration of the church transforms the holy space of St. Peter's into a holy time that harbors an Eden of separable delicious elements; Catholicism permits a retrospective contact with this time while Protestantism enforces a disagreeable forward motion toward death. Thus inverting typically anti-Catholic views of Rome's fraudulent proximity to art, views that led the Unitarian Orville Dewey to explain that Catholicism's greatest evil is "that imagination and sentiment are substituted for real feeling and virtue,"[2] Lowell claims that in Catholic aestheticism lies its superior authenticity, for its materiality supplies, like the new geology, a record of the "climbing generations" (290). Such consoling gradualism enables Lowell, the religious connoisseur, to gain access to an apostolic past, aesthetically speaking. If one can no longer ingest Christ, one can at least handle those who did, those generations of the faithful displayed before the connoisseur-tourist. Lowell's revealingly commodified sacred (one contained in his freighted abstraction "The Roman Church") permits the ambiguous pleasures of dissection—the pleasures, in short, of the "mosaic" that can be poetically reassembled after the deciphering consumer has taken it apart.

For Lowell, the Church's veiled glories facilitate a positive release of the truth, one associated with the curative effects of bloodletting and implicitly contrasted with the debilitating loss of blood from the barely tinctured Protestant body. Continuing his revision of New England suspicions about Roman enclosures, Lowell sees in Catholicism's "veiled" (290) glories the pleasures, not the terrors, of enclosure. Whether through the aesthetics of its noonday interior, where sunlight mixes with "ever-burning lamps" (299), or through its theology of transubstantiation, Catholicism offers mixture without pollution, embrace without captivity. Or, in the summary terms of the narrator's diagnosis: "The secret of her power is typified in the mystery of the Real Presence" (290).

The most compelling interiority thematized in Lowell's tourism through European Catholicism is finally neither the cathedral, with its light-entangled sublimities, nor the "Real Presence" but an abstracted "man" who represents both himself and his American Protestant reader; both claim psyches divided between the imagination and the "iconoclast Understanding" (290–91), a division built upon a gendered opposition between the female Church, clinging to "her faith in the imagination," and the masculine intellect. As the "only church that has been loyal to the heart and soul of man" (290), Catholicism abides as the loving mother, staving off the dangers of the father and the specter of parental abandonment.

It is finally Lowell's preoccupation with analyzing the constituent parts of the whole, with breaking open the commodity to feel the history of its making, with going back in a controlled intimacy of contact with past generations ("making us pass over and feel beneath our feet all the golden rounds of the ladder" [290]) that motivates his praise for this loyal and maternal Catholicism. Both he and "she" understand the virtues of the mosaic, of inlaid separable pieces, over potentially exclusionary wholes. Maternal Catholicism feeds the Protestant tourist's "kitchen longings and visions" with the "visible, tangible raw material of imagination" (291). Like Thoreau's famous confession of longing for the raw woodchuck, Lowell's swift progress from "visible" to "raw" voices the connection between the oracular and the oral.

This religious travelogue describes conversion, then, as an alchemical linguistic procedure of which Catholicism is the mistress and Protestantism, like Hawthorne's Aylmer, the deviant practitioner. "Protestantism reverses the poetical process I have spoken of above, and gives not even the bread of life, but instead of it the alcohol, or distilled intellectual result" (292). Instead of the "sacramental claret of southern France" or the "Real Presence" of Italy, Protestantism offers grain alcohol, a toxic distillation whose dangers are those of aggressive extraction and depletion. In performing his own alchemical transmutation, punning on the "Bread of Life" so that it no longer functions as "Eucharist" but simply as bread (eventual source of Protestantism's grain alcohol), the tourist narrator attempts his own conversion of Catholicism into the matter for his art of surveillance, decipherment, and poetic reconstruction. Performing a self-professed "ceremony" (295) of measurement, the tourist confesses finally that the heart of St. Peter's cathedral looks to him like a gigantic bedroom; the remembered proportions of an infant's world resurface in his concluding dreamlike vision, in which he is "brought to terms at once by being told that the canopy over the high altar (looking very like a four-post bedstead) was ninety-eight feet high. If he still obstinates himself, he is finished by being made to measure one of the marble *putti,* which look like rather stoutish babies, and are found to be six feet, every sculptor's son of them" (294–95). Dwarfed amid this gigantic bedroom with its marble sons, the poet-tourist turned surveyor busies himself by estimating their monetary worth. Before leaving the cathedral, Lowell returns one last time to its twilight shadows, where he waits in this childhood terrain, whose maternal features conform to the hallucinatory measurements of Romanism, romantic naturalism, and American domesticity: "Then, standing in the desert transept, you hear the far-off vespers swell and die like low breathings of the sea on some conjectured shore" (299).

4

FOUR CONVERTS

FOURTEEN

Elizabeth Seton: The Sacred Workings of Contagion

Sometime during the last quarter of the eighteenth century, the famous revivalist preacher George Whitefield leaned over the prostrate body of a fourteen-year-old black boy and breathed, "Jesus Christ has got thee at last." Soon after this moment of divine seizure and conversion, the boy, John Marrant, a free black, fled his South Carolina town and family for the wilderness. He later described his adventures in one of the three most popular captivity narratives published in America, *A Narrative of the Lord's Wonderful Dealings with John Marrant, a Black (Now Gone to Preach the Gospel in Nova-Scotia).*[1] Marrant's story of evangelical enlightenment and ensuing captivity—first as a prisoner of the Cherokee Indians and then, on his return to the settlements, as an impressed sailor in the British Navy—articulates the complex interaction between captivity and conversion in American culture. Edited by the white Reverend Aldridge, who claims that "no more alterations . . . have been made, than were thought necessary" (180), Marrant's conversion and captivity narrative remains inescapably dual, for its conversion heroics are represented through Aldridge—a narrative situation of double inscrutability that both underscores the racial dominion asserted by white spectator over black prodigy and recapitulates the vexed rhetorical status of all convert prose, which dedicates itself to describing the indescribable.

Speaking worldly language to publicize its heavenly discoveries, convert prose characteristically wrestles with its own representations, vehemently intent on language but suspicious of the mimesis so hard won.[2] Marrant's story, in its association of God with symbolic disguise, abrupt role reversal, and violent transit between civilization and wilderness, interweaves his conversion with white America's triadic struggle against Britain, Africa, and the Indian nations. Instigating and then resolving into an elaborately patterned series of further self-transformations, captivities, and deliverances, Marrant's tent-meeting conversion functions as a trope through which the black convert and (implicitly) the white reader organize and master the national and racial conflicts that jointly menace them. The radically unknowable God of evangelical Methodism serves paradoxically to control the abrupt transformations of the Revolutionary era while the drama of the interior life, its abysses, reversals, paradoxes, and triumphs, asserts the virtuosity of the black convert, whose "enslavement" to Whitefield's Christ issues into a proliferation of escapes.

Like the originating mystery of the Incarnation—the Godhead's paradoxical and always provisional allegiance to the flesh—Marrant's tale of conversion and captivity oscillates between transcendence and embrace of the sensuous world. The strange agreements and interchanges between the profane and the sacred suggestively implied by the Incarnation manifest themselves in the consummate theatricality of his story of the spirit, his narrative unfolding further dramas of disguise and transformation, play and crisis, as he converts himself from free black to adopted Indian, to British soldier, and finally to Methodist missionary. Having, like other spiritually motivated captives, virtually engineered his abduction by the Cherokees, the prisoner avoids his torture-death by converting his Indian executioner at the sacrifice site—a feat performed by spontaneously praying "with remarkable liberty" (190) in the Cherokee tongue, by quoting Scripture charismatically spoken to the literally and spiritually uncomprehending Cherokees, and, at hints of each deliverance, by singing Watts's hymns. The successful replication of Whitefield's conversion technology not only confirms his own saved status, his mastery, as it were, of his own enslavement, but also advertises the evangelical economy of the Holy Spirit; for like Marrant's various identities, the spirit functions as a volatile commodity amenable to duplication, distribution, and exchange at moments of crisis.

Eventually casting off his adopted princely status, Marrant returns to the town from which he had fled, disguised as a "savage" to proselytize among whites and blacks, first holding revival meetings in the back settlements and, by doing so, coming to know his true vocation. As free black disguised as Indian, Marrant describes his "head . . . set out in the savage manner, with a long pendant down my back, a sash round my middle, without breeches, and a tomahawk by my side" (194). Thus transformed, he preaches the Gospel of Jesus to the white man from whom it came, the convert turning and turning again inside the constraints of early American culture, extracting power from oppression, liberty from captivity, authentic dissemblance from inauthentic being. He is as visible and invisible as the Lord whom he represents. "The singularity of my dress drew everybody's eyes upon me, yet none knew me" (195). If the return home brings on the expected struggle with spiritual complacency, Marrant uses the occasion to warn the reader, "Don't forget our Lord's exhortation, 'What I say unto you, I say unto all, *WATCH*'" (197). We are of course to watch for the coming of Christ and for the continuation of Marrant's narrative, to submit our potentially errant attention to his authorial capture.

When impressed by the British for seven years' service during the Revolutionary War, Marrant (now the involuntary servant of his oppressor) undergoes a final displacement and doubling. From "redskin" to "redcoat," the black man submerges himself in cultural conflict; all oppression becomes inscribed on him so that he, like his crucified Lord, might become a strategist of deliverance. Freed in England, he is ordained in the newly rejected Mother Country and concludes his career on another cultural margin, in Nova Scotia, as a Methodist missionary. Thus this virtuoso of New World culture and his adventures in the political and spiritual picaresque proclaim that unity abides beneath the worst of conflicts. As he assumes and sheds the guises of America, he develops into a cross-cultural, interracial, evangelized force who asserts the continuity of the spiritual over the violent and random impact of the cultural.

In Marrant's spiritual autobiography, conversion constitutes a crucial intersection of charismatic agency and coercive historical event. In both the extremity of its events and its representation, his conversion narrative prefigures and provisionally contains political and racial schism. Alternating between black, white, and red man, profane musician and sanctified captive, impressed soldier and charismatic preacher, Marrant embodies fundamental oppositions and inequities in Revolutionary America between the Old and the New World, the savage and the civilized, the slave and the free man, "Old" and "New" lights. Thus his career improbably testifies to the emergent myth of the New Republic— that no social enslavement need be permanent. The sheer availability of liberty—of deliverance—in the spiritual dimension argues for freedom's plenitude in the temporal. There is finally no tangled alliance (or antagonism) between the two, but rather a mimetic accord, one narratively registered with the symbolic precision and splendor of ritual. Marrant's narrative concludes on the eve of his voyage to Nova Scotia, for which he entreats our prayers that "Indian tribes may stretch out their hands to God; that the black nations may be made white in the blood of the Lamb" (200).

〰️

In antebellum America the issue of conversion was no less engaged with the drama of the marginal self and the threat of national disunity.[3] But the site for the representation of transcendence and its conflicted negotiation between the mysteries of interiority and the burdens of the historical self broadened to include the novel and ideologically suspect domain of the Roman Catholic church. With the increasing standardization of Protestant conversion to a nondenominational "saving faith in Jesus," conversion to Catholicism assumed an obliquely radical position in America; like Marrant's Methodism, Roman Catholicism afforded a sanctified deviance from mainstream culture, offering antebellum converts a paradoxical deliverance from Protestant hegemony through the proverbial captivity to Old World orthodoxy. As Marrant had expertly "converted" captivity into liberty, racial marginality into evangelical authority, so many nineteenth-century Americans found in "popery" their joy, salvation, and regenerated cultural identity.

Those antebellum citizens who converted to one or another denomination of Protestant Christianity were both leaving the world and subscribing to one of their culture's most prized values. Indeed, from the Puritan migration onward, spiritual rebirth had been a primary means of cleansing the community of heterogeneous elements and, for individuals, of attaining status in its purified precincts.[4] Those antebellum Americans who chose Catholicism, however, adopted what their peers defined as corrupt and defiled. Emerging from the intersection of intense cultural prejudice and an often overwhelming subjective conviction of Catholicism's truth, Protestant converts to Rome consolidated their religious identities through the experience of cultural resistance that not only confirmed their decision but consoled them for its inevitable costs. Wrote one convert: "It seems to me that the difference between my embracing the Roman Catholic Church and any other is the same as the difference between remaining as I am, and selling all that I have and following Christ."[5] For Catholic converts, the process entailed a series of radical ideological inversions in which the Whore of Babylon became the Mother Church and the Antichrist became the venerated pope—a transformation so amazing that Stowe, fascinated by the submission of her own character, Father Francesco, to "antichrist," could only attribute it to "some metaphysical process of imaginative devotion."[6]

Because they were both insiders and outsiders, such nineteenth-century American Catholic converts as Elizabeth Ann Seton (1774–1821), Isaac Hecker (1819–1888), Sophia Ripley (1803–1861), and Orestes Brownson (1803–1876) developed a distinctive critical capacity to diagnose the majority culture they had repudiated.[7] Their effort to resituate themselves within but not inside that abandoned culture involved an intricate battle with its familiar but now "heretical" influences and at times a subversive reappropriation of Protestant America for Rome. As the eighteenth-century minister John Thayer argued in his conversion narrative, the Roman church was precisely that "City built upon a mountain" memorialized in John Winthrop's sermon aboard the *Arbella*. The true church was not the one so eloquently envisioned and laboriously pursued by Winthrop and company; rather, it had been elsewhere all along and "visible" for all the world to see.[8]

Proponents of the mid-century doctrine of Manifest Destiny argued that Protestant purity and redemption were central to the domestic and international expansionist politics of the Republic. American missionaries set off not only for the Hawaiian Islands, but for Catholic Europe, seeking to offset there the presumed machinations of Jesuits and other papal agents in America by proselytizing on the streets of Rome.[9] At the very time such Protestant missionary efforts were occurring, however, American Protestants in sizable numbers were defecting to Rome. Of the estimated 350,000 conversions to Catholicism in nineteenth-century America, some 57,400 took place between 1831 and 1860.[10] Although several prominent converts were drawn from the ranks of High Episcopalianism, antebellum conversions were not traceable to any one ideological center, such as the Oxford movement provided in England.[11] Instead those conversions of which we have written descriptions developed as individual (and regionally diffuse) responses to cultural and individual pressures indigenous to pre–Civil War America. As such, Catholic converts articulated a distinctive indictment of and alternative to the economic and domestic pressures of middle-class life—pressures characteristically experienced as an emptiness within, an absence remedied only by the redemptive "substance" of Catholic dogma. The defection in the ranks provoked some of the culture's most profound and revealing comment on the nature of authority and subversion, interpretation and truth, corruption and regeneration. Indeed, contemporary accounts of Catholic conversion elicited explanatory strategies that pointed to significant ideological tensions in mainstream Protestant culture. Impelled by their adopted faith, many converts struggled to domesticate their decision, to accommodate themselves and their audiences to foreign modes of ecclesiastical polity and piety. Simultaneously, convert writing, which included conversion narratives, periodical essays, personal correspondence, fiction, and poetry, transcended its struggle to communicate with its surrounding "heretical" culture. Hence, the language of Catholic conversion variously incorporated liberal Protestant (and especially Transcendentalist) views of the spirit and the nativist language against which conversions shaped themselves.

Many Catholic converts were fleeing the psychologically coercive extremes of Calvinism, whose insistence on the worthlessness of human effort appeared increasingly tyrannical and implausible. If the famous eighteenth-century Puritan missionary David Brainerd comfortably lamented that his prayers were like *"paddling* with my hand in the water," and if Marrant pursued precisely such evangelicalized impotence in the wilderness, later generations resisted such abasement as an unseemly enslavement. Holmes's memorable revulsion at being taught as a child that "we were a set of little fallen wretches" was shared by the Catholic convert and prolific novelist Joshua Huntington, who recalled that his Calvinist education produced only religious indifference. "I constantly heard the doctrine taught that every action, even the prayer, of the unconverted man is wholly sinful, an abomination in the sight of God; so I made none."[12]

Long-standing theological and clerical debates over the proper morphology of conversion generally followed one of two models: the gradual education of the struggling soul, a spiritual evolution influentially put forth in John Bunyan's *Pilgrim's Progress,* or the stunning transformation of the worldly soul, an experience typified by Paul on the road to Damascus. Was conversion to be a "natural" and noninstitutional product of the new cult of domesticity and family nurture, as liberal Protestants like Horace Bushnell argued in *Christian Nurture* (1847)?[13] Or were the revivalists the correct model, with their increasingly nondenominational but "conservative" terrain of radical impotence, vitiated nature, and blinding grace? Converts to Rome frequently articulated their conversion experiences as an alternative to this debate; they resisted the instantaneous captivity of evangelical revivalism epitomized by John Marrant and systematized by such nineteenth-century revivalists as Peter Cartwright and Charles Grandison Finney; they also resisted the cult of domesticity, choosing a path of gradual enlightenment that had little to do with the "Angel in the House." In claiming that they traveled a "gradual path," these converts denied notions of innate depravity and transformative domesticity while accepting the use of reason and the possibility of celibacy. Because Catholic doctrine validated the careful use of reason in cooperation with grace, the foreign church was especially attractive to such figures as Orestes Brownson, who spoke for many converts in describing the forcefully cerebral nature of his developing belief in the claims of Rome: "I have disputed the ground inch by inch, and have yielded only when I had no longer any ground on which to stand."[14]

Catholics were not, of course, averse to marketing the Pauline dynamic of conversion. An influential spiritual autobiography of the period, *The Conversion of Marie-Alphonse Ratisbonne: Original Narrative of Baron Theodore de Bussières,* reported that "a man, in full possession of all his senses and faculties, entered a church an obstinate Jew; and, by one of those swift flashes of grace which laid Saul prostrate at the gates of Damascus, he came forth, ten minutes afterwards, a Catholic in heart and in will."[15] If Catholics advertised such miraculous transformations, Protestant converts to Rome typically emphasized the time-consuming complexity of their repudiation of Protestantism. *The Apology for the Conversion of Stephen Cleveland Blythe, to the Faith of the Catholic, Apostolic, and Roman Church, Respectfully Addressed to Protestants of Every Denomination* (1815) records one pilgrim's exhaustive travels through Episcopalianism, Deism, Moravianism, Swedenborgianism, and Unitarianism. "But, as if I were doomed to be the victim of my own fastidious delicacy," Blythe writes, "and endlessly to roam in quest of what I should never find, I soon discovered in the simplest form of Christianity, the most palpable inconsistencies."[16] Finally returning to Boston after his prolonged spiritual search, Blythe joined the Catholic church in 1809.

The convert Joshua Huntington found that the illogicalities of Princeton seminary training destroyed his respect for Calvinist theology and thus the very basis of his Christian faith. The Reformers' appeal to a pure scriptural rather than (corrupt) apostolic authority was finally a spurious solution, he declared in his *Gropings After Truth: A Life Journey from New England Congregationalism to the One Catholic and Apostolic Church* (1868), for scriptural interpretation was itself thoroughly shaped by human mediation. "The simple fact is, that the Bible is a rule of faith to Protestants to this extent, and no further, that, having received their faith from the oral instruction of their parents and teachers, without the Bible, they have recourse to it in after-years, merely to find in it the things which they have been taught, and which they already believe."[17] Training for the ministry, Huntington failed in his struggle to experience the desired descent of the spirit; his "conviction became gradually fixed that this notion of conversion was wholly a delusion" (25), and he finally abandoned his fledgling clerical career to become a schoolmaster. Sometime later, he found himself reading issues of the *Catholic World,* "merely from curiosity, to see how the advocates of this absurd superstition would attempt to defend it in the brilliant light of this nineteenth-century" (89). The conversion that ensued from this studiously casual exploration conscientiously opposes the antirational morphology of evangelical pietism. "At length, I began to think her [the church's] claims might be well founded, and by a gradual process of change, my admission of the possibility of this was converted, through the operations of my own mind, into a conviction of its probability, and finally into a full belief in its truth" (93). Huntington's defense of the "operations of my own mind" is characteristic of antebellum convert prose, an effort to reassert the legitimacy of the reasoning (or feeling) self against Protestant cultural validations of the *willing* self, one capable of entrepreneurial, revivalistic, or Emersonian transformations through a sheer assertion of will.

Writing usually in the tradition of Christian apologetics, rather than in the intimate confessional mode of spiritual autobiography, converts like Stephen Blythe and Joshua Huntington at times confirmed contemporary suspicions of Catholic piety. Sharply contrasted to the abasements of Calvinism or the intuitions of liberal Unitarianism, their Catholic conversion narratives characteristically focused less on a saving grace than on a saving epistemology and politics, a way of knowing and of being in society. Converts also unintentionally buttressed pejorative associations between Rome and worldliness by trying to prove the reasonableness of their decision. They struggled to convey that grace was an "objective" as well as a "subjective" matter and that the true church was a visible institution that embodied the living, invisible Christ but whose claims were accessible to human reason.

This stress on objectivity was such a puzzling redefinition of spirituality that some Protestant reviewers of convert authors often found no religion at all in their accounts of spiritual illumination; their narratives seemed hopelessly "outside" the spirit to Protestant readers. They might be stories of fraud or folly, but not of an authentic piety; Bishop Levi Silliman Ives's widely read narrative *The Trials of a Mind in Its Progress to Catholicism* (1854) deviated so far from conventional representations of spiritual progress that it was judged "utterly deficient in those qualities of solemn and penetrating earnestness which will so profoundly engage our sympathies when we read of the real struggles of a soul with facts and mysteries."[18] This reviewer's bewilderment was not entirely a matter of anti-Catholic prejudice, for his inability to credit Ives's narrative with any spiritual sincerity whatever reveals deeply held differences not only about the procedures and fruits of conversion but also about the nature of the interior life. Could that life include sanctified elements of the exterior world, or were such elements an inevitable corruption of the questing spirit? As suggested by Maria Monk's depictions of monastic obedience as a pathological debasement of reason, the divergence between Protestant and Catholic devotional practices signaled deep disagreement over not only what interior life was but also who was to be in it. If, as a writer explained in the Catholic *Metropolitan,* "in divinizing authority, Catholicity has sanctified obedience," that view inflamed resistance from those preoccupied with the dangers of submission and the perils of intellectualism in a democratic, individualist culture.[19]

To antebellum readers preoccupied with the expansionist menace of slavery or "unionism"—both threats to the sovereignty of the American citizen—converts spoke a baffling language of interiority, enclosure, and reasoned submission, a vocabulary that inevitably entangled itself with traditional republican anxieties about abuse of authority and the Protestant insistence on the primacy of private judgment. As supposed victims of Catholicism's "false glitter which dazzled and betrayed men into worship of their destroyers," converts were accorded the marginal, if threatening, status of the mesmerized and self-destructive soul.[20] Converts could respond with their own version of the captivity ethos, declaring of those who persisted in their delusions of independence that "they who have not been illumined by the faith, though they think themselves free, are slaves to the greatest of all tyrants—pride, and the degraded servants of the most base of all masters—self."[21]

The varied and often vital articulations of Catholic converts belied the nativist Nicholas Murray's confident claim that "if there is any moral position on which the mind of this age is satisfied, it is that Popery is the mystery of iniquity."[22] Quarreling with the age's developing validation of an increasingly isolate and emancipated subjectivity, antebellum converts used "sanctified" reason to contain the perilous reflexivity of "private judgment." Dismissing Protestant claims for the controlling authority of Scripture, one writer for the *Catholic World,* in words reminiscent of Melville's portrait of the maddened Ahab, described the Protestant Bible reader as both victim and blasphemous executor of private judgment: "He holds the sacred book before the mirror of his reason. The image it presents, however imperfect or deformed, becomes to him the truth of the Eternal Word. He casts the pure wheat of God between the millstones of his human judgments and his human loves. The grist they grind is all the bread he has whereon to feed his soul."[23] For readers familiar with the perils of psychological captivity—from the pyrotechnic catastrophe of Brockden Brown's *Wieland* to Nat Turner's discovery of insurrectionary directives in the dew drops of the corn, this was a powerful image of the dangers of self-involvement. As the writer of the above passage reiterated, submission to the church's teaching authority meant escape from this imprisonment, from the human grist-mill of interpretation. "It is to his deliverance from this spiritual state that the name *conversion* alone properly belongs."[24]

There, you read what I w[oul]d have carried to the grave,
only I wish you to know well . . . the impossibility of a
poor protestant to see our meaning without being led step
by step & the veil lifted little by little.
          Elizabeth Seton to her spiritual director

In October 1803 William and Elizabeth Seton sailed for Italy, accompanied by the eldest of their five children, eight-year-old Anna. While many Americans were already migrating west, the New York couple had set themselves on an opposite course: to recuperate health and possibly fortune in the Old World. In flight from the American winter and the collapse of the family trading business, the young Setons sought therapy in Italy. The warm air might arrest William's advanced tuberculosis, and his loyal Italian friends, the Filicchis, might rescue the family from poverty. Bankrupt and dying, William Seton embodied the mercantile vulnerability of the body in the young capitalist economy—its shameful vulnerability to "reversal" and collapse.[25]

Elizabeth Seton knew that the voyage was a hopeless one; William was in the final, acute, stage of a disease already famous for its romantic languor, a languor whose alternation between "hectic" and "pallor" visibly enacted the psychomachia fundamental to the Christian's development—the soul's struggle against the seductions and confinements of the flesh.[26] An ardent Episcopalian, twenty-nine-year-old Elizabeth wrote a spiritual journal during the voyage. Like the English Puritans two centuries back, she understood her transatlantic migration in scriptural terms. Only for Seton, the Promised Land lay not in the American wilderness but in the benevolent climate of Italy. Sea voyages, country air, and dry climates were common prescriptions, along with bloodletting and the application of blisters to drain the body of its "congestion." Notwithstanding the shift from corporate Puritanism to individual therapeutic quest, Seton's devotional language in her journal performs the conventional mediatory function between two orders of petition—that of the invalid body and that of the infirm soul. Hers was a language that sought to control illness by consenting to its presence everywhere, to use disease as an emblem not so much of civic disorder (as yellow fever functioned in the politically divisive 1790s) as of disordered subjectivity, independent of political era. The journal "passage" and the sea passage jointly articulated and interconnected the primary issues of her devotional and social experience: exposure, contamination, corruption, sacrifice, and reunion. She wrote:

> Considering the *Infirmity* and corrupt nature which would overpower the Spirit of Grace, and the enormity of the offense to which the least indulgence of them would lead me—in the anguish of my Soul shuddering to offend my Adored Lord—I have this day solemnly engaged that through the strength of His Holy Spirit I will not again expose that corrupt and Infirm nature to the Smallest temptation I can avoid—and therefore if my Heavenly Father will once more *reunite us all* that I will make a daily Sacrifice of every *wish* even the most *innocent,* least [sic] they should betray me to a deviation from the Solemn and Sacred vow I have now made—[27]

Seton addressed these words to her husband's half sister Rebecca Seton, who remained in America. That Elizabeth Seton bestowed such complex intimacies on her sister-in-law points to the role her female relatives would increasingly assume for her.[28] Rebecca, Harriet, and Cecilia Seton (members of her husband's family), as well as Elizabeth's two older daughters, Anna and Rebecca, came to function as precocious saints; recipients and favored exempla of Seton's writing, these young women and girls played a central narrative and devotional function in both her interior and her social life. Amplifying her parental role, Seton fashioned maternity into a spiritual enterprise while her piety correspondingly depended on familial obedience and affectional union. But the actions of Seton as mother and as Christian creature were laced through with imitation and the consequent struggle toward an ever greater authenticity. In her self-portrait as powerful infantilized subject recorded in her journal "vow," Seton propitiates her "heavenly Father," thus enacting before her sister-in-law Rebecca a filial drama of obedience. Negotiating between the deviant and the gracious, the journal entry confirms the Christian truth that submission masters infirmity while also displaying the mother's authority over her female relatives and children; her self-portrait as an infirm, potentially deviant, self-sacrificing mother who submits to God implicitly represents the child (ever potentially wayward) who reads her text.

It was a frankly intentional and, as the years proceeded, increasingly elaborate strategy of parental discipline and celebration. While Seton was disappointed in her sons, her daughters would fully absorb the spiritual training in the years to come. Three years after her Italian trip, Elizabeth recorded of her daughter Rebecca's precocious piety in "A Journal of the Soul," written for Cecilia Seton: "The innocent ones are playing in a corner Rebecca appealed to me with most powerful eloquence hands and eyes all in motion 'did I not tell Amelia right, if we have the crown of thorns in this World will we not have the roses in the next'—dear love if at 5 years you know the truth, that is, the lesson of the cross what may not an experience of their precious thorns produce in you."[29] The mother's speculation about her daughter's body pierced by "precious thorns" would soon enough materialize for Rebecca, who later suffered the torments of an injured, perhaps tubercular hip and those of heroic therapeutic intervention.

The immediate reader of Seton's ship diary was, of course, Seton herself. While her text addresses her sister-in-law (who, as mute auditor, symbolically represents Elizabeth's "adored Lord"), Seton is the first witness and recipient of her own "solemn and sacred vow." The artifice that perplexes all confessional prose (the activity of revealing to one's self what one already knows) is especially at issue here, where Seton transcribes her indirect confession to an omniscient Lord by way of the distant Rebecca. Her revelation and vow are simultaneously already known and never knowable—their solemnity, however earnest, a theatrical one, held up before herself for scrutiny and renewed acts of imitation. While the dying William Seton provided the context for such devotional activity, Elizabeth addressed it in particular to his sister Rebecca, also ill from tuberculosis. The very plethora of causes and treatments accorded tuberculosis a horror of the infinite to which Seton's journal fully testifies in her repeated, if implicit, parallels between the workings of the sacred and those of disease. Seton, pressed on either side by dying beloveds, recorded a situation that became a typical one in her life.

In its revelation of the already known and its anxious preoccupation with images of submission and control, Seton's passage metaphorically registered the peculiar impossibilities of the voyage—a journey in search of reprieve from an already-known death that was yet an ongoing contagion. Like the ship carrying her tubercular husband, Seton's entry contains in a single hypotactic sentence a potentially overpowering content, the diseased "enormity" of her own nature. Against a series of future conditionals ("would overpower," "would lead me," "should betray me") that convey the latent treachery of contaminated nature, Seton's language posits the humbly militant subject who combats potential evil with a definitive past ("I have . . . solemnly engaged," "I have now made") and a definitive future ("I will not again expose," "I can avoid," "I will make a daily sacrifice"). Her humility stands as subversive substitute for her husband's humiliation, her language of exposure, avoidance, and sacrifice that of the penitent bankrupt assuming renewed control.

The specificity and control manifest in both the past and future tenses of Seton's "solemn and sacred vow" issue, then, from a generalized infirmity of the body—whose uninterrupted perils Seton both acknowledges and minimizes in the ongoing present of her opening, "Considering the *infirmity* and corrupt nature"; her concluding reassertion of the "sacred vow I have now made" confirms the dominion of this new spiritual present over the potentially unregulated dimension of the body. The vow—her statement to God that is both anterior to the journal entry and reiterated in the passage's linguistic transit from deviance to control—bisects Seton's troubled subjectivity with linear precision. Cordoning off the threatening topography of "exposure" and "deviation" from a purged and newly constrained self ("I will not again expose that corrupt and infirm nature to the smallest temptation"), Seton's vow articulates the linear norm implied by her imagery of deviance.

Like the vow, the voyage was meant to provide a linear control over the family's situation, an exodus from William's bankruptcy and tuberculosis. To preserve the ritual space newly organized by her promise, Seton commits herself to a continuous purgation. Since wishes lead to deviance, the proposed "sacrifice of every wish" is tantamount to the expulsion of every threat; to give up is also to get rid of—a devotional drama that closely allies renunciation to more aggressive activities of decontamination and banishment. Indeed, in imitating the social and financial banishment performed on her and her husband, Seton's renunciations compete against those prior exclusions and diminish their impact. The enormity of the social damage is suggested in the psychological remedy—a daily self-purification, extending into the indefinite future; in continued opposition to the persistent threat of the deviant, this repeated expulsion will ward off the perils of proximity and incorporation, the perils, in Seton's words, of "the least indulgence."

From its opening opposition between the "enormity of the offense" and the "least indulgence," the entry concludes with a corresponding and equally portentous antithesis between "even the most *innocent*" wish and a traitorous "deviation." The object of her ritually controlled interior purity is the reunion of the family ("if my Heavenly Father will once more *reunite us all*")—a reunion that will motivate and reward the new unity of a self purged of wishes and closed to exposure. Behind such a petition lay difficult adolescent years as a homeless stepdaughter and, even more painful, the childhood loss of her mother. Years later, Seton recorded as her first memory: "At 4 years of age sitting alone on a step of the door looking at the clouds while my little sister Catherine 2 years old lay in her coffin they asked me did I not cry when little Kitty was dead?—no because Kitty is gone up to heaven I wish I could go too with Mamma—."[30]

Seton's vow, however, did not produce its desired effect; nor did the voyage. On landing, the couple were confined to the lazaretto in Leghorn, quarantined as suspected carriers of yellow fever. They subsisted in this "dungeon" for a month as untouchables, excluded from Italy and America, waiting to manifest their symptoms. But all that occurred in the lazaretto was the rapid advance of William's tuberculosis. Maddeningly, their flight from New York had landed them in the symbolically exact zone for consumption: a stony, damp, and windy dungeon. The point was not lost on Seton, who wrote home: "Consider—My Husband who left *his all* to seek a milder climate confined in this place of high and damp walls exposed to cold and wind which penetrates to the very bones, without fire except the kitchen charcoal which oppresses his Breast so much as to Nearly convulse him."[31] This imprisonment confirmed the fundamental structures of Seton's interior life. The quarantine, like Indian captivity for New England settlers, translated metaphoric captivity and corruption into a reality at once terrifying and reassuring. Seton's rhetorical and psychic investment in the topos of any "least indulgence" producing an enormity of corruption reflected not just the terrors of fallen nature but also the particular ones of disease—specifically, the contagious, inscrutable workings of yellow fever and consumption. It was no accident that on board ship for Italy she had prayed and written in the language of avoidance, purgation, and self-seclusion, within the linear boundaries of a vow. Nor was it accidental that this world of contagion, cataclysmic suffering, and mute surveillance of the dying body should produce, in turn, her conversion to the Catholic church and illuminate her later career as Mother Seton, first American-born woman saint.

Quarantine was already familiar to Seton, for as the daughter of Richard Bayley, Columbia University's first professor of anatomy and New York

City's chief health officer, she had often witnessed her father's zealous efforts to control yellow fever outbreaks. With her husband's bankruptcy, she and the children moved increasingly in Richard Bayley's world and in particular spent two summers at his Health Establishment on Staten Island.

During the summer of 1801, boatloads of immigrants unloaded at the island, dying of yellow fever and malnutrition. Striving to quell the panic among New York's citizens, Bayley had already published an important treatise, *An Account of the Epidemic Fever* (1796). Although Bayley did not understand the bacterial etiology of the fever, he correctly suspected the role played by environmental causes and argued that the disease spread because of poor sanitary conditions and lack of ventilation. Like many physicians familiar with the paranoia surrounding epidemics, Bayley's principal concern was to reclassify yellow fever victims as non-contagious, and hence safe to care for. As he explained in his pamphlet: "Indeed, I have been anxious about nothing so much as to fix upon the mind, the great and obvious distinction betwixt contagious diseases, and those which, under very peculiar circumstances, may assume much of that character."[32] During the last summers of the eighteenth century, circumstances conspired to render the disease seemingly contagious: boatloads of immigrants (Bayley estimated only 150 out of the 800 victims were New York citizens, the rest being immigrants) and hot, wet weather. Bayley's treatment for the disease consisted of providing adequate ventilation, purgatives for the stomach and bowels, occasional use of the lancet (especially if the disease struck a robust person who *"had just arrived from the purer and cooler air of the country"* [114]), and, in severe cases, the application of blisters to the stomach.

Uncertainty whether the disease was contagious nonetheless continued in the Bayley-Seton household during the summer of 1801. According to one biographer, Seton's father "would not permit her past the extra white railing he had erected to protect his beloved family from contagion."[33] Seton's correspondence during that summer oscillates between an Enlightenment rhetoric of controlled sensibility and an emergent romantic Christian language of empathy and vicarious agony. Watching the dying immigrants being carried to shore, she spoke like a Gothic heroine, practicing, like Emily de St. Aubigné of Radcliffe's *Mysteries of Udolpho,* a rational virtue to contain her fears: "To me who possesses a frame of fibres strong and nerves well strung, it is but a passing scene of nature's sufferings, which when closed will lead to happier scenes."[34] But if she proffered such a language of distanced control to her friend Julia Scott (whom she feared might otherwise "swoon"), she wrote with abandon to her spiritual intimate, her sister-in-law Rebecca Seton. One letter in particular to Rebecca expresses this critical shift from controlled surveillance to barely disciplined identification, from metaphors of spectacle to those of possession.

> Rebecca, I cannot sleep. The dying and the dead possess my mind. Babies perishing at the empty breast of the expiring mother. And this is not fancy, but the scene that surrounds me. Father says such was never known before, that there is [*sic*] actually 12 children that must die for mere want of sustenance, unable to take *more* than the breast, and from the wretchedness of their parents, deprived of it, as they have lain ill for many days on the ship without food, air, or *changing*. *Merciful Father!* Oh, how readily would I give them each a turn of Kit's treasure if in my choice! But, Rebecca, they have a Provider in Heaven Who will smooth the pangs of the suffering innocent.
>
> Father goes up early in the morning to procure all possible comforts for the sufferers. . . . My side window is open, and wherever I look there are lights. Tents are pitched over the yard of the convalescent house, and a large one . . . joined to the dead house.[35]

The escalation of Seton's language from a controlled sensibility into the release of her agony reflects the psychic configuration of an island divided between healthy and contaminated enclosures. Having recently survived her own fifth "confinement," Seton supervised a busy domestic circle while looking beyond the white railing to the tents that contained, in perilous proximity, the diseased, the dead, and her idolized father, her sole remaining parent. Both obliged and anxious to assert domestic order against the immigrant horror, Seton suffered an increasing sense of illicit plenitude, her mother's milk ("Kit's treasure") literally and figuratively representing her moral plight. Underscoring the distressing presence of the famished immigrant infants, Seton's breast milk, a "treasure" effortlessly produced by her body, pointed to the confused commingling of impotence and moral responsibility provoked by witnessing such suffering.

Like the spontaneous but finally restricted abundance of her milk, Seton's access to the suffering was immediate but curtailed—a vision of the dead house through an open "side window." The longing for release from this burden surfaces in her cry, "Oh, how readily would I give them each a turn of Kit's treasure if in my choice!" Moral equilibrium of a sort was finally achieved when her exhausted father contracted the fever and died on August 17, 1801. The contagion had penetrated the barrier of the white railing and seeped into the domestic precinct, bringing Elizabeth Seton into uninterrupted contact with it. But while, as her father's nurse, she could now touch and soothe the suffering, the maddening sense of exclusion and helplessness deepened. Having imagined a regulation of the suffering through distributing her precious milk, Seton, faced with a dying parent who persisted in his Deist ways, turned from the notion of distribution to that of destruction. Sacrifice might perhaps control the contagion, a vow might rail it off again. Thus, walking outside with her baby Kit, she "offered the life of the sleeping child in exchange for her father's soul."[36] If her father's body had already been claimed for death, his disturbingly skeptic soul might possibly achieve immortality through the offered body of his granddaughter.

Seton's proffered sacrifice of her newborn initiated a series of agonized engagements with contagious disease that occurred throughout her life. In the twenty years that remained to her, she would lose her husband, two sisters-in-law (Rebecca and Cecilia) and two beloved daughters (Anna and Rebecca) to consumption—a disease that, like yellow fever, was sometimes susceptible to cure but more often not and whose crisis stages of ague and fever recalled the shorter-lived course of the fever that had killed her father. The early instance of the fantasied sacrifice of her child (whom she frequently described as her "dearest self") anticipated her developing strategy of control—to contain the suffering body by taking its contagion within. This psychic alliance between contagion and incorporation found expression and legitimation in Seton's devotional life, specifically the enormous importance she attached as an Episcopalian (and later as a Catholic) to communion. Her devotion to the Eucharist organized an otherwise eclectic spirituality that prior to her Catholic conversion included bits and pieces of the American religious mosaic. According to one of her biographers, she "wore a Catholic crucifix, looked kindly on the life of the cloister, subscribed to the doctrine of angels, liked Methodist hymns, the quietism of the Quakers, and the emotionalism of Rousseau, read general Protestant works, practiced meditation, was inclined to the narrow Calvinism of her ancestors in the matter of sin and punishment, and attended the Episcopal Church."[37] The Eucharist focused such dispersed denominational affiliations; more profoundly, contagion, community, and communion were inextricably linked in this liturgical rite that enabled her to ingest the wounded body.

After the death of her father, Seton moved back to Manhattan, followed by the fever, which began to claim victims in the city. But if New York represented a renewed threat of infection, it also meant the precious opportunity to attend the Episcopal service. As if to urge herself on as well as her sister-in-law, Seton wrote to Rebecca in the fall of 1801: "The terror of our fellow citizens seems to be so awakened that I do not believe you ought to come to town, as prudence says; *but I say*, 'Come dear, let us keep the feast' with sincerity and truth."[38] Seton's interpolation from 1 Corinthians 5:7–8 emphasizes the nourishment of communion and its symbolic opposition to both the famished immigrant and the citizen too afraid to partake of either community or communion. In Seton's reported response to the Eucharist we understand how the ritual symbolically duplicated the dreaded yellow fever, its ague and its extremities of thirst. "So great was her devotion to the Episcopalian remembrance of the Last Supper, that her teeth chattered against the cup of wine in an ecstasy of trembling awe when she received; and after the service she [and a close friend] would ask the sexton for the remnants of the sacramental wine, that they might renew their devotion in receiving again."[39]

When Seton and her husband sailed for Italy two years after this, the configuration of her devotional being had achieved its fundamental shape: the informally conventual relationship with younger women (performing their Episcopalian charity work, she and Rebecca Seton had already been dubbed Protestant Sisters of Charity); an almost topographical sense of fidelity and deviance that resisted the contagious disorders of open space: "The misfortune of the afternoon will, I hope, be a lesson for life to my darling sister," wrote Seton to Rebecca, "that you should never violate the strict rule, not to leave home on any persuasion on Sacrament Sunday, and to say openly to whoever may request it that it is your rule"; and finally a profound association between the enclosure of rules and one's proximity to God. Thus, sailing out of New York harbor for Italy, she wrote to her young sister-in-law Cecilia Seton:

> Still my heart would dictate to you many anxious requests respecting your habitual observance of that Heavenly Christian life you have so early begun—in order to persevere in this your first attention must be to make yourself a few particular Rules which you must not suffer anything on Earth to divert you from as they relate immediately to your sacred duty to God.[40]

The lazaretto in Leghorn intensified and partially resolved many of these issues, for it provided the desired access to an enclosed suffering, a captivity whose mythic clarity gave purpose to Seton's transit from the New to the Old World. Along with her eight-year-old daughter and her acutely ill husband, she was finally inside "an immense Prison bolted in and barred with as much ceremony as any monster of mischief might be—a single window double grated with iron thro' which, if I should want any thing, I am to call a centinel, with a fierce cocked hat, and long riffle gun, that is that he may not receive the dreadful infection we are supposed to have brought with us from New York."[41] She was now the immigrant, imprisoned, contagious, a feared spectacle. The relief was enormous, its spiritual utility clear from her first description of their confinement in a "room with high arched cielings like *St. Paul's*—brick floor naked walls and a jug of water."[42] The family's implicit martyrdom gained daily visual confirmation in William's suffering, displayed before his attentive wife as mute tableau for recording in her Lazaretto Journal: "William could not sit up—his ague came on and my Souls agony with it,—my Husband on the cold bricks without fire, shivering and groaning lifting his dim and sorrowful eyes with a fixed gaze in my face while his tears ran on his pillow without one word—."[43]

As the suffering icon, William reenacts Christ's crucifixion and its demands; he is both the tubercular husband, entirely dependent on her, and the weighty image of Christ's Passion willingly borne. On November 23, her husband worsening, she began her journal entry with a sentence fragment that swiftly compacted the invalid and her Lord: "Not only willing to take my *cross* but kissed it too."[44] From her successful maternal confinements and the plenteous "treasure" of her mother's milk, she now approached the crucifixional center of her captivity in her husband's suffering: "I find my present opportunity a Treasure—and my confinement of Body a liberty of Soul which I may never again enjoy while they are united." Positioned as spectator before her dying husband, Seton recognized that she, along with her husband, had become a spectacle in turn for outsiders. Caged like the animals in New York's zoo, they were prodded by the guard's stick to keep them from getting too close to their visitors. "It reminded me," wrote Seton in her journal, "of going to see *the Lions*."[45]

The lazaretto made manifest the ritual space of Seton's developing interior life that her shipboard journal had rhetorically anticipated. Bounded and marked by suffering, her life found expression in the quarantine chambers, their own past recapitulated theatrically by the guard, whose reminiscences she recorded: "In this room what suffering have I seen—*there*, lay an Armenian beging an knife to end the struggles of Death—*there* where the Signora's bed is, in the frenzy of Fever a Frenchman insisted on shooting himself, and died in agonies."[46] Like American tourist accounts of walking atop the dead in Rome, Seton's transcription of the guard's litany is alive with religious melodrama; her bed on the site of a former suicide, she duly notes her own tenuous control of mortality. Seton resists the weight of the lazaretto's visual testimony to its Gothic history with the alternative significance of her spirituality: "Little billets of paper pasted on the doors mark how many days different persons have staid and the *shutter* is all over Notched. . . . I do not mark ours—trusting they are marked *above*."[47] If celestially located, these marks of suffering indelibly imprint themselves on her consciousness, their invisibility to mortal eyes the sign of their heavenly visibility.

In her rhetorical play on economic and spiritual gain and loss and the shifting visibility and invisibility of suffering, Seton monitored her husband's illness. The corruption and confinement of William's body, the sight of her radical impending loss, became necessary pretexts for his spiritual expansion. Impeded breathing and hemorrhage, the inhalation of the spirit and the exhalation of earthly life interlaced into a single lazaretto activity of conversion and dying. On December 5, Seton wrote: "He drew himself towards me and said 'I breathe out my Soul to you,' the exertion he made assisted Nature's remaining force and he threw a quantity from his Lungs, which had threatened to stop their motion, and so doing experienced so great a revolution that in a few hours afterwards he seemed nearly the same as when we first entered the Lazaretto."[48]

The pattern of crisis and recovery, loss and gain ended within the next three weeks. The ceaseless toil of William's previous trading life, which he had so bemoaned (returning home from a sermon in New York, he had said to his wife, "I toil and toil and what is it, what I gain, destroys me daily Soul and Body I love without God in the world, and shall die Miserably"), was now translated into the inefficient toil of his breathing.[49] But the extension of bankruptcy's patterns of futile expenditure was intercepted by William's growing capacity for his wife's paradoxical discursive mode. Wrote his wife in her journal, "He very often says *this* is the period of his life which if he lives or dies he will always consider as Blessed—the only time which he has not lost."[50] The process of William's conversion in turn translated their joint captivity into contemplative retreat, for, overjoyed at her husband's spiritual development, Seton confessed, "Oh if I was in the dungeon of this Lazaretto I should Bless and Praise my God for these days of retirement and abstraction from the world which have afforded leisure and opportunity for so blessed a Work."[51] The transformation of William's physical collapse and disintegration into spiritual wholeness is thus allied with monastic retreat, the crises of bankruptcy, tuberculosis, and quarantine providing an ironic leisure for a powerfully efficacious activity dependent on the hidden liberties of captivity, a "work" of sublime import that supplants the frantic and futile work of New York days.

On December 19 the family was freed, and they immediately traveled to their friends, the Antonio Filicchis in Pisa. On December 27 William died. Elizabeth herself prepared her husband's body for burial, as she had her father's, since others feared to touch the allegedly contagious corpse. William Seton was buried on December 28 in the Protestant cemetery in Leghorn.

These dear people [the Catholic Filicchis] are so strange about religion.

Elizabeth Seton

While variously impressed by her sight-seeing of cathedral interiors and religious art, Seton did not become a Catholic during her protracted stay abroad, although the Filicchis tried to convert her.[52] But her friendship with them as well as her encounter with Italian Catholic culture profoundly impressed her, the "elegance of cielings in carved gold, altar loaded with gold, silver, and other precious ornaments, pictures of every sacred subject and the dome a continued representation of different parts of Scripture—all this can never be conceived by description—nor my delight in seeing old men and women, young women, and all sorts of people kneeling promiscuously about the Altar."[53] Attending mass at the monastery chapel at Montenaro, she confronted the stark deficiencies of English Protestant culture when at the elevation of the Host an English tourist whispered loudly, "This is what they call there real *Presence*." Seton's vivid record of that moment voices a fundamental tension between the spiritual obtuseness of Protestantism and the mystery of transubstantiation. For Seton, the Catholic doctrine of transubstantiation led inevitably back to her own experience with the mystery of pregnancy and motherhood.

> My very heart trembled with shame and sorrow for his unfeeling interruption of their sacred adoration for all around was dead silence and many were prostrated—involuntarily I bent from him to the pavement and thought secretly on the word of St. Paul with starting tears "they discern not the Lords body" and the next thought was how should they eat and drink their very damnation for not *discerning* it, if indeed it is not *there*— yet how should it be *there,* and how did he breathe my Soul in me, and how and how a hundred other things I know nothing about.
>   I am a *Mother* so the Mothers thought came also how was my GOD a little babe in the first stage of his mortal existence *in*

Mary, but I lost these thoughts in my babes at home, which I daily long for more and more.[54]

On the eve of their departure for America, her daughter Anna and then Seton herself came down with scarlet fever; once again in the midst of a potentially fatal illness, she acknowledged to her sister-in-law and spiritual confidante Rebecca her growing fascination with Catholicism. Confined to her bed and longing for home, the widow recorded her frustrated proximity to the Catholic Host. As before when she had stared across the white railing to the immigrant tents, she now looked down from her window on a physical representation and potential resolution of suffering.

> How happy would we be if we believed what these dear souls believe, that they *possess God* in the Sacrament and that he remains in their churches and is carried to them when they are sick, oh my—when they carry the Blessed Sacrament under my window while I face the full loneliness and sadness of my case I cannot stop the tears at the thought my God how happy would I be even so far away from all so dear, if I could find you in the church as they do (for there is a chapel in the very house of Mr. F.) how many things I would say to you of the sorrows of my heart and the sins of my life—[55]

Seton's acute topographical sense of God's presence and her exile from that presence increased on her arrival in New York with her daughter Anna on June 4, 1804, for the next month Rebecca Seton died of consumption. Bereaved once again, Seton entered on a yearlong struggle over the competing claims of Catholic and Protestant Christianity, dutifully reading polemical defenses of Protestantism such as Thomas Newton's *Dissertation on the Prophecies,* as suggested by her much-loved pastor, Henry Hobart, and similar defenses of Catholicism such as Robert Manning's *England's Conversion and Reformation Compared,* as suggested by Antonio Filicchi. These various polemics left her fully instructed but maddeningly unconvinced, while repeated reading of Thomas à Kempis, St. Francis of Sales, and *The Lives of the Saints* left her still reluctant to join the Catholic church. Suffering increasing opprobrium from her family for her errant theological proclivities, the indecisive widow also faced disapproval from her Catholic friends, some of whom suggested that her protracted uncertainty might be due to an insufficiently purified soul. Once again Seton's tormented situation curiously duplicated her exclusion from the suffering on Staten Island. In the journal of her conversion that she kept for Amabilia Filicchi, she wrote of her continuing but increasingly uncomfortable attendance at Episcopal service: "Yet I got in a side pew which turned my face towards the Catholic Church in the next street, and found myself twenty times speaking to the blessed Sacrament *there* instead of looking at the naked altar where I was."[56]

In the middle of January 1805 she wrote to Amabilia of her decision to become a Catholic, having (like many other converts) finally lost faith in her Episcopalian bishop's capacity to absolve sins. As much as she looked for apostolic authority, she sought as well the Real Presence, no longer satisfied with the Protestant Episcopalian formulation of communion.[57] By Ash Wednesday in February 1805 Seton had found her authentic interiority. In the journal of her conversion, she wrote of going for the first time to a Catholic church to worship, a decision she knew would likely cost her the crucial financial support of her New York family and friends. Her description of entering St. Peter's Church resonates with the intense excitement of crossing into an unexplored place of spectacular dimensions in which divinity was both grandly exhibited and carefully enclosed: "—when I turned the corner of the street it is in, here my God I go said I, *heart all to you*—entering it, how that heart died away as it were in silence before the little tabernacle and the great Crucifixion over it—Ah My God here let me rest said I—and down the head on the bosom and the knees on the bench."[58]

The picture beneath which Seton sank in relief was *The Crucifixion* by the Mexican artist José Maria Vallejo; displayed above the "little tabernacle," Vallejo's portrait of Christ's naked and suffering body created a heretical and, for Seton, utterly compelling pictorial space in which God was both visually explicit and intimately framed. On March 14, 1805, when she formally joined the church, Seton returned again to Vallejo's painting suspended above the hidden Christ, whose visual and emotional impact vanquished her intellectual doubts and provided a bodily location for her formerly vagrant subjectivity.

> For as to going a walking any more about what all the different people believe, I cannot, being quite tired out. and I came up light at heart and cool of head the first time these many long months, but not without begging our Lord to wrap my heart deep in that opened side so well described in the beautiful crucifixion, or lock it up in his little tabernacle where I shall now rest forever.[59]

Pointedly reversing the captivity imagery conventional to anti-Catholic discourse, Seton not only prayed to be locked within the "little

Tabernacle" but also acknowledged to Amabilia the emancipation of her first confession—"How awful those words of unloosing after a 30 years bondage."[60] Such liberation led directly to an experience of ecstatically possessing God that again found topographical expression in Seton's description of attending her first communion, a passage into a physicalized interiority that dramatically contrasted with her prior "walking . . . about" among different beliefs: "—The long walk to town, but every step counted nearer that street—then nearer that tabernacle, then nearer the moment he would enter the poor poor little dwelling so all his own" (167). Ever afterward the heart of Jesus would be her "asylum into which she would retreat, the Eucharist her medicine against all illness." Three years after her conversion, she mourned the "naked unsubstantial" Protestant faith, "founded on Words of which they take the Shadow while we enjoy the adored Substance in the center of our Souls."[61]

In June 1808 Seton left New York for Baltimore with her five children, having been invited by the superior of the Baltimore Sulpicians, Father William Dubourg, to found a girls' school. In opening the Paca Street School, Seton founded the American parochial school system. Writing to her young sister-in-law Cecilia, who had converted by this time as well, Seton described the first communion of one class of her schoolgirls as a moment of subterranean descent and emotional liberation like that American tourists exploring the catacombs in Italy imagined of the early Christians: "This morning in the subteraneous Chapel of the Blessed Virgin in the very depth of solitude . . . he celebrated the adorable sacrifice and despensed the sacred Passover—his tears fell fast over his precious hands while he gave it, and we had liberty to sob aloud unwitnessed by any, as no one had an idea of our going there."[62]

On March 25, 1809, Seton took vows of poverty, chastity, and obedience and thereafter became known as Mother Seton. Permitted to keep her children with her until they came of age, Mother Seton quickly attracted a small band of women who wished to become nuns under her supervision. On June 1, 1809, Seton and four others assumed the habit of the American Sisters of Charity; that same month, the small group removed to the remote Catholic village of Emmitsburg, Maryland, where during the next ten years they constructed the permanent house for their order. The regularity, rural seclusion, and maternal intensity of convent life brought Seton great happiness. From Sabbath picnics in the woods to teaching in the school to regulating the spiritual development of her children and "daughters," Seton experienced a powerful combination of contemplative retreat and community. She recalled these early days in Emmitsburg as a time of aesthetic, social, and spiritual coherence:

"Woods, rocks, walks—Harriet's first anxieties to go to Mass, evening Adoration—our visit at 11 to the church the bright moon light night of St Mary Magdaline—the Evening I ran from the woods to meet Nina, Jos, and Rebec—oh oh oh how sweet—."[63] Such pastoral intimacy and maternal spontaneity rotated around the austere regulations of convent life, whose rules (particularly those requiring an initially difficult submission in turn to three different Sulpician male superiors) led Seton to express the joy of subordinating her will: "I am so in love now with rules," she wrote to her close spiritual friend Gabriel Bruté, "that I see the *bit* of the bridle all gold, or the *reins* all of silk."[64]

But during these same years, Seton also endured the deaths of her most intimate female companions. Her sister-in-law Harriet Seton died suddenly of "an inflammation of the brain" in December 1809.[65] But no horror equaled that of her eldest daughter Anna's death from tuberculosis at age sixteen on March 12, 1812. As Seton had recorded her husband's illness and death, so she registered the torturous progress of her daughter "Annina's" disease in a deathbed journal. As the tuberculosis spread through her lungs and bones, Annina called in the schoolgirls to reveal her tortured flesh as religious exemplum: "Pulling up her sleeve to show her bony arm to one of the boarders she said gaily 'Oh when you see that in the resurrection' to the little ones when they came to see her she said, 'You come to look at what the worms will soon devour and see how soon you may die, remember how short a time ago I was playing with you all—Love Our Lord'—."[66] A cord, known then as a "Seton," was daily pulled under the child's skin to keep a passage open for drainage; the terrible painfulness of this procedure was converted as well by this intensely religious girl into a cause for her spiritual development and the salvation of her family. Or in her words: "All my cough and distress in continual spitting I seem to suffer for you, and the pains of my side and breast and the poor Seton for my brothers dear William and Richard. How much I think of their souls."[67] On November 3, 1816, Seton's younger daughter Rebecca died in an equal agony; having long suffered the crippling effects of a hip injury (and probably tuberculosis in the hip joint), the child finally succumbed to her disability, nursed throughout by her mother. Seton wrote a journal for this daughter's death as well. On April 18, 1820, she wrote to her old and close friend Antonio Filicchi of her own impending death from tuberculosis. She was trying, she wrote, "to make my very breathing a continual thanksgiving."[68]

Sophia Ripley: Rewriting the Stony Heart

As the later writings of Isaac Hecker, Sophia Ripley, and Orestes Brownson demonstrate, the effort to reposition antebellum culture in the "interiors" of Roman Catholic orthodoxy was no less radical than the questioning of Protestant orthodox conventions by writers of the American Renaissance. As evident in Sophia Ripley's unpublished correspondence; in Hecker's journals, letters, *Questions of the Soul* (1855), and *Aspirations of Nature* (1857); and in Brownson's periodical essays, *The Spirit-Rapper* (1854), and *The Convert* (1857), the imposition of a Catholic discourse on preexistent modes of perception and articulation produced conceptual innovations that both paralleled and subverted those of American romanticism and utopian thought. "Mr. Emerson's maxims must be converted," wrote Hecker in *Questions of the Soul*. "Substitute humility to obey, for 'self-reliance'; courage to believe, for 'trust thyself';—deny thyself, for 'act out thyself';—master thy instincts, for 'obey thy instincts';—self-sacrifice, for 'self-culture';—surrender thyself to God, for 'be thyself.'"[1]

As suggested by Hecker's reformulation, the distinctive position of these Catholic converts in their native culture—a position of internal exile—produced a unique and often penetrating criticism of the ideological and rhetorical conventions of liberal American Protestantism. Indeed, as their biographies suggest, the two religious worlds, Rome and New England, were closely, even competitively, intertwined. Brook Farm in particular provided the ground where several key figures met and separated. There Hecker and Sophia Ripley first met; the conversations between the educated Ripley and the mystically inclined young baker from New York who would found the Paulist Fathers eventuated in their conversion and lasting closeness. Referring to their Brook Farm reading

course in Dante, Ripley reportedly said to Hecker when he returned from
Europe a newly ordained Redemptorist priest: "I am without doubt the
only convert you and Dante have made between you."[2] Greatly admired
by George Ripley and almost venerated by Sophia, Hecker served as her
father confessor from 1851 until her death in 1861. From the 1840s
onward, Brownson and Hecker were also close friends and maintained
an active correspondence; at one point, Brownson credited Hecker with
converting him: "I am more indebted to you for having become a Catholic than to any other man under heaven, and while you supposed I was
leading you to the Church, it was you who led me there. I owe you a debt
of gratitude I can never repay."[3] Although he converted in 1844 and was
already a devastating critic of Transcendentalism, Brownson nonetheless
sent his son Orestes to the Brook Farm School; still later, in his spiritual
autobiography, *The Convert* (1857), the militant anti-Protestant declared his deep love for Brook Farm's founder George Ripley:

> One man, and one man only, shared my entire confidence, and
> knew my most secret thought. Him, from motives of delicacy, I
> do not name; but, in the formation of my mind, in systematizing
> my ideas, and in general development and culture, I owe more to
> him than to any other man among Protestants. We have since
> taken divergent courses, but I loved him as I have loved no
> other man, and shall so love and esteem him as long as I live.[4]

For his part, George Ripley tried to recall Hecker to Brook Farm by
advertising the spiritual aspirations of the community: "When will you
come back to Brook Farm? Can you do without us? Can we do without
you? Oh! That you would come as one of us, to work in the faith of the
divine idea, to toil in loneliness and tears for the sake of the Kingdom
which God may build up by our hands."[5] On escorting her converted
niece, Sarah Stearns, to the Mount St. Vincent Sisters of Charity, Sophia
Ripley vividly recalled the uncanny resemblance of the two worlds: "We
sat on the rocks under some trees and talked over old times before she
took the irrevocable step of entering the house. . . . Something within and
without seemed so like Brook Farm, that the whole was more a revival
of some former experience than anything new and strange."[6]

So sweetly linking at every point the visible with the invisible . . .
    Sophia Ripley on Easter Mass, Flatbush, New York, 1855

"What glorious summer weather we have had, particularly the last two
or three weeks," wrote Sophia Ripley to her cousin Ruth Charlotte Dana

from Brook Farm in September 1846. With energetic lyricism, Ripley continued:

> I cannot describe to you the joy of my physical existence these hottest days. It seemed to me I had a glimpse of that angelic state with a body as glorified, and the soul aided and supported by it in its highest action. I trod on air, my brain was clear, my spirit serene. No amount of labor was too great for me, four or five hours of sleep was all I required. I rose at 4 1/2 and went through the woods in the fields, a most lovely walk, to the river with the girls, and there we were in the river awaiting the sunrise. All the long evegs [sic] were spent in the woods or walking in the garden, and the golden, brilliant light of the moon turned night into day, put to shame all the recently announced theories of the ruined condition of that planet.[7]

Ripley's description of her summer days at Brook Farm, like those of Seton at Emmitsburg, breathes with the excitement of an attained faith in which the "glorified" body no longer contradicts but fully mobilizes the powers of the soul. If Hawthorne was exhausted and depressed by manual work at Brook Farm, Sophia achieved (however momentarily) an invigorated union both of soul and body and of that integrated self in a community. After long days directing the Brook Farm School, or nursing the sick, or ironing sometimes for ten hours straight, Ripley enjoyed a signal aesthetic alertness, registered by her presence at those inopportune hours of dawn and midnight when nature revealed her feminine self most splendidly. Exploring the illumined landscape of the river at sunrise or the garden in moonlight, Ripley portrays herself as an angelic being, her powers of discernment and articulation perfectly equilibrated with a body freed from the debilitating purities of middle-class domesticity. Easefully converting her masterful energies into intimate, inspirational prose, Ripley completed the Transcendentalist circuit, elevating her reader into those heights where she, as author, claimed a continued dwelling. Short of the Emersonian essay, no better format existed to convey the elliptical features of Transcendentalist spirituality than the abbreviated confessional mode of the private letter to an intimate friend.

But while her passage testifies to the early success of the utopian experiment, Ripley was simultaneously engaged in strangely different pursuits. As cousins in the prominent (Unitarian) Dana family and soon-to-be Catholic converts, Sophia and Charlotte were well aware of the subversive nature of their developing intimacy. Thus Sophia confided to

Charlotte in the same letter that her romantic pastoralism was already linked to Rome, for she had consecrated her Brook Farm School to "our Blessed Mother," who has "tenderly" guarded it ever since.

In September 1846 Ripley sent some issues of the *Harbinger* to her cousin, urging her to take special care of her husband's Fourierist journal: "*The Harbinger* is like a precious child to me, and I would not see it used for curl-papers, or lamp-lighters, except to light a torch before the Image of our Holy Mother." In referring to her husband's journal as a potentially sacrificial offspring, the childless Ripley aptly conveyed her precarious position in antebellum New England. Jealously guarding her reform ideology (an increasingly uneasy amalgam of Brook Farm associationism and Fourier's doctrines of "universal unity"), she was also willing to offer her soul's progeny—improbably enough—to the Virgin Mary.[8] Ripley wrote these words a full year or more before officially joining the Catholic church. If the *Harbinger* would still be, several years later, a treasured possession in a crass industrial culture, it was therefore only the more fit for sacrificial burning. But notwithstanding her ambivalent possessiveness toward the journal, Ripley's position was hardly a confused one. In artfully opposing the vain waste of a modernizing economy (the back issues used to curl hair and light lamps) to an alternative productive sacrifice (the paper flaring in honor of the Virgin), Ripley's language is charged with purpose and the secret pleasure of unorthodox conclusions—in this case those of Roman Catholic orthodoxy. As Ripley drew nearer to the church, confidential references in her letters to her cousin increased. Although she had not yet officially converted, her sense of community was clearly shifting from the girls in the river to the "little band" of communicants she observed at mass in a Boston church, of whom she wrote to Charlotte in September 1846: "I seemed to partake more largely of the depths of its richness, and I truly longed to follow the little band, *without saying a word or . . . being asked a question,* who had the privilege of partaking of the Blessed Sacrament."[9] For "Sacrament," Ripley had originally written "Sacrifice"— her emendation illustrating her self-conscious struggles with the vocabulary of a novel Catholic piety. And like Seton before her, Ripley longed to circumvent the polemical arena for an intensified relation to the heart, to regain the "heart religion" of Edwardsian revivalism while conspicuously denying its Calvinist roots.

The intensity of her correspondence with Charlotte during these years was undoubtedly fueled by the familial and marital isolation Ripley suffered because of her unseemly conversion.[10] From Brook Farm in 1846, Sophia had expressed her love for Charlotte in the Transcendentalist vernacular of affinity: "Meanwhile we are not separated. I feel you always near to me. It *is* true that where there is any sympathy between beings of the same kindred, there is a mystic tie of union that binds them; each soul has a fragrance for the other, that does not breathe from merely selected friendships."[11] In the manuscript, Sophia originally wrote that "each has a fragrance for the other" only to insert "soul" later in order to assure the ideality of her love. After she and her husband had reorganized Brook Farm into a Fourierist phalanx in a last attempt to finance the community, they saw the expensive phalanstery burn down in March 1846.[12] It was a time of exhaustion and increasing poverty and, for Sophia Ripley in particular, a time of growing alienation from all reformism. As early as 1843 Ripley had voiced her frustration with the passivity and self-absorption of Brook Farmers to Emerson, himself a sympathetic visitor to the community: "This worship of beauty and unceasing life search for it is it not, after all, only living in the outskirts of truth. Beauty and truth are sometimes told to us to be one, but my increasing conviction is, that beauty is the attitude of truth, not truth itself."[13] Ripley's disavowal of romantic aestheticism marked the beginning of her transition from idealism to a more objectivist epistemology, a reorientation simply described by Isaac Hecker: "It is not the mind that creates things, or originates their qualities or characteristics, but it is these which inform and shape the mind."[14]

The fierce enmities of anti-Catholic literature, as we have seen, inhabited a terrain of ambivalent observation and imitation that contained the cultural mystery of conversion to this "objective" truth. With characteristic acuity Sophia Ripley, herself on the verge of joining the church, articulated the complexities of attending mass with an unnamed anti-Catholic friend—a Brook Farm excursion into a Boston immigrant church that unfolded a fascinating drama of domestic tourism and transgression.

> I accepted the cross of going with a person of my acquaintance who has always had in the greatest degree that mixture of hatred and contempt for the Catholic Church, so common among Protestants. A person of the coolest, keenest and most subtle intellect and one who out Emersoned Emerson, in his skepticism. He for the first time, on this visit, spoke respectfully of the Church, so much so, that I was able to tell him all that was in my soul about it, which could be spoken out; for he has spiritual tendencies, and many other fine traits which have always bound me to him. I could hardly believe my senses when I actu-

ally found him there. He says he was deeply impressed by the service, and bore with the meekness of a child Father O'Brian's public reproof of his unholy use of his opera glass—*he*—who is more keenly alive to reproof than anyone I know.[15]

The ironic implications of this triangulated watching unfold when the Protestant spectator becomes the main spectacle in turn, subject to "public reproof," to exposure and priestly evaluation. The emotional transactions and ambivalent bondings between Ripley, her unnamed friend, and Father O'Brian circulate between two competing cultural models, Emersonian distance and Irish-Catholic engagement. Himself the original object of surveillance by a native member of the elite culture, the immigrant priest reverses the embarrassment of spectacle by performing his own judgmental scrutiny. As a woman, a near-convert, and a member of Brook Farm, Ripley arguably possessed the greatest cultural marginality of the three. Although witness to both spectacles (the mass watching and the reproof), Ripley is vulnerable to both audiences: as a "pro-Catholic," she forms part of the service surveyed by her friend, while as one "bound" to her companion, she shares his humiliation, just as surely as she still retains the memory of her own "heretical" skepticism. Culturally allied to him who watches, she articulates the moral drama of the spectacle in a way that reveals her uncomfortable negotiation of this terrain of shifting intimacies and distances. The sudden embarrassing inversion of cultural authority uncovers not only the peculiar burdens of the convert (and of the priest in an anti-Catholic culture) but the complexities of the Protestant-Catholic gaze, caught in a mutual surveillance. The borders between spying, prayerful "witness," and conversion were volatile ones made all the more so by the possibility of ethnic, class, and gender transgression.

Ripley joined the Catholic church sometime between September 1847 and March 1848.[16] Moving with her husband to New York in search of employment after the collapse of Brook Farm, she spent the remaining thirteen years before her death from cancer teaching and translating religious texts while her husband pursued an increasingly successful career as literary critic for the *New York Tribune*. Sophia's Catholicism both created and compensated for her occupational and cultural marginality during these years. She quickly moved toward an informally cloistered existence by joining a lay order that permitted her to develop an iconographic self whose symbolic intentions anticipated Hawthorne's characterization of Hester Prynne. She wrote to Charlotte in 1848: "I have joined the Gray Sisters, in a slate colored linen embroidered so as to shew that I am not yet wholly withdrawn from the world."[17] Committed to her membership in this lay order of Franciscans (which required neither vows nor seclusion but submission to certain rules and the practice of charity), Ripley adopted and, like Hawthorne's Hester, carefully modified a costume of conspicuous cultural resistance. Ripley's highly stylized process of identity reformation transpired with frequent, often subversive, reference to her liberal Bostonian background; her most Catholic writing invariably registered her abandoned Transcendentalism. Thus in one anecdote she mentions an Irish priest who "congratulated us . . . upon having transcended a great deal of transcendental trash."[18] From her converted perspective, nature was no longer a spiritual reality that transcended and negated the confines of theology. Spiritual illumination was not bestowed on those who stood in the river at Brook Farm to await the sunrise but was reserved for those who stood in the illumined interiors of the Catholic church, with its "countless blazing lights" and the "retirement & shadowy stillness of Lent."[19]

In addition to its evident compensatory function, Sophia's epistolary relationship to her cousin, which continued through the New York years, provides a fascinating record of ongoing cultural conflict and identity struggle. The correspondence itself provided countless opportunities for the witty subversion of Protestant conventions of self-formation. Writing to "Dear Lotty" in 1856, Sophia opened on a characteristic note of religious whimsy: "I really feel some self-reproach at not having written you for a long time, but as that condition is the very best for me, I shall look upon it as a 'happy fault,' bringing the sweet fruits of compunction."[20] Such whimsy rested on a serious but very private work of self-revision. Frequently composed in cross-hand, Ripley's letters to Charlotte record the development of her new piety and even reenact the private drama of the confessional in her struggle to overcome a reserve and temperamental "coldness" that plagued her throughout her life. Her belief in church dogma and discipline and her excited exploration of new devotional practices increasingly excluded her, along with other converts, from mainstream culture, an isolation that intensified the church's reality for her. As she wrote to Charlotte in 1855, her life in New York City divided itself between Protestant work weeks and Catholic Sabbaths, a division that symbolically confirmed one of her operative distinctions between the enervating worldliness of Protestantism and the sublimities of her new faith.

> It is a strange life I live here. Not a word ever heard during the week that could in the most indirect manner imply the existence of the Catholic Church & everything around so Protestant, that I have to go alone to realize that the beautiful life of the Church is not a dream, & then Sunday comes, when we are all bathed in the sea of joy that pours in like a flood with the worship of Holy Church.[21]

Notwithstanding her isolation, Ripley's new faith often motivated significant commentary on key concerns in that Protestant society. She in fact ironically assumed the oppositional role that her reformer husband was gradually abandoning as he moved into his position as primary literary reviewer for the *New York Tribune*. Such vexed issues as the nature of religious authority, of ecclesiastical community, of sinfulness and justification underwent an informal revision in her correspondence. While her husband, George, busily reviewed new books, Sophia used her own language skills to translate Catholic texts. The two major works she translated were St. Catherine of Genoa's *Life and Writings* and St. Alphonsus de Liguori's *Glories of Mary,* a defense of the devotion to Mary directed against the Jansenists and originally published in 1750.[22] As suggested by the works she chose to translate, Ripley was deeply engaged by Catholicism's sanctification of womanhood. Speaking of her literary efforts, she acknowledged the formative opposition in her life between her motherless and disapproving earthly family (Sophia's father had abandoned the family years before only to return and disinherit her) and the kinship of her Catholic community, sustained by the intercessory love of the Virgin Mother. "I accept with thankfullness the mortification of the unqualified condemnation of my small share of the work by my family," Ripley wrote to Charlotte of her translation efforts, "though I must confess I did not look to them for much sympathy in this my first literary enterprise."[23] With Charlotte she shared "the double bond of kindred and faith" and could confide her painful alienation from both father and husband.[24]

Ripley's application of the language of mortification and confession to the difficult issue of familial rejection illustrates the strategy by which she developed her new sense of identity. Deprived of her Brook Farm association and alienated from the Dana clan, she gingerly appropriated the freighted language of a still alien church. Through its vocabulary of penance, she simultaneously accused her family and acknowledged her slightly insincere use of the term "mortification." Ripley continued to express her sublimated hostility toward her Boston family by conspicuously using Catholic theological terms in reference to them. Discussing her father, for example, she was careful to distinguish between actual sin and Original Sin, just as Bishop Hughes of New York had done for her during various crises. While such a distinction had virtually "saved" Ripley, in her angry hands it became the instrument of entombing her father. "It fills my heart with sadness to think of my poor father, so lonely in every sense of the word, sinking under the burden of old age, with the accumulated and cumulating burden of actual and original sin still heavier upon him."[25] If the past of her familial times stretched behind her like a troubling void, she carefully and even graphically delineated for her own enjoyment the new experience of time made available to her as a convert. Her sense of time newly pervaded by the Catholic liturgical calendar, Ripley frequently dated her letters by Latin salutations to the Holy Family or to the day's patron saint. Her delighted appropriation of the ecclesiastical calendar and the novel sense of an intercessory community now revealed to her a shapelessness and insincerity in her prior Protestant reformism and family life.

Writing to "Dear Lotty," Sophia lampooned the pretensions of her abandoned culture: "Let us congratulate our Protestant friends that they at length have a saint in their calendar. The minister says 'Daniel Webster has left the senate of earth to join the senate of the skies—& is already admitted into the Councils of God! We shall find things going on much better I presume now he is there!'"[26] In turn, her converted perspective reframed long-standing problems of gender, vocation, and epistemology that Brook Farm had failed to resolve. Linked to the church's corporate liturgical time, her daily life became a disciplined routine. "Although my life exteriorly and interiorly is far from bearing any resemblance to a religious, yet my daily work is planned for me by my director (who does the same for all his penitents), with the same exactness, as if we were under a superior, and very little time is given us for letter writing."[27] Spurned by her family, she was suddenly and intensely visible to herself.

> I had a nice little mortification Sunday morng, which seemed at the time a very great one. The Bishop told me to go to the Sacristy to confession as usual on Sunday morng, and as I sat there waiting, in came the Western Bishop, then priest after priest, til they seemed Legion & almost all Jesuits! There sat the poor lone woman, without even being allowed the chance of excusing herself, by saying "I am performing an act of obedience, it is not my boldness that leads me to intrude here." I wished the floor would open and swallow me up, but it did not, & I am preserved to tell the tale.[28]

The rhetorical impact of this passage derives partially from Ripley's self-conscious (and self-delighted) inversion of anti-Jesuit discourse. As the chief emblem of the duplicitous seductive power of the papacy, Jesuits attracted great enmity in Ripley's America. Ripley's situation of her lone self within the Jesuit "Legions" is energized by her still Protestant fascination with Loyola's soldiers. She is the individual, gloriously terrified and distinct, they the representatives of European absolutism and collectivity, fascinatingly uniform and quiet. It is a moment of exhilarating contact with the formerly taboo interiors of the alien faith. It is, moreover, a moment of suspenseful juxtaposition of her womanhood and their malehood, an encounter that records not only a woman's successful trespass on masculine terrain but also an encounter between two transforming sexualities. They are celibate, she a wife abandoning the Protestant ideology of the hearth.

In letter after letter, Ripley informally outlined a new language that revised customary boundaries between "inside" and "outside," individual and community. These letters, now that the Catholic church mediated the intimate bond between the cousins, drawing them together as it divided them from their Unitarian origins, constructed a powerful exile that was yet a protective interiority. They looked out on the unchurched world from the redemptive enclosure of their new theology. It was a strategy that operated in self-conscious opposition to its twin and rival: the Protestant evangelical ideology of the hearth and the sacred enclosure of the home. The world disclosed by Sophia's letters to Charlotte was well described by René de Montalembert in his intensely nostalgic biography of St. Elizabeth of Hungary, a volume (and a saint) treasured by Ripley. Before recounting Elizabeth's life of legendary piety, the author depicts a thirteenth century safely ensconced in its faith and inextricably connected to the other world: "It would be an endless task to specify all the innumerable bonds which thus connected heaven and earth; to penetrate into that vast region, where all the affections and all the duties of mortal life were mingled and intertwined with immortal protection."[29] If Montalembert's thirteenth century differed almost point by point from bourgeois antebellum America, American converts such as Seton and Ripley struggled to re-create the communalism of the Age of Faith in their own lives. Writing to Charlotte in 1857, Ripley expressed her hopes that "the holy guardian angels and saints have surrounded you in close circle, interposing their blessed presence between you and this moving panorama of men and women."[30]

No longer Sophia Willard Dana Ripley, she now signed her correspondence Sophia Elizabeth Ripley, adopting her confirmation name from her favorite saint, Elizabeth of Hungary, whose own two daughters, as Ripley delightedly discovered, both bore the name Sophia.[31] But such happy identifications struggled against a persistent and penetrating isolation; for all her rebirth, she remained problematically unchanged, her transformation still haunted by her original identity. These troubling, even shameful, continuities of personality were mercifully disrupted with her confirmation, whose cordoning off of the past provided a momentary euphoria: "There is no moment since that could possibly be mistaken for the moment before; so entirely is our state changed by it."[32] But Ripley's correspondence records as well the more strenuous reality of disavowing her husband's initially progressive but finally bourgeois culture for an alternative and principally female Catholic community. Of all her letters, one in particular vividly conveys the culturally specific suffering involved in that pilgrimage. Throughout her years as a Catholic, Sophia struggled against the lingering and, for her, malign presence of Protestantism, which she even detected in the vehemence of Orestes Brownson's conversion polemics.[33]

In March 1848, the new convert wrote a lengthy and passionately confiding letter from her new home in Flatbush, Long Island, to her cousin. With its narrative coherence and exacting self-examination, Ripley's letter powerfully condenses her conversion experience. Scrawled across the fourth page in cross-hand, Ripley's "No one" (Fig. 11) signaled the urgent privacy of her communication. Like other letters to Charlotte, this one extended and confirmed the activities of the confessional by reporting what occurred within it. Skillfully negotiating between the spontaneous intimacy of the epistolary context and the psychological immensity of her subject, Ripley brings a traditional Christian language of retrospection and prophetic enlightenment to bear on her particular spiritual crisis. Before Charlotte, she redescribes her labored ascent from a terrain of spiritual inferiority and cultural alienation to a redemptive discharging of her burden in the confessional. Her beginning narration of her confrontation with unworthiness suggests the obsessional intensity of her self-exploration, an intensity produced by her conflation of her deficiencies with those of Protestantism.

> Sunday morng I woke long before light, & my thoughts fastened themselves on a subject, I often mentioned to you when you were here, the coldness of heart of Protestantism, & my own very cold heart in particular. A clear revelation of myself was made to me as never before. I saw that all through life my ties with others were those of the intellect & imagination & not warm human heart ties; that I do not love anyone & never did,

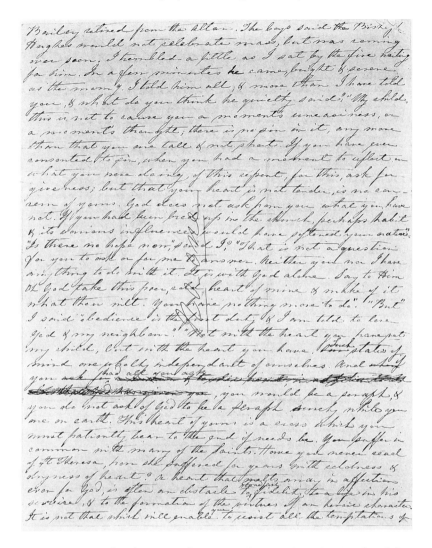

Fig. 11. Facsimile of a page of correspondence written in cross-hand from Sophia Dana Ripley to her cousin Ruth Charlotte Dana. The page discusses Ripley's momentous spiritual conversation with New York's Bishop Hughes. Courtesy, The Massachusetts Historical Society.

with the heart & of course never could have been worthy in any relation.[34]

Sophia's poignant confession at age forty-five of never having loved invokes the familiar preoccupation of many antebellum New Englanders with the coldness of their culture and themselves. Hawthorne's repeated fictional examinations of sinful separation from the obligations of the heart, Melville's haunting portrait of Bartleby the Scrivener, and Emerson's repudiation of corpse-cold Unitarianism and his own terrible confession of emotional numbness in his essay "Experience" are well-known instances of a regional malaise.[35] For Sophia Ripley, the burdens of this culturally constructed reserve became identified with the traditional evangelical burden of the unconvicted heart, reserved because of its own torpor and sterility. Ripley fought against the deadness (and the anxieties suppressed and controlled by that deadness) of the carnal self by indicting the cold Protestantism of New England. During one of her difficult visits to her family, she again conflated her fallen self and her Boston home to reject them both outright: "Protestant life is very dreary, and Protestant thought very shallow, and Protestant feeling has no worthy objects."[36] Such projection facilitated her cure, for each distancing from her native culture enabled her to recontextualize the coldness of her own heart; recalling long-standing theological debates over how Christ's grace is either imputed to or infused in the regenerate, Sophia struggled to have the "warmth" of Catholicism not only extended to her but incorporated within her. Ripley's 1848 "No one" letter proceeds to reveal the mutual implication of problems of "grace," of competing religious and cultural affiliations, and of familial relationships; these theological, political, and familial terrains were all involved in an urgent cultural project to rejoin subject to object, the suffering soul to Christ, the emotional interior to the cultural exterior.

Borrowing prophetic imagery to convey her enlightenment to Charlotte, Sophia continued her confession of emotional distance:

> I saw what had caused my greatest difficulties & trials. I saw
> above all that my faith in the Church was only a reunion of
> my intellect with God; I saw that faith requires to strike root
> in the heart, & if the stony soil refuses to receive it, it has no-
> where to plant itself & therefore has no root at all. I saw how,
> all through my life I had been trying to do good to people, to
> repair the injury of this deathlike coldness & yet it never
> brought me into kind & equal relations.

Ripley's use of Christ's parable (Matthew 13:20–21) to convey the culpability of her stony heart suggests the terrible failure of Brook Farm (abandoned the summer before), whose stony soil had resisted cultivation, and whose bankruptcy signaled the abrupt end of Ripley's vocation as utopian reformer. Recognizing that her stoniness persisted beneath the "gratified imagination," which, according to her, she shared with so many converts, she struggled to move beyond the warmth of a newly satisfied aesthetic sensibility to the truer warmth of a "sanctified heart." Ripley's quest voices her anxious response to Christ's warning against those who receive "the seed into stony places" and therefore will be unable to endure any challenges to their faith.

Behind her fear that her heart was not sufficiently rich to anchor her new faith and behind her failed efforts at self-cultivation at Brook Farm lay an unspecified early wounding that had left her icy and denatured. The stark dissociation of her nocturnal introspection, in which she "looked on it as a dreadful fact that the heart of a human being should be turned to stone," reenacts this severance from feeling as she gazes Medusa-like onto her guilty, inadequate self. In memorable contrast to the ardor of Elizabeth Seton, Ripley can only acknowledge numbly her disconnection and lack of spiritual potential.

Ripley's letter dramatically recounts her resolution of this crisis when the next morning she sets out to unveil her stony isolation to her "Blessed Director." Reenacting her dread and suspense for Charlotte, she portrays herself as a "beast of burden" walking through the still and sunlit streets of lower New York, her sin of emotional deadness ironically increased by her failure to feel "wretched, though I thought I ought to be." For all her supposed lack of emotion, Ripley's short pilgrimage is laden with a fearful anxiety of rejection. Will the priest banish the new convert, disgusted by her inadequate and still "Protestant" uncertainties? Tormented by the conflict between her habitual self-restraint and her longing for intimacy, Ripley, in her imagery of stone, covers an ongoing familial crisis of paternal rejection so profound that she later described the spiritual direction given her by Isaac Hecker and by the mother superior of the Sisters of St. Catherine as enabling her to be "a child for the first time, one of their children."[37]

But the passage from psychological orphanhood to such a regained childhood entailed a painful confrontation with her defensive emotional dissociation from that past. Abandoned as a child by her father and later scorned by him until his death, Ripley felt a profound sense of personal culpability for this rejection. It was this, arguably, that formed her cold heart, and in desperation she resolved to expose what she had hidden within: "I determined to make a clean breast of it to my Blessed Director, take this heart out & let him see that it was all of stone; & calmly take the consequences." Ripley's ensuing encounter with Bishop Hughes produced an epiphany in her life. The bishop's response to his convert's confession of coldness—as she recounts it—constructs a new familial narrative of paternal acceptance whose intimacy she extends in turn to Charlotte:

> My child, this is not to cause you a moment's uneasiness, or a moment's thought; there is no sin in it, anymore than that you are tall & not short. If you have ever consented to sin, when you had a moment to reflect on what you were doing, of this repent, for this, ask forgiveness; but that your heart is not tender, is no concern of yours. God does not ask from you what you have not. If you had been bred up in the church, perhaps habit & its various influences would have softened your nature.

Ripley's narrative of Hughes's response opposes her still lingering, virtually Calvinist ethos of vitiated human nature to her adopted Catholic theology that limited the effects of Original Sin and further distinguished those effects from those of actual sin. The Catholicism made available to her through her momentous conversation with Bishop Hughes removes from her the burden of her personality, proffering a radical solution to her urgent sense of inadequacy and emptiness by declaring the matter beyond her control. The bishop responds to Ripley's anxious bewilderment about how her "cold" heart is to fulfill the commandment to love God and neighbor by tellingly connecting her painful isolation to that suffered even by the sainted. He explains that we are told to love, "Not with the heart you have *not* my child, but with the heart you have. Such states of mind are wholly independent of ourselves.... This heart of yours is a cross which you must patiently bear to the end if need be. You suffer in common with many of the Saints. Have you never read of St. Theresa, how she suffered for years with coldness & dryness of heart?"

To Ripley, these therapeutic words came with the force of divine assurance and ushered her "as it were from death unto Life." Even so, Ripley proceeded to press Bishop Hughes on whether "one who could read over the mysteries of the Passion of our Lord without emotion, was worthy of partaking of his Blessed Body." The bishop's response resolves Ripley's anxiety over her emotionlessness by claiming it for the Gospel accounts as well: "'What' said he, 'could be more cold than the narration itself. The narrators did not feel it in its fullness. They relate it as they would something they met at a crossing of the road. Did you never notice this. Go to the communion, my child, in peace.'"

Cultivating the heart by accommodating its coldness led Ripley in turn to find in Catholicism's "blessed books" a cure for her related struggle with the deadness of the written word. Ripley's conversation with Hughes finally consolidated her "Transcendentalist" concerns with "cultivating" a self freed from both Calvinist liabilities and Unitarian emptiness. Concluding her account of the encounter for Charlotte, she describes "with what a gentle shudder and tone of profound compassion the Bishop spoke in his instructions of the horrible doctrines of original sin and total depravity so diffused through Protestantism, 'that even those who have never believed in them feel their withering power.'" The stoniness of her heart, the thieving coldness of Protestantism (especially the repressive effects of its Calvinist and Unitarian extremes), and the coldness of "narration itself" all constitute a barren world to be abandoned for the cultivated and forgiving substance of Catholicism, whose novel materiality released the emotions: Ripley described a requiem mass she later heard as an experience that "would have drawn tears from stones."[38]

Issuing from the stony self, such tears break through bodily boundary, not, as in sentimental fiction, to ease the woman's renewed submission to the domestic cult of purity, but to claim a foreign model of expressivity for a previously pallid selfhood, one pained by its own absence from itself. Writing from New York to console Charlotte for the pain she suffered in her back, Sophia emphasized the sweet meaningfulness of such pain by turning to a significant metaphor: "Is not every new leaf of life as we turn it over by the light of the sanctuary lamp more richly illuminated than the last?"[39] Her life newly lit by the aesthetic constructions of her new faith, Ripley moved increasingly in a world of womanly piety dedicated to the overcoming of inhibition. Fascinated, Ripley pondered the rare, even magnetic, self-presentation of her niece Sarah Stearns (soon to become a Sister of Charity), that enabled her while still a Protestant to be taken for a Catholic and accordingly given access to the foreign domestic interiors of the Catholic immigrant community. "I believe with all these Protestant sins she has a more Catholic look than any of us, for all the Catholic men, women and children in the street speak to her, and give her seats in churches, and take her home, and refresh her with cold water, and present her with nice little books of devotion and choice spiritual reading, such as cannot be procured at any price in this country."[40] If Sarah Stearns, by virtue of her "Catholic look," enjoyed a series of novel and nourishing attentions that included "choice" books otherwise unavailable to Protestant Americans, the Catholic convert Julia Metcalf surpassed even this achievement, managing indeed to be seen not as a convincing imitation but as the original itself. Sophia wrote of her singular achievement of authenticity:

> Tell Julia she passes for a *born Catholic* I find & and I am devoured with envy. She is said to be the only one among the new

converts who by her voice, manner & expression of countenance could be mistaken for one! Though I am a little cheered
by having been asked at Radde's yesterday where I went to en-
quire for pictures, if I did not wish for Catholic ones; & certainly they had no reason to suspect this except from the expression of my countenance![41]

As Ripley's repeated discussion of sanctified womanhood suggests,
the Catholic veneration of Mary and the intercession of the saints enabled her to resist the angers of Protestant womanhood by focusing on
the Church's "consecration" of the feminine. A "Miss B——" served as
one instance of the secular feminism to be abandoned:

> I was as explicit with her as language would permit, talked to
> her fully of the fall of woman, and consequently the fall of
> man; told her instead of allowing her imagination to dwell
> upon the sins of men, she was to fill it with celestial pictures of
> the virginal purity of saints, by whom mankind is to be re-
> deemed; that every woman must share in this sanctity . . . and
> she can only attain it, by accepting the consecration of woman-
> hood offered in the church, through our Blessed Mother.[42]

Ripley's confident embrace of woman's original culpability and redemptive powers directs female attention away from the "sins of men" to an
empowering focus on the sins of woman. Her numerous references to the
Virgin suggest how the Madonna enabled her to practice a repeated, even
scheduled, loss and recovery of Mary as well as Christ. Lamenting the
passing of the month of May, Sophia confessed that "it makes one feel
sad to have this sweet month close, and yet if we did not separate from
Her as well as from our dear Lord at this season, the spirit would not
come to us."[43] An intriguing, if brief, description of heaven in which
Ripley imagines the dead "sitting at the feet of our Blessed Lady, listening
to the tale of her holy childhood,"[44] enables her to enjoy the closeness
and hearth-side storytelling so central to the Protestant cult of domesticity while avoiding its debilitating subordination to the authority of the
husband and (absent) "Papa." Ripley's holy women, be they the Virgin
and female saints or the nuns of her acquaintance, enjoy an institutional
sanction that permits them to exert their redemptive feminine influence
outside the home. Thus, accompanying the sisters on their prison rounds,
Ripley gained entry to an otherwise inaccessible masculine region and
vicariously enjoyed a feminine control over its latent violence and the
stoniness of human nature beneath. "We went to the cells of the convicts

and there are six under sentence—and stood by the side of the most
ferocious murderers in the narrow gallery and no keeper near—but one
cannot fear under their holy protection. Their conversation and prayers
with these poor fellows would almost have melted the stones upon which
we knelt."[45]

To Ripley's confessor and close friend Isaac Hecker, her Brook Farm
utopianism led naturally to her conversion and ensuing vocation as a
lay sister. "I believe," declared Hecker in his tribute written the year
following Ripley's death, "that the grace to believe was accorded to her
by Heaven in reward for the straightforwardness, earnestness and purity with which she labored at Brook Farm to carry out the precepts of
this charity."[46] Ripley's intense identification with nuns and fallen
women led to her work for the Sisters of the Good Shepherd, an order
dedicated to the rehabilitation of prostitutes. To raise the thousand
dollars per year the order needed to support its work, Ripley spent the
last three years of her life begging eight hours daily on the streets of
New York. Far from the ecstatic summer days of Brook Farm, Ripley
ended in the heart of immigrant New York, practicing the mendicancy
Emerson so vehemently warned against in "Self-Reliance." But the
sense lingered of an internal unworthy Protestantism, of exile from the
"warmth" of the Catholic interior. Directing Charlotte what to say to
some new converts for example, Ripley wrote in 1855: "Tell them I am
one of the door-keepers, and never expect to be anything else; for daily
is my mind more and more impressed with our worthlessness as Catholics. The Church, with all her power may just save us, but nothing
more, and we can do nothing for her. We are too hardened in our old
ways."[47]

While Sophia frequently expressed hopes for her husband's conversion, the closest she came was to an implicit parallel between her church
and his literary project, the *American Cyclopedia*. As her husband reportedly said, "The Church has a place for everything and everything is
in its place."[48] But much to her disappointment, his "church" never
materialized beyond the encyclopedic confines of his book, which finally
brought him financial stability. Ill with breast cancer, Sophia retreated
to Staten Island in 1860 and returned, however partially, to the rural
seclusion and beauty she had known at Brook Farm. In an image of the
final recovery of a pastoral refuge, she wrote to Charlotte on July 5,

1860: "All ordinary objects of interest have faded in the distance, & our Lord has led me around to the other side of life, where helpless, and passive, I find myself lying in the cool shade at his feet."[49] She died in February 1861. In a final and fitting irony, funeral services were held at Boston's Purchase Street Church, where her husband had been Unitarian pastor for ten years before leaving to found Brook Farm. In 1855 the church had been sold to a Catholic parish.

SIXTEEN

Isaac Hecker: The Form of the Missionary Body

*Brownson Alcott dead! I saw him coming from Rochester
on the cars. I had been a Catholic missionary for I don't
know how many years. We sat together. "Father Hecker,"
said he, "why can't you make a Catholic of me?" "Too
much rust here," said I, clapping him on the knee. He got
very angry because I said that was the obstacle. I never saw
him angry at any other time. He was too proud.*

Isaac Hecker, March 5, 1888

Confiding in his diary in 1843 that "I would not take it on myself to
say I have been 'born again,' but I know that I have passed from death
to life,"[1] Isaac Hecker voiced his increasing experience of internal transformation that ineluctably forced his withdrawal from his family and
business obligations, his retreat to Brook Farm, and his eventual conversion to the Catholic church. Hecker's reception into the Catholic
church on August 2, 1844, concluded a decade-long interrogation of
various political, Protestant evangelical, and finally utopian communitarian solutions to social reform and internal regeneration. His diary of
1843 and 1844 reveals how these cultural struggles interacted with the
intensity of his interior emotional life, its "flow," its estrangements, and
its violence. Hecker's passage from death to life—a passage that soon led
him to identify life with Catholic truth—entailed a lifelong involvement
with opening the way for others to join the church; he confessed at one
point that "I feel that I am a pioneer in opening and leading the way. I
smuggled myself into the *Church,* and so did Brownson."[2] Acutely aware
of the transcendent validity and cultural peculiarity of his new faith, Isaac
Hecker, like Sophia Ripley, for whom he served as confessor, also remained complexly indebted to his home culture, dedicating himself after
his own conversion and ordination to the conversion of other Americans:
"I believe that Providence calls me . . . to America to convert a certain
class of persons amongst whom I found myself before my conversion."[3]

Hecker's preoccupation with his own conversion and that of his fellow Americans is recorded not only in his diary but in his two works of the 1850s, *Questions of the Soul* (1855) and *Aspirations of Nature* (1857). The diary and these two works reveal a fascinating and recurrent problem of negotiating the boundary between his worldly and spiritual selves, as well as the boundary between his divided self and the "spiritual presence" of others. Often solitude and radical community were strangely welded together for him: "I feel in better health than I ever have both mind and body at the same time having an increased sensitiveness so that the touch of anyone I cannot bear," he wrote in his diary; but he continued: "Also I am conscious of a more constant and spiritual communion, feel more vividly and distinctly the . . . spiritual presence of others."[4]

Like the writings of Elizabeth Seton and Sophia Ripley, Hecker's diary, correspondence, and two published works are nostalgically, sometimes angrily, engaged with the Protestant culture left behind, a culture fully identified as the "world" repudiated by the spiritual pilgrim yet still at the core of his distinctive converted selfhood. Abandoning the Unitarian-Transcendentalist argument for self-sufficiency, whose three spokesmen Bronson Alcott, Ralph Waldo Emerson, and Henry David Thoreau he dubbed "three consecrated cranks,"[5] as well as the doctrine of Calvinist depravity, Hecker early experienced a dreamlike dissociation from his New York origins and the New England associations later established by his stays at Brook Farm and, briefly, at Fruitlands. "My past seems to me like a dream," he wrote to his close friend and mentor Orestes Brownson in 1843, "and so it is but a day dream. The deeper we drink of life the more mysterious it seems."[6]

Hecker's dreamlike past and mysterious present were alike informed by a series of decisive confrontations between the marketplace and the monastery that led to his transformation from a morally troubled worker in his family's increasingly successful bakery enterprise to a charismatic missionary preacher, a transformation that for Hecker was instigated by the "heathenish selfishness of business competition."[7] Recorded in the diary that he began in April 1843 while at Brook Farm (to which he had gone, with his family's support, to pursue his studies), Hecker's disengagement from the conventional matrimonial and business expectations of the American male involved a protracted effort to extract himself not only from the contaminations of capitalism but from those of the body itself—all in order to ingest what he called the "true eternal food of life."[8]

Returning to New York from Brook Farm in 1843, Hecker persevered in his Thoreauvian enterprise of self-purification—only his project was conspicuously guided by a concern for achieving union with what he called "the Spirit" that was always pressing within him, leading him he knew not where, and always suggesting to him the insufficiencies of his contemporary existence. Frustrated by his efforts to continue the prayerful, abstemious life he had practiced at Brook Farm and had witnessed at Fruitlands, Hecker questioned in his diary the very possibility of extricating the body from culture: "What yet remains? My diet is all purchased and all produced by hired labor. My dress I suppose the most of it by Slave Labor. And I cannot say that I am rightly conditioned until all that I eat and drink or wear is produced by *Love*."[9] Only twenty-four years old at the time he recorded this entry, Hecker berated himself for missing out on the heavenly life that, paradoxically, he continually felt within yet could not, as he understood it, achieve; he longed to enjoy this heavenly life in his temporal self, although its internal presence, labeled the Spirit, continually urged him forward in a maddeningly uncertain direction. Fleeing the distractions of the family business, Hecker went to board at the Thoreau home in Concord to study languages. From there he wrote a letter home pointedly directed at his family's immigrant industriousness in terms that Thoreau would soon make famous in *Walden:* "What is it that costs so much labor of mind and body? Is it not that which we consume on and in our bodies? Then, if we reduce the consumption there will be less need of production."[10] But Hecker's ruminations about how best to purify the self through disciplined abstention were intricately challenged, even thwarted, by an equally powerful passivity that at times removed him from control of his ascetic project, simultaneously estranging him from himself and somehow leading him closer to himself. At times expressive of profound inhibition, a maddening inability to study or write or do the task at hand, this passivity also bordered on release and even Adamic regeneration, a regeneration dependent on a developing distinction between a "willfullness" that "locks up" and a "willingness" that "unlocks the portal to the divine mysteries of God."[11] He recorded in May 1844 the following acknowledgment of this interior sense of ceaseless passage toward an unknown destination.

> My life is beyond my grasp, and bears me on will-lessly to its
> destined haven. Like a rich fountain it overflows on every side;
> from within flows unceasingly the noiseless tide. . . . It is to me
> now as if I had just been born, and I live in the Sabbath of

creation. . . . It is a singular fact that, although conscious of a more interior and potent force at work within, I am now more quiet and will-less than I was when it at first affected me. I feel like a child, full of joy and pliability.[12]

Such flowing passages covered a tremendous, even violently compacted, energy, a warring closeness with the "constant presence of invisible beings": "If I remain where I am still, it by collecting its scattered rays burns in my soul so deeply, bringing forth deep sighs groans and at times making me almost utter an unnatural howl which to repress takes all my energy."[13]

Hecker's return to an original, pliant, childlike self coincided with his joining the Catholic church. Against the pressured psychological interiors of an increasingly secular nineteenth-century psyche, converts like Hecker argued for the highly structured but "flowing" interiority of the church. Many, having suffered the emptiness of a post-Unitarian existence, knew precisely the torments of Melville's Pierre, who suffered, if with unrepresentative vehemence, in his bondage to the void: "Appalling is the soul of a man! Better might one be pushed off into the material spaces beyond the uttermost orbit of our sun, than once feel himself fairly afloat in himself!"[14] In several intriguing respects, Hecker's diary and even his later proselytizing works register the agonies of Pierre, afloat in an unconfined and undetermined space of subjectivity, only Hecker pointedly redirected those very pressures of boundlessness into a subordination to the authority of the church. Entering the Catholic enclosure represented an ideological break not only from the agonies of Pierre but also from the culture's various Protestant versions of the unmediated spirit and the invisible church. While antebellum popular fiction urged an increasingly nondenominational development of one's soul in the privacy of the "closet," popular Catholic literature, apologetics, and convert writing like Hecker's insisted that the Catholic church was the one true enclosure; it and it alone, according to another convert, exhibited the "*positive marks of the true Church, namely, 'Unity, Sanctity, Catholicity, and Apostolicity.'*"[15] For Hecker, such abstractions were far less important than the developing urgency of the spirit within that led him finally into the church, not because it offered "Unity," but because it appealed powerfully to his personal enterprise of both controlling and releasing the body. Salvation, in short, depended on membership in a public and consecrated "bodily" space at once visible and invisible.

Convert prose repeatedly diagnosed torments like Pierre's as a cultural problem, an unfortunate result of Protestantism's private judgment, sectarian controversies, and debilitating theologies of human depravity.

As a largely uneducated twenty-four-year-old, Hecker decisively—and with aggressive insight—attributed life's ambiguities to the willful flaws of the elite culture's Protestantized human consciousness: "The reason why men are perplexed and in darkness about their being and the questions which their being often asks, is not that these are insoluble, but that the disposition and spirit in which a solution is attempted is so contrary to that in which they may be solved, that they appear as hidden mysteries."[16] This formulation on Hecker's part is crucial, for his diary indeed records an extended, even painfully protracted, process of inter-rogation—interrogation often wrongly phrased, as one might surmise from this quotation. The rhetorical structure of the diary is characterized by a restless alternation between a relentless interrogatory and a series of declarative outbursts. In Hecker's understanding of antebellum cul-tural perplexity, conversion to the alien faith was as much a new way of asking the question as the discovery of an answer.

For some, this new mode of phrasing the question meant, as it did for Sophia Ripley, the redescription of culture entire as Protestantism. For the convert author Joshua Huntington, the conversion process entailed a cognitive resolution that systematically reconceptualized various "truths" as the heretical errors of an errant subjectivity. Somewhat disingenuously, Huntington suggested to his readers that his devastating critique of Calvinist depravity and predestination "may, perhaps, awaken a suspicion in your mind that some other things which you have always taken for granted are equally false."[17] The doctrine of private judgment now led in the works of these various converts directly to the modern, implicitly insipid, ethos of sincerity; according to Huntington, it "has led vast numbers of persons to the conclusion that, since there are very few articles of the Christian creed which can be established with certainty, it is of no importance what a man believes, so long as he is sincere, and acts according to his own convictions of duty."[18]

It remained for Orestes Brownson in his 1857 spiritual autobiography *The Convert* to indict even this notion of sincerity. According to Brown-son, the emptying of any rationality from Protestantism meant in turn a pervasive hypocrisy in the culture, the inability of the average Prot-estant American to believe in anything and a further inability to stand up for any convictions, should he or she have any. Like Huntington and Brownson, Hecker found it frustrating as well to witness how the Amer-ican struggle against Calvinist depravity and the rejection of reason could become what was for him a disreputable argument for a meaningless progressive benevolence or Pelagianism. Of Catharine Beecher's *Com-mon Sense Applied to the Gospels* (1857), Hecker wrote to Brownson (with whom he remained in active correspondence throughout his life, both prior to his conversion and throughout his career as a Paulist):

> Miss C. confounds the Jansenistic interpretation with the true interpretation of St. Augustine, consequently confounds the Catholic doctrine of original sin with that of Calvin. She is strangely ignorant for one who writes in theology, ignorant of what the Catholic Ch[urch] teaches, and seeing no escape from Calvinism except in Pelagianism she embraces it in preferrence [sic]. . . . To this class of minds it seems to me, we have the task to show that it is not necessary to repudiate nature to be a Xtian, on the contrary, Xtianity supposes nature, & esteems it at its real & true value.[19]

Hecker's critique of Catharine Beecher isolates what perhaps remained for him the single most persuasive point about Catholicism: that it allowed the union of nature and spirit and indeed, as Hecker claimed, the completion, the perfection of nature through the jointly romantic and ascetic workings of spirit. Antebellum discussion of Catholic piety continued to be informed by disagreement about the relation not only between the converted individual and the redeemed community but between the individual spirit and the recalcitrant body. Just as Protestants attributed enormous power to priests, they acknowledged in the Catholic church a successful, if deeply alien, form of embodied community, hierarchically organized around the living Christ. No image better conveyed the highly systematic but organic structure of the rival church than the illustration of the "Apostolical Tree" that figured at the center John Milner's *End to Religious Controversy* (1818), the age's most influential polemical work, used extensively by American Catholics to defend and to explain their faith (Fig. 12).[20] Convinced that "the most fruitful source of conversions to the Catholic Church, are the detected calumnies and misrepresentations of her bitterest enemies" (xxviii), Milner wrote a series of studiously congenial letters disproving various accusations against the church. Throughout, he insisted that no community could be established without a centralized authority, the most legitimate one available in this world being that faithfully and organically transmitted from the apostles.

Milner's emphasis on the organicity and continuity of Catholic community received brilliant scholarly exposition in Johann Adam Möhler's *Symbolism; or, Exposition of the Doctrinal Differences between Catholics and Protestants* (1832). Explained Möhler, whose book Isaac Hecker read carefully while at Brook Farm (the volume being loaned to him by none other than Theodore Parker), the true church both conceals and embodies Christ, and each mass serves as both commemoration and renewed sacrifice. "If Christ, concealed under an earthly veil, unfolds, to the end of time, his whole course of actions begun on earth, he, of necessity, eternally offers himself to the Father as a victim for men; and the real permanent exposition hereof can never fail in the Church, if the historical Christ is to celebrate in her his entire imperishable existence."[21] By 1845 Isaac Hecker himself was pondering what he called the

> strange fact [of] this faith in a Sacrifice. Nothing but blood will satisfy. I know not how it is this thing seems different to me now from what it has. I never could contemplate this faith of the past in a favorable light until now. . . . It is true that true love is most cruel. See what Abraham in will at least did do. . . . These and many such facts I have not been able to give a right account of until now. They are strange but nothing truer. Revenge & Love do act alike. We would kill that we most love—shed its blood. This is the virtue of a Sacrifice that it be that which is pure and of our deepest affection.[22]

Möhler, regarded as the founder of the historical school of theology in the nineteenth century, first published his *Symbolism* in America in 1844; in Europe it had gone through five large editions within six years of its publication. The Tübingen professor's penetrating analyses of the creedal distinctions between Roman Catholicism, Lutheranism, Calvinism, Quakerism, and even Swedenborgianism addressed contemporary concerns over the proper relation between spirit and letter, subjectivity and objectivity, faith and its institutional embodiment. Outlining the ironic development by which rationalism emerged from the Reformers' repudiation of reason and "infidel" liberalism from Calvin's excessive emphasis on depravity, Möhler diagnosed Swedenborgianism as a misguided effort to reestablish objectivity, "as subjectivity, striving after objectivity, became to itself an outward thing, in order to replace the external, visible Church founded by Christ" (427). Möhler's extended defense of Catholicism continually recurs to the church's blending of substance and interior spirit. "Everything which is truly interior must, according to Catholic doctrine, be outwardly expressed" (301). Indeed, it was precisely this image of a fully externalized and substantial form of Catholicity that inspired the "paranoid" depictions of the church in anti-Catholic discourse. In the words of one "escaped nun":

> Every part of the great machine called popery, is of such a nature as to require study to be fully understood. Every part is

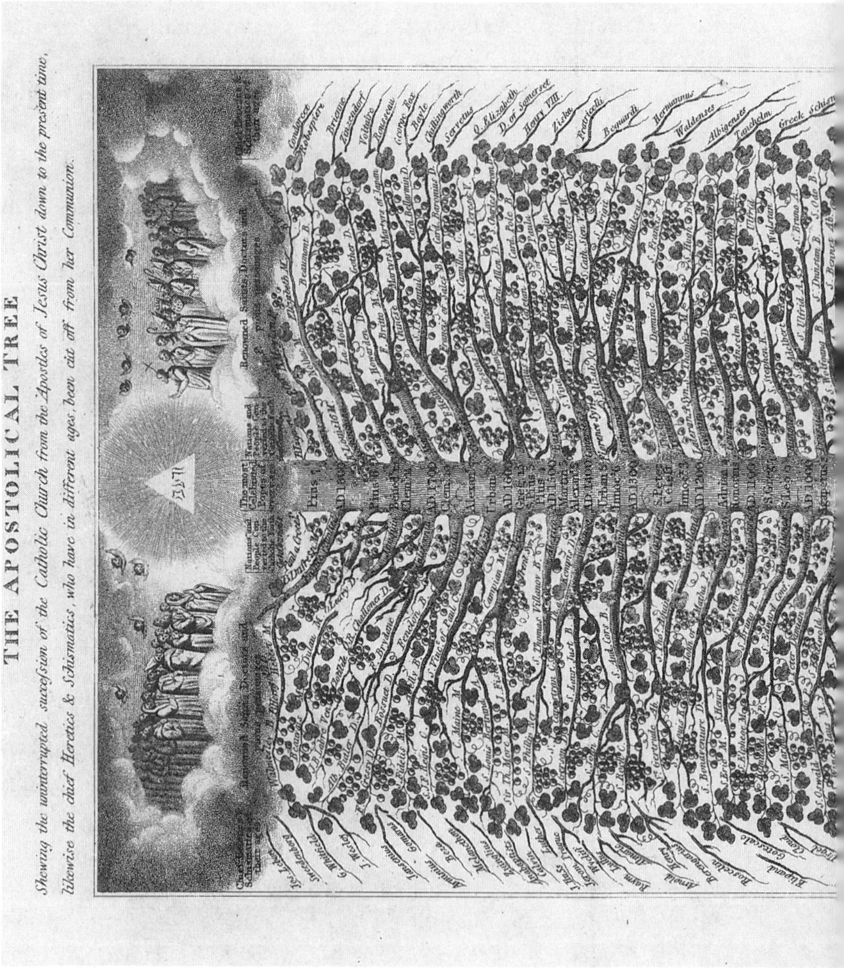

Fig. 12. "The Apostolical Tree." From John Milner, *The End of Religious Controversy, in a Friendly Correspondence between a Religious Society of Protestants, and a Roman Catholic Divine* (London, 1818). Courtesy, Boalt Law School Library, University of California, Berkeley.

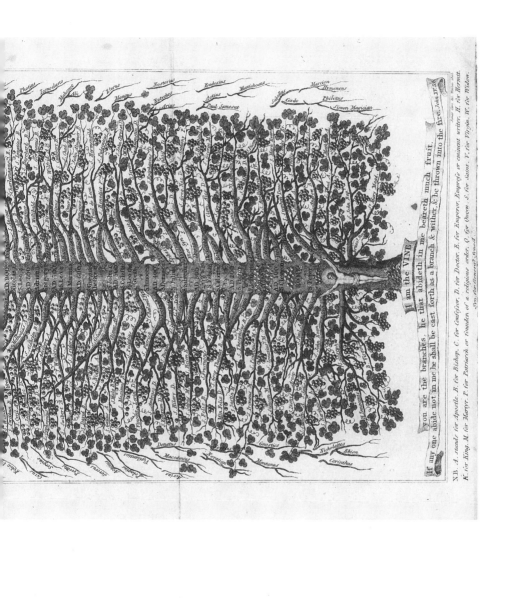

I am the VINE

you are the branches. he that abideth in me beareth much fruit. If any one abide not in me he shall be cast forth as a branch & wither, & be thrown into the fire. John XV.

N.B. A. stands for Apostle. B. for Bishop. C. for confessor. D. for Doctor. E. for Emperor. Empress or eminent writer. H. for Hermit. K. for King. M. for Martyr. P. for Patriarch or founder of a religious order. Q. for Queen. S. for Saint. V. for Virgin. W. for Widow. Syn. for Synod. Synod.

complex, & adapted to operate in particular ways, upon particular classes of people, and for particular ends, though subservient to the whole system, and secretly directed by the same head. Every part has also an exterior and an interior; the former is assumed and false, but protruded upon public attention in order to make deceitful impressions; and the other is secret, concealed and difficult of discovery, cautiously guarded and surrounded with arrangements invented, prepared, and ready to be used, to quiet suspicion or to mislead it.[23]

If this image of a highly mechanized, secretive, and excessively organized Catholicism characterized the anxiety of such "escaped nuns," it was precisely such organic systemization that formed the primary ingredient of Möhler's defense of Catholicism. From his perspective, Protestant theology was characterized throughout by a rupture between internal and external that left the human creature only partially regenerated, the church insufficiently materialized, and the relation between body and spirit antagonistic. Explains Möhler: "The Protestants conceive justification to be a thing chiefly external, and the Church to be a thing chiefly internal, so that, in either respect, they are unable to bring about a *permeation* of the inward and the outward" (188). It was of course precisely such "permeation" that troubled nativist fiction of the period. Because of what Möhler understood as an unnatural separation born of Luther's personal despair of sanctification, Protestantism (especially Lutheranism) necessarily curtailed the possibility of conversion. An irreducible duality was lodged at the heart of Protestant regeneration. "In the Lord's supper, Luther could not find Christ alone,—bread and wine ever recurred to his mind, because, in the will of those regenerated in Christ, he saw a permanent dualism, a perpetual co-existence of a spiritual and a carnal inclination, so that the latter—evil principle in man—could never be truly converted into the former" (320).

Anticipating Andrews Norton's objection to the Transcendentalists, Möhler charged that the Reformers "entirely merged the objective historical Christianity into their own subjectivity" (407). In contrast to the Reformation's deviation from an objective truth, Roman Catholicism remained loyal to the essential and eternal meaning of the Incarnation. "As from the beginning, the abstract idea and positive history, doctrine and fact, internal and external truth, inward and outward testimony were organically united; so must religion and Church be conjoined, and this for the reason, *that God became man*" (342). In contrast to the fearful interiorities projected by anti-Catholic rhetoric, this language of Catholic apology emphasized a redemptive corporeality available to human beings, an embodiment that disgusted or perplexed many Protestant observers. But as the missionary Isaac Hecker rhetorically inquired of his American Protestant audiences: "For what else is the Church, but God made manifest to the hearts and minds of men—his Body."[24] Like other converts, Hecker labored to demonstrate that truth was an organic "body" independent of and superior to any linguistic expression or book. To ground one's faith solely in Scripture was to endanger this embodied truth, since "no account of Christ is Christ." Teaching people to read the Bible "broke Christendom into fragments, multiplied jarring Christian sects, [and] produced swarms of doubters."[25] Converts and sympathetic observers of the church increasingly voiced their opposition to the divisiveness of a mass print culture by appealing to the human need for spiritual substance and sustenance, substances implicitly antitextual. Liberal Protestants frequently conceded their hunger, frankly admitting that they were "word-ridden Anglo-Saxons, thirsting for forms of beauty which they cannot devise."[26]

Writing home from New England on June 11, 1844, to declare his intention of joining the church, Hecker appealed precisely to this cultural idiom of bodily need: "I feel like affirming, in the spirit of the man whom Christ made to see, I know not whether this Church be or not be what certain men call it, but this I know: it has the life my heart is thirsting for, and of which my spirit is in great need."[27] In a thirty-nine-page manuscript account of conscience written in October 1848, Hecker refined his expression of this appetite in terms that recall Seton's hunger for the Eucharist: "I have a constant hunger and thirst for Our Lord in the sacrament of His body and blood. If it were possible I would desire to receive no other food than this, for it is the only nourishment that I have a real appetite for."[28]

Finding themselves happily externalized into a populated, "objective" region, converts like Isaac Hecker confirmed Möhler's formulations about the body's relation to the spirit. That space, densely inhabited by the interconnected members of the church "militant," the church "suffering," and the church "triumphant," functioned for them as an all-embracing and significantly inhabited interiority. But emanating from the mystery of the Incarnation as embodied and expounded by the supernatural teaching authority of the visible church, that interiority reached into the public world as well. Explained one American Catholic in an essay entitled "The Two Sides of Catholicism," the church's invisible faith and visible papal hierarchy were two necessary halves of the whole: "The most profound and supersensual characteristic of the Church is, therefore, closely though mysteriously allied with the palpable

exterior."[29] Like many converts, Isaac Hecker employed this Catholic
vision to criticize the disembodied and unnecessarily conflicted vision of
union expounded by Transcendentalists. Indeed Hecker's critique of
some Transcendentalists, especially Emerson, focused precisely on the
aberrant notion of the body created by the doctrines of Transcendentalism:

> A Transcendentalist is one who has a keen sight but little
> warmth of heart: Fine conceits but destitute of the rich glow of
> Love. He is in rapport with the Spiritual world, unconscious of
> the celestial one. He is all nerve and no blood [—] colour less.
> He talks of self reliance but fears to trust himself to Love. He
> never abandons himself to Love, but always is on the look out
> for some new facts[.] His nerves are always tightly stretched
> like the string of a bow, his life is all effort. In a short period
> they loose their tone. Behold him sitting in a chair! He is not
> sitting but braced upon its angles as if his bones were of iron
> and his nerves of steel. Every nerve is drawn his hands are
> clinched like a miser it is his lips and head that speaks not his
> tongue and heart.[30]

Hecker's extraordinary formulation of the Emersonian body as a
mechanized, and profoundly uncomfortable construction perched
tensely on his chair, a creature whose self-alienation is so profound that
his body is no longer body but a miserly machine hoarding its human
affections from expression, remains perhaps his most powerful criticism
of the Protestant culture from which he was gradually extricating himself. As late as the years immediately following the Civil War, Hecker
returned to the phenomenon presented by Emerson, writing to Brownson that a lecture recently delivered by Emerson once again falsely
repudiated the connection between the internal and external worlds:
"You will find a passage in Emerson's speech which I have marked. He
professes to find a contradiction between 'the without' and 'the within'—an imaginary one—as between faith and science, or revelation and
reason."[31] Influenced by such apologists as John Milner and, especially,
Johann Möhler, Hecker continued to insist that genuine conversion
meant not a rupture from the world but the completion of its promise.
There need be no irremediable gap between spirit and letter, between
ascetic discipline and affective expressivity.

The rhetorical structure of Hecker's *Aspirations of Nature,* its chapters headed by epigraphs from such antidogmatic spokesmen of a divine
spirit emancipated from denominational constraints as William Ellery
Channing, William Cullen Bryant, and even Emerson, underlines the

continuing interaction between his converted sensibility and that of American romanticism. Hecker's understanding of his own conversion and continuing obligation to the unconverted of New England's liberal elite recurrently thematized itself around the dynamics of captivity through which the reunion of inner and outer was to be accomplished. Thus one chapter's epigraph, from Bryant, implicitly posits Hecker, the son of German immigrants and new advocate for the papacy, as New England's mythic deliverer:

> My spirit yearns to bring
>   The lost ones back—yearns with
>   desire intense—
> And struggles hard to wring
>   The bolts apart, and pluck thy
>   captives thence.[32]

That Hecker, himself profoundly influenced by European romanticism, used its emancipatory rhetoric for his own apologias demonstrates provocatively that various Protestant theological tenets were indeed excerpts from the Catholic whole.

Concluding his *Aspirations of Nature* with an argument for the primacy of the Holy See, Hecker subversively borrows from Emerson his own Transcendentalist dictum: "The world is awakening to the idea of union" (358). Hecker had developed his Transcendentalist interest in "union" from his close friendship with the Associationist George Ripley, who several years earlier had published the following description in the *Harbinger* of a Catholic mass he had attended: "It is to me the embodiment of that instinctive aspiration for unity, which the heart clings to so fondly, that not even the perversions of modern society,—of an antagonistic, dollar-worshipping, common-place age, can quite expel. I love to regard it as an anticipation of the choral harmonies of a better day."[33] To Hecker, as to Sophia Ripley, George Leach, and Sarah Stearns (the other Brook Farmers who converted), the Catholic church anticipated no such future unity but embodied it at the present moment. The church's various and interrelated forms of community, particularly the intercessory bonds between the living and the saints, led Hecker to admit at one point that he "seem[ed] to feel their presence much more intimately and really than that of those around me."[34] It was finally this supernaturally sensed community that disciplined Hecker's otherwise boundless communings with the spirit, for it provided (like Hawthorne's "ideal reader") a loving but manageably distant audience that enabled his vocation to emerge.

Writing home from Holy Cross College in June 1844, Hecker presented his decision to join the church in the familiar antebellum language of "influence": "There is a conviction which lies deeper than all thought or speech, which moves me with an irresistable influence to take this step, which arguments cannot reach, nor any visible power make to falter."[35] In light of Hecker's unorthodox plans, such language effectively removed his decision from the polemical (and family) arena that proved such a trial for both Seton and Ripley. Depicting himself as uncontrollably subject to such mysterious persuasions, Hecker skillfully thwarted any possible family attempts to dissuade him. To declare himself beyond the reach of family and friends, he portrayed himself as beyond his own reach. Throughout his ensuing Catholic career, Hecker frankly luxuriated in the indeterminate influences of his newfound church, for as he argued, the very susceptibility of human consciousness to apparently extramundane desires and influences was the most persuasive proof of God's existence; the truthfulness of Catholicism was correspondingly confirmed by the presence of these persuasive mysteries. Even to the antimystical Brownson, Hecker insisted on these vital forces as a necessary protection against the "charnal" vision typical in nativist depictions of a morbid Catholicism: "We feel ever an imperceptible influence in attending the mysteries of the Church. The mysteries of the Church are the mediums of the mystic life. A church without mysteries is without a Soul, a congregation of corpses."[36]

While still a new member of the church, Hecker recorded in his diary the continuing quandary that had precipitated his conversion, namely "how to live a life which shall be conformable to the life within and not separate from the persons and circumstances around me."[37] Following his brief stay at Brook Farm and his entry into the church shortly thereafter, he finally decided to train for the priesthood, sailing in 1845 for Europe, where, in Belgium, he took vows in the Congregation of the Most Holy Redeemer on October 15, 1846. After three difficult years struggling to apply himself to his studies, he was ordained a priest on October 23, 1849. Returning to America in January 1851, he became a missionary priest and writer, founding the Missionary Society of St. Paul the Apostle, known as the Paulists. In his books and articles, he practiced what he felt to be his divinely inspired urge to convert his fellow Protestants, convinced that the Calvinist repudiation of reason and of the redemptive potential of the body had no place in the optimistic ideology of the American Republic. Catholicism's defense of reason and its more cooperative relation between spirit and flesh, by contrast, made it the ideal religion for America. What he was up against is suggested by

Thoreau's rejection of Hecker's invitation to journey through Europe together on a pilgrimage to Rome: "I remember you, as it were, with the whole Catholic Church at your skirts. And the other day, for a moment, I think I understood your relation to that body; but the thought was gone again in a twinkling, as when a dry leaf falls from its stem over our heads, but is instantly lost in the rustling mass at our feet."[38]

Overcoming Thoreau's chilling dismissal, Hecker became an influential priest who held missions throughout America that often attracted large crowds. Having been released from his Redemptorist vows by the pope, Hecker in 1858 established his Paulist community, held together not by vows but by American republican principles of voluntary agreement. It was, in Hecker's view, the long-awaited solution to the problem of how to live in America: "The civil and political state of things of our age, particularly in the United States, fosters the individual life. But it should do so without weakening the community life: this is true individualism. The problem is to make the synthesis. The joint product is the Paulist."[39]

For many years, Hecker enjoyed success as a missionary priest and an interior life that brought him sustained and ardent spiritual happiness. He had long felt himself peculiarly blessed with intuitive apprehensions of the presence of the Lord, his angels, and his saints. As he himself frequently acknowledged, Catholicism gave structure and purpose to an otherwise undisciplined visionary nature that threatened to succumb to excesses of enthusiasm and passivity. But toward the end of his life, Hecker met with the terrors of spiritual dryness and the physical debility of what was probably chronic leukemia.[40] No longer could he find God within himself or the divine energy and glory he had celebrated for so many years. That "inseparable synthesis" between the "action of the Holy Spirit embodied visibly in the authority of the Church, and the action of the Holy Spirit dwelling invisibly in the soul" had broken apart.[41]

Father Hecker left New York in 1873 to travel in Europe, seeking out health spas and shrines. During these years he traveled up the Nile and returned to the Continent via the Holy Land. Still faithful to the church and to his brother Paulists, Hecker endured a profound loss of spiritual and physical vigor; writing from Switzerland in the autumn of 1874, he expressed his desolation over the loss of God's presence: "The only words which come to my lips are 'my soul is sad unto death' and these I repeat and repeat again."[42] Hecker's allusion to Hezekiah's lament, the same that Poe had selected to introduce his hero's plight in "The Pit and the Pendulum," shows his poignant descent into a suffering captivity, one mysteriously welded of bodily and spiritual exhaustion. Wandering in the vague and humiliating terrain of this ennui, he recorded in his memoranda the fracture of his sublimely integrated being into competing voices of lamentation and sardonic self-depreciation. "I used to say, Oh Lord! I feel as if I had the whole world on my shoulders; and all I've got to say is, Oh Lord! I am sorry you have given me such small potatoes to carry on my back. But now—well, when a mosquito comes in I say, Mosquito, have you any good to do me? Yes? Then I thank you, for I am glad to get good from a mosquito."[43]

Hecker continued his European travels, seeking to recover the spiritual consolations he had known so abundantly in his youth. Like Melville's Clarel, he painfully combined the tourist and the pilgrim, attempting to experience God in a wandering travail of sight-seeing, struggling in the seemingly inextricable bonds of a physical and spiritual malaise that greatly tested but did not destroy his faith. No longer directing his assured apologetics for Catholicism toward his benighted Protestant countrymen, Hecker took up a new genre, that of the captivity narrative:

> I have taken to writing fables. Here is one: Once upon a time a bird was caught in a snare. The more it struggled to free itself, the more it got entangled. Exhausted, it resolved to wait with the vain hope that the fowler, when he came, would set it at liberty. His appearance, however, was not the signal for its restoration to smiling fields and fond companions, but the forerunner of death at his hands. Foolish bird! Why did you go into the snare? Poor thing; it could not find food anywhere, and it was famishing with hunger; the seed was so attractive, and he who had baited the trap knew it full well, and that the bird could not resist its appetite. The fowler is our Lord. The bait is Divine Love. The bird is the soul. Oh skilfull catcher of souls! Oh irresistable bait of Divine Love! Oh pitiable victim! But most blessed soul; for in the hands of our Lord the soul only dies to self to be transformed into God.[44]

Returning to America, Hecker spent the last thirteen years of his life in an invalid state, sitting dejected and apart during community recreations, infrequently officiating at mass and doing so only with great emotional difficulty. According to his original biographer Walter Elliott, Father Hecker sought to avoid becoming oppressed with his fear of Judgment Day by "mending old clocks, a pretty well mended collection of which he kept in his room against such occasions."[45] Isaac Hecker died on December 22, 1888.

SEVENTEEN

Orestes Brownson:
The Return to Conspiracy

Threatened and perplexed by Catholic conversion, liberal Protestants typically trivialized the phenomenon. As the Transcendentalist James Freeman Clarke assured his readers in his critique of Orestes Brownson's conversion from Transcendentalism to the Roman faith: "The conversions to Romanism are mere eddies in the stream,—dimples of water turning backward, and showing thereby the power with which the main current is setting forward. For all reaction merely proves the strength of the action. It is the wave falling back a little, that it may return again, farther up the shore."[1]

But no one knew better than Brownson himself the enormous difference between all versions of Protestantism and Roman Catholicism or the energy it took to fight this "main current." He offered an extraordinary description of what lay behind his theological struggles:

> To pass from one Protestant sect to another is a small affair, and is little more than going from one apartment to another in the same house. We remain still in the same world, in the same general order of thought, and in the midst of the same friends and associates. We do not go from the known to the unknown; we are still within soundings, and may either return, if we choose, to the sect we have left, or press on to another, without serious loss of reputation, or any gross disturbance of our domestic and social relations. But to pass from Protestantism to Catholicity is a very different thing. We break with the whole world in which we have hitherto lived; we enter into what is to us a new and untried region, and we fear the discoveries we may make there, when it is too late to draw back. To the Protestant mind this old Catholic Church is veiled in mystery, and

leaves ample room to the imagination to people it with all manner of monsters. . . . We enter it, and leave no bridge over
which we may return. It is a committal for life, for eternity. To
enter it seemed to me, like taking a leap in the dark; and it is
not strange that I recoiled, and set my wits to work to find out,
if possible, some compromise, some middle ground on which I
could be faithful to my Catholic tendencies without uniting myself with the present Roman Catholic Church.[2]

Brownson failed entirely in his effort to find such a middle ground;
indeed, as a Catholic convert he developed a sustained career as a
vehement controversialist. For him, as for Hecker, the debate between
an autonomous subjectivity and an authoritative objectivity, the effort
to reunite nature and grace, was the core spiritual and epistemological
issue. As a convert, he fought strenuously for the legitimate place of
reason and objective reality in the spiritual life, arguing that to reject
reason was to eventually (and rather quickly) reject faith. "Unhappily,
the religious belief of my Protestant countrymen," he wrote in his 1857
spiritual autobiography *The Convert,* "as far as religious belief they
have, is built on scepticism, and hence, if they think at all, they have a
perpetual struggle in their minds between faith and reason."[3] For Brownson, such skepticism derived from the Kantian claim that the subject
finally determines the object; once dependent on subjective thoughts and
sensations, human consciousness will inevitably degenerate into the
mental and spiritual indifference of "modern pantheism, which represents God as realizing or actualizing himself in idea, idea as realizing itself
in the race, the race as realizing itself in individuals, and individuals as
realizing themselves in the act of thinking, that is, feeling, knowing, and
loving: a superb system of transcendental nullism."[4]

How to reconcile inner and outer, the individual and the community,
logic and intuition? Like Hecker's distaste for the "heathenish competition" of the business world, Brownson's initial motivation to join the
church was his quest for a just society; "it was not in seeking to save my
soul, to please God, or to have the true religion, that I was led to the
Catholic Church, but to obtain the means of gaining the earthly happiness of mankind."[5] Brownson's political reformism was closely but
problematically allied with a profound personal alienation from his local
New England culture. The son of an impoverished Vermont couple who
was given over to foster care between the ages of six and fourteen,
Brownson was indelibly imprinted by his orphaned youth, later claiming
that he had "had no childhood."[6] During his years as a Presbyterian, then
Unitarian, then Transcendentalist preacher and writer in New England,

he remained the outsider—accepted into the inner circles of the New England clergy and literati but never really one of them. If his intellectual project during these years was to reconcile subject and object through careful philosophical study of Kant, Victor Cousin, Benjamin Constant, and finally Pierre Leroux, he was also struggling to make himself at home in Boston's antebellum culture. Working to free himself from his filial dependence on William Ellery Channing, Brownson made an extraordinary confession of the isolation and lack of understanding he endured during these Boston years.

> In my happiest moments my thought has never been clear to myself, and I have felt that there was more in it than I had mastered. With more than tolerable powers of utterance, both as a speaker and as a writer, I have never been able to utter a thought that I was willing to accept when reflected back from another mind. Neither friend nor enemy has ever seemed to understand me; and I have never seen a criticism from a friendly or an unfriendly hand, with but one single exception, in which there was the remotest allusion to the thought I seemed to myself to have had in writing the piece criticized.[7]

Almost ten years prior to his conversion in 1844, Brownson had argued for the reunion of subject and object, spirit and letter in his *New Views of Christianity, Society, and the Church* (1836), where as a Unitarian he expounded, with passionate anti-Calvinist vagueness, his Church of the Future. Unlike Protestantism's excessive secularism or Catholicism's excessive supernaturalism, his church would unite spirit and letter and hence encourage the "illimitable progress" of a humankind that, like Jesus, would incarnate the progressive principles of divinity.[8] In his seminal letter, "The Mediatorial Life of Jesus" (1842), addressed to his "spiritual father" William Ellery Channing, Brownson first publicly repudiated this personal theology of Christian progress for a doctrine of "communion" derived from the ethical theories of Pierre Leroux. Against Channing's Unitarian stress on subjective individualism, Brownson now insisted on the more authentic reality of mediated existence and, following Leroux, argued that the individual lived only through communion with the other:

> Now man's object, by communion with which he lives, is other men, God, and nature. With God and nature he communes only indirectly. His direct, immediate object is other men. His life, then, is in himself and in other men. All men are brought by this into the indissoluble unity of one and the same life. All

become members of one and the same body, and members one of another. The object of each man is all other men. Thus do the race live *in solido,* if I may use a legal term, the objective portion of each man's life being indissolubly in all other men, and, therefore, that of all men in each man.[9]

Through this doctrine of communion adapted from the work of Leroux, Brownson argued himself into agreeing with the Christian dogma of Original Sin, for to him it was the objective nature of the human community that made logical the theological position on transmissible sin. Original Sin "is hereditary by virtue of the fact stated, that the preceding generation always furnishes the objective portion of the life of the succeeding generation, and without the objective portion the subjective portion would be as if it were not."[10] Brownson's doctrine of communion served as the turning point in his intellectual and spiritual career, for not only did it provide him for the first time with "a doctrine to preach," but it also persuaded him of the existence and necessity of the historical Christ: "And as he by living by the Father lives the life of God immediately, so they by living by him so live the life of God, mediately."[11] Thus this open letter to Channing (which Emerson termed "local and idolatrous"), in its thorough critique of individualism and perfectionism, entirely revised Brownson's former understanding of political reform.[12] Reform was no longer a matter of revolutionary action against the structures of a nascent industrial capitalism, as he had argued in his controversial essay "The Laboring Classes" (1840). Brownson now argued that man "cannot lift himself, but must be lifted, by placing him in communion with a higher and elevating object."[13]

But this new theology of communion did not mean that Brownson had no interest in the affective dimension of faith. On the contrary, his spiritual autobiography records an epiphanous discovery of God's freedom that meant in turn that he was "no longer fatherless," no longer "an orphan left to the tender mercies of inexorable general laws."[14] As a loving subjective force, this free God pierced through nature's objective order to rescue his child.

If to those outside the Protestant consensus its claims were obviously biased, from Brownson's Catholic perspective the nation's "truth" was deformed by the distortions of its own rampant individualism. As one Catholic journalist declared, public opinion in the United States was not a "product of our free institutions" but an "*olla podrida*" of old English prejudice, Irish party feeling, French infidelity, German rationalism and modern paganism [that] is decidedly against Catholics."[15] Brownson became the most significant spokesman for this Catholic counterconsensus view, devoting his polemical talents to elucidating and defending the "foreign Church" (and his doctrine of communion) to largely suspicious Protestant audiences in his own *Quarterly Review* and his two most significant literary ventures, *The Spirit-Rapper: An Autobiography* (1854) and *The Convert.*

As America's most prominent and vocal Catholic convert, Brownson readily detected and criticized the artfulness of such self-professedly realistic romantic historians as George Bancroft, William H. Prescott, and Francis Parkman. Having stepped outside the Unitarian-Transcendentalist circle by converting, Brownson knew firsthand the Brahmin culture from which their histories emerged. Liberal Protestant New England and its national historians alike suffered from dangerous self-deceptions from which Brownson himself had only recently been rescued. Subscribing to a view of the northern imperial genius considerably less sanguine than that of New England historians, Brownson berated them for their liberal Protestant or, worse yet, agnostic progressivism that transformed history into a chain of providential events—events that finally depended more on the ostensible "genius" of the Anglo-Saxon than on God or any instituted church. For its confusion of historical facts with "speculative science," George Bancroft's democratic Transcendentalism especially irked Brownson. Adept at turning the tables on his liberal adversaries, Brownson even hurled the traditional anti-Catholic accusation of idolatry at Bancroft: "The worship of humanity has taken, in the uncatholic world, the place of the worship of God, and become the dominant idolatry or superstition of the age."[16]

The accusation carried particular force in light of Prescott's and Parkman's shared fascination with Indian "idolatry" and Catholic "papadolatry." To what extent were their accounts a distorted reflection of their own Protestant or even agnostic idolatries? Brownson's subversive reading of Protestant historiography on America accused it of a covert agenda: the celebration of man's power over God, a celebration only faintly disguised by the historians' habitual reference to Providence. The nation that understood itself as singled out for especial sanctity, as righteously triumphant over the diabolic and the savage, was in Brownson's newly militant reality an atheist culture whose reformist essence was the true demon. Just as many anti-Catholic Americans were indulging in fantastic visions of papal conspirators subverting America's republican traditions, Brownson, for whom "Satan was the first Protestant,"[17] argued that Reformed Christianity was a global demonic plot against the pope and his flock. But such a potentially powerful critique of official culture did not inspire in Brownson any especial sympathy for conquered native groups. A strong nationalist, Brownson defended America's providential mission, simply insisting that it be a Catholic, not a Protestant one. Until America submitted to the dominion of Mother Church, its seeming victory over the diabolic would remain a self-delusion, the achievement of its Manifest Destiny a failed effort. Seeking to inspire (and advertise) American Catholic patriotism, Brownson argued that America's Manifest Destiny was available to Catholic immigrants as well as Protestant natives:

> Especially should [this manifest destiny] endear the country to every Catholic heart, and make every Catholic, whatever his race or native land, a genuine American patriot; for it is the realization of the Christian ideal of society, and the diffusion through all quarters of the globe, for all men, whatever their varieties of race and language, of that free, pure, lofty, and virile civilization which the church loves, always favors, and has from the first labored to introduce, establish, and extend, but which, owing to the ignorance, barbarism, and superstitions retained, in spite of her most strenuous exertions, from pagan Rome and the barbarian invaders of the empire, she has never been able fully to realize in the Old World.[18]

As a militant anti-Protestant, Brownson felt continuously compelled to challenge his New England culture's liberal assumptions and especially its increasing post-Calvinist optimism about humankind. "Man is not naturally progressive," Brownson insisted, opposing Emersonian romanticism and its efforts to divinize the human, if not humanize the Deity.[19] True Brownsonian progress could occur only through a human agency sanctioned and controlled by the Roman church. By the same reasoning, Catholic dogma, as a continuous and undistorted account of temporal and supernatural reality, provided the only starting point for an accurate American history. Reform theology, being of human fabrication, was necessarily biased and headed for extinction; Catholicism, being of divine origin, was impartial and eternal. "Facts are never to be feared," declared Brownson, "for they can never come into conflict with religion."[20]

In writing history himself, Brownson revealed a strong penchant for extravagant explanation that oddly mirrored the prior extravagances of such Protestant apologists as John Foxe and Cotton Mather. The age's skepticism and theological liberalism signaled nothing less than demonic possession. Brownson's own major attempt at narrative history, *The Spirit-Rapper: An Autobiography,* unfolds the story of an American social reformer who becomes an evil mesmerist and sets out to radicalize the world by hypnotizing its masses. In certain respects, the Spirit-Rapper represents Brownson's alternative and former self, whose liberalism is now diagnosed as pathogenic evidence of satanic possession. Not only does the mesmerist utterly fail in his insurrectionary schemes to perfect society, but his skills with animal magnetism also invite literal satanic invasion. Brownson's egomaniacal hero eventually confirms antebellum conservative progressivism: as Stowe and Thoreau also argued, no true social reform can occur without individual spiritual regeneration. Repenting his "demonic" radicalism, the mesmerist eventually converts to Catholicism, exposing his emancipatory politics as tyrannous egotism in disguise. Brownson's narrative trajectory from spiritualism to Catholicism enables a panoramic review of nineteenth-century Western culture, a reexamination of Transcendentalism, reformism, and spiritualism from the Roman perspective, his portrait of the radical mesmerist particularly aimed at the pretensions of liberal and utopian New England thought.

The most recent development in a long train of post-Reformation catastrophes, the spread of mesmerism powerfully indicated to Brownson the godlessness and consequent vulnerabilities of modern culture. To him, the lust to control and be controlled inevitably issued from an abandonment of Catholicism's ecclesiastical policy of sanctified authority and obedience; contemporary America, in its faddish pursuit of spiritualism, demonstrated the enslavement, not the advance, of Western culture. Brownson's curious book is one of the few historical texts to internationalize antebellum America, for in it he labored to demonstrate that theological liberalism and the European revolutions of 1848 were insidiously, indeed satanically, connected. For Brownson, a man of refined religious distrust, contemporary American fascination with mesmerism and spiritualism indicated a developing network of dangerous revolutionary trends: "The connection of spirit-rapping or the spirit manifestation, with modern philanthropy, visionary reform, socialism and revolutionism, is not an imagination of my own."[21]

Strongly influenced by Hawthorne's critique of mesmerism in *The Blithedale Romance*, Brownson in *The Spirit-Rapper* extended his deterministic Catholic analysis of his domestic culture to all Europe. In this sense, his text represents an ironic instance of the expansionism characteristic of American national politics. America's degeneration is now cast as part of a global struggle between Satan and Christ for control, not just of the New World, but of world history. Brownson's Catholic mouthpiece Merton explains to the Spirit-Rapper that the past is "little else but the history of the conflict between these invisible powers" (220). Brownson's Augustinian vision struggled against what he thought a hubristic progressivism that celebrated man's interventionist role in history. Such attempts, whether by mild philanthropist or wild revolutionist, would soon issue in the dominion of Satan, not Christ.[22]

But Brownson's energetic critique of the Spirit-Rapper's various forays into the avant-garde of socialism and spiritualism persuaded few readers. With studied contempt for Brownson's provocatively reactionary history, the Unitarian press found in the work "many old legends disinterred and exhibited as unquestionable truths."[23] Indeed, most of his New England readership was already convinced, in the wake of 1848, that European radicalism was as distasteful as European repression; there was little need to satanize its excesses. Certainly Brownson's argument that American reformism was conspiratorially connected to such foreign socialism was little more than dogmatic excess on his part. But it was less Brownson's attack on the occult than his proffered remedy that alienated his Protestant readership. Like many New England liberals, Emerson viewed the spiritualist craze as the "rat-hole of revelation" but hardly saw a return to ecclesiastical authority as the solution. And while Hawthorne's *Blithedale Romance* subtly exploited anti-Catholic anxiety in its portrait of the nunlike veiled Priscilla bonded by mesmerism to Westervelt/Hollingsworth, Brownson vigorously denied any such connection between monastic and mesmeric subordination. In stark contrast to Hawthorne's ironic vision, Brownson insisted that the Catholic church afforded the only reliable protection against a malleable human nature, one that Brownson, like the theoreticians of the new domesticity, understood as inherently susceptible to dangerous influences. As a convert, Brownson was himself no longer interested in accepting the compromised resistance to mesmerism offered by *The Blithedale Romance*. If Hawthorne's unchurched vision offered the petty and commingled servitudes of ordinary life in exchange for the exaggerated bondage of mesmerism, Brownson insisted on a reality free of both imprisonments. The church afforded refuge not only from Satan but also from the pressures of a desiring and dependent human nature.

Scorning Calvinism's simultaneous insistence on private judgment and human depravity, Brownson's Catholic vision argued for the utopian potential of a human reason guided by the church's teaching authority. Notwithstanding the original Fall, the historical church provided an avenue back into near-Edenic unity. Those who joined could recover soul, mind, and homeland all at once. Thus Merton, the novel's young Catholic layman, persuades the dying Spirit-Rapper that because the

Roman church fulfills the ancient tradition of monotheism, it is the vessel for true history and hence serves as man's most original home. Subsequent religious developments occurring outside the church's domain are at best flawed imitations of this original Catholic monotheism.

Brownson's historical vision provided a novel understanding of the reasons for declension and the possibilities for progress—novel, that is, to his antebellum Protestant readership. Against Prescott's and Parkman's argument for a providential American power, Brownson and other Catholic controversialists asserted a contrasting vision of apostasy and decline. This conservative Catholic position (one that strenuously advocated the papacy's own increasing conservatism), ironically resembled the "underground" vision of nineteenth-century culture articulated by such disaffected observers as Thoreau and Melville. Indeed, Orestes Brownson continued to support the radical social reformer Fannie Wright, notwithstanding his new defense of the pope. In its strenuous materialism and fractured allegiances, Protestant modernity was contaminated, if not demonically tinged, for such outsiders. Brownson's vociferous historical critique illustrated continued orthodox Catholic dismay with Reformed Christianity.

The Reformation, which Americans from John Winthrop on had seen as the European preamble to the settlement of America, was in truth a calamitous and perhaps a satanically inspired departure from Catholic unity. Instead of bringing liberation, the Reformation initiated a renewed and more terrible bondage to temporal powers from which emerged, in turn, the various maladies of nineteenth-century modernism, particularly the evils attendant on industrialism, political radicalism, and religious experimentation. As William Cobbett remonstrated in *The History of the Protestant "Reformation" in England and Ireland Showing How That Event Has Impoverished and Degraded the Main Body of the People in Those Countries* (1824): "What that is evil, what that is monstrous, has not grown out of this . . . Protestant 'Reformation!'"[24] Although Brownson disdained Cobbett's political subversiveness, regretting to "see any alliance of Catholics with vulgar radicals, whose proffered aid should be spurned rather than accepted," he basically agreed with and even amplified Cobbett's alarmist antimodernism.[25] If for the Anglo-American Cobbett such disturbing aspects of the Industrial Age as jails, factories, standing armies, poor rates and pauper houses, the stock exchange, and England's national debt all resulted haphazardly from the Reformation's destruction of the feudal order, this tangle of interrelated problems was menacing enough to Brownson to amount to a contemporary Protestant conspiracy. Arguing that the church was the only site for an authentic eternity *and* temporal history, Brownson concluded by 1854 that the opposition must necessarily be supernatural as well. Satan masterminded all historical forces that militated against Catholic unity. "Mahomet," Calvin, Knox, and Luther were no "hypocrites" but, like the Greeks and Romans, were "demonically infected." Leaders of the Puritan and French revolutions were alike "driven onward by infuriated demons" (*Spirit-Rapper,* 220).

The Reformation had traumatized human beings by cutting them off from history and leaving them exposed to a virulent present, according to the newly enlightened Spirit-Rapper. Thus does he diagnose his countrymen's faddish pursuit of mesmerism as a response to their displacement from the Catholic fold:

> They have been transplanted from the old homestead, are without ancestors, traditions, old associations, or fixed habits transmitted from generation to generation through a long series of ages. They have descended, in great part, from the sects that separated in the seventeenth century from the Anglican Church, which had in the sixteenth century itself separated from the Church of Rome, and to a great extent broken with antiquity. (15)

This three-century-old act of separation defines the Protestant temperament. Rootlessness, rebelliousness, and isolation are part of the Protestant's genetic equipment as the false creed blights each successive generation. Ironically, the only historical continuity in such a world is that provided by the devil, who in his interlocking conspiracies reorganizes, however fatally, the synthesis shattered by the Reformation.

If for Cobbett, England "became, under a Protestant Church, a scene of repulsive selfishness,"[26] for Brownson the Reformation produced an even more problematic modern character. Lutheran and Calvinist theology had not only spoiled the ethical nature of Americans but also deeply damaged their interpretive capacities, for the Reformation's rejection of authority opened up a "Pandora's Box" of unrestricted individual interpretations of the Word. Premised on the validity of private judgment, Protestantism finally reduced to the single absurd principle that "each and every man is in himself the exact measure of truth and goodness."[27] For Brownson, this fate (which was precisely Emerson's goal), led simply to disease; unless an absolute standard constrained the human mind, it would degenerate into chronic confusion and eventual nihilism. The Spirit-Rapper speaks as a typical Brownsonian Protestant casualty when he recalls of his secular days: "My freedom and inde-

pendence of mind were in denying, not in believing" (226). Neurosis as
well as eternal damnation inevitably result from such a life based on the
"infidel premise . . . that liberty is the absence of all restraints" (230).

Unlike the conspiratorial vision of anti-Catholic Protestants, Brownson's vision of satanic plots strangely protects human beings from serious
moral condemnation. In Brownson's cosmos, man is more victim than
villain, an unwitting dupe of the devil's machinations. Thus does his
imperialist supernaturalism produce a kind of tenderness toward human
foibles that adds dimension to his cultural critique. Having utterly repudiated any secular vision of human agency, Brownson deprives his
historical actors in *The Spirit-Rapper* of any innate power to change
history; when they manage such a feat, it is only thanks to Satan. By
contrast, progressive Protestants were increasingly dispossessing the
devil of agency; but as the ascendant historical agent, humanity unwittingly laid claim to malignant as well as divine attributes. Endowed with
such proto-numinous power, Americans could become agents of regress
as well as progress: it was supremely villainous humanity in the form of
scheming Jesuits, lecherous confessors, and despotic popes who frightened nineteenth-century Protestants.

Having suffered satanic invasion, Brownson's Spirit-Rapper finally
regains his senses when he converts to Catholicism. Continuing perfect-
ibility, the Unitarian-Transcendentalist program for American society,
eventually strikes him as a Sisyphean absurdity that deprives him of all
desire to continue living. Like Melville's Ishmael in *Moby-Dick,* the
Spirit-Rapper flirts with suicidal longings before being saved, not by a
sea voyage but by conversion. Like other antebellum Catholic apologists,
Brownson drew parallels between the integrity of the individual psyche,
the unity of the Catholic church, and the fate of the nation. Only by
becoming Catholic could America expect to heal those sectarian and
sectional disputes that threatened to disband the Union. The shattered
Spirit-Rapper prior to his conversion resembles antebellum America, an
imperiled nation, splintered by democratic liberalism into conflicting
ideologies, corrupted by materialism, enervated by rampant ecclecticism.
The material affluence and religious pluralism of mid-century life (which
many Americans were celebrating) only confirmed Brownson's orthodox
perspective. Unless bonded to the Lord and his one church, men and
women would inevitably suffer a cultural bondage, captured and enslaved by the sheer variety of contemporary ideologies.

Spurred by his converted perspective, Brownson used *The Spirit-
Rapper* to scrutinize marginal as well as significant nineteenth-century
movements, repudiating each in turn. If to the romantic historians most

events kept time to the progressive march, to Brownson post-Reformation history dimly and distortedly reflected an original but now abandoned Catholic unity. The past four centuries aped the true past. Protestantism disguised its atheism in a "livery stolen from Catholicity,"[28] and all that it produced was a false imitation. Such a view arrested the dynamism of Protestant liberation into repetitive historical examples of the demonic conspiracy to overthrow Catholicism. Brownson's "history" consequently depicts a curiously leveled nineteenth century, crowded and motionless like Irving's Westminster Abbey, each "liberal" event encased as a separate instance of demonic invasion. As this veteran of antebellum America's major cultural trends tours the ruins of his recent past through the persona of the mesmerist, one senses the profound alienation of his adopted Catholic sensibility from both past and present. Externalizing his isolation, Brownson assigns non-Catholics to a void resembling the one he himself endured as the alienated convert. The most adequate refuge from a present whose very essence is Protestant lies in the aggression of an obsessive polemical discourse.

Buoyed by the victory of Union forces in the Civil War, Brownson initially put forward a more optimistic diagnosis of American culture in his postwar political treatise *The American Republic: Its Constitution, Tendencies, and Destiny* (1865). As he reasoned in that work, America would eventually become Catholic because the country was "dialectically constituted, and founded on real Catholic, not sectarian or sophistical principles."[29] But this optimism soon subsided into the alienated vision that had characterized *The Spirit-Rapper.* The more secure Brownson's own rescue, the less he predicted salvation for his culture. While, like Hecker, he argued energetically throughout the 1850s that Catholicism and American democracy shared basic affinities and needed only each other to produce the just society on earth, his confidence finally wavered. By 1870 his politics of community had virtually repudiated the public sector for the sustaining interiors of Roman Catholic orthodoxy; Catholicism and democracy were fundamentally at odds with one another, the spirit and the flesh enemies once again. Convinced, finally, that America was to be "permanently Protestant," the aging Brownson concluded his career as a revisionist historian committed to the political relevance of a repudiated Catholic past.[30] Writing to Hecker in 1870, Brownson implicitly acknowledged that he had abandoned the project of a lifetime, the reunion of interior and exterior, self and culture.

> I defend the republican form of government for our country, because it is the legal & only practicable form, but I no longer

hope anything from it. Catholicity is theoretically compatible with democracy, as you and I would [e]xplain democracy, but practically, there is, in my judgment, no compatibility between them. According to Catholicity all power comes from above and descends from high to low; according to democracy, all power is infernal, is from below, and ascends from low to high. This is democracy in its practical sense, as politicians & the people do & will understand it. Catholicity & it are as mutually antagonistic as the spirit & the flesh, the Church and the World, Christ & Satan.[31]

Conclusion:
"Heaps of Human Bones"

The incorporation of Romanism into authorial domains of narratological complexity lies behind the era's most significant Protestant fiction of Rome: Hawthorne's *Marble Faun; or, The Romance of Monte Beni* (1859). The story of two American artists and their adventures in Rome, Hawthorne's novel has been judged the most ambitious failure of his career. In this final Hawthornian romance, religious difference figures not only as ethnic and existential alienation but, more damaging, as narrative crisis. Vagrant, alternately too controlled and insufficiently so, *The Marble Faun* represents a well-known dispersal of Hawthorne's aesthetic powers in the face of cultural and psychological conflicts that a decade before had produced great works of fiction. A similar constellation of antebellum issues—a longing for the Old World, a resistant embrace of Victorian patriarchy, a fascination with sexual crime and confession—"work" for *The Scarlet Letter* and against *The Marble Faun*. As the strange underside to the earlier masterly romances in which narrative ambiguity and secrecy create powerfully confidential texts whose characters are weighty in their evanescence, this last completed romance of Rome is narrated not by an artful dodger but by a voice that cannot seem to get out of the way and confides only conventions, not original literary creations. Certainly there was no lack of effort on Hawthorne's part, as he confessed to William D. Ticknor: "If I have written anything well, it should be this Romance; for I have never thought or felt more deeply or taken more pains."[1] Narrative inhibition over revealing the history of its characters and an often overtly expressed difficulty integrating the allegorical and the psychological, the pictorial and the dramatic make *The Marble Faun* a fascinating instance of a painstaking, ultimately failed, Protestant effort to comprehend Catholicism. If Hawthorne's earlier use of romance aimed at a purposeful, even aggressive, defamiliarization, the same techniques operate in his last completed romance as unwitting de-realization.

In contemporary cultural criticism of *The Marble Faun,* a vital language of crisis, conflict, and conclusion replaces that of the novel's own artificial and inconclusive speech. Recent readings include as relevant narratives of cultural crisis those at work in antebellum fears of conspiracy, or in the formation of the antebellum literary marketplace, or in the maintenance of middle-class marriage.[2] Hawthorne's conflicted expressions of emergent (and constricting) cultural forces of canon production or of the proliferating modes of gender necessary to middle-class companionate marriage are the significant features on which this new scholarship of repression focuses. The character of Hilda, high priestess of high art and exemplar of psychological and sexual sublimation, a character dubbed the Dove (Hawthorne's nickname for his wife, Sophia) illustrates the literary convergence of these differing modes of repression. Economic, political, and sexual coercion, in the logic of this recent cultural criticism, issues in the novel's own repressed aesthetic, one in which vitalized representations are excluded by psychologically (and culturally) motivated literary artifices that preclude the mimetic unreality of successful romance. The sheer unlifelikeness of Hilda's character (among others) ironically registers the authenticity of the extratextual cultural narratives at work behind her construction; if the novel is dead, there is a vital cultural life behind it that partially remedies its awkward impairments.

The narrative's fragmentations, although they are clearly disabled representations of various cultural and psychological forces of inhibition, have something further to tell us about how cultural and psychological problems can produce not only schism but also a stasis and artifice born of religious conflict. Differences in *The Marble Faun,* whether thematized in the hybrid figure of Donatello, or in the narratorial voices of tourism and fiction, or in the novel itself as writing, sculpture, and painting, are not in conflict so much as adjacent to one another, strenuously segregated from contact. In this novel, antebellum anxieties about sexuality and class produce a Roman romance that is hostile not only to the "flesh" but to itself as organic narrative. The contents of these extratextual cultural concerns spill over into the world of the text's own making, enough so that the narrative voice palpably resists creating an embodied text; as the narrator admits, his novel's "idea grows coarse, as we handle it, and hardens in our grasp" (10). Instead of constructing the illusion of autonomous story, Hawthorne's narrative voice recurrently intervenes to disrupt the mimetic relations it simultaneously struggles so hard to construct.

Hawthorne's inability to release his materials into an interactional space of representation, to allow them to *become aesthetic*, has arguably less to do with the various ideological issues mentioned than with the situation of those issues in Rome. In his preface to the novel, Hawthorne explains that he chose Italy as a "sort of poetic or fairy precinct, where actualities would not be so terribly insisted upon" (3), as a place, then, that would enable his romance to embody itself, as seventeenth-century Boston did for his making of *The Scarlet Letter*. But it turned out quite otherwise, for in selecting Italy, Hawthorne painfully tangled his own authorial practices with a competing, conspicuously religious, romance tradition: that of the antebellum Protestant encounter with Rome. Hawthorne selects this Protestant romance as the subject for his own romance techniques, his story recounting the stay of two young American (and very much Protestant) artists in Rome, their witness of a crime, the conventual captivity of the Protestant heroine, and finally their return home to marriage and homemaking.

But the recounting of this ultimately anti-Catholic romance unleashes a disabling narrative conflict. The Protestant romance tradition—one articulated by Elizabeth Seton as well as Maria Monk—interferes with Hawthorne's idiosyncratic romance techniques, those forged in his famous twelve-year seclusion from the world after college. For the Protestant romance of Rome endows the Eternal City, as we have seen, with an obdurate material excess, composed of heaps of ruins, images, and "ponderous remembrances" (6), a materiality resistant to translation, let alone to Hawthornian etherealization. Such a city precipitates an anorectic crisis in this American romance: after wandering the palaces, churches, and galleries of Rome, Hawthorne confessed in his notebooks to his "misery": to "see sights after such repletion is, to the mind, what it would be to the body to have dainties forced down the throat long after the appetite was satiated."[3] The Eternal City's aggressive, finally unassimilable, materiality in *The Marble Faun* suggests that its difference is entirely other than that of Hester Prynne's Boston, where sparseness paradoxically encloses a richness of sexual, theological, and political conflict. Italy, it turns out, is not a "fairy precinct" but the opposite: a region of excessive representation, of gorgeous, decadent, or even morbid representations of the body that clog the romance's efforts to distill and rearrange them. By mid-century, the Protestant romance tradition imaged both Italian and American Catholicism as a region of seductive but finally contaminated embodiment, there to intrigue and capture an ascetic Protestant spirituality with the tangible visual splendors of transubstantiation and of crucifixes inhabited by visually powerful bodies of Jesus—its various self-representations serving as embodiments that not only sensually engaged the Protestant tourist, as we have seen, but also rivaled the tourist who happened to be an author.

In Hawthorne's view, New England Protestantism was jointly compromised by the patriarchal repressions of Calvinism and the matriarchal coercions of Victorian Protestantism. Against both repressive parental alternatives, Hawthorne posited a postdenominational, overtly domestic language of "spirit" that dovetailed with his signature rhetoric of "romance" to create his "fairy precinct." This precinct is removed from the toxic embodiments of realism; but once situated in Rome (rather than, say, in Boston), these sexual, theological, and narrative vocabularies of "spirit" and (Hawthornian) "romance" form a style not of subversive de-realization but of orthodoxy, artifice, and literary inhibition. The narrative action, segregated from the place of its own telling by an anxiously intervening narrator, cannot etherealize its location into "fairy precinct" and so instead pictorializes it and hence excludes it from the narrative's verbal plane.

It is through this Protestant adventure with Romanism that Hawthorne images Rome as a monolithic corpse being slowly buried by time, as Capuchin cemeteries disgustingly crowded with monkish skeletons, as the sexualized interiors of confessionals and convents. His four tourist characters descend into the catacomb of St. Calixtus and "wandered by torch-light through a sort of dream, in which reminiscences of church-aisles and grimy cellars—and chiefly the latter—seemed to be broken into fragments and hopelessly intermingled" (24). These dismantled and commingled cellar images are not just those of emotional disturbance before embodiment but also those of a repulsed professional fascination with the representational practices of a foreign religion, whose foreignness depends on its uncanny familiarity as the parent religion to Protestantism. Hawthornian romance, the idiosyncratic construction of a symbolically saturated but always linear ideality that provocatively resists the confusions of "actuality," tries in *The Marble Faun* to subsume this engagement with Romanism in plot and scenic precinct. But Romanism's self-representational powers as theme continually threaten to overwhelm Hawthorne's own romance powers as technique. Hence our narrator, besieged by the Eternal City's rival authorial splendors, remorselessly deadens Rome—not just by pathologizing it as corpse but by artificializing it with didactic literary conventions that deny it membership in the suggestive representational space of New England romance.

Rome's materiality and provocative representations urge the narrative, not into an evasive and symbolically resonant asceticism (the logic of *The Scarlet Letter*), but rather into an obsessive self-purification and self-regulation, obsessions registered in the recurrent appeal to melodramatic event, stylized dialogue, obtrusive narrative interventions, and overguided interpretation. To write a Hawthornian romance about a Protestant romance in Rome demands a narrative vigilance over this Roman subject matter, "rising foglike from the ancient depravity of Rome, and brooding over the dead and half-rotten city" (412); there can be no mixings and distillations with this "fog," no etherealizations, but rather only anxious segregations, not only of the teller from the tale but also of the action from the setting. The novel's recurrent musings on transformation and interchangeability between animate and represented beings signal precisely the absence of such transformative powers in the novel, formally speaking.

The Marble Faun, then, is a post-Calvinist seeing into, gazing onto, and internal speculation on its own romance of Roman Catholicism. Thus viewed as a competitive aesthetic, Rome cannot deepen the antebellum Protestant representational space of this novel, as it does in *Middlemarch* or *The Portrait of a Lady*, but instead crowds into and engulfs it. Overpoweringly "real," this Catholic background for the novel's action is therefore forced constantly back into the pictorial and didactic, then to the implausible, and finally into the disjoined, as the narrative itself is dismembered into "the fragments of a letter, which has been torn and scattered to the winds" (92–93). Assimilation of this Roman context can only go so far as a qualified Protestant appropriation of Catholic vocabulary, an appropriation still so risky that the narrator feels himself compelled to take it from his own character. Thus Kenyon cannot reflect on meeting a veiled penitent, a foreign religious figure, without suffering the Protestantizing intervention of his narrator: "It occurred to him that there is a sanctity (or, as we might rather term it, an inviolable etiquette) which prohibits the recognition of persons who choose to walk under the veil of penitence" (393). Thus the narrator enforces religious difference by renaming "sanctity" as "inviolable etiquette," cordoning off his Protestant American character from even this fleeting exploration of Catholic practice. These parenthetical interventions accumulate to damage the mimetic aura of Hawthornian romance; with them, Kenyon lapses into a fictional artifact that cannot compete with the projected charismatic lure of Catholic artifacts. Kenyon's overtly contrived quality bespeaks Hawthorne's efforts to rival Catholic representation with the purified representation of his romance techniques. But having given over all the powers of embodiment to Rome, his only representational recourse is toward the dubious purity of convention and metafictional interruption. Kenyon and his friends thus wander, not through Rome but through the pages of the book.

Catholicism is further refused access to the temporal narration and the narrator's own belief in his narrative when cordoned off into gently mocked convention. Thus the narrator imagines Hilda in a convent where "Innocence might shriek in vain" (412). As the taboo site designed to make palpable Hilda's studiously pure Protestant sensibility, one that might otherwise have great difficulty knowing and sensing itself, the convent interior as a scene of captivity makes Protestant subjectivity real to itself: substantial yet pure. Structured by conventions of diseased or seductive embodiment, this unredeemed matter of convent and confessional enabled Protestant tourists, authors, ministers, and readers to reformulate their felt sense of emptiness, ghostliness, and weakness as energized, form-making purity. *The Marble Faun*, however, displays the novelistic difficulty of this enterprise.

The disturbance arises in incorporating this Protestant dynamic of self-substantiation as a convention, one whose acknowledged artifice will illuminate the originality and aesthetic power of Hawthornian romance. But even incorporated as convention, Hilda's confessional and convent captivities are engaged with a Catholicism still imagined as overpoweringly original and toxic. Rome, particularly the Rome of the catacombs and monastic burial grounds, verges beyond metaphor into the literal embodiment of decaying flesh and bones. It doesn't stand for, it *is* the region of creative mixture, of excessive materiality that Hawthornian romance must distill. Hence the characters are ghostlike, not saintlike, continually on the point, not of an aesthetic disciplining of matter, but of simply vanishing within it or falling into and finally under it. As Miriam explains to Hilda in reference to Curtius's chasm: "A footstep, a little heavier than ordinary, will serve; and we must step very daintily, not to break through the crust, at any moment. By-and-by, we inevitably sink!" (162). Miriam's perilous walk across the artificial surface of life, a covert critique of Victorian womanhood, offers a picture of dainty stepping that will fail, notwithstanding the vigilance, deference, and delicacy of her transit. Miriam's bodily self-control of her fleshly weight and anger not only dramatizes Victorian American sexuality but also mirrors the narrative's fearful clinging to its own surface, its reluctance to engage with its setting, its apprehensiveness at its impending engulfment.

Religious difference between the Protestant narrator, Kenyon, and Hilda, on the one hand, and the Catholicized regions of plot, of setting, and of the hybrid characters Donatello and the Model, on the other, enforces the novel's unintegrated generic differences and finally propels the narrator's efforts to escape his own fiction, to seek respite from a narrative whose material elements are imaged as oppressive Catholic clutter. Thus in the Capuchin cemetery the narrator intrudes himself between his characters and their setting, forbidding them (and hence the reader) any unmediated contact with the narrative moment while voicing his own need to look from and outside his own fiction. "The cemetery of the Capuchins is no place to nourish celestial hopes; the soul sinks, forlorn and wretched, under all this burthen of dusty death. . . . Thank Heaven for its blue sky; it needs a long, upward gaze, to give us back our faith! Not here can we feel ourselves immortal, where the very altars, in these chapels of horrible consecration, are heaps of human bones!" (194).

The ideological motivations behind this antebellum Protestant romance of a bone-filled Catholicism force the narrator to overthematize the distinctions between his evanescent characters and their corporeal environment. Such didactic excess is meant to dramatize the vitality, agency, and substance of their spiritual purity in the face of Catholicism's multiple sensory representations. But this liberal, virtually postdenominational Protestantism feels acutely its own disabled incarnational powers, and thus it authors its romance of Rome in the hopes that it might vicariously identify with Rome's incarnational powers, not to possess but to deny them. Thus Hawthorne imagines a magically efficacious Catholicism in which confession is a bodily restorative: afterward, penitents rise, "unburthened, active, elastic, and incited by fresh appetite for the next ensuing sin" (412). Such an envious portrait of resilience, appetite, and unburdened selfhood automatically expels these Catholic worshipers from the "real" of prior Hawthornian romance, constituted opposingly of burden, torpor, and sinfulness.

Theologically and spiritually split in its narrative structure, *The Marble Faun* is in a religiously fearful relation with itself as narrative. Defensively positioned on the borders of his own story, the narrator maintains his telling of the Protestant romance by reducing Catholic Italy to a "land of picture." A tremendous not-seeing is necessary to keep Italy at this distance, to keep it there in such a way that it cannot participate in the action, repeatedly killed off to unleash the self-purifying mobility of Protestant subjectivity. But it is precisely that self-purifying mobility—a trait enabled by the religious romance tradition—that disrupts the authenticity of Hawthornian romance by advertising the "writtenness" of the characters. Their ideological verisimilitude, in other words, cancels their fictional persuasiveness.

Thus Hilda's liminal position between New England Protestantism and Italian Catholicism, her tending of the Virgin's shrine, her transit through confessional and convent, and her sympathetic copying of the Old Masters, does not signal the breakdown of religious antipathies, finally, but their continuance in the form of narrative crisis. It is not just that she purifies corrupt environments by passing through them without being passed through but that such touristic impenetrability is encoded in the artifice of Hawthorne's depiction of her character. And thus we have Kenyon stultify what little representational vitality remains to Hilda's disappearance by enclosing the episode within the weary platitudes of convent incarceration.

The novel's Catholicism, then, is a hybrid construct disjointedly composed of visually described artifacts and a series of unconvincingly narrated episodes. This discourse yokes a threatening, eroticized materiality—repulsive altars of bones and fat "leering" priests—with the unreal literary conventions of confessional and convent captivity, a hybrid vision fashioned from divisions internal to Hawthorne's own spirituality: his post-Calvinist sympathy for an anciently suppressed Catholic materiality, maternalism, and ceremony and his ethnic, regional, and sexual distaste for contemporary Italian (and Irish) Catholic practices and urban spaces. The religious anxieties that motivate Hawthorne's flattening of Rome into a touristic prose of pictorialized units and the conventions of confessional and convent captivity narrative disable the renowned powers of his voyeurist prose. In this final, failed, romance, the voyeur-narrator images Roman Catholicism as the secret interior to his fiction, but he wants not only to stay outside but to look outside. Thus he moves Hilda through Catholicism's secret spaces while resolutely thwarting his own engagement with these episodes. Hawthornian interiority gives way to the artifice of interiority at the conventional heart of anti-Catholic romance, a convention that functions aesthetically and politically to maintain a surface relation to the foreign faith. That surface relation prevents authentic contact, hence any genuinely dimensional representation of Protestant character in a Catholic setting, and as a result the narrative stays supremely on its own surface, both formally and ideologically. Its melodramatic imaging of Catholicism as illicit bodily interior that empowers a purified Protestant subjectivity—an ideological positioning that is shaped by the conventions of anti-Catholicism—forbids precisely what Hawthornian romance requires: a contact of character, setting, and narrator so commingled that it can risk the repeated evasions and concealments of narrative disembodiment.

The novel's generic crises of boundary between description and narration, between the visual space of artifacts and the verbal space of storytelling, between the obtrusive autobiographical voice of tourism and the ideally evasive voice of romance testify finally to a barely survived competition of religiously discordant powers of representation. Hawthornian romance ingests but cannot assimilate Italy as Romanism. For all his effort, Hawthorne's construction of a representational interior for *The Marble Faun* using the material of foreign religious interiorities led inescapably to the surface conventions and stasis of religious difference.

The double exhibition of what seems almost like two
religions . . .
> "Modern Saints, Catholic and Heretic,"
> North American Review, 1853

The Catholic-Protestant debate produced a generically diverse literature, one preoccupied with issues of imitation, appropriation, and sometimes subversive doubling.[4] The uncanny sense of a suppressed identification between Catholic and Protestant implicit in Prescott's history of the sacerdotal Aztec and Parkman's of the Jesuit missionaries, like Hawthorne's disabled ruminations on Rome, underscores the complexity of masculine Protestant affinities to a Catholicism imagined as antidote to and rival of a (virile) purity harbored within. The writings of Mother Seton and Sophia Ripley testify in their turn to a repudiation of the felt emptiness and inhibitions of Protestantism for the intensities of a female expression conspicuously different from the constraints of domesticated sentiment. "By *the heart*," wrote Mother Seton toward the end of her life, "we understand the most secret part of the Soul, Where joy, and sadness, fear, or desire, and whatever we call sentiments or affections is formed— then the love of God *in the heart* is that sweet attraction which draws us incessantly to him."[5] Seton's efforts to keep the affections of the heart connected to those of the soul remain a saintly eccentricity in nineteenth-century culture, which moved steadily toward their separation, a separation that in large part motivated Protestantism's entanglements with the sentimental attractions and menace of Romanism.[6]

In 1847 Brownson, in a rhetorical performance that was one of the age's most haunting expressions of the convert's investment in his secular double, appealed to Emerson to leave off Satan and embrace God:

> One who was as proud as thyself, and who had wandered long
> in the paths thou art beating, and whose eye was hardly less

keen than thy own, and who knew by heart all thy mystic lore, and had as well as thou pored over the past and the present, as well as thou had asked

> The fate of the man-child
> The meaning of man,

and had asked the heavens and the earth, the living and the dead, and in his madness, hell itself, to answer him, and whose soul was not less susceptible to sweet harmonies than thy own, though his tones were harsh and his speech rude,—nay, one who knows all thy delusions and illusions, assures thee that thou shalt not in this be deceived, and thy confidence will not be misplaced or betrayed.[7]

Alternately imperious, visionary, and brotherly, Brownson's promise to Emerson verbalizes the multiple tensions of antebellum Catholic conversion. If Brownson had been initially deceived by Emerson, he would not deceive in turn; the convert's precarious management of his own disappointed love depends, finally, on exposing Emerson rather than himself as the vulnerable child who is afraid to extend his trust and who is fearful of adult betrayal. As a Christian who has found his true father, Brownson refrains from exercising his child's rage against the teacher whose Transcendentalist wisdom had betrayed his confidence. But as the liberated underling, he speaks a language of precarious charity as well. Directed to the ideologue of independent manliness, Brownson's invitation to Emerson is an instance of expertly tailored rhetorical irony, the competitive pressures of the exchange between the convert and his Emersonian "double" all the more poignant in light of Brownson's lifelong admiration for Emerson.

Inverting stereotypical anti-Catholic imagery of spellbinding priests and deluded worshipers, other Catholics asserted that it was Protestants, not themselves, who suffered from the mesmerist bonds of false belief. As Brownson had suggested to Emerson and as he advertised in *The Spirit-Rapper*, Protestants were victims of their own conspiratorial vision, which needlessly alienated them from Rome and rendered them pathetic (and dangerous) orphans. Another Catholic commented on the propagandizing of Protestants with lies about the Holy Church: "This is only, or mainly to be deplored on account of the poor victims who are duped and deluded; yet who, at the very moment . . . are betraying the symptoms of those who think themselves the *witnesses* of a delusion practiced upon others, and not the subjects of it themselves, as in fact they are."[8] In his influential indictment of Brownson's conversion, the Transcendentalist James Freeman Clarke had himself resorted to a similar rhetoric of projection and doubling, arguing that "It is an old trick of proselytes to ascribe to the party they have left, all the blunders and errors which were peculiar to themselves. . . . [Brownson] believes himself to be describing the gyrations of Protestantism, when he has given us merely the natural history of his own intellectual instability."[9]

The mimetic dynamics of this Protestant quarrel with Catholicism are well illustrated not only in criticisms of conversions but also in short fiction like "My Confession," published in *Harper's New Monthly Magazine* in 1855, a tale that captures the peculiar embarrassments of the rivalry.[10] The narrator recounts how as a child he accidentally murdered his best friend and thereafter endured a tormented inability to confess his crime, "the secret always . . . clogging on my tongue" (767). Like the deep ambivalence toward Elizabeth Seton, whom one writer elsewhere described as a "lovely woman, possessed of almost genuine and undoubted piety, yet whose mind, in many respects so clear and luminous, 'rayed out darkness' of the intensest quality wherever penance was in question," this *Harper's* story debates the legitimacy of bodily mortification and the possibility of expiation.[11] Although the narrator becomes a devoted doctor in hopes of atoning for his crime, he still wonders whether "deeds of reparation [could] dispel that darkness which a mere objectless punishment—a mere mental repentance—could not touch" (768). The answer is both yes and no; for through his medical skill, he heroically saves the life of a young woman to whom he is mysteriously drawn, and who, predictably enough, turns out to be his murdered friend's twin sister. Thus mythic themes of doubling, expiation, and sacrifice serve to articulate the incestuous nature of antebellum Protestant struggles with the Catholic rival.

Casting off his professional authority, the doctor kneels before his patient and confesses his childhood crime. Although quickly forgiven by the redemptive mercy of the female invalid, he carefully emphasizes that this is a Protestant, not a Catholic, scene: he is forgiven, but not absolved. He didactically insists that his crime "still shades my life; but as a warning, not as a curse—a mournful past, not a destroying present" (769). Such blunt distinctions record his simultaneous disavowal of the burden of a Protestant sin that can never be relieved by confession and repudiation of the Catholic doctrine of absolution. From his conflicted appropriation and dismissal of the confessional emerges a brave (although somewhat unconvincing) pre-Freudian resolution: "Work and love: by these may we win our pardon, and by these stand out again in the light" (769).

The pressure toward trivialization imposed by such simplified contrasts between "Catholic" penance and "Protestant" repentance at times
resulted in overtly absurdist pieces. Four years after "My Confession,"
Harper's published "One of the Nunns," which again approached the
alternative discourse of Catholicism through the theme of the double.[12]
Undoubtedly influenced by Poe's "Pit and the Pendulum," this story
unfolds in a context of improbable, even ludicrous, captivity: the narrator, a young journalist, describes how he climbed inside the huge bell
of Notre Dame Cathedral in Montreal—one in a long line of American
tourists fascinated by the immensities of a Catholic "interior." The
reporter succeeds in his attempt to examine the inside of the bell but
emerges slightly injured, and a girl whom he has been told is "one of the
nuns" nurses him back to health. The mystery of her identity is comically
developed. When sailing back to America, he unexpectedly encounters
her and says that he thought her "a real nun; not only by name, but—."
To his perplexed silence she coyly responds: "Oh, no Sir; I am none-
such" (805). This confusion of names, like that of Maria Monk, mirrors
the commingled taxonomies at the heart of Protestant Romanism. End-
ing on the hint of possible marriage between the two, this vaguely
Shakespearean moment of mistaken identity reduces religious schism to
punning farce, the image of the nun yielding finally to the culturally
ascendant perception that behind nuns lurked the specter of "none-such"
and nothingness.

Reviewing the Reverend Charles White's 1853 biography of Elizabeth Seton, the *North American Review* used the occasion to contrast
female Catholic saintliness to its Protestant counterpart in the Unitarian
Mary Lovell Ware. Widow of the Reverend Henry Ware, Mary Ware
lived a life of charitable labors, suffering all the while a personal life full
of illness and the tragic loss of children. Fascinated by the prodigious
goodness of both Seton and Ware, the writer approvingly notes that
both meet his anticontemplative specifications for pragmatic labor in
the world. "The Saint is especially a worker. He is somebody who *does*
something; not who fasts, or prays, or talks, or preaches merely, but
who does what he finds to do for his fellow-creature."[13] The similarity
between the two "saints" however, begins and ends there, for what
ensues is an extended rumination on the factors that explain the extreme differences between the two women—differences that continually
threaten to topple Seton from the "niche" provided for her by the
conspicuously tolerant author. Having declared that "canonization is
not, in our day, the privilege of popes and counsels" (149), the author
labors to discredit the Catholic church that produced the excessively

penitential but still admirable Seton: "But the system, with its will-worship, its egotism under the transparent disguise of self-abasement, its passionateness, induced by a friction no less obvious than that by which we heat sealing-wax til it will attract to itself all the needle-points that are near enough—this is what strikes us painfully throughout the account of Mrs. Seton's life, her sufferings, her labors and her excellencies" (159). Intent on proving that each sect has its "own natural, inseparable genius" (165), the author then unreservedly celebrates the "cool" saintliness of Mary Ware.

Such predictable defenses of a temperate Protestantism yield in turn to an intriguing moment of authorial identification with both women when the author attempts to imagine their attitudes toward one another, independent of his masculine evaluation. Mrs. Seton, he theorizes, would have mourned for Mrs. Ware "all the more surely lost for those deluding virtues which would soothe the conscience that needed rather wounding; while Mrs. Ware, calm, reasonable, and self-governed, would look with a tender pity, scarcely consistent with respect, on the dramatic virtues and ecstatic devotions of the more tropical Saint" (165). What produced such a fascinating "double exhibition" (165)? Could such radical distinctions possibly emerge from a single Christianity? Or was Christianity itself producing progeny each with its own "natural, inseparable genius" (165)? Faced with such riddles, the author resorts finally to the influence of family heredity, suggesting that if each woman had had the other's childhood environment, their characters would have been accordingly modified. The author speculates that Seton's ardent piety was a temperamental and environmental inheritance from her good but "violent" father, while Ware's father, shy, delicate, and literary, similarly imprinted himself on the reserved saintliness of his daughter. Thus does the author suggest, as Holmes argued in *Elsie Venner,* that Catholicism and Protestantism are finally derivative systems obeying the superior determinant of heredity. Paternal (not maternal) inheritance is the true influence and one that operates more powerfully than individual aspirations or institutionalized theologies, an argument that effectually displaces the transformative influence of supernatural grace and conversion with that of heritable bodily transmissions. Dispelling the threatening specter of two religions and their competing communities, such a biological view translates the issue of salvation or damnation into that of family heredity and nurture. Thus the two "saints" are doubles in the safe sense that all human beings are alike while the dread sense that their "double exhibition" might signify a profound metaphysical disagreement is gingerly laid aside.

The proximity between the physical and moral not only elucidates the frightened assessments of Catholic power but also suggests the impending redescription of all religion in terms originally dedicated to ostracizing Catholicism. Already in 1833, George Ripley (then a Unitarian minister) was using the dogma of transubstantiation to discuss what to him seemed the even more irrational notion of the Trinity. In his letter to a Trinitarian friend, *The Doctrines of the Trinity and Transubstantiation Compared,* Ripley argued that the Trinity had even less scriptural basis than transubstantiation. In his Unitarian view, the Trinity emerges as yet another Catholic idea, one surrounded by the appropriate rhetorical imagery of fictionality and rank fertility: "I should place it among those fictitious creatings, of a strange fancy, of which the dark ages were fertile."[14] The dilemma such a position could lead to surfaced even in Bishop William Whittingham's bewildered and indignant question about how to proceed if one indeed still felt the power of the spirit:

> Must we be claimed as advocates for monkery with all its abominations, or for Jesuitism with its unspeakable iniquities, because we laud the "Catholic feelings" of self-renunciation, mortification, subjection of the individual will, and devotion to the life and work of Christ, that furnished the spark of life with which these monsters stalked abroad to conquest?[15]

Whittingham's somewhat rhetorical question suggests the developing cultural perception that religion in any form was beginning to participate not only in the pathologies of Catholicism but in those of the body as well.

Edward Beecher's evangelical attack on the evil organizational genius of the Roman church ironically anticipates this same fear that religion in any form is diseased. "For holy as religion is, all the bad passions gather about its perverted standard, and under the sanctions of its hallowed name, and by all the augmented motives of eternity, let loose the malignant passion of the desperately wicked heart."[16] Beecher's unease about the unsavory aspects of religion qua religion led many in postbellum America to deny religion any place whatever in developing taxonomies of what constituted the healthy human being. The "mental physiologist" William Carpenter argued, like Holmes in *Elsie Venner,* for a new unity of mind and body against the harmful dualisms of metaphysics, claiming in his *Principles of Mental Physiology* that "it is the high prerogative of Science to demonstrate the *unity* of the Power which is operating through the limitless extent and variety of the Universe, and to trace its *continuity* through the vast series of ages that have been occupied in its evolution."[17]

In this newly scientific controversy about the role of the body (not the spirit) in the evolutionary production of union, Catholicism's incarnational theology presented a unified discourse that still bore a strange resemblance to the new physiology, for it too was self-perpetuating, mysterious, yet accessible to rational exploration. But when the British "mental pathologist" Henry Maudsley (1835–1918) published his *Body And Mind: An Inquiry into Their Connection And Mutual Influence, Specifically in Reference to Mental Disorders* in an effort to dispel "the metaphysical haze which still hangs over the functions of the supreme centres," he spoke like Oliver Wendell Holmes against all religion in the terms of a transposed Calvinism. "Multitudes of human beings come into the world weighted with a destiny against which they have neither the will nor the power to contend; they are the step-children of Nature, and groan under the worst of all tyrannies—the tyranny of a bad organization."[18] As Elsie Venner's death makes clear, the physicalization of the doctrine of Original Sin was hardly a liberation, the transition from the confinements of theology to the captivity of the body still creating an unduly coercive community, one now of an uncontrollable heredity. In "The Anatomist's Hymn," Holmes bids readers look for God neither in the world outside nor in the traditional, if fearful, interior of the soul, but in the new, sacralized space of the body itself: "Look in upon thy wondrous frame,— / Eternal wisdom still the same!" In Holmes's anti-creedal celebration, the body emerges as the new pastoral landscape, one whose automatic processes of self-purification remove it from its prior religious associations with corruption:

> The smooth, soft air with pulse-like waves
> Flows murmuring through its hidden caves
> Whose streams of brightening purple rush
> Fired with a new and livelier blush,
> While all their burden of decay
> The ebbing current steals away,
> And red with Nature's flame they start
> From the warm fountains of the heart.[19]

Although the biological heart is now the fountainhead for this new sacred, a sacred that is warm, pure, and effortlessly autonomous, it still is a "slave" to its task, its freedom from external authority consigning the person to the new constraints of gratitude for (and fear of) invisible processes of circulation. Like the woman at the hearth of the 1850s domestic novel, Holmes's heart nourishes and ennobles but can never leave its task, its own captivity disguised beneath its cleansing powers. After marveling at the body's strong exterior that protects its inward flame, the poet goes on to portray this wondrous human as a chained beast, one ceremonialized with Homeric imagery, but captive nonetheless:

> Its living marbles jointed strong
> With glistening band and silvery thong,
> And linked to reason's guiding reins
> By myriad rings in trembling chains,
> Each graven with the threaded zone
> Which claims it as the master's own.

In this celebratory anatomy, we still ponder whether the flesh is a sacred mediation of spirit or a site for renewed captivity. Although the poet applauds the body's capacity to produce that quintessential Protestant product—white light—from the spectrum of deviant color, this very act of purification is still one of authoritarian control:

> See how yon beam of seeming white
> Is braided out of seven-hued light,
> Yet in those lucid globes no ray
> By any chance shall break astray.

The body struggles here to assert its new primacy within the terms of an abandoned sacred and its attendant evils. Thus Holmes's celebration of the "cloven" brain is still mediated through an ancient Luciferian imagery. The brain's covert identification with the devil's proverbial cloven hoof transposes into another dubious image of an abandoned religious interiority—the "cell." The word's traditional associations with asylum or monastery chambers cling to Holmes's new conception of the cerebral landscape as an electrical field; the brain of "The Anatomist's Hymn" advertises biologized powers still structured according to a pictorial tradition reminiscent of Protestantism's vision of Catholicism: a light-infused but dim interior that encloses within it monastic intensities:

> Think on that stormy world that dwells
> Locked in its dim and clustering cells!
> The lightening gleams of power it sheds
> Along its slender glassy threads!

Holmes's use of what we recognize as imagery born of profound theological conflict in the decades prior to the Civil War points to the developing postbellum conviction that religion was in fact only an analogy to the more genuine and pressing concerns of human physiology and psychology. Melville's 1876 poem of religious quest, *Clarel,* in its depiction of a tour to the Holy Land, deposits its readers in a sterile Palestinian landscape that insists on the desiccation at the heart of theology. Melville's Holy Land is not so much putrescent, like antebellum descriptions of Rome that focus on the charnel aspects of Christendom, as utterly sterile, empty even of decomposing flesh. In the step beyond Rome to Palestine, the evidences for a true Christianity vanish in *Clarel*'s bleached and bone-filled landscape. As an extended example of the postbellum Protestant movement toward and through a sacred past, Clarel's directionless pilgrimage embodies the anxiety of a theological search that has become futile before it has even begun. His exploration of the historical Jerusalem's barrenness suggests the weariness of his search, the terrible irrelevance of any incarnational aesthetic. If such futility is also the generating motive for Melville's postwar poetry, the repeated failure of the poem's characters to find resolution forming the very material of his plot, it offers an image of what would become the paradox of so much postbellum fiction, an ambiguous indebtedness to the faith it eschewed, the duress of literary creation a mimesis of the rigors of prayer but certainly not that activity itself. Maudsley's Victorian resignation is one Melville shared; it is a resignation to a postreligious cosmos—"The cage may be a larger or a smaller one," ventures Maudsley of his physiological vision, "but its bars are always there."[20] Such a sensibility is entirely different from that of antebellum Americans, for whom captivity, and even the bars of the cage, always promised to dissolve into the light with the resolution of theological dispute.

Notes

1. The single most significant book on American antebellum Catholicism remains Ray Allen Billington, *The Protestant Crusade 1800–
1860,* first published in 1938. Brownson's essay "The Laboring Classes"
is reprinted in Perry Miller, ed., *The Transcendentalists,* 436–46.

2. Horace Bushnell, *"Barbarism the First Danger": A Discourse for
Home Missions,* 24. My investigation of what Catholicism meant to the
antebellum Protestant imagination is indebted to Edward W. Said's
Orientalism, an inquiry into the imaginative contours and political functions of Orientalism for the European mind, functions that exceed "mere
political subject matter or field" to constitute a range of discursive
gestures, "a certain *will* or *intention* to understand, in some cases to
control, manipulate, even to incorporate, what is a manifestly different
(or alternative and novel) world" (12).

3. David Brion Davis, "Some Themes of Counter-Subversion: An
Analysis of Anti-Masonic, Anti-Catholic, and Anti-Mormon Literature," in David Brion Davis, *From Homicide to Slavery: Studies in
American Culture* (New York: Oxford University Press, 1986); Richard
Hofstadter, *The Paranoid Style in American Politics and Other Essays*
(New York: Random House, 1967). A recent application of the "conspiratorial" and "paranoia" thesis to nineteenth-century American literature is Robert S. Levine, *Conspiracy and Romance.* For a fine piece
arguing that conspiratorial thought was natural to the Enlightenment
pursuit of understanding human motivation, see Gordon S. Wood,
"Conspiracy and the Paranoid Style." The great benefit of this essay is
that it does not stigmatize conspiratorial thought but instead illuminates
it as a logical outgrowth of the eighteenth-century celebration of ratio-

nality. For Bishop England's discussion of the nicknames for Catholicism, see *The Works of the Right Reverend John England*, 4:415–30.

4. Examples of such scholarship include Lawrence Buell, *New England Literary Culture;* Myra Jehlen, *American Incarnation;* Donald E. Pease, *Visionary Compacts.* For an intriguing critique of New England's bid for national primacy, see Anne Norton, *Alternative Americas.* All this scholarship builds on the work of Perry Miller's *New England Mind: The Seventeenth Century* and *New England Mind: From Colony to Province;* and Sacvan Bercovitch's *Puritan Origins of the American Self* and *American Jeremiad.* For a brief treatment of these issues, see Russell Reising, *The Unusable Past,* especially chap. 2, "The Problem of Puritan Origins in Literary History and Theory."

5. David M. Potter, *The Impending Crisis, 1848–1861,* ed. Don E. Fehrenbacher; Michael F. Holt, *The Political Crisis of the 1850s;* David H. Bennett, *The Party of Fear;* Kenneth M. Stampp, *America in 1857.* Stampp notes that "by 1857 the northern wing of the American party, though still exerting considerable power in several states, was rapidly losing its membership to the Republicans" (38).

6. Sydney E. Ahlstrom, *A Religious History of the American People,* 540–54; Edwin Scott Gaustad, *Historical Atlas of Religion in America.*

7. For a comprehensive argument against the notion that there was any such thing as a single Protestant Way in nineteenth-century America, see Michael Zuckerman, "Holy Wars, Civil Wars," *Prospects* 16 (1991): 205–40. Antebellum Protestants, notwithstanding the proliferation of Protestant sects, frequently used the term "Protestant Way," however, precisely to distinguish from Rome what they felt was a core Protestantism. For a recent argument against there being any standard Christianity widely practiced by Americans, see Jon Butler, *Awash in a Sea of Faith,* an example of newly pluralized church denominational history. Philip Gleason argues in a corresponding vein that antebellum Catholicism had no single identity. Discussing German Catholic immigrant struggles with liberal German immigrants of the "Forty-Eighter type" (19), whose anticlericalism led them to endorse the anti-Catholicism of the Know-Nothing party, Gleason writes that in nineteenth-century Milwaukee "anticlericals mocked the Catholic religion by leading a cow to the walls of a convent and baptizing it amid the grossest of vulgarities" (20). Gleason provides a useful discussion of the internal dissensions among immigrant Catholics and particularly the conflicts between the liberal "Americanizers" and conservative thinkers anxious to preserve ethnic and linguistic identity (*The Conservative Reformers,* chap. 2).

8. The most comprehensive discussion of the Indian captivity genre remains Richard Slotkin, *Regeneration through Violence;* see also his *Fatal Environment.* For a recent discussion of Indian captivity, see Mitchell R. Breitwieser, *American Puritanism and the Defense of*

Mourning, especially chap. 4. James Axtell, *The Invasion Within,* remains the single best ethnohistorical treatment of English and French missionary efforts in North America. See also his *After Columbus,* especially chaps. 1, 2, 8.

9. Bercovitch, *The American Jeremiad;* Ann Douglas, *The Feminization of American Culture;* Jane Tompkins, *Sensational Designs.* Studies of nineteenth-century Catholicism, principally sociological in focus, include Patrick W. Carey, *People, Priests, and Prelates;* Jay P. Dolan, *Catholic Revivalism* and *The Immigrant Church;* Philip Gleason, *Keeping the Faith;* James Hennesey, *American Catholics.* A good brief treatment of the theological and philosophical divergences in Catholic and Protestant thought is James M. Gustafson, *Protestant and Roman Catholic Ethics;* see also Robert McAfee Brown and Gustave Weigel, *An American Dialogue.*

10. "Sulla Morale Cattolica Osservazioni di Alessandro Manzoni," *Christian Examiner* 25 (1839): 274.

CHAPTER I

1. "Europe and America," *American Quarterly Review* 9 (June 1831): 419.

2. Cotton Mather, *Selections,* 3. Jonathan Edwards, from the *History of the Work of Redemption* (1739), as quoted in Alan Heimert & Perry Miller, eds., *The Great Awakening,* 25.

3. Edwards, *History of the Work of Redemption,* 22. Edward's implicit association of Roman Catholicism with indifference would prove crucial in the later antebellum struggle against "popery."

4. My understanding of nineteenth-century American religion has been informed by the following works: Sydney E. Ahlstrom, *A Religious History of the American People;* Ray Allen Billington, *The Protestant Crusade, 1800–1860;* Robert N. Bellah & Frederick E. Greenspahn, *Uncivil Religion;* Nathan O. Hatch, *The Democratization of American Christianity,* especially chap. 6, "The Right to Think for Oneself"; R. Laurence Moore, *Religious Outsiders and the Making of Americans,* especially chap. 2; Jon Butler, *Awash in a Sea of Faith.* My understanding of the Reformation is additionally indebted to A. G. Dickens and John M. Tonkin, *The Reformation in Historical Thought;* and Claude Welch, *Protestant Thought in the Nineteenth Century, 1799–1870,* vol. 1. Further afield, studies that have significantly shaped my approach to the study of religion are Rudolf Otto, *The Idea of the Holy,* especially chaps. 1–9; Mary Douglas, *Purity and Danger* and *Natural Symbols;* Clifford Geertz, *The Interpretation of Cultures,* especially part 3; Peter L. Berger, *The Sacred Canopy;* Kenneth Burke, *The Rhetoric of Religion;* René Girard, *Violence and the Sacred;* Geoffrey Galt Harpham, *The Ascetic*

Imperative in Culture and Criticism; Roland Barthes, *Sade, Fourier, Loyola;* Elaine Scarry, *The Body in Pain.*

5. "De Maistre and Romanism," *North American Review* 79 (Oct. 1854): 373. See also Ruth Miller Elson, *Guardians of Tradition,* for numerous examples of the Protestant consensus that pervaded nine-teenth-century schoolbooks. Elson notes of these texts: "The mingling drops in the American ocean are assumed to be male, white, Protestant, and from Northern European shores" (263).

6. Referring to the romantic historians, David Levin, in *History as Romantic Art,* writes: "They all believed that the essential libertarian gene was Teutonic" (74). See also Tuveson's discussion of the Anglo-Saxon myth at the base of the concept of Manifest Destiny, in Ernest Lee Tuveson, *Redeemer Nation,* 125. Archbishop Martin J. Spalding of Baltimore gives the counterversion of the Teutonic myth by arguing that only the Roman church could save European society from the barbarians of the north. See his *History of the Protestant Reformation* (1866), 1:19. A superb recent treatment of racialism and millennial thought is Reginald Horsman, *Race and Manifest Destiny.*

7. R. G. Collingwood, *The Idea of History,* 42–50. Charles L. San-ford, *The Quest for Paradise,* notes that "Luther's interpretation [his second commentary on the Revelation of John], partaking of the opti-mistic futurism of New World idealism, became extremely influential among Protestant reformers" (79). See also William A. Clebsch, *Chris-tianity in European History.* As Clebsch notes, while Christianity put history into motion, the meaning of that history was declared constant: "To Augustine belongs the credit or blame, as one may choose, for the Christian theory that the present age was the last age, a time of waiting, the *saeculum senescens.* Time passed. Life went on for men and women, but the meaning of history sat still. Nothing would importantly change" (94). Nineteenth-century American Protestants, while subscribing to this understanding, newly insisted on the dynamism of Protestantism and projected onto Roman Catholicism many of the politically and psycho-logically unsavory aspects of the Christian stasis, or "time of waiting." For a discussion of Protestant millennialism and its impact on nine-teenth-century American historiography, see Dorothy Ross, "Historical Consciousness in Nineteenth-Century America," *American Historical Review* 89, no. 1 (1984).

8. "Michelet's *Life of Luther,*" *North American Review* 63 (Oct. 1846): 434. Cf. Tuveson: "The Discovery of America, and later the American Revolution were placed in a sequence of victories beginning with the Reformation" (24). Such Hegelian views were of course current in Europe as well. As Peckham argues, "One can interpret the function of nineteenth-century historicism as redeeming by restoration and pu-rification whatever is subjected to historical explanation. The pattern that now emerges is "redemption by history" or, more properly, "redemp-

tion by historicizing" (Morse Peckham, *Romanticism and Behavior,* 33. For a careful discussion of the schisms in New England Protestantism's historicizing of its Puritan past, see Lawrence Buell, *New England Literary Culture,* chap. 9, "The Politics of Historiography." Buell argues that the disagreement between Arminian and orthodox approaches was formative; he describes the embattled religious scene of mid-century New England: "Intradenominational warfare had begun to subside, as orthodoxy started to liberalize, Unitarianism moved in a temporarily more conservative direction in recoil from the Transcendentalist menace, and Congregationalists of all stripes began to perceive that the rise of the Baptists, Methodists, and Catholics, not to mention the 'nothingarians,' had created a permanent state of denominational pluralism" (226). Buell's analysis, although it does not treat the issue of Catholicism, is useful for understanding the often bitter local conflicts behind Protestant historicizing. For Emerson's statement about the buffalo-hunter from his 1849 essay "Power," see *The Complete Works,* 6:348.

9. Studies of the impact of those divisions on nineteenth-century American literature include Gillian Brown, *Domestic Individualism;* Anne Norton, *Alternative Americas;* Donald E. Pease, *Visionary Compacts;* John P. McWilliams, Jr., *Hawthorne, Melville, and the American Character;* Larzer Ziff, *Literary Democracy;* Sacvan Bercovitch, *The Office of the Scarlet Letter;* Lauren Berlant, *The Anatomy of National Fantasy.*

10. Spalding, *The History of the Protestant Reformation,* 1:66. Subsequent references are given parenthetically in the text.

11. The best single discussion on Protestant iconoclasm remains John Phillips, *The Reformation of Images.* For an intriguing religious argument about the historical formation of "idolatry," see Owen Barfield, *Saving the Appearances.* See also, W. J. T. Mitchell, *Iconology,* especially chap. 6, "The Rhetoric of Iconoclasm." Two recent treatments of iconoclasm in relation to American culture are Ann Kibbey, *The Interpretation of Material Shapes in Puritanism;* and Dell Upton, *Holy Things and Profane.* My thinking on the relation between New World "history" and the "flesh-bound" powers of Rome is additionally indebted to Walter J. Ong, *The Presence of the Word* and *Interfaces of the Word.* See also Margaret R. Miles, *Image as Insight,* especially chap. 5. Miles discusses competing Protestant and Catholic understandings of the visual.

12. *Foxe's Book of Martyrs,* ed. G. A. Williamson, 87. Further citations of this work appear parenthetically in the text. In Foxe's description of the burning of Thomas Haukes in 1555, the theatrical narrativizing of the persecution is gruesomely apparent in the audience's sudden acquisition of a shared interpretation with the sufferer:

In the which [flames] when he continued long, and when his speech was taken away by violence of the flame, his skin also drawn together, and his fingers consumed with the fire, so that now all men thought certainly he had bene gone, sodainely and contrary to all expectation, the blessed servant of GOD, beyng myndfull of his promise afore made, reached up his hands burning on a light fier (which was marvueilous to behold) over his head to y living God, and with great rejoyling, as seemed, strooke or clapped them three tymes together. At the sight whereof there followed such applause & outcry of the people, and especially of them which understode the matter, that the like hath not comonly bene heard. (*Actes and Monuments of Martyrs* [1583 edition], 2:1592–93)

Foxe insists that he is a historian: "In speaking whereof I take not upon me the part of the moral or divine philosopher, to judge of things done, but only keep me within the compass of an historiographer" (*Foxe's Book of Martyrs,* 457).

13. See Buell, *New England Literary Culture,* for the nineteenth-century quarrel over Mather's reputation (218–24). Mather's implicit appropriation of Foxe's role is in Mather, *Selections,* 5.

14. For a description of one such Bible burning, see Billington, *The Protestant Crusade,* 158.

15. Elson, *Guardians of Tradition,* 295. See also Stanley K. Schultz, *The Culture Factory,* for a discussion of the pedagogical achievement of this American optimism.

16. Miles, *Image as Insight,* provides an especially thorough explanation for the intrusive power of counter-Reformation imagery. For an analysis of post–Civil War America's quest for authentic images that would bestow verisimilitude, if not authenticity, on American experience, see Miles Orvell, *The Real Thing.*

17. Ann Douglas, *The Feminization of American Culture,* broadly treats the Protestant culture's diminishing effectiveness as a wide-spread "feminization"—a declension in part due to the encroachment of female fiction on masculine clerical discourse. On the earlier Franklinian project of effacing the self into republican America's "print culture" and from thence into civic virtue, see Michael Warner, "Franklin and the Letters of the Republic." Although Warner depicts the Franklinian project as politically powerful, by the antebellum decades many Americans were uncomfortably aware of the depleted power of the written.

18. "History of the Great Reformation of the Sixteenth Century in Germany, Switzerland, etc.," *Christian Examiner* 32 (1842): 27.

19. See Elizabeth Eisenstein, *The Printing Press as an Agent of Change.* For an imaginative and historically dense discussion of the ideological impact of reading Scripture and, more particularly, novels on female "private judgment," see Cathy N. Davidson, *Revolution and the Word.*

20. Benjamin Franklin, *Autobiography*, 4–5.

21. Susanna Rowson, *Charlotte Temple*, 31.

22. Billington, *The Protestant Crusade*, 157–59. Billington does not discuss the impact of John Foxe but notes that "Cheever also attacked the [Champlain Bible] burning in his *Hierarchical Despotism*, 144, as a revival of the Spanish auto-da-fé in the United States" (165 n.101). For Roman Catholic perceptions about the beauties of the Protestant Bible, see Kenneth Cmiel, *Democratic Eloquence*, 97.

23. See Levin, *History as Romantic Art*, for the association of artifice and immorality. David Noble makes much the same point in discussing America's vision of itself: "Romanticism and democracy must replace rationalism and republicanism before the artificial complexities of historical culture were transcended and progress reached in its culmination in mankind's organic harmony with nature" (*Historians against History*, 15).

24. Speaking of the colonial preacher Thomas Shepard, Bercovitch notes: "Shepard's equation of new life with New World, and of baptism with the Atlantic as a greater Red Sea, became a staple of early colonial autobiography. It has its counterpart in the sermons on grace, with their recurrent application of nautical language to the process of conversion. To be sure, the application is traditional. Yet as several critics have observed, its frequency, specificity, and poignancy in colonial writing is [*sic*] extraordinary" (*The Puritan Origins of the American Self*, 118).

25. "Neander's Church History," *North American Review* 80 (Jan. 1855): 205.

26. "The Errors and Superstitions of the Church of Rome," *Christian Examiner* 55 (1853): 51.

27. W. C. Brownlee, "The Importance of American Freedom to Christianity," *The Christian Review* 1, no. 2 (1836): 201. As editor of the *American Protestant Vindicator*, Brownlee, a pastor of the Dutch Reformed Church, was one of our most prominent nativists.

28. See Cmiel, *Democratic Eloquence*, for an account of the Unitarian Leicester Sawyer's rewriting of the Bible (97–106). On Horace Bushnell, the era's most important theorist of a "romantic" and "symbolic" Christianity, see Conrad Cherry, ed., *Horace Bushnell: Sermons*; H. Shelton Smith, *Changing Conceptions of Original Sin*, chap. 7; James O. Duke, *Horace Bushnell*. For an analysis of Bushnell's position concerning Unitarianism, Transcendentalism, and writers of the American Renaissance, see Philip F. Gura, *The Wisdom of Words*, chap. 2.

29. "Sacrifice," *Christian Examiner* 65 (1858): 318. My reference to the effect of disestablishment on Virginia church architecture is indebted to Upton, *Holy Things and Profane*, 96.

30. See Hatch, *The Democratization of American Christianity*, on the spirit newly available to the American masses. I am not aware of any

study that satisfactorily theorizes the relation between such religious democratization and the practices of often brutal exclusion involved in the formation of American selfhood, as discussed by Francis Jennings, *The Invasion of America,* and Ronald Takaki, *Iron Cages.*

31. "Balmes on Civilization," *Christian Examiner* 52 (1852): 184.

32. "A Roman Beatification," *Christian Examiner* 58 (1855): 107, 117.

33. *Selections from Ralph Waldo Emerson,* ed. Stephen E. Whicher, 312.

34. "Orestes A. Brownson's Argument for the Roman Catholic Church," *Christian Examiner* 47 (1849): 247.

35. "De Maistre and Romanism," *North American Review* 79 (Oct. 1854): 375.

36. Samuel F. B. Morse, *Foreign Conspiracy against the Liberties of the United States,* 52, 136. Morse's fellow nativist William Nevins sounded an uncharacteristically hesistant note on this issue. Speaking of the Roman Catholic church, he wrote: "I think I see her *going down* already, although I know many suppose she is rising in the world" (*Thoughts on Popery,* 85).

37. "Reaction in Favor of the Roman Catholics," *Christian Examiner* 23 (1838): 26.

38. Nicholas Murray [Kirwin, pseud.], "*The Decline of Popery and Its Causes,*" 20. Cf. Murray's more hostile image that popery is "like a vessel bound by a heavy anchor and a short iron cable to the bottom of the stream, while the tide of knowledge and freedom are rising around it" (32).

CHAPTER 2

1. "Bartol's Pictures of Europe," *North American Review* 82 (Jan. 1856) [A review essay on C. A. Bartol's *Pictures of Europe*]: 33.

2. "Burgos and Its Cathedral," *Illustrated Magazine of Art* 1 (1853): 269. See also William L. Vance, *America's Rome,* a magisterial presentation of American perceptions of classical, Catholic, and contemporary Rome. Joy S. Kasson, *Artistic Voyagers,* more broadly investigates the impact of Europe on writers and painters of the American Renaissance.

3. *The Journals of Francis Parkman,* ed. Mason Wade, 1:141. My use of the term *interiority* to describe the young Parkman's experience of the cave and hidden shrine is one that will recur throughout the book and is meant to suggest how antebellum Protestants experienced the peculiar quality of the Catholic aesthetic—composed not only of sublime or claustrophobic architectural enclosures (literal "interiors," into which Protestants actually or imaginatively traveled) but also of an emotional state of being caged or sheltered in an imagined Catholic container. As

I hope my argument will make clear, antebellum Protestants were very much concerned with rendering such "interiority" available to the public gaze.

4. This was primarily a New England, not a southern phenomenon. The most intriguing recent work on the different sensibility of southerners in antebellum America remains Anne Norton, *Alternative Americas*. On the complex dynamics involved in the New England authorial search for a past, see Eric J. Sundquist, *Home as Found;* John T. Irwin, *American Hieroglyphics;* Myra Jehlen, *American Incarnation*.

5. For a discussion of this filial dynamic at work in the eighteenth-century American revolutionary consciousness, see Jay Fliegelman, *Prodigals and Pilgrims*. For a discussion of white perceptions of savagery, see Roy Harvey Pearce, *Savagism and Civilization*.

6. C. A. Bartol, *Pictures of Europe Framed in Ideas* (Boston: Crosby, Nichols and Co., 1855), 204 (as quoted in "Bartol's Pictures of Europe," *North American Review* 82 [Jan. 1856], 61).

7. Harriet Beecher Stowe, *The Minister's Wooing*, 250.

8. George Stillman Hillard, *Six Months in Italy*, 1:203.

9. *The Journals of Francis Parkman*, 1:132.

10. Alice Chandler, *A Dream of Order*, 20. Ambivalence toward this Catholic feudal past found a powerful expression in the following passage from the *Christian Examiner:*

> The visitor, musing over the remains of a feudal castle, trampling under his feet towers and battlements levelled to the ground, and arches, and monuments, and fragments of armor, cannot repress a pang of regret, as his fancy runs back to the days of greatness, of valor, and of courtesy that are no more; and in his chivalrous enthusiasm he forgets that from that rocky nest the bloody falcon rushed forth, the pirate of the air, the terror of the valley, and that while he wheeled his indefatigable course through the firmament, at every uttering of his ominous shriek, at every shaking of his mighty pinions, a harmless flock was quaking with anguish and terror within the inmost recesses of their foliage.

("Sulla Morale Cattolica Osservazioni di Alessandro Manzoni," *Christian Examiner* 25 [1839]: 304). For a discussion of neomedievalism in postbellum America, see T. J. Jackson Lears, *No Place of Grace*. In antebellum America the influential architect Andrew Jackson Downing appropriated Gothic design for the American Protestant home; his style, Carpenter's Gothic, was immensely successful. Catharine Beecher even selected the Gothic style as the ideal one for the Christian home in her influential domestic treatise, *The American Woman's Home*, 23–42. In antebellum America, the interest in medieval church design was less nostalgic than anxious, an anti-Catholic quest for a pure, invincible union of spirit and flesh that avoided the perils of literal or figurative miscegenation or, in the theological sense, the perils of transubstantiation. For a Catholic reading of neomedievalism, see Philip Gleason, "American Catholics and the Mythic Middle Ages" in *Keeping the Faith*.

11. Quoted in Merton M. Sealts, Jr., *Melville as Lecturer*, 130. As Sealts explains, Melville's lectures are "composite texts," paraphrased and summarized by professional reporters (viii).

12. Martin J. Spalding, *The History of the Protestant Reformation*, 1:214.

13. See Jonathan Culler, "Semiotics of Tourism," 129–30. Culler discusses the historical distinction between "traveller" and "tourist" as the "terms of an opposition integral to tourism" (130). Antebellum accounts reveal significant confusion on the part of tourists; if they are semioticians in Culler's sense ("The sightseer confronts the symbolic complex head on and explores the relation of sight to its markers" [134]), they are dazed ones. See also Dean MacCannell, *The Tourist*.

14. "Michelet's *Life of Luther*," *North American Review* 63 (Oct. 1846): 445; "Remarks on Mystery," *Christian Examiner* 17 (1835): 216. Or as the nativist William Nevins put it: "The advantage is, that we have daily and hourly the opportunity to *consult the Author* of the Bible on the meaning of it" (William Nevins, *Thoughts on Popery* [1836], 9).

15. Nathaniel Hawthorne, *The Marble Faun*, 101. I am indebted to Professor Jay Fliegelman of Stanford University for this allusion to antebellum epistolary cross-writing.

16. Harvey Wish, *The American Historian*, 4. For the millennialist impulse fueling such divisions, see Ruth H. Bloch, *Visionary Republic*.

17. Nicholas Murray, *"The Decline of Popery and Its Causes,"* 23. Murray, writing under the pseudonym Kirwan, became so popular for his anti-Catholic polemics that converts to Catholicism became known as Kirwanites. See Ray Allen Billington, *The Protestant Crusade, 1800–1860*, 261 n.82.

18. "The Romish Hierarchy," *North American Review* 82 (Jan. 1856): 111.

19. "The doctrine of the New Testament is onward, and forever onward" ("The Churches and the Church," *Christian Examiner* 41 [1846]: 196).

20. "The Holy Week at Rome," *Harper's New Monthly Magazine* 9 (1854): 322. The article was probably written by James Jackson Jarves since the same phrase appears in his *Italian Sights and Papal Principles As Seen through American Spectacles*, 297.

21. Mme de Staël, *Corinne; or, Italy*, 81.

22. Walt Whitman, "Preface to the 1855 Edition of 'Leaves of

Grass,'" in *Complete Poetry and Selected Prose,* 411; the quotation also appears in Frederick Somkin, *Unquiet Eagle,* 58.

23. Washington Irving, "Westminster Abbey," in *The Sketch Book of Geoffrey Crayon,* 140. As if implicitly addressing the contrast between English abbey and Roman catacomb, Irving writes of the former: "It is the place, not of disgust and dismay, but of sorrow and meditation" (138).

24. "The Holy Week at Rome," *Harper's New Monthly Magazine,* 324.

25. *The Journals of Francis Parkman,* 1:142.

26. On the Gothic in American literature and culture, see J. Gerald Kennedy, *Poe, Death, and the Life of Writing;* Donald A. Ringe, *American Gothic;* and, more generally, the collection of essays in Juliann E. Fleenor, ed., *The Female Gothic.* On the Gothic as daughterly confinement within the remembered maternal body, see Claire Kahane, "The Gothic Mirror," in Shirley Nelson Garner et al., eds., *The Mother Tongue,* 334–51. My use of the term *Gothic* in describing antebellum tourist responses to Rome is indebted to the feminist and psychoanalytic arguments of the essays collected in Garner et al.'s volume.

27. John O'Sullivan, "The Democratic Principle," *Democratic Review* 17 (1845); Reginald Horsman, *Race and Manifest Destiny,* discusses O'Sullivan's essay, 219–20. For Melville's observation on the earth as monastery, see "The Encantadas, or Enchanted Isles," in *The Piazza Tales and Other Prose Pieces, 1839–1860,* 172.

28. Paul R. Baker, *The Fortunate Pilgrims,* 120.

29. John Calvin, as quoted in Colleen McDannell and Bernhard Lang, *Heaven,* 148. For "nurseries of piety," see "Burial of the Dead," *Christian Examiner* 31 (1842): 151.

30. For a wide-ranging discussion of Protestant piety and its domestic setting, see Kathryn Kish Sklar, *Catherine Beecher.* For an account of Catholic piety in the home, see Ann Taves, *The Household of Faith.* For the nineteenth-century denial of death's physicality, its sentimental repudiation of the suffering body, and consequent changes in graveyard art and visiting habits, see David E. Stannard, *The Puritan Way of Death,* 167–96.

31. George W. Greene, "Visits to the Dead in the Catacombs of Rome," *Harper's New Monthly Magazine* 10 (1855): 579.

32. "A Reminiscence of Rome," *Harper's New Monthly Magazine* 15 (1857): 742. Further references appear parenthetically in the text. This hysteria was not just a literary event. Anatomical remains left about the grounds by students of a St. Louis medical school nearly touched off a riot among fearful Protestants. See Billington, *The Protestant Crusade,* 237 n.52.

33. Chandler, *A Dream of Order,* discusses the early eighteenth-century custom of constructing artificial Gothic ruins: "The false past,

almost as well as the true past, could teach a sense of the sublime" (185).

34. "The Catacombs of Rome," *Atlantic Monthly* 1 (1858): 815.

35. "The Catacombs of Rome," 815. A related form of ancestral bonding appeared in the antebellum spiritualist movement, which, in fashioning a world of concerned spirits to whom one could appeal, offered a Protestant version of intercession to spiritually beleaguered Americans. See Russell B. Nye, *Society and Culture in America, 1830–1860*, 283–320, for an account of the movement. See also Richard Silver, "The Spiritual Kingdom in America: The Influence of Emmanuel Swedenborg on American Society and Culture, 1815–1860." See also Howard Kerr, John W. Crowley, and Charles L. Crow, eds., *The Haunted Dusk*, especially Carolyn L. Karcher, "Philanthropy and the Occult in the Fiction of Hawthorne, Brownson, and Melville," 67–97.

36. "The Catacombs and the Church of Rome," *Christian Examiner* 43 (1847): 284.

37. Willis, *Pencillings by the Way*, 1835 (New York: Scribner, 1852), p. 398, as quoted in Vance, *America's Rome*, 1:75. In glimpsing the skeletal remains of martyrs, these affluent and increasingly liberal Protestants felt closer to Christ; to visit the catacombs offered empirical support for their wavering faith in Revelation.

38. "Kate O'Connor. A Story of Mixed Marriages," *Metropolitan* 2 (1854): 537.

39. "The Catacombs of Rome," 520. Further references to this article appear parenthetically in the text. Many writers also tried to prove that Catholic saints had really been Protestants. See for example, W. C. Brownlee, *The Religion of the Ancient Irish and Britons not Roman Catholic, and the Immortal Saint Patrick Vindicated from the False Charge of being a Papist*, 2d ed. (New York, 1841). I am indebted to Ray Allen Billington, *The Protestant Crusade* (371 n.36), for this reference.

40. Nevins, *Thoughts on Popery*, 33.

CHAPTER 3

1. Edward Everett, *The Discovery and Colonization of America and Immigration to the United States*, 8.

2. Francis Parkman, *The Jesuits in North America in the Seventeenth Century*, vii.

3. Hayden White, *Metahistory*, describes the fictionality that attends such historical truthfulness. "Historical 'stories' tend to fall into the categories elaborated by Frye precisely because the historian is inclined to resist construction of the complex peripeteias which are the novelist's and dramatist's stock in trade. Precisely because the historian is not (or claims not to be) telling the story 'for its own sake,' he is inclined

to emplot his stories in the most conventional forms—as fairy tale or detective story on the one hand, as Romance, Comedy, Tragedy, or Satire on the other" (8). For a recent treatment of the vexed issue of impartiality in nineteenth-century historiography, see Peter Novick, *That Noble Dream*, 1–108.

4. William Hickling Prescott, *The History of the Conquest of Mexico*. Further references to this work appear parenthetically in the text. The best single account of America's romantic historians remains David Levin, *History as Romantic Art*.

5. Adolph de Circourt to William Hickling Prescott (hereafter WHP), June 7, 1847, in *The Correspondence of William Hickling Prescott, 1833–1847*, ed. Roger Wolcott, 645.

6. For WHP's letter home about the naval purchase of his history, see *Correspondence*, 590. Prescott's biographer, C. Harvey Gardiner, claims that *Mexico* was "included in the library of every American fighting ship" after sailors on the USS *Delaware* petitioned for a copy. See Gardiner, *William Hickling Prescott*, 249.

7. WHP to Gen. Cushing, as quoted in George Winston Smith and Charles Judah, *Chronicles of the Gringos*, 407.

8. As quoted in Reginald Horsman, *Race and Manifest Destiny*, 238. An account of American animus against such "idol worship" is contained in Samuel E. Chamberlain's memoirs of the Mexican War; describing a grisly massacre of Mexican civilians in a cave, Chamberlain writes: "A fire was burning on the rocky floor, and threw a faint flickering light on the horrors around. . . . A rough crucifix was fastened to a rock, and some irreverent wretch had crowned the image with a bloody scalp" (*My Confession*, 88). Chamberlain's manuscript, written between 1855 and 1861, was not published until 1956 in a condensed version for *Life* magazine.

9. Prescott, "Bancroft's United States" (1841), in *Biographical and Critical Essays*, as quoted in Dale T. Knobel, *Paddy and the Republic*, 51.

10. WHP to his sister, May 30, 1847, *Correspondence*, 643.

11. "The Mexican War," *Massachusetts Quarterly Review* 1 (1847): 51. Having inherited significant holdings in banking, insurance, and railroad stocks, Prescott was less than sympathetic to the agricultural expansionism of slaveholding interests. "The Texas project is very distasteful to most of the North," he wrote to the Mexican statesman Lucas Alamán in 1845, "and the party to which I belong view it with unqualified detestation" (*Correspondence*, 533–34). Hearing of congressional sanction for the annexation of Texas, Prescott described it "as the most serious shock yet given to the stability of our glorious institutions." See "Bancroft's United States," in *Biographical and Critical Essays*, 164.

12. *The Literary Memoranda of William Hickling Prescott*, 2:32.

13. For a discussion of opposition to the Mexican War, see John H. Schroeder, *Mr. Polk's War.*

14. "Prescott's History of the Conquest of Mexico," *Christian Examiner* 35–36 (1844): 210. The review was written by George Ticknor Curtis. Levin, *History as Romantic Art,* treats the various anti-Catholic traits in Prescott's work to demonstrate the opposition of the romantic historians to reactionary European power.

15. "Spanish Devotional Poetry," *North American Review* 34 (Apr. 1832): 292.

16. Prescott, "Bancroft's United States," 180. For "another, yet the same," see the review of William Hickling Prescott, *History of the Conquest of Mexico, North American Review* 58 (Jan. 1844): 169.

17. Prescott, "Bancroft's United States," in *Biographical and Critical Essays,* 181.

18. As quoted in Horsman, *Race and Manifest Destiny,* 239.

19. WHP to Fanny Calderón de la Barca, Feb. 28, 1844, in *Correspondence,* 447; Prescott also eagerly anticipated that shortly after its publication *Mexico* could be abridged for school use.

20. Prescott, *Literary Memoranda,* 2:86.

21. WHP to Edward Everett, Sept. 28, 1840, *Correspondence,* 162.

22. Writing in 1844 of the tariff debates and the territorial disputes over Texas and Oregon, Prescott claimed to "take refuge from these political squabbles among the Andes, where I am trying to dig out a few grains of Peruvian gold" (WHP to Lord Morpeth, Nov. 30, 1844, *Correspondence,* 520).

23. Prescott, *Representative Selections,* ed. William Charvat and Michael Kraus, cxiii. Such an affection for adolescent virility configures Prescott's account of the sixteenth-century conquest, in which the forward motion of conquistadorial energy confronts Mexico, whose femininity is either modestly concealed or frankly displayed. Both forms of the feminine invite possession. "At their feet," Prescott writes of Cortés's army, "lay the city of Tezcuco, which, modestly retiring behind her deep groves of cypress, formed a contrast to her more ambitious rival on the other side of the lake, who seemed to glory in the unveiled splendors of her charms, as Mistress of the Valley" (*Mexico,* 402). That antinomy between labor and recreation is a gendered one as well, for Aztec culture and landscape claim the seductions and perils of the feminine, against which "the genius and enterprise of man have proved more potent than her spells" (10). Later, comparing Montezuma's pomp and bigotry to those of Louis XIV, Prescott provides a portrait of the Aztec monarch less as vitiated Mexican than as helpless woman. "He might be said to forego his nature; and, as his subjects asserted, to change his sex and become a woman" (438).

American soldier accounts of the 1846 campaign testify to the continuing feminization of Mexico. If some Mexican women "were public in their open admiration of the . . . fair skin [and] blue eyes" of the American invaders, as one soldier memoirist claimed, such preferences for American men only confirmed the dubious virility of the Mexican male. Chamberlain's account of the torture deaths of twenty-three "Yankedos" (Mexican women who consorted with American troops) confirms the feminine degeneracy of the Mexican priest and layman. The Yankedos were "violated, ears cut off, branded with the letters 'U.S.' and in some cases impaled by the cowardly 'greasers,' who thus wreaked their vengence on defenceless women" (*My Confession,* 237).

Even critics of the war appealed to Mexico's sexual inferiority as a defense against the masculine expansionism of the United States. "Why, if the United States were to conquer all Mexico, viewed as a military exploit the glory of the deed would be nothing. As well might the Horseguards at London claim glory because they had chased a crowd of women from Billingsgate, and driven them up Ludgate Hill" ("The Mexican War," *Massachusetts Quarterly Review* 1 [1847]: 51). Prescott's *Mexico*—with its crucial introduction of native American cultures—afforded its author the opportunity to exteriorize the contradictions he had earlier isolated in the figure of Spain's Queen Isabella. While conflicts between an emancipatory nationalism and a persecutorial Catholicism are uneasy constituents of his portrait of Isabella, Prescott naturalized them in that text by appealing to a transcultural mythology of contradictory womanhood.

24. Review of Prescott's *History of the Conquest of Mexico,"* *North American Review* 58 (Jan. 1844): 209.

25. Theodore Parker, "The Character of Mr. Prescott as an Historian," *Massachusetts Quarterly Review* 2 (1849): 247–48.

26. "Prescott as an Historian," *North American Review* 83 (July 1856): 96. Parkman's work was similarly praised: "The air of verity is over his pages," declared the *Christian Examiner* 51, in "Parkman's Conspiracy of Pontiac" (1851): 381. The view that Parkman is a realist has long prevailed, with critics mistaking his irony for impartiality. Thus Parkman's biographer distinguishes him from Gibbon by claiming that the American historian was "under no compulsion to discredit the reality of the forces that had attracted him to its opposite" and that he therefore "achieved a unique kind of historical impartiality." See Howard Doughty, *Francis Parkman,* 85–86.

27. Review of Prescott's *History of the Conquest of Mexico, North American Review* 58 (Jan. 1844): 181–82.

28. As quoted in Lawrence Buell, *New England Literary Culture,* 203.

29. Review of Prescott's *History of the Conquest of Mexico,* 179.

30. As quoted in Gardiner, *William Hickling Prescott,* 209. Prescott's works were especially indebted to the novels of Walter Scott, expert resurrectionist of a feudal past whose submission to a centralizing Protestant modernity is both inevitable and tragic. "*Waverley,*" said Prescott, was "Shakespeare in prose" ("Sir Walter Scott," *North American Review* [Apr. 1838], in *Essays from the North American Review,* ed. Allen Thorndike Rice, 24).

31. Ruminating on the Gospel in his journal, for example, Prescott voiced his skepticism about the Bible: "It is in vain to look for moral certainty in an affair of historic testimony" (*Literary Memoranda,* 1: 209).

32. Buell, *New England Literary Culture,* briefly suggests that the romantic historians saw the "purely narrative . . . as a guarantee of objectivity" (209). See also Lionel Gossman, "History as Decipherment," for an intriguing argument that "the historical imagination of the nineteenth century was drawn to what was remote, hidden, or inaccessible: to beginnings and ends, to the archive . . . [to] the so-called mute peoples . . . whose language and history remained an enigma" (25). I am indebted to Gossman's larger claim that nineteenth-century romantic historiography is typified by "tension between veneration of the Other" and the desire to "domesticate and appropriate it" (40).

33. Referring to the "moral standard" (6) of his day, Prescott reasons in the introductory pages of his history that such progress enables his impartiality. "I have endeavored not only to present a picture true in itself, but to place it in its proper light, and to put the spectator in a proper point of view. . . . to surround him with the spirit of the times" (6). Although concluding that the historian must judge historical actions by eternal standards but actors by the standards of their time, Prescott did not extend such tolerance to all his historical actors. As much as Cortés benefits from his author's relativism, Montezuma suffers, for his time was not properly a historical era but rather a timeless "twilight" outside the providential continuum, a dusk that images the stasis of the "barbarian" condition. Much as Jefferson's *Notes on the State of Virginia* positions blacks in a static category of fixed inferiority while according Indians a measure of participation in the white culture's progressive destiny, Prescott's *Mexico* immobilizes the Aztec while granting partial developmental potential to the Spaniard. What Archbishop Hughes did not acknowledge was that this toleration of the white Catholic was necessary to justify the conquest of the Indian Catholic.

34. Prescott, *Literary Memoranda,* 2:145.

35. *Literary Memoranda,* 2:32.

36. WHP to Lucas Alamán, March 30, 1846, in *Correspondence,* 583; also see Pascual de Gayangos to WHP, *Correspondence,* 107,

specifically his praise for WHP's "freedom from all political as well as religious bias."

37. Review of Prescott's *History of the Conquest of Mexico, North American Review* 58 (Jan. 1844): 177.

38. As quoted in Horsman, *Race and Manifest Destiny*, 215–16, 246.

39. Horace Bushnell, *"Barbarism the First Danger": A Discourse for Home Missions*, 5, 12.

40. "The character of the native population . . . [is] also fruitful in the elements of the poetical and the picturesque, and enable[s] the writer to throw the charm of fiction over his pages, while adhering scrupulously to the unvarnished truth." Review of Prescott's *History of the Conquest of Mexico*, 161.

41. Ibid., 179.

42. Prescott, *Literary Memoranda*, 2:69. Prescott concludes his "Bancroft's United States" as follows: "Truth, indeed, is single, but opinions are infinitely various, and it is only by comparing these opinions together that we can hope to ascertain what is truth" (*Biographical and Critical Essays*, 182).

43. Prescott, *Representative Selections*, lxvii. In a style that "has no marked character at all" (Review of Prescott's *History of the Conquest of Mexico, North American Review* 58 [Jan. 1844]: 208). Prescott's layered and contradictory meditations on Spanish and Aztec character and a universalized human nature also register nineteenth-century culture's growing preference for racial over environmental explanations of character. The earlier environmental paradigm, which stressed the improvability of national character with the shift from a degenerate European context to a regenerate American one, optimistically located a potential for change at the very heart of the individual. Prescott's ethnocentric revision of this earlier environmental paradigm denies any possibility of improvement to the Aztec while allowing the Aztec all the capacities for degeneration. "These pure and elevated maxims, it is true, are mixed up with others of a puerile, and even brutal character, arguing that confusion of the moral perceptions, which is natural in the twilight of civilization" (41). For a discussion of the antebellum subordination of environmental to racial conceptions of character, see Knobel, *Paddy and the Republic*.

44. As quoted by Charvat in Prescott, *Representative Selections*, xx.

45. Prescott, *Literary Memoranda*, 2:163. Habitually describing his authorship in the terms of the conquest his history records, Prescott complained in his journal of the obligations of book reviewing that interrupted him in the later stages of composing *Mexico*: "Nothing but a friend could have dragged me so soon—if ever—into harness again,— and just as I am storming the Aztec capital! Within a few days only of its fall" (*Literary Memoranda*, 2:97). Such an unimpeded transit from

historiography to politics had already been enacted at the text's origins as well—origins characterized by a proprietary struggle between Prescott and the senior historian Washington Irving. Irving's *History of the Life and Voyages of Christopher Columbus* (1828) and *Chronicle of the Conquest of Granada* (1829) had established him as antebellum America's chief interpreter of Spanish culture. Having chosen Spanish history as his particular subject in 1826, Prescott found himself in an uncomfortable (because largely doomed) rivalry with the popular Irving, whose history of Columbus had already deprived Prescott of some of his most "dramatic" material (Charvat, in Prescott, *Representative Selections*, xxvii). Prescott consoled himself with the greater literary power of Cortés's exploit: "The Conquest of Mexico though very inferior in the leading idea, which forms its basis, to the story of Columbus, is on the whole, a far better subject; since the event is sufficiently grand, and as the catastrophe is deferred—the interest is kept up—through the whole" *Literary Memoranda*, 2:68). But when Prescott turned to the writing of *Mexico*, he once again encountered Irving, who again ceded the terrain to the younger historian. The preface to *Mexico* graciously acknowledges Irving's retreat from their contested historical territory. "By a singular chance," writes Prescott, "I have found myself unconsciously taking up ground which he was preparing to occupy. It was not till I had become master of my rich collection of materials, that I was acquainted with this circumstance; and, had he persevered in his design, I should unhesitatingly have abandoned my own, if not from courtesy, at least from policy" (6–7). Irving later wrote: "I doubt whether Mr. Prescott was aware [that I] gave him up my bread" (as quoted by Charvat, xxxiv).

46. Prescott, *Literary Memoranda*, 2:69.

47. *Literary Memoranda*, 1:52. The phrase "effeminate native of Hispaniola" is taken from *Mexico;* in context it reads: "The ferocious Goth, quaffing mead from the skulls of his slaughtered enemies, must have a very different mythology from that of the effeminate native of Hispaniola, loitering away his hours in idle pastimes, under the shadow of his bananas" (36).

48. *Literary Memoranda*, 2:145. The remark refers to *The Conquest of Peru*.

49. WHP to Professor Nippoli, March 5, 1869 (Bancroft Papers, Massachusetts Historical Society), as quoted in Levin, *History as Romantic Art*, 125.

50. Prescott, "Madame Calderón's *Life in Mexico*," in *Biographical and Critical Essays*, 184. For a brief discussion of Madame Calderón's life, see *The Correspondence of William Hickling Prescott, 1833–1847*, xv–xvi.

51. Prescott, "Madame Calderón's *Life in Mexico*," 184.

52. Thomas D'Arcy McGee, *The Catholic History of North America.* Striving to legitimate Catholicism, McGee writes: "In the character of the first archbishop and the first president we find many points of personal resemblance, which we cannot think either trivial or fanciful" (92). But McGee's courting of mainstream culture disguises a more genuine hostility, which surfaces in later descriptions of his enterprise: "The work of historical retribution has only begun; but with the blessing of God it will be followed up, until we show our boastful Anglo-Saxon theorists that the race they thought politically dead in Europe had a resurrection in America, and that from America it can still send its strong voice across the waves, to tell our motherland to be of good cheer, for the day of her deliverance also will assuredly come round" (121). Further references to McGee are given parenthetically in the text.

53. *The American Protestant Vindicator,* December 25, 1834, as quoted in Ray Allen Billington, *The Protestant Crusade, 1800–1860,* 120.

54. "Sulla Morale Cattolica Osservazione di Alessandro Manzoni," *Christian Examiner* 25 (1839): 273.

55. Parkman, *The Jesuits in North America in the Seventeenth Century,* 99. Further references to this volume are given parenthetically in the text. For his part, the nativist W. C. Brownlee explained the ubiquity of the Jesuit in terms subscribed to by Parkman's history of the Jesuits: "The truth is, human nature is at best a popish sort of thing,—prone to erect itself into a supreme arbiter, eager to gain the ascendancy, ready to 'deal damnation' upon every foe or rival; and studious of preëminence even in that religion which teaches humility and self-denial" (W. C. Brownlee, "The Importance of American Freedom to Christianity," *Christian Review* 1, no. 2 [1836]: 214).

56. Doughty, *Francis Parkman,* discusses Parkman's "instinct for the baroque" (257).

57. Quoted in Doughty, 252–53.

58. "Balmes on Civilization," *Christian Examiner* 52 (1852): 180.

59. In *History as Romantic Art,* David Levin discusses how the romantic historians (Bancroft, Prescott, Motley, and Parkman) all "worked out the affinity of Catholic and infidel" along the lines of sensuality and superstition. According to Levin, their most significant similarity was that both groups were reactionary, a cardinal flaw to the progressive historians. For Bancroft (whose work Parkman studied carefully), the Indian was savage, not "natural," and, like the Catholic church, "inflexibly attached to the past" (129). Levin's summary of perceived Indian traits suggests even closer parallels to antebellum stereotypes of Catholics: "He is baffled by abstractions, dominated by his senses, limited to materialism, difficult to improve, addicted to treachery,

loose in morals, irresolute in formal combat" (133). One of Parkman's biographers suggests the context for this symbolic identification of Catholic and Indian in observing of Parkman's youthful Italian and American expeditions: "Parkman's Roman days with their climax in his stay at a Passionist convent were in a lesser way comparable to his Magalloway expeditions or, later, his sojourn among the Oglala Sioux" (Doughty, *Francis Parkman*, 78). I disagree with Doughty's estimation that Parkman's Roman experience "was less direct in its bearings on what he was to do, and was not of a particularly dramatic cast" (78). A later biographer claims uncritically that Parkman was "right, in the main, to make the impracticality of the Jesuits and their co-workers the butt of irony and invective" (Robert L. Gale, *Francis Parkman*, 129).

60. Francis Parkman, "European Journal," Dec. 24, 1843, in *The Journals of Francis Parkman*, ed. Mason Wade, 1:125. The passage is also quoted by Doughty, 69.

61. Parkman, journal entry, Feb. 27, 1844, *Journals*, 1:180. For a further example of Parkman's integration of his early tourist experiences in Italy into his historical account of Jesuit missionizing, see the footnote where Parkman reminisces about his stay in a Passionist monastery while touring Italy (*Jesuits*, 197 n.2). It is worth noting that Parkman entertained himself during his monastery visit by reading Cooper's *Pioneers*.

62. R. W. B. Lewis, *The American Adam*, 170. For a recent and largely unsympathetic examination of Parkman's strenuous masculinity, see David Leverenz, *Manhood and the American Renaissance*, chap. 7. For an insightful argument that Parkman's illness was born of the cultural imperative to be manly, so that the historian "conceived of his own body and so worked it into the context of his definition of ideal manhood as to make it an inescapable prison," see Kim Townsend, "Francis Parkman and the Male Tradition," 100.

63. Francis Parkman to Mary Dwight Parkman, as quoted in Doughty, 394.

64. Parkman, journal entry, 1843–44, *Journals*, 1:130.

65. As quoted in Wilbur R. Jacobs, "Francis Parkman's Oration 'Romance in America,'" *American Historical Review* 68, no. 3 (1963): 695, 697.

66. "The Founder of the Jesuits," *North American Review* 59 (Oct. 1844): 420. Catholic apologists simply reversed the insult. See Martin J. Spalding's character sketch of Luther that detailed his decline into sensuality: "His own deterioration, and the work of the Reformation were both gradual; and they went hand in hand" (*The History of the Protestant Reformation*, 1:78). For a more recent example, see Jacques Maritain, *Three Reformers: Luther, Descartes, Rousseau* (New York: Thomas Y. Crowell, 1929).

67. Quoted in Sister Marie Leonore Fell, *The Foundations of Nativism in American Textbooks,* 31.

68. For Parkman's bias against the Indians and its detrimental effect on his histories, see W. J. Eccles, "The History of New France According to Francis Parkman," *William and Mary Quarterly* 18 (1961): 163–75; and the more persuasive article by F. P. Jennings, "A Vanishing Indian: Francis Parkman versus His Sources," *Pennsylvania Magazine of History and Biography* 87 (1963): 306–23. In a more favorable vein, Parkman's bias has been analyzed as integral to the creation of his powerful narrative voice. See Richard C. Vitzhum, "The Historian as Editor," *Journal of American History* 53 (1966): 471–83.

69. "Woman in Her Psychological Relations," *Journal of Psychological Medicine* 4 (1851): 32.

70. W. Newnham, *Essay on Superstition,* 229.

71. Francis Parkman, "A Convent at Rome," *Harper's* 81 (1890): 448–54.

72. D. C. Stange, "Abolition as Treason," *Harvard Library Bulletin* 28 (1980): 159.

73. *Letters of Francis Parkman,* ed. Wilbur R. Jacobs, 1:178. I agree with Doughty's perplexed appraisal that "there is something almost uncanny in the way his complex of maladies shaped his life to the best deployment of his powers, and ruthlessly fitted its lines to a profounder realization of his purpose than he could have otherwise achieved" (*Francis Parkman,* 224). Doughty is moved to speculate that Parkman's illness functioned as his demon or muse without pondering the cultural contexts for such a "daemonic" (225) illness.

74. Francis Parkman, *Vassall Morton,* 405. Cf. Parkman's letter of September 4, 1861, to the editors of the *Boston Daily Advertiser:* "There is a close analogy between the life of nations and of individuals. Conflict and endurance are necessary to both, and without them both become emasculate" (*Letters,* 1:142).

75. Orestes A. Brownson, "Rome or Reason," in *The Works of Orestes A. Brownson,* 3:298. Brownson's review of Parkman's *Jesuits* originally appeared in the *Catholic World* (1867).

76. The "Autobiography of Francis Parkman," in "Remarks by the President," Special Meeting, Nov. 1893, Massachusetts Historical Society, proceedings, 352. For those interested in the history of American mania this "Autobiography," actually a letter Parkman wrote to George Ellis in 1864, made public only posthumously at Parkman's request, is a fascinating and important piece. Parkman's third-person description of the imperialist expansion of his impulses—"Labor became a passion, and rest intolerable. . . . Despite of judgment and of will, his mind turned constantly towards remote objects of pursuit, and strained vehemently

to attain them" (353)—recalls Charles Brockden Brown's portraits of the Wieland father and son. Parkman wrote a second autobiographical letter in 1886 to Martin Brummer that largely repeats his earlier letter.

77. "The Founder of the Jesuits," *North American Review* 59 (Oct. 1844): 420.

78. Parkman, "Autobiography," 355.

79. Parkman, "Autobiography," 353. Parkman recurs to the term *vehemence* to diagnose the attitude that brought on his illness and impelled his historical studies. Hence my use of it in quotes.

80. Little work has been done on nineteenth-century masculinity on the order of T. Walter Herbert's provocative new study on Hawthorne, *Dearest Beloved: The Hawthornes and the Making of the Middle-Class Family* (Berkeley and Los Angeles: University of California Press, 1993). An early study that remains invaluable is Philip Greven, *The Protestant Temperament.*

81. Francis Parkman, "Autobiography," 357.

CODA TO PART I

1. Paul R. Baker, *The Fortunate Pilgrims,* 201.

2. John S. C. Abbott, *"Conquest of Mexico," Harper's New Monthly Magazine* 12 (1855): 3.

CHAPTER 4

1. On the subversive potential of the Gothic in antebellum fiction, see especially David S. Reynolds, *Beneath the American Renaissance,* part 2; Michael Denning, *Mechanic Accents,* chaps. 6–8.

2. Martin Luther, "The Pagan Servitude of the Church," in *Martin Luther,* ed. John Dillenberger, 284.

3. *The Journey of Alvar Núñez Cabeza de Vaca and His Companions from Florida to the Pacific, 1528–1536.* (Subsequent references to this volume are given parenthetically in the text.) Cabeza de Vaca refers to himself as "naked" in his dedicatory preface. The first American edition of this captivity narrative was printed in 1851 by Buckingham Smith for private distribution. See also Rolena Adorno, "The Negotiation of Fear in Cabeza de Vaca's *Naufragios," Representations* 33 (1991): 163–99.

4. "Captivity of Father Isaac Jogues of the Society of Jesus Among the Mohawks," in Richard VanDerBeets, ed., *Held Captive by Indians.* Subsequent references to this work are given parenthetically in the text. Following his ransom, the mutilated missionary was granted papal dispensation to celebrate mass. Returning to New France, Jogues was captured and killed by Mohawks on October 18, 1646. Along with seven

of his companions, he was canonized in 1930. See *New Catholic Encyclopedia,* s.v. "North American Martyrs." Even if Jogues's focus did not include Protestantism, Jesuit missionaries in Maryland were already involved in such polemics. See James Axtell, "White Legend: The Jesuit Missions in Maryland," in *After Columbus;* Axtell notes that missionary efforts with Indians were delayed because of the "large number of Protestants who arrived in 1638 [who] needed to be saved from heresy" (77).

5. Francis Parkman, *The Jesuits in North America in the Seventeenth Century,* 195. Indeed, Parkman's representation of Jogues's torture, by resisting the enumeration of its details, "which would be as monotonous as revolting" (*Jesuits,* 317), thereby shifts the focus of Jogues's experience from the numinous closer to the depravities of the "savage." Parkman's continuing discomfort with Jogues's piety surfaces in his concluding focus on the martyr's laudable aggressiveness: "We have seen how, during his first captivity, while humbly submitting to every caprice of his tyrants and appearing to rejoice in abasement, a derisive word against his faith would change the lamb into the lion, and the lips that seemed so tame would speak in sharp, bold tones of menace and reproof" (403).

6. For a profound meditation on Mary Rowlandson's ambivalent embrace of her captivity, see Mitchell R. Breitwieser, *American Puritanism and the Defense of Mourning.* The conflict provoked by a trauma resistant to exegetical purification and ordering that characterizes Rowlandson's narrative is powerfully absent in Jogues's account of his traumatic captivity, where bodily torments and loss are continually energized by the promise of martyrdom. As a Puritan minister's wife, needless to say, Mary Rowlandson had no access to the psychological support Jogues enjoyed in a celibate fraternity whose elite members were spiritually enthralled by the "Canadamania" that swept France and fueled such missionary ventures. The best single study of the Jesuits in Canada is James Axtell, *The Invasion Within.*

7. Parkman also includes this particular detail from Jogues's narrative, otherwise titled "Captivity of Father Isaac Jogues, of the Society of Jesus, among the Mohawks," describing the missionary "carving the name of Jesus on trees, as a terror to the demons of the wilderness" (*Jesuits,* 322).

8. For a contemporary study of bodily pain's insidious defeat of language and of the subject's potentially consolatory, if not redemptive, power to gain control, see David B. Morris, *The Culture of Pain.* My thinking about the rhetorical representation of bodily pain remains indebted to the work of Elaine Scarry, *The Body in Pain,* especially chap. 4, "The Structure of Belief and Its Modulation into Material Making"; and Geoffrey Galt Harpham, *The Ascetic Imperative in Culture and Criticism,* especially part 1, "The Ideology of Asceticism."

9. Isaac Penington, *Works*, 2:371. The quotation is also cited by H. Richard Niebuhr, *The Kingdom of God in America*, 50. Penington (1616–1679) became a Quaker in 1657 and suffered repeated imprisonment for refusing to take oaths. His is a classic example of the righteous exploitation of captivity for spiritual and political power.

10. Richard Slotkin, *Regeneration through Violence*, chaps. 3–5. As Slotkin notes of the Puritans: "Their concept of the city on the hill had been based on the principle of resistance to the forces of superstition, paganism, passion, nature and unreason symbolized by Catholicism and tribalism" (121).

11. My account of such a theological family romance draws on Sigmund Freud, "The 'Uncanny'" (1919), in *The Standard Edition of the Complete Psychological Works*, 17:219–56; and René Girard's analysis of "fascination with the insolent rival" (12) in *Deceit, Desire, and the Novel*.

12. John Williams, "The Redeemed Captive Returning to Zion," in *Puritans among the Indians*, ed. Alden T. Vaughan and Edward W. Clark. Subsequent references to this work are given parenthetically in the text. Williams's narrative saw eight editions between 1707 and 1800.

13. For an account of Eunice Williams's life, see Alexander Medlicott, Jr., "Return to the Land of Light," *New England Quarterly* 38 (1965): 202–16. Eunice's statement about losing her soul appears in Slotkin, *Regeneration through Violence*, 100–101. Several other New England girls taken as captives to Canada during the Indian wars became Catholics; some, like Lydia Langley of Groton and Mary Ann Davis of Salem, went on to become nuns. See Mary Ewens, *The Role of the Nun in Nineteenth Century America*, 24ff. For a discussion of the daughterly struggles of another New England captive-turned-convert, see Alice N. Nash, "Two Stories of New England Captives," 39–48.

14. "Memoirs of Odd Adventures, Strange Deliverances, etc., in the Captivity of John Gyles, Esq.," in VanDerBeets, ed., *Held Captive by Indians*, 98.

CHAPTER 5

1. *The Escaped Nun and Other Narratives*, 154.

2. John Hughes, *"The Decline of Protestantism and Its Cause,"* 26. Barbara Welter, "From Maria Monk to Paul Blanshard," discusses the episodic resurgence of nativist hostilities. Welter usefully seeks to examine Protestant hostility without undue reference to "paranoia."

3. Lyman Beecher, *A Plea for the West*, 141, 116. Bryan Le Beau, "Saving the West from The Pope," discusses nativist anxiety about the vulnerability of the Mississippi River Valley and the establishment of successful Catholic schools. St. Louis University had nearly three hundred students, Protestant and Catholic, by 1855.

4. Eric Foner, *Free Soil, Free Labor, Free Men,* 230. An account of the sectional politics of nativism that remains useful is W. Darrell Overdyke, *The Know-Nothing Party in the South.*

5. *Pope or President?* 350. The notion of hidden government appears in a favorable light, however, in contemporary discussions of the family. William A. Alcott's *Young Wife* suggests that the husband's eduction of the wife should proceed "by indirect means—silent, gentle, and often unperceived, but always operative" (24). The parallel to the hated methods of alleged papal intrigue is a close one.

6. For the roots to American civil religion, see the classic study by Max Weber, *The Protestant Ethic and the Spirit of Capitalism;* and Henry F. May, *The Enlightenment in America.*

7. Helen Dhu [pseud.], *Stanhope Burleigh,* ix.

8. Ibid., xiii.

9. Isaac Taylor, *Loyola,* 16. Popular novels reiterated the image of Jesuit control extending from individual psyche across the entire globe. Overhearing the conspiratorial plans of his superiors, one Jesuit novitiate claimed: "The veil withdrawn, I beheld myself face to face with one of the most mysterious powers which has ever been known to reduce to system, on a vast scale, the art of subjugating all sorts of passions—the passions of the mass, and the passions of sovereigns—to the obtaining of a fixed and immutable purpose" (*The Jesuit Conspiracy,* 27).

10. Horace Bushnell, *A Letter to His Holiness Pope Gregory XVI,* 8. Bushnell's letter is a fascinating example of the passive-aggressive rhetorical stance assumed by many genteel Protestants when discussing Roman Catholicism. The letter to the pope concludes: "If I would not have you go to lay up accusations against me, I ought as earnestly to hope that you may so discharge the responsibility laid upon you, by this letter, as not to be required to accuse yourself" (24).

11. Michael F. Holt, "The Politics of Impatience," 309–31.

12. "The Church of Rome in Her Theology," *Christian Examiner* 65 (1858): 2.

13. "Notices of Recent Publications," *Christian Examiner* 47 (1849): 322. The remark appears in a review of Isaac Taylor's *Loyola; and Jesuitism in its Rudiments.*

14. Foner, *Free Soil, Free Labor, Free Men,* 260. Foner concludes: "The events of the 1850s clearly demonstrated that the Republican ideology, which identified the South and slavery as the enemies of northern 'free labor' and which offered immigrants a place in the economic development of the nation, had a far broader appeal to the native-born Protestants who made up the bulk of the northern population than did anti-foreign and anti-Catholic animus." See also David Brion Davis, ed., *The Fear of Conspiracy,* 102, and his classic piece: "Some Themes of Counter-Subversion, *Mississippi Valley Historical Review* 47 (1960–

61). The essay is reprinted in David Brion Davis, *From Homicide to Slavery: Studies in American Culture* (Oxford University Press, 1986). For a study of abolitionist rhetoric (and its anti-Catholic bias), see Peter F. Walker, *Moral Choices,* parts 1 and 2.

15. David M. Potter, *The Impending Crisis, 1848–1861,* 251. For the view that anti-Catholicism functioned as a scapegoat, see the *New Catholic Encyclopedia,* s.v. "American Nativism," where the author observes that "the Know-Nothing uproar was used to distract the public from the slavery controversy." Potter points out that the rural Protestant North was "sympathetic to anti-slavery and temperance and nativism and unsympathetic to the hard drinking Irish Catholics." For an account of the Louisville riot see Richard Hofstadter and Michael Wallace, eds., *American Violence,* 314. The quotation in the text is from the anti-Know-Nothing journal the *Louisville Courier,* as reprinted in the *New York Times,* Aug. 10, 1855.

16. Ray Allen Billington observes: "In the south the ever-present fear of a slave insurrection was played upon by writers who conjured up supposed evidence of a Catholic-Negro alliance against Protestant whites." Billington notes that such southern fears were seemingly legitimized by Bishop England's establishment of his school (*The Protestant Crusade, 1800–1860,* 139 n.56).

17. Davis, analyzing antebellum fears of conspiracies emanating from the slave power, the banking power, Freemasons, Mormons, and Catholics, notes that the significant factor was "that the ultimate peril was always conceptualized as 'slavery.'" He speculates, persuasively I think, that "this may have reflected a deep-seated guilt over the expansion of Negro slavery at a time of widening freedom and opportunity for white Americans" (*The Fear of Conspiracy,* 68).

18. Harriet A. Jacobs, *Incidents in the Life of a Slave Girl,* 35.

19. Ned Buntline [Edward Zane Carroll Judson], *The Jesuit's Daughter,* 163.

20. See J. V. Ridgely, "George Lippard's *The Quaker City*," *Studies in the Literary Imagination* 7, no. 1 (1984), for a helpful breakdown of the novel's entangled plots, which Ridgely reads as representing the "convolutions" of the "mass mind" (79). Ridgely further observes that the novel's message is one of ubiquitous enslavement: "The road of the Republic had led from Independence Hall to Monk Hall, from the liberated spirit of man proclaimed by the patriots to the enchained minds and bodies of the Monks" (94).

21. My figures are from Ray Allen Billington, "Tentative Bibliography of Anti-Catholic Propaganda in the United States (1800–1860)," *Catholic Historical Review* 18 (1932–33).

22. *Western Monthly Magazine* 3 (June 1835), quoted in Billington, *The Protestant Crusade,* 346.

23. "Are We to Have Fiction?" *Metropolitan* 1 (1853): 294.

24. "The Priest—the Wife—the Family," *United States Magazine and Democratic Review* 17 (1846): 131.

25. Calvin Colton [pseud.], *Protestant Jesuitism,* 30–31. Billington cites this passage as well (*The Protestant Crusade,* 244).

26. David Meredith Reese, *Humbugs of New-York,* 225.

27. Davis, *The Fear of Conspiracy,* xx. Frederick Somkin, *Unquiet Eagle,* makes a similar point in discussing the generalized fear of America's impending doom: "In thus weaving a web of significance, the idea of the cataclysm paradoxically served the function of building a sense of security" (46). The pseudo-religion of anti-Catholicism bore evidence of the increasing heterogeneity and secularization of American society. As an accusatory structure that covertly promoted the complacency and prosperity it ostensibly attacked, anti-Catholic sentiment expressed nostalgia for the order and authority of the system it so strenuously opposed.

28. Taylor, *Loyola,* preface. Davis, "Some Themes of Counter-Subversion," also relates nativism to the anxieties provoked by modernization; the literature of countersubversion served a "double purpose of vicariously fulfilling repressed desires, and of releasing the tension and guilt arising from rapid social change and conflicting values" (220).

29. Beecher, *A Plea for the West,* 130.

30. Nicholas Murray [Kirwan, pseud.], "*The Decline of Popery and Its Causes,*" 6.

31. "Sacrifice," *Christian Examiner* 65 (1858). References to this essay are given parenthetically in the text.

32. Samuel F. B. Morse, *Foreign Conspiracy against the Liberties of the United States,* 131–32.

33. John Adams, *Letters,* 1:35, quoted in Howard Mumford Jones, *America and French Culture,* 371 n.63.

34. Morse, *Foreign Conspiracy,* 186.

CHAPTER 6

1. On the sentimentalization of antebellum Christianity, see Ann Douglas, *The Feminization of American Culture;* Jane Tompkins, *Sensational Designs;* David Reynolds, *Faith in Fiction,* especially chap. 4. The best discussion of middle-class sentiment and its struggles with insincerity remains Karen Halttunen, *Confidence Men and Painted Women.*

2. For a nineteenth-century defense of affective religion, see Friedrich Schliermacher, *On Religion: Speeches to Its Cultured Despisers.* See also William A. Clebsch, *American Religious Thought.*

3. Finney, "Sinners Bound to Change Their Own Hearts" (1836), 8. The crucial point of Finney's "heart religion" is not (as it was for

revivalists of the Great Awakening a century earlier) to dispute ratio-nalistic piety but rather to emphasize moral agency, the individual's voluntary powers and consequent spiritual obligation to (paradoxically enough) will the surrender of his or her will.

4. Charles Stearns, ed., *Narrative of Henry "Box" Brown.* An illustration of Brown and his box appears in Potter, *The Impending Crisis.* See also D. G. Mitchell's description of his implied reader of the 1850s best-seller *Reveries of a Bachelor:* "You sob over that poor dumb heart within you, which craves so madly a free and joyous utterance" (119).

5. On the early American novel's creation of sentimental commu-nion with women readers, see Cathy N. Davidson, *Revolution and the Word.*

6. Scholars of the Indian captivity narrative have traditionally de-scribed its reorientation toward sentiment and sensationalism as a cor-ruption of the genre and hence have tended to dismiss later examples. See, for example, Richard VanDerBeets, ed., *Held Captive by Indians,* in-troduction; James D. Hart, *The Popular Book,* 41.

7. On the antebellum literary marketplace, see R. Jackson Wilson, *Figures of Speech;* Michael T. Gilmore, *American Romanticism and the Marketplace.* For Hawthorne's struggles with commercial pressures, see especially Richard H. Brodhead, *The School of Hawthorne,* chaps. 1–4.

8. R. B. Stratton, *Captivity of the Oatman Girls.* Stratton's tale concludes by thanking God for the blessings of civilization that normally shield us from the sufferings of Indian captivity. Gone is the structure of merciful affliction.

9. Grimsted, *Melodrama Unveiled,* notes a similar development in American drama: "What did happen in the nineteenth-century theater repeated the pattern Tocqueville constantly found in American manners generally: democracy freed drama from its literary conventions, but this liberty begot a conformity or voluntary compliance with other conven-tions that was at least as strict as anything imposed before" (171). For *The Narrative of the Capture and Subsequent Sufferings of Mrs. Rachel Plummer, Written by Herself,* see VanDerBeets (333–66). Parenthetical page references in the text are to this edition.

10. W. B. Carnochan, *Confinement and Flight,* notes a similar con-stellation of images in Crusoe's adventures: "The cave within a cave, the womb at the end of the tunnel, turns into a vaulted cathedral full of sparkle and opulence" (42).

11. David Meredith Reese, *Humbugs of New-York,* 238.

12. As quoted in Ray Allen Billington, *The Protestant Crusade, 1800–1860,* 57.

13. Jules Michelet, *Priests, Women, and Families,* 268n.

14. John Claudius Pitrat, *Paul and Julia.* Pitrat's anti-Catholic tale of seduction by priests and eventual gravesite death offers an intriguing

masculine counterpart to Susanna Rowson's *Charlotte Temple*. Carol Z. Wiener, "The Beleaguered Isle," *Past and Present* 51 (1971), notes that "the abstract notion of man's corruptibility was confused inextricably with the concrete problem of his inability to resist the lures of the Catholic Church" (46). The phrase, "prisons of confiding girls" is from Nicholas Murray [pseud. Kirwan], *Romanism at Home,* 206. Murray's appeal to Chief Justice Taney's professional mastery over the problem of human corruptibility reflects a gradual nineteenth-century shift in cultural authority from the clergy to the law. Taney is Murray's object of professional appeal who, even if Roman Catholic, can be encouraged to uncover Catholic duplicity because his training has presumably overcome his religion: "Brought up to a profession which proverbially sharpens the intellect for just discrimination . . . you are as capable of separating the false from the true, the fiction from fact, the seeming from the real, as any other American citizen" (18).

15. The gender issues fueling antebellum convent agitation prefigure those at work in twentieth-century female Gothics. Tanya Modleski, *Loving with a Vengeance,* argues that the novelistic interiors that trap the twentieth-century Gothic heroine represent women's "most intimate fears, or, more precisely, their fears about intimacy—about the exceedingly private, even claustrophobic nature of their existence" (20). The Fourierist phalanstery, imagined by a nineteenth-century utopian like John Adolphus Etzler as offering "the greatest comforts . . . to the greatest sum of individuals in the smallest space," clearly rivaled the domestic project, as did Thoreau's ideal house, envisioned as a spartan and uncompartmentalized space that would reveal him as living life "sincerely." For a discussion of Etzler and Thoreau, see Steven Fink, "Thoreau and the American Home," *Prospects* 2 (1987): 330–31.

16. Samuel M. Hopkins, "John Knox and Mary, Queen of Scots," in *The Christian Parlor Book,* n.p.

17. Jules Michelet, *Priests, Women, and Families,* 164. Subsequent page references are given parenthetically in the text. Michelet and Michel Foucault (*The History of Sexuality*) agree that confession played a prime role in the sexualization of the idle bourgeois woman. But Michelet, from his paranoid vision, interpreted the phenomenon as indicating the overweening ambition of priests to rule. Foucault, applying more diffuse conspiratorial notions of "power," argues that confession (particularly in the eighteenth and nineteenth centuries) was a self-reflexive event by which the bourgeoisie distinguished and affirmed itself as a class by endowing itself with a verbose sexuality. Protestant conviction that confessional discourse seduced female penitents anticipated Foucault's analysis of the "science" of confession and its influence on the developing discourse of sexuality. In Foucault's words, the rite of confession developed after the Council of Trent into "the nearly infinite task of telling—telling oneself and another, as often as possible, every-

thing that might concern the interplay of innumerable pleasures, sensations, and thoughts which, through the body and the soul, had some affinity with sex" (20).

18. *The Escaped Nun and Other Narratives,* 19.

19. For an illuminating discussion of the precariousness of the middle-class family in nineteenth-century America, see Richard H. Brodhead, "Sparing the Rod: Discipline and Fiction in Antebellum America," *Representations* 21 (1988): 67–96.

20. Orestes A. Brownson, "Madness of Antichristians," in *The Works of Orestes A. Brownson,* 14:415.

21. Josephine M. Bunkley, *The Testimony of an Escaped Novice,* 25–26.

22. Murray, *Romanism at Home,* 167.

23. As quoted in Oliver W. Larkin, *Art and Life in America,* rev. ed. (New York: Holt, Rinehart and Winston, 1960), 180. See also T. Walter Herbert, "The Erotics of Purity," *Representations* 36 (1991).

24. *The Escaped Nun and Other Narratives,* 77.

25. Rosamond Culbertson, *Rosamond; or, a Narrative of the Captivity and Sufferings of an American Female under the Popish Priests . . . ,* 261. Ewens, *The Role of the Nun in Nineteenth Century America,* states that there is no evidence that Culbertson actually existed; hence my use of quotation marks around her name.

26. Henry M. Field, *The Good and the Bad in the Roman Catholic Church,* 25.

27. Joseph F. Berg, *The Great Apostacy,* 88.

28. Father Chiniquy, *The Priest, the Woman, and the Confessional,* 119, 125.

29. Charles W. Frothingham, *The Haunted Convent,* 23.

30. "Female Convents," *Christian Examiner* 19 (1836): 55.

31. Bunkley, *The Testimony of an Escaped Novice,* 34.

32. "Sulla Morale Cattolica Osservazioni di Alessandro Manzoni," *Christian Examiner* 25 (1839): 289.

33. Bunkley, *The Testimony of an Escaped Novice,* 35.

34. Field, *The Good and the Bad in the Roman Catholic Church,* 10. Rising nativist sentiment in the 1830s and 1840s submerged even these tentatively positive images of monastic life. Ruth Miller Elson, *Guardians of Tradition,* notes that "in 1839, S. Goodrich offers a pleasant picture of life in a convent, and a story of a monk heroically offering his own great artistic talent to God. In 1853 the same author presents a violently biassed picture of the Catholic Church in which he accuses it of approaching idolatry" (52). See also Philip Gleason, "Mass and Maypole Revisited," *Catholic Historical Review* 57 (1971): 265.

35. My thinking on the constrictions of Protestant selfhood is indebted to Max Weber, *The Protestant Ethic and the Spirit of Capital-*

ism; John Owen King III, *The Iron of Melancholy;* Ronald Takaki, *Iron Cages;* Philip Greven, *The Protestant Temperament.*

36. Auguste Carlier, *Marriage in the United States,* 32. Carlier convincingly disputes Tocqueville's appeal to democracy as the principal explanation for the independence and virtue of American women, citing instead the influence of Anglo-Saxon culture and Protestantism. My analysis of the convent's deviation from the mobile and self-reliant ways of American women is indebted to Ewens, *The Role of the Nun.*

37. *Foxe's Book of Martyrs,* ed. G. A. Williamson. Subsequent page references are given parenthetically in the text.

38. Jay Fliegelman, *Prodigals and Pilgrims.*

39. As quoted in Ewens, *The Role of the Nun,* 97.

40. Michelet, *Priests, Women, and Families,* 204.

41. For discussions of this maternal power, see Nancy F. Cott, *The Bonds of Womanhood;* Katherine Kish Sklar, *Catharine Beecher.* Gillian Brown, "The Empire of Agoraphobia," *Representations* 20 (1987), is a fine study of the psychic (and spatial) constraints of such affectional domesticity.

42. Edward Beecher, *The Papal Conspiracy Exposed,* 150. The literature of antebellum no-popery had no conception of the priest's possible parenting skills, such as those of the missionary priest Charles Nerinckx, remembered by Archbishop Martin Spalding; in church, Spalding recalled, Nerinckx, "surrounded by the little children, who so dearly loved him, . . . knelt down, and, with his arms extended in the form of a cross,—the children raising also their little arms in the same manner—he recited prayers in honor of the five blessed wounds of our Divine Saviour" (as quoted in Ann Taves, *The Household of Faith,* 15).

43. In discussing the surprising popularity of Warner's novel, one reviewer explained that "papas were not very difficult to convert, for papas like to feel their eyes moisten, sometimes, with emotions more generous than those usually excited at the stock-exchange or in the counting-room" (*North American Review,* n.s. 67 (1853): 113. On the "quiet" of domestic novels, see Nina Baym, *Novels, Readers, and Reviewers,* 204. For two good discussions of the novel, see Susan S. Williams, "Widening the World," *American Quarterly* 42 (1990); and Isabelle White, "Anti-Individualism, Authority, and Identity," *American Studies* 31 (1990).

44. Donald Grant Mitchell, *Reveries of a Bachelor,* 79. Subsequent references are given parenthetically in the text.

45. My argument about Ik Marvel's fantasies of destruction is indebted to the following works on the idolatrous or iconoclastic imagination: John Phillips, *The Reformation of Images;* Margaret R. Miles, *Image as Insight;* Dell Upton, *Holy Things and Profane;* Ann Kibbey, *The Interpretation of Material Shapes in Puritanism,* especially chap. 3.

46. "Social Influence of Catholic Theology," *Metropolitan* 1 (1853): 79.

47. James Jackson Jarves, *Italian Sights and Papal Principles*, 334.

48. "The Artistic and Romantic View of the Church of the Middle Ages," *Christian Examiner* 45 (1849): 362.

49. "The Ladies of the Sacred Heart," *Harper's New Monthly Magazine* 17 (1858): 205–6. Subsequent page references to this article are given parenthetically in the text.

50. "Margaret—the Lay Sister," *Harper's New Monthly Magazine* 17 (1858): 806–13. Page references to this article are given parenthetically in the text.

51. "Discourse at the Habiting of an Ursuline Nun," in *The Works of the Right Reverend John England*, 4:203.

CHAPTER 7

1. *Trial Documents of the Convent Riot* (1870), 20 (hereafter referred to as *Trial Documents*).

2. For the connection between this 1833 revival and the 1834 convent burning, see Louisa G. Whitney, *The Burning of the Convent*, 18.

3. James T. Austin, *"Argument" before the Supreme Judicial Court in Middlesex*, 9. For a cogent, if unsuccessful, argument that the government must indemnify the Ursulines in order to guard against mob destruction of private property, see George Ticknor Curtis, *The Rights of Conscience*.

4. The incident is recounted in Mary Ewens, *The Role of the Nun in Nineteenth Century America*, 150. See also Peter Condon, "Constitutional Freedom of Religion and the Revivals of Religious Intolerance," *U.S. Catholic Historical Society Records and Studies* 4, part 2 (1906).

5. Capt. Frederick Marryat, *Diary*, 78.

6. On the convent burning, see *Documents Relating to the Ursuline Convent in Charlestown*; "Destruction of the Charlestown Convent," *U.S. Catholic Historical Society Records and Studies* 12 (1918) and 13 (1919); John England, "Documents Relating to the Imposture of Rebecca T. Read [*sic*], and the Burning of the Ursuline Convent, at Charlestown, Mass," *The Works of the Right Reverend John England*, vol. 4; "Mob Law," *American Quarterly Review* 17 (1835); and Ewens, *The Role of the Nun*. Ray Allen Billington, *The Protestant Crusade, 1800–1860*, also contains extensive accounts of the episode. On the ritual aspect to Catholic-Protestant violence, see Natalie Zemon Davis, *Society and Culture in Early Modern France*, chap. 6. A good account of why Jacksonian America suffered from so much mob violence is Michael Feldberg, *The Turbulent Era*.

7. Whitney, *The Burning of the Convent*, 106.

8. *Report of the Committee Relating to the Destruction of the*

Ursuline Convent, August 11, 1834, 12. See also David Grimsted, "Rioting in Its Jacksonian Setting," *American Historical Review* 77 (1972): 361–97.

9. James T. Austin, *"Argument,"* 7.

10. *Trial Documents,* 82.

11. Whitney, *The Burning of the Convent,* 58.

12. Ibid., 123.

13. Ibid.

14. *Supplement to "Six Months in a Convent,"* 128. Another student, Lucy Thaxter, remembers in her "Account" that "for some days previous to the riot we had heard rumors of an excited state of feeling among the people in consequence of a story which was going about of a nun having been buried alive at the convent" (n.p.). Thaxter escaped early during the riot.

15. Whitney, *The Burning of the Convent,* 37.

16. *Trial Documents,* 36; *Trial of the Convent Rioters,* 12.

17. *Trial Documents,* 27.

18. Ibid., 36.

19. Ibid., 23.

20. Whitney, *The Burning of the Convent,* 18.

21. Charles W. Frothingham, *The Convent's Doom,* 12.

22. From a handbill included in *Trial Documents.*

23. James T. Austin, *"Argument,"* 9.

24. *Trial Documents,* 43.

25. *Trial of the Convent Rioters* [newspaper clippings], 2.

26. *Report of the Committee Relating to the Destruction of the Ursuline Convent, August 11, 1834,* 11.

27. *Trial Documents,* 80.

28. *Trial of the Convent Rioters,* 21.

29. *Trial Documents,* 33.

30. *Trial of the Convent Rioters,* 14.

31. For Reed's account of her escape, see *Six Months in a Convent,* 172–74. Subsequent page references are given parenthetically in the text. Sales figures are from Billington, *The Protestant Crusade,* 90. My account of Reed's work disputes his claim that it was important, "not because of its contents . . . but because of the controversy which it aroused" (91).

32. Whitney, *The Burning of the Convent,* 53; see also Billington, *The Protestant Crusade,* 71.

33. Mary Anne Ursula Moffatt [Mother Mary Edmond St. George], *An Answer to Six Months in a Convent Exposing Its Falsehoods and Manifold Absurdities by the Lady Superior.* Subsequent references are given parenthetically in the text. For another example of the interrelated themes of convent captivity, orphanhood, and morbid sensibility, see *Sister Agnes; or, The Captive Nun.*

34. The quoted terms are those of Reed's editor in the introduction, 31. If such popular texts as the dime novel or popular history like Reed's *Six Months in a Convent* can be read, in Fredric Jameson's terms, as the "dream work of the social" (an approach recently extended to antebellum popular literature by Michael Denning)—as symbolic disclosures and at least provisional resolutions of intractable social inequities and confusions—such a reading can (perhaps unwittingly) reinscribe such texts with the very coherence characteristic of middle- and upper-middle-class discourse, an imposition justified by the alleged subversiveness of popular working-class literature. It becomes plausible to ascribe coherence as long as it is adversarial. Reed's work urges us to engage more seriously with the social function of incoherence. See Denning, *Mechanic Accents,* especially the introduction and chaps. 3 and 5.

35. See Billington, *The Protestant Crusade,* 73–74. After the bishop bought the land, the Charlestown selectmen asked the legislature to authorize them to make rules regulating burials; acting on that authority, they passed regulations governing the transport and burial of bodies, which had to be done with permits; Fenwick, realizing the only effect was to discriminate against Catholics, ordered the burial of the two children and was then prosecuted. On the issue of trespass, Eve Sedgwick observes of the Gothic novel: "Thus violence seems to pertain much less to a sojourn in the depths of monastery, convent, Inquisition, castle, or hiding place than to an approach—from within or without—to the interfacing surface" (*The Coherence of Gothic Conventions,* 24).

36. *Report of the Committee Relating to the Destruction of the Ursuline Convent,* 5.

37. "Sacrifice," *Christian Examiner* 65 (1858): 318.

38. *Supplement to "Six Months in a Convent,"* 69.

39. Brownson, "Protestantism Ends in Transcendentalism," *Brownson's Quarterly Review* 3 (1846): 369–99; reprinted in *Works,* vol. 6.

40. Theodore Dwight, *Open Convents,* 116.

41. James D. Hart, *The Popular Book,* claims that both Maria Monk's and George Lippard's novels were aimed at a working-class male audience. Leslie A. Fiedler supports this interpretation in his introduction to *The Monks of Monk Hall,* where he claims that demi-pornographic fiction was "not merely produced by men only but intended for an exclusively male audience" (xiii). The collaborative male and female authorship of several such demi-pornographic works, their frequent use of the persona of the sentimental heroine, and the difficulty of establishing precise reader demographics all make these claims debatable.

42. Maria Monk, *Awful Disclosures of the Hotel Dieu Nunnery,* 4. Further references are given parenthetically in the text.

43. William L. Stone, *Maria Monk and the Nunnery of the Hotel Dieu,* 10. Further references are given parenthetically in the text.

44. Quoted in Ralph Thompson, "The Maria Monk Affair," *Colophon,* part 17 (1934): n.p.

45. As reprinted in John England, "Documents Relating to the . . . Burning of the Ursuline Convent," in *Works,* 4:418.

CHAPTER 8

1. For an explication of such "dream logic" at work in dime-novel fiction, see Michael Denning, *Mechanic Accents.* The best scholarship on connections between "low," "middle," and "high" culture includes Lawrence W. Levine, *Highbrow, Lowbrow.* For a sustained treatment of these issues in the literary marketplace of the American Renaissance, see David Reynolds, *Beneath the American Renaissance.*

2. Herman Melville, *Benito Cereno,* in *The Piazza Tales and Other Prose Pieces, 1839–1860.* Parenthetical page references in the text are to this edition. Edgar Allan Poe, "The Pit and the Pendulum," in *Collected Works of Edgar Allan Poe,* vol. 2. Parenthetical page references in the text are to this edition.

3. Mary Rowlandson, "The Sovereignty and Goodness of God," in Alden T. Vaughan and Edward W. Clark, *Puritans among the Indians,* 75.

4. "The Artistic and Romantic View of the Church of the Middle Ages," *Christian Examiner* 45 (1849): 377.

5. As reported by Ray Allen Billington, *The Protestant Crusade, 1800–1860,* 375 n.68.

6. *The History of the Inquisition of Spain . . . of D. Juan Llorente,* preface.

7. For a discussion of Poe's interest in premature burial and its impact on narration, see J. Gerald Kennedy, *Poe, Death, and the Life of Writing,* especially chap. 2. For an analysis of Poe's "supererogatory verbosity," see Louis A. Renza, "Poe's Secret Autobiography."

8. Hawthorne, *The French and Italian Notebooks,* 48.

9. Joseph F. Berg, *The Confessional; or, an Exposition of the Doctrine of Auricular Confession As Taught in the Standards of the Romish Church,* 75.

10. The best account of these masculine struggles remains Philip Greven, *The Protestant Temperament.* For an account of the nativist Jane Swisshelm and her accusations of unbridled sexuality in the Church of Rome, see Peter F. Walker, *Moral Choices.* Swisshelm further observed: "To be a member of the Roman church was to be a friend of Southern interests." Walker links the abolitionist Moncure Conway's

diatribes against Jesuitism to "pure naked rage, but it is a rage that has not been unequivocally focused on its real object" (73)—for Conway a "safe" attack. Swisshelm's attack on unions, slavery, and Catholicism is finally, according to Walker, a defense of the "individual workingman entrepreneur" (165) and the "competitive marketplace" (166)—a defense of sovereign selfhood against effeminizing tyrannies.

11. See Michael Zuckerman, "Holy Wars, Civil Wars," for an account of the troubled acceptance of economic pressures on the part of Americans still believing in Christian norms of moderation, communality, and moral values. For an account of the volatile gender dynamics at work in Douglass's critique of slavery, see my "Punishment of Esther: Frederick Douglass and the Construction of the Feminine," in *Frederick Douglass: New Literary and Historical Essays,* ed. Eric Sundquist (New York: Cambridge University Press, 1991).

12. *The Diary of George Templeton Strong,* 2:140.

13. For one example of southern musings on the inner feelings behind the black "masks" of slaves, see Mary Chestnut's numerous entries in C. Vann Woodward, ed., *Mary Chestnut's Civil War Diary,* especially the "Witherspoon Murder Case," 209–19.

14. Gloria Horsley-Meacham, "The Monastic Slaver," *New England Quarterly* 56 (1983): 261.

15. Eric J. Sundquist, "Suspense and Tautology in *Benito Cereno,*" *Glyph* 8 (1981): 109. See also Sundquist, "*Benito Cereno* and New World Slavery," in Sacvan Bercovitch, ed., *Reconstructing American Literary History,* 93–122. For a reading of the novella that stresses contemporary political ramifications, see Levine, *Conspiracy and Romance,* 165–233.

CHAPTER 9

1. Rev. Cyrus Mason, *A History of the Holy Catholic Inquisition Compiled from Various Authors,* 14.

2. "De Maistre and Romanism," *North American Review* 79 (Oct. 1854): 377.

3. Nathaniel Hawthorne to Sophia Hawthorne, December 13, 1858, in *Love Letters of Nathaniel Hawthorne, 1841–1863,* 268.

4. Herman Melville, "The Two Temples," in *The Piazza Tales and Other Prose Pieces, 1839–1860.* Parenthetical page references in the text are to this edition. James Duban, "Satiric Precedent for Melville's 'The Two Temples,'" *American Transcendental Quarterly* 42 (1979), describes Melville's satire as directed against "exclusive church worship, its anti-democratic tendencies, its Pelagian implications, and its affront to the myth of America's messianic identity" (138).

5. Beryl Rowland, "Melville Answers the Theologians," *Mosaic* 7 (1974): 4–6.

6. Ibid., 11–12.

7. "Reaction in Favor of the Roman Catholics," *Christian Examiner* 23 (1838): 14.

8. As quoted in Ray Allen Billington, *The Protestant Crusade, 1800–1860*, 252.

9. Isaac Taylor, *Loyola*, 203.

10. See Arnold Lunn, *Roman Converts*, 53.

11. Nathaniel Hawthorne, *The French and Italian Notebooks*, 60. Hawthorne's voyeurism achieved its most memorable expression in his account of watching the practice of confession: "Yesterday morning, in the Cathedral, I watched a woman at confession, being curious to see how long it would take her to tell her sins, the growth of a week or two, perhaps. I know not how long she had been at it, when I first observed her; but I believe nearly an hour passed, before the priest came suddenly out of the confessional, looking weary and moist with perspiration, and took his way out of the Cathedral. The woman was left on her knees. This morning, I watched another woman, and she, too, was very long about it, and I could see the face of the Priest, behind the curtain of the Confessional, scarcely inclining his ear to the perforated tin through which the penitent communicated her outpourings. . . . it cannot be often that these [commonplace iniquities] are re-deemed by the treasure-trove of a great sin" (ibid., 458).

12. As quoted by Joseph I. Dirvin, *Mrs. Seton*, 165.

13. Charles Eliot Norton, *Notes of Travel and Study in Italy*, 211.

14. *The Journals of Francis Parkman*, 1:208–9.

15. As quoted by John Dillenberger, *The Visual Arts and Christianity in America*, 144.

16. Sophia Dana Ripley to Ruth Charlotte Dana, Flatbush, 1855, Dana Family Collection, Massachusetts Historical Society.

17. As quoted in Dillenberger, *The Visual Arts and Christianity in America*, 143. Dillenberger notes: "It is interesting, if not ironic, that the reservations about Catholicism on the part of Morse and Weir is [*sic*] counterbalanced by a fascination that resulted in an exquisite painting by each of a Catholic subject" (143). Dillenberger also notes of Weir's neo-Gothic friends: "The Gothic Revival proponents had little appreciation of the place of painting and sculpture within a liturgical context" (143). The Roman Catholic painter John LaFarge was largely responsible for reintroducing religious paintings and the Christ figure to Boston and New York churches (150).

CHAPTER 10

1. Orestes A. Brownson, *The Convert*, 161.

2. Sophia Dana Ripley to Ruth Charlotte Dana, September 12, 1856, Dana Family Collection, Massachusetts Historical Society.

3. "The New Editor's Introductory," *Metropolitan* 2 (1854): 4.

4. *New Catholic Encyclopedia,* s.v. "Conversion." The article opposes a "situational" Protestantism to a "transformational" Catholicism.

5. Jedidiah Vincent Huntington, *St. Vincent De Paul, and the Fruits of His Life,* 6. Philip Schaff, German-American theologian and spokesman for the Mercersburg movement, argued that the current "growing disposition to insist on outward visible unity and historical continuity of the church, on altar-service, on the idea of sacrifice, on a more compact form of Government" did not necessarily mean conversions. On the contrary, such tendencies, Schaff argued, may "form a strong barrier against this extreme, as well as against infidelity" (*America. A Sketch of the Political, Social, and Religious Character of the United States of North America,* 230).

6. Nathaniel Hawthorne, *The French and Italian Notebooks,* 136.

7. E. Rameur, "The Progress of the Church in the United States," *Catholic World* 1 (1865): 16.

8. Samuel F. B. Morse, *Foreign Conspiracy against the Liberties of the United States,* 48.

9. Morse is discussed briefly in Barbara Novak, *American Painting of the Nineteenth Century.* See also Oliver W. Larkin, *Samuel F. B. Morse and American Democratic Art.* Paul J. Staiti, "Ideology and Politics," discusses (without theorizing the connection between) the "private, continental Morse" and the "public, nativist Morse" (28).

10. Henry M. Field, *The Good and the Bad in the Roman Catholic Church,* 28.

11. Isaac Hecker to Brownson, June 24, 1844, in *The Brownson-Hecker Correspondence,* 106.

12. C. Sparry, *Papacy in the 19th Century; or, Popery—What It Is, What It Aims at, and What It Is Doing,* 25.

13. Ralph Waldo Emerson to Margaret Fuller, January 8, 1843, in *The Letters of Ralph Waldo Emerson,* ed. Ralph L. Rusk, 3:116.

14. Emerson, journal entry for November–December 1862, in *Emerson in His Journals,* 508.

15. Theodore Parker, "The Life of Saint Bernard of Clairvaux," *Christian Examiner* 30 (1841): 24.

16. "St. Ambrose and the Church of the West," *North American Review* 81 (Oct. 1855): 434.

17. For the publication history of *Evangeline,* see Newton Arvin, *Longfellow,* 102–8.

18. As quoted in Manning Hawthorne and H. W. Longfellow Dana, "The Origin of Longfellow's *Evangeline,*" *Papers of the Bibliographical Society of America* 41 (1947): 171. Although written in a spirit of

uncritical praise, this article contains a great deal of information on the genesis and writing of *Evangeline*.

19. Henry Wadsworth Longfellow, *Evangeline,* I,i,53–54, in *The Complete Poetical Works of Henry Wadsworth Longfellow.* Further references are given parenthetically in the text.

20. As quoted in Hawthorne and Dana, "The Origin of Longfellow's *Evangeline*," 184.

21. As quoted in *Poetical Works of Longfellow,* ed. George Monteiro (Boston: Houghton Mifflin, 1975), introduction to *Evangeline.*

22. Orestes A. Brownson, "Religious Novels," 152.

23. As quoted in Hawthorne and Dana, "The Origin of Longfellow's *Evangeline*," 199–200.

24. Sophia Dana Ripley to H. W. Longfellow, January 23, 1848, quoted in Henrietta Dana Raymond, "Sophia Willard Dana Ripley," 72.

25. As quoted in Hawthorne and Dana, "The Origin of Longfellow's *Evangeline*," 172.

26. On Longfellow's use of Postl's volume, see Hawthorne and Dana, 188 n.40.

27. Longfellow to Hawthorne, November 29, 1847, as quoted in Hawthorne and Dana, 200.

28. Hawthorne and Dana, 178.

29. As quoted in Hawthorne and Dana, 187.

30. Levi Silliman Ives, *The Trials of a Mind in Its Progress to Catholicism,* 22.

31. Sophia Hawthorne to H. W. Longfellow, July 24, 1864, as quoted in Hawthorne and Dana, 200 n.68.

32. Sparry, *Papacy in the Nineteenth Century,* 18.

33. Channing, "Letter on Catholicism" [1836], 432. Further references to this essay are given parenthetically in the text. For Emerson's description of Channing, see Emerson, "Historic Notes of Life and Letters in New England," in *The Transcendentalists,* ed. Perry Miller, 500.

34. Hawthorne, *The Scarlet Letter,* Centenary Edition, 1:33. On Channing's ambivalent politics, see Delbanco, *William Ellery Channing.*

35. Channing, "*The Church,*" 14. Further references to this sermon are given parenthetically in the text.

36. For Channing's friendship with Bishop Cheverus, see Jack Mendelsohn, *Channing,* 192–94.

37. Daniel Barber, *Catholic Worship and Piety Explained,* 29.

38. Levi Silliman Ives, *The Trials of a Mind,* 227.

39. Ibid., 20, 160, 63.

40. "The Artistic and Romantic View of the Church of the Middle Ages," *Christian Examiner* 45 (1849): 371.

41. Hecker to Brownson, July 24, 1845, in *The Brownson-Hecker Correspondence,* 130.

42. Victor Turner, "Passages, Margins, and Poverty," *Worship* 46 (1972), discusses the "mystical power over the fertility of the earth and of all upon it ascribed to a conquered, 'autochthonous' people" (395). A classic earlier account of such ritual power is Mary Douglas, *Purity and Danger.*

43. James Russell Lowell, *Fireside Travels,* 288.

44. Horace Bushnell, *Common Schools* (Hartford Press of Case Tiffany, 1853), 2. See also Jay P. Dolan, *The Immigrant Church.*

45. "De Maistre and Romanism," *North American Review* 79 (Oct. 1854): 374.

46. Bunkley, *The Testimony of an Escaped Novice,* 286n. Harriet Beecher Stowe to the Duke of Sutherland, February 23, 1860, unpublished correspondence in H. B. Stowe manuscript collection, The Stowe-Day Foundation, Hartford, Connecticut.

47. Bushnell, *"Barbarism the First Danger,"* 24.

48. Field, *The Good and the Bad in the Roman Catholic Church,* 1.

49. James Jackson Jarves, *Italian Sights and Papal Principles As Seen through American Spectacles,* 350.

50. Hugh Quigley, *The Prophet of the Ruined Abbey,* as quoted in Willard Thorp, "Catholic Novelists in Defense of Their Faith, 1829–1865," *Proceedings of the American Antiquarian Society* 78 (1968): 53.

51. John D. Bryant, *The Immaculate Conception of the Most Blessed Virgin Mary, Mother of God; a Dogma of the Catholic Church,* 300–301.

52. David Meredith Reese, *Humbugs of New-York,* 219.

53. John Hughes, *"The Decline of Protestantism and Its Cause": A Lecture Delivered in St. Patrick's Cathedral, November 10, 1850,* 15. For a contemporary reformulation of Archbishop Hughes's point, see Robert McAfee Brown and Gustave Weigel, *An American Dialogue:* "The center of Protestantism is not within itself but in the Catholic Church" (191).

CHAPTER 11

1. Nathaniel Hawthorne, "The Minister's Black Veil," in *Twice-Told Tales,* 39. Further references to this edition are given parenthetically in the text.

2. For a comprehensive explication of the tale's eighteenth-century historical context, see Michael Colacurcio, *The Province of Piety,* chap. 6, "The True Sight of Sin."

3. Nathaniel Hawthorne, journal entry for 1842, in *The American Notebooks.* The entry is also quoted by Henry G. Fairbanks, *The Lasting Loneliness of Nathaniel Hawthorne,* 54.

4. Brownson to Hecker, November 8, 1843, in *The Brownson-Hecker Correspondence,* 76 (hereafter referred to as *Correspondence*).

5. "The Port-Royalists." *Edinburgh Review* (July 1841), as quoted in William Ellery Channing, "*The Church,*" 57.

6. Andrew Delbanco, *William Ellery Channing,* 73.

7. Calvin Colton [pseud.], *Protestant Jesuitism,* 23, 17.

8. Hecker to Brownson, July 23, 1845, in *Correspondence,* 127–28.

9. Hecker, *Aspirations of Nature,* 296.

10. Ralph Waldo Emerson, "Self-Reliance," in *Selections from Ralph Waldo Emerson,* ed. Stephen E. Whicher, 162.

11. "Balmes on Civilization," *Christian Examiner* 52 (1852): 187.

12. "A Roland for an Oliver," *Christian Examiner* 7 (1830): 240.

13. "Sphere of Human Influence," *Christian Examiner* 45 (1848): 426.

14. Harriet Beecher Stowe, *Uncle Tom's Cabin,* 218.

15. Lydia Maria Child, *The Mother's Book,* 4.

16. Horace Bushnell, "Unconscious Influence," *The American National Preacher* 20 (1846). Further references to this sermon are given parenthetically in the text.

17. For a useful exposition of Bushnell's linguistic theories, see James O. Duke, *Horace Bushnell.* Contrast Bushnell's insistence on the metaphoric character of scriptural language to the Catholic convert Peter H. Burnett's view of Christ: "When He used language as a medium of communication, He did not rob it of its established character" (*The Path Which Led a Protestant Lawyer to the Catholic Church,* 115).

18. Hawthorne's projected image of unmediated communion in the afterlife, expressed in an early letter to Sophia ("In Heaven, I am very sure, there will be no occasion for words;—our minds will enter into each other, and silently possess themselves of their natural riches") was to Bushnell already a reality, if a slightly less benign one (Hawthorne to Sophia Hawthorne, April 6, 1840, in *Love Letters of Nathaniel Hawthorne, 1839–1841,* 173).

19. Edward Beecher, *The Papal Conspiracy Exposed, and Protestantism Defended in the Light of Reason, History, and Scripture,* 378.

20. Emerson, "Behavior," in *The Complete Works,* 6:178–79.

21. "Female Convents," *Christian Examiner* 19 (1836): 82. The St. Leopold Foundation was an Austro-Hungarian missionary society founded in 1829 to further the growth of the Catholic church in America. Morse's *Foreign Conspiracy* was directed against the alleged conspiracies of the foundation. See Ray Allen Billington, *The Protestant Crusade, 1800–1860,* 121–23; Robert S. Levine, *Conspiracy and Romance.*

CHAPTER 12

1. "De Maistre and Romanism," *North American Review* 79 (1854): 400.

2. "On the Gothic Style in the Fine Arts," *Putnam's Monthly* 2 (Aug. 1853): 192.

3. "A Roland for an Oliver," *Christian Examiner* 7 (1830): 231.

4. As quoted in Jane Dillenberger and Joshua C. Taylor, *The Hand and the Spirit*, 48. Discussing the painting's immense popularity in America, Taylor points to its implicit doubleness of focus. "The 'Transfiguration on the Mount' was the perfect example of a moment in which the corporeal aspect of man was suddenly seen in its spiritual context" (16).

5. As quoted in Neil Harris, *The Artist in American Society*, 362 n.41.

6. "Narrative of Miss Emma Forbes Cary," in Georgina Pell Curtis, ed., *Some Roads to Rome in America*, 74.

7. Sophia Dana Ripley (hereafter SDR) to Ruth Charlotte Dana (hereafter RCD), March 1848, in Dana Family Collection, Massachusetts Historical Society.

8. Ralph Waldo Emerson, "Power," in *The Complete Works of Ralph Waldo Emerson,* vol. 6. The relationship between Emerson's notions of what constituted "power" and his interest in Catholicism is suggested by his letter to Margaret Fuller, January 8, 1843, on attending mass: "It is so dignified to come where the priest is nothing, and the people nothing, and an idea for once excludes these impertinences" (*Selections from Ralph Waldo Emerson,* ed. Stephen E. Whicher, 217).

9. John Adam Moehler, *Symbolism; or, Exposition of the Doctrinal Differences between Catholics and Protestants As Evidenced in Their Symbolical Writings,* 534.

10. "Debates on the Roman Catholic Religion," *Christian Examiner* 23 (1838): 62.

11. "Fanaticism," *Christian Examiner* 21 (1837): 301.

12. Orville Dewey, *The Old World and the New,* 1:119.

13. Helen Dhu, *Stanhope Burleigh,* xiii.

14. William Nevins, *Thoughts on Popery,* 194.

15. SDR to RCD, Flatbush, 1855, Dana Family Collection, Massachusetts Historical Society.

16. Nevins, *Thoughts on Popery,* 60.

17. SDR to RCD, April 1851, Dana Family Collection, Massachusetts Historical Society. In her letter, Ripley underlines her phrase, "all classes of persons."

18. Orestes A. Brownson, "New England Brahminism," *Brownson's Quarterly Review* (1863); reprinted in *Works,* 4:445.

19. Nathaniel Hawthorne, *The French and Italian Notebooks,* 99.

20. *Emerson in His Journals,* entry dated June–July 1842, 286.

21. John Chipman Gray, "Review of *La Divina Commedia*," as quoted in Giamatti, *Dante in America*, 21–22. Gray's review originally appeared in *North American Review* 8 (1819): 322–47.

22. Review of *Le Prime Quattro Edizioni della Divina Commedia Letteralmente Ristampate per Cura di G. G.* Warren Lord Vernon, *Atlantic Monthly* 5 (1860): 629.

23. Emerson, "The Poet," in *Selections from Ralph Waldo Emerson*, ed. Stephen E. Whicher, 238.

24. Longfellow, "Review of *A History of the Italian Language and Dialects*," *North American Review* 35 (Oct. 1832): 41. By April 1863 Longfellow had translated all of the *Commedia*, publishing it privately in 1865 and then publicly in May 1867. During this time he also began the Dante Club, which initially consisted of weekly meetings with Lowell and Norton to read and critique Longfellow's translation efforts. The Italian poet compelled an extensive imaginative investment from all three of these writers, one that is discussed by T. J. Jackson Lears, *No Place of Grace*.

25. Lowell, "Dante," in *Among My Books*, 123. Further references to Lowell's essay are given parenthetically in the text.

26. Oliver Wendell Holmes, *Elsie Venner*. Further references to this work are given parenthetically in the text.

27. Holmes was well aware of the parallel between his story and Hawthorne's, claiming in his preface that he had not read *The Marble Faun* when composing his novel. His image of a bone-ridden "Romanism" was shared of course not only by Hawthorne but also by many other New England "tourists" of Catholicism.

28. O. W. Holmes to H. B. Stowe, September 13, 1860, in John T. Morse, Jr., *Life and Letters of Oliver Wendell Holmes*, 263.

29. O. W. Holmes to H. B. Stowe, November 17, 1867, *Life and Letters*, 224.

30. O. W. Holmes, "autobiographical notes," *Life and Letters*, 45.

31. O. W. Holmes to H. B. Stowe, May 29, 1869, *Life and Letters*, 226; O. W. Holmes to H. B. Stowe, September 25, 1871, 253.

32. O. W. Holmes to H. B. Stowe, undated letter, 252. Suggestive parallels exist between Holmes's emphasis on hereditary predisposition and the emphasis placed on apostolic succession by many Catholic converts. Bishop Ives writes: "Christ's religion is not the result of a mental process—not a thing wrought out or perfected in the laboratory of human reason—but a mysterious, superhuman fact, a thing brought down as a gift from heaven to earth, and handed on through the successive generations of earth by the power of heaven" (Levi Silliman Ives, *The Trials of a Mind in Its Progress to Catholicism*, 107–8). For his part, Brownson observed that Holmes's "writings and those of Mrs. Stowe

are more Catholic than they are aware of, and in fact, no one can appreciate their meaning so fully as a Catholic of New England birth, especially if he be a convert." In "New England Brahminism," 436.

33. Harriet Beecher Stowe, *Agnes of Sorrento.* Further references to this work are given parenthetically in the text.

34. For a useful discussion of the antebellum development of racist ethnologies and their impact on literature, see Carolyn L. Karcher, *Shadow over the Promised Land.* For a good illustration of contemporary attitudes toward climate and its political significance, see "Italy," *North American Review* 78 (Apr. 1854), where the author observes that climate explains why Protestantism is the "religion of will" and "Romanism . . . a system of acquiescence" (458).

35. "The Gardens of the Vatican," lines 12–14, in *Collected Poems of Harriet Beecher Stowe,* ed. John Michael Moran, 47.

36. This conflicted missionary impulse was shared by the Mercersburg theologian Philip Schaff, who, like Stowe, understood Catholic Europe as both patient and doctor to American evangelical Protestantism: "Why may not Europe, if she should ever decay, be likewise regenerated by America? As the setting sun throws back its golden beams to the eastern horizon, as the pledge of his return in the east; so history shows likewise its reacting influences. But at all events, Europe still stands on the summit of Christian civilization, and will certainly yet long remain there . . . and long continue to furnish her youthful, vigorous daughter beyond the ocean with the richest nourishment of her spiritual life" (*America,* xvii).

37. H. B. Stowe, "The Ministration of Departed Spirits," 4; as quoted in Jane Tompkins, *Sensational Designs,* 129. John A. Coleman observes that "the Christian notion of sainthood assumes . . . a tradition built upon vital links between past, present, and future. It requires a world in which the living and dead commingle in an intercourse of mutual challenge and sustenance" ("Conclusion: After Sainthood?" in *Saints and Virtues,* ed. John Stratton Hawley, 207). In *Agnes of Sorrento* (and her other major novels), Stowe is occupied much more by the promise of sustenance than the notion of challenge.

38. "The Other World," *Collected Poems of Harriet Beecher Stowe,* lines 11–12.

39. Isaac Hecker, "Memorandum," as quoted in Walter Elliott, *The Life of Father Hecker,* 163.

40. James Jackson Jarves, *Art-Hints,* 355; quoted in David Alan Brown, *Raphael and America,* 27. Neil Harris's discussion of Protestant clerical writings on Italian art analyzes them as renewed conversion experiences, without pondering the gender implications of such viewing experiences. Harris notes of the responses of such ministers as Henry Ward Beecher, Horace Bushnell, and C. A. Bartol that "art could pro-

pagandize, but this was only to the good, for it could produce arguments as amenable to Protestantism as to Catholicism" (*The Artist in American Society,* 135). Harris's brief discussion of the European tour's lessening of the American Protestant tourist's anti-Catholicism, while usefully arguing that Protestantism's "moral declension" made it receptive to the potential conversionary powers of art (149), does not explore these appropriate dynamics in detail. For a wide-ranging historical discussion of the Virgin, see Marina Warner, *Alone of All Her Sex.* Warner notes of the Virgin's intercessory function precisely what troubled nineteenth-century Americans:

> There is tension, nevertheless, between the theory of the Virgin's intercession and the cult practices that attempt to secure it. For the flowers arrayed before her image or her statue, the smoking candles and sanctuary lamps, the rising incense swung from censers, the implorations of the choir, the numberless paintings and churches, poems and songs made in her honor are offered to her, for her own glorious sake, because the beauty and perfection of womanhood she represents has enchanted men and women for centuries. And underneath all this undiluted flattery runs the courtier's usual ulterior motive. (289)

Warner's view, it is worth noting, is that the ideal of the Virgin is a "particular misogynist web" (337).

41. Orestes A. Brownson, "The Worship of Mary," in *Works,* 8:66. On the relationship between this essay and Brownson's struggle against spiritualism, see Edward Day, "Orestes Brownson and the Motherhood of Mary," *American Ecclesiastical Review* 129 (1953). Bonaventure Stefun, "The Mother of God in Brownson's Writings," *American Ecclesiastical Review* 134 (1956), notes: "The Incarnation meant for him the font of faith, and the Incarnation meant that a woman had become the mother of God. The light of the Star of Bethlehem would ever be tinted with the glorious blue of virgin motherhood" (316). Addressing Protestant anxieties that Mary's creaturehood adulterated the purity of the Christ child, the convert John Bryant appealed to the logical necessity of her immaculate conception: "Is it credible that He who could create, at a word, pure from impure, clean from defiled,—He who is bound by no law, and can except from law whom He will,—would clothe His immaculate purity with sinful flesh?" (*The Immaculate Conception of the Most Blessed Virgin Mary, Mother of God; a Dogma of the Catholic Church,* 57). See also James P. Walker, *Book of Raphael's Madonna,* as evidence for the sentimental Protestant appropriation of the Virgin.

42. O. W. Holmes to H. B. Stowe, November 17, 1867, in John T. Morse, Jr., *Life and Letters,* 225.

43. For this estimate of the number of antebellum church burnings, see David Potter, *The Impending Crisis, 1848–1861,* 241–65. Discussing the connections between antislavery and anti-Catholicism, Potter observes that "in some ways, the anti-Catholic impulse seemed to have more psychological voltage than the antislavery impulse" (253). My study is in large part an attempt to answer why this should be so.

44. "Female Convents," *Christian Examiner* 19 (1836): 57.

45. James Freeman Clarke, "Joan of Arc," *Christian Examiner* 45 (1848): 26.

46. Isaac Taylor, *Loyola,* 29.

47. [Ellery Channing,] "Ernest the Seeker," *Dial* 1 (1841). References to this tale will be given parenthetically in the text.

48. See Robert N. Hudspeth, *Ellery Channing.*

49. *The Brownson-Hecker Correspondence,* introduction, 14.

50. William Ellery Channing II, *Conversations in Rome: Between an Artist, a Catholic, and a Critic.* References to this volume are given parenthetically in the text.

CHAPTER 13

1. Nathaniel Hawthorne, *The Scarlet Letter.* Citations are given parenthetically in the text.

2. Frederick Newberry, "Tradition and Disinheritance in *The Scarlet Letter,*" emphasizes the novel's alternations between a vestigial Anglo-Catholicism and a bleakly triumphant Puritanism. Ronald J. Gervais, "Papist among the Puritans: Icon and Logos in *The Scarlet Letter,*" extends Newberry's reading to argue that "restoring a qualified and tenuous connection between the icon [Hester] and logos [Dimmesdale] is the burden of the novel" (13).

3. David Leverenz, *Manhood and the American Renaissance,* chap. 9: "Mrs. Hawthorne's Headache: Reading *The Scarlet Letter,*" remains the best single essay on the shifting "inquisitorial" complexities of the novel's narrative structure. Recent readings that argue for the novel's cultural engagement with the construction of (and resistance to) national identity include Sacvan Bercovitch, *The Office of the Scarlet Letter;* Lauren Berlant, *The Anatomy of National Fantasy.*

4. Hawthorne's *Italian Notebook* contains repeated instances of his discomfort with various canvases in which the painter's model (and often mistress) was used to represent the Madonna.

CODA TO PART 3

1. Lowell, *Fireside Travels,* 288–99. Subsequent references to "A Few Bits of Mosaic" are given parenthetically in the text. The book is a collection of magazine essays originally published during the 1850s—

hence my reference to the author's "magazine audience." Lowell's most comprehensive account of the allure of European Catholicism is his lengthy poem "The Cathedral," published in 1870, in which Chartres cathedral serves as locus for the poet's romantic struggles with nostalgia and alienation. Lowell's earlier travel sketches speak more directly, however, to the bodily anxieties involved in Protestant spectating upon (and consuming) the Catholic "whole." Hence my focus upon the sketches rather than the later poem.

2. Orville Dewey, *The Old World and the New*, 170.

CHAPTER 14

1. *A Narrative of the Lord's Wonderful Dealings with John Marrant, a Black, (Now Gone to Preach the Gospel in Nova-Scotia) Born in New-York, in North-America, Taken down from his own Relation, Arranged, Corrected and Published By the Rev. Mr. Aldridge,* in Richard VanDerBeets, ed., *Held Captive by Indians,* 183. Further page references appear parenthetically in the text.

2. See Wayne Proudfoot, *Religious Experience,* especially introduction and part 1, "Expression."

3. My use of the term *marginal* derives from Victor Turner's analysis of cultural liminality and marginality in his "Passages, Margins, and Poverty," *Worship* 46 (1972). Summarizing themes from his previous major works, Turner underscores the special burdens of the marginal figure: "Marginals like liminars are also betwixt-and-between, but unlike ritual liminars they have no cultural assurance of a final stable resolution of their ambiguity" (395).

4. Patricia Caldwell, *The Puritan Conversion Narrative,* discusses conversion narratives in relation to church membership. While Caldwell sensitively analyzes much seventeenth-century American and British conversion prose, her argument that the "obliquely anguished tone" (132) of the former defines it as peculiarly American remains unpersuasive. The attempt to demonstrate the "American-ness" of Puritan conversion narratives contributes to the Protestant bias in American cultural and literary studies and leaves us unequipped to explain the different paradigm that structured antebellum Catholic convert prose. See also Christine M. Bochen, "Personal Narratives by Nineteenth-Century American Catholics," for discussion of some of the differences between the two conversion models.

5. Isaac Hecker, letter to the Hecker family, June 11, 1844, quoted in Rev. Walter Elliott, *The Life of Father Hecker,* 152.

6. Harriet Beecher Stowe, *Agnes of Sorrento,* 339.

7. For brief biographical information on these converts, see Sydney E. Ahlstrom, *A Religious History of the American People; Dictionary of American Religious Biography;* and the *New Catholic Encyclopedia.*

My selection of these four converts for study was based on their intimate connections with significant institutional or cultural developments in nineteenth-century America: Seton founded the American Sisters of Charity as well as the American parochial school system and became the first American-born woman saint; Hecker founded the Congregation of Missionary Priests of Saint Paul (C.S.P.) in 1858 as well as the widely read periodical the *Catholic World* in 1865; Ripley was cofounder of Brook Farm and after her conversion was instrumental in the American establishment of the Order of the Good Shepherd; and Brownson, a prolific essayist and widely known (if highly controversial) apologist for the Catholic church, published his incisive *Brownson's Quarterly Review* from 1843 for thirty years thereafter (with some interruption).

8. *An Account of the Conversion of the Reverend Mr. John Thayer*, 1.

9. Ray Allen Billington, *The Protestant Crusade, 1800–1860*, discusses the European missionary activities of the American and Foreign Christian Union, 270–80.

10. My figures are taken from Bochen, "Personal Narratives by Nineteenth-Century American Catholics," 57ff.

11. See Clarence E. Walworth, *The Oxford Movement in America; or, Glimpses of Life in an Anglican Seminary*, for a Catholic convert's analysis of the impact of Tractarianism on his and his seminary colleagues' progression toward Rome. See also Vanbrugh Livingston, *A Letter to the Hon. and Rev. George Spencer on the Oxford Movement in the United States*, for the argument that the American Protestant Episcopal church was far less likely to go toward Rome than the Anglican church. Robert Gorman, *Catholic Apologetical Literature in the United States, 1784–1858*, chap. 9, provides an informative history of American conversions during the years between 1840 and 1858. The 1846 pamphlet *The Late Conversions to the Catholic Church; Being a Reply to Recent Statements Made by Bishop de Lancey*, reprinted in *Miscellanea Catholica America*, vol. 6, asserts against Protestant accusations of conspiracy that "there is a peculiar characteristic belonging to these conversions. It is this:—in these changes, *almost every individual acted singly and alone*" (50). For an overview of this issue, see Ahlstrom, *A Religious History of the American People*, "Catholic Movements in American Protestantism," 615–36.

12. *Memoirs of the Rev. David Brainerd, Missionary to the Indians . . . Chiefly Taken from His Diary by Rev. Jonathan Edwards . . .* , ed. Serena Edwards Dwight (New Haven, 1822), as quoted in *Conversions*, ed. Hugh T. Kerr and John M. Mulder, 78. Brainerd's phrase "*paddling with my hand in the water*" is italicized in Kerr's transcription. Oliver Wendell Holmes, autobiographical notes, as quoted in John T. Morse,

Jr., *The Life and Letters of Oliver Wendell Holmes*, 1:38. Joshua Huntington, *Gropings after Truth*, 24.

13. Bushnell's efforts to domesticate religious piety were anticipated by William Ellery Channing in his famous 1819 sermon "Likeness to God." Arguing for an even more imperceptible continuum between creature and God, Channing effectively redefined conversion from rebirth to a simple continuation of life. Piety involved the pursuit of union via identity, not communion: "This likeness [between God and creature] does not consist in extraordinary or miraculous gifts, in supernatural additions to the soul, or in any thing foreign to our original constitution." Channing's text is excerpted in Perry Miller, ed., *The Transcendentalists*, 22–25.

14. Orestes A. Brownson, "The Mediatorial Life of Jesus," in *The Works of Orestes A. Brownson*, 4:142.

15. *The Conversion of Marie-Alphonse Ratisbonne: Original Narrative of Baron Theodore de Bussieres*, 21.

16. *An Apology for the Conversion of Stephen Cleveland Blythe, to the Faith of the Catholic, Apostolic, and Roman Church . . .* , 10.

17. Huntington, *Gropings after Truth*, 60. Where clarity permits, further quotations from this volume appear parenthetically in the text.

18. "Notices of Recent Publications," *Christian Examiner* 56 (1854): 463.

19. The phrase is quoted from "Social Influence of Catholic Theology," *Metropolitan* 1 (1853): 79. To Hecker and Brownson, not just the nature of interior life but its very existence was at issue. "Brownson was firmly persuaded," reported Hecker to his first biographer, "and so am I, that the great fault of men generally is that they deem the life of their souls, thoughts, judgments, and convictions, yearnings, aspirations, and longings to be too subject to illusion to be worthy their attentive study and manly fidelity; that even multitudes of Catholics greatly undervalue the divine reality of their inner life, whether in the natural or supernatural order" (as quoted in Elliott, *The Life of Father Hecker*, 122). For an intriguing discussion of the differing Catholic and Protestant models of domestic piety and spiritual sensibility, see Colleen McDannell, *The Christian Home in Victorian America, 1840–1900*.

20. The phrase is from Joseph Story, "Character of the Puritans," in Ebenezer Bailey, *The Young Ladies' Class Book* (Boston, 1831), 213; as quoted in Sister Marie Leonore Fell, *The Foundations of Nativism in American Textbooks, 1783–1860*, 67.

21. Isaac T. Hecker, *Questions of the Soul*, 236.

22. Nicholas Murray [pseud. Kirwan], *Romanism at Home*, 236. Murray's confident position was just as confidently dismissed by John Henry Newman, *An Essay on the Development of Christian Doctrine:*

"Whatever be the historical Christianity, it is not Protestantism. If ever there were a safe truth, it is this" (5). Such formulations ignored the salient preoccupation of nineteenth-century Anglo-American religious culture with degrees of religious affiliation, rather than simply wholesale commitment.

23. "The Philosophy of Conversion," *Catholic World* 4, no. 22 (1867): 466.

24. Ibid., 467.

25. This account of Elizabeth Seton depends largely on excerpts from her writings included in the following texts: *Memoir, Letters, and Journal of Elizabeth Seton, Convert to the Catholic Faith, and Sister of Charity* (hereafter referred to as *Memoir*); Charles I. White, *Life of Mrs. Eliza A. Seton, Foundress and First Superior of the Sisters or Daughters of Charity* (hereafter referred to as White); Joseph I. Dirvin, *Mrs. Seton* (hereafter referred to as Dirvin); *Elizabeth Seton: Selected Writings,* ed. Ellin Kelly and Annabelle Melville (hereafter referred to as *ES*). The epigraph appears in *ES,* 67; date and addressee remain unspecified. To my knowledge little recent scholarship on Seton exists beyond the work of Kelly and Melville. Amanda Porterfield, *Feminine Spirituality in America,* discusses Seton as one example in the American "spectrum of feminine religious power" (110). While I agree that Seton's maternal sensibility was central to her devotional life, I do not share Porterfield's understanding of a female religious taxonomy. To put it briefly, Seton was far more Catholic than she was "female"; indeed, her Catholicism so profoundly affected her "femaleness" that to place Seton in a continuous spectrum composed of other devout women from various denominations and historical eras misleadingly implies, I think, that her faith was secondary to an essentialized category of gender.

26. On tuberculosis as a cultural symbol, see Susan Sontag, *Illness as Metaphor.* One medical dictionary argued that the hereditary "predisposition" to tuberculosis received its main encouragement from an error in marriage: "There can be no question, that from errors in the contraction of this great engagement of life, much of the hereditary tendency to consumption is developed, and especially when the union is between parties nearly related by blood; doubly so if the predisposition already exists in the family." See Spencer Thomson, *A Dictionary of Domestic Medicine and Household Surgery,* 135. The connections Seton drew between consumption, contagion, her family, and her spiritual life were not unusual for the age. What is exceptional is the rhetorical intensity and complexity with which she formulated them. For the consumptively inclined, the two crucial coordinates were vocation and location, for these could allegedly cause and remedy the disease. Such an antebellum poem as James Gates Percival's "Consumption," in *The Poetical Works,* typically linked the corrosive progress of tuberculosis

to a suppressed eroticism and a "saint's desires." The poem's opening assertion, "There is a sweetness in woman's decay / When the light of beauty is fading away," forms part of the nineteenth-century literary tradition developed by Washington Irving, Edgar Allan Poe, and Harriet Beecher Stowe of sacramentally disposing of women. As with later authors, tuberculosis was a prime literary "carrier" for ideological assertions of female sanctity and frailty. In Percival's poem, the unnamed masculine celebrant of the female invalid testifies to the disease's aesthetic transformation of woman, first into landscape and then into saint: "And there is a blending of white and blue / Where the purple blood is melting through / The snow of her pale and tender cheek." The saturation of the "snow" with the "purple blood" situates this feminized pastoral in a larger erotic terrain of virginity's blushes and bloody loss. Such loss doesn't occur; indeed consumption prevents the maiden's entry into life and hence is crucial to her transition from a biological to a sacred power. Consumption figured in just such language of a stealthy preservation of purity that imitated the mysterious comings of grace. But both life and tuberculosis are finally "hectic"—a false illumination that opposes heavenly repose: "But dearer the calm and quiet day / When that heaven-sick soul is stealing away." Poets and medical men were fascinated by the disease in part because of its curious gap in representation; its presence both did and did not signify a suffering death.

27. *ES*, 102. Subsequent quotations follow Seton's text without editorial comment.

28. Carroll Smith-Rosenberg argues in her now classic article "The Female World of Love and Ritual: Relations Between Women in Nineteenth-Century America" that eighteenth- and nineteenth-century women enjoyed close affectional ties with one another—an intimate, supportive world generated by the separation of the sexes into their separate spheres (reprinted in Smith-Rosenberg, *Disorderly Conduct*, 53–76).

29. "A Journal of the Soul," August 19, 1807, *ES*, 222.

30. Seton, "Dear Remembrances," *ES*, 344.

31. Seton, "The Italian Journal," November 25, 1803, *ES*, 110.

32. Richard Bayley, *An Account of the Epidemic Fever Which Prevailed in the City of New York, during Part of the Summer and Fall of 1795*, 119. Further references are given parenthetically in the text.

33. Dirvin, 91.

34. Seton to Julia Scott, June 11, 1801, in *Letters of Mother Seton to Mrs. Julianna Scott*, 88.

35. Letter from Seton to Rebecca Seton, as quoted in Dirvin, 91.

36. I have relied here on Dirvin's description of this incident; however, he provides no substantiating evidence for the episode (96–97).

37. Dirvin, 84.

38. Letter from Seton to Rebecca Seton, October 14, 1801, as quoted in Dirvin, 100.

39. The description of Seton's response to Communion is Dirvin's (106).

40. Letter from Seton to Rebecca Seton, October 14, 1801, as quoted in Dirvin, 87; letter from Seton to Cecilia Seton, October 1, 1803, *ES*, 81.

41. *ES*, 103–4, entry for November 19, 1803.

42. *ES*, 105, entry for November 19, 1803.

43. *ES*, 106, entry for November 20, 1803.

44. *ES*, 109, entry for November 23, 1803.

45. Ibid.

46. *ES*, 110, entry for November 25, 1803.

47. Ibid.

48. *ES*, 118, entry for December 12, 1803.

49. *ES*, 113, entry for November 30, 1803.

50. *ES*, 120, entry for December 13, 1803.

51. Ibid.

52. The importance of Seton's friendship with the Filicchis in dismantling her anti-Catholic prejudices is underscored by her later acknowledgment to Amabilia Filicchi: "Oh my the Worshipper of images and the Man of Sin are different enough from the beloved souls I knew in Leghorn to ease my mind in that point, since I so well knew what you worshipped my Amabilia" ("The Journal for Amabilia Filicchi," entry for August 28, 1804, *ES*, 160. The epigraph for this section is in *ES*, 131).

53. "The Italian Journal," *ES*, 126.

54. *ES*, 132. In her 1807 *Journal of the Soul*, written for Cecilia Seton, Elizabeth Seton recorded a dream that suggests how profoundly she had internalized the specter of Protestant disdain: "What are the workings of Fancy in sleep whose secret finger weaves the web—it was but a web—yet I sensibly pressed the *Adored Host* close to my heart after saving it from the hand of one who ridiculed my faith in its *Divine* essence" (*ES*, 220). The nightmarish counterpart to Seton's bodily identification with Catholicism is recorded in an 1808 entry in "Journal for Cecilia Seton": "In the midst of my uneasy slumbers I was busily employed in extracting my large Crucifix from the back of *StM*—it was fastened with needles which were under the back bone—what an imagination" (*ES*, 234).

55. *ES*, 133.

56. "The Journal for Amabilia Filicchi," *ES*, 161.

57. See Dirvin, 163n.

58. "Journal for Amabilia Filicchi," entry for February 27, 1805, *ES*, 165.

59. Ibid., 166.

60. Ibid.

61. Ibid., 167, 227. On Jesus as her asylum, cf. Father Tisserant's advice to Seton: "You have told me that the Heart of Jesus was your refuge. . . . Retired within that asylum, what have you to fear?" (as quoted in Dirvin, 189). On the Eucharist as medicine, Seton later exclaimed: "That *he* [Jesus] *is there* . . . is as certainly true as that Bread naturally taken removes my hunger—so this Bread of Angels removes my pain, my cares, warms, cheers, sooths, contents and renews my Whole being—" (*ES*, 226–27).

62. Letter from Seton to Cecilia Seton, April 3, 1808, *ES*, 255.

63. Seton, "Dear Remembrances," *ES*, 352.

64. As quoted in Dirvin, 331.

65. Dirvin, 294.

66. "Annina's Diary," unpublished ms. in Seton archives, Order of the Sisters of Charity, Emmitsburg, Maryland.

67. Ibid.

68. Seton to Antonio Filicchi, April 18, 1820, *ES*, 290.

CHAPTER 15

1. Isaac Hecker, *Questions of the Soul*, 282.

2. As quoted in Katherine Burton, *In No Strange Land*, 39. Burton provides no source for her quotation of Ripley.

3. Letter from Orestes Brownson to Isaac Hecker, March 28, 1851, in *The Brownson-Hecker Correspondence*, 148 (hereafter referred to as *Correspondence*).

4. Orestes A. Brownson, *The Convert; or, Leaves from My Experience,* in *Works,* 5:81. Thomas R. Ryan, *Orestes A. Brownson,* notes of this passage: "By almost common consent reference is here made to George Ripley" (98).

5. Letter from George Ripley to Isaac Hecker, September 18, 1843; as quoted in Walter Elliott, *The Life of Father Hecker,* 91.

6. Letter from Sophia Ripley to Ruth Charlotte Dana, April 29, 1849; as quoted in Henrietta Dana Raymond, "Sophia Willard Dana Ripley," 88–89.

7. Letter from Sophia Dana Ripley (hereafter referred to as SDR) to Ruth Charlotte Dana (hereafter referred to as RCD), Brook Farm, 1846, Dana Family Collection, Massachusetts Historical Society. The epigraph to this section is from a letter (SRD to RCD, November 5, 1855) in the same collection. Unless otherwise stated, subsequent quotations from letters of SDR to RCD are from the Dana Family Collection and follow the original without editorial comment.

8. SDR to RCD, September 1846. See also Anne C. Rose, *Transcendentalism as a Social Movement, 1830–1850,* on Ripley's decision to convert shortly after Brook Farm's turn toward Fourierism: "Intellectually, her decision was perfectly consistent with the community's new commitment to universal unity" (196).

9. SDR to RCD, September 1846.

10. Rose, *Transcendentalism as a Social Movement,* 185n., briefly discusses the compensatory function of Ripley's correspondence with her cousin Charlotte. My account of Ripley's isolation is developed almost entirely from her confidential letters to Charlotte.

11. SDR to RCD, Brook Farm, September 12, 1846.

12. My account of Brook Farm's demise is drawn from Charles Crowe, *George Ripley;* and Lindsay Swift, *Brook Farm.*

13. SDR to Ralph Waldo Emerson, July 29, 1843, as quoted in Lisette Riggs, "George and Sophia Ripley," 174.

14. Isaac Hecker, *Aspirations of Nature,* 17.

15. SDR to RCD, September 3, 1847.

16. According to Raymond, "Sophia Willard Dana Ripley," 62.

17. SDR to RCD, June 7, 1848.

18. SDR to RCD, September 15, 1848.

19. SDR to RCD, February 21, 1860. Ripley's revised aesthetic extended from church interiors and liturgical calendars to the deathbed scenes of Protestant friends. Recounting the death from tuberculosis of one such friend, the ex-Transcendentalist wrote, like Seton before her, of the desolating absence of ritual help in Protestant dying: "The clouds from chloroform dispersed wonderfully—but the cloud from the spirit, there was no assured hand to lift & the sun could not shine out as it set in this world, I trust to rise in glory. 'A glory to which' Aunt E truly said, 'the poor child was a stranger.' A short time before death, after an attack of suffocation, she said, 'Netta it is impossible but I must die, it is impossible but I must die'—& Netta answered Don't be afraid dear Helen & this was her last sacrament!" (SDR to RCD, June 28, 1851).

20. SDR to RCD, August 5, 1856.

21. SDR to RCD, 1855, "Dearest Daughter," Dana Family collection.

22. Caryl Coleman, "A Forgotten Convert," *Catholic World* 122, no. 728 (Oct. 1925–Mar. 1926). St. Alphonsus's celebration of the Virgin repeatedly emphasized her maternal, merciful intercession for all who addressed her. Speaking of God's division of his government, Alphonsus explained: "Justice He reserved to Himself; mercy He transmitted to Mary, ordaining that all mercies which come to man should come through Mary's hands, and that these mercies should be distributed according to her choice." See Ligouri, *The Glories of Mary,* part 1, 14.

Like Seton before her, Ripley intensely identified with such a merciful (and powerful!) maternity.

23. SDR to RCD, September 26, 1850.

24. SDR to RCD, letter fragment [1855?] beginning, "Do you know I can see."

25. SDR to RCD, undated letter from New York headed "Octave of St. John."

26. SDR to RCD, [1855?] dated only "Monday Morning."

27. SDR to RCD, December 9, 1855.

28. SDR to RCD, Flatbush, [1855?], "Ever dear little Mother & Sister."

29. Count de Montalembert, *The Life of St. Elizabeth, of Hungary, Duchess of Thuringia,* trans. Mary Hackett, 2d edition (New York: D. and G. Sadlier and Co., 1888), 91. St. Elizabeth was Sophia Ripley's favorite saint. Melville was also attracted to this saint and sent Montalembert's biography to his favorite cousin, Kate. Joseph G. Knapp, *Tortured Synthesis,* notes that Melville's correspondence during the 1870s revealed a "special fondness for Catholic saints" (99).

30. SDR to RCD, September 18, 1857.

31. SDR to RCD, May 1, 1848.

32. SDR to RCD, July 9, 1848.

33. "When I crossed the threshold of Our Holy Church," Ripley wrote of Brownson, "I did not expect to meet this form of evil, a Protestant Reformer, at the very outset, within those Sacred precincts. I thought I had left them forever behind. If abuses have crept into the Church, may they be reformed quietly & with all delicate consideration, by experienced & thorough Catholics but not to be trumpeted in the ears of new converts, by these rash & *undiscriminating* fanatics. There is a slumbering power in the church which should protect us & other new converts from their rude assaults for no man does us so great an injury as he who gives us a painful association with those we revere, or undermines our confidence in them. It is a cruel robbery" (SDR to RCD [Flatbush, 1855]).

34. SDR to RCD, March 1848.

35. For an intriguing analysis of Emerson's rhetorical and psychological management of the perils of emotion, see David Leverenz, "The Politics of Emerson's Man-Making Words," *PLMA* 101, no. 1 (1986): 38–53.

36. SDR to RCD, October 26, 1850.

37. SDR to RCD, June 28, 1851.

38. SDR to RCD, December 2, 1853.

39. SDR to RCD, September 26, 1858.

40. SDR to RCD, May 1, 1848.

41. SDR to RCD, May 17, 1848.
42. SDR to RCD, March 1848, Flatbush, Long Island.
43. SDR to RCD, June 1, 1851.
44. SDR to RCD, November 28, 1853.
45. SDR to RCD, June 28, 1851.
46. Isaac Hecker, "Tribute to Mrs. George Ripley," as quoted in Raymond, "Sophia Willard Dana Ripley," appendix.
47. SDR to RCD, Flatbush, 1855.
48. SDR to RCD, December 6, 1857.
49. SDR to RCD, July 5, 1860.

CHAPTER 16

1. Isaac Hecker, diary entry, January 11, 1843, in *The Diary,* ed. John Farina, 89 (hereafter referred to as *Diary*).
2. As quoted in Walter Elliott, *The Life of Father Hecker,* 344 (hereafter referred to as Elliott). The epigraph for this section is excerpted from a reminiscence by Father Hecker as quoted in Elliott, 81.
3. Hecker to Mon. T. R. Pere [Rev. Michael Heilig, C.S.S.R.], May 30, 1848; as quoted in *The Brownson-Hecker Correspondence,* 20 (hereafter referred to as *Correspondence*).
4. *Diary,* 149. John Farina attempts to normalize such entries of Hecker's by suggesting that by "spiritual presence" Hecker intends his former close friends at Brook Farm. I would argue, however, that Hecker indeed means the spiritual presence of spiritual bodies since his diary and other writings frequently record an intimate sense of the presence of the supernatural as personal beings.
5. This phrase is recorded in a reminiscence of 1888 by his first biographer, Walter Elliott, 82.
6. Hecker to Brownson, December 14, 1843, in *Correspondence,* 79.
7. As quoted in Elliott, 32.
8. *Diary,* 141; see also the entry on 129.
9. *Diary,* 135.
10. Hecker to his family, May 2, 1844; as quoted in Elliott, 141.
11. *Diary,* 142.
12. *Diary,* May 19, 1844, 188.
13. *Diary,* November 1843, 147.
14. Herman Melville, *Pierre; or, The Ambiguities,* 284.
15. *The Reasons of John James Maximilian Oertel, Late a Lutheran Minister for Becoming a Catholic,* 10. Even Catholic converts dedicated to a rational explication of their decision at times portrayed themselves as victims of unknown influences; Bishop Ives, for example, explained

his conversion experience as emanating from an anonymous persuasion: "In the outset, let me recall the fact, that for years a mysterious influence, which I could neither fully comprehend nor entirely throw off, visited my mind, unsettling its peace and filling it with yearnings for something in religion more *real* than I had hitherto experienced" (13).

16. As quoted in Elliott, 108.

17. Joshua Huntington, *Gropings after Truth*, 144.

18. Ibid., 111.

19. Hecker to Brownson, February 19, 1860, in *Correspondence*, 211. I have followed the editors' practice, and hence Hecker's frequent abbreviation of "Christian" to "Xtian" appears without bracketed explanation in my text, as does spelling in subsequent quotations.

20. John Milner, *The End of Religious Controversy, in a Friendly Correspondence between a Religious Society of Protestants and a Roman Catholic Divine*, 122–23. Completed in 1802, Milner's "letters" were a highly influential contribution to Catholic-Protestant polemics. Most of the points by Huntington, Ives, and Brownson can be found in Milner's volume. See, for example, Milner's assertion that Protestants have been inculcated from infancy in the belief that their faith is scriptural. "Hence, when they actually read the Scriptures, they fancy they *see there* what they have been otherwise taught to believe" (62). For Milner's influence on American converts, see Robert Gorman, *Catholic Apologetical Literature in the United States, 1784–1858*, 53ff. Gorman relies on Peter Guilday, "Two Catholic Bestsellers," *America* 54 (1935): 177–79, for his information on Milner. Further references to Milner are given parenthetically in the text.

21. John Adam Moehler [Johann Adam Möhler], *Symbolism; or, Exposition of the Doctrinal Differences between Catholics and Protestants*, 312. Further references to Möhler are given parenthetically in the text.

22. *Diary*, January 14, 1845, 289.

23. *The Escaped Nun and Other Narratives*, 269.

24. Isaac Hecker, *Questions of the Soul*, 289.

25. As quoted in Elliott, 134.

26. "Ritual," *Christian Examiner*, 69 (1860): 321.

27. Hecker to his family, June 11, 1844; as quoted in Elliott, 151.

28. As quoted in Elliott, 224.

29. "The Two Sides of Catholicism," *Catholic World* 1, no. 1 (1865): 746.

30. *Diary*, [Spring?] 1844, 206–7.

31. Hecker to Brownson, August 26, 1869, in *Correspondence*, 277. Hecker is referring to Emerson's "Speech at the Second Annual Meeting of the Free Religious Association at Tremont Temple, Friday, May 28,

1869." Brownson cites Emerson's address in his "Free Religion," *Catholic World* 10, no. 56 (1869).

32. Isaac Hecker, *Aspirations of Nature*, 3.

33. "Christmas in Philadelphia," *Harbinger* 6 (Jan. 1, 1848).

34. As quoted in Elliott, 227.

35. Hecker to his family, June 1844; as quoted in Elliott, 165.

36. Hecker to Brownson, August 17, 1844, in *Correspondence*, 111.

37. Hecker, diary entry, August 20, 1844; as quoted in Elliott, 187.

38. Thoreau to Hecker, August 14, 1844; as quoted in *Autobiography of Brook Farm*, 121.

39. As quoted in Elliott, 296. Describing Hecker's success as a missionary priest, Sophia Ripley wrote to Ruth Charlotte Dana: "He instructs at 6 a.m. every day and by five the Church is so thronged by all classes of persons that it is difficult to get in" (letter dated April 1851, Dana Family Collection, Massachusetts Historical Society).

40. John Farina, *An American Experience of God*, 141.

41. Hecker, *The Church and the Age* (1887); as quoted in Elliott, 313.

42. As quoted in Elliott, 376.

43. As quoted in Elliott, 381.

44. As quoted in Elliott, 385.

45. For Hecker's difficulties at mass, see memorandum entry for Christmas 1885, quoted in Elliott, 413. The citation is from Elliott, 405.

CHAPTER 17

1. James Freeman Clarke, "Orestes A. Brownson's Argument for the Roman Catholic Church," *Christian Examiner* 47 (1849): 247.

2. Orestes A. Brownson, *The Convert; or, Leaves from My Experience*, in *Works*, 5:158–59. Subsequent references give pages only.

3. Brownson, *The Convert*, 16. The lawyer and future governor of Oregon Peter Burnett was among several converts whose vision of Catholic community clearly derived from Milner, Moehler, and Brownson. In 1859 Burnett published an eight-hundred-page treatise on the reasonableness of his new faith. For Burnett, Protestantism maintained " 'its painful preeminence' . . . [only] through mighty crimination, and by wading through the moral slaughter of the Christian world" (Peter H. Burnett, *The Path Which Led a Protestant Lawyer to the Catholic Church*, 725). Such crimes demanded extensive countermeasures. With an attention to detail bordering on mania, Burnett expounded the analogies between Anglo-American jurisprudence and the Roman Catholic church to prove the reasonableness of the latter's structure and claims. For lawyer Burnett, the "mixed codes of jurisprudence" (12) represented by the oral and written traditions of common and statutory law operated

like tradition and Scripture in the church. With a somewhat perverse ingenuity, he argued that English law confirmed the validity of papal claims. "That tradition . . . is a safe, certain, and efficient means of transmission, is demonstrated in the case of the common law of England" (15). In Burnett's reasoning, a tribunal of last resort (like the United States Supreme Court) was necessary to construe the meaning of Christ's law; the Savior naturally provided for such a judicial body by establishing the Roman church. Because Christ, as legislator, spoke the language of precedent and legislative clarity, the scriptural passage granting Peter the keys to heaven fully justified the Roman church's literal interpretation of that passage.

Brownson correctly predicted that most readers would be offended by Burnett's conversion narrative precisely because of its insistent (and voluminous) logic. Said Brownson of American readers: "They are not accustomed to find or to expect certainty in matters of religion, and they feel it a sort of insult to their understanding when you present them a religion which demands and seems to have certainty" (Brownson, "Burnett's Path to the Church," in *Works*, 20:95). Bent on demonstrating that Christ intended a perfect and visible unity, Burnett consciously opposed the era's various experimental utopian communities, which based themselves on the ties of intuitive affinity between their members, with his vision of the church as "that sacred union which holds men together, not merely as constituents of a community, but as members of one mystical body; not cemented together by the sense of mutual want, or strung one unto the other by the ties of the flesh, or the interests of the world, but firmly united by the headship of One, in whom the sublimest thought reposes, as in its proper sphere, and inly communicating through the circulation of vital influences, passing from one unto the other" (59).

In striking contrast to the liberal Protestant investment in skepticism and ambivalence, Burnett's argument forcefully appealed to the validity of human testimony and mediation. Not only Christ and his apostles but one's fellow creatures were worthy of trust. In his chapter on miracles, for example, he accuses Hume and Paley of a "distrust of human veracity" (245) and seeks to defend the Church's confidence in those who witnessed the prodigies of her saints. To do otherwise was to consign oneself to a mean-spirited dimension reserved for those who chose one or another Protestant sect. "The convert from the Catholic Church seems conscious that he is embracing an inferior and lower grade of faith, and adopting a colder and more suspicious estimate of human veracity" (738).

4. *The Convert*, 143.
5. Ibid., 48.
6. Ibid., 4.

7. Orestes A. Brownson, "The Mediatorial Life of Jesus," in *Works*, 4:142. See also Donald Capps, "Orestes Brownson," *Journal for the Scientific Study of Religion* 7 (1968); Henry F. Brownson, *Orestes A. Brownson's Early Life*; Thomas R. Ryan, *Orestes A. Brownson*; and John A. Coleman, *An American Strategic Theology*, especially chap. 4.

8. Orestes A. Brownson, *New Views of Christianity, Society, and the Church* (Boston, 1836), in *Works*, 4:54. See also Brownson to Victor Cousin, November 15, 1836: "Your work Sir, found me sunk in vague sentimentalism, no longer a sceptic, but unable to find any scientific basis for my belief. I despaired of passing from the subjective to the objective. You have corrected and aided me; you have enabled me to find a scientific basis for my belief in Nature, in God and Immortality, and I thank you again and again for the service you have done me" (as quoted in Daniel R. Barnes, "An Edition of the Early Letters of Orestes Brownson," 135).

9. Brownson, "The Mediatorial Life of Jesus," 155.

10. Ibid., 156.

11. Ibid., 169, 165.

12. Ralph Waldo Emerson to Elizabeth Peabody, as quoted in Ryan, *Orestes A. Brownson*, 112.

13. Brownson, "The Mediatorial Life of Jesus," 129.

14. Brownson, *The Convert*, 140.

15. "Catholic Literature in the United States," *Metropolitan* 2 (1854): 69.

16. Orestes A. Brownson, "Bancroft's History of the United States," in *Works*, 19:411. Years later, in *The American Republic*, Brownson would describe humanism as a Satanic conspiracy: "His [Satan's] favorite guise in modern times is that of philanthropy. He is a genuine humanitarian, and aims to persuade the world that humanitarianism is Christianity, and that man is God" (362).

17. Orestes A. Brownson, "Archbishop Spalding," in *Works*, 14:513.

18. Orestes A. Brownson, "The Mission of America," *Brownson's Quarterly Review* (1856), in *Works*, 11:567–68.

19. Orestes A. Brownson, "The Philosophy of History," in *Works*, 4:419. The article originally appeared in the *United States Magazine and Democratic Review* 12 (1843). See also Thomas A. Ryan, "Orestes A. Brownson and Historiography." R. G. Collingwood, in *The Idea of History*, aptly describes the confusion surrounding humanity's role in history and the Christian notion of Providence:

> In one sense man is the agent throughout history, for everything that happens in history happens by his will; in another sense God is the sole agent, for it is only by the working of God's providence that the operation of man's will at any given moment leads to *this* result, and not to a different one. In one sense, again, man is the end for whose sake historical events

happen, for God's purpose is man's well-being; in another sense man exists merely as a means to the accomplishment of God's ends, for God has created him only in order to work out His purpose in terms of human life. But this new attitude to human action gained enormously, because the recognition that what happens in history need not happen through anyone's deliberately wishing it to happen is an indispensable precondition of understanding any historical process. (48)

20. Brownson, "Bancroft's History," 386.

21. Orestes A. Brownson, *The Spirit-Rapper: An Autobiography,* preface. Further references to this volume are given parenthetically in the text.

22. According to the *New Catholic Encyclopedia,* for Augustine "the struggle between faith and unbelief is the master theme of world history" (s.v. "Ecclesiastical Historiography"). On Brownson and Hawthorne, see Carolyn L. Karcher, "Philanthropy and the Occult," in Howard Kerr et al., eds., *The Haunted Dusk,* 69–97.

23. "Notices of Recent Publications," *Christian Examiner* 56 (1854): 449.

24. William Cobbett, *A History of the Protestant Reformation in England and Ireland Showing How That Event Has Impoverished and Degraded the Main Body of the People in Those Countries* . . . (London, 1824), Letter IV.

25. Orestes A. Brownson, "Cardinal Wiseman's Essays," *Brownson's Quarterly Review* (1853), in *Works,* 10:452.

26. Cobbett, Letter IV.

27. Orestes A. Brownson, "Protestantism Ends in Transcendentalism," *Brownson's Quarterly Review* 3 (1846): 382.

28. Ibid., 383.

29. Orestes A. Brownson, *The American Republic,* 423.

30. For Brownson's views on America becoming "permanently Protestant," see Thomas T. McAvoy, "Orestes A. Brownson and American History," *Catholic Historical Review* 40 (1954).

31. Brownson to Hecker, August 25, 1870, in *Correspondence,* 291.

CONCLUSION

1. Nathaniel Hawthorne, *The Marble Faun; or, The Romance of Monte Beni.* The title of the concluding chapter, "Heaps of Human Bones," is from this work (194). Further citations appear parenthetically in the text. Nathaniel Hawthorne to William D. Ticknor, in *Letters of Hawthorne to William D. Ticknor,* 99–100. My argument diverges from that of critics who claim that the novel's partial disclosures and competing pictorial, sculptural, and verbal representations induce readerly partic-

ipation. For the best example of such an "optimistic" reading of the novel, see Jonathan Auerbach, "Executing the Model: Painting, Sculpture, and Romance-Writing in Hawthorne's *The Marble Faun*." Marga C. Jones, "*The Marble Faun* and a Writer's Crisis," attributes the novel's awkwardness to Hawthorne's "uncontrolled acceptance of his material" (109). In fact, it is quite the reverse, an inability to approach it. For an excellent discussion of the biographical factors pressing against the composition of this novel, see Gloria C. Erlich, *Family Themes and Hawthorne's Fiction*. Walter Herbert develops a brilliant reading of *The Marble Faun* in relation to the Hawthorne family's entangled struggles with female "purity," the Roman winter, and Una's malaria during the novel's composition. See his "Erotics of Purity," *Representations* 36 (1991): 114–32.

2. See Richard Brodhead, *The School of Hawthorne*; Joel Pfister, *The Production of Personal Life*; Robert S. Levine, *Conspiracy and Romance*; T. Walter Herbert, *Dearest Beloved* (Berkeley and Los Angeles: University of California Press, 1993). For a reading of the novel that explores the "dilemma of American individualism" (159), see Myra Jehlen, *American Incarnation*, 153–84.

3. Nathaniel Hawthorne, *The French and Italian Notebooks*, 49.

4. My analysis of the imitative relationship between antebellum Catholics and Protestants draws on the following works: René Girard, "*To Double Business Bound*"; Mary Douglas, *Natural Symbols*; Kenneth Burke, *A Rhetoric of Motives* (Berkeley and Los Angeles: University of California Press, 1969). I am especially indebted to Burke's notion that "competition itself is but a special case of imitation" (131). The epigraph for this section is from "Modern Saints, Catholic and Heretic," *North American Review* 77 (July 1853): 165.

5. *Elizabeth Seton: Representative Selections*, ed. Kelly and Melville, 356.

6. This separatism infiltrated from Protestant sentimental writing into Catholic novels. For the adaptation of Catholic novelists to the devices of Protestant popular fiction as well as a discussion of anti-Catholic fiction, see David S. Reynolds, *Faith in Fiction*, 180–87.

7. Orestes A. Brownson, "R. W. Emerson's Poems," *Brownson's Quarterly Review* (1847), in *Works* 19:202.

8. "A Brief History of Weglij Hockwer, a Jewess of Constantinople, Who Became a Convert to the Catholic Religion, and Was Baptised during the Holy Week of 1853," *Metropolitan* 1 (1853): 567.

9. James Freeman Clarke, "Orestes A. Brownson's Argument for the Roman Catholic Church," *Christian Examiner* 48 (1849): 230.

10. "My Confession," *Harper's New Monthly Magazine* 10 (1855). References to this article are given parenthetically in the text.

11. "Modern Saints, Catholic and Heretic," *North American Review* 77 (July 1853): 158.

12. "One of the Nunns," *Harper's New Monthly Magazine* 19 (1859). References to this article are given parenthetically in the text.

13. "Modern Saints, Catholic and Heretic," 147. Further references to this article are given parenthetically in the text.

14. George Ripley, *The Doctrines of the Trinity and Transubstantiation Compared*, 3.

15. As quoted in Ray Allen Billington, *The Protestant Crusade, 1800–1860*, 179–80.

16. Edward Beecher, *The Papal Conspiracy Exposed, and Protestantism Defended in the Light of Reason, History, and Scripture*, 50.

17. William B. Carpenter, *Principles of Mental Physiology with their Applications to the Training and Discipline of the Mind, and the Study of Its Morbid Conditions*, 697.

18. Henry Maudsley, *Body and Mind*, 17, 43.

19. Oliver Wendell Holmes, "The Anatomist's Hymn," in *Collected Works*, 1:175. Subsequent quotations from this poem are from 1:176.

20. Maudsley, 162.

Selected Bibliography

Abbott, John S. C. *"Conquest of Mexico." Harper's New Monthly Magazine* 12 (1855).

Ahlstrom, Sidney E. *A Religious History of the American People.* New Haven: Yale University Press, 1972.

Alcott, William A. *The Young Wife; or, Duties of Woman in the Marriage Relation.* 1837. Reprint. New York: Arno Press, 1972.

Alexander, Jon. *American Personal Religious Accounts, 1600–1980: Toward an Inner History of America's Faiths.* New York and Toronto: Edwin Mellen Press, 1983.

Alterton, Margaret. "An Additional Source for Poe's 'The Pit and the Pendulum.'" *Modern Language Notes* 48 (1930).

Altschuler, Glenn C. "Whose Foot on Whose Throat? A Re-examination of *Benito Cereno." College Language Association Journal* 18 (1975): 383–92.

"American Nativism." *New Catholic Encyclopedia,* vol. 10. New York: Mc-Graw-Hill, 1967.

Angus, David L. "Detroit's Great School Wars: Religion and Politics in a Frontier City, 1842–1853." *Michigan Academician* 12 (1980).

"Antiquities—the Museum of Georgetown College, D.C." *Metropolitan* 1 (1853).

An Apology for the Conversion of Stephen Cleveland Blythe, to the Faith of the Catholic, Apostolic, and Roman Church. . . . New York: Joseph Desnoues, 1815.

"Are We to Have Fiction?" *Metropolitan* 1 (1853).

Arnstein, W. L. "The Great Victorian Convent Case." *History Today* 30 (1980): 46–50.

Arthur, T. S. "Saint Barbara." *Harper's New Monthly Magazine* 22 (1860–61).

"The Artistic and Romantic View of the Church of the Middle Ages." *Christian Examiner* 45 (1849).

Arvin, Newton. *Longfellow: His Life and Work.* Boston: Little, Brown, 1962.

Ashe, Geoffrey. *The Virgin.* London: Routledge and Kegan Paul, 1976.

Auerbach, Jonathan. "Executing the Model: Painting, Sculpture, and Romance-Writing in Hawthorne's *The Marble Faun." ELH* 47 (1980): 103–20.

431

Austin, James T. *"Argument" before the Supreme Judicial Court in Middlesex, on the Case of John R. Buzzell, One of the Twelve Individuals Charged with Being Concerned in Destroying the Ursuline Convent at Charlestown.* Boston: Ford and Damrell, 1834.

Autobiography of Brook Farm. Edited by Henry W. Sams. Englewood Cliffs, N.J.: Prentice-Hall, 1958.

Axtell, John. *After Columbus: Essays in the Ethnohistory of Colonial North America.* New York: Oxford University Press, 1988.

———. *The Invasion Within: The Contest of Cultures in Colonial North America.* New York: Oxford University Press, 1985.

Bailey, Ebenezer. *The Young Ladies' Class Book.* Boston, 1831.

Baird, Robert. *Religion in America; or, An Account of the Origin, Progress, Relation to the State, and Present Condition of the Evangelical Churches in the United States.* New York: Harper and Brothers, 1844.

Bakan, David. *Disease, Pain, and Sacrifice: Toward a Psychology of Suffering.* Chicago: University of Chicago Press, 1968.

Baker, Paul R. *The Fortunate Pilgrims: Americans in Italy, 1800–1860.* Cambridge: Harvard University Press, 1964.

"Balmes on Civilization." *Christian Examiner* 52 (1852).

Barber, Daniel. *Catholic Worship and Piety Explained.* Washington City, 1821.

Barfield, Owen. *Saving the Appearances: A Study in Idolatry.* New York: Harcourt, Brace and World, n.d.

Barish, Jonas. *The Antitheatrical Prejudice.* Berkeley and Los Angeles: University of California Press, 1981.

Barnes, Daniel R. "An Edition of the Early Letters of Orestes Brownson." Ph.D. diss., University of Kentucky, 1970.

———. "Brownson and Newman: The Controversy Re-examined." *Emerson Society Quarterly* 50 (1968).

Barthes, Roland. *Sade, Fourier, Loyola* [1971]. Translated by Richard Miller. New York: Hill and Wang, 1976.

"Bartol's Pictures of Europe." *North American Review* 82 (Jan. 1856).

Baughman, Ernest W. "Public Confession and *The Scarlet Letter*." *New England Quarterly* 40 (1967).

Bayley, Richard. *An Account of the Epidemic Fever Which Prevailed in the City of New York, during Part of the Summer and Fall of 1795.* New York: T. and J. Swords, 1796.

Baym, Nina. *Novels, Readers, and Reviewers: Responses to Fiction in Antebellum America.* Ithaca, N.Y.: Cornell University Press, 1984.

———. *Woman's Fiction: A Guide to Novels by and about Women in America, 1820–1870.* Ithaca, N.Y.: Cornell University Press, 1978.

Beaver, Harold. "Parkman's Crack-Up: A Bostonian on the Oregon Trail." *New England Quarterly* 48 (1975).

Bedford, Henry. *The Life of St. Vincent de Paul.* New York: D. and J. Sadlier and Co., 1858.

Beecher, Catharine E. and Harriet Beecher Stowe. *The American Woman's Home: or, Principles of Domestic Science; Being a Guide to the Formation and Maintenance of Economical, Healthful Beautiful and Christian Homes.* 1869. Reprint. Hartford: The Stowe-Day Foundation, 1987.

Beecher, Edward. *The Papal Conspiracy Exposed, and Protestantism Defended in the Light of Reason, History, and Scripture.* 1855. Reprint. New York: Arno Press, 1977.

Beecher, Lyman. *A Plea for the West.* Cincinnati, 1835.

"Belief and Imagination: Religious Traditions in Literature." Special Issue. *Notre Dame English Journal* 12 (1978–79).

Bell, Rudolph M. *Holy Anorexia.* Chicago: University of Chicago Press, 1985.

Bellah, Robert N., and Frederick E. Greenspahn, *Uncivil Religion: Interreligious Hostility in America.* New York: Crossroad, 1987.

Bennett, David H. *The Party of Fear: From Nativist Movements to the New Right in American History.* Chapel Hill: University of North Carolina Press, 1988.

Bercovitch, Sacvan. *The American Jeremiad.* Madison: University of Wisconsin Press, 1978.

———. *The Office of the Scarlet Letter.* Baltimore: Johns Hopkins University Press, 1991.

———. *The Puritan Origins of the American Self.* New Haven: Yale University Press, 1975.

———, ed. *Reconstructing American Literary History.* Cambridge: Harvard University Press, 1986.

Berg, Joseph F. *Answer to the Lecture of Archbishop Hughes, on the Decline of Protestantism.* Philadelphia: C. Collins, Jr., 1850.

———. *The Confessional; or, An Exposition of the Doctrine of Auricular Confession As Taught in the Standards of the Romish Church.* 3d ed. Philadelphia, 1841.

———. *The Great Apostacy, Identical with Papal Rome; or, An Exposition of the Mystery of Iniquity, and the Marks and Doom of Antichrist.* Philadelphia, 1842.

Berger, Peter L. *The Sacred Canopy: Elements of a Sociological Theory of Religion.* New York: Anchor Books, 1969.

Berlant, Lauren. *The Anatomy of National Fantasy: Hawthorne, Utopia, and Everyday Life.* Chicago: University of Chicago Press, 1991.

Berthold, Dennis. "Hawthorne, Ruskin, and the Gothic Revival: Transcendental Gothic in *The Marble Faun.*" *Emerson Society Quarterly* 20 (1974).

Bezanson, Walter Everett. "Herman Melville's *Clarel.*" Ph.D. diss., Yale University, 1943.

Billington, Ray Allen. *The Protestant Crusade, 1800–1860: A Study of the Origins of American Nativism* [1938]. Chicago: Quadrangle Books, 1964.

———. "Tentative Bibliography of Anti-Catholic Propaganda in the United States (1800–1860)." *Catholic Historical Review* 18 (1932–33).

Bloch, Ruth H. *Visionary Republic: Millennial Themes in American Thought, 1756–1800.* Cambridge: Cambridge University Press, 1985.

Bochen, Christine M. "Personal Narratives by Nineteenth-Century American Catholics: A Study in Conversion Literature." Ph.D. diss., Catholic University of America, 1980.

Bostrom, Irene. "The Novel and Catholic Emancipation." *Studies in Romanticism* 2 (1963).

Bottomley, Frank. *Attitudes to the Body in Western Christendom.* London: Lepus Books, 1979.

Bourne, George. *Lorette. The History of Louise, Daughter of a Canadian Nun: Exhibiting the Interior of Female Convents.* New York: 1833.

Boyce, John. *Mary Lee; or, The Yankee in Ireland.* Baltimore: Kelly, Hadian and Piet, 1860.

Breitwieser, Mitchell R. *American Puritanism and the Defense of Mourning: Religion, Grief, and Ethnology in Mary White Rowlandson's Captivity Narrative.* Madison: University of Wisconsin Press, 1990.

Brengle, Phil. "Father Francis; a Tale of the Spanish Inquisition." *The Christian Parlor Book.* Vol. 5. New York, 1849.

Brewer, E. Cobham. *A Dictionary of Miracles Imitative, Realistic, and Dogmatic.* Philadelphia: Lippincott, 1855.

"A Brief History of Weglij Hockwer, A Jewess of Constantinople, Who Became a Convert to the Catholic Religion, and was Baptised during the Holy Week of 1853." *Metropolitan* 1 (1853).

Brodhead, Richard H. *The School of Hawthorne.* New York: Oxford University Press, 1986.

———. "Sparing the Rod: Discipline and Fiction in Antebellum America." *Representations* 21 (1988): 67–96.

———. "Veiled Ladies: Toward a History of Antebellum Entertainment." *American Literary History* 1, no. 2 (1989).

Brooks, Peter. "Virtue and Terror: *The Monk.*" *ELH* 40 (1973).

Brooks, Van Wyck. *The Dream of Arcadia: American Writers and Artists in Italy, 1760–1915.* New York: Dutton, 1958.

Brown, David Alan. *Raphael and America.* Washington, D.C.: National Gallery of Art, 1983.

Brown, Gillian. *Domestic Individualism: Imagining Self in Nineteenth-Century America.* Berkeley and Los Angeles: University of California Press, 1990.

———. "The Empire of Agoraphobia." *Representations* 20 (1987): 134–57.

Brown, Jerry Wayne. *The Rise of Biblical Criticism in America, 1800–1870.* Middletown, Conn.: Wesleyan University Press, 1969.

Brown, Robert McAfee, and Gustave Weigel. *An American Dialogue: A Protestant Looks at Catholicism and a Catholic Looks at Protestantism.* Garden City, N.Y.: Anchor Books, 1961.

Browne, Henry J. "Catholicism in the United States." In *The Shaping of American Religion,* edited by James Ward Smith and A. Leland Jamison. Princeton, N.J.: Princeton University Press, 1961, 72–121.

Brownlee, W. C. "The Importance of American Freedom to Christianity." *Christian Review* 1, no. 2 (1836).

Brownson, Henry F. *Orestes A. Brownson's Early Life: From 1803 to 1844.* Detroit: H. F. Brownson, 1898.

Brownson, Orestes A. "American Literature." *Brownson's Quarterly Review* (1847). In *The Works of Orestes A. Brownson.* 20 vols. Detroit: Thorndike Nourse, 1883, vol. 19.

————. *The American Republic: Its Constitution, Tendencies, and Destiny.* New York: P. O'Shea, 1866.

————. "Archbishop Spalding." In *The Works of Orestes A. Brownson,* vol. 14.

————. "Bancroft's History of the United States." In *The Works of Orestes A. Brownson,* vol. 19.

————. "Burnett's Path to the Church." In *The Works of Orestes A. Brownson,* vol. 20.

————. *The Convert; or, Leaves from My Experience.* In *The Works of Orestes A. Brownson,* vol. 5.

————. "Free Religion." *Catholic World* 10, no. 56 (1869).

————. "Madness of Antichristians." A review of *The People* by Jules Michelet. *Brownson's Quarterly Review* (1847). In *The Works of Orestes A. Brownson,* vol. 14.

————. "The Mediatorial Life of Jesus." In *The Works of Orestes A. Brownson,* vol. 4.

————. "The Mission of America." *Brownson's Quarterly Review* (1856). In *The Works of Orestes A. Brownson,* vol. 11.

————. "Native Americanism." *Brownson's Quarterly Review* (1845). In *The Works of Orestes A. Brownson,* vol. 10.

————. "New England Brahminism." *Brownson's Quarterly Review* (1863). In *The Works of Orestes A. Brownson,* vol. 4.

————. *New Views of Christianity, Society, and the Church.* Boston, 1836. In *The Works of Orestes A. Brownson,* vol. 4.

————. "Novel-Writing and Novel-Reading." *Boston Quarterly Review* 3, ser. 1 (January 1848).

————. "The Philosophy of History." In *The Works of Orestes A. Brownson,* vol. 4.

————. "Protestantism Ends in Transcendentalism." *Brownson's Quarterly Review* 3 (1846): 369–99.

————. "R. W. Emerson's Poems." *Brownson's Quarterly Review* (1847). In *The Works of Orestes A. Brownson,* vol. 19.

————. "Religious Novels." *Brownson's Quarterly Review* (1847). In *The Works of Orestes A. Brownson,* vol. 19.

————. Review of *History of the United States,* by George Bancroft. *Brownson's Quarterly Review* (1852). In *The Works of Orestes A. Brownson,* vol. 19.

————. Review of *The Scarlet Letter,* by Nathaniel Hawthorne. *Brownson's Quarterly Review* 7 (1850).

————. "Rome or Reason." *Catholic World* (1867). In *The Works of Orestes A. Brownson,* vol. 3.

————. *The Spirit-Rapper: An Autobiography.* Detroit: Thorndike Nourse, 1884.

————. "The Works of Daniel Webster." *Brownson's Quarterly Review* (1852). In *The Works of Orestes A. Brownson,* vol. 19.

The Brownson-Hecker Correspondence. Edited by Joseph Francis Gower, Jr., and Richard M. Leliaert. Notre Dame, Ind.: University of Notre Dame Press, 1979.

"Brownson's Writings." A review of *Charles Elwood; or, The Infidel Converted,* by Orestes A. Brownson. *The Dial: A Magazine for Literature, Philosophy, and Religion* (1841–44).

Bryant, John D. *The Immaculate Conception of the Most Blessed Virgin Mary, Mother of God; a Dogma of the Catholic Church.* Boston: Patrick Donahoe, 1855.

———. *Redemption, A Poem.* Philadelphia: John Penington and Son, 1859.

Buell, Lawrence. *New England Literary Culture: From Revolution through Renaissance.* Cambridge: Harvard University Press, 1986.

Bunkley, Josephine M. *The Testimony of an Escaped Novice.* New York, 1855.

Buntline, Ned [Edward Zane Carroll Judson]. *The Jesuit's Daughter: A Novel for Americans to Read.* New York, 1854.

"Burgos and Its Cathedral." *Illustrated Magazine of Art* 1 (1853).

"Burial of the Dead." *Christian Examiner* 31 (1842).

Burke, Kenneth. *Language as Symbolic Action: Essays on Life, Literature, and Method.* Berkeley and Los Angeles: University of California Press, 1966.

———. *The Philosophy of Literary Form: Studies in Symbolic Action.* Berkeley and Los Angeles: University of California Press, 1967.

———. *The Rhetoric of Religion: Studies in Logology.* Berkeley and Los Angeles: University of California Press, 1961.

Burnett, Peter H. *The Path Which Led a Protestant Lawyer to the Catholic Church.* New York: Benziger Brothers, 1872.

Burton, Katherine. *In No Strange Land: Some American Catholic Converts.* Freeport, N.Y.: Books for Libraries Press, 1942.

Bushnell, Horace. *"Barbarism the First Danger": A Discourse for Home Missions.* New York, 1847.

———. *Christian Nurture* [1847]. Grand Rapids, Mich.: Baker Book House, 1979.

———. *Common Schools.* Hartford Press of Case Tiffany, 1853.

———. *A Letter to His Holiness Pope Gregory XVI.* London, 1846.

———. "The Moral Uses of Great Pestilences" [1849]. In *Moral Uses of Dark Things.* New York: Scribner, 1868.

———. "Unconscious Influence." *American National Preacher* 20, no. 8 (1846).

Butler, Jon. *Awash in a Sea of Faith: Christianizing the American People.* Cambridge: Harvard University Press, 1990.

———. "The Future of American Religious History: Prospectus, Agenda, Transatlantic *Problematique.*" *William and Mary Quarterly* 42 (1985).

Byrd, Max. "The Madhouse, the Whorehouse, and the Convent." *Partisan Review* 44 (1977).

Cabeza de Vaca, Alvar Núñez. *The Journey of Alvar Núñez Cabeza de Vaca and His Companions from Florida to the Pacific, 1528–1536.* Translated by Fanny Bandelier. New York: A. S. Barnes and Co., 1905.

Caldwell, Patricia. *The Puritan Conversion Narrative: The Beginnings of American Expression.* Cambridge: Cambridge University Press, 1983.

Callcott, George H. *History in the United States, 1800–1860.* Baltimore: Johns Hopkins University Press, 1970.

Cameron, Kenneth W. "Thoreau and Orestes Brownson." *Emerson Society Quarterly* 51 (1968).

Camp, James Edwin. "An Unfulfilled Romance: Image, Symbol and Allegory in Herman Melville's *Clarel*." Ph.D. diss., University of Michigan, 1965.

Canavan, Thomas L. "Robert Burton, Jonathan Swift, and the Tradition of Anti-Puritan Invective." *Journal of the History of Ideas* 34 (1973).

"Cant of the Anti-Catholic Press." *Metropolitan* 2 (1854).

Capps, Donald. "Orestes Brownson: The Psychology of Religious Affiliation." *Journal for the Scientific Study of Religion* 7 (1968).

Carey, Patrick W. *People, Priests, and Prelates: Ecclesiastical Democracy and the Tensions of Trusteeism*. Notre Dame, Ind.: University of Notre Dame Press, 1987.

———. "Republicanism within American Catholicism, 1785–1860." *Journal of the Early Republic* 3, no. 4 (Winter 1983).

Carlier, Auguste. *Marriage in the United States*. 1867. Reprint. New York: Arno Press, 1972.

Carnochan, W. B. *Confinement and Flight: An Essay in English Literature of the Eighteenth Century*. Berkeley and Los Angeles: University of California Press, 1977.

Carpenter, William B. *Principles of Mental Physiology with Their Applications to the Training and Discipline of the Mind, and the Study of Its Morbid Conditions*. New York: D. Appleton and Co., 1875.

Carthy, Mary P. "English Influences on Early American Catholicism." *Historical Records and Studies* 46 (1958).

Cartwright, Peter. *A Letter Purporting to Be from His Satanic Majesty, the Devil: With an Answer Annexed*. Cincinnati, 1859.

Cary, Emma Forbes. "Narrative of Miss Emma Forbes Cary." In *Some Roads to Rome in America*, edited by Georgina Pell Curtis. St. Louis, Mo.: B. Herder, 1909.

"The Catacombs and the Church of Rome." *Christian Examiner* 43 (1847).

"The Catacombs of Rome." *Atlantic Monthly* 1 (1858).

"Catholic Literature in the United States." *Metropolitan* 2 (1854).

Chadwick, Owen, ed. *The Mind of the Oxford Movement*. Stanford, Calif.: Stanford University Press, 1961.

Chamberlain, Samuel E. *My Confession: The Recollections of a Rogue*. Lincoln: University of Nebraska Press, 1987.

Chandler, Alice. *A Dream of Order: The Medieval Ideal in Nineteenth-Century English Literature*. Lincoln: University of Nebraska Press, 1970.

Channing, William Ellery. *"The Church." A Discourse Delivered in the First Congregational Unitarian Church of Philadelphia*. Philadelphia, 1847.

———. "Letter on Catholicism." In *Essays, Literary and Political*. Glasgow, 1837.

———. *Slavery*. 1835. Reprint. New York: Arno Press, 1969.

Channing, William Ellery, II [Ellery Channing]. *Conversations in Rome: Between an Artist, a Catholic, and a Critic*. Boston: William Crosby and H. P. Nichols, 1847.

The Charlestown Convent; Its Destruction by a Mob, on the Night of August 11, 1834. With a History of the Excitement before the Burning, and the Strange and Exaggerated Reports Relating Thereto; the Feeling of Rage and Indignation Afterwards; the Proceedings of the Meetings, and Expressions of the Contemporary Press. Also, the Trials of the Rioters, the Testimony, and the Speeches of Counsel. With a Review of the Incidents, and Sketches and Record of the Principal Actors; and a Contemporary Appendix. Compiled from Authentic Sources. Boston: Patrick Donahoe, 1870.

Chateaubriand, Viscount de. *The Genius of Christianity; or, The Spirit and Beauty of the Christian Religion.* Translated by Charles I. White. Facsimile reprint. New York: Howard Fertig, 1976.

Chavez, John R. *The Lost Land: The Chicano Image of the Southwest.* Albuquerque: University of New Mexico Press, 1984.

Cherry, Conrad, ed. *Horace Bushnell: Sermons.* New York: Paulist Press, 1985.

Chestnut, Mary. *Mary Chestnut's Civil War.* Edited by C. Vann Woodward. New Haven: Yale University Press, 1981.

Child, Lydia Maria. *The Mother's Book.* 1831. Reprint. New York: Arno Press, 1972.

"Chillingworth." *Christian Examiner* 30 (1841).

Chiniquy, Father. *The Priest, the Woman, and the Confessional.* New York, 1880.

Chinnici, Joseph P. "Organization of the Spiritual Life: American Catholic Devotional Works, 1791–1866." *Theological Studies* 40 (1979).

"The Christian Duty of Granting the Claims of the Roman Catholics." *Christian Examiner* 7 (1830).

"Christmas in Philadelphia." *Harbinger* 6 (1848).

"The Churches and the Church." *Christian Examiner* 41 (1846).

"The Church in the Catacombs." *National Magazine* 1 (July–Dec. 1852).

"The Church of Rome in Her Theology." *Christian Examiner* 65 (1858).

Clarke, James Freeman. "Joan of Arc." *Christian Examiner* 45 (1848).

———. "Orestes A. Brownson's Argument for the Roman Catholic Church." *Christian Examiner* 47 (1849).

Clebsch, William A. *American Religious Thought: A History.* Chicago: University of Chicago Press, 1973.

———. *Christianity in European History.* New York: Oxford University Press, 1979.

Clendinnen, Inga. "'Fierce and Unnatural Cruelty': Cortés and the Conquest of Mexico." *Representations* 33 (1991): 65–100.

Clifton, Robert. "The Popular Fear of Catholics during the English Revolution." *Past and Present* 52 (1971).

"Climatology." *North American Review* 91 (Oct. 1860).

Cline, Howard F., C. Harvey Gardiner, and Charles Gibson, eds. *William Hickling Prescott: A Memorial.* Durham, N.C.: Duke University Press, 1959.

Cmiel, Kenneth. *Democratic Eloquence: The Fight over Popular Speech in Nineteenth-Century America.* Berkeley and Los Angeles: University of California Press, 1990.

Cobbett, William. *A History of the Protestant Reformation in England and Ireland Showing How That Event Has Impoverished and Degraded the Main Body of the People in Those Countries. . . .* London, 1824.

Colacurcio, Michael J. *The Province of Piety: Moral History in Hawthorne's Early Tales.* Cambridge: Harvard University Press, 1984.

Coleman, Caryl. "A Forgotten Convert." *Catholic World* 122, no. 728 (Oct. 1925–Mar. 1926).

Coleman, John A. *An American Strategic Theology.* New York: Paulist Press, 1982.

Collingwood, R. G. *The Idea of History.* Oxford: Clarendon Press, 1946.

Colton, Calvin [pseud.]. *Protestant Jesuitism. By a Protestant.* New York: Harper and Brothers, 1836.

Condon, Peter. "Constitutional Freedom of Religion and the Revivals of Religious Intolerance." *U.S. Catholic Historical Society Records and Studies* 4 (1906).

Conrad, Susan. *Perish the Thought: Intellectual Women in Romantic America, 1830–1860.* New York: Oxford University Press, 1976.

The Conversion of Marie-Alphonse Ratisbonne; Original Narrative of Baron Theodore de Bussières. Edited by W. Lockhart. New York: Edward Dunigan and Brother, 1856.

Conversions: The Christian Experience. Edited by Hugh T. Kerr and John M. Mulder. Grand Rapids, Mich.: William B. Eerdmans Co., 1983.

Cooper, James Fenimore. *Gleanings in Europe: Italy.* Edited by John Conron and Constance Ayers Denne. Albany: State University of New York Press, 1981.

Cott, Nancy F. *The Bonds of Womanhood: "Woman's Sphere" in New England, 1780–1835.* New Haven: Yale University Press, 1977.

Cross, Andrew B. *Priests' Prisons for Women.* Baltimore, 1854.

Crowe, Charles. *George Ripley: Transcendentalist and Utopian Socialist.* Athens: University of Georgia Press, 1967.

[Culbertson, Rosamond]. *Rosamond; or, A Narrative of the Captivity and Sufferings of an American Female under the Popish Priests, in the Island of Cuba.* New York: Leavitt, Lord, and Co., 1836.

Culler, Jonathan. "Semiotics of Tourism." *American Journal of Semiotics* 1, nos. 1–2, (1981).

Curran, Francis X. *Catholics in Colonial Law.* Chicago: Loyola University Press, 1963.

Curran, Robert Emmett, ed. *American Jesuit Spirituality: The Maryland Tradition, 1634–1900.* New York: Paulist Press, 1988.

Curtis, George Ticknor. "Prescott's *History of the Conquest of Mexico.*" *Christian Examiner* 35–36 (1844).

———. *The Rights of Conscience and of Property; or, The True Issue of the Ursuline Convent Question.* Boston: Charles C. Little and James Brown, 1842.

Curtis, Georgina Pell, ed. *Some Roads to Rome in America.* St. Louis, Mo.: B. Herder, 1909.

"Daily Miracles." *Christian Parlor Book* 5 (1849).

Da Porte, Lorenzo. "Critique on Certain Passages in Dante." *New York Review and Atheneum Magazine* 1 (1825).

Darling, Arthur B. *Political Changes in Massachusetts, 1824–1848: A Study of Liberal Movements in Politics.* New Haven: Yale University Press, 1925.

Davidson, Cathy N. *Revolution and the Word: The Rise of the Novel in America.* New York: Oxford University Press, 1986.

Davis, Andrew Jackson. *The Approaching Crisis.* New York, 1853.

Davis, David Brion. *The Fear of Conspiracy: Images of Un-American Subversion from the Revolution to the Present.* Ithaca, N.Y.: Cornell University Press, 1971.

———. "Some Themes of Counter-Subversion: An Analysis of Anti-Masonic, Anti-Catholic, and Anti-Mormon Literature." *Mississippi Valley Historical Review* 47 (1960–61).

———, ed. *Antebellum American Culture: An Interpretive Anthology.* Lexington, Mass.: D. C. Heath and Company, 1979.

Davis, Natalie Zemon. *Society and Culture in Early Modern France.* Stanford, Calif.: Stanford University Press, 1965.

Day, Edward. "Orestes Brownson and the Motherhood of Mary." *American Ecclesiastical Review* 129 (1953).

"Debates on the Roman Catholic Religion." *Christian Examiner* 23 (1838).

Delbanco, Andrew. *William Ellery Channing: An Essay on the Liberal Spirit in America.* Cambridge: Harvard University Press, 1981.

"De Maistre and Romanism." *North American Review* 79 (Oct. 1854).

Demos, John. "Images of the American Family, Then and Now." In *Changing Images of the Family,* edited by Virginia Tufte and Barbara Myerhoff. New Haven: Yale University Press, 1979, 43–60.

Denning, Michael. *Mechanic Accents: Dime Novels and Working-Class Culture in America.* New York: Verso, 1987.

"Destruction of the Charlestown Convent." *U.S. Catholic Historical Society Records and Studies* 12 (1918) and 13 (1919).

Dewey, Orville. *The Old World and the New; or, A Journal of Reflections and Observations Made on a Tour in Europe.* 2 vols. New York: Harper and Brothers, 1836.

Dhu, Helen [pseud.]. *Stanhope Burleigh: The Jesuits in Our Homes.* New York: Stringer and Townsend, 1855.

Dickens, A. G., and John M. Tonkin. *The Reformation in Historical Thought.* Cambridge: Harvard University Press, 1985.

Dillenberger, Jane, and Joshua C. Taylor. *The Hand and the Spirit: Religious Art in America, 1700–1900.* Berkeley, Calif.: University Art Musuem, 1972.

Dillenberger, John. *The Visual Arts and Christianity in America: The Colonial Period through the Nineteenth Century.* Chico, Calif.: Scholar's Press, 1984.

Dirvin, Joseph I. *Mrs. Seton: Foundress of the American Sisters of Charity.* New York: Farrar, Straus and Cudahy, 1962.

Documents Relating to the Ursuline Convent in Charlestown. Boston: Samuel N. Dickinson, 1842.

Dolan, Jay P. *The American Catholic Experience: A History from Colonial Times to the Present.* New York: Doubleday, 1985.

———. *Catholic Revivalism: The American Experience, 1830–1900.* Notre Dame, Ind.: University of Notre Dame Press, 1978.

———. *The Immigrant Church: New York's Irish and German Catholics, 1815–1865.* Baltimore: Johns Hopkins University Press, 1975.

Doody, Terrence. *Confession and Community in the Novel.* Baton Rouge: Louisiana State University Press, 1980.

Doughty, Howard. *Francis Parkman.* New York: Macmillan, 1962.

———. "Parkman's Dark Years: Letters to Mary Dwight Parkman." *Harvard Library Bulletin* 4 (1950).

Douglas, Ann. *The Feminization of American Culture.* New York: Avon Books, 1978.

Douglas, Mary. *Natural Symbols: Explorations in Cosmology.* New York: Random House, 1982.

———. *Purity and Danger: An Analysis of the Concepts of Pollution and Taboo.* London: Routledge and Kegan Paul, 1966.

Duban, James. *Melville's Major Fiction: Politics, Theology, and Imagination.* De Kalb: Northern Illinois University Press, 1983.

———. "Satiric Precedent for Melville's 'The Two Temples.'" *American Transcendental Quarterly* 42 (1979).

Dugmore, C. W. *The Mass and the English Reformers.* London: Macmillan; New York: St. Martin's Press, 1958.

Duke, James O. *Horace Bushnell: On the Vitality of Biblical Language.* Chico, Calif.: Scholar's Press, 1984.

Durandus, William. *The Symbolism of Churches and Church Ornaments: A Translation of the First Book of the Rationale Divinorum Officianum.* Edited by John Mason Neale and Benjamin Webb. Leeds, England: T. W. Green, 1843.

Durkheim, Emile. *The Elementary Forms of the Religious Life* [1915]. Translated by Joseph Ward Swain. New York: Free Press, 1965.

Dwight, Theodore. *Open Convents: or, Nunneries and Popish Seminaries Dangerous to the Morals, and Degrading to the Character of a Republican Community.* New York: Van Nostrand and Dwight, 1836.

———. *The Roman Republic of 1849.* New York, 1851.

Eccles, W. J. "The History of New France according to Francis Parkman." *William and Mary Quarterly* 18 (1961).

Eisenstein, Elizabeth. *The Printing Press as an Agent of Change.* Cambridge: Cambridge University Press, 1979.

"Elizabeth Bayley Seton." *New Catholic Encyclopedia.* Vol. 13. Washington, D.C.: Catholic University of America, 1967.

Elliott, Walter. *The Life of Father Hecker.* 1891. Reprint. New York: Arno Press, 1972.

Ellis, John Tracy. *American Catholicism.* Chicago: University of Chicago Press, 1969.

———. *Perspectives in American Catholicism.* Baltimore: Helicon, 1973.

———, ed. *Documents of American Catholic History.* Milwaukee: Bruce Publishing Co., 1956.

Elson, Ruth Miller. *Guardians of Tradition: American Schoolbooks of the Nineteenth Century.* Lincoln: University of Nebraska Press, 1964.

Emerson, Ralph Waldo. *The Complete Works of Ralph Waldo Emerson.* Centenary Edition. 12 vols. Boston: Houghton Mifflin, 1903.

———. *The Letters of Ralph Waldo Emerson.* Edited by Ralph L. Rusk. 6 vols. New York: Columbia University Press, 1939.

———. *Selections from Ralph Waldo Emerson.* Edited by Stephen E. Whicher. Boston: Houghton Mifflin, 1957.

Emerson in His Journals. Edited by Joel Porte. Cambridge: Harvard University Press, 1982.

England, John. "Documents Relating to the Imposture of Rebecca T. Read [*sic*], and the Burning of the Ursuline Convent, at Charlestown Mass." In *The Works of The Right Reverend John England.* Cleveland: Arthur H. Clark Co., 1908, vol. 4.

"The English Reformation." *Christian Examiner* 37 (1844).

Epstein, Barbara L. *The Politics of Domesticity: Women, Evangelism, and Temperance in Nineteenth Century America.* Middletown, Conn.: Wesleyan University Press, 1981.

Erikson, Erik. *Young Man Luther: A Study in Psychoanalysis and History.* New York: Norton, 1958.

Erlich, Gloria C. *Family Themes and Hawthorne's Fiction: The Tenacious Web.* New Brunswick, N.J.: Rutger's University Press, 1986.

"Ernest the Seeker." *Dial* 1, no. 1 (1841).

"The Errors and Superstitions of the Church of Rome." *Christian Examiner* 55 (1853).

The Escaped Nun and Other Narratives. New York: De Witt and Davenport, n.d.

Essays from the North American Review. Edited by Allen Thorndike Rice. New York: D. Appleton and Co., 1879.

Everett, Edward. *The Discovery and Colonization of America and Immigration to the United States.* Boston: Little, Brown, 1853.

Ewens, Mary. *The Role of the Nun in Nineteenth Century America.* 1971. Reprint. New York: Arno Press, 1978.

Fairbanks, Henry G. *The Lasting Loneliness of Nathaniel Hawthorne.* Albany, N.Y.: Magi Books, Inc., 1965.

"Fanaticism." *Christian Examiner* 21 (1837).

Farina, John. *An American Experience of God: The Spirituality of Isaac Hecker.* New York: Paulist Press, 1981.

Farrell, Bertin. *Orestes Brownson's Approach to the Problem of God: A Critical Examination in the Light of the Principles of St. Thomas Aquinas.* Catholic University of America Studies in Sacred Theology, 2d. ser., no. 34. Washington, D.C.: Catholic University of America Press, 1950.

"The Fathers of the Desert." *Metropolitan* 1 (1853).

Feldberg, Michael. *The Turbulent Era: Riot and Disorder in Jacksonian America.* New York: Oxford University Press, 1980.

Fell, Sister Marie Leonore. *The Foundations of Nativism in American Textbooks, 1783–1860.* Washington, D.C.: Catholic University of America Press, 1941.

"Female Convents." *Christian Examiner* 19 (1836).

Ferguson, Robert A. *Law and Letters in American Culture.* Cambridge: Harvard University Press, 1984.

Field, Henry M. *The Good and the Bad in the Roman Catholic Church: Is That Church to Be Destroyed or Reformed? A Letter from Rome.* New York: Putnam, 1849.

Fink, Steven. "Thoreau and the American Home." *Prospects* 2 (1987).

Finney, Charles Grandison. "Sinners Bound to Change Their Own Hearts." In *Sermons on Important Subjects.* New York: John S. Taylor, 1836.

Fleenor, Juliann, ed., *The Female Gothic*. Montreal: Eden Press, 1983.

Flibbert, Joseph. "The Dream and Religious Faith in Herman Melville's *Clarel*." *American Transcendental Quarterly* 50 (1981).

Fliegelman, Jay. *Prodigals and Pilgrims: The American Revolution against Patriarchal Authority, 1750–1800*. Cambridge: Cambridge University Press, 1982.

Fogle, Richard H. *Melville's Shorter Tales*. Norman: University of Oklahoma Press, 1960.

Foner, Eric. *Free Soil, Free Labor, Free Men: The Ideology of the Republican Party before the Civil War*. New York: Oxford University Press, 1970.

Foster, Charles H. *The Rungless Ladder: Harriet Beecher Stowe and New England Puritanism*. Durham, N.C.: Duke University Press, 1954.

Foucault, Michel. *Discipline and Punish: The Birth of the Prison*. Translated by Alan Sheridan. New York: Random House, 1979.

———. *The History of Sexuality*. Vol. 1. Translated by Robert Hurley. New York: Random House, 1980.

———. *The Order of Things: An Archaeology of the Human Sciences*. New York: Random House, 1973.

———. *Power/Knowledge: Selected Interviews and Other Writings, 1972–1977*. Translated by Colin Gordon, Leo Marshall, John Mepham, and Kate Soper. Edited by Colin Gordon. New York: Harvester Press, 1980.

Fourier, Charles. *Design for Utopia: Selected Writings of Charles Fourier*. Translated by Julia Franklin. Edited by Charles Gide. New York: Schocken Books, 1971.

Foxe, John. *Actes and Monuments of Martyrs*. London, 1583.

Foxe's Book of Martyrs. Edited by G. A. Williamson. Boston: Little, Brown, 1965.

Franklin, Benjamin. *Autobiography*. Edited by J. A. Leo Lemay and P. M. Zall. New York: Norton, 1986.

Freedman, Estelle B. *Their Sisters' Keepers: Women's Prison Reform in America, 1830–1930*. Ann Arbor: University of Michigan Press, 1981.

Freud, Sigmund. "The 'Uncanny.'" In *The Standard Edition of the Complete Psychological Works of Sigmund Freud*. 24 vols. London: Hogarth Press, 1955, 17:219–56.

Frothingham, Charles W. *The Convent's Doom: A Tale of Charlestown in 1834*. 5th ed. Boston: Graves and Weston, 1854.

———. *The Haunted Convent*. Boston: Graves and Weston, 1854.

Frothingham, Octavius Brooks. *Transcendentalism in New England*. New York: Harper and Row, 1959.

Frye, Northrop. *The Great Code: The Bible and Literature*. New York: Harcourt Brace Jovanovich, 1982.

Fuller, John Douglas Pitts. *The Movement for the Acquisition of All Mexico, 1846–1848*. Baltimore: Johns Hopkins University Press, 1936.

Gale, Robert L. *Francis Parkman*. New York: Twayne, 1973.

Gallagher, Catherine, and Thomas Laqueur, eds. *The Making of the Modern Body: Sexuality and Society in the Nineteenth Century*. Berkeley and Los Angeles: University of California Press, 1987.

Gardiner, C. Harvey. *Prescott and His Publishers*. Carbondale: Southern Illinois University Press, 1959.

——. *William Hickling Prescott: A Biography*. Austin: University of Texas Press, 1969.

Garner, Shirley Nelson, Claire Kahane, and Madelon Sprengnether, eds. *The Mother Tongue: Essays in Feminist Psychoanalytic Interpretation*. Ithaca, N.Y.: Cornell University Press, 1985.

Gausted, Edwin Scott. *Historical Atlas of Religion in America*. Rev. ed. New York: 1976.

Gavin, Anthony. *The Great Red Dragon; or, The Master-Key to Popery*. New York, 1856.

Geertz, Clifford. *The Interpretation of Cultures*. New York: Basic Books, 1973.

Gerber, David A. "Modernity in the Service of Tradition: Catholic Lay Trustees at Buffalo's St. Louis Church and the Transformation of European Communal Traditions, 1829–1855." *Journal of Social History* 15 (Summer 1982).

Gerson, Noel B. *Harriet Beecher Stowe*. New York: Praeger, 1976.

Gervais, Ronald J. "Papist among the Puritans: Icon and Logos in *The Scarlet Letter*." *ESQ* 25 (1979): 11–16.

Giamatti, A. Bartlett, ed. *Dante in America: The First Two Centuries*. Binghamton, N.Y.: Medieval and Renaissance Texts and Studies, 1983.

Gilhooley, Leonard, ed. *No Divided Allegiance: Essays in Brownson's Thought*. New York: Fordham University Press, 1980.

Gilmore, Michael T. *American Romanticism and the Marketplace*. Chicago: University of Chicago Press, 1985.

Girard, René. *Deceit, Desire, and the Novel: Self and Other in Literary Structure*. Translated by Yvonne Freccero. Baltimore: Johns Hopkins University Press, 1965.

——. *"To Double Business Bound": Essays in Literature, Mimesis, and Anthropology*. Baltimore: Johns Hopkins University Press, 1977.

——. *Violence and the Sacred*. Translated by Patrick Gregory. Baltimore: Johns Hopkins University Press, 1977.

Gleason, Philip. *The Conservative Reformers: German-American Catholics and the Social Order*. Notre Dame, Ind.: University of Notre Dame Press, 1968.

——. *Keeping the Faith: American Catholicism Past and Present*. Notre Dame, Ind.: University of Notre Dame Press, 1987.

——. "Mass and Maypole Revisited: American Catholics and the Middle Ages." *Catholic Historical Review* 57 (1971).

Goen, C. G. "Broken Churches; Broken Nation: Regional Religion and North-South Alienation in Antebellum America." *Church History* 52 (1983).

Goodrich, Samuel Griswold. *Lights and Shadows of American History*. Boston: George C. Rand, 1855.

——. *Peter Parley's First Book of History*. New York, 1831.

Gorman, Robert. *Catholic Apologetical Literature in the United States, 1784–1858*. Washington, D.C.: Catholic University of America Press, 1939.

Gossman, Lionel. "History as Decipherment: Romantic Historiography and the Discovery of the Other." *New Literary History* 18, no. 1 (1986): 23–57.

Grabo, Norman S. "Catholic Tradition, Puritan Literature, and Edward Taylor." *Papers of the Michigan Academy of Science, Arts and Letters* 45 (1960).

Gray, John Chipman. "Review of *La Divina Commedia*." In A. Bartlett Giamatti, *Dante in America: The First Two Centuries*. Binghamton, N.Y.: Medieval and Renaissance Texts and Studies, 1983.

Greene, George W. "Visits to the Dead in the Catacombs of Rome." *Harper's New Monthly Magazine* 10 (1855).

Greven, Philip. *The Protestant Temperament: Patterns of Child-Rearing, Religious Experience, and the Self in Early America*. New York: Knopf, 1977.

Griffin, David E. "'The Man for the Hour': A Defense of Francis Parkman's *Frontenac*." *New England Quarterly* 43 (1970).

Grimsted, David. *Melodrama Unveiled: American Theater and Culture, 1800–1850*. Berkeley and Los Angeles: University of California Press, 1987.

———. "Rioting in Its Jacksonian Setting." *American Historical Review* 77, no. 2 (1972): 361–97.

———, ed. *Notions of the Americans, 1820–1860*. New York: Braziller, 1970.

Guilday, Peter. *John Gilmary Shea: Father of American Catholic History*. New York: United States Catholic Historical Society, 1926.

———. "Two Catholic Bestsellers." *America* 54 (1935).

Gura, Philip F. *The Wisdom of Words: Language, Theology, and Literature in the New England Renaissance*. Middletown, Conn.: Wesleyan University Press, 1981.

Gustafson, James M. *Protestant and Roman Catholic Ethics*. Chicago: University of Chicago Press, 1978.

Haller, William. *The Elect Nation*. London: Jonathan Cape, 1963.

Halttunen, Karen. *Confidence Men and Painted Women: A Study of Middle-Class Culture in America, 1830–1870*. New Haven: Yale University Press, 1982.

Hann, R. R. "Sabotage Indeed: The Alleged Plot against the Bible." *Journal of Ecumenical Studies* 20 (1983).

Harpham, Geoffrey Galt. *The Ascetic Imperative in Culture and Criticism*. Chicago: University of Chicago Press, 1987.

Harris, Neil. *The Artist in American Society: The Formative Years, 1790–1860* [1966]. Rev. ed. Chicago: University of Chicago Press, 1982.

Hart, James D. *The Popular Book: A History of America's Literary Taste*. New York: Oxford University Press, 1950.

Hasenmueller, Christine. "'A Picture Is Worth a Thousand Words': How We Talk about Images." *Semiotica* 73 (1989).

Hatch, Nathan O. *The Democratization of American Christianity*. New Haven: Yale University Press, 1989.

Havran, Martin J. *The Catholics in Caroline England*, Stanford, Calif.: Stanford University Press, 1962.

Hawley, John Stratton, ed. *Saints and Virtues*. Berkeley and Los Angeles: University of California Press, 1987.

Hawthorne, Manning, and H. W. Longfellow Dana. "The Origin of Longfellow's *Evangeline*." *The Papers of the Bibliographical Society of America* 41 (1947).

Hawthorne, Nathaniel. *The American Notebooks*. Edited by Claude M. Simpson. Centenary Edition. Columbus: Ohio State University Press, 1972.

———. *The French and Italian Notebooks*. Edited by Thomas Woodson. Centenary Edition. Columbus: Ohio State University Press, 1980.

———. *Letters of Hawthorne to William D. Ticknor, 1851–1864*. Newark, N.J.: Carteret Book Club, 1910.

———. *Love Letters of Nathaniel Hawthorne, 1839–1841*. Chicago: Society of The Dofobs, 1907.

———. *Love Letters of Nathaniel Hawthorne, 1841–1863*. Chicago: Society of the Dofobs, 1907.

———. *The Marble Faun; or, The Romance of Monte Beni*. Edited by William Charvat et al. Centenary Edition. Columbus: Ohio State University Press, 1968.

———. *The Scarlet Letter*. Edited by William Charvat et al. Centenary Edition. Columbus: Ohio State University Press, 1962.

———. *Twice-Told Tales*. Edited by William Charvat et al. Centenary Edition. Columbus: Ohio State University Press, 1974.

Hecker, Isaac. *Aspirations of Nature*. New York: James B. Kirker, 1857.

———. *The Diary: Romantic Religion in Ante-Bellum America*. Edited by John Farina. New York: Paulist Press, 1988.

———. *Questions of the Soul*. 6th ed. New York: Catholic Publication House, 1855.

Heimert, Alan, and Perry Miller, eds. *The Great Awakening: Documents Illustrating the Crisis and Its Consequences*. Indianapolis: Bobbs-Merrill, 1967.

Hennesey, James. *American Catholics: A History of the Roman Catholic Community in the United States*. New York: Oxford University Press, 1981.

Herbert, James C. "William Perkins's 'A Reformed Catholic': A Psycho-Cultural Interpretation." *Church History* 51 (1982).

Herbert, T. Walter. *Dearest Beloved: The Hawthornes and the Making of the Middle-Class Family*. Berkeley and Los Angeles: University of California Press, 1993.

———. "The Erotics of Purity: *The Marble Faun* and the Victorian Construction of Sexuality." *Representations* 36 (1991): 114–32.

Hewit, A. F. "Pure vs. Diluted Catholicism." *American Catholic Quarterly Review* 20 (1895).

Higham, John. *Send These to Me: Immigrants in Urban America*. Rev. ed. Baltimore: Johns Hopkins University Press, 1984.

Hillard, George Stillman. *Six Months in Italy*. 2 vols. Boston: Ticknor, Reed, and Fields, 1853.

Hirsch, David H. "Another Source for 'The Pit and the Pendulum.'" *Mississippi Quarterly* 23 (1969–70).

"History of the Great Reformation of the Sixteenth Century in Germany, Switzerland, etc." *Christian Examiner* 32 (1842).

The History of the Inquisition of Spain . . . Abridged and Translated from the Original Works of D. Juan Antonio Llorente. Philadelphia, 1843.

Hobson, Barbara Meil. *Uneasy Virtue: The Politics of Prostitution and the American Reform Tradition*. New York: Basic Books, 1987.

Hofstadter, Richard, and Michael Wallace, eds. *American Violence: A Documentary History*. New York: Vintage Books, 1970.

Holden, Vincent F. *The Yankee Paul: Isaac Thomas Hecker*. Milwaukee: Bruce Publishing Co., 1958.

Hollis, C. Carroll. "Brownson on Native New England." *New England Quarterly* 40 (1967).

Holmes, J. Derek. *The Triumph of the Holy See: A Short History of the Papacy in the Nineteenth Century.* London: Burns and Oates, 1978.

Holmes, Oliver Wendell. *The Collected Works of Oliver Wendell Holmes.* 13 vols. Boston: Houghton Mifflin, 1892.

———. *Elsie Venner: A Romance of Destiny* [1861]. New York: New American Library, 1961.

Holt, Michael F. *The Political Crisis of the 1850s.* New York: Norton, 1978.

———. "The Politics of Impatience: The Origins of Know Nothingism." *Journal of American History* 60 (1973).

"The Holy Week at Rome." *Harper's New Monthly Magazine* 9 (1854).

"Home Life of the Brook Farm Association." *Atlantic Monthly* 42 (1878).

Hopkins, John Henry. *The History of the Confessional.* New York, 1850.

Hopkins, Samuel M. "John Knox and Mary, Queen of Scots." In *The Christian Parlor Book.* New York, 1849.

———. "Monks and Monasteries." *The Christian Parlor Book.* New York, 1849.

Horsley-Meacham, Gloria. "The Monastic Slaver: Images and Meaning in *Benito Cereno.*" *New England Quarterly* 56 (1983).

Horsman, Reginald. *Race and Manifest Destiny: The Origins of American Racial Anglo-Saxonism.* Cambridge: Harvard University Press, 1981.

Howe, Daniel Walker, ed. *Victorian America.* Philadelphia: University of Pennsylvania Press, 1976.

Hudson, Winthrop S. *Religion in America.* New York: Scribner, 1965.

Hudspeth, Robert N. *Ellery Channing.* New York: Twayne, 1973.

Hughes, John. "An Account of the Conversion of an American Family." In *Tracts Published under the Superintendence of the Catholic Institute of Great Britain.* Tract 38. London: 1838–41.

———. *"The Decline of Protestantism and Its Cause": A Lecture Delivered in St. Patrick's Cathedral, November 10, 1850.* New York: Edward Dunigan and Brother, 1850.

Huntington, Jedidiah Vincent. *Rosemary; or, Life and Death.* New York: D. and J. Sadlier, 1860.

———. *St. Vincent De Paul, and the Fruits of His Life.* Philadelphia, 1852.

Huntington, Joshua. *Gropings after Truth: A Life Journey from New England Congregationalism to the One Catholic and Apostolic Church.* New York: Catholic Publication Society, 1868.

The Illustrated Magazine of Art. New York: Alexander Mongomery, 1853.

"An Interview with Martin Luther." *Harper's New Monthly Magazine* 22 (1861).

Irving, Washington. *The Sketch Book of Geoffrey Crayon, Gent.* Edited by Haskell Springer. Vol. 8 of *The Complete Works of Washington Irving.* Boston: Twayne Publishers, 1978.

Irwin, John T. *American Hieroglyphics: The Symbol of the Egyptian Hieroglyphics in the American Renaissance* [1980]. Baltimore: Johns Hopkins University Press, 1983.

"Italy." *North American Review* 78 (Apr. 1854).

Ives, I. M. *Two Lectures on the Inquisition.* Milwaukee: Rufus King and Co., 1853.

Ives, Levi Silliman. *The Trials of a Mind in Its Progress to Catholicism: A Letter to His Old Friends.* Boston: Patrick Donahoe, 1854.

Jacobs, Harriet A. *Incidents in the Life of a Slave Girl. Written by Herself.* Edited by Jean Fagan Yellin. Cambridge: Harvard University Press, 1987.

Jacobs, Wilbur R. "Francis Parkman's Oration 'Romance in America.'" *American Historical Review* 68, no. 3 (1963).

———. "Some of Parkman's Literary Devices." *New England Quarterly* 31 (1958).

Jameson, Anna Brownell. *History of Our Lord As Exemplified in Works of Art.* London, 1864.

———. *Sisters of Charity, Catholic and Protestant, and the Communion of Labor.* Boston: Ticknor and Fields, 1857.

Jarves, James Jackson. *Art-Hints: Architecture, Sculpture and Painting.* New York, 1855.

———. *Italian Sights and Papal Principles As Seen through American Spectacles.* New York: Harper and Brothers, 1856.

Jehlen, Myra. *American Incarnation: The Individual, the Nation, and the Continent.* Cambridge: Harvard University Press, 1986.

Jennings, Francis. *The Invasion of America: Indians, Colonialism, and the Cant of Conquest.* Chapel Hill: University of North Carolina Press, 1975.

———. "A Vanishing Indian: Francis Parkman versus His Sources." *Pennsylvania Magazine of History and Biography* 87 (1963).

"The Jesuit." *National Magazine* 3 (July–Dec. 1853).

The Jesuit Conspiracy. The Secret Plan of the Order. Detected and Revealed by the Abbate Leone. London, 1848.

The Jesuit Relations and Allied Documents: Travels and Explorations of the Jesuit Missionaries in New France, 1610–1791. . . . Translated and edited by Reuben G. Thwaites. 73 vols. Cleveland: Burrows Brothers, 1896–1901.

Jones, Howard Mumford. "The Allure of the West." *Harvard Library Bulletin* 28 (1980).

———. *America and French Culture, 1750–1848.* Chapel Hill: University of North Carolina Press, 1927.

Jones, Marga C. "*The Marble Faun* and a Writer's Crisis." *Studi Americani* 16 (1970): 81–123.

Judd, Sylvester. *Margaret, a Tale of the Real and Ideal.* Boston, 1845.

Karcher, Carolyn L. *Shadow over the Promised Land: Slavery, Race, and Violence in Melville's America.* Baton Rouge: Louisiana State University Press, 1980.

———. "Spiritualism and Philanthropy in Brownson's *The Spirit-Rapper* and Melville's *The Confidence-Man.*" *Emerson Society Quarterly* 25 (1979).

Kasson, Joy S. *Artistic Voyagers: Europe and the American Imagination in the Works of Irving, Allston, Cole, Cooper, and Hawthorne.* Westport, Conn.: Greenwood Press, 1982.

"Kate O'Connor. A Story of Mixed Marriages." *Metropolitan* 2 (1854).

Keen, Benjamin. *The Aztec Image in Western Thought.* New Brunswick, N.J.: Rutgers University Press, 1971.

Kelley, Mary. "The Sentimentalists: Promise and Betrayal in the Home." *Signs* 4 (1979).

Kennedy, J. Gerald. *Poe, Death, and the Life of Writing.* New Haven: Yale University Press, 1973.

Kenney, Alice P. "Necessity of Invention: Medievalism in America." *Literary Review* 23 (Summer 1980).

Kenny, Vincent. *Herman Melville's "Clarel": A Spiritual Autobiography.* Hamden, Conn.: Shoe String Press, Archon Books, 1973.

Kenrick, Francis Patrick. *Letter on Christian Union, Addressed to the Bishops of the Protestant Episcopal Church.* Philadelphia: Eugene Cummiskey, 1841.

Kerr, Howard, and Charles L. Crow, eds. *The Occult in America: New Historical Perspectives.* Urbana: University of Illinois Press, 1983.

Kerr, Howard, John W. Crowley, and Charles L. Crow, eds. *The Haunted Dusk: American Supernatural Fiction, 1820–1920.* Athens: University of Georgia Press, 1983.

Kibbey, Ann. *The Interpretation of Material Shapes in Puritanism: A Study of Rhetoric, Prejudice, and Violence.* Cambridge: Cambridge University Press, 1986.

Kimball, Gayle. *The Religious Ideas of Harriet Beecher Stowe: Her Gospel of Womanhood.* Studies in Women and Religion, vol. 8. New York and Toronto: Edwin Mellen Press, 1982.

King, John Owen, III. *The Iron of Melancholy: Structures of Spiritual Conversion in America from the Puritan Conscience to Victorian Neurosis.* Middletown, Conn.: Wesleyan University Press, 1983.

Kirk, Martin J. *The Spirituality of Isaac Thomas Hecker: Reconciling the American Character and the Catholic Faith.* New York: Garland, 1988.

Knapp, Joseph G. *Tortured Synthesis: The Meaning of Melville's "Clarel."* New York: Philosophical Library, 1971.

Knobel, Dale T. *Paddy and the Republic: Ethnicity and Nationality in Antebellum America.* Middletown, Conn: Wesleyan University Press, 1986.

La Capra, Dominick. *Rethinking Intellectual History: Texts, Contexts, Language.* Ithaca, N.Y.: Cornell University Press, 1983.

"The Ladies of the Sacred Heart." *Harper's New Monthly Magazine* 17 (1858): 205–6.

Lankford, John. "An End and a Beginning: Reflections on Ahlstrom's Religious History." *Anglican Theological Review* 41 (1974).

La Piana, Angelina. *Dante's American Pilgrimage: A Historical Survey of Dante Studies in the United States, 1800–1944.* New Haven: Yale University Press, 1948.

Larkin, Oliver W. *Art and Life in America.* Rev. ed. New York: Holt, Rinehart and Winston, 1960.

———. *Samuel F. B. Morse and American Democratic Art.* Edited by Oscar Handlin. Boston: Little, Brown, 1954.

The Late Conversions to the Catholic Church; Being a Reply to the Recent Statements Made by the Bishop de Lancey. Philadelphia: M. Fithian, 1846.

Lea, Henry Charles. *A History of Auricular Confession and Indulgences in the Latin Church.* 2 vols. Philadelphia, 1896.

"Leading Theories on the Philosophy of History." *North American Review* 95 (July 1862).

Lears, T. J. Jackson. *No Place of Grace: Antimodernism and Tradition in the Nineteenth Century.* Chicago: University of Chicago Press, 1985.

Le Beau, Bryan. "Saving the West from the Pope: Anti-Catholic Propaganda and the Settlement of the Mississippi River Valley." *American Studies* 32, no. 1 (1991).

Leland, Henry P. *Americans in Rome.* New York: Charles T. Evans, 1863.

"The Lessons of Modern History." *North American Review* 80 (Jan. 1855).

"Letters on the Holy Eucharist." *United States Catholic Magazine* (June 1842).

Leverenz, David. *Manhood and the American Renaissance.* Ithaca, N.Y.: Cornell University Press, 1989.

———. "The Politics of Emerson's Man-Making Words." *Proceedings of the Modern Language Association* 101, no. 1 (1986): 38–53.

Levin, David. "Forms of Uncertainty: Representation of Doubt in American Histories." *New Literary History* 8 (1976).

———. *History as Romantic Art.* Stanford, Calif.: Stanford University Press, 1959.

Levine, Lawrence W. *Highbrow, Lowbrow: The Emergence of Cultural Hierarchy in America.* Cambridge: Harvard University Press, 1988.

Levine, Robert S. *Conspiracy and Romance: Studies in Brockden Brown, Cooper, Hawthorne, and Melville.* New York: Cambridge University Press, 1989.

Lewis, Matthew Gregory. *The Monk* [1796]. London: Oxford University Press, 1973.

Lewis, R. W. B. *The American Adam: Innocence, Tragedy, and Tradition in the Nineteenth Century.* Chicago: University of Chicago Press, 1955.

Light, Dale. "The Reformation of Philadelphia Catholicism, 1830–1860." *The Pennsylvania Magazine of History and Biography* 112 (1988).

Ligouri, Saint Alphonsus Maria de'. *The Glories of Mary* [1750]. In *Ascetical Works,* edited by Charles G. Fehrenbach. Baltimore: Helicon Press, 1962, vol. 1.

Lippard, George. *Quaker City; or, The Monks of Monk Hall* [1845]. Edited by Leslie Fiedler. New York: Odyssey Press, 1970.

Livingston, Vanbrugh [Americo-Catholicus, pseud.]. *A Letter to the Hon. and Rev. George Spencer on the Oxford Movement in the United States.* New York, 1842.

Loewenberg, Bert James. *American History in American Thought: Christopher Columbus to Henry Adams.* New York: Simon and Schuster, 1972.

Longfellow, Henry Wadsworth. *The Complete Poetical Works of Henry Wadsworth Longfellow.* 1863. Reprint. Boston: Houghton Mifflin, 1902.

———. "Review of *A History of the Italian Language and Dialects.*" *North American Review* 35 (Oct. 1832).

Lough, A. G. *The Influence of John Mason Neale.* London: S.P.C.K., 1962.

Lowell, James Russell. *Fireside Travels* [1864]. 6th ed. Boston: Houghton Mifflin, 1882.

———. *Letters of James Russell Lowell.* Edited by C. E. Norton. 2 vols. New York: Harper and Brothers, 1893.

————. *The Poetical Works of James Russell Lowell.* 5 vols. Boston: Houghton Mifflin, 1904.

Lunn, Arnold. *Roman Converts.* Freeport, N.Y.: Books for Libraries Press, 1924.

Luther, Martin. "The Pagan Servitude of the Church." In *Martin Luther: Selections from His Writings,* edited by John Dillenberger. Garden City, N.Y.: Anchor Books, 1961, 249–359.

McAvoy, Thomas T. *A History of the Catholic Church in the United States.* Notre Dame, Ind.: University of Notre Dame Press, 1969.

————. "Orestes A. Brownson and American History." *Catholic Historical Review* 40 (1954).

MacCannell, Dean. *The Tourist: A New Theory of the Leisure Class.* New York: Schocken Books, 1976.

McDannell, Colleen. *The Christian Home in Victorian America, 1840–1900.* Bloomington: Indiana University Press, 1986.

McDannell, Colleen, and Bernhard Lang. *Heaven: A History.* New Haven: Yale University Press, 1988.

McGee, Thomas D'Arcy. *The Catholic History of North America: Five Discourses to Which Are Added Two Discourses on the Relations of Ireland and America.* Boston: Patrick Donahoe, 1855.

McWilliams, John P., Jr. *Hawthorne, Melville, and the American Character: A Looking-Glass Business.* Cambridge: Cambridge University Press, 1984.

Maistre, Joseph de. *The Pope: Considered in His Relations with the Church, Temporal Sovereignties, Separated Churches, and the Cause of Civilization.* Translated by Aeneas Dawson. London, 1850.

Manning, Henry Edward. "The Workings of The Holy Spirit in the Church of England." *Catholic World* 1, no. 3 (1865).

Manross, William W. *A History of the American Episcopal Church.* New York: Morehouse, 1935.

Marraro, Howard R. "American Travellers in Rome, 1811–1850." *Catholic Historical Review* 29 (1944).

Marryat, Capt. Frederick. *Diary.* In *Diary in America,* edited by Jules Zanger. Bloomington: Indiana University Press, 1960.

Marshall, Hugh. *Orestes Brownson and the American Republic.* Washington, D.C.: Catholic University of America Press, 1971.

Martineau, Harriet. *Society in America.* Edited by Seymour Martin Lipset. Gloucester, Mass.: Peter Smith, 1968.

Mason, Rev. Cyrus. *A History of the Holy Catholic Inquisition Compiled from Various Authors.* Philadelphia, 1835.

"Massacre of St. Bartholomew." *Harper's New Monthly Magazine* 17 (1858).

Mather, Cotton. *Selections.* Edited by Kenneth B. Murdock. 1926. Reprint. New York: Hafner Press, 1973.

Maudsley, Henry. *Body and Mind: An Inquiry into their Connection and Mutual Influence, Specially in Reference to Mental Disorders.* 2d ed. New York: D. Appleton and Co., 1874.

May, Henry F. *The Enlightenment in America.* New York: Oxford University Press, 1976.

Medlicott, Alexander, Jr. "Return to the Land of Light: A Plea to an Unredeemed Captive." *New England Quarterly* 38 (1965).

Melville, Herman. *Clarel: A Poem and Pilgrimage in the Holy Land* [1876]. Vols. 14 and 15 of *The Works of Herman Melville*. New York: Russell and Russell, 1963.

———. *Journal of a Visit to Europe and the Levant, October 11, 1856–May 6, 1857*. Edited by Howard C. Horsford. Princeton, N.J.: Princeton University Press, 1955.

———. *The Letters of Herman Melville*. Edited by Merrell R. Davis and William H. Gilman. New Haven, Conn.: Yale University Press, 1960.

———. *The Piazza Tales and Other Prose Pieces, 1839–1860*. Evanston, Ill.: Northwestern University Press, 1987.

———. *Pierre; or, The Ambiguities* [1852]. Evanston, Ill.: Northwestern University Press, 1971.

Mendelsohn, Jack. *Channing: The Reluctant Radical*. Boston: Little, Brown, 1971.

"The Mexican War." *Massachusetts Quarterly Review* 1 (1847): 8–54.

Michelet, Jules. *Le Prêtre, La Femme, La Famille* [1845]. Published in English as *Priests, Women, and Families*. Translated by C. Cocks. London, 1845.

"Michelet's *Life of Luther*." *North American Review* 63 (Oct. 1846).

Miles, Margaret R. *Image as Insight: Visual Understanding in Western Christianity and Secular Culture*. Boston: Beacon Press, 1985.

Miller, Perry. *Errand into the Wilderness*. Cambridge: Harvard University Press, 1956.

———. *The New England Mind: The Seventeenth Century* [1939]. Boston: Beacon Press, 1961.

———. *The New England Mind: From Colony to Province* [1953]. Boston: Beacon Press, 1961.

———, ed. *The Transcendentalists: An Anthology* [1950]. Cambridge: Harvard University Press, 1971.

Miller, Randall M., and Thomas D. Marzik. *Immigrants and Religion in Urban America*. Philadelphia: Temple University Press, 1977.

Milner, John. *The End of Religious Controversy, in a Friendly Correspondence between a Religious Society of Protestants and a Roman Catholic Divine*. 2d ed. London: Keating, Brown, and Co., 1819.

Mintz, Steven. *A Prison of Expectations: The Family in Victorian Culture*. New York: New York University Press, 1983.

Mitchell, Donald Grant. *Reveries of a Bachelor; or, A Book of the Heart* [1850]. New York, 1884.

Mitchell, W. J. T. *Iconology: Image, Text, Ideology*. Chicago: University of Chicago Press, 1986.

"Mob Law." *American Quarterly Review* 17 (1835).

Modern Catholic Dictionary. Edited by John A. Hardon. Garden City, N.Y.: Doubleday, 1980.

"Modern Saints, Catholic and Heretic." *North American Review* 77 (July 1853).

Modleski, Tania. *Loving with a Vengeance: Mass-produced Fantasies for Women*. New York: Methuen, 1982.

Moehler, John Adam [Johann Adam Möhler]. *Symbolism; or, Exposition of the Doctrinal Difference between Catholics and Protestants As Evidenced in*

Their Symbolical Writings. Translated by James Burton Robertson. New York: Edward Dunigan, 1844.

[Moffatt, Mary Anne Ursula] Mother Mary Edmund St. George. *An Answer to Six Months in a Convent Exposing Its Falsehoods and Manifold Absurdities by the Lady Superior.* Boston: J. K. Eastburn, 1835.

Monk, Maria. *Awful Disclosures of the Hotel Dieu Nunnery. Revised, with an Appendix.* New York: Published by Maria Monk, 1836.

———. *Awful Disclosures of the Hotel Dieu Nunnery.* Facsimile of the 1836 edition. Hamden, Conn.: Archon Books, 1962.

Montalembert, Count [Charles-Forbes-René] de. *The Life of St. Elizabeth, of Hungary, Duchess of Thuringia.* Translated by Mary Hackett. New York: D. and J. Sadlier and Co., 1888.

Montgomery, David. "The Shuttle and the Cross: Weavers and Artisans in the Kensington Riots of 1844." *Journal of Social History* 5 (1972).

Moore, R. Laurence. *In Search of White Crows.* New York: Oxford University Press, 1977.

———. "Religion, Secularization, and the Shaping of the Culture Industry in Antebellum America." *American Quarterly* 41, no. 2 (1989).

———. *Religious Outsiders and the Making of Americans.* Oxford: Oxford University Press, 1986.

Morris, David B. *The Culture of Pain.* Berkeley and Los Angeles: University of California Press, 1991.

———. "Gothic Sublimity." *New Literary History* 16 (1985).

Morse, John T., Jr. *The Life and Letters of Oliver Wendell Holmes.* 2 vols. London: Sampson Low, 1896.

Morse, Samuel F. B. *Foreign Conspiracy against the Liberties of the United States.* 1835. Reprint. New York: Arno Press, 1977.

Moss, Michael E. *Robert W. Weir of West Point.* West Point, N.Y., 1976.

Murray, Nicholas [Kirwan, pseud.]. *"The Decline of Popery and Its Causes": An Address delivered in the Broadway Tabernacle on January 15, 1851.* New York: Harper and Brothers, 1851.

———. *Romanism at Home. Letters to the Hon. Roger B. Taney, Chief Justice of the United States.* 6th ed. New York: Harper and Brothers, 1852.

"My Confession." *Harper's New Monthly Magazine* 10 (1855).

Myerson, Joel, ed. *The Transcendentalists: A Review of Research and Criticism.* New York: Modern Language Association of America, 1984.

Narrative of Don Juan Van Halen's Imprisonment in the Dungeons of the Inquisition at Madrid and His Escape in 1817 and 1818. New York, 1828.

Narrative of Henry "Box" Brown, Who Escaped from Slavery Enclosed in a Box 3 Feet Long and 2 Wide. Written from a Statement of Facts Made by Himself with Remarks upon the Remedy for Slavery By Charles Stearns. Edited by Maxwell Whiteman. Afro-American History Series. Philadelphia: RHistoric Publications, 1969.

A Narrative of the Lord's Wonderful Dealings with John Marrant, a Black, (Now Gone to Preach the Gospel in Nova-Scotia) Born in New-York, in North-America, Taken Down from His Own Relation, Arranged, Corrected and Published, by the Rev. Mr. Aldridge. In *Held Captive by Indians: Selected*

Narratives, 1642–1836, edited by Richard VanDerBeets. Knoxville: University of Tennessee Press, 1973, 177–201.

Nash, Alice N. "Two Stories of New England Captives: Grizel and Christine Otis of Dover, New Hampshire." In *New England / New France, 1600–1850: The Dublin Seminar for New England Folklife,* edited by Peter Benes. Boston: Boston University, 1989.

"Neander's Church History." *North American Review* 80 (Jan. 1855).

Nevins, William. *Thoughts on Popery.* 1836. Reprint. New York: Arno Press, 1977.

Newberry, Frederick. "Tradition and Disinheritance in *The Scarlet Letter.*" *ESQ* 23, no. 1 (1977): 1–26.

"The New Editor's Introductory." *Metropolitan* 2 (1854).

Newman, John Henry. *Apologia Pro Vita Sua* [1864]. Edited by David J. De-Laura. New York: Norton, 1968.

———. *An Essay in Aid of a Grammar of Assent* [1870]. New York: Oxford University Press, 1985.

———. *An Essay on the Development of Christian Doctrine.* 2d ed. London, 1846.

Newnham, W. *Essay on Superstition: Being an Inquiry into the Effects of Physical Influence on the Mind, in the Production of Dreams, Visions, Ghosts, and Other Supernatural Appearances.* London: J. Hatchard and Son, 1830.

"New York Church Architecture." *Putnam's Monthly* 2 (Sept. 1853).

Niebuhr, H. Richard. *The Kingdom of God in America.* Hamden, Conn.: Shoe String Press, 1956.

Noble, David. *Historians against History: The Frontier Thesis and the National Covenant in American Historical Writing since 1830.* Minneapolis: University of Minnesota Press, 1965.

Norman, E. R. *Anti-Catholicism in Victorian England.* New York: Barnes and Noble, 1968.

"North American Martyrs." *New Catholic Encyclopedia,* vol. 10. New York: McGraw-Hill, 1967.

Norton, Anne. *Alternative Americas: A Reading of Antebellum Political Culture.* Chicago: University of Chicago Press, 1986.

Norton, Charles Eliot. "*The New Life* of Dante." *Atlantic Monthly* 3 (1859).

———. *Notes of Travel and Study in Italy.* Boston: Houghton Mifflin, 1859.

"Notices of Recent Publications." *Christian Examiner* 47 (1849).

"Notices of Recent Publications." *Christian Examiner* 56 (1854).

Novak, Barbara. *American Painting of the Nineteenth Century: Realism, Idealism, and the American Experience.* New York: Harper and Row, Icon Editions, 1979.

Novick, Peter. *That Noble Dream: "The Objectivity Question" and the American Historical Profession.* Cambridge: Cambridge University Press, 1988.

Nye, Russell B. *George Bancroft: Brahmin Rebel.* New York: Knopf, 1944.

———. *Society and Culture in America, 1830–1860.* New York: Harper and Row, 1974.

Oates, Mary J., ed. "'Lowell': An Account of Convent Life in Lowell, Massachusetts, 1852–1890." *New England Quarterly* 61, no. 1 (1988): 101–18.

Oertel, John James Maximilian. *The Reasons of John James Maximilian Oertel, Late a Lutheran Minister for Becoming a Catholic.* New York: P. Kavanagh, 1840.

"One of the Nunns." *Harper's New Monthly Magazine* 19 (1859).

"On Exterior Worship." *Metropolitan* 1 (1853).

Ong, Walter J. *Interfaces of the Word: Studies in the Evolution of Consciousness and Culture.* Ithaca, N.Y.: Cornell University Press, 1977.

———. *The Presence of the Word: Some Prolegomena for Cultural and Religious History.* Minneapolis: University of Minnesota Press, 1967.

"On the Gothic Style in the Fine Arts." *Putnam's Monthly* 2 (Aug. 1853).

"On the Uses of Communion, and the Propriety of a General Attendance upon It." *Christian Examiner* 31 (1842).

Ortner, Sherry, and Harriet Whitehead. *Sexual Meanings: The Cultural Construction of Gender.* New York: Cambridge University Press, 1981.

Orvell, Miles. *The Real Thing: Imitation and Authenticity in American Culture, 1880–1940.* Chapel Hill: University of North Carolina Press, 1989.

Otto, Rudolf. *The Idea of the Holy.* Oxford: Oxford University Press, 1923.

Overdyke, W. Darrell. *The Know-Nothing Party in the South.* Baton Rouge: Louisiana State University Press, 1950.

"Oxfordism and the English Church." *Christian Examiner* 36 (1844).

Parker, G. "Fornicating with the Devil." *History Today* 30 (1980).

Parker, Theodore L. "The Character of Mr. Prescott as an Historian." *Massachusetts Quarterly Review* 2 (1849).

———. "The Life of Saint Bernard of Clairvaux." *Christian Examiner* 30 (1841).

Parkman, Francis. "A Convent at Rome." *Harper's* 81 (1890): 448–54.

———. *The Jesuits in North America in the Seventeenth Century* [1867]. Williamstown, Mass.: Corner House Publishers, 1980.

———. *The Journals of Francis Parkman.* Edited by Mason Wade. 2 vols. New York: Harper and Brothers, 1974.

———. *The Letters of Francis Parkman.* Edited by Wilbur R. Jacobs. 2 vols. Norman: University of Oklahoma Press, 1960.

———. *Vassall Morton.* Boston: Phillips, Sampson and Co., 1856.

———. "The Woman Question." *North American Review* 129 (Oct. 1879).

"Parkman's Conspiracy of Pontiac." *Christian Examiner* 51 (1851).

Parry, Stanley J. "The Premises of Brownson's Political Theory." *Review of Politics* 16 (1954).

Parsons, Wilfred. *Early Catholic Americana, 1729–1830.* New York, 1939.

Pearce, Roy Harvey. *Savagism and Civilization: A Study of the Indian and the American Mind* [1953]. Rev. ed. Berkeley and Los Angeles: University of California Press, 1988.

———. "The Significance of the Captivity Narrative." *American Literature* 19 (1947).

Pease, Donald E. *Visionary Compacts: American Renaissance Writings in Cultural Context.* Madison: University of Wisconsin Press, 1987.

Pease, Otis A. *Parkman's History: The Historian as Literary Artist.* New Haven: Yale University Press, 1953.

Peckham, Morse. *Romanticism and Behavior: Collected Essays*. Columbia: University of South Carolina Press, 1976.

Pelikan, Jaroslav, ed. *Interpreters of Luther*. Philadelphia: Fortress Press, 1968.

Penington, Isaac. *Works*. 2 vols. 4th ed. Philadelphia, 1863.

Percival, James Gates. *The Poetical Works*. Boston, 1865.

Perry, J. *The Protesting Christian*. Cincinnati: Catholic Society for the Diffusion of Useful Knowledge, 1840.

Pettit, Norman. *The Heart Prepared: Grace and Conversion in Puritan Spiritual Life*. New Haven: Yale University Press, 1966.

———. "Lydia's Conversion: An Issue in Hooker's Departure." *Publications of the Cambridge Historical Society* (1964–66).

Pfister, Joel. *The Production of Personal Life: Class, Gender, and the Psychological in Hawthorne's Fiction*. Stanford, Calif.: Stanford University Press, 1991.

Phillips, John. *The Reformation of Images: Destruction of Art in England, 1535–1660*. Berkeley and Los Angeles: University of California Press, 1973.

"The Philosophy of Conversion." *Catholic World* 4, no. 22 (1867).

"Picture-Buying." *Crayon* 1 (1855).

Pinto, Holly Joan. *William Cullen Bryant, the Weirs, and American Impressionism*. Roslyn, N.Y.: Nassau County Museum of Fine Art, 1983.

Pise, Charles Constantine. *Father Rowland: A North American Tale*. 1831. Reprint. New York: Arno Press, 1978.

Pitrat, John Claudius. *Paul and Julia; or, The Political Mysteries, Hypocrisy, and Cruelty of the Leaders of the Church of Rome*. Boston: Edward W. Hinks and Co., 1855.

Pius IX. *The Papal Syllabus of Errors* [1864]. Wilmington, N.C.: McGrath Publishing Co., 1981.

Poe, Edgar Allan. *Collected Works of Edgar Allan Poe*. Edited by Thomas Ollive Mabbot. Cambridge: Harvard University Press, 1978.

"The Poet of Puseyism." *Christian Examiner* 33 (1843).

Pope or President? Startling Disclosures of Romanism as Revealed by Its Own Writers. 1859. Reprint. New York: Arno Press, 1977.

"Popery and Our Common Schools." *National Magazine* 3 (July–Dec. 1853).

Porterfield, Amanda. *Feminine Spirituality in America: From Sarah Edwards to Martha Graham*. Philadelphia: Temple University Press, 1980.

Portier, William L. *Isaac Hecker and the First Vatican Council*. Lewiston, N.Y.: Edwin Mellen Press, 1985.

Potter, David M. *The Impending Crisis, 1848–1861*. Edited by Don E. Fehrenbacher. New York: Harper and Row, 1976.

Prescott, William Hickling. *Biographical and Critical Essays*. London: Routledge, 1856.

———. *The Correspondence of William Hickling Prescott, 1833–1847*. Edited by Roger Wolcott. Boston: Houghton Mifflin, 1925.

———. *The History of the Conquest of Mexico* [1843]. New York: Modern Library, 1936.

———. *The History of the Reign of Ferdinand and Isabella the Catholic* [1837]. 2 vols. Philadelphia, 1868.

———. *The Literary Memoranda of William Hickling Prescott.* Edited by C. Harvey Gardiner. 2 vols. Norman: University of Oklahoma Press, 1961.

———. *Representative Selections.* Edited by William Charvat and Michael Kraus. New York: American Book Co., 1943.

———. "Sir Walter Scott." In *Essays from the North American Review;* edited by Allen Thorndike Rice. New York: D. Appleton and Co., 1879.

"Prescott as an Historian." *North American Review* 83 (July 1856).

"Prescott's *Conquest of Mexico.*" *Massachusetts Quarterly Review* 2 (1849).

"The Present Tendencies of the Church." *Christian Examiner* 35 (1843).

"The Priest—the Wife—the Family." *United States Magazine* 17 (1846).

"Protestantism." *Christian Examiner* 41 (1846).

Proudfoot, Wayne. *Religious Experience.* Berkeley and Los Angeles: University of California Press, 1985.

"Quakerism and Catholicism." Review of *Reasons for Becoming a Roman Catholic; Addressed to the Society of Friends,* by Frederick Lucas. *Christian Examiner* 30 (1841).

Quigley, Hugh. *The Prophet of the Ruined Abbey; or, A Glance of the Future of Ireland.* New York: Edward Dunigan and Brother, 1855.

Quinn, Arthur Hobson. *Edgar Allan Poe.* New York: Appleton-Century-Crofts, 1941.

Radcliffe, Ann. *The Mysteries of Udolpho* [1794]. New York: Dutton, 1962.

Ralls, W. "Papal Aggression of 1850: A Study in Victorian Anti-Catholicism." *Church History* 43 (1974).

Rameur, E. "The Progress of the Church in the United States." *Catholic World* 1 (1865).

Ramsey, Albert C. *The Other Side; or, Notes for the History of the War between Mexico and the United States.* New York, 1850.

Raymond, Henrietta Dana. "Sophia Willard Dana Ripley: Co-Founder of Brook Farm." Master's thesis, Columbia University, 1949.

"Reaction in Favor of the Roman Catholics." *Christian Examiner* 23 (1838).

"The Real and the Ideal in New England." *North American Review* 84 (Apr. 1857).

Reardon, B. M. G. *Religious Thought in the Nineteenth Century.* Cambridge: Cambridge University Press, 1966.

Reed, Rebecca Theresa. *Six Months in a Convent; or, The Narrative of Rebecca Theresa Reed, Who Was under the Influence of the Roman Catholics about Two Years, and an Inmate of the Ursuline Convent. . . .* Boston: Odiorne and Metcalf, 1835.

Reese, David Meredith. *Humbugs of New-York: Being a Remonstrance against Popular Delusion; Whether in Science, Philosophy, or Religion.* New York: John S. Taylor; Boston: Weeks, Jordan and Co., 1838.

Reidy, John P. "Orestes Augustus Brownson: Conservative Mentor to Dissent." *American Benedictine Review* 21 (1970).

Reising, Russell. *The Unusable Past: Theory and the Study of American Literature.* New York: Methuen, 1986.

"Religion, Love, and Marriage in Italy." *Harper's New Monthly Magazine* 14 (1857).

"Remarks on Mystery." *Christian Examiner* 17 (1835).

"A Reminiscence of Rome." *Harper's New Monthly Magazine* 15 (1857).

Renza, Louis A. "Poe's Secret Autobiography." In *The American Renaissance Reconsidered,* edited by Walter Benn Michaels and Donald E. Pease. Baltimore: Johns Hopkins University Press, 1985.

Report of the Committee Relating to the Destruction of the Ursuline Convent, August 11, 1834. Boston: J. H. Eastburn, 1834.

Review of William Hickling Prescott, *History of the Conquest of Mexico, North American Review* 58 (Jan. 1844).

Reynolds, David S. *Beneath the American Renaissance: The Subversive Imagination in the Age of Emerson and Melville.* New York: Knopf, 1988.

———. *Faith in Fiction: The Emergence of Religious Literature in America.* Cambridge: Harvard University Press, 1981.

Reynolds, Larry J. *"The Scarlet Letter* and Revolutions Abroad." *American Literature* 57 (1985).

Ricci, Scipio de. *Female Convents. Secrets of Nunneries Disclosed.* New York, 1834.

Ridgely, J. V. "George Lippard's *The Quaker City:* The World of the American Porno-Gothic." *Studies in the Literary Imagination* 7, no. 1 (1984).

Riggs, Lisette. "George and Sophia Ripley." Ph.D. diss. University of Maryland, 1942.

Ringe, Donald A. *American Gothic: Imagination and Reason in Nineteenth-Century Fiction.* Lexington: University Press of Kentucky, 1982.

———. "The Artistry of Prescott's 'The Conquest of Mexico.'" *New England Quarterly* 26 (1953).

Ripley, George. *The Doctrines of the Trinity and Transubstantiation Compared.* Boston, 1833.

Ripley, Sophia Dana. "Letters to Ruth Charlotte Dana." Unpublished correspondence. Dana Family Collection, Massachusetts Historical Society.

"Ritual." *Christian Examiner* 69 (1860).

Roddan, John T. *John O'Brien; or, The Orphan of Boston, a Tale of Real Life.* Boston: Patrick Donahoe, 1850.

"A Roland for an Oliver." *Christian Examiner* 7 (1830).

"A Roman Beatification." *Christian Examiner* 58 (1855).

"Romanism and Protestantism." *Christian Examiner* 47 (1850).

"The Romish Hierarchy." *North American Review* 82 (Jan. 1856).

Rose, Anne C. *Transcendentalism as a Social Movement, 1830–1850.* New Haven: Yale University Press, 1981.

Rosenzweig, Paul. "The Search for Identity: The Enclosure Motif in Pym." *Emerson Society Quarterly* 26 (1980).

Ross, Dorothy. "Historical Consciousness in Nineteenth-Century America." *American Historical Review* 89, no. 1 (1984).

Rothstein, William G. *American Physicians in the Nineteenth Century: From Sects to Science.* Baltimore: Johns Hopkins University Press, 1972.

Roundy, Nancy. "Present Shadows: Epistemology in *Benito Cereno." Arizona Quarterly* 34 (Winter 1978).

Rowland, Beryl. "Melville Answers the Theologians: The Ladder of Charity in 'The Two Temples.'" *Mosaic* 7 (1974).

Rowlandson, Mary. "The Sovereignty and Goodness of God." In *Puritans among the Indians: Accounts of Captivity and Redemption 1676–1724,* edited by Alden T. Vaughan and Edward W. Clark. Cambridge: Harvard University Press, 1981, 31–75.

Rowson, Susanna. *Charlotte Temple* [1794]. New York: Oxford University Press, 1986.

Ruether, Rosemary R., and Rosemary S. Keller. *Women and Religion in America.* 2 vols. San Francisco: Harper and Row, 1981.

Ryan, Mary P. *Women in Public: Between Banners and Ballots, 1825–1880.* Baltimore: Johns Hopkins University Press, 1990.

Ryan, Thomas A. *Orestes A. Brownson: A Definitive Biography.* Huntington, Ind.: Our Sunday Visitor, 1976.

———. "Orestes A. Brownson and Historiography." *Irish Ecclesiastical Record* (Dublin) 81 (1956): 10–17, 122–30.

"Sacrifice." *Christian Examiner* 65 (1858).

Said, Edward W. *Orientalism.* New York: Vintage Books, 1978.

"St. Ambrose and the Church of the West." *North American Review* 81 (Oct. 1855).

"Saints, and Their Bodies." *Atlantic Monthly* 1 (1858).

"Saint Theresa and the Devotees of Spain." *Christian Examiner* 45 (1849).

Sams, Henry W., ed. *Autobiography of Brook Farm.* Englewood Cliffs, N.J.: Prentice-Hall, 1958.

Sanchez-Eppler, Karen. "Bodily Bonds: The Intersecting Rhetorics of Feminism and Abolition." *Representations* 24 (1988): 28–59.

Sanford, Charles L. *The Quest for Paradise: Europe and the American Moral Imagination.* Urbana: University of Illinois Press, 1961.

Saum, Lewis O. *The Popular Mood of Pre–Civil War America.* Westport, Conn.: Greenwood Press, 1980.

Scarry, Elaine. *The Body in Pain: The Making and Unmaking of the World.* New York: Oxford University Press, 1985.

Schaff, Philip. *America. A Sketch of the Political, Social and Religious Character of the United States of North America.* New York: Scribner, 1855.

———. *Principles of Protestantism.* Philadelphia, 1845.

Schleirmacher, Friedrich. *On Religion: Speeches to Its Cultured Despisers* [1799]. New York: Harper and Row, 1986.

Schlesinger, Arthur M., Jr. *Orestes A. Brownson: A Pilgrim's Progress.* Boston: Little, Brown, 1939.

Schroeder, John H. *Mr. Polk's War: American Opposition and Dissent, 1846–1848.* Madison: University of Wisconsin Press, 1973.

Schultz, Stanley K. *The Culture Factory: Boston Public Schools, 1789–1860.* Oxford: Oxford University Press, 1973.

Scribner, B. "Popular Propaganda for the German Reformation." *History Today* 32 (1982).

Scudder, Horace Elisha. *James Russell Lowell: A Biography.* 2 vols. Boston: Houghton Mifflin, 1901.

Sealts, Merton M., Jr. *Melville as Lecturer.* Cambridge: Harvard University Press, 1957.

Sedgwick, Eve Kosofsky. *The Coherence of Gothic Conventions* [1980]. Rev. ed. New York: Methuen, 1986.

"Seduction." *Christian Examiner* 15 (1834).

Seton, Elizabeth. *Letters of Mother Seton to Mrs. Julianna Scott.* Edited by Joseph B. Code. New York: The Father Salvator M. Burgio Memorial Foundation, 1960.

———. *Memoir, Letters and Journal of Elizabeth Seton, Convert to the Catholic Faith and Sister of Charity.* Edited by Robert Seton. 2 vols. New York: P. O'Shea, 1869.

———. *Selected Writings.* Edited by Ellin Kelly and Annabelle Melville. New York: Paulist Press, 1987.

Shea, John Gilmary. "Where Are the Remains of Christopher Columbus?" *Magazine of American History with Notes and Queries* 9 (1883).

Shea, Leo Martin. *Lowell's Religious Outlook.* Washington, D.C.: Catholic University of America Press, 1926.

Shuffleton, Frank. "Nathaniel Hawthorne and the Revival Movement." *American Transcendental Quarterly* 44 (1979).

Silver, Richard. "The Spiritual Kingdom in America: The Influence of Emmanuel Swedenborg on American Society and Culture, 1815–1860." Ph.D. diss., Stanford University, 1983.

Sister Agnes; or, The Captive Nun. By a Clergyman's Widow. New York: Riker, Thornes and Co., 1854.

Sittler, Joseph. "Space and Time in American Religious Experience." *Interpretation: A Journal of Bible and Theology* 30 (1976).

Sklar, Katherine Kish. *Catharine Beecher: A Study in American Domesticity.* New York: Norton, 1976.

Slotkin, Richard. *The Fatal Environment: The Myth of the Frontier in the Age of Industrialization, 1800–1890.* Middletown, Conn.: Wesleyan University Press, 1985.

———. *Regeneration through Violence: The Mythology of the American Frontier, 1600–1860.* Middletown, Conn.: Wesleyan University Press, 1973.

Smith, George Winston, and Charles Judah. *Chronicles of the Gringos: The U.S. Army in the Mexican War, 1846–1848. Accounts of Eyewitnesses and Combatants.* Albuquerque: University of New Mexico Press, 1968.

Smith, H. Shelton. *Changing Conceptions of Original Sin.* New York: Scribner, 1955.

Smith-Rosenberg, Carroll. *Disorderly Conduct: Visions of Gender in Victorian America.* New York: Oxford University Press, 1985.

"Social Influence of Catholic Theology." *Metropolitan* 1 (1853).

Somers, Paul P., Jr., and Nancy Pogel. "Pornography." In *Handbook of American Popular Culture,* edited by M. Thomas Inge. 3 vols. Westport, Conn.: Greenwood Press, 1981, 3:291–319.

Somkin, Frederick. *Unquiet Eagle: Memory and Desire in the Idea of American Freedom, 1815–1860.* Ithaca, N.Y.: Cornell University Press, 1967.

Sontag, Susan. *Illness as Metaphor.* New York: Vintage Books, 1979.

Spalding, Martin J. *The History of the Protestant Reformation in Germany and Switzerland and in England, Ireland, Scotland, the Netherlands, France, and Northern Europe* [1860]. 2 vols. Baltimore: John Murphy and Co., 1866.

Sparry, C. *Papacy in the Nineteenth Century; or, Popery—What It Is, What It Aims at, and What It Is Doing.* New York: C. Sparry, 1846.

"Sphere of Human Influence." *Christian Examiner* 45 (1848).

Spierenburg, Pieter. *The Spectacle of Suffering: Executions and the Evolution of Repression: From a Preindustrial Metropolis to the European Experience.* Cambridge: Cambridge University Press, 1984.

Sprague, William. *Annals of the American Unitarian Pulpit.* New York, 1865.

Staël, Mme de. *Corinne; or, Italy.* Translated by Emily Baldwin and Pauline Driver. London: George Bell and Sons, 1888.

Staiti, Paul J. "Ideology and Politics in Samuel F. B. Morse's Agenda for a National Art." In *Samuel F. B. Morse: Educator and Champion of the Arts in America.* Exhibition catalogue. New York: National Academy of Design, 1982.

Stampp, Kenneth M. *America in 1857: A Nation on the Brink.* Oxford: Oxford University Press, 1990.

Stange, D. C. "Abolition as Treason: The Unitarian Elite Defends Law, Order, and the Union." *Harvard Library Bulletin* 28 (1980).

Stannard, David E. *The Puritan Way of Death: A Study in Religion, Culture, and Social Change.* New York: Oxford University Press, 1977.

Stansell, Christine. *City of Women: Sex and Class in New York, 1789–1860.* New York: Knopf, 1986.

Stanton, Phoebe B. *The Gothic Revival and American Church Architecture: An Episode in Taste, 1840–1856.* Baltimore: Johns Hopkins University Press, 1968.

Stefun, Bonaventure. "The Mother of God in Brownson's Writings." *American Ecclesiastical Review* 134 (1956).

Stern, Milton R. *Contexts for Hawthorne: "The Marble Faun" and the Politics of Openness and Closure in American Literature.* Urbana: University of Illinois Press, 1991.

Stone, William L. *Maria Monk and the Nunnery of the Hotel Dieu, Being an Account of a Visit to the Convents of Montreal and Refutation of the "Awful Disclosures."* New York, 1836.

Stowe, Harriet Beecher. *Agnes of Sorrento* [1862]. In *The Writings of Harriet Beecher Stowe.* 16 vols. New York, AMS Press, 1967, vol. 7.

———. *Collected Poems of Harriet Beecher Stowe.* Edited by John Michael Moran. Hartford, Conn.: Transcendental Books, n.d.

———. *The Minister's Wooing.* Hartford, Conn.: Stowe-Day Foundation, 1988.

———. *The Ministration of Departed Spirits.* Boston: American Tract Society, n.d.

———. *Uncle Tom's Cabin; or, Life among the Lowly* [1852]. New York: Penguin Books, 1981.

Stratton, R. B. *Captivity of the Oatman Girls: Being an Interesting Narrative of Life among the Apache and Mohave Indians . . .* [1859]. Upper Saddle River, N.J.: Literature House, Gregg Press, 1970.

Strong, George Templeton. *The Diary of George Templeton Strong.* Edited by Allan Nevins and Milton Halsey Thomas. 2 vols. New York: Macmillan, 1952.

"Sulla Morale Cattolica Osservazioni di Alessandro Manzoni." *Christian Examiner* 25 (1839).

Sullivan, William. "Roads to Rome." *American Ecclesiastical Review* 120 (1949).

Sundquist, Eric J. *Home as Found: Authority and Genealogy in Nineteenth-Century American Literature.* Baltimore: Johns Hopkins University Press, 1979.

————. "Slavery, Revolution, and the American Renaissance." In *The American Renaissance Reconsidered,* edited by Walter Benn Michaels and Donald E. Pease. Baltimore: Johns Hopkins University Press, 1985.

————. "Suspense and Tautology in *Benito Cereno.*" *Glyph* 8 (1981).

Supplement to "Six Months in a Convent" Confirming the Narrative of Rebecca Reed . . . by the Testimony of More Than One Hundred Witnesses. Boston, 1835.

Sweeney, K. "Rum, Romanism, Representation, and Reform: Coalition Politics in Massachusetts, 1847–1853." *Civil War History* 22 (1976).

Swidler, Arlene. "Brownson and the 'Woman Question.'" *American Benedictine Review* 19 (1968).

Swift, Lindsay. *Brook Farm: Its Members, Scholars, and Visitors.* 1900. Reprint. New York: Corinth Books, 1961.

Swinson, William. *An Expose of the Know Nothings: Their Degrees, Signs, Grips, Passwords, Charges, Oaths, Initiations Together with Their Objects, Tendencies, and Increase.* Philadelphia: W. Ferguson Davis, 1854.

Takaki, Ronald. *Iron Cages: Race and Culture in Nineteenth Century America.* New York: Oxford University Press, 1990.

Taves, Ann. *The Household of Faith: Roman Catholic Devotions in Mid-Nineteenth Century America.* Notre Dame, Ind.: University of Notre Dame Press, 1986.

Taylor, Isaac. *Loyola: And Jesuitism in Its Rudiments.* New York: Robert Carter and Brothers, 1857.

Taylor, William R. "A Journey into the Human Mind: Motivation in Francis Parkman's *La Salle.*" *William and Mary Quarterly* 19 (1962).

Thayer, John. *An Account of the Conversion of the Reverend Mr. John Thayer.* 5th ed. Baltimore: William Goddard, 1788.

Thaxter, Lucy W. "An Account of Life in the Ursuline Convent at Mt. Benedict, Charlestown, Mass. and of the Events of the Night on Which the Convent was Destroyed" (January 1843). Unpublished ms. Houghton Library, Harvard University.

Thomas, Keith. *Religion and the Decline of Magic.* New York: Scribner, 1971.

Thompson, G. R. *Poe's Fiction: Romantic Irony in the Gothic Tales.* Madison: University of Wisconsin Press, 1973.

Thompson, George [Greenhorn]. *Anna Mowbray: or, Tales of the Harem.* New York: Henry R. J. Barkley, n.d.

Thompson, Ralph. "The Maria Monk Affair." *Colophon,* part 17 (1934), n.p.

Thomson, Spencer. *A Dictionary of Domestic Medicine and Household Surgery.* 10th Edition. Philadelphia: Claxton, Remsen and Haffelfinger, 1877.

Thorp, Willard. "Catholic Novelists in Defense of Their Faith, 1829–1865." *Proceedings of the American Antiquarian Society* 78 (1968).

Tompkins, Jane. *Sensational Designs: The Cultural Work of American Fiction, 1790–1860.* New York: Oxford University Press, 1985.

"To Rome, Buried in Her Ruins." *Christian Examiner* 62 (1857).

Townsend, Kim. "Francis Parkman and the Male Tradition." *American Quarterly* 38, no. 1 (1986): 97–113.

"Tracts for the Times." *Christian Examiner* 27 (1840).

"The Trial and Execution of John Huss." *Harper's New Monthly Magazine* 17 (1858).

Trial Documents of the Convent Riot ["The Charlestown Convent; Its Destruction by a Mob . . . also the Trials of the Rioters, the Testimony, and the Speeches of the Counsel . . . Compiled from Authentic Sources"]. Boston: Patrick Donahoe, 1870.

Trial of the Convent Rioters [newspaper clippings]. Cambridge, Mass., 1834.

Tribble, Joseph L. "The Paradise of the Imagination: The Journeys of *The Oregon Trail.*" *New England Quarterly* 46 (1973).

Turner, Victor. *The Forest of Symbols: Aspects of Ndembu Ritual.* Ithaca, N.Y.: Cornell University Press, 1967.

———. "Passages, Margins, and Poverty: Religious Symbols of Communitas." *Worship* 46 (1972).

Tuveson, Ernest Lee. *Redeemer Nation: The Idea of America's Millennial Role.* Chicago: University of Chicago Press, 1959.

———. "Space, Deity, and the 'Natural Sublime.'" *Modern Language Quarterly* 12 (1951).

"The Two Sides of Catholicism." *Catholic World* 1, no. 1 (1865).

Upton, Dell. *Holy Things and Profane: Anglican Parish Churches in Colonial Virginia.* Cambridge: MIT Press, 1986.

Vance, William L. *America's Rome.* 2 vols. New Haven: Yale University Press, 1989.

Van Der Beets, Richard. "The Indian Captivity Narrative as Ritual." *American Literature* 43 (1972).

———, ed. *Held Captive by Indians: Selected Narratives, 1642–1836.* Knoxville: University of Tennessee Press, 1973.

Vanderhaar, Margaret M. "A Re-Examination of *Benito Cereno.*" *American Literature* 40 (1968–69).

Van Tassel, David D. *Recording America's Past: An Interpretation of the Development of Historical Studies in America, 1607–1884.* Chicago: University of Chicago Press, 1960.

Vaughan, Alden T., and Edward W. Clark. *Puritans among the Indians: Accounts of Captivity and Redemption, 1676–1724.* Cambridge: Harvard University Press, 1981.

Vidler, Anthony. *The Architectural Uncanny: Essays in the Modern Unhomely.* Cambridge: MIT Press, 1992.

Vitzhum, Richard C. *The American Compromise: Theme and Method in the Histories of Bancroft, Parkman, and Adams.* Norman: University of Oklahoma Press, 1974.

———. "The Historian as Editor: Francis Parkman's Reconstruction of Sources in Montcalm and Wolfe." *Journal of American History* 53 (1966): 471–83.

Walker, James P. *Book of Raphael's Madonna*. New York: Leavitt and Allen, 1860.

Walker, Peter F. *Moral Choices: Memory, Desire, and Imagination in Nineteenth-Century American Abolition*. Baton Rouge: Louisiana State University Press, 1978.

Walworth, Clarence E. *The Oxford Movement in America; or, Glimpses of Life in an Anglican Seminary*. New York: Catholic Book Exchange, 1895.

Warner, Marina. *Alone of All Her Sex: The Myth and the Cult of the Virgin Mary*. New York: Vintage Books, 1976.

Warner, Michael. "Franklin and the Letters of the Republic." *Representations* 16 (1986): 110–30.

Weber, Max. *The Protestant Ethic and the Spirit of Capitalism*. Translated by Talcott Parsons. New York: Scribner, 1958.

Webster, Noah. *History of the United States*. New Haven, Conn., 1832.

Weiner, Carol Z. "The Beleaguered Isle: A Study of Elizabethan and Early Jacobean Anti-Catholicism." *Past and Present* 51 (1971).

Weiskel, Thomas. *The Romantic Sublime: Studies in the Structure and Psychology of Transcendence*. Baltimore: Johns Hopkins University Press, 1976.

Welch, Claude. *Protestant Thought in the Nineteenth Century, 1799–1870*. 2 vols. New Haven: Yale University Press, 1972.

Welsh, Howard. "The Politics of Race in *Benito Cereno*." *American Literature* 46 (1974).

Welter, Barbara. "The Cult of True Womanhood, 1820–1860." *American Quarterly* 18, no. 2 (1966).

———. "From Maria Monk to Paul Blanshard: A Century of Protestant Anti-Catholicism." In *Uncivil Religion: Interreligious Hostility in America*, edited by Robert N. Bellah and Frederick E. Greenspahn. New York: Crossroad, 1987, 43–71.

White, Charles I. *Life of Mrs. Eliza A. Seton, Foundress and First Superior of the Sisters or Daughters of Charity*. Baltimore: John Murphy and Co., 1859.

White, Hayden. *Metahistory: The Historical Imagination in Nineteenth-Century Europe*. Baltimore: Johns Hopkins University Press, 1973.

White, Isabelle. "Anti-Individualism, Authority, and Identity: Susan Warner's Contradictions in *The Wide, Wide World*." *American Studies* 31, no. 2 (1990).

White, Joseph Blanco. *Extracts from Blanco White's Journal and Letters*. Printed for the American Unitarian Association. Boston: William Crosby and H. P. Nichols, 1847.

———. *A Letter to Protestants Converted from Romanism*. Oxford, England: W. Baxter, 1827.

———. *The Life of the Rev. Joseph Blanco White, Written by Himself with Portions of his Correspondence*. London: John Chapman, 1845.

Whitman, Walt. *Complete Poetry and Selected Prose*. Edited by James E. Miller, Jr. Boston: Houghton Mifflin, 1959.

Whitney, Louisa G. *The Burning of the Convent. A Narrative of the Destruction, by a Mob, of the Ursuline School on Mount Benedict, Charlestown, As Remembered by One of Her Pupils*. Cambridge, Mass., 1877.

Willard, Emma. *History of the United States*. New York, 1828.

Williams, John. "The Redeemed Captive Returning to Zion." In *Puritans among the Indians: Accounts of Captivity and Redemption, 1676–1724,* edited by Alden T. Vaughan and Edward W. Clark. Cambridge: Harvard University Press, 1981, 167–226.

Williams, Susan S. "Widening the World: Susan Warner, Her Readers, and the Assumption of Authorship." *American Quarterly* 42, no. 4 (1990).

Wilson, R. Jackson. *Figures of Speech: American Writers and the Literary Marketplace from Benjamin Franklin to Emily Dickinson.* Baltimore: Johns Hopkins University Press, 1989.

Winsor, Justin, ed. *The Memorial History of Boston.* 3 vols. Boston, 1882.

Wish, Harvey. *The American Historian: A Social-Intellectual History of the Writing of the American Past.* New York: Oxford University Press, 1960.

Wolf, Bryan Jay. *Romantic Re-Vision: Culture and Consciousness in Nineteenth-Century American Painting and Literature.* Chicago: University of Chicago Press, 1982.

Wolff, George D. "The Mercersburg Movement: An Attempt to Find Ground on Which Protestantism and Catholicity Might Unite." *American Catholic Quarterly Review* 3 (1878).

Wolff, Robert Lee. *Gains and Losses: Novels of Faith and Doubt in Victorian England.* New York: Garland, 1977.

"Woman in Her Psychological Relations." *Journal of Psychological Medicine* 4 (1851).

Women in American Religion. Edited by Janet Wilson James. Philadelphia: University of Pennsylvania Press, 1980.

Wood, Gordon S. "Conspiracy and the Paranoid Style: Causality and Deceit in the Eighteenth Century." *William and Mary Quarterly* 39 (1982).

Wright, Nathalia. *American Novelists in Italy: The Discoverers: Allston to James.* Philadelphia: University of Pennsylvania Press, 1965.

Wright, Richardson. *Forgotten Ladies.* Philadelphia: Lippincott, 1928.

Ziff, Larzer. *Literary Democracy: The Declaration of Cultural Independence in America.* New York: Penguin Books, 1981.

Zuckerman, Michael. "Holy Wars, Civil Wars: Religion and Economics in Nineteenth-Century America." *Prospects* 16 (1991).

Index

Huntington, Jedediah, 199
Huntington, Joshua, 214, 282, 283–84, 325
Hurons, in Parkman's history, 36, 66, 69, 72, 73, 74, 135
Hysteria, 28, 106, 173, 204, 377n32

Illustrated Magazine of Art, 18
Images, Catholic: and Protestant historiography, 6–7, 9; and Protestant tourism, 17, 19, 22
Immigration, Catholic, xvii, xviii, xix; and conversion to Catholicism, 226, 227, 245; and Hawthorne's "Minister's Black Veil," 221, 224; nativist struggle against, xx, 15, 99, 102, 174, 202, 221, 392n15; in New England, 40, 55, 62, 103; and patriotism, 341; and political conspiracy, 100, 101; and Protestant historiography, 5, 6, 40–41, 55, 62; and Protestant liberalism, 212, 215; and Protestant tourism, 20, 21. *See also* German immigrants; Irish immigrants
Imperialism, 11, 35, 100, 281; and Melville's *Benito Cereno*, 175, 176, 179; Prescott's legitimation of, 39–40, 41–42, 56, 83
Inauthenticity: and anti-Catholic discourse, 106, 107, 264; and captivity narrative, 115, 164; and conversion to Catholicism, 198–99, 212; and Protestant nativism, 198
Incarnationalism, 199, 238, 278, 330, 331, 364, 411n41
Individualism: xxi, 108–9, 117, 126, 251–52, 285, 335, 339, 340

Industrialization: xxi, 6, 21, 127, 142, 165, 345
Influence, rhetoric of, 228–32, 238, 239, 246, 247, 270, 334; in Bushnell's writings, 229–33, 238, 249
Inquisition, Catholic, 99, 105, 216, 257; and Melville's *Benito Cereno*, 173, 174, 175, 176, 178; and Poe's "Pit and the Pendulum," 165, 166–67, 169, 170, 186
Interiority: and captivity narrative, 105, 108, 149, 173, 174, 182; and Catholic architecture, 17, 83, 121, 173, 182, 215, 270, 374n3; and Catholic morbidity, 17, 28, 83; and conversion to Catholicism, 299–300, 324, 331; and eroticism, 17, 83, 183; and Hawthorne's *Marble Faun*, 357, 358; of Jesuits, 78, 83; and Melville's *Benito Cereno*, 173, 174, 176, 178, 179, 180, 181, 182; and Möhler's *Symbolism*, 327, 330; and national identity, xxi; and Protestant spirituality, 184; and Protestant tourism, 17, 25, 28, 83, 183, 374n3; and public/private sphere, 182, 183; and superstition, 44–45, 61, 83, 183; and women, 121, 123, 183
Invalidism: of Hecker, 335, 336; of Parkman, xxiv, 66, 69, 70, 75, 77–79, 81, 83, 386n62, 387n73, 388n79; poetic representation of, 417n26; of Prescott, xxiv, 57, 83; Protestant characterized by, 271; and Seton's

52, 153, 400n34; and thematics of artifice, 162; and Ursuline convent riot, 139, 143, 145–46, 147, 148, 150, 151
Reese, David, 109, 218, 220
Reform, social, 225, 226, 321; and Orestes Brownson, xvii, 338, 339, 343–45; and Sophia Ripley, 305, 306, 309, 310, 314
Reformation: and anti-Catholic discourse, xx; Catholic critique of, 6, 345–46; and Indian captivity narrative, 91, 94, 96; and Luther's character, 386n66; and Protestant historiography, 3–5, 6, 38; and Protestant tourism, 21, 31, 34
Republican party, 100, 102, 368n5, 391n14
Restorationism, 31
Revelation, Book of, 34, 182
Ricci, Scipio de, 106
Ridgely, J. V., 392n20
Riots, xviii, 103, 172; at Ursuline convent, xxii, 136–42
Ripley, George, 303–9 *passim*, 312, 319, 333, 363
Ripley, Sophia, 191, 240; and Brook Farm, 302–7, 314, 319, 414n7, 420n8; and Calvinism, 316, 317; and Catholic community, 311–12, 333; and Catholic mass, 306, 317; and Catholic saints, 309, 311, 312; and comments on Brownson, 312, 421n33; and communion sacrament, 305; and conversion to Catholicism, xxvi, 198–99, 237, 302, 307, 312, 420n8; and correspondence with Ruth Char-

lotte Dana, 303–20 *passim*; and cultural identity, 281, 302, 307, 308, 310, 312, 314, 322; death of, 307, 319, 320; and Fourierism, 305, 306; and gender identity, 311; lay order joined by, 307–8, 319; on Longfellow's *Evangeline*, 206; and objectivism, 306; and original sin, 310, 316, 317; prose style of, 304; Protestant coldness battled by, 314–17, 358; and reformism, 305, 306, 309, 310, 314; and relations with family, 309–10, 315; and relations with Isaac Hecker, 302–3, 315, 319, 321; and relations with John Hughes, 310, 315–16; and relations with husband, 305, 306, 307, 309, 312, 319; and sanctification of womanhood, 309, 318; and Transcendentalism, 304, 305–6, 308, 316; translations by, 307, 309; and Virgin Mary, 305, 309, 318, 421n22
Ritualism: and Indian captivity narrative, 90, 99; and Protestant historiography, 36, 45–46, 72–73, 80; and Protestant nativism, 107; and theatrical spectacle, 189–90
Romance narrative, 201–2, 243; and Hawthorne's *Marble Faun*, 350–58; and Hawthorne's *Scarlet Letter*, 264–65, 266; and Longfellow's *Evangeline*, 203–11; and Stowe's *Agnes of Sorrento*, 248, 249, 251
Romanticism, 25, 26, 224, 259, 262, 271, 326, 333, 342; and

Romanticism (*continued*)
rhetoric of influence, 228, 230;
and utopianism, 302, 306
Romanticism, historiographic,
xxvi, 37–38, 48, 150, 153,
341, 370n6, 382n32,
385n59; and Parkman's *Jesuits*, xxi, 65, 66–67, 68, 70,
81–82; and Prescott's *Mexico*, xxi, 38, 50, 51–52, 61,
62
Rome, city of, 22–29, 31–34,
217, 258, 259, 352–58
Rowlandson, Mary, 91, 164,
389n6
Rowson, Susanna, 10, 124,
147, 394n14

Said, Edward, *Orientalism* by,
367n2
Saints, Catholic, 117, 203, 251,
252, 253, 256, 410n37
Salem, witchcraft in, 9, 98
Sanford, Charles L., 370n7
Satanism, and Brownson's Catholicism, 341, 343–49, 358
Scarlet fever, 298
Schaff, Philip, 404n5, 410n36
Science: and mind-body relation, 363–66; and Protestant
historiography, 26, 31, 33–
34, 70
Scott, Walter, 21, 43, 65, 66,
382n30
Scott, Winfield, 39
Scripture, Protestant: and Bushnell's theories, 230, 407n17;
Catholic critique of, 283,
285, 331, 423n20; and Hawthorne's "Minister's Black
Veil," 222; and historiography, 6–12, 48; and tourism,
21, 22. *See also* Word, Protestant scriptural

Sculpture, xxiii, 125, 191, 235
Sectarianism, Protestant: and
Catholic conspiracy, 109; and
conversion to Catholicism,
198, 225–26, 228, 233, 324,
337, 347; and historiography,
4, 5, 9, 51, 52–53, 370n8;
and pluralism, 258; and social class, 138, 147
Secularism, xix, xxvii, 4, 120,
182
Sedgwick, Eve Kosofsky,
400n35
Seduction, priestly, xxv, 122–25,
126, 147, 155, 171, 182,
201, 394–95n14
Selfhood, Protestant: and captivity narrative, 88, 114, 118,
132, 167; and conversion to
Catholicism, 198, 284, 285,
302, 322; democratic division
of, 184; Emerson's view of,
270, 284, 302, 319; fictional
privatization of, 324; narrative coherence of, 35, 42–43;
and Parkman's writings, 17,
35–37, 69, 81; and Prescott's
writings, 35–37; and rhetoric
of influence, 230, 232; and
sentimentality, 114; and
Stowe's writings, 252; and
tourism, 17, 69, 270. *See also*
Subjectivity, Protestant
Sentimentality: and anti-Catholic
discourse, 117, 182, 231; and
captivity narrative, 113–17,
126, 132, 147, 148, 152,
154, 162, 164, 394n6; Ca-
tholicism characterized by,
120–21; and commercial fiction, 131–32; and conversion
to Catholicism, 198, 358; and
domestic sphere, 113, 120,
131–32, 229, 266, 317, 358;

and eroticism, 123–24; and family, 117, 120; and female body, xxv, 124–25; and femininity, 113, 115, 117, 120–21, 123, 124, 131, 147; and Hawthorne's *Scarlet Letter*, 266, 268; and Holmes's *Elsie Venner*, 243; and Longfellow's *Evangeline*, 205, 207, 208, 209, 212; and marriage, 131; and medievalism, 127; and middle class, 114, 115, 117, 125; and motherhood, 229; and Protestant selfhood, 114; and Protestant spirituality, 113; and Stowe's *Agnes of Sorrento*, 248

Seton, Elizabeth Ann: American Sisters of Charity founded by, 300–301, 414n7; and bodily infirmity, 286–87, 288, 289, 293, 295, 301; Catholic conversion of, xxvi, 197, 198, 298–300; and Catholic culture, 297; and Catholic interiority, 299–300; and Catholic mass, 190, 297; and Catholic penance, 360, 362; and cultural identity, 281, 322; and devotion to Eucharist, 293, 294, 331; and domestic sphere, 292, 293; and epidemic disease, 290–93, 416n26; and Episcopalianism, 286, 293, 294, 299; and financial instability, 286, 289, 296; maternalism of, 287–88, 292–93, 295, 297, 416n25; as "Mother Seton," 290, 300; parochial school system founded by, 300, 414n7; Protestant emptiness repudiated by, 358; and quarantine in Italy, 290, 294–97; and

relations with family, 287–88, 289, 290, 293, 299, 300, 301; and relations with father, 290–91, 292, 293; and relations with husband, 286, 288, 290, 293–97; and travel to Italy, 286, 294; Mary Lovell Ware contrasted with, 361–62; White's biography of, 361

Sexuality: and Catholic confessional, 100, 120–26, 268, 395n17; and Catholic morbidity, 17, 19, 24; and Catholic spectacle, 190–91, 239; and convent captivity narrative, 111, 125, 154, 155, 157; and Hawthorne's *Marble Faun*, 355; and Hawthorne's *Scarlet Letter*, 246, 260, 263, 268; and middle class, 191, 395n17; and public/private sphere, 117; and slave captivity narrative, 104, 105; and Stowe's *Agnes of Sorrento*, 253–54; and transvestism, 222; and women's solitary reading, 10. *See also* Eroticism; Gender

Shaw, Lemuel, 140, 143
Shea, John Gilmary, 62–63
Shepard, Thomas, 373n24
Skepticism: xxvii, 338, 342, 425n3
Slavery: and anti-Catholic discourse, 102–5, 171–72, 173, 174, 391n14, 412n43; and Fugitive Slave Law, 136; and Melville's *Benito Cereno*, 163, 172–81 *passim*; and Protestant historiography, 6, 9, 41, 42; and Protestant nativism, 102–4, 171–72; and Spanish Catholicism, 175,

Designer: Ina Clausen
Compositor: Braun-Brumfield, Inc.
Text: 10/12 Sabon
Display: Sabon
Printer: Braun-Brumfield, Inc.
Binder: Braun-Brumfield, Inc.